Special Edition

USING

MICROSOFT SQL
SERVER 6.5
SECOND EDITION

Special Edition

USING

MICROSOFT SQL

SERVER 6.5

SECOND EDITION

Written by Stephen Wynkoop

Special Edition Using Microsoft SQL Server 6.5
Second Edition

Library of Congress Catalog No.: 97-65014

ISBN: 0-7897-1117-6

99 98   6 5 4 3 2

Interpretation of the printing code: the rightmost double-digit number is the year of the book's printing; the rightmost single-digit number, the number of the book's printing. For example, a printing code of 97-1 shows that the first printing of the book occurred in 1997.

Screen reproductions in this book were created by using Collage Plus from Inner Media, Inc., Hollis, NH.

Credits

PRESIDENT
Roland Elgey

PUBLISHER
Stacy Hiquet

PUBLISHING MANAGER
Fred Slone

SENIOR TITLE MANAGER
Bryan Gambrel

EDITORIAL SERVICES DIRECTOR
Elizabeth Keaffaber

MANAGING EDITOR
Sandy Doell

ACQUISITIONS EDITOR
Kelly Marshall

SENIOR EDITOR
Mike La Bonne

EDITORS
Kelly Brooks
Kristen Ivanetich
Jean Jamison
Sydney Jones
Anne Owen
Andy Saff
Kathy Simpson
Heather Stith

TECHNICAL EDITOR
Nelson Howell

DIRECTOR OF MARKETING
Lynn E. Zingraf

STRATEGIC MARKETING MANAGER
Barry Pruett

PRODUCT MARKETING MANAGER
Kristine Ankney

ASSISTANT PRODUCT MARKETING MANAGERS
Christy M. Miller
Karen Hagen

TECHNICAL SUPPORT SPECIALIST
Nadeem Muhammed

ACQUISITIONS COORDINATOR
Carmen Krikorian

EDITORIAL ASSISTANTS
Andrea Duvall
Chantal Mees Koch

BOOK DESIGNERS
Ruth Harvey

COVER DESIGNER
Dan Armstrong

PRODUCTION TEAM
Michael Beaty
Amy Gornik
Kay Hoskin
Angela Perry

INDEXER
Eric Brinkman
Kevin Fulcher

Composed in *Century Old Style* and *Franklin Gothic* by Que Corporation.

This book is dedicated to Brennan and Caitlin. I hope you continue to find computers more fun than work!

About the Authors

Stephen Wynkoop is an author and lecturer working extensively with Microsoft-based products and technologies, with an emphasis on Internet and client/server technologies. Stephen has been developing applications and consulting in the computer industry for more than 15 years. He is author or co-author of several other titles from Que and other publishers, including *Que's Running a Perfect Web Site Second Edition, Special Edition Using Windows NT Server 4.0,* and *The BackOffice Intranet Kit.* Stephen is a regular speaker at Microsoft's technical conferences and has written books on Microsoft Access and Microsoft Office development and integration. Stephen is also a Microsoft Certified Professional. You can reach Stephen via the Internet at **swynk@pobox.com**, or visit his Web site at **http://www.pobox.com/~swynk**.

Chris Lester is a software support engineer in Microsoft Premier Support. He has dabbled in UNIX-based databases, XBase, dBase, and data design (as well as several programming languages). He has extensive experience with LAN-based messaging systems and Microsoft Exchange in particular. When Chris is not working he can be found eating, sleeping, or dreaming about a Porsche.

Acknowledgments

The crew on this book has been fantastic to work with. Nelson Howell, diligently pointing out my errors and making suggestions on the technical side, Kelly Marshall and Mike La Bonne at Que moving the project forward as quickly as possible, and the many, many copy editors and layout teams have been a lot of fun to work with. Without such a team, these projects are impossible.

I'd also like to say "Thank You!" to my wife, Julie, and family, Brennan and Caitlin. They put up with a number of tirades when things didn't work as expected, and Julie in particular makes sure the work is actually readable, generally a good thing in books! This book gains a whole level of better understandability with her involvement in the editing cycles.

Finally, but certainly not lastly, this Second Edition of the *Special Edition Using SQL Server 6.5* book would surely not be possible without the prior efforts of the original author team of Bob Branchek, Peter Hazlehurst, and Scott L. Warner. The work put forward on the original version shows through on this new expanded edition and shows how well these folks know their stuff.

Stephen Wynkoop

We'd Like to Hear from You!

As part of our continuing effort to produce books of the highest possible quality, Que would like to hear your comments. To stay competitive, we *really* want you to let us know what you like or dislike most about this book or other Que products.

Please send your comments, ideas, and suggestions for improvement to:

Rosemarie Graham
Macmillan Computer Publishing
201 West 103rd Street
Indianapolis, IN 46290-1097

You can also visit our home page on the World Wide Web at:

http://www.quecorp.com

Thank you in advance. Your comments will help us to continue publishing the best books available in today's market.

Contents at a Glance

Table of Contents

II | Up and Running with SQL Server

III | Server-Side Logic and Capabilities

IV | SQL Server Administration Topics

20   SQL Server Security   575

Appendixes

Introduction

All of data processing is involved with the operations of storing and retrieving data. A database, such as Microsoft SQL Server, is designed as the central repository for all the data of an organization. The crucial nature of data to any organization underlines the importance of the method used to store it and enable its later retrieval.

Microsoft SQL Server uses features similar to those found in other databases and some features that are unique. Most of these additional features are made possible by SQL Server's tight integration with the Windows NT operating system. SQL Server contains the data storage options and the capability to store and process the same volume of data as a mainframe or minicomputer.

Like most mainframe or minicomputer databases, SQL Server is a database that has seen an evolution from its introduction in the mid-1960s until today. Microsoft's SQL Server is founded in the mature and powerful relational model, currently the preferred model for data storage and retrieval.

Unlike mainframe and minicomputer databases, a server database is accessed by users—called clients—from other computer systems rather than from input/output devices, such as terminals. Mechanisms must be in place for SQL Server to solve problems that arise from the access of data from perhaps hundreds of computer systems, each of which can process portions of the database independently from the data on the server.

Within the framework of a client/server database, a server database also requires integration with communication components of the server in order to enable connections with client systems. Microsoft SQL Server's client/server connectivity uses the built-in network components of Windows NT.

Unlike a stand-alone PC database or a traditional mainframe or minicomputer database, a server database, such as Microsoft SQL Server, adds service-specific middleware components—such as *Open Database Connectivity (ODBC)*—on top of the network components. ODBC enables the interconnection of different client applications without requiring changes to the server database or other existing client applications.

SQL Server also contains many of the front-end tools of PC databases that traditionally haven't been available as part of either mainframe or minicomputer databases. In addition to using a dialect of *Structured Query Language (SQL)*, GUI applications can be used for the storage, retrieval, and administration of the database.

Now, with the addition of new database-aware components, you can also use your SQL Server with your Internet-based applications. Tools such as the Internet Database Connector, or IDC, and the Advanced Data Connector, or ADC, are available that will help you integrate SQL Server database information into your Web pages. Depending on the tool or approach you select, you'll have access that ranges from static Web pages to dynamic, Visual Basic-enhanced Web pages. These exciting tools are making Web-based applications a reality. ■

Who Should Use This Book

This book is written for users of Microsoft SQL Server—from database users and developers to database administrators. It can be used by new users to learn about any feature of Microsoft SQL Server. It can also serve as a reference for experienced users who need to learn to use a feature of the product that they haven't yet employed.

The CD-ROM that accompanies this book offers example Transact-SQL statements and demonstration applications provided by many third-party vendors to give you a feeling for many of the products and services available in the market, as well as ideas for using SQL Server in your organization. You'll also find additional links to tools, articles, and other resources on the Web at **http://www.pobox.com/~swynk**, the author's site, or at the Que Publishing site, **http://www.quecorp.com**, where you can find additional books online as well.

In addition, you can use the electronic version of this book included on the CD. The electronic version will enable you to reference the information in the book on your monitor alongside an actual SQL Server database.

How to Use This Book

This book is divided into six sections. The sections are intended to present the use of SQL Server as a logical series of steps in the order in which the reader would most likely use the product. Ideally, you will go through the chapters and their sections in sequence.

Part I: Understanding the Basics

Part I discusses the basic features of Microsoft SQL Server and provides an overview of its capabilities. In this part, you'll learn about necessary information related to Microsoft SQL Server. The background information about SQL Server is recommended for all new and current users of SQL Server who may be unfamiliar with it.

In Chapter 1, "Introducing Microsoft SQL Server," you'll learn the origin and evolution of SQL Server and its implementation as a relational database. You'll also learn about the components of SQL Server, including the installation and configuration of the database and its client components.

Chapter 2, "Understanding the Underlying Operating System, Windows NT," explains the features of the operating system that SQL Server takes advantage of to obtain optimal performance. The SQL Server database components are designed solely for implementation on the Windows NT system.

Chapter 3, "Installing and Setting Up the Server and Client Software," covers the physical installation and configuration of the server engine and the tools you'll use with it. This covers both the server installation and the setup of the tools from the client system.

In Chapter 4, "Data Modeling, Database Design, and the Client/Server Model," you'll learn how to design a database. Moreover, you'll become familiar with the terminology associated with a relational database, such as SQL Server.

Chapter 5, "Creating Devices, Databases, and Transaction Logs," explains how to create the storage areas on a disk where you create your database and backups of your database.

Chapter 6, "Creating Database Tables and Using Datatypes," provides you with instructions on how to create database tables and choose the datatypes of the table columns. You can also read about the considerations involved in your choice of table and table column characteristics.

Part II: Up and Running with SQL Server

In Part II, you'll learn how to start working with SQL Server, extracting the information in your tables to make the best use of it. You'll also learn to manipulate the stored data, including combining data from multiple sources. If you are already familiar with SQL or the previous version of SQL Server, you'll still want to read the chapters in this section to learn how this version differs from the earlier version. You'll also want to learn about the additions that support the ANSI SQL standard.

Chapter 7, "Retrieving Data with Transact-SQL," provides instruction in the use of the SELECT statement and the addition of clauses to the SELECT statement for controlling the retrieval of targeted data.

Chapter 8, "Adding, Changing, and Deleting Information in Tables," continues the instruction on retrieving data begun in Chapter 7. Included in the discussion is instruction on how to combine data from multiple tables.

Chapter 9, "Using Functions," provides a comprehensive treatment of the functions you can use in Transact-SQL. The examples presented in the chapter are simple and direct, which facilitate the understanding of how to use the functions.

In Chapter 10, "Managing and Using Views," you'll learn the definition and use of stored SELECT statements subsequently used like an actual table. You'll also learn about the problem of disappearing rows, a phenomenon that occurs with the storage of rows through a view.

In Chapter 11, "Managing and Using Indexes and Keys," you'll learn how to define the database objects used to ensure fast retrieval of the rows of database tables. In addition, you'll learn to use the database object that is a basis for ensuring referential integrity in a database.

Chapter 12, "Understanding Transactions and Locking," provides an understanding of the synchronization mechanism used by SQL Server to ensure the integrity of database tables and operations.

Part III: Server-Side Logic and Capabilities

The client/server model requires that you have intelligence on the part of both sides of the equation. SQL Server provides several different tools in this arena, including the most prominent—stored procedures. In Part III, you'll learn about these and other capabilities managed and executed by the server-side of the client/server equation.

Chapter 13, "Managing and Using Rules, Constraints, and Defaults," contains information on how to restrict the values that may be inserted into database tables and other database structures.

Chapter 14, "Managing Stored Procedures and Using Flow-Control Statements," and Chapter 15, "Creating and Managing Triggers," discuss the capability of creating a set of Transact-SQL statements that can be stored and subsequently executed as a group. You can use flow-control statements, including conditional statements, to effectively write a SQL program that manipulates your database. In addition, you'll learn to create a set of SQL statements that are automatically activated when SELECT, INSERT, UPDATE, or DELETE statements are executed on a database.

Chapter 16, "Understanding Server, Database, and Design Query Options," allows you to configure your server and database for various uses and situations. In addition, you'll also learn to configure your queries against the database.

Chapter 17, "Setting Up and Managing Replication," discusses how you implement the automatic creation and maintenance of multiple copies of a database to enhance performance in the access of data.

Chapter 18, "Using the Distributed Transaction Coordinator," tells you how to extend the capabilities included in transactions across servers. This chapter explains the setup, use, and troubleshooting associated with these extended transaction capabilities.

Part IV: SQL Server Administration Topics

When your server is up and running, and during the forming of your ongoing maintenance plans, you'll find that several topics will come up. The chapters in this section will include management of security and backup approaches, as well as the art of optimizing your server.

Chapter 19, "SQL Server Administration," provides you with information about how to keep data consistently available to the users of client systems. Availability of data from a database is ensured by a combination of fault-tolerant mechanisms and the duplication of data before it's lost.

Chapter 20, "SQL Server Security," continues the discussion of maintaining data availability by explaining the implementation of proper security for SQL Server and its databases.

Chapter 21, "Optimizing Performance," explains how you can enhance a database and the retrieval of information from the database by using important calculations based on different storage factors. Moreover, you'll learn to use the built-in monitoring tool of the Windows NT system to monitor the performance of SQL Server components and applications.

Part V: Developing Applications and Solutions

This part of the book focuses entirely on development issues. This ranges from the use of db-lib to how you access SQL Server using the Advanced Data Connector technology just arriving on the development scene. These chapters will give you a great look at the different ways you can go about working with some of the more popular tools available for client-side applications development.

Chapter 22, "Developing Applications to Work with SQL Server," provides you with information about the client and server components used for the interconnection of systems. The network components and protocols are the basis on which SQL Server and client applications depend for communication.

"Understanding SQL Server and the Internet" is the subject of Chapter 23, which offers full coverage of how to work with the Internet Database Connector (IDC) and a look at emerging technologies that let you create more dynamic Web pages for your site.

Chapter 24, "Creating and Using Cursors," provides you with instruction on the use of a feature of SQL Server that enables you to perform selection operations on individual rows of a database table. You can also randomly access an individual row and manipulate it without affecting other rows.

Chapter 25, "Accessing SQL Server Databases Through Front-End Products," discusses the access of a SQL Server database through programming and non-programming applications. The chapter uses representative examples of the most prevalent client products.

Chapter 26, "Upsizing Microsoft Office 97 Applications to SQL Server," goes into detail on how you can migrate your application from Access 97 to SQL Server. This includes setting up views from queries, working with tables, and working through the details associated with the up-sizing effort.

Part VI: Appendixes

The eight appendixes provide additional information on supporting topics that you'll want to know for your installation. From RAID configurations to working with the software included on the CD, the information is all here.

There is also a complete reference to the Data Access Objects, or DAO. This comprehensive guide is useful regardless of the host language you choose to develop in.

Conventions Used in This Book

Que has over a decade of experience developing and publishing the most successful computer books available. With that experience, we've learned what special features help readers the most. Look for these special features throughout the book to enhance your learning experience.

The following font conventions are used in this book to help make reading it easier:

- *Italic type* is used to introduce new terms.
- Screen messages, code listings, and command samples appear in monospace type. For more details about syntax, see the following section, "Syntax Guidelines."
- Code that you are instructed to type appears in **monospace bold type**.
- Shortcut keys are denoted with underscores. For example, "choose File, Edit" means that you can press Alt+F, then press E to perform the same steps as when you click the File menu and then click Edit.

TIP Tips present short advice on a quick or often overlooked procedure. These include shortcuts.

NOTE Notes present interesting or useful information that isn't necessarily essential to the discussion. A note provides additional information that may help you avoid problems or offers advice that relates to the topic. ▦

CAUTION

Cautions warn you about potential problems that a procedure may cause, unexpected results, or mistakes to avoid.

This icon indicates that you can also find the related information on the enclosed CD-ROM.

On the CD

Syntax Guidelines

It's important to have a clearly defined way of describing Transact-SQL commands. In this book, the following rules apply:

- Anything in *italics* means that you have to substitute the italicized text with your own text.
- Anything placed inside square brackets "[...]" means that it can be optionally left out of the command.
- Anything placed inside curly braces "{ ... }" means that one of the values must be chosen to complete the syntax.
- The available values are separated by the bar (or pipe) character "|" (meaning "OR"). Consider the following example:

```
{DISK | TAPE}
```

It would be translated as "DISK or TAPE."

■ If you see "…" after any bracketed block in a Transact-SQL statement, it means that section can be repeated as many items as is appropriate.

■ Finally, cross-references are included that refer you quickly to specific sections throughout the book.

Understanding The Basics

CHAPTER 1

Introducing Microsoft SQL Server

As the computer industry moves to more distributed environments and moves its data from mainframe to servers, you need to understand the concepts behind a client/server database environment.

In several respects, server databases such as Microsoft SQL Server are identical to mainframe databases. The overwhelming majority of databases used on computer systems are relational databases. Also, server databases such as relational databases on mainframe or minicomputer systems support the use of Structured Query Language (*SQL*), as well as proprietary tools for accessing data.

Where you start to see differences in a PC-based client/server solution is in the architecture and physical implementation of the system. With a SQL Server solution, your users have intelligent client systems, such as personal computers. In a mainframe or minicomputer environment, users are likely to use a terminal or a PC running terminal-emulation software.

With more intelligent client systems, users can retrieve information from the server and manipulate it locally. This type of implementation optimizes the processing of the information, allowing each component to work on the information independently in the manner best suited for

What language SQL Server uses to implement and maintain the relational model

Transact-SQL is a subset standard of SQL that SQL Server uses to implement, maintain, and access databases.

What software is used to access SQL Server

SQL Server comes with several utilities that allow you to access its services. You can use these utilities locally or remotely to manage a SQL Server system.

How to obtain help

With a system as complex as SQL Server, knowing every detail is very difficult. Online help is available in an easy-to-search book-type format.

that component. The server focuses on the database processes, and the client focuses on the presentation of the information. ■

Making the Move to SQL Server

Two key features of a server database become important because of the client access to data. The first feature provides a single point of access to the data in the database. The second feature divides processing and manipulation between the client and server systems.

SQL Server permits client applications to control the information retrieved from the server by using several specialized tools and techniques, including options such as stored procedures, server-enforced rules, and triggers that permit processing to be done on the server automatically. You don't have to move all processing to the server, of course; you still can do appropriate information processing on the client workstation.

Because mainframe and minicomputer systems traditionally do all processing at the host side, it can initially be simpler to implement systems in this environment than in a true client/server implementation. It's simpler because users work at terminals that are directly connected to the mainframe or minicomputer and work directly with the database by using the processing power of the mainframe or minicomputer.

Although organizations routinely use SQL Server to manipulate millions of records, SQL Server provides several tools that help you manage the system and its databases and tables. The Windows- and command-line-based tools that come with SQL Server allow you to work with the many aspects of SQL Server. You can use these tools to

- Perform the administration of the databases
- Control access to data in the databases
- Control the manipulation of data in the databases

You also can use a command-line interface to perform all operations with SQL Server.

A dialect of the SQL language is used with SQL Server for interactive and application program access to data. SQL is the de facto standard for database operations, and every vendor's database product should include a version of it.

N O T E   The *Microsoft Open Database Connectivity model* (ODBC) uses SQL to connect to databases even when the underlying database doesn't natively support SQL. In those cases, SQL is translated into a set of commands that accomplish the requested call for the given database. After you master SQL, you can work with any ODBC data source that you need to access, and you can use ODBC to make the translations needed for the underlying database engine. ■

Although this book explains how to use the command-line tool for issuing interactive SQL commands, remember that you can perform most operations with the application tools that use the Windows Graphical User Interface (GUI). You can use either interface or both interfaces, depending on your interest. If you're familiar with another SQL dialect, you may initially find that issuing direct SQL commands from the command-line for all operations is simpler.

Understanding Relational Features of SQL Server

A key characteristic of SQL Server is that it is a relational database. You must understand the features of a relational database to effectively understand and access data with SQL Server. You can't construct successful queries to return data from a relational database unless you understand the basic features of a relational database.

▶ **See** Chapter 2, "Understanding the Underlying Operating System, Windows NT," for more information about relational databases and establishing database structures, **p. 33**.

Dr. E.F. Codd designed the model for relational databases in 1970, as a means of storing, retrieving, and manipulating data more easily than in hierarchical and network databases. Hierarchical and network databases were difficult to design, and it sometimes was difficult to write proper queries for access to data.

Hierarchical and network databases were difficult to work with for several reasons. One reason was that the physical and logical definitions of data storage in hierarchical and network databases had to be written in a cryptic syntax. Another difficulty of working with data definitions came from the fact that different types of internal pointers, numeric references to data locations, and other low-level details had to be set up and stored through the database. The pointers were used for the subsequent direct retrieval of data.

In Codd's relational database model, the data is referenced as though it were stored in a two-dimensional table. The actual physical storage of the data—although significant for the time required to store, change, or retrieve data—is insignificant syntactically for reference. The two-dimensional table model permits data to be referenced as the rows and columns of the table.

In a relational database, data is referenced as the rows and columns of a table. You can easily visualize data stored as a table, because you often encounter data stored in tables in everyday life. You reference train and plane schedules as a table, for example, and you create typical worksheets as a table. See Figure 1.1.

FIG. 1.1
This is an example of a common table, showing flights out of the Tucson area.

Flights out of Tucson - Que Airways

Time	Dest.	Flt.	Gate
6:45a	Indianapolis	2332	3
8:30a	Phoenix	617	4
9:15a	Los Angeles	4325	3
12:00p	San Carlos	17	7
5:45p	Seattle	7548	4
7:30p	Las Vegas	777	7

The rows of a table are unordered in Codd's relational model. In the relational model implemented in Microsoft SQL Server, the rows of a database table are also unordered unless you create a clustered index for the table. After you create a clustered index for a table, the rows are stored in ascending order by the one or more columns that you use to create the index.

▶ **See** Chapter 11, "Managing and Using Indexes and Keys," for more information about clustered indexes and the other types of indexes supported by SQL Server, **p. 325**.

It's important, however, that the statements you use in the retrieval language to access table rows be independent of the order of the rows. If you require the rows of a table to be retrieved and displayed in some order, the statement that you issue to retrieve the rows must specify the row order. The rows are sorted as they're retrieved for your query.

The original relational model required each row to be uniquely defined by at least one column of a table: the unique key. The unique-row requirement ensures that each row is accessed or changed independently and uniquely from other rows of the table. The query language used to access table rows can use only data stored within each row to separate one row from another.

SQL Server, however, doesn't require you to define unique table rows. You can create two or more rows of a table that can't be referenced separately from one another. Although you may not find a use for duplicate rows, some users feel that such rows are desirable in certain applications.

In Chapter 2, "Understanding the Underlying Operating System, Windows NT," you learn more about relational-design concepts and techniques. For now, though, it's important to understand what is possible, if not practical. If you want to prevent duplicates, you can add to tables a constraint that prevents duplicate rows.

> **CAUTION**
>
> As you see in Chapter 2, unless you're absolutely certain that you must allow the storage of duplicate rows, you should ensure that table rows are unique. In the absence of enforced uniqueness, accidentally adding one or more duplicates to the table is too easy. After you add duplicate rows, removing or updating them is difficult.

In the relational database model, data that's stored across tables in one or more databases is combined during the access of the rows during an inquiry. If the Employees table contains columns such as Name, Department, and Badge, for example, a second table named Pays can contain the columns Hours_Worked, PayRate, and Badge.

You can define the Badge column in both tables. This way, you can subsequently retrieve column values from both tables in a single query. You combine columns from multiple tables by using statements that call out the columns you need and specify (in the Where clause) the information that is common to both tables. You read more about the syntax of this operation later in this book. For now, it's important to understand only that this pulling together of information based on common values is known as a *join*.

▶ **See** Chapter 7, "Retrieving Data with Transact-SQL," for more information on using Where clauses, **p. 175**.

The example in the Employees and Pays tables uses the relational capabilities of SQL Server to retrieve information from each table by using the corresponding badge numbers. Following is an example SELECT statement:

```
SELECT * from Employees, Pays where Employees.Badge = Pays.Badge
```

Not surprisingly, if you modify or delete a badge number in the Employees table, you must update the corresponding badge number in the Pays table. The process of ensuring that corresponding values of related tables are maintained to keep table relationships intact is called *referential integrity*. This process can even include deleting related information in other tables. For example, if you remove a master record, as would be the case if the Employees record were deleted and it referred to records in the Pays table.

Maintaining referential integrity is easiest if table rows are unique. This practice ensures that a second table will have only a single row. Make sure that you maintain the badge number if it is modified or deleted in the first table. If you don't, you'll end up with *orphaned records*, those with a detail record but no master record.

In the relational database model, the column, or set of columns, that uniquely defines the rows of a table is referred to as a *key*.

N O T E A key that uniquely defines the rows of a table is called a *primary key*. If you add a column that is a primary key in one table to a second table, the column added to the second table is called the *foreign key*.

The column is a foreign key because the new columns referencing the first table are used only to allow the matching of corresponding rows between the tables. For more information, see Chapter 11, "Managing and Using Indexes and Keys." ▪

In earlier database systems, internal pointers were created and maintained within the database to link the corresponding rows stored in the tables. The pointer mechanism created a problem however, because of the maintenance issues associated with keeping the pointers accurate.

N O T E Older hierarchical and network databases don't use terms such as *table* and *row*. Hierarchical and network databases use their own terminology to describe data. The equivalent of a row in a relational database is a *record*, and the equivalent of a column in a relational database is a *data item* or *field*. ▪

If you neglected to identify data that must be combined later, during retrieval, you couldn't do it after the database structure was created; you had to re-create the logical and physical structure of the database. The main problem involved with using hierarchical and network databases was that changes in data-retrieval combinations were impossible to make without redesigning the database.

In relational databases such as SQL Server, you can add a new column to a table at any time. This capability allows you to create relationships with other tables. Unlike typical hierarchical or network databases, a relational database doesn't need to be redefined if you add a new column to a table; only a single table must be redefined. You don't need to unload the rows of the table and later reload the table to add a new column; you can use SQL's ALTER TABLE statement to make modifications in existing tables.

▶ **See** Chapter 8, "Adding, Changing, and Deleting Information in Tables," for more information about the ALTER TABLE statement, **p. 225**.

Exploring Client/Server Features of SQL Server

Client/server computing is a type of distributed model for data storage, access, and processing. In a distributed processing system, multiple computers collectively perform a set of operations. A client/server system uses at least two computers, one of which nearly always is a personal computer.

N O T E Distributed processing was introduced in minicomputer systems to provide the capabilities of large mainframe computers. By working together, several minicomputers could match the data storage, access, and processing capabilities of a mainframe computer in some operations. ■

Each system in a client/server model performs one or more of the data storage, access, or processing operations. Client/server computing can't be done with a system that uses terminals or PCs running terminal emulators that are connected to another computer. In this arrangement, the terminal or the PC that's used as a terminal is simply too passive; it only sends and displays sets of characters.

When PCs and servers are connected, the overall processing should be divided between the server, mainframe, or minicomputer system and the client system. The client and the server each process work within its own capabilities—a form of teamwork that contributes to the efficiency and speed of the overall operation.

Client/server, as the name implies, also involves an unequal division of processing. The inequality results from the processing disparity between the server and the client. The larger and faster server computer transfers data faster, stores greater quantities of data, and typically performs more extensive processing than the client system.

N O T E Client/server computing is quickly becoming the backbone of the Internet, for good reason. Client/server optimizes the processing on the side of the transaction that makes the most sense, whether it be displaying information to the end user or sorting through information that should be returned for display.

By using client/server technology on the Internet, many mainstream applications are coming online. At the same time, these applications are not causing the same level of bandwidth use that you would see in a completely client-side application environment because smaller amounts of data are transferred between the systems using the applications.

You can find out more about this application of the client/server approach on the Internet in Chapter 23, "Understanding SQL Server and the Internet." ■

Smaller PC systems are used as clients in client/server systems because the PCs perform proportionally less of the overall work, relying primarily on the server for heavy-duty data manipulation. Also, the PC's keyboard and monitor allow it to work as an input device, by generating commands and data, and as an output device by displaying data to the user.

N O T E   A client and a server also are defined by the direction of the data flow and operational responsibilities. A large, powerful PC system can function as a server if it receives commands and data from one or more PC systems, processes the data, and returns information to other PC systems. The server is the computer system that receives requests for processing or information from other computer systems.

You can use large, powerful PCs as servers with less powerful PCs as clients and still qualify as using client/server technology. In this environment, the servers usually are more powerful models, a fact that helps them process requests from many clients. ■

Microsoft SQL Server is a perfect example of a client/server system. The SQL Server database must be installed on the Windows NT platform. The Windows NT operating system provides an extremely broad range of processor systems that you can use as your server. Windows NT is supported on I86-processor-based systems, PPC, MIPS, and Alpha AXP RISC-processor-based systems.

SQL Server provides the server software that's installed on the server system and some client software that's installed on the client PC systems. Windows GUI application tools allow you to create, maintain, and access the database and all objects from the client.

The network software components required for the interconnection of clients and the server computer are built into the Windows NT system. Windows NT also provides a choice of network protocols for communication between the client and server systems. A client can run Windows 95, which also contains built-in network software for connection with the Windows NT server system. The Windows 95 client and Windows NT server systems support a wide range of network cards.

In a client/server system in which the server application is a database such as SQL Server, the server is responsible for creating and maintaining database objects such as the table and indexes. The server maintains referential integrity and security, and ensures that operations can be recovered in the event of numerous types of failures.

The client application performs all user interaction, including displaying information and allowing manipulation of the application with the graphical user interface. After rows of data are retrieved from the server, the application can create copies to be held locally, and the data can be manipulated. You also can control the type of access to the information. Read-only access often is an excellent option, insulating users from the master copies of the information that they work with on the server.

If you work with local copies of the information, you can work with the information locally without communicating with the server. After you complete your work, you can send changes back to the server or (if you used the information only for review) simply discard the working databases. You can manipulate the data directly in the SQL Server database from the client, of course, if necessary and if your application allows. You must be sure to update the server with all changes so that other users can access the most recent data in the database.

You also can access SQL Server directly from the server. Direct server access is convenient, especially for administrative operations, but it isn't a client/server approach, because the operations occur locally rather than across the network. Microsoft SQL Server comes with 32-bit versions of the SQL Windows application tools for the Windows NT server that are normally used on the clients.

Although you can have client applications validate new or updated data, the validation should optimally be done at the server. A column such as Badge, for example, can be checked to ensure that each new or updated badge number is unique and falls within a specified range. It's safer for the data to be validated at the server as a part of a SQL Server-defined mechanism. If the validation is defined at the server, it is always in force, whether or not the connected client performs a validation.

N O T E   A big benefit of using server-side validation is that it protects the database from access by applications that may access the database in nonstandard manners. These include applications such as Excel, Access, and Word, which can connect to the database by using ODBC. In each case, rules and integrity checks that you implement on the server are still enforced, even though the client application may be unknown. ■

If you rely on client applications to validate data before the data is sent to the server, you must ensure that all the client applications do it consistently. You also must ensure that changes aren't made directly at the server, where no validation mechanism has been defined.

A simple, reliable solution is to implement server-side validation, especially given the current industry-wide push to standardize interfaces and to allow third-party applications to access company information systems for additional analysis.

 T I P   You also can perform validation in client applications. Client validation can be specific to the client application and should include those checks that aren't enforced by server validation mechanisms. When the updates are sent to the server, it still enforces its own validation.

Examining SQL Server Features and Components

The core components of SQL Server are the relational database and its structure. SQL Server is a powerful, comprehensive database environment. This section points out certain parameters for using SQL Server.

SQL Server allows you to define up to 32,767 databases. If you realize that a database is a centralized repository for the storage of information, being overly constrained by the 32,767-database limit is difficult; you're not likely to encounter any situation in which you need to define more than this very liberal limit. If you do, consider adding servers to your network to help balance the load. In a typical production installation, fewer than five application-oriented databases (and often, only one) are in service on any given server.

You can define up to two billion tables within each of your 32,767 databases. You're not likely to need anywhere near two billion tables in a database, however. With most typical systems, you have no more than several hundred tables in a database.

You can define up to 250 columns for each table. In Chapter 4, when you learn about database design, you see that when you normalize your database tables, you largely overcome this limitation. SQL Server allows you to combine columns from as many as 16 tables in a single query.

The number of rows in a table is effectively unlimited for SQL Server. You're limited in practice by the capacity of the storage medium on which tables are stored; databases and their tables can be stored across multiple physical disks. SQL Server allows databases to expand to include up to 32 physical disks.

N O T E The 32-disk limit is imposed indirectly through subordinate logical structures. You store SQL Server databases, transaction logs, indexes, and tables in logical structures called *segments.* You can expand a database by adding segments that are created on devices. A database can include up to 32 segments. See Chapter 5, "Creating Devices, Databases, and Transaction Logs," for information about creating databases and segments. ▪

For each table, you can define up to 250 indexes, only one of which can be defined as a clustered index. An *index* is a structure that allows table rows to be retrieved quickly. In a *clustered index*, the table rows are sorted and maintained in storage in a physically ordered state—that is, rows that are sorted before and after one another are stored in that sorted order. An index is often defined for the columns that are referenced in retrieval statements. You should find that 250 indexes provide fast retrieval of table rows.

Indexes require additional storage space in the database for the index structure that must be created and stored. One performance recommendation is to define only as many indexes as you need because of the space that indexes take up. You need to define enough indexes to allow for the rapid retrieval of rows, however. You should define the minimum number of indexes that you require. Needing more than 250 for a single table would be unusual.

Devices and Databases

You store databases and all the objects within them in disk files. SQL Server calls your database files *devices*, but they're logical units rather than physical devices. You create a database in the logical devices. Remember that you can create up to 32,767 databases.

Each database is created with a set of system tables in which SQL Server records data about the database objects, such as tables or indexes that you subsequently create. Like a relational-database product, SQL Server keeps the control information about your database objects in a relational database, which is the set of system tables.

Transact-SQL

Structured Query Language (SQL), the query language developed by IBM in the 1970s, has become the de facto standard database query language for relational databases. The dialect of SQL that you use with SQL Server is Transact-SQL, which Microsoft implements as a core component of SQL Server.

Transact-SQL adds to the original SQL keywords for the formation of data retrieval, storage, and manipulation statements. When SQL Server's implementation of SQL was put into place, Microsoft, like other database vendors, added features and extensions to the language.

Compared with other vendors' SQL dialects, Transact-SQL has less unique syntax. Arguably, the SQL dialect SQL-PLUS, used with the relational database Oracle, has the most vendor-specific, additional unique syntax. Although the large set of unique syntax in some SQL dialects is useful, the use of dialect-specific syntax makes stored sets of SQL commands nonportable and can cause you many headaches when you move your systems between RDBMS systems.

N O T E   Remember that some SQL dialect is used with all relational databases. If you work with more than one relational database, or if you must convert from one to another, using the SQL syntax that's the most generic is easiest. Stored sets of SQL statements, if they use generic syntax, can be easily converted or used across relational databases. ■

Transact-SQL is best characterized as lean and mean. You have just enough enhancements to basic SQL to write functional queries. Transact-SQL contains statements that create logical storage units (the devices), as well as the databases that reside on the devices. You can also use Transact-SQL statements to create the objects, such as tables, that are stored within the databases.

Not surprisingly, you can use Transact-SQL statements to add and manipulate data and other database objects. Four keywords are used to form statements that perform all basic data storage, retrieval, and manipulation:

- Use INSERT to add new rows to a database table.
- Use DELETE to delete rows from a table.
- Use UPDATE to change the rows of a table.
- Use SELECT to form various statements for retrieving data from one table or multiple tables.

The INSERT, DELETE, UPDATE, and SELECT statements, as well as other statements, use a generic form of SQL for data manipulation. The extensions to Transact-SQL principally provide flow control to direct the execution order of statements. Use flow-control statements in organized sets of SQL statements that are stored as objects within your database.

Stored sets of Transact-SQL statements contained in the SQL Server database are called *stored procedures*, which are compiled so that they execute SQL statements rapidly. You can use stored procedures in addition to programs for database access and manipulation because the procedures can use variables and parameters, return errors and status, and use flow control to control the execution order of SQL statements.

▶ **See** Chapter 14, "Managing Stored Procedures and Using Flow-Control Statements," for more information on stored procedures, **p. 403**.

A *trigger* is a special type of stored procedure used to maintain referential integrity in a SQL Server database. You can create insert, delete, and update triggers to control addition, deletion, or updates in corresponding rows of related tables for which the trigger is defined. Triggers are an excellent way to maintain referential integrity, because they give you complete control of the operations that they perform and because they're server-based.

You also use several additional objects including rules, defaults, and constraints to help control or to apply values to table columns automatically.

You use a *default* to supply a value to a column of a database table when the insertion of a new row doesn't specify a value for the column. A *rule* constrains the values that can be entered in the column of a table. A *constraint* defines a characteristic of a table column, such as requiring unique values.

Two Windows NT processes are part of the SQL Server set of components. You issue Transact-SQL statements that are conveyed to and performed by the two server processes. You can use a tool such as the Performance Monitor to display the characteristics of the SQL Server processes.

Figure 1.2 shows the working set for the SQL Server processes SQLSERVR and SQLEXEC. (The *working set* of a process is the percentage of processor time that's directly allocated to a process.)

FIG. 1.2
The Performance Monitor displays the characteristics of the SQL Server processes and helps you watch for out-of-the-ordinary system-level occurrences.

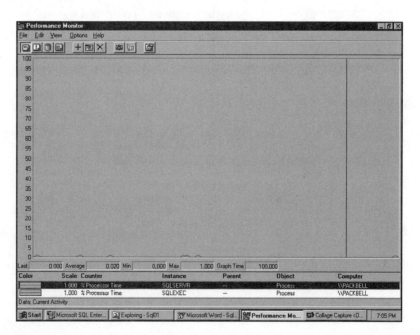

The SQLSERVR process is divided into multiple threads for execution. *Threads* are the separate units of execution on a Windows NT system. The division of one of the two SQL Server processes into multiple threads allows multiple execution in a multiprocessor environment such as Windows NT. If your server has more than one processor, different operations on the SQL Server databases can be executed simultaneously.

 TIP You can buy a wide range of computer systems with multiple processors and increased memory to enhance the Windows NT version of SQL Server and to increase the speed of transactions.

You can use Windows NT's Performance Monitor not only to monitor the performance of SQL components, but also to learn about the function of components. You can perform different Transact-SQL statements and use the Performance Monitor to determine which component is activated to perform the operation.

Command-Line Applications

You can issue SQL statements through the Interactive Structured Query Language (*ISQL*) utility. *ISQL/w* is the Windows tool that allows you to use Transact-SQL with SQL Server from a graphical interface (for more information, see "ISQL/w" later in this chapter). If you become familiar enough with Transact-SQL syntax, or if you prefer working at the DOS command line, you can perform all operations on your databases through ISQL command lines.

From a command-line session, you invoke ISQL with the command isql. You can use several parameters in the ISQL command line. You can enter the user name and password after ISQL to take you directly to an ISQL command session, for example.

The following example shows the initiation of a command session:

```
isql /Usa /P<password> /S<server>
1>
```

The command prompt is successively numbered until the execution (GO) command is entered.

You can use the -? or /? switch to display the syntax for the ISQL command, as shown in the following example:

```
usage: isql [-U login id] [-e echo input]
       [-p print statistics] [-n remove numbering]
       [-c cmdend] [-h headers] [-w columnwidth] [-s colseparator]
       [-m errorlevel] [-t query timeout] [-l login timeout]
       [-L list servers] [-a packetsize]
       [-H hostname] [-P password]
       [-q "cmdline query"] [-Q "cmdline query" and exit]
       [-S server] [-d use database name]
       [-r msgs to stderr] [-E trusted connection]
       [-i inputfile] [-o outputfile]
        [-b On error batch abort]
        [-O use Old ISQL behavior disables the following]
             <EOF> batch processing
             Auto console width scaling
             Wide messages
```

```
        default errorlevel is -1 vs 1
   [-? show syntax summary (this screen)]
```

N O T E ISQL command-line parameters are case-sensitive. Be sure to observe the uppercase and lowercase indications provided by the help from ISQL, also detailed in Table 1.1. ■

Table 1.1 summarizes the functions of the parameters. Each parameter (also called a *switch* in the Microsoft SQL Server documentation) is preceded by a forward slash (/) or a hyphen (-). The command isql /? displays the hyphens (-), although the hyphen or forward slash can be used. The use of the hyphen in command-line ISQL is inherited from the Sybase version of SQL Server.

Table 1.1 ISQL Command-Line Parameters

Parameter	Function
a *packet_size*	Indicates packet size for data transfer 512 through 65535; NT default is 8192
b	On error batch abort
c *cmdend*	Specifies the command terminator; default is GO
d *dbname*	Issues a USE dbname command on entry into ISQL
E	Uses trusted connection
e	Echoes input
H *wksta_name*	Specifies the workstation name
h *headers*	Provides the number of rows to print between column headings
i *inputfile*	Specifies an input batch file for execution
L	Lists the local and remote servers
l *timeout*	Sets the login timeout
m *errorlevel*	Sets error-level displays to this level or higher
n	Omits prompt line numbers
O	Uses old behavior
o *outputfile*	Specifies file to which statement output is directed
P *password*	Specifies password; prompted for if not specified
p	Displays performance statistics
Q *"query"*	Executes an .SQL batch file and exits the ISQL session
q *"query"*	Executes an .SQL batch file
r [0¦1]	Controls redirection of error-level messages

continues

Table 1.1 Continued

Parameter	Function
S *servername*	Specifies the server name; default is local
s *colseparator*	Sets column separator; default is blank
t *timeout*	Sets the command timeout in seconds; default is no timeout
U *login_id*	Provides the case-sensitive SQL Server user account name
w *columnwidth*	Sets column width; default is 80
?	Shows syntax

Table 1.2 lists the set of commands used after you enter ISQL. You must use these commands at the beginning of a command line, which is a 1> prompt.

Table 1.2 ISQL Commands

Command	Purpose
GO	Default command terminator; executes a statement
RESET	Clears statements before execution
ED	Invokes the default system editor
!! *command*	Executes a Windows NT command
QUIT or EXIT()	Exits ISQL
Ctrl+C	Terminates a query without exiting ISQL
SHUTDOWN	Stops the SQL Server and exits ISQL

 TIP You can use the command-line recall feature of Windows NT—the ↑ key—to recall commands that you have entered within ISQL. Your ISQL commands are limited to 1,000 characters per line.

Applications

Four GUI applications are available for accessing and managing SQL Server installations:

■ The first application allows you to enter Transact-SQL statements.

■ The SQL Client Configuration Utility allows you to define the set of database and network library routines for database operations performed from a client system.

■ SQL Server Books Online provides a complete set of SQL Server manuals organized for retrieval through the Books Online browser.

- The final major tool is the Enterprise Manager. You're likely to spend a fair amount of time with this utility, which provides access to the core administrative functions of SQL Server.

Each of these is covered in the next sections.

ISQL/w   A Windows version of ISQL called ISQL/w issues Transact-SQL statements. You enter Transact-SQL commands in a separate query window inside the ISQL/w main window. You can cut, copy, paste, print, save, and edit previous queries more easily in ISQL/w than you can through an ISQL command line.

After you start the ISQL/w application from the SQL Server 6.5 program group, you sign in to SQL Server by indicating your user name, your password (if necessary), and the server that you want to use. SQL Server maintains its own list of users who can connect to a server from a client system by using a valid login ID and user name.

▶ **See** Chapter 20, "SQL Server Security," for more information on implementing and managing SQL Server security, **p. 575**.

Figure 1.3 shows a SELECTSELECT statement used to retrieve all rows from the system table SysDatabases, which contains a list of all defined databases. The tabular list of columns of information kept for the databases is displayed in the Results window.

FIG. 1.3
SQL statements are entered in the Query page of ISQL/w. Press Ctrl+E to execute the statements.

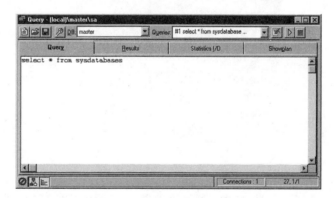

 If you have several statements in the Query page, you can select the statements that you want to execute and then press Ctrl+E to execute them. Only the selected statements are submitted to SQL Server.

Your query output is displayed in a separate Results window, which you can reach by clicking the Results tab. In addition, when you submit a query, ISQL/w automatically switches the current view to the Results tab. The Results tab shows information such as the rows returned by query and error messages. You can use the scroll bars to view the entire query output. Figure 1.4 shows the tables that are created automatically when SQL Server is installed.

The SQL Client Configuration Utility   The SQL Client Configuration Utility defines the Net-Library and DB-Library used for communication between the client and server. Figure 1.5

shows the SQL Server Client Configuration Utility dialog box. Click Locate to check for multiple copies of client libraries on your client or server system. You must consult the documentation of your client product to confirm that the correct version of the DB-Library is selected.

FIG. 1.4
You can use ISQL/w from both the client and server systems to submit configuration commands, as well as query statements.

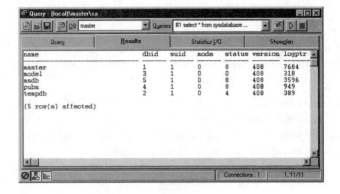

FIG. 1.5
Establish the client configuration in the appropriate tab of the setup dialog box.

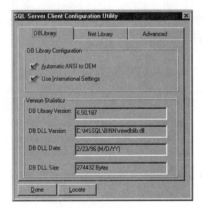

N O T E You should use the latest version of the network and database libraries on your system. If you have a mixed-version environment, consider upgrading all servers to the most recent server software or attempting to use previous-version drivers with the newer servers. Although this method works in most cases, you may experience some problems in using new features. ■

Net-Library is set to Named Pipes when you install the SQL Server client application tools on a client system. *Named pipes* is the default communication mechanism used for communication between the client application and the SQL Server system. You can choose a different network library to use an alternative communication mechanism from named pipes. As Figure 1.6 shows, you can choose alternative mechanisms for the TCP/IP, IPX/SPX, and Banyan VINES transport protocols.

N O T E The SQL Client Configuration Utility is helpful because a client may need to connect to more than one server. If you install all the necessary protocols, the client workstation can access the routines located in network and database libraries. ■

FIG. 1.6
You can choose among the most popular network protocols when you set up the software.

SQL Server Books Online   The SQL Server Books Online help facility contains the contents of 13 books and a glossary on SQL Server (see Figure 1.7). Like ISQL/w and the SQL Client Configuration Utility, the SQL Server Books Online application can be installed automatically on a client or server system. You'll find it extremely convenient to have quick access to such extensive documentation without leaving your computer system. These books include the entire text of the SQL server documentation provided by Microsoft.

FIG. 1.7
You can print or copy pages or complete sections of the Books Online information.

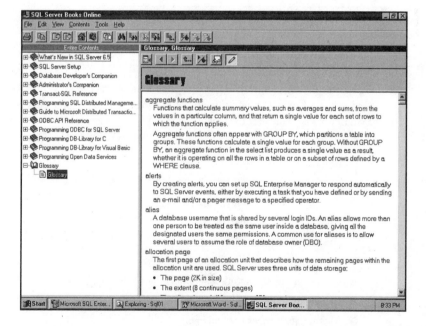

SQL Service Manager   The SQL Server Manager is one of the only utilities likely to be most valuable to you when physically working on the server. The SQL Service Manager application starts, stops, or pauses the SQL Server processes. You must start SQL Server before you can perform any operations with the databases. The SQL Service Manager is the easiest way to start either a local or remote server. Figure 1.8 shows the SQL Service Manager dialog box after the MSSQLServer service is started.

FIG. 1.8
If you pause the MSSQLServer service, no additional client or server connections are permitted.

Status also shown here

N O T E   Services in Windows NT, such as the MSSQLServer and SQLExecutive of SQL Server, are system processes that run in the background within NT. These background processes are used by SQL Server and client systems that require their functions. ■

The traffic-light metaphor simplifies starting, stopping, and pausing SQL Server. Double-click Stop or the red-light symbol to stop SQL Server. Double-click Pause or the yellow-light symbol to pause SQL Server if the server has been started.

 T I P   You can minimize the SQL Service Manager and still observe the traffic lights to determine whether server service is stopped, as with a red light, or started, with a green light.

The icon that represents the Service Manager displays the appropriate traffic light.

SQL Enterprise Manager   SQL Enterprise Manager is the server application that you use to perform nearly all administrative operations with local or remote servers. You can even use SQL Enterprise Manager to start and stop both SQL Server services mentioned earlier, rather than use the SQL Service Manager. You also use SQL Enterprise Manager to do the following:

- Manage user-account and server logins
- Back up and restore databases and transaction logs
- Start, stop, and configure servers
- Check database consistency
- Display server statistics
- Set up and manage database replication
- Create and manage database objects and tasks
- Create and control user accounts and groups
- Manage the access-control lists

You also may find it convenient to perform queries by using Transact-SQL commands from within SQL Enterprise Manager. Click the SQL Query Tool toolbar button in SQL Enterprise Manager's main window to display a window in which you can issue ISQL statements, as shown in Figure 1.9. Unlike ISQL/w, you won't have to connect and log in, because you connected when you started SQL Enterprise Manager.

FIG. 1.9
In this window, you can issue ISQL statements directly by clicking the Query Analyzer button.

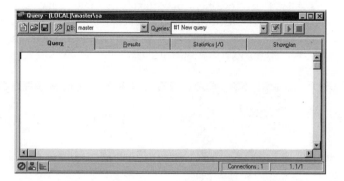

Although you can perform all the administrative operations for SQL Server through ISQL, SQL Enterprise Manager allows you to perform the operations by using pull-down menus and dialog boxes rather than a command line. In Figure 1.10, the grouping of server objects in folders has been expanded to display several types of server entities.

FIG. 1.10
Server objects are displayed in hierarchical fashion in the Server Manager window.

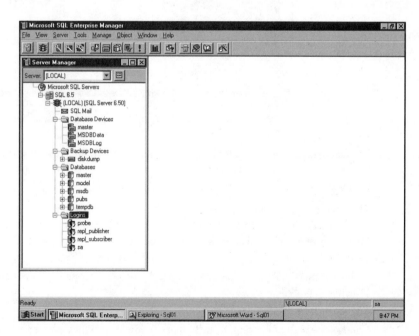

SQL Performance Monitor   The SQL Performance Monitor is a standard administrative application of the Windows NT operating system. SQL Server was written to allow SQL Server objects and counters to be displayed in the Performance Monitor with Windows NT object counters. For convenience, an additional icon has a predefined set of objects and counters that you can use to monitor SQL Server.

Figure 1.11 shows a chart of several important SQL counters that you can use to monitor the performance of SQL Server on your system. The integration of the SQL Server objects, counters—like those shown for the cache hit ratio—and user connections enables you to select and display SQL Server statistics with NT objects and counters.

FIG. 1.11
The Performance Monitor is used to display statistics on the performance of both the system and SQL Server.

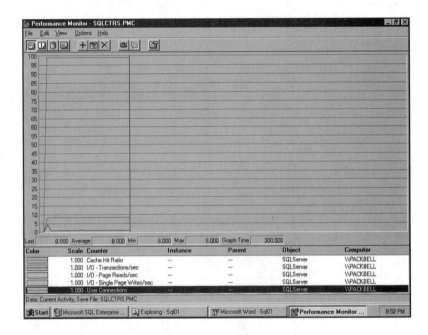

You can dynamically switch to display the counter information as a vertical-bar graph rather than a chart. You can also record object counters in a log for later display, or you can display the information as a tabular report.

The Performance Monitor also allows you to set threshold values for SQL Server counter values. When the threshold value is reached, an alert is displayed within an Alert view of the Performance Monitor. Also, an alert message can be sent to you even if you're working on a client workstation.

▶ **See** Chapter 21, "Optimizing Performance," for more information on performance-monitoring techniques, **p. 593**.

SQL Security Manager The SQL Security Manager administers SQL Server accounts. Choose one of the following security types to implement on your system during the installation of SQL Server:

■ **Standard security.** Standard security requires you to log in to SQL Server by using a user name and ID.

■ **Integrated security.** Integrated security requires you to log in only to Windows NT; you don't need to log in a second time when you access SQL Server. You'll still be prompted to sign in, but your user name in SQL Server is taken from your network login ID.

■ **Mixed security.** Mixed security allows you to log in to SQL Server or to use the integrated login of Windows NT. Integrated logins can be used only with connections to the server from clients using named pipes.

Figure 1.12 shows the SQL Security Manager dialog box. The Security Mode is standard for the Windows NT domain PACKBELL. Login access through named pipes has been granted to users who are members of the SQL Server group Administrators.

FIG. 1.12
Integrated security provides the simplest account management in SQL Server, but it also requires the most comprehensive user-setup.

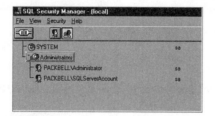

The SQL Security Manager graphically maps Windows NT groups and users to SQL Server accounts and passwords. You can also use the SQL Security Manager to find SQL Server access permissions for mapped accounts.

Distributed Transaction Coordinator   The Distributed Transaction Coordinator (DTC) can break up transactions across servers, allowing you to implement truly distributed applications and database integration. Although transactions are a standard part of a SQL server-based application, using transactions across more than one physical server has traditionally been a problem.

With the Distributed Transaction Coordinator, or DTC you can control these types of transactions, and you have the tools to diagnose performance and bottleneck situations that arise. In addition, you can roll-back failed transactions that include different servers.

▶ **See** Chapter 18, "Using the Distributed Transaction Coordinator," to find out more about the Distributed Transaction Coordinator, **p. 533**.

Other Utilities   Many other utilities are helpful with your SQL Server installation. With Microsoft's Office products, for example, you can use the Microsoft Query (MSQUERY) application to execute queries against tables managed by SQL Server.

This utility is much like the query function in Microsoft Access, allowing you to build and see the results of your SQL statements. MSQUERY also is a key tool for learning to use the SQL language. You can visually build the query that produces the result you need and then have the application show you the SQL statements that are used to create that result.

Microsoft Excel, Microsoft Access, and Visual Basic also work closely with Microsoft SQL Server, as do other third-party languages. Borland's Delphi development environment provides close-knit connectivity with SQL Server. You can use each of these products as a foundation for developing client/server applications for your users.

▶ **See** Chapter 26 for more information on upsizing your application from Access to SQL Server, **p. 709**.

▶ **See** Chapter 25 for information on using other applications to access SQL Server, including different development environments, **p. 693**.

From Here...

Now that you know how to implement SQL Server in your organization, you're ready to begin working with the topics that really make SQL Server work for you. (Be sure to review Chapter 3, "Installing and Setting Up the Server and Client Software," so that you understand what will be installed and where it will be located on your system.)

For more information about selected topics, see the following chapters:

- Chapter 11, "Managing and Using Indexes and Keys," shows you how to create and use keys and indexes.

- Chapter 13, "Managing and Using Rules, Constraints, and Defaults," shows you how to create and use rules and defaults.

- Chapter 15, "Creating and Managing Triggers," shows you how to create and use triggers to maintain referential integrity in the database.

- Chapter 24, "Creating and Using Cursors," shows you how to use cursors in a programming language to manipulate rows of a database table one at a time.

CHAPTER 2

Understanding the Underlying Operating System, Windows NT

Windows NT, the operating system that SQL Server runs under, has several mechanisms that you should understand to use SQL Server more effectively. *Operating-system components* or *processes* are sections of computer code that control how the computer's hardware and other software is used.

Some NT components, for example, control how applications use one or more central processors. The MSSQLServer and MSQLExecutive processes of SQL Server use Windows NT processes to service client systems.

Windows NT is also responsible for managing the security of the network and its associated resources. You create system users for the server and can control their access to resources, including SQL Server, on that system.

Although reviewing the entire Windows NT security model is beyond the scope of this book, having a comprehensive understanding of how your network is set up is important. This understanding includes how users are defined and whether you plan to use the same security model in your SQL Server implementation.

Understand the Windows NT features multiprocessors and multithreading

By taking advantage of multiprocessor and multithreading environments, Windows NT offers significant performance improvements over environments that don't have these capabilities.

Understand and use the built-in networking components

Windows NT supports the interconnection of client systems to the SQL Server database.

Use the reporting facilities of Windows NT

Windows NT contains built-in monitoring and reporting tools that you can use to monitor SQL Server.

In addition to Windows NT processes that control the use of resources such as the CPUs, several system applications control aspects of the operating system affect SQL Server. You can monitor the use of Windows NT and SQL Server processes through the Performance Monitor and change usage based on the statistics collected. Through the Event Viewer, you can display errors and other events returned as the result of SQL Server's activity and use the returned information to interpret and correct those errors.

It's also helpful to understand the configurations of interconnections among the Windows NT servers that SQL Server is on. The interconnection of server and client is accomplished primarily through network software, which you use to communicate between client and server or between server and server.

In the NT domain section later in this chapter, you see how you work with users on your system, how you set up new users, and how you assign rights. ■

▶ **See** Chapter 20, "SQL Server Security," for information about how to establish SQL Server security, **p. 575**.

Understanding Multiprocessing, Multitasking, and Multithreading

Many times, the differences among the terms *multiprocessing*, *multitasking*, and *multithreading* are confusing. These processes are important in your use of SQL Server, however, because they affect the performance and scalability of the system.

Multitasking and *multiprocessing* are two mechanisms of an operating system (such as Windows NT) that are used to share one or more central processors of the computer system. Earlier operating systems permitted only one application at a time to use a computer's resources. Before long, operating-system designers realized that the core resources of a computer system, such as the CPU, could be shared by multiple applications.

In its simplest form, multiprocessing occurs when an operating system switches the use of a computer system's CPU among multiple applications. The operating system must keep track of where each program leaves off so that the program can start again at that spot when the program receives use of the central processor again. This is *round-robin scheduling*. Round-robin scheduling permits each process to use a CPU for a given period, rather than allowing one process to use a CPU exclusively.

Each application must receive use of a CPU long enough to get a reasonable amount of work done. Also, the switching of the CPU must be accomplished quickly. If an operating system gives each application enough time to use a CPU, and if the switch among applications is performed quickly enough, a user who is interacting with one application may work as though the CPU were dedicated to his exclusive use. This performance can be influenced by having too many applications waiting to use the CPU(s).

N O T E The interval of time during which Windows NT exchanges use of the central processor is several hundred milliseconds. Windows NT maintains an elaborate technique to determine what program receives the use of the central processor next. Programs are assigned a priority from 0 to 31. NT grants use of the central processor to the program that has the highest priority—the one that has been waiting the longest to use the central processor—and works down the list of priorities in order. ▪

Operating systems such as Windows NT perform a more sophisticated sharing of the use of a central processor than the simple round-robin approach. A program on Windows NT can be written in several functional sections, each of which can receive use of a central processor independently. One definition of the term *multitasking* refers to the sharing of the use of a central processor by multiple sections of a program simultaneously.

A complete application program that can use the resources of a system is called a *process* in the Windows NT system. Each program section that can receive use of a Windows NT central processor is called a *thread*. One key attribute of a thread is that it must have its own priority for Windows NT to schedule use of system resources separately for each thread. In Windows NT, the term *multitasking* also refers to the use of the central processor of an NT system by multiple threads of the same process or different processes.

N O T E The two types of multiprocessing capabilities are symmetric and asymmetric. Windows NT uses s*ymmetric multiprocessing*, which is the most commonly implemented. Symmetric multiprocessing spreads the processes for both the operating system and applications among all available system CPUs. *Asymmetric multiprocessing* allows the operating system to be placed on a single CPU and applications to be spread among others. ▪

A feature such as multitasking with multiple threads is most advantageous when more than one processor is available to be shared. An application that's written in several threads can have each thread execute simultaneously on Windows NT. This is referred to as a *multiprocessor environment*.

You can use a powerful single-processor system for SQL Server, such as a Digital Alpha AXP, MIPS R4000, PowerPC, or Intel Pentium Pro system. Windows NT can use multiple-CPU systems because of its symmetric multiprocessing capability. Symmetric multiprocessing allows several threads to execute simultaneously, regardless of whether they're running application or operating-system code.

N O T E Multiple-CPU systems are particularly advantageous for use as servers for a SQL Server database, because I/O requests from client systems can be handled while other operations, such as account validation, are performed by a second processor of the system. Multiple-server requests can be handled at one time, greatly increasing the number of workstation clients that can be served by the server. ▪

Part

I

Ch

2

Understanding Multi-Architecture

An important characteristic of Windows NT is its multi-architecture feature. The term *architecture* refers to different hardware components that can be used on a computer system, especially central processors. Windows NT runs on computer systems that use different microprocessors for their central processing units.

Windows NT can run on systems that use Intel 386, 486, or Pentium processors, as well as on x86 clones produced by such vendors as Cyrix and AMD. Windows NT also runs on Digital's Alpha AXP, MIPS R4000 series processors, and the PowerPC. The Windows NT distribution CD-ROM contains the separate versions of the installation software for all four systems; more compatible systems are planned.

As you can see, a key advantage of using SQL Server with Windows NT as the operating-system platform is that you have many choices of computer systems to use as a server for a SQL Server database. Windows NT and SQL Server are scalable from a desktop PC to a large Alpha AXP or MIPS system. They even scale to systems with one or more processors that have enough power to replace a minicomputer or even a large mainframe system.

Understanding the Multiple-User Environment of SQL Server on Windows NT

Traditional mainframe and minicomputer system databases are accessed by users sitting in front of input/output devices. Windows NT is unlike minicomputer and mainframe systems, in that users don't use dumb terminals as input or output devices. Instead, each user gains access to an NT system running SQL Server by using a computer system that has its own operating system. As discussed in Chapter 1, this system is referred to as the *client system*. The multiple users of a Windows NT server access an application such as SQL Server from their own client computer system.

> **N O T E** *Dumb terminals* got their nickname because they simply transfer characters to and from the CPU, using the CPU to perform the work with the information. Dumb terminals, unlike PCs and other workstations, can't do any processing. Dumb terminals replaced the card readers and printers that were used as input and output devices in early computer systems. A dumb terminal combines separate input and output devices in a simple device for input and output. ■

Each user typically runs Windows for Workgroups, Windows 95, DOS, OS/2, or Windows NT Workstation on a client workstation system. Each operating system allows a user to run applications independently of a central server system. A user at a workstation uses connectivity software (usually, the network operating system) to establish a connection to a central server computer running Windows NT Server.

Understanding the Windows NT Network Components

Windows NT enables you to establish networks and to connect to other computer systems. The connectivity feature of Windows NT serves several purposes:

- You can make a network connection for the purpose of sharing the resources of different systems.
- You can create the connection to access information on a remote disk of another Windows NT or a non-Windows NT system.
- You may need to transfer data between two systems. When you access the SQL Server database on the server system from a client system, you're wholly dependent on the communication connections that are established by the NT system.
- You can perform administrative operations through network connections to Windows NT. You use commands to learn the connection status of systems, monitor the flow of control and user data between connections, and alter the characteristics that affect the connections.
- You can change the size of network and disk buffers—the space in RAM used to temporarily store the data coming from one system and received by a second system.

You can use the connectivity components of Windows NT to connect an application on a client workstation to the SQL Server database on the NT server. All the specified uses of client/server connectivity, such as remote administration, monitoring, and data transfer, are necessary in a system using SQL Server.

▶ **See** Chapter 19, "SQL Server Administration," for more information on administration of SQL Server, **p. 547**.

▶ **See** Chapter 21, "Optimizing Performance," for a more detailed discussion of Using NT performance monitoring, **p. 593**.

Sharing Resources

Windows NT networks are set up as domains, each of which can have several workgroups.

A *domain* is one form of a Windows NT network. Before a computer can be added to a domain, an account must be set up. The administrator controls rights for this account.

Workgroups are logical groupings of systems in a network, arranged by department, task, or some other method. Users are placed in workgroups to make locating and using shared resources easier.

Both methods of sharing resources could work for sharing a SQL Server resource. Workgroups are geared toward users and, therefore, don't offer sophisticated or versatile security measures. Windows NT offers excellent built-in security through its use of domains for implementation and administration. SQL Server can take full advantage of this security.

▶ **See** Chapter 20, "SQL Server Security," for more information on how SQL Server uses the built-in security of Windows NT, **p. 575**.

Part

I

Ch

2

Installing Network Software

You add network protocols to allow access to and from different network types through the Network Properties dialog box (see Figure 2.1). To access this dialog box, choose Settings, Control Panel from the Start menu, and double-click the Network icon. (Alternatively, you can right-click the Network Neighborhood icon on the Desktop and then choose Properties.) You can add, remove, configure, or update components in this dialog box.

FIG. 2.1
You can manipulate several network software properties at the same time.

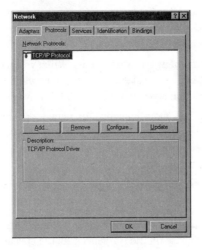

After entering new configuration information for a network component, you are prompted to either reboot the system or leave the system up and running (see Figure 2.2). Your network components won't be available until you reboot.

FIG. 2.2
After the installation is complete, you need to reboot the system for the changes to take effect.

If you're adding the additional network software that comes with Windows NT, you need to confirm or change the path for the NT distribution. If you're installing optional network software, enter the path for its distribution.

Configuring Adapter Cards

If your NT workstation has a built-in network hardware interface or an installed network interface card, or NIC, its associated network software is installed during the Windows NT Workstation or Server installation. You can add or change network interface cards on PC workstations that don't have network interfaces on their motherboards.

The manufacturers of network interface cards use software programs, referred to as *drivers,* for their NICs. If you change from one NIC to another, you have to change the driver software. You may need to change network adapters for several reasons—to upgrade as faster cards become available, to replace a faulty card, or to add a new special-function card to the system, for example.

One reason to update your card is to improve network performance. You can change from a slower 8-bit NIC to a faster 16- or 32-bit NIC. The 16- and 32-bit NICs perform some network operations faster than 8-bit NICs do. Other NIC characteristics can also affect performance, including the buffer sizes and the types of media supported.

You may need to change the NIC on the server system to get adequate performance for queries made against your SQL Server database. You also may change the NIC on selected client systems that require faster access to the server database.

Click the Add button in the Adapters tab of the Network Properties dialog box to display the Select Network Adapter dialog box. Then select the network adapter card in the Network Adapter card list. In Figure 2.3, the selected adapter card is the 3Com Etherlink II Adapter.

Part

I

Ch

2

FIG. 2.3

You need to add adapter-card software if you add a second or different NIC to your system.

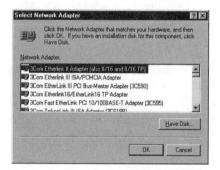

Network adapter cards typically require you to specify an IRQ level and an I/O base address when you add adapter software. The IRQ level and I/O base address should match the ones specified by the manufacturer.

Windows NT can detect and configure some adapter cards automatically. Before buying a NIC, you should consult a reputable dealer, who can tell you whether the card can be set up by Windows NT automatically. You can also check with Microsoft to learn about NICs that Windows NT can configure automatically.

Some major manufacturers provide NICs that allow you to set the IRQ and addresses by using software rather than jumpers on the card. Cards that can be set up automatically can be advantageous, especially if you have a large number of other interface cards installed in your PC workstation.

The more cards you install in your system, the more likely it is to have conflicts. Two cards that have identical default IRQ or address settings will not work as expected if those settings aren't changed. Some interface cards allow few changes to be made in their IRQ or address settings. If you can use software to set some of your interface cards to a large number of values, you can prevent many card-setting conflicts.

Ideally, you should check the specification of all cards that you want to use in your PC workstation to determine whether all IRQ and address conflicts can be eliminated. If you don't do this, you may have to change one or more cards later to eliminate conflicts and to allow all cards—including your network card—to work.

You should also ascertain whether the interface cards, including the network interface cards that you buy for NT, are supported by Windows NT. Microsoft provides a list of the supported interface cards, including network NICs that can be used with Windows NT.

You should know the factory default settings for your network adapter card, as well as the current settings, if you changed them from the factory defaults. You should also run any diagnostic program to learn quickly whether the network adapter cards function properly.

Select the adapter card from the Installed Adapter Card list in the control panel application and then click OK to install the network adapter by using the default NT driver, or click Have Disk to use a manufacturer's driver. The user's involvement in the installation of adapter cards depends on the capabilities of the card and the sophistication of the driver software. Most of the settings may be determined automatically; other settings may need to be supplied by you during installation.

N O T E Many manufacturers repackage network adapter cards for PC workstations that are manufactured by other companies. If your network adapter card doesn't appear in the list, it may be listed under a different name. Check with the vendor from whom you bought the card. Also check the documentation that came with the card, the diagnostic display of the card's characteristics, or the labeling on the adapter board itself to find the card's designation. ■

 Consider buying identical network adapter cards for PC workstations. Several adapter manufacturers provide additional software for diagnosing and monitoring network interface card operation, but only if you have matching NICs among PCs.

Understanding Workgroups

The capability to form workgroups is one of the built-in network features of Windows NT. Windows NT allows the interconnection of Windows NT systems in groups that can share resources. As mentioned earlier, a *workgroup* is a logical set of workstations that share resources with one another. This sharing of resources is the basis for designating workstations as the members of the same workgroup.

The members of a workgroup typically can share the resources equally. Examples of resources that workgroup members can share equally are a disk drive and the directories and files on it.

The capability to share resources among workstations without a designated server system is called *peer-to-peer networking*. Each system can access another system's resources after they become shared. In such an arrangement, the systems function as both clients and servers. In this case, a *server* is a workstation that makes a resource (such as a disk) available to another workstation. A *client* is a workstation that accesses the resources of another workstation.

Workstations in a network that share resources should be placed in a logical organization, which is the NT workgroup. You must designate which NT workstations become members of the group. After you form workgroups, you can set up the resources for sharing. The underlying capability of peer-to-peer networking of workgroups permits workgroup client access to a SQL Server database. The peer-to-peer features of a workgroup can also be used to share related information about SQL Server, such as the documentation, which could reside on any shared disk in a workgroup.

After the disk-sharing feature, for example, is enabled on each system, you can access another workgroup member's disks. You can execute applications, read or write databases, create documents and spreadsheets, and delete or rename files on the shared disk of another workstation in the workgroup.

A disk drive that's a hardware component of a workstation is called a *local drive*. Local disk drives are directly connected to a workstation.

A *remote drive* is a disk drive that's accessible to a workstation but isn't one of its hardware components. The remote drive is the local drive of another workstation. The physical connection to a remote drive is through the LAN.

Workstations that are part of the same network can be made members of the same workgroup. Workstations that need to access the others' resources should be made members of the same workgroup. This is the basic criterion for the formation of workgroups.

You can, however, define a workgroup based on your own criteria. The placement of two or more workstations in a workgroup is arbitrary, which means that an administrator has full control of designating members of the workgroup. You can have groups of only two members each, for example, if you need such a configuration. You can even place workstations that share no resources in the same workgroup, although this situation is unlikely.

You'll find that there's a practical limit on the number of systems that can be members of the same workgroup. A constraint results from the speed of the workstation's hardware, including its disk drives, memory, processor, and system bus. The individual hardware components of a workstation that is used as a server in a workgroup may not be fast enough to allow that workstation to serve many workgroup members.

Members of a workgroup may access a SQL Server database in a different workgroup as well as in their own. More likely, however, the SQL Server database will be installed on a Windows NT server system in a domain.

Members of a workgroup can access the SQL Server database, even though it is placed in a different type of logical organization, the domain.

In a server-based, domain-model network system, you can buy a large, powerful, fast single system that's the only server in a group of workstations. If your server system has a Pentium,

MIPS R4000, or Alpha AXP processor, or multiple i486 processors, it can function as a server for a much larger number of workstations.

In traditional networks, the network configuration is either a workstation/server network or a peer-to-peer network—usually not both. With the introduction of Windows for Workgroups and continuing with Windows 95 and Windows NT Workstation, however, systems are more typically a mixture of server-based and peer-to-peer-based networks. The appeal of the peer-to-peer type of network often is cost. You don't have to implement a huge system to act as a server to other workstations in the network in this environment. The disadvantage is that you typically won't be running hard-core server applications, such as SQL Server, on the workstations of these environments.

Also, as you implement your workgroups, you'll find that logical groupings of your users begin to emerge, even beyond the groups that you've already established. You should consider Windows NT domains if you have difficulty administering workgroup networks. Domains allow you to group users in logical cross-sections and then use these groups to manage security, access to the network, user names, and more.

The latter type of centralized organization provides some of the features of a client/server-based network. If you require more of a client/server configuration for your workstations, including the capability to serve dozens or hundreds of clients, you'll want to use the additional features provided by the Windows NT Server.

A simple rule of thumb for peer-to-peer configured workgroups is to limit their members to 20 or so. Microsoft suggests that you define fewer than 20, but the number of members who interact with one another simultaneously determines the actual limit. You can deviate from the suggested limit of 20 workstations, although you should keep the recommended values in mind as you configure your workgroups.

You may want to limit the members of a workgroup to fewer than 20 to allow for the occasional load put on your system by connections to your resources from outside your workgroup. Unlike the domain model mentioned earlier in this chapter, a workgroup isn't a security mechanism and doesn't serve to restrict access to the resources of member workstations. Other members of the network can access the resources of workstations outside their own workgroups after they know their share names and optional passwords.

It may help you understand workgroups to think of them as being a loosely organized confederation rather than an integrated republic. The members of a workgroup log on to their workstations, establishing their user names for the network. Their user names and passwords are checked in an account database that resides on a local disk. You administer each workstation separately, including defining a separate account for each workstation.

You designate a workstation as a member of a workgroup or domain when you install Windows NT. (You can use the Network Control Panel later to change your membership in a workgroup.) You can designate a workstation as a member of only one workgroup at a time.

A new workgroup is created the first time that you use its name. This situation occurs when you install a Windows NT system or when you change the name of your workgroup later.

Members of the same workgroup are displayed together when you examine the workstations of your network.

Members of a workgroup are displayed together to simplify the sharing of resources. There's no restriction on the workstations that can become members of a workgroup provided by Windows NT. You define the criteria for workstation membership.

A workgroup can include workstations with faster processors or multiple processors and large fast disks to extend the 20-workstation practical limit of the workgroup network. Faster processors and faster disks help extend the limit by performing server tasks faster, thereby allowing more workstations to interact as clients and servers and to have acceptable performance.

You cannot extend your network to a configuration in which your servers support 10,000 or more NT workstations, however. Although you can have tens of thousands of interconnected NT systems, the maximum number in a given network is far smaller and is limited by the number of systems that can perform well while interconnected. Real-life tests indicate that approximately 250 workstations, used in a busy network, comprise a realistic network goal.

In a workgroup, you create and administer a user account on each workstation. You log on to each workstation, and your user name and password are validated at the local workstation. If you are responsible for the administration of more than one workstation, you must log on to each workstation to maintain its account database. This is particularly inconvenient if a user has accounts on several workstations and you must make changes in each one.

Another possibility to help better manage your user base is to specify a domain for your computer rather than a workgroup. As mentioned earlier in this chapter, a domain is a more tightly administered group of workstations. You can read about domains in the following section, "Understanding Windows NT Domains."

 TIP If you cannot locate a workgroup or domain system that you want to connect to, you're probably experiencing a conflict with the network drivers on your system. Make sure that you installed the correct drivers and that you matched your network configuration with the settings on your network card.

Also, if you find that you can see other workstations on your network but cannot gain access to the server, check your user name and password. The password that you used to log on to your workstation may not be the same as the password established for your NT domain account.

Understanding Windows NT Domains

Domains are the fundamental architecture that controls how your client systems access the server, whether they are on your local-area network or on the Internet. Domains provide a means of logically grouping systems and users to facilitate administering the systems, accessing your server, and interacting with one another.

Windows for Workgroups introduced peer-to-peer networking for Microsoft platforms. *Peer-level networking* means that workstations share information stored on their local hard disks with other users on the network. Although this arrangement is a great way to share small to medium amounts of information on a few workstations, a serious bottleneck arises as the number of workstations—and the traffic that they generate—grow.

The bottleneck results from the requirement to manage access to the information and balance performance on a given user's system. You must balance this requirement against access to the information over the network. In systems in which the number of workstations and the amount of shared information becomes a burden on the network, you should consider implementing a more industrial-strength solution. With Windows NT, domains become part of the network picture.

Figure 2.4 shows a sample domain configuration with a two-server domain and a single-server domain.

FIG. 2.4

Servers belong to a single domain, whereas users and systems can use more than one domain.

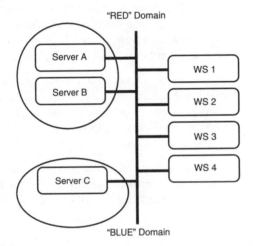

At first, system administrators may disagree with the configuration shown in Figure 2.4, on the ground that workstations belong in one domain or another. The point of the figure is that servers belong to one domain and one domain only. Workstations and users can sign into and out of different domains as needed, as long as they are authorized in other domains. The important thing is that when you enter, or log into, a given domain, you must abide by the domain's rules and security parameters.

You set up and administer user rights from the User Manager for Domains (see Figure 2.5), which is listed in the Administrative Tools menu in NT.

The User Manager enables you to work with both users and groups, and to assign all rights recognized by the system to those users. When you create the necessary users and groups, apply rights to your system and control access to the files and directories on it.

TIP   You can work with more than one user at a time. If you manage existing users and want to set up the group associations, logon times, and other attributes, first select the users from the list by Shift+clicking and Ctrl+clicking the names in the list; then choose User, Properties.

FIG. 2.5

Users belong to groups, and you control access to resources either by these group assignments or by the individual users.

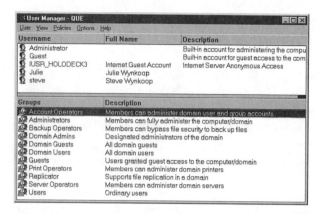

Part

I

Ch

2

> **CAUTION**
>
> Be wary of one particular user: GUEST. Strongly consider disabling the account. The GUEST account is dangerous, because any user who logs on to your system without a valid user name and assigned password is assigned to this account. Therefore, any privileges given that account are automatically provided to any user who signs on to the system without otherwise defined access.
>
> The built-in group EVERYONE is also in the system. Every user and group belongs to this group. In addition, the group's settings provide the default privileges to all resources when they are created, unless user access is explicitly revoked or modified. This means that you can assign rights to limit access to your users, but unless you remove the rights for the group EVERYONE from the resource that you set up, all users still have access to it.

In almost all cases, your best option is granting group rights to resources rather than to users, even when you are granting access to a resource to a single user. This procedure will save you time and effort later, when the user is replaced or gains an assistant who needs to have the same level of access. In that case, you need only modify the members of the group; you won't need to change access privileges for resources in your system. Consider the following steps in implementing your system's user database:

- Decide whether to allow access to your system via the GUEST account. If you decide not to allow access, disable the account. If you are concerned about security, it is highly recommended that you never leave the GUEST account enabled.

- Define the users who are required in your system.

- Create the individual user accounts.

- Define the security-rights profiles that you will apply to the system.

- Create groups containing the users to whom you granted the security rights.

- Apply security to the resources. Use the groups as the means of indicating access, or lack of access, to the resource.

■ Apply security to the resources based on individual users, in those rare cases in which this method is warranted or required.

> **CAUTION**
>
> Windows NT assigns user rights based on a Lleast rRestrictive model. If you belong to two profiles, for example, and if one profile indicates that you have no access to a resource but the other indicates that you do have access, you can gain access to the resource. The least restrictive of the two profiles indicates that you are allowed access.
>
> Put simply, any user whom you assign to the NOACCESS group, but whom you do not remove from other groups, may have more access rights than you planned. The effect of the NOACCESS group may be weakened because the other groups allow overriding user rights, granting user rights to certain resources. When you revoke a user's access, be sure to review the associated account; make sure that it does not belong to other groups that may influence effective rights.

Working with NT Users

The User Manager for Domains enables you to create new users in several ways. One way of creating new users that offers you the most leverage for your time is choosing the Copy command (User menu) to copy the rights of an existing user. As you can see in Figure 2.6, you set up several options for users who may access your system.

FIG. 2.6

When you copy an existing user, the copy inherits the groups and privileges of the original.

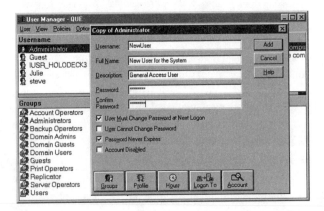

N O T E If you choose the Must Change Password option, an additional step is required the first time that a user logs onto the system: Each person must change his or her password. This practice may seem to be a good idea at first, but be wary of the user's particular type of system.

In some environments—specifically, Windows 3.x systems—the system may not allow users to change their passwords. In such cases, you effectively lock the users out of the system, because NT bars them from the system until the passwords have been changed.

If you have a user blocked from signing onto the system, review the account and make sure that this option is not checked. Also make sure that the Account Disabled option is not selected. This option also prevents access to your system. ▪

The following sections briefly cover the various aspects of user accounts.

Assigning Groups

The Groups button enables you to set up the groups to which the user belongs. Figure 2.7 shows the Group Memberships dialog box.

FIG. 2.7
Work with users in groups to simplify management tasks.

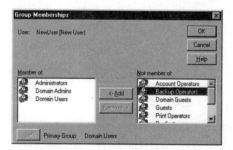

When you assign a user to a group, he gains the rights and privileges associated with that group. By double-clicking groups listed in the Member Of and Not a Member Of list boxes, you add and remove membership in groups. After the user is assigned to the appropriate groups, choose OK to save the changes and return to the new user's Properties dialog box.

Controlling Access to Resources

After you create your users and groups, you must assign permissions. Assigning permissions is the final step toward securing your system at a general level. This section shows you the basics of applying permissions to system resources.

Windows Explorer is the key to applying security to various resources on your system. Select the directory resource that you want to share, and right-click it. The shortcut menu that appears (see Figure 2.8) has an option that establishes sharing for the resource.

Choose Sharing from the menu. This option not only sets up the share name and the number of users accessing the resource, but also offers the option to set permissions on the resource by clicking the Permissions button. Figure 2.9 shows the dialog box in which you set the initial options.

FIG. 2.8

Choose Sharing from the shortcut menu to set up or maintain sharing options for the selected resource.

FIG. 2.9

Setting up the initial share information is a straightforward process.

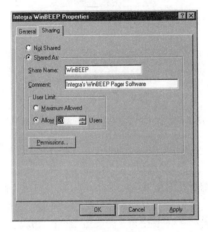

N O T E This information on securing share-level security on your system pertains to setting up shares on the server. Remember that share-based security is different from NTFS-based security. If you establish rights based on a share, the rights are not enforced unless the share is accessed.

If you use the directory that the share relates to without using the share, the rights have no effect.

If you need to protect content on the server, you must use NTFS for the file system. You also must set rights based on the permissions for the directory, not the share. ■

N O T E If you select a share name that is longer than the DOS-standard format, some DOS workstations may not be able to access the resource. If you select such a name, you are warned about this fact as you apply the share information for the resource. ■

If you click OK or Apply at this point without setting permissions in the permissions dialog box, all users who have access to the resource via a share, a parent directory, and so on have open, Full Control access to the resource. Be sure to click the Permissions button.

The underlying file system dictates how permissions change. If the NTFS (the NT File System) is installed, you gain additional options. These options enable you to apply specific permission subsets, rather than just generic permission categories. The following list shows the general access permission categories that you can assign:

- **No Access.** Users are unable to access, read from, or write to the resource.
- **Read.** Read users and groups can read the directory, load and execute files located in the directory, and so on. These users and groups cannot delete objects or add new objects to the resource.
- **Change.** Change users can read, modify, and execute existing objects, but they cannot insert or delete objects.
- **Full Control.** Full Control users have all rights to the resource.

When you choose Add, you have two options:

- You can select single or multiple users and groups.
- You can assign rights that apply to a set of users as a set.

When you choose OK, the users are listed in the Permissions text box. If the permissions are properly applied, choose OK again to save and apply the changes. Now the resource is available with your declared permissions.

Understanding the NT Performance Monitor

You must be able to monitor the use of system resources by applications, including the components of SQL Server, to properly control the system. The Windows NT system provides extensive performance-monitoring capability.

The Performance Monitor administrative tool, which controls the monitoring and display of the use of system resources, graphically displays the performance of one or more computers in a network. Resources or entities that can be monitored are called *objects*. Objects can include processes, threads, processors, and memory. Counters are used with objects to record usage statistics. You can record and, later, review performance information displayed in a chart.

You can closely monitor the characteristics of the main resources of the computer system, the CPU(s), RAM, and disks in Windows NT by using the Performance Monitor. You can, for example, collect and display the percentage of time that both system code and user code use the CPU, such as the SQL Server and SQL Monitor processes.

▶ **See** Chapter 21, "Optimizing Performance," for more information on how to use the information returned by the Performance Monitor, **p. 593**.

The chart window, which is one of four displays called *views*, appears in an initialized state. Open the Performance Monitor from the Windows NT Administrative Tools group. Figure 2.10 shows the main window of the Performance Monitor.

FIG. 2.10

The statistics are collected from the currently running system automatically after you select them.

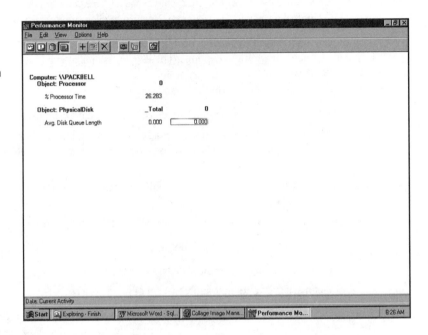

N O T E You need to start the logging process manually after you select the components that you want to monitor. By default, when the monitor is loaded, the logging isn't yet active. ▪

Logging isn't enabled when the Performance Monitor starts, so no information is displayed. The three additional views that you can display are Alert, Log, and Report. To select objects to be monitored and displayed, or to be recorded in a log file, choose Add to Chart from the Edit menu.

Selecting Objects and Counters in a Chart View

You choose objects for monitoring from the Object drop-down list. You choose a counter for an object from the Counter list. Each object has a different default counter. The default object is Processor, with a default counter of % Processor Time.

In the preceding section, the percentage of processor time for the CPU of the system PACKBELL is selected for monitoring and display.

You can use the <u>E</u>xplain button to display an explanation of the selected counter. The counter % Processor Time, for example, is explained at the bottom of the Add to Chart dialog box as the percentage of time that a processor is executing an executable thread of code.

After you choose an object counter, click the <u>A</u>dd button to add the counter line to the display. After you choose all object counters, click the <u>D</u>one button to display the chart view. The Cancel button changes to <u>D</u>one when you choose a counter for display. The chart view in Figure 2.11 shows the percentage of time that the processor was busy executing code.

FIG. 2.11
Each counter is assigned a different color automatically.

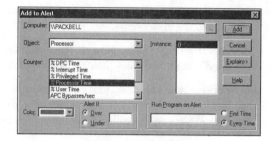

Displaying Information in a Report View

You can display the information collected by the Performance Monitor for object counters in a report rather than a chart. A report view presents the information in tabular format. You may find a report format to be preferable for viewing statistics, because the numeric representation of all counters is displayed. You can create a report by choosing <u>R</u>eport from the <u>V</u>iew menu.

A new report is blank because you haven't selected any object counter information. You select the object counters for a report by choosing <u>A</u>dd to Report from the <u>E</u>dit menu. Only object counter values are displayed in the report. In the Add to Report dialog box, the counter % Processor Time for the object Processor on the system PACKBELL is added to the report (see Figure 2.12).

FIG. 2.12
Multiple counters are available for monitoring most objects in the Performance Monitor.

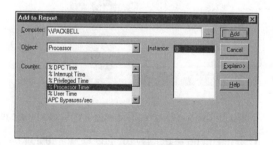

After you choose the object counters, click the Done button to display the report view. The report is organized by objects, with all counters for the same object grouped below a column header. Instances of the same object are displayed across the page, rather than in a single column.

The report view shown in Figure 2.12 shows the counters for each of the three objects to be included in the report. For the Processor and PhysicalDisk, the second column shows the instance. PhysicalDrive 0 denotes the first hard drive of the system. Instance 0 of the Processor denotes the first and only CPU of the computer system NT486.

Selecting Objects and Counters in an Alert View

An *alert* is a line of information displayed in the alert view of the Performance Monitor when the value of an object counter is above or below a value that you define. The entry in the log includes a date and time stamp, the actual object counter value, the criteria for returning the entry, the object value counter, and the system.

Choose Alert from the View menu to display an alert view, which is initialized by default. Choose Add to Alert from the Edit menu to display the Add to Alert dialog box.

You choose the computer, object counter, color, and instance (if appropriate), similar to the way that you choose these elements for chart views. Alerts are different in that they result in the display of information only if the object counter value is greater than or less than a value that you define.

Selecting Objects in a Log View

The log view allows the selection of objects and their counters to be logged for subsequent display and analysis. You display the log view by choosing Log from the View menu. Like the other views, the log is initialized by default. No object counters are defined for it.

Choose Add to Log from the Edit menu to open the Add To Log dialog box (see Figure 2.13). You can choose objects in this dialog box. Click the Done button to display the log view with your selected objects.

FIG. 2.13

You can log the performance statistics from another Windows NT system running SQL Server by entering its name in the Computer text box.

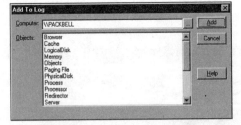

The selected objects appear in the view with all counters collected for each object.

Choose Log from the Options menu to display the Log Option dialog box, in which you can specify the name to be given the log file, its location, and the interval at which counters will be written to the log file.

You can pause the log by clicking the Pause button or stop it by clicking the Stop button. Counters for the objects included in the log file are available for subsequent viewing.

Displaying and Interpreting SQL Server Events

You can use an integrated logging tool in Windows NT to log information about application, system, and security operations called *events*. This tool, called the Event Viewer, controls the logging and subsequent display of information about all events.

The Event Viewer records the date and time of the occurrence, source, type, category, ID number, user name, and computer system for Windows NT and application-defined operations. You can display these events by various categories, order, and amount of detail. Information about operations related to the use of Microsoft SQL Server is recorded primarily in the application log. Information recorded in the system section may be related to the use of SQL Server's system processes.

Events are occurrences you should know about that occur during the execution of user or system code. The events are logged in the event log file, which is enabled automatically at system startup. You can keep event logs and examine them later as printed reports. You can disable event logging through the Control Panel's Services item.

> **CAUTION**
>
> You shouldn't disable event logging when you use SQL Server. If you do, you lose the information recorded about database operations, which could help you correct problems later.

The first time you use the Event Viewer, its window displays events from the system log. In the example shown in Figure 2.14, the window is large enough to display one-line listings of 21 system events. The most recent event, which is listed first, is selected. If you choose Save Settings on Exit from the Options menu, the last log viewed appears in the Event Viewer window when you run it again.

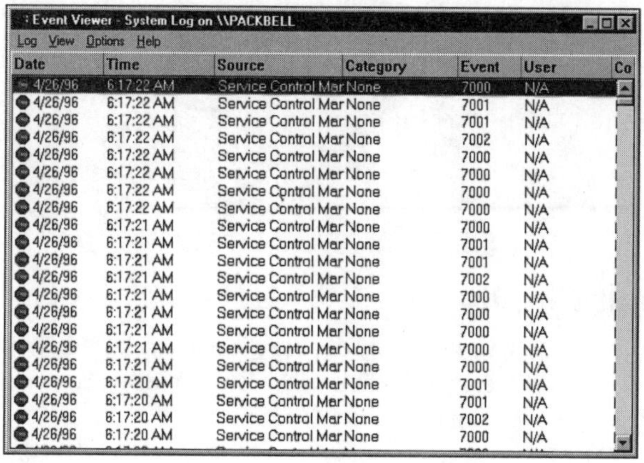

FIG. 2.14

The Event Viewer can display information from the last log that you examined.

The Log menu allows you to view events from the System, Security, or Application log (see Figure 2.15).

FIG. 2.15

Information about SQL Server events is recorded in the application log.

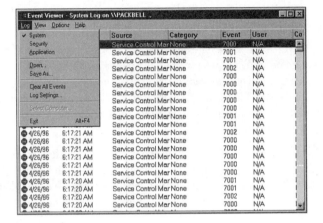

Configuring the Application Event Log

You should configure the application log of the Event Viewer after you install SQL Server. Choose Log Settings from the Log menu to display the Event Log Settings dialog box. You can set the maximum size of the log file (in kilobytes) and the period of time during which events should be recorded, and indicate whether to overwrite events if the log file is full. Separate settings are kept for each of the three logs: system, security, and application. In Figure 2.16, the system log file is set to a maximum size of 512K, and events are set to be overwritten in a week.

FIG. 2.16

You may choose Overwrite Events as Needed to ensure that no new events are lost at the expense of the oldest recorded events.

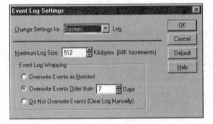

Displaying Event Details

You can view details about an event by double-clicking a selected event or by choosing Detail from the View menu in the main window of the Event Viewer. You must examine the detail of an event to learn the meaning of the event numbers.

The information at the top of the detail display is similar to an event line in the initial display of events. The description section of the Event Detail dialog box provides additional information about the event. Figure 2.17 shows the detail for an event from the application log recorded about a SQL Server event.

FIG. 2.17
If the Type field displays Information or Success, the event isn't an error—just the record of an event that occurred on the system.

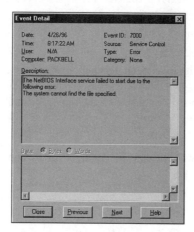

For each logged event, several items of information are displayed. The items of information recorded for each event are date, time, user, computer, event ID, source, type, and category.

Table 2.1 can help you interpret the information displayed in the Event Detail dialog box for events in all application logs.

Table 2.1   Item Descriptions for Logged Events

Item	Description
Event	Windows NT-assigned event number
Category	Event source; security source can be Login, Logoff, Shutdown, Use of User Rights, File, Print, Security Changes, or None
Computer	Name of computer on which error occurred
Date	Date of event
Event ID	Unique number for each source to identify event
Source	Program that was logged—for example, an application or a system component, including a driver
Time	Time of event
Type	Severity of error, such as Error, Warning, Information, Success, Audit, or Failure Audit displayed as an icon
User	User name when error occurred; can be blank (N/A)

The Event Detail dialog box shows information about a normal stop of the SQL Server process, probably issued through the SQL Service Manager. The Type field shows the entry Information, specifying that the event isn't an error. You can scroll the Description list to display additional information, if any, for an event.

▶ **See** Chapter 1, "Introducing Microsoft SQL Server," for further discussion of the SQL Service Manager, **p. 11**.

The last section of information in the Event Detail dialog box displays a byte dump in hexadecimal. Not all events display a dump—only those in which the information is relevant. The information in the dump can be interpreted by someone who knows the application code or the Windows NT system that is noted in the event log. You can click the Words option button to display the dump in words rather than bytes.

Click the Previous and Next buttons to display the detail for the preceding and following events, respectively, in the current log.

Using the View Menu

You can use the commands in the View menu to control other characteristics of the display of events in the main window of the Event Viewer. The newest events are listed second in the window, for example (see Figure 2.18).

FIG. 2.18

The newest events are listed second in the window.

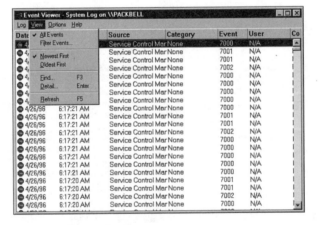

Choose Find from the View menu to display the Find dialog box, shown in Figure 2.19. Use Find to locate events by criteria that you specify in the Find dialog box. You can enter various items for an event in the Find dialog box, including the source, category, event ID, computer, user, and any part of the description. If the event is found, the main Event Viewer window appears with the specified error selected. If the event isn't found, you see a Search failed error message.

FIG. 2.19
Use the Direction
option buttons to
define the direction
of the search through
the log.

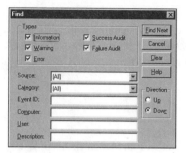

You can display the Filter option to choose events by using criteria based on one or more items of an event. You can choose events based on the date and time of all events or based on the first and last events of a range of dates and times. You also can enter the source, category, user, computer, and event ID to filter the events that are displayed.

By default, Information, Warning, Error, Success Audit, and Failure Audit are selected; you can deselect these options to restrict the events that are returned. Success Audit and Failure Audit are valid only for the security log.

Clearing the Event Log

Choose Clear All Events from the Log menu to empty a log file of all recorded events. If you choose Clear All Events, a precautionary dialog box appears. Click the Cancel button to cancel the emptying of the event log.

N O T E If you look through the event log and notice transactions that are being completed when SQL Server starts, these events are being rolled back or rolled forward to synchronize with the time when the server was shut down. This is how SQL Server maintains a consistent database in times of unexpected shutdowns. SQL Server examines the database to determine where it left off and ensures that the databases are at the last possible point of consistency. ■

Reality Check

While you are implementing Windows NT and the users on your system, you can easily forget to remove or control the members in the EVERYONE group. In many implementations, this situation leads to unwanted access to resources on the server. Carefully review the groups to which you assign your users.

As a precaution, in our implementations, we create a user who represents the rights that we want to assign on a general basis. Later, when we add users to the system, we copy that original user, update the user name, and update the password, so we are assured that the user rights are appropriate. In some cases, of course, you want to grant specific additional or lesser rights to a given user, but starting with the copied user provides a good basis for additions.

In addition, if you're using Remote Access Services (RAS) on your server, be sure to remove the GUEST account. If you don't, you may be opening your system to an additional means of logging into and searching your systems. If a person calls in and then logs in with an unknown user name and password, that person is assigned to the GUEST account and given the corresponding rights.

From Here...

In this chapter, you learned about the relevant characteristics of Windows NT, on which you install Microsoft SQL Server. Windows NT's multithreaded design and support for multiple processors is ideally suited for an application such as SQL Server. In addition, the built-in network support of the Windows NT system makes possible a simple, straightforward connection from clients to SQL Server. Last, you learned that information returned by SQL Server is returned to the built-in reporting facilities of Windows NT: the Performance Monitor and the Event Viewer.

For information on selected aspects of the topics mentioned in this chapter, review the following chapters:

- Chapter 21, "Optimizing Performance," teaches you how to optimize the performance of SQL Server, including using SQL Server-specific information returned by the Performance Monitor.
- Chapter 26, "Upsizing Microsoft Office 97 Applications to SQL Server," teaches you how to use client-workstation-based applications to access the server database.

CHAPTER 3

Installing and Setting Up the Server and Client Software

The installation of SQL Server is relatively simple and similar to the installation of other Microsoft products. In this chapter, you learn about the different steps and considerations to keep in mind as you set up your server system and the clients that will access it. ■

Learn what you need to know about installing the server-side software

Find out about the different options and what they mean for your installation in terms of functionality and development considerations.

See how to install client-side applications and libraries

After the server software is installed, you'll need to set up each of the client systems that will be accessing it. See how you can install the utilities that you'll use to connect to and manage your SQL Server.

Learn about the utilities that are installed and how they are used from both the client and the server

Several of the utilities are available on both the client and server computers on your network—find out how you use these applications and which are available in the different environments.

Understanding Server Hardware and Software Requirements

The computer system for your SQL Server installation should be on the list of supported Windows NT systems. If your system is an Intel x86-based processor, it should be 33 MHz or faster, according to Microsoft documentation. In practice, it's not recommended that you implement SQL Server in a production environment on anything less than a Pentium 75 MHz with 32M of RAM. Of course the faster the processor speed and more memory you have, the better the performance will be.

Also, according to the documentation, you must have a minimum of 16M of RAM for x86-based systems, although additional memory is recommended. A minimum of 16M is suggested for a Windows NT Server system, but 32M is more appropriate. Most RISC-based systems are usually configured with a minimum of 64M and often are configured with 128M of memory.

N O T E These stated minimums are just that: minimums. As you bring up systems, there are a number of factors that will impact these numbers. Be sure to pay special attention to any replication tasks you may want to run and to the number of client systems that you'll be allowing to access the server during peak periods.

One of the biggest performance boosts you can offer in the SQL Server world is the addition of memory. This simple enhancement can improve performance by twofold or more in many cases.

These recommendations aren't unreasonable for a server system. Memory has become very inexpensive in recent years. In 1977, a quarter of a megabyte of memory for at least one manufacturer's system was priced at $17,000. In recent times, you can buy 1M of memory for less than $50.

Although you might be using an Intel x86-based processor in your server system, its processing power and speed far exceeds the large minicomputer systems of ten to 15 years ago. Physically, your server might be only as large as a client system, but don't be deceived by that. ■

You need to have at least 70M of disk space to complete the installation, and if you install the book's online feature of SQL Server, you'll need to add 15M to this requirement. If you have only 70M, however, you don't have any space to create additional logical devices on which to create your databases. You should count on a minimal SQL Server installation requiring approximately 150M to start.

Note that although you *can* create your database tables and other objects within the master database, you shouldn't. Try to keep your core objects, those installed when you first bring up SQL Server, on a common logical device. As you'll see in Chapter 5, "Creating Devices, Databases, and Transaction Logs," when you create additional devices, databases and tables, you can designate different storage devices for those if your primary location does not have the disk space available.

You also need a floppy-disk drive for 3 1/2-inch, high-density disks or a CD-ROM drive to read the installation media.

▶ **See** Chapter 5, "Creating Devices, Databases, and Transaction Logs," for more information on creating new devices, **p. 91**.

Load the SQL Server software from your installation media onto a Microsoft Windows NT workstation or Windows NT Server system. You don't need any additional network software because the Windows NT system contains built-in network software. You need a network interface card (NIC) that's supported by Windows NT. If you access SQL Server directly only from the server system, without using a network for access, you don't need an NIC.

You can install SQL Server on a partition that uses either the FAT or NTFS file systems. You'll probably want to take advantage of the recovery and security features of a NTFS disk partition rather than the older and simpler FAT disk system, although your installation might have other considerations for other installed software that dictate this installation parameter.

▶ **See** Que's *Special Edition Using Microsoft Windows NT Server* by Roger Jennings, for more information on the installation of NT Server.

Part

I

Ch

3

Running Setup

Installing SQL Server for Windows NT is simple. The installation is similar to the installation of nearly all Microsoft Windows products, and it'll appear familiar to you if you've installed a Windows application. You must run the setup program using an NT account that has Administrative privileges, such as the NT Administrator account.

To perform the installation, follow these steps:

1. Choose Run from the Start menu.

2. Type the drive letter of your floppy or CD-ROM drive, followed by **setup** in the run combo list box.

   The setup program displays one or more message boxes after checking whether you're working from an Administrative account and whether SQL Server already is installed. Figure 3.1 shows the Welcome dialog box that appears when the SQL Server setup program is invoked.

3. When you continue, you'll be prompted to enter a Name, Company, and Product ID in the Enter Name and Organization dialog box. Then click Continue.

4. A second dialog box appears, asking you to confirm the name and company. If you want to change the name, click Change. If not, click Continue.

5. The SQL Server 6.5 Options dialog box appears. The Install SQL Server and Utilities option is automatically selected.

   When you first install SQL Server, only the Install SQL Server and Utilities, Upgrade SQL Server, and Install Utilities Only options are available. Install SQL Server and Utilities installs all the SQL Server software, including the 32-bit version of the client utilities on the server. Click Continue.

FIG. 3.1

You can change a characteristic such as the security mode only by running SQL Setup.

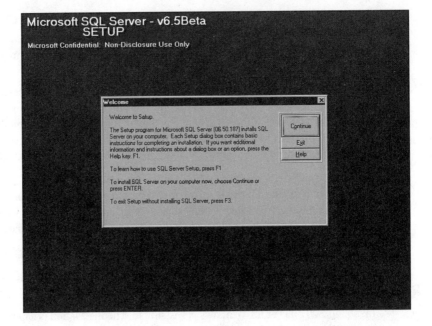

6. In the Choose Licensing Mode dialog box, you must enter the way in which you've bought licenses for the use of SQL Server, as well as the number of clients that may connect to the server. Figure 3.2 shows the entry of a server-based license that will permit a maximum of 20 connections. After you click Continue, an additional dialog box appears that requires you to confirm that you've bought the number of client licenses that you've entered.

7. In the SQL Server Installation Path dialog box that appears, confirm or change the drive and directory path for SQL Server files and click Continue. Drive C is the default.

8. The MASTER Device Creation dialog box that appears allows you to confirm or change the entries for the MASTER device drive, directory, and the size of the MASTER device.

   The default size of 25M for the MASTER Device Size may be inadequate. If you anticipate creating many devices, databases, or other objects, you can initially allocate a master device of perhaps 40M to 60M.

   The master device contains the master database and transaction log, which holds several system tables. You should avoid creating any objects in the master database, unless you want the objects to be available throughout the server system to all databases. SQL Server adds Rows to the system tables to reference objects that you create. Click Continue.

9. The SQL Server Books Online dialog box appears, enabling you to define whether you want to install the online documentation to run from the hard disk or the CD (see Figure 3.3). You should install the documentation on a hard drive of the server, unless you're short on disk space.

FIG. 3.2
Client licensing permits you to buy the exact number of client connections that you need.

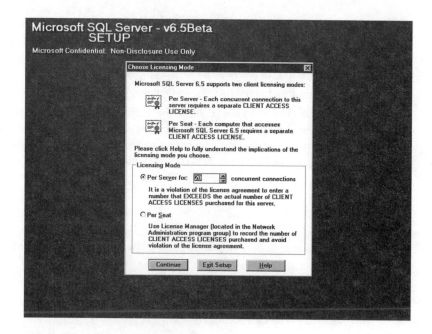

FIG. 3.3
You can share the online documentation from the server, saving disk space on the client systems. You can also install copies on client systems.

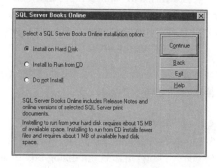

10. The Installation Options dialog box appears, shown in Figure 3.4, enabling you to define the Character Set, Sort Order, and Additional Network Support. Click Sets.

FIG. 3.4
Select Auto Start SQL Server at Boot Time to automatically start SQL Server when the system is restarted. You should also select Auto Start SQL Executive at Boot Time to start the Executive processes when the server is booted.

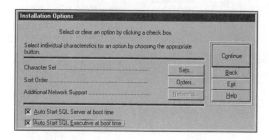

11. In the Select Character Set dialog box, select a language. If you're working only in English, you can choose 437 US English in the Select Character Set list box. If you're working in another language or storing information in multiple languages, you should select 850 Multilingual or ISO Character Set (Default). Click OK.

12. You're returned to the Installation Options dialog box. Click Orders.

13. In the Sort Order list box, confirm the default sort order or change it. If, for example, you select Binary Order, Order By clauses in Select statements are sorted by the direct binary representation of the column values. You can also select Dictionary Order, Case-Insensitive, the default, to treat corresponding upper- and lowercase letters as identical values.

CAUTION

If you must change your character set or sort order later, you'll have to rebuild the master database, so be sure you select carefully. Unless you have a compelling reason to do otherwise, you'll typically select the Case-Insensitive option.

---

14. Click OK. You're again returned to the Installation Options dialog box. Click Networks to set up the protocols that will be used.

15. You can install additional Net-Libraries to Named Pipes in the Select Network Protocols dialog box. For example, you can enter one or more additional Net-Libraries, such as the IPX/SPX or TCP/IP communication mechanisms. If you don't select additional Net-Libraries during installation, you can install them later.

N O T E If you have the desktop version of Microsoft SQL Server, you can't select alternate Net-Libraries. Only Named Pipes may be installed. ■

16. Click OK to return to the Installation Options dialog box.

17. Click Continue. Enter a Windows NT account and password to be used by SQL Executive Service in the SQL Executive Log On Account dialog box (see Figure 3.5).

FIG. 3.5

You should enter a password for the SQL Executive Service account that contains at least eight characters.

TIP It's a good idea to use a separate NT account for this service rather than share the NT Administrator account. If you later change the NT Administrator account, or change the password associated with the account without realizing it's being used by SQL Executive Service, the Executive Service will be unable to start.

18. Click Continue. A File Copy in Progress dialog box appears, showing the progress of server files as they're copied from the distribution. As the installation proceeds, additional feedback is displayed on your monitor telling you that SQL Server is installing SQL Server.

After you've indicated the different setup options, if you're installing from CD, the process will complete without further intervention. If you install SQL Server from floppy disks, you'll be prompted to change disks as each is copied to the server. When the installation is completed successfully, click Reboot if you want to begin using SQL Server; otherwise SQL Server will start the next time your NT Server is restarted.

NOTE Remember to manually start the SQL Server services after you reboot if you haven't defined automatic SQL Server startup; otherwise, the service won't be started and you won't be able to log in to start working with it. ■

Part
I
Ch
3

Starting the Server

You have several options available for starting SQL Server on the system. You can configure the SQL Server services system to start automatically each time the Windows NT server system is booted. You also can use the SQL Service Manager to start the SQL Server services. Several Windows application tools can optionally start SQL Server when the applications try to connect to the server. Finally, the server can be started by using a command line.

Using Automatic Service Startup

You can enable the automatic startup of SQL Server each time the Windows NT system is started. To start up SQL Server each time the server is booted, select the Auto Start SQL Server at Boot Time check box in the Installation Options dialog box. This is shown in Figure 3.4. You also can define an automatic startup for SQL Server after installation.

If you don't define SQL Server processes to automatically start up, you can later change it to automatic by using the Control Panel's Services option. To do so, follow these steps:

1. Open the Control Panel.
2. Double-click Services.
3. In the Services dialog box, scroll down the Service list box to find MSSQLServer.

4. Select MSSQLServer. The Startup should be Manual. A manual service isn't automatically started.

5. Click Startup to open the Service dialog box (see Figure 3.6).

FIG. 3.6

You can change the Windows NT account that a service uses through the Service dialog box.

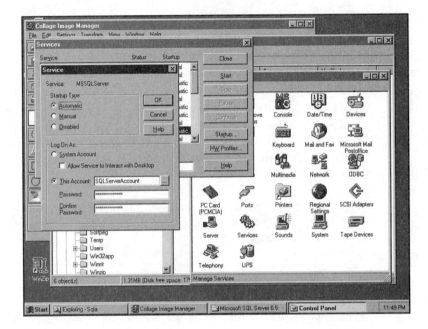

6. In the Startup Type section, select Automatic.

   You can also specify that the MSSQLServer process created by the automatic startup of the service use an account other than the Administrator system account. If you use another account, you must specify the Password Never Expires characteristic in the NT Server's User Manager utility. You don't need to specify a different account from the system account for SQL Server.

CAUTION

It's very important that you consider your future uses for SQL Server as you install it with regard to user identities for the SQL processes.

If you're using, or will be using in the future, the e-mail capabilities of SQL Server and the post office resides on a Novell server, you won't be able to access the mail system unless you establish a separate account for SQL Server.

7. Click OK in the Service dialog box. The MSSQLServer Startup column should have changed from Manual to Automatic.

8. If you want to immediately start SQL Server, click Start. A message box appears, telling you that SQL Server is starting. If the SQL Server service is successfully started, Started is added in the Status column of the Services dialog box for the SQL Server service.

9. Click Close.

Starting SQL Server with SQL Service Manager

You can use the SQL Service Manager to start MSSQLServer on the Windows NT server system. To start MSSQLServer by using the SQL Service Manager, follow these steps:

1. Click the SQL Service Manager icon in the SQL Server for Windows NT group.

2. Click Start/Continue or double-click the green light.

   The status message at the bottom of the SQL Service Manager dialog box should change from The service is stopped to The service is starting. After SQL Server is started, the message changes to The service is running.

3. Either Close the SQL Service Manager or minimize it to an icon. Note that, even if you close the service manager, SQL Server will continue running.

If you leave the SQL Server Service Manager minimized, you can easily Stop or Pause SQL Server as needed.

Starting SQL Server Through Windows Applications

You can optionally start up SQL Server when you connect to the server locally from the server or remotely from a client system. For example, a client-side version of the SQL Service Manager can be invoked from the toolbar of the SQL Enterprise Manager, allowing you to start and stop the server engine.

Starting SQL Server Through a Command Line

To start up SQL Server by using a command line, follow these steps:

1. Open a command prompt.

2. At the command prompt, enter this command line:

```
sqlservr /d drive:\directory\data\master.dat
```

Use /d to specify the name of the SQL Server master database.

The *drive* is the drive letter you entered in the Drive text box of the SQL Server Installation Path dialog box. The *directory* is the directory you entered in the Directory text box of the same dialog box. The default for the directory is SQL and the default for the drive is C.

Master.dat is the name of the data file that's the SQL Server master device. The master database is located on the master device and contains the set of system tables that defines SQL Server. Master.dat is located in the DATA subdirectory of the SQL directory.

Part

I

Ch

3

N O T E The sqlservr command line actually starts two system processes, both of which can have multiple threads. ■

Installing the Client Software

Many of the SQL Server utilities that you use to manage the server, issue queries against it, and develop and debug your applications are available not only as server-based applications, but also as client-side applications. The utilities installed will vary depending on the client environment you are installing into. If you're using a 16-bit client, such as Windows for Workgroups, you'll have fewer options installed than if you're using a 32-bit environment like Windows 95 or Windows NT.

For the 16-bit Windows clients, the following utilities are installed:

- *ISQL/W—the ISQL client for Windows.* This application allows you to issue SQL statements to the server just as you can from the command line. This application uses a graphical user interface to present the query, results, and any optional trace and analysis settings you may want to establish.

- *SQL Client Configuration Utility.* This allows you to set up the different configuration options for the client software. These options include network topology and any custom DLLs required to access the server. This utility is identical in function to the Client Configuration Utility installed on the server, although dialog boxes are slightly different in presentation.

- *SQL Server Books Online.* As the name implies, this option provides you with a fully searchable online version of the SQL Server book set. This item is also the same as the version installed on the client when the SQL Server is installed.

For the 32-bit client, the following utilities are installed:

- *ISQL/W—the ISQL client for Windows.* As with the server and 16-bit versions, this application allows you to issue SQL statements to the server just as you can from the command line. This application uses a graphical user interface to present the query, results, and any optional trace and analysis settings you may want to establish.

- *SQL Client Configuration Utility.* This allows you to set up the different configuration options for the client software. These options include network topology and any custom DLLs required to access the server. This utility is identical in function to the Client Configuration Utility installed on the server, although dialog boxes are slightly different in presentation.

- *SQL Server Books Online.* As the name implies, this option provides you with a fully searchable online version of the SQL Server book set. This item is also the same as the version installed on the client when the SQL Server is installed.

- *SQL Enterprise Manager.* As you'll learn throughout this book, this application is the central command center for administering SQL Server. This includes managing the devices, databases, replication, and other features and facets of SQL Server. Chances are very good that you'll become very well versed in the use of the Enterprise Manager as you administer your SQL Server system.

- *SQL Security Manager*. As with the server-installed version, this application allows you to manage the users and groups that access the SQL Server system.

- *MS Query*. This tool, long included with the Office applications suite as the query tool for ODBC data sources, is not only a great tool to create queries against data sources, but also one of the best hands-on tools for learning the SQL language. You can graphically create a query, and then review the SQL statements that are created to carry out the request.

- *SQL Help*. This help file contains the details of the Transact-SQL dialect used by SQL Server. You can use this help file to understand the different commands you can issue against the server above and beyond the typical standard SQL commands.

- *SQL Trace*. This facility helps you manage the flow of transactions to and from your server. You'll be using this utility with the Distributed Transaction model in SQL Server 6.5.

- *SQL Web Page Wizard*. The Web Page Wizard allows you to create interactive, single-instance or trigger-oriented Web pages to be accessed from your Web site. The wizard will create the HTML and database interface code for you, saving time when you're developing database-centric pages for your Web site.

Steps to Installing the Software for 32-Bit Clients

If you're installing the software on a 32-bit client such as Windows 95 or Windows NT, you can take advantage of the added utilities mentioned previously. To start setup, select the processor subdirectory on the CD that corresponds to your system. It's most likely that you'll be installing using the i386 subdirectory. This corresponds to the 32-bit installation of the utilities.

> **N O T E** To avoid conflicts with system files, you should exit all other software applications prior to running the setup program. If you don't, you might receive an error message as the files are copied to your system. This error message will prevent you from completing the installation successfully. Pay special attention to less-obvious applications such as the Office toolbar or other applications that run in the background. When in doubt, use the Windows task manager to verify the processes that are active on your system. ■

Here are the steps to installing the software:

- Start SETUP.EXE to begin.
- Click Continue at the prompt.
- If you are upgrading from a prior version of the client utilities, you'll be prompted to choose between installing the new utilities and removing the old version of the utilities on your system.

TIP If you're upgrading your client software, it's a good idea to remove prior versions of the utilities before you install the newer 6.5 versions on your system. If you do uninstall your old utilities, you'll need to restart the setup process to continue with the installation of the new utilities.

■ You'll be prompted to specify the utilities you want to install. Your control over the installation is complete, allowing you to fine-tune your requirements based on disk space constraints or your need for a specific utility.

■ The final phases of installation are automatic. The setup program will copy the routines to your system and update your system files.

■ At the end of the routine, you'll be prompted to reboot the system, which will complete the process.

Once completed, you'll be able to use the client workstation to administer, inquire into, and manage the different aspects of your SQL Server system.

Installing the Software for 16-Bit Clients

As mentioned previously, the 16-bit client software offers fewer, although just as useful, utilities for your SQL Server installation. When you install the software on your system, you'll be following similar prompts as other Windows installations that you might have completed.

The first step is to open the Clients subdirectory on the CD containing SQL Server. Select your operating system, which should be either DOS or Win16 for the 16-bit Windows client software.

If you're running the Windows setup, select and run the SETUP program. Installation of the DOS client software simply requires copying the files to a directory of your choice.

The Windows setup program will prompt you for the destination of the files and will then ask you to confirm which utilities you want to install.

When you click Install, the utilities will be copied to your system. A program group will be created and you'll be ready to start using the utilities with your system.

SQL Server can be installed in an environment with many different chip sets and variations of the Windows operating system. All of the software needed to install and run the server, as well as to install and configure client machines, comes on the SQL Server CD. The process of installing software on the clients should be planned and consistent on clients running the same version of Windows to make maintenance and troubleshooting easier.

From Here...

In this chapter you've learned about the different options you have for installing the software on your systems, both from a client and a server point of view. For more information about these and other related topics, please see the following chapters:

■ Chapter 2, "Understanding the Underlying Operating System, Windows NT," contains information about how to set up the operating system portion of your server. This will integrate into your selections for where and how to install SQL Server on your system.

■ Chapter 19, "SQL Server Administration," covers the different tasks that you'll need to be considering as you work with your server. These include backing up the system and more.

■ Chapter 20, "SQL Server Security," goes into the details of securing your server and controlling access to the objects in your databases.

Part
I

Ch
3

CHAPTER 4

Data Modeling, Database Design, and the Client/Server Model

Chances are good that when you started learning about development in the programming world, you began with flow-charting. Flow-charts are great tools for diagramming programmatic flow and for laying out the components of your system. The purpose is to discover logic flaws and missing functionality before coding, rather than during the cycle.

The reality is that flow-charts are rare. How many times have you been in a crunch to pull a flow-chart together for a project, but waited to do the chart until the project was completed? This situation is more common than any of us like to admit. Pulling a flow-chart together after the fact is easy, because you already know what you've designed in the program, and you're not going to flow-chart something that you opted not to include. This approach is fairly safe, provided that you reviewed the program along the way to ensure that its functions meet your customer's needs.

How you approach database design and architecture

Designing and implementing a database involves many issues. These issues can vary widely, depending on the scope of a project.

What normalization is and how to accomplish it

Normalization is a way to guarantee that data is available and flexible.

What client/server is and what pieces of the SQL Server system can be used to help implement it

Client/server systems can share the resources of many systems within an organization and even beyond the boundaries of the organization.

How to make design easier and faster

Many tools can aid in the design and even the implementation of a database system.

Database design, however, isn't as open to modification along the way. Because changing a database table after the fact alters the foundation of all other parts of the system, even in subtle ways, it often requires major overhaul work in the balance of the system. A simple change in a table can mean that entire portions of the application stop functioning.

Probably the most important thing that you can do when you bring up a database-oriented system is diagram and design the database structure that will support the application. If you don't do this, you end up making some subtle (or not-so-subtle) changes in the structure later—probably at a time when the changes are far more expensive in the development cycle.

When you decide to develop a system based on Microsoft SQL Server, you've taken the first step toward implementing two separate architectures in your software: client/server and relational database tables. Both architectures are powerful if they are used correctly, and they present a real advantage to your system if you pay attention to the rules along the way.

This chapter introduces those rules, including the theory and practice of a client/server system, such as determining the best location to implement a given function and breaking apart procedural flow.

Because the decision to move to client/server depends heavily on the flow of the application and where things are physically being completed, SQL Server is an ideal component to provide server-side functionality and to bring client/server to your applications. You need to understand what pieces of the database design dovetail with your desire to move to the client/server world. ■

Understanding the Basics of Normalization

When you start working with relational databases, you inevitably hear about data normalization and bringing things into third normal form. *Normalization* refers to how you implement the relationships and storage of data in your database tables. When you normalize a table, you try to limit the redundant data in the table. Many levels, or types, of normalization exist.

Your overall goal is likely to be a *3NF*, or *third normal form*, database. In most cases, this level of normalization is the best compromise between extremes when it comes to normalization versus functionality and ease of implementation. Levels exist beyond 3NF, but in practice, they can cloud the database with more design issues than functional issues.

When you delve into the world of normalized databases, you are, by definition, starting down the road of relational databases. Before normalized databases, structures used a series of *pointers* to retain relationships between different tables and values. You may recall implementing *linked lists*, in which each row of a database table contains a pointer to both the following and preceding rows. To traverse the database, you simply walked up and down this list of links between records.

In the relational world, you define columns that relate to each other between tables. These columns are *keys* to other values. Keys are used to uniquely define a relationship to another instance or set of information. This chapter discusses keys in the definitions of the normalization levels.

What's in a Name?

A key difference between SQL Server-type database implementations and other, more traditional PC-based databases is the terminology that describes the databases and their information. Keep in mind that a device, or physical file on the disk drive of the server, contains one or more databases. Databases contain one or more tables, and tables contain one or more columns of information. For each table of columns, one or more rows may exist.

In more traditional terms, there was no concept of a database, as in SQL Server. Instead, you had a file that contained records of fields. The following table shows a basic comparison of terms between a SQL Server implementation and a more traditional database, such as Btrieve or dBASE:

New Term	Old Term
Device	N/A
Database	File
Table	N/A
Column	Field
Row	Record

You need to keep these terms in mind. If you use the new terms in describing the tables that you're designing, you can prevent problems of ambiguity between developers and designers.

With relational databases, you don't use ordered, or sorted, rows. You use real-time statements—those that are evaluated when they are called or issued—to control the presentation of the information. You also use joins and views to control the way that information is retrieved, rather than try to store the information in the most advantageous format possible at the outset. This method allows for more dynamic access to the information in the database tables; it also allows you to simply store the information and then retrieve it in any manner.

The next few sections examine the different types of normalization, from the first through the third normal form.

First Normal Form

In *first normal form*, or *1NF*, the foundation for the relational system is put into place. In 1NF, you don't have multiple values represented in any single column. In database terms, each value in the database table is *atomic*, or represented only one time.

In the past, you may have implemented a database in which you stored the item code for each item ordered with the order record, as in a point-of-sale system. Later, when your program queried the order, it retrieved and parsed this field, and could determine what was ordered with that order record. Figure 4.1 shows an example of this type of table. You have the opportunity to store one or more item numbers with the order record.

FIG. 4.1

Without 1NF, you could store more than one logical item in a physical record. This approach isn't valid when you normalize your database.

OrderNum	OrderItems	OrderTotal
1	1320, 1405, 1602, 1201, 1000	$1,453.00
2	2001, 1001, 2345	$23.45
3	3021, 4000	$225.46
(AutoNumber)		$0.00

N O T E These examples were created in Microsoft Access working with SQL Server, because it's a good tool for creating tables quickly and easily. The tool that you use is entirely up to you. The SQL Enterprise Manager, although a bit less visual, can still serve as an excellent design and testing tool. ■

In 1NF, duplicates aren't allowed. You need to create a schema in which only one item is recorded for each order record on file. To implement the point-of-sale solution mentioned earlier in this section, you would have an order represented by one to *n* records containing the item-code information that made up the order. This solution provides a slightly different challenge in retrieving the information for the record. You must have a means of retrieving each record associated with the order and making sure that you've retrieved only those records—no more or less. This leads to order numbers called out in each record, of course.

Figure 4.2 shows the result of this first pass at normalizing a database table.

FIG. 4.2

In a 1NF table, each row is a single atomic record that must be capable of standing alone.

OrderNum	OrderItem	Description
1	1320	Milk
1	1405	Cookies
1	1602	Bread - French
1	1201	Bread - Italian
1	1000	Bread - American
2	2001	Cheese
2	1001	Bread - Swedish
2	2345	Bologna
3	3021	Paper Towels
3	4000	Eggs
0		

For now, simply remember that in 1NF, each row must contain only one instance of the information and all column values must be atomic.

Second Normal Form

The first requirement of *second normal form*, or *2NF*, is that it fulfill the requirements of 1NF. The second requirement is that each instance or row in the database table be uniquely identifiable. To do this, you must often add a unique ID to each row. In the example in the preceding section that breaks apart the orders table, it looks at first as though the structure fits this rule. You have, after all, instituted an order ID, and if you combine the order ID and the item code, you have a unique handle in the row. Right?

Not exactly. You could conceivably have a single order with more than one instance of an item. Consider an example: When you do your grocery shopping and buy your milk for the week, you may buy multiple half-gallons of milk in the same order.

You need to add an OrderItemID column to the table to fulfill the requirements of 2NF (see Figure 4.3). You keep the OrderNum, but OrderItemID is the primary unique identifier for the item in a given row.

FIG. 4.3

After you add a unique row ID for each line item, this table fits the 2NF model.

OrderItemID	OrderNum	OrderItem	Description
1	1	1320	Milk
2	1	1405	Cookies
3	1	1602	Bread - French
4	1	1201	Bread - Italian
5	1	1000	Bread - American
11	1	1320	Milk
6	2	2001	Cheese
7	2	1001	Bread - Swedish
8	2	2345	Bologna
9	3	3021	Paper Towels
10	3	4000	Eggs
(AutoNumber)	0		

Record: 1 of 11

N O T E Notice that although a new item has been added as item 11, it can still be related to the order based on the order number. What has been done is to provide a way to uniquely identify the row within the table.

Third Normal Form

Third normal form, or *3NF,* is a life-saver for the developer. All the work of normalizing your database tables really pays off when you move to the 3NF model. As 2NF relies on first being in 1NF, 3NF requires that you be compliant with the 2NF model. In short, when you have a table that's in 3NF, you won't have redundant nonkey information in your table that relies on nonkey information in another table.

That definition seems to be strange until you understand what's really happening. The goal of normalizing your tables is to remove redundant nonkey information from your tables. In Figure 4.3 earlier in this chapter, the model is broken nicely. Because you're storing descriptions in the table, and because these descriptions probably are used elsewhere in the database, storing them individually in the table is a problem.

Here's where you start to see the real advantages of moving to 3NF. The simple examples in this chapter relate to a grocery store.

Imagine that you're storing your information as shown in Figure 4.3 and need to change the description of Milk to Milk 3%, because your vendor has maliciously introduced Milk 1% into the mix. You need to write a utility that updates the sales database tables and any other table that ever referenced Milk to show the correct percentage. A real nightmare that often leads to problems is inconsistent information in the database. Forgetting about, or not knowing about, only one table that needs to be updated can invalidate your use of an item for the sales history.

Part

I

Ch

4

Normalization is the key to taking care of this problem. In Figure 4.4, the problem is corrected simply by removing the description from the table.

FIG. 4.4
To fit the 3NF model, the description column is removed from the order items table.

3NF : Table

OrderItemID	OrderNum	OrderItem
1	1	1320
2	1	1405
3	1	1602
4	1	1201
5	1	1000
6	2	2001
7	2	1001
8	2	2345
9	3	3021
10	3	4000
11	1	1320
(AutoNumber)	0	0

Record: 1 of 11

Because an item code is already assigned to Milk, you have the information that you need to set up the Inventory table shown in Figure 4.5.

FIG. 4.5
By creating an Inventory table, you create a "home base" to refer to and use any time you reference inventory items.

Inventory : Table

ItemCode	Description	Cost	Retail	SalePrice	SaleStart	SaleEnd
1000	Bread - American	$0.54	$0.99	$0.00		
1001	Bread - Swedish	$0.54	$0.99	$0.00		
1201	Bread - Italian	$0.54	$0.99	$0.00		
1320	Milk 2%	$1.25	$1.89	$0.00		
1321	Milk 1%	$1.10	$1.79	$1.50	12/31/95	1/15/96
1405	Cookies	$2.43	$3.29	$0.00		
1602	Bread - French	$0.54	$0.99	$0.00		
2001	Cheese	$0.69	$1.19	$0.00		
2345	Bologna	$1.72	$2.19	$0.00		
3021	Paper Towels	$0.34	$0.59	$0.00		
4000	Eggs	$0.52	$0.69	$0.00		
0		$0.00	$0.00	$0.00		

Record: 1 of 11

After you begin normalizing your table, you begin to wonder how to get a complete picture of the item sold. How can you find out all the information about the line item—its description, the sale price, and so on? This is where relational databases and their use of views come into play. In the example, you can create a query that returns the information that you need quickly and easily. Figure 4.6 shows what a sample view returns to your application for the table examples.

You can see that by using the combined information between the tables, you still have the same full data set to work with, but you're limiting the sources of information. Often, the way that you end up working with the information does not change—only the methods used behind the scenes to retrieve that information. This is the case with the 3NF table in this example. You're still storing the same information base. You're just retrieving the information by using a different method—in this case, a logical view of the two related tables.

FIG. 4.6

When you create a relational view of the database tables, you can retrieve and work with a complete picture of the information, although the information may be dispersed across several tables.

	OrderNum	OrderItem	Description	Retail
▶	1	1320	Milk 2%	$1.89
	1	1405	Cookies	$3.29
	1	1602	Bread - French	$0.99
	1	1201	Bread - Italian	$0.99
	1	1000	Bread - American	$0.99
	2	2001	Cheese	$1.19
	2	1001	Bread - Swedish	$0.99
	2	2345	Bologna	$2.19
	3	3021	Paper Towels	$0.59
	3	4000	Eggs	$0.69
	1	1320	Milk 2%	$1.89
*				

Record: 1 of 11

Understanding the Client/Server Model

Before you start designing your database, you need to understand where the functional components of your system will reside. It's important to understand where data manipulation is done and what should be stored in the database compared with what should be calculated or determined on-the-fly.

With SQL Server, you can implement true client/server systems. These systems can adhere to the concepts of client/server, allowing you to divide functional components into cooperative operations that accomplish your application's goal. This sounds strange, but what it amounts to is dividing processing between the client and server in a way that makes sense to the application. In database-oriented systems—especially those in which the database subsystem is open and accessible from many points—implementing an intelligent database layer to manage the data makes sense. This layer is responsible only for storage and inquiries as they relate to the information; it has no responsibility for the presentation of information.

The next couple of sections review the types of functions and operations that reside in the client and server sides of the client/server model. Although these concepts aren't exhaustive, you need to understand them.

For many people, *client/server* is just a fancy term for a PC database that resides in a common location and is accessed by many workstations. After reading this chapter, you should understand that client/server is much more than a common storage location. You can't create a client/server system by using Microsoft Access database tables, for example, whether the tables are stored on a file server or a local system, because no intelligent engine can process the database independently of your application. The logic controlling the data is still driven by your client-side application.

N O T E You can create Access-based client/server systems by creating linked or attached tables to an Access database. These tables can be based in a server-based intelligent database system and can help you create a client/server system in Access. The statement that Access database tables aren't client/server refers only to the native Access database tables, which typically are contained in physical files that have the .MDB extension. ■

Part

I

Ch

4

Typical Roles of the Client Side

Client-side applications are responsible for displaying information to users, manipulating information in the database and on the user's screen, displaying reports, and providing for user-interruptible operations. Any operation that you submit to the server component of your system should never require users to intervene to complete the operation.

The client application typically is written in a host language, such as Delphi, PowerBuilder, Visual Basic, C, and C++. These applications allow users to perform, add, change, and delete operations against the database, when applicable.

The client application should avoid, at nearly all costs, having to work with the entire contents of the database tables. When a set of information is worked with by the client application, you should always think of it as being a *results set*, not the entire data set that is available to you. A results set indicates that you should ask the server application to filter and limit the information that will be presented to you, so that the operations you carry out are completed against as small a set of information as possible.

One of the best comparisons of older systems and client/server compares a file cabinet and a folder. In older systems, you typically do the equivalent of asking for a file cabinet full of information, so you can take the time to sift through the contents to find the file that you want. In this scenario, your client-side application is the piece that does the sifting. All information from the database table is passed through the client, with does the filtering to find the information that you want to work with.

In the client/server world, however, you simply request the file folder that you want. You don't filter through the file cabinet; the server process does. This arrangement limits network traffic, because only the results set is passed back over the network. Another significant benefit of this arrangement is that it also increases performance for your application. Typically, server systems are powerful computing platforms. Because this optimized server platform can work with all information locally, it can do so at top speed, processing the information at the best rate possible.

In short, your client-side application should be optimized to work with the results sets. This fact works hand-in-hand with database structure and design, because you need to make sure that you create the database in such a way that it supports this requirement. You have to define in the contents of the database the joins, queries, stored procedures, and table structures that support this optimized query.

In summary, following are some guidelines for the client side of your application:

- The client should gather all needed information before making a request of the server.
- The client is responsible for all display of data to the user.
- The client should work with results sets rather than tables.
- The client should handle all data-manipulation operations.
- The client provides all formatting of data and presentation of information in reports.

Typical Roles of the Server Side

The server side of the client/server equation typically is task-oriented, which means that operations are broken into logical components. This process is what you're starting to see now with Microsoft's BackOffice offerings. You have server-side components that control mainframe connectivity with the SNA (Systems Network Architecture) Server, database access with SQL Server, electronic mail with the Exchange Server, Internet and intranet access with Internet Information Server, and more products on the horizon that continue in this vein.

With SQL Server, your goal is to create the results sets that the client-side applications require. The database engine is responsible for carrying out information storage, updating, and retrieval in the system. When you start working with SQL Server, you'll notice that it has no user interface (UI) at all. Utilities are available to help you manage it, but SQL Server in and of itself has no UI. This situation occurs by design. SQL Server exists to fulfill requests made of it to the point of returning the results from those requests. Unlike Access, dBASE, FoxPro, and similar products, SQL Server has no involvement in showing users the results of these queries.

When you design your database structures, you need to keep close watch on the way that you implement informational control in your system. Different people may need different access levels to the information, for example, so security should be a major issue in querying the database. In such a case, your table structures and joins need to reflect this requirement.

Also keep in mind the way that users are going to access your information. In today's open systems, new challenges exist in presenting and controlling information. As you create your database tables and the rules that govern them, you need to assume absolutely nothing about the client side of the application. A good question to ask yourself is, "When I receive this information, what needs to happen with it?" You can answer this question by saying, "It needs to be stored for later retrieval."

If you're storing sales information, you should validate the item code of the item that is being sold. Does it exist in the inventory database? Is sufficient stock on hand to sell this item? Do you force sufficient stock levels, or do you allow a "negative stock" situation to occur and simply log the discrepancy in a suspected transactions table?

Each issue requires work on the database side through rules and triggers that allow you to define the functions carried out automatically by the server, based on database values. True, you could expect the client application to complete these tasks, but what if someone is accessing your database from Excel or Word? Can you really assume that the user has made sure that these checks are taking place? The server should carry out these important tasks to make sure that they are done, regardless of the point of entry.

N O T E For additional information about rules and triggers, see Chapter 15, "Creating and Managing Triggers." In Chapter 13, "Managing and Using Rules, Constraints, and Defaults," you can find out more about server-side automation. In addition, see Chapter 25, "Accessing SQL Server Databases Through Front-End Products." ■

Part

I

Ch

4

Exceptions to the Rules and Roles

There are exceptions to every rule, and the client/server model certainly is subject to this fact. These may be times where you need to do more processing on the client, or cases on the server where you want to blindly store information received. You need to address these situations on a case-by-case basis, but keep in mind that the client/server model is there to help and guide your efforts. Always be cautious when you develop systems that fall outside the model, because more often than not, you're asking for trouble.

> **CAUTION**
>
> While you're implementing an intricate trigger or rule, it may seem to be the right thing to do, but it can become a nightmare if you try to move too much functionality to the wrong side of the client/server model.
>
> Think long and hard about other ways that you can implement something if you put into place an operation that breaks the client/server model. You'll be glad that you did.

Establishing a Road Map to Your Database

At the start of this chapter, it was stated that one way you can design your database is diagram it and work out the relationships between tables on paper first. This practice helps point out any flaws in the points of information that you may need to extract from the system.

Database flow-charts consist of *entity relationship diagrams,* or *ERDs*. ERDs show exactly how a database is structured, what the relationships between the tables are, what rules and triggers are involved in maintaining referential integrity, and so on. One benefit of the ERD is that you can sit down with the client and take a logical walk through the database, making sure that the system serves the client's needs.

N O T E It's beyond the scope of this book to provide an all-encompassing view of the intricacies of entity relationship diagramming. The information provided in this chapter is meant to fit 90 percent of the cases for what you'll be doing. In some cases, you need to implement slightly different or less frequently used facets of the ERD systems. In those cases, you'll be best served by consulting the capabilities of your design software and database back end, as well as the resources available on the Internet and in other sources of information on the world of ERD. ■

Entity Relationships are Diagramming the Flow Charts of the Database World

Entity relationships are shown by drawings that include several objects. These objects include entities, attributes, and relationships. You can depict each aspect of your system in a specific way. Figure 4.7 shows a basic diagram for the point-of-sale system discussed in this chapter.

The customer table was added to track an order for a customer, but apart from this addition, the table structure reflects the earlier tables and relationships. Look at the way that these basic objects—the entities, attributes, and relationships—apply to the simple model.

FIG. 4.7
This diagram shows a relational diagram for the grocery sales system.

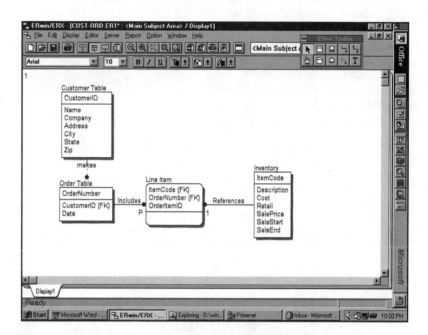

Using and Referencing Entities   Figure 4.8 shows four boxes, each of which represents a table, or entity. These entities will become the tables in the database, and each box includes the columns that will be created for the table. Each entity's object has two sections, with a portion above the dividing line and a portion below it.

 When you name entities, you should always make their names singular. This practice helps reinforce the fact that an entity contains only one instance of the object it represents.

The portion above the dividing line represents the identifying portion of the row. Remember that to have a normalized database in 3NF, you need to be able to uniquely identify each row instance in the database table. By placing the identifying characteristics above the line, it's easy to read and determine how the record will be retrieved in most cases.

In Figure 4.8, you can see that by the definition for the customer table, you'll most likely retrieve records from it by using the CustomerID.

N O T E   Although a record may usually be retrieved by this identifier, it's not an exclusive handle to the row. In most systems, you need to provide other means of retrieving rows. In the Customer table, for example, you probably will need to implement some name searches.

continues

continued

These searches won't include the Customer ID, but after you find the customer that the user wants to work with, you are likely to retrieve the Customer ID for the selection and then retrieve the entire customer record that was selected. ■

FIG. 4.8

The basic entity is represented by a box that typically contains two sections.

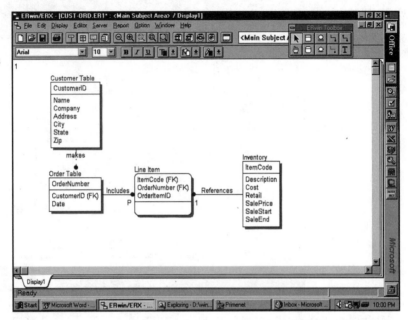

Using and Referencing Attributes   Attributes go hand in hand with the entity objects. *Attribute* is the term for the different column elements that make up the entity object—the table in the database. Attributes for the Customer table include CustomerID, Name, Company, and so on.

Attributes are described as *key* or *non-key*. As the name implies, non-key attributes are those items that make up the entity that don't depend on any other entity. In other words, non-key attributes don't make up, or constitute part of, a key that's used in the entity.

Key attributes come in two types: primary and nonprimary. *Primary keys* are always shown above the line, indicating that they're identifying attributes for this entity. If the attribute is a key to the entity but not part of the identifying structure for the entity, it's placed below the line.

If an item refers to a key value in another table, it's known as a *foreign key*. Again, if you reference the basic model, as shown in Figure 4.9, you can see that the Customer table doesn't have any foreign-key segments, but the Order table does, as indicated by (FK). The foreign keys in the Order table are nonidentifying, but they help designate the customer to whom the order refers.

Moving from the Order table to the Line Item table, you see that the OrderNumber *is* listed as an identifying component of the Line Item table. To find a specific instance of an order line item, then, you need to know the OrderItemID, the ItemCode, and the OrderNumber. In this implementation, the Line Item table is an associative table between the Inventory table and the Order table.

FIG. 4.9

The basic ERD shows foreign keys as primary (identifying) and non-primary (nonidentifying) columns in the sample tables.

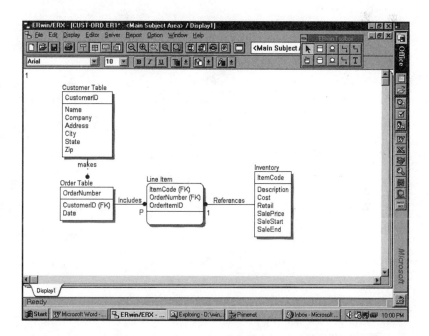

Using and Referencing Relationships If a "proof-is-in-the-pudding" segment of database design ever existed, it's in the relationships that you define between the different entities. It's easiest and most descriptive to look to your database ERDs to tell a story, in plain English, about what's happening in the database. In Figure 4.9, you see verbs between the entities. These verbs describe the relationships between the two entities and are indicated by the relationship line between them.

A customer makes orders in the Order table, and an order includes line items that reference inventory items. You can also read the diagram in the other direction. You could also say that inventory items are referenced by line items. In any event, you should be able to show concise paths for information to follow when you are trying to reach an end result.

The examples use ERwin by Logic Works. This tool allows you to define the different objects and then place the relationships between the objects appropriately. In the relationship between the Customer and Order tables, Figure 4.10 shows that the relationship is nonidentifying and that the relationship is a zero, one or more relationship.

You can also see that the key in the Order table that will be used to retrieve the customer information is CustomerID. This key is automatically added to the Order table and to the non-key portion of the record. If you define an identifying relationship, CustomerID is moved to the top portion, or identifying-key portion, of the Order table entity.

FIG. 4.10

ERwin allows you to define the relationship between the Customer and Order tables easily.

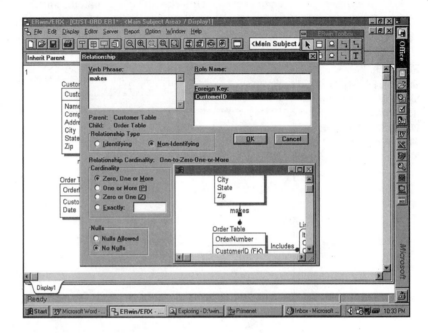

Each of the other relationships is defined in a similar manner. You can walk down the table structure and determine exactly how the different entities will interact. The following sections guide you through the design process with the customer.

System-Architecture Definition

Creating a solid definition for a database structure involves several steps. In many cases, you can point to flaws in the database design, only to realize that if the customer were more completely involved in the process, the problem could have been averted.

While you are bringing a customer up to speed, terminology, methodology, and approach aren't the goal of client reviews. The goal of any system that you'll endeavor to write is to ensure that the database structure supports the functionality of the system. This is where the maxim "Determine the output first; then input will follow" comes to bear on a project. It's certainly true that the test of any system is the output. If you created the best system ever devised to allow input of information but didn't provide a way to get meaningful information out of the system, you wasted your time.

Defining User's Goals for the System

The first thing that you need to do is decide what you'll be providing for the customer. Reports and output nearly always are a developer's least favorite part of a system to develop and implement. Often, one of the first statements that a developer makes to a customer is, "We'll give you reporting tools to create your own reports. All we need to do now is figure out what needs to happen in the program." This statement is a formula for problems.

If you don't know that the users need to have an aging report from their point-of-sale system's accounts-receivable subsystem, for example, would you automatically store the date on which the original invoice went out?

N O T E Involving the user may seem to prolong the development process. But many studies and personal experiences have proved otherwise. Spending the time now pays off many times over later in the project, in terms of more accurate deadlines, correct designs, and the like. ■

Truly, the only way you can ensure that you're not coding in vain is to make sure that you fulfill the output needs for the system.

Following is a general set of guidelines that not only allows you to ensure that you've hit at least the high points of your target audience, but also relates nicely to the database-design topics covered in this chapter:

- Meet with your users, and get a good overview of what they need from the system. Make the discussion as specific as possible. Get copies of current forms, reports, screen shots of what they may have on their current systems, and so on.

- Create a functional overview of the system. An overall system flow-chart is a good component of the overview, allowing the customers to review the system and ensuring that you understand what's happening at different steps in the flow of work through the system.

- Present the functional overview to the users. Walk through the system carefully to make sure that it's correct.

- Create a set of tables by using a good ERD tool. Don't worry about foreign keys and the like initially. At this point, it's more important to simply make sure that you're gathering the right information for the users.

- Present the database tables to the users—not from the perspective that they should understand how and why you've laid out the tables the way you have, but more from the standpoint of "OK, ask me any question about where some bit of information will be stored. We want to make sure that we can show you all the information you need." The first thing that you should do, even before meeting with the customers, is review the reports and samples that you obtained early on, to make sure that you're addressing them appropriately.

- Next, put into place the relationships between the tables, as needed. Make sure that you can walk down all the logical paths that you expect the users will need, based on your needs analysis. More information about resolving many-to-many joins appears in the following section of this chapter.

- Present this schema to the users with a challenge. Ask them to present a query for information from the system. Can you satisfy that query with identifying or non-identifying relationships? Can you get there from here?

These questions are the test of your database design. You should be able to address each of the stated intentions for the system.

> **N O T E** Systems get very complex very fast. The importance of reviewing systems with users can't
> be overemphasized. In one such case, working with the users prevented a substantial
> design rewrite. Although the information to determine a specific-case customer was available, the
> database tables hadn't provided for the relationships correctly. Preventing this oversight early on saves
> many, many hours of development time in the long run. ■

Avoiding Many-to-Many Joins

In some cases, you face a join situation that won't resolve to a single instance on either side of the database-table equation. In such a case, consider implementing an associative table that provides a link between the tables. You can see a simple example of this technique in the sample system, because you could just add ItemCode to the Order table.

> **N O T E** A *join* is a way of creating a logical view of your data. You specify how the information is
> retrieved, and what information you want to see. Then SQL Server returns the results set to
> your client application in the form of a set of data from the tables as you've requested. ■

If you didn't have the associative table between the Order Table and the Inventory table, you would end up with a many-to-many relationship between the two tables. This isn't a good way to accomplish the relationship, because you wouldn't have a singular path for identifying an instance of an order record. Figure 4.11 shows the associative table, the Line Item table.

When to Break the Mold

Sometimes, fully normalizing the database tables just doesn't work with the model that you're putting into place. You're most likely to encounter this situation in terms of performance. You may end up with a join to return information that simply takes too long to complete.

If you're working with static tables in your application (as may be the case with the inventory table in the example), you may want to load that table to a local Access table for access by your application. If you were to do this once a day, you'd be reasonably assured of having the correct, up-to-date information at the workstations.

You may be loading down tables that, when considered alone, don't provide a complete picture. If you have a customer table, an account-balance table, and a sales-representative table related by means of customer number, you end up with a three-way join to return a complete picture of the information.

You may want to consider denormalizing this set of tables at the client. In this case, you could create a single table that holds the information from all three tables as a single row of information. Thereafter, when you request information for customer X, you receive all the information that you need, and a further join isn't required.

FIG. 4.11

An associative table has been implemented to remove the many-to-many relationship problem imposed by the Order and Inventory tables.

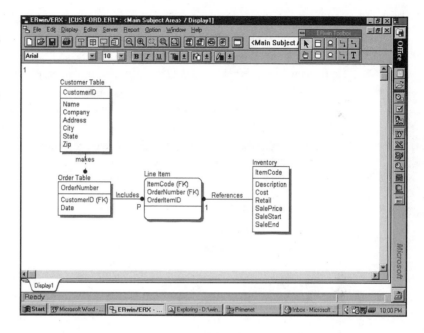

NOTE In reality, you wouldn't want to manipulate something as potentially dynamic as the customer-account balance in a remote mode. As a rule, you should use this method of denormalization only for static tables, or at least for those that change infrequently. ■

From Here...

In this chapter, you reviewed a great deal of information that can pay off in the long run for your applications. Be sure to normalize your database tables to the highest degree possible. If you find exceptions to the normalization goals, you should make sure that you're not overlooking some other method of accomplishing the same task.

Review your plan carefully with your customers, whether the customers are internal or external clients. This review provides substantial leverage in your projects and helps you come in on time and on budget.

The following chapters provide additional information that you'll find useful in your database-design efforts:

■ Chapter 7, "Retrieving Data with Transact-SQL," shows you how to create the joins that this chapter talks about. The chapter also shows you how to create the SQL statements that you need to retrieve the information in the format, order, and filtered results sets that you can work with most optimally.

Part

I

Ch

4

- Chapter 10, "Managing and Using Views," shows you how to create the logical data sets that you'll be working with in SQL Server's relational environment.

- Chapter 13, "Managing and Using Rules, Constraints, and Defaults," shows you how to implement business rules and data integrity in your database tables.

- Chapter 15 "Creating and Managing Triggers," helps you add referential integrity to your applications by enabling server-side processes when certain data-driven events occur.

- Chapter 20, "SQL Server Security," helps you determine the best approach for securing your database and the objects that it contains.

CHAPTER 5

Creating Devices, Databases, and Transaction Logs

The storage of physical data in SQL Server is controlled through the creation of Devices. *Devices* are areas of disk that are preallocated for the use of SQL Server, and appear as files on your system. SQL Server can use devices for the storage of data, logs, or database dumps.

Databases are logical areas that SQL Server reserves for the storage of tables and indexes. One or more databases can be created on a given device; the only gating factor is that the overall size of the databases on a device can't exceed the size of the device.

Transaction logs, covered in Chapter 12, "Understanding Transactions and Locking," are the work areas that SQL Server uses to manage a sort of picture of the information on your system in a before-and-after state. This before-and-after information is used to control transaction rollbacks, should the need arise, and they are also used to recover a database, should it need to be restored or restarted unexpectedly. ■

- **Learn how to create and use devices**

  SQL Server places databases onto devices. Devices must be created on a computer system's storage device, usually a hard drive.

- **Learn how to create and use databases and transaction logs**

  Databases store data and are where you create the tables that you use in SQL server. Transaction logs store transactions that were made against a database, providing for the rollback and other fault-tolerant capabilities of SQL Server.

- **Become familiar with tempdb and its use**

  SQL Server uses a temporary database as an electronic scratch pad to work with information requests. There are several things that can be done to tempdb to enhance performance.

- **Learn how to create and use removable media databases**

  Many applications are sent to a remote site to be executed or are for temporary applications. Databases stored on removable media might be more efficient and cost-effective for such applications.

Defining Devices

Devices are the physical files that SQL Server creates on-disk for storing databases and logs. Devices must be created before databases can be created. A device can be of two types: a *database device* is used for storing databases, and a *dump device* is used for storing transaction logs.

Devices can store more than one database or transaction log in them. However, you often get better performance with a single database per device. This performance increase results from the fact that each device is managed by a single I/O thread from the operating system. By allocating only a single database per device, you're, in effect, setting up your system so that it can service each database with a different I/O thread, instead of sharing these threads between databases.

A database can span multiple devices if it needs to grow, and this can be an optimizing method due to striped physical disk access over multiple drives.

The optimization comes from being able to split a database across devices. This gives you two distinct advantages. First, you can place the different devices on different physical drives. By doing so, you allow the different disk drives to service the device, effectively giving you more than one set of read/write heads working on a database request. This can be an especially big benefit in a larger database with large amounts of random requests for information that tend to span the database, or impact it at different points.

The performance increase can be less in a case where your application is largely responsible for inserting new records. This is because the new records are likely to be maintained on the expanded portion of the database and to reside on the same device and physical disk as the database grows.

The second optimization from splitting the database across devices comes from the I/O threads used by the operating system. Because each device is managed by a different I/O thread, when you put different portions of your database on different devices, you allow the system to allocate more than one I/O thread to support your database. Once again, this can be a real benefit to larger databases.

Creating Database Devices

You can create a disk device in SQL Server in two ways. Graphically, you create a disk device by using the SQL Enterprise Manager. Another process is Transact-SQL, T-SQL, using either the ISQL command-line utility or the ISQL/W Windows-based utility.

The Transact-SQL method is performed using the DISK INIT command. Both the Enterprise Manager and T-SQL methods are discussed in the following sections.

Using SQL Enterprise Manager   *SQL Enterprise Manager* is a versatile tool that permits Database Administrators (DBAs) to perform most of the administrative functions of SQL Server without knowledge of the often cryptic Transact-SQL commands required.

In some cases, when you create your SQL Server system, you'll want to use an ISQL Script, which enables you to run an essentially unattended installation. One drawback to the Enterprise Manager is that it does not permit this type of unattended installation. Although you can load the installation scripts and run them easily, you cannot run the Enterprise Manager from the command-line. It's meant to be more of an interactive tool for management of the server.

To use SQL Enterprise Manager to create a device, follow these steps:

1. Start SQL Enterprise Manager from the Microsoft SQL Server 6.5 group. Figure 5.1 shows SQL Enterprise Manager just after it has been started.

FIG. 5.1
Note that no server is selected, and that most of the main toolbar buttons are disabled.

2. Select the server that is going to be managed. Then, from the Manage menu, choose Database Devices. The Manage Database Devices window appears, as shown in Figure 5.2.

3. Click the New Device toolbar button, located farthest to the left on the Manage Database Devices dialog box, to create a new device. The New Database Device dialog box appears (see Figure 5.3).

4. Enter the details about the device being added, including the name, where the device should be placed, and its size (see Figure 5.4).

Part
I

Ch
5

FIG. 5.2
Each existing device is shown as a bar on the graph, with the dark area representing unused space in the device.

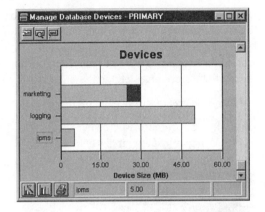

FIG. 5.3
With the New Database Device dialog box, you can use the slider to specify how big the device should be by dragging it to the right to indicate the size you need.

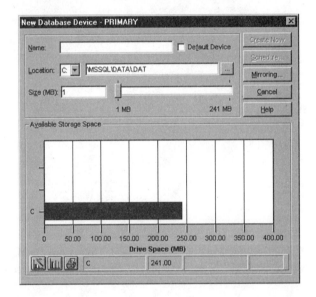

5. Click Create Now to begin creating the device. The length of time that this process takes depends on the size of the device being created and the speed of the physical drives being used. After the device is successfully created, you see the message box shown in Figure 5.5.

> **N O T E**   This device can be scheduled to be created by using the Schedule button. This option lets the user enter a time—a single or recurring instance—for the operation to be performed. In addition, the Transact-SQL script that SQL Server uses to complete the operation can be edited. Additions or modifications can make the scheduled operation more powerful than simply creating a table. ▪

FIG. 5.4
The information entered creates a 50M device called Demodevice on the C drive using the physical file C:\MSSQL\DATA\ demodevice.DAT.

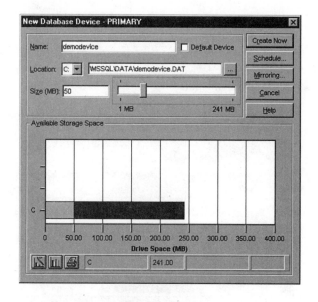

FIG. 5.5
This message indicates that no errors occurred during the allocation of disk space for the database device's creation.

 TIP If you remove a device, you need to restart SQL Server before you can create a new device with the same physical file name. For example, if you create a test device, remove it; then try to re-create it again. SQL Server fails during the second creation step. You receive an error message indicating that the file could not be opened/accessed (see Figure 5.6).

FIG. 5.6
You may receive an error message if you try to create a new device with the same name as a previously existing device.

T I P After you restart SQL Server, you can create the new device as needed.

After successful creation of the device, SQL Enterprise Manager will add it to the graph of devices. This graph is shown in Figure 5.7.

FIG. 5.7
The NewDevice device
has been added and is
now empty, as indicated
by the dark graph bar.

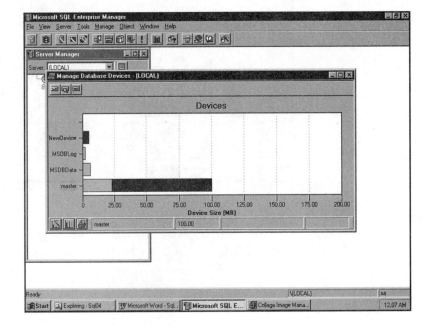

N O T E SQL Server creates a physical file on the drive when the device is created. If you are using NT File System, NTFS, the operating system returns control to SQL Enterprise Manager immediately after executing the create command because of the way NTFS represents files to calling programs. Don't be concerned if device creation that took a long time on FAT or OS/2 HPFS is very quick. This speed is one of the blessings of NT's new file system. ■

Using *DISK INIT* DISK INIT is the T-SQL equivalent of creating a device through SQL Enterprise Manager. In fact, SQL Enterprise Manager's graphical front end is actually just creating the right DISK INIT command to be sent to the server. The syntax for the use of DISK INIT is as follows:

```
DISK INIT
    NAME = 'logical_name',
    PHYSNAME = 'physical_name',
    VDEVNO = virtual_device_number,
    SIZE = number_of_2K_blocks
    [, VSTART = virtual_address]
```

The options for the T-SQL command DISK INIT are as shown in Table 5.1.

TIP Before you run the DISK INIT command, run SP_HELPDEVICE. This stored procedure shows you what device numbers are already in use. Device 0 is reserved for the main, default device on your system, but all other non-used values are available for your new device.

By running SP_HELPDEVICE first, you can avoid getting an error message when you run the DISK INIT indicating that the device number is already in use.

Table 5.1 DISK INIT Parameters

Parameter	Description
logical name	Any valid SQL Server identifier. A shorter name is helpful as it has to be used each time a database is created.
physical name	The full path and file name of the file to be used on the hard disk to store the data.
virtual device number	The unique system identifier for the device. It can range from 0 to 255. Zero (0) is reserved for the master database, but it cannot duplicate any existing virtual device number in your system.
number of 2k blocks	This is how a device is sized, which is the minimum value of 512, equivalent to 1M.
virtual address	This parameter controls the virtual paging of the data device and how SQL Server accesses it. This parameter should be used only when you're working closely with a product support technician at Microsoft and is not typically something you'll need to work with.

Using the DISK INIT command, the following SQL statement creates the same data device that was created earlier by using the SQL Enterprise Manager.

```
DISK INIT
    Name = 'NewDevice',
    PhysName = 'C:\SQL60\DATA\NewDevice.DAT',
    VDevNo = 6,
    Size = 2500
```

Understanding Device Options

There are two different options that you can consider for devices you create. Though not required, these options may be helpful depending on the environment you are setting up. The options control how devices are used after you've created them. These options, *mirroring* and *default devices*, let you indicate to SQL Server how the devices will be used, and you provide information about how SQL Server can apply special processing to the devices.

One option, that of creating a mirroring device, is provided to give you a fault tolerant option. The other option, creating a default device, can save time when you create databases on your system.

The specifics of these options are covered in the next two sections.

Mirroring   When you set up a device for *Mirroring,* you indicate to SQL Server that it should write transactions to databases on the device twice. This is done once on the primary device defined for the database and once on the mirror device.

Take care in selecting the location of the mirror. You'll be doing yourself little or no good if you place the mirror device on the same physical drive as the source device. If you do, and the drive fails, you will lose both the source device and the mirror.

Because hard drives are the most likely candidate for a system failure that impacts data, you may want to consider this option to protect your databases.

N O T E   Windows NT also supports several fault-tolerant options that are enforced at the operating system level. For more information, please refer to Que's *Special Edition Using Microsoft Windows NT Server* and see the information topics regarding striped disk storage.

In most cases, the operating system's implementation of mirroring provides better performance and options than SQL Server. These options might include various implementations of Redundant Arrays of Inexpensive Drives, RAID. There are six levels of RAID, zero(0) to five(5), that can be implemented and they provide different methods of distributing physical data across multiple drives. ■

Overview of Mirroring

Mirroring is done when SQL Server writes changes to a device to two locations at once. The primary location is your standard device. This is the database that you are normally using and have incorporated in your system's applications. Because both devices are identical, if a switch is required from the main device to the secondary device, there is no data loss, and the users of your system will not be interrupted in their use of the system.

Another key aspect of mirroring and the device change that happens when the system recovers from a device failure is that it is completely transparent to your applications. They can still access the system with the same database references and programmatic statements and require no changes in the code to reference the substituted device.

▶ **See** Appendix B, "Understanding RAID," **p. 731,** for more information about levels of RAID.

As SQL Server uses a device, if it can no longer access the main device, it automatically switches to the mirror device, making all future changes to the mirror. When you've recovered the drives containing the problem device, you can move the information back to the original device and restart SQL Server using the corrected devices as the default once again.

SQL Server performs mirroring by installing a mirror-handling *user* on the server. This user is listed as spid 1 in the system processes, which you can list by running the system procedure sp_who. Mirroring is a continuous operation and provides maximum redundancy in the event of a failure.

You can also set up mirroring to be handled by the underlying Windows NT Operating System and with some hardware-only solutions. For more information on these options, be sure to review the documentation for the product you are considering to ensure that it is compatible with up-time requirements for your system.

Setting Up Mirroring with Enterprise Manager

When you create a device, or if you edit a device, you'll notice an option to establish mirroring. In Figure 5.8, you can see the options that enable you to work with a device.

FIG. 5.8
Right-click a device and select Edit to modify mirroring options.

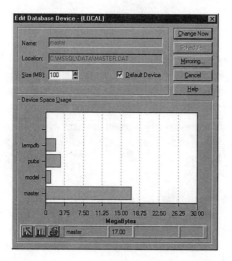

Click Mirroring to indicate where the mirror file will be located. Remember, the paths you designate are relative to the server. If you're working from a workstation, be careful to keep this in mind. You can select a location that is either on the current server or on a fully qualified network path (see Figure 5.9).

FIG. 5.9
When you select the location of the mirror file, SQL Server mirrors the requested database.

Part
I

Ch
5

> **CAUTION**
>
> If you're using long file names for your devices (such as *NewDevice*), be aware that there seems to be a bug in the way that SQL Enterprise Manager assigns the name of the mirror device. SQL Enterprise Manager defaults the name to be limited by the old FAT 8.3 limitations and truncates *NewDevice* to *NewDevic*. This isn't a major problem, but it could result in SQL Server attempting to create duplicate files because the difference in the name is not considered until after the eighth byte of the file.
>
> For example, *NewDevice* and *NewDevice2* will have an identical default mirror name created, which will cause an error condition in SQL Enterprise Manager.

After the process is completed, the device is mirrored and SQL Server takes care of the rest. From that point on, any informational changes to the primary device are also reflected in the mirror device.

> **CAUTION**
>
> If you implement mirroring for a device, be sure you also mirror the Master database. This database is responsible for maintaining the system information necessary to continue processing should mirroring become necessary for any device. When you mirror the Master database, you're ensuring that you'll be able to enable SQL Server to recover the mirrored devices that have failed.
>
> If you do not mirror the Master database, you may find that you cannot utilize the mirrors for other devices, as this information (the information about the mirrored devices managed by SQL Server) is maintained in the Master database and could be lost.

The final step is to tell SQL Server about the mirrored device in the case of the Master database. Because the Master database is used to start the server, you need to indicate to the server where the mirror can be found if it is needed. Other devices are managed automatically, so this step is only required for the Master database.

There are two parameters required at SQL Server startup that control the Master database's mirrored state: -r and -d. Figure 5.10 shows the SQL Server Configuration/Options dialog box. Choose Server, SQL Server, Configure to open this dialog box. Click the Parameters button on the Server Options page and then add the startup parameters.

Add a new parameter,-r<mirror location>, which indicates the location of the mirror for the master device. Note that, even after SQL has switched to the mirror device during normal use, when you restart the system, it must still first try the primary Master device. This means that you must leave the -d specification that is showing the location of the "normal" Master device. When you add the -r option, you're specifying the fallback position that SQL should use when it has determined the master device to have become unusable.

Click the _Add_ button to create a new parameter, and be sure to specify the entire path and file name to the mirror device file when you create the -r parameter.

FIG. 5.10
Startup options that enable mirroring the Master database can be set in the SQL Server configuration sub-system.

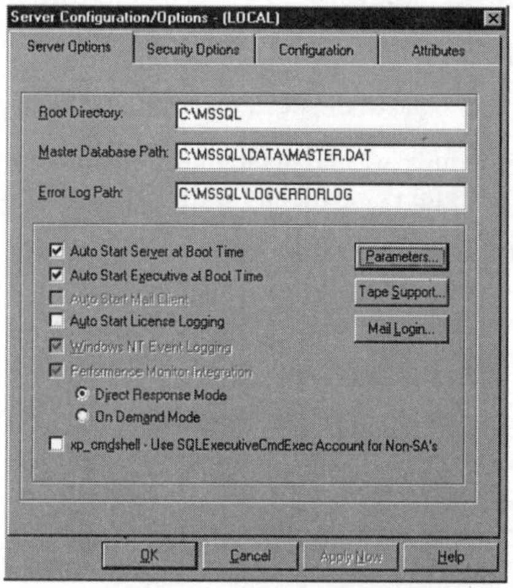

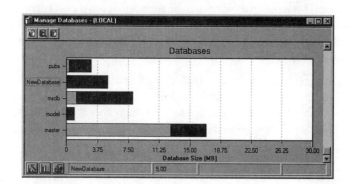

Figure 5.11 shows the dialog box that enables you to indicate the startup options.

FIG. 5.11
Be sure to specify both -r and -d options for the Master device. If both are not found, the mirroring will not work correctly.

Part

I

Ch

5

Setting Up Mirroring Using Transact-SQL

When you set up mirroring using T-SQL, you'll use the DISK MIRROR command.

The DISK MIRROR command's syntax is as follows:

```
DISK MIRROR
     NAME = 'logical_name',
     MIRROR = 'physical_name'
     [, WRITES = {SERIAL ¦ NOSERIAL }]
```

The parameters shown in Table 5.2 are available for the DISK MIRROR command:

Table 5.2 *DISK MIRROR* **parameters**

Parameter	Description
logical name	This is the name of the device that will be mirrored.
physical name	This is the full path and file name of the mirror device. Use an extension of MIR for compatibility with SQL Enterprise Manager.
WRITES	This option is provided for backward compatibility with earlier versions of SQL Server for operating systems other than NT. It is not used with Windows NT.

The following example shows how to mirror the NewDevice created earlier:

```
DISK MIRROR
    Name = 'NewDevice',
    Mirror = 'C:\SQL60\DATA\NEWDEVICE.MIR'
```

What to Do When Mirroring Is in Force

When SQL Server has switched to a mirror, it automatically suspends mirroring with the original device. This frees up the device to be replaced or otherwise corrected. When the mirroring is active, the users of your system will not notice any difference in the functioning of their applications. They'll be able to continue working just as they did before the problem was found with the original device.

After you've replaced the original device, or otherwise corrected the problem that was detected, you can re-mirror the active device back to the primary device. Re-mirroring is identical to the original job of mirroring a device. You simply specify the file name that will contain the mirror, and SQL Server takes care of the rest.

N O T E Mirroring can have a significant impact on performance on your system. Since SQL Server is forced to write the information to two devices instead of one, you'll quickly find that the overhead involved can be substantial. There are a few things you can consider to help lessen this impact, specifically:

- Don't mirror devices that hold transaction logs. These devices are the highest volume of the different components of your SQL Server system and, therefore, the impact imposed by the mirroring can be extreme.
- Consider hardware solutions that enable you to install more than one hard disk adapter and let the system manage the mirroring of the hard disk drives in your system. Using this approach, you'll significantly decrease the overall impact on your system. ■

If you want to switch from a current device to the mirror, as may be the case where you've just brought a replacement for a failed device online, the following are the steps you'll follow, from the creation of the original mirror through failure of the device to replacement of it and re-mirroring to return to the original state:

1. Mirror the original device.
2. The device fails; SQL Server switches to the mirror device and continues processing.
3. Replace or correct the original device.
4. Re-mirror the active device back to the original.
5. Unmirror the device, selecting the option to Switch to Mirror Device—Replace option.
6. Mirror the device, now the replacement for the original, back to the backup device.

At this point, you're back where you started with the original device being the active device and the mirror standing by as needed to back it up.

As you can see, mirroring your devices can provide powerful backup capabilities to your key production systems.

▶ **See** Chapter 19, "SQL Server Administration" in the section, "Backing Up and Restoring Databases and Transaction Logs" **p. 555**, for more information about backup techniques and approaches.

Establishing Default Devices   Default devices are used by SQL Server when the CREATE DATABASE command isn't accompanied by a specific device on which it should be placed. Many devices can be specified as default. SQL Server uses them alphabetically until each device is filled.

When SQL Server is installed, the MASTER device is set up as the default device. This means that if you inadvertently create a new database and do not indicate the device on which to place it, it will be created on the MASTER device. This is never a good thing.

The full syntax is explained in the next portion of this chapter, but one of the first things you should do on a new system is create a new device that you can use as a starting point for all databases. Then, issue the command that will make the MASTER device a non-default device:

```
sp_diskdefault Master, defaultoff
```

and make the newly created device the new starting default device:

```
sp_diskdefault newdevice, defaulton
```

It might be a good idea to make this second, newly defined default device extremely small. This way, if you ever forget to indicate a default device when you create a database, the call will fail because it will run out of space. Think of it as a string around your finger, reminding you that you need to indicate the device you want to use for new databases.

To make a device a default device, select the Default Device check box on the Edit Database Devices dialog box in SQL Enterprise Manager. Alternately, use the sp_diskdefault system-stored procedure. The syntax for sp_diskdefault is as follows:

```
sp_diskdefault device_name, {defaulton ¦ defaultoff}
```

Device_name is the logical device name that's being made the default or not. If your device name has special characters you will need to enclose the device name in single quotes so that SQL Server recognizes it.

In the following example, the device NewDevice is made a default device:

```
sp_diskdefault NewDevice, defaulton
```

Displaying Device Information

There are two ways to find information about the devices that are now installed/active on a SQL Server. This can be done by using SQL Enterprise Manager or by using the system-stored procedure sp_helpdevice.

The syntax for sp_helpdevice is as follows:

```
sp_helpdevice [logical_name]
```

logical_name is the name of the device that's to be inspected. If no device is specified, sp_helpdevice reports information on all the devices on the SQL Server.

N O T E　The sp_helpdevice command must be entered through Transact-SQL. See the command line applications section of Chapter 1, "Introducing Microsoft SQL Server," for help on starting a command line ISQL session. There is also a graphical interface for ISQL/w. Transact-SQL commands can be entered in SQL Enterprise Manager by choosing Tools, SQL Query Tool. ■

CAUTION

If you use the command line ISQL application, remember to enter a go command to perform the commands entered to that point. The go command is the default command end identifier. This identifier can be changed by using a switch when starting the ISQL session. Again, see the command line applications section in Chapter 1.

Listing 5.1 shows the output and use of sp_helpdevice to view all the devices on the server:

Listing 5.1 Sample *sp_helpdevice* Results

```
/*-----------------------------
sp_helpdevice
------------------------------*/
device_name    physical_name            description
➥status cntrltype device_number low      high
-------------------------------------------------
diskdump       nul                      disk, dump device
➥16     2        0             0          20000
diskettedumpa  a:sqltable.dat           diskette, 1.2 MB, dump device
➥16     3        0             0          19
```

```
diskettedumpb   b:sqltable.dat                    diskette, 1.2 MB, dump device
➡16      4        0                0                19
master            C:\SQL60\DATA\MASTER.DAT        special, default disk, physical
➡disk, 40 MB
➡3       0        0                0                20479
MSDBData          C:\SQL60\DATA\MSDB.DAT          special, physical disk, 2 MB
➡2       0        127              2130706432       2130707455
MSDBLog           C:\SQL60\DATA\MSDBLOG.DAT       special, physical disk, 2 MB
➡2       0        126              2113929216       2113930239

(1 row(s) affected)
```

Creating Dump Devices

Dump devices are special devices that SQL Server uses to perform backups and to *dump*, or clear out, the transaction logs on databases. By default, SQL Server creates dump devices for the use of backups and log clearing. Several types of dump devices can be created, based on the medium to which the data is being written:

- *Disk.* A disk device can be a local disk device or a network disk device that is used for dumping data from the database as a backup. If the device is on the network, make sure that the NT server that is running SQL Server can access the network share where the device is placed.

- *Tape.* A tape dump device is used to back up a database directly to a tape device attached to the local computer. It isn't possible to dump to a tape attached to a remote computer.

- *Diskette.* A diskette dump device is provided for backward compatibility with earlier versions of SQL Server.

- *Named pipe.* SQL Server has a named pipes interface to perform backups; this interface allows third parties to hook in custom backup software and utilities. Named pipe devices aren't managed by SQL Enterprise Manager and must be explicitly referenced in a manual DUMP or LOAD command issued through ISQL or ISQL/W.

  ▶ **See** the Chapter 1, "Introducing SQL Server," in the section entitled "Command-Line Applications," **p. 11**.

- *NULL.* This is the special device used to dump the transaction logs of a database so that they're freed for more transactions to be posted against the server. Performing a dump to a NULL device removes log entries from the database/log without adding data to the device itself. The NULL device is named DISKDUMP and is added to the system automatically when SQL Server is created. You can't manually add a NULL device to an existing SQL Server.

You can add a dump device to the system through SQL Enterprise Manager, or by using the system-stored procedure sp_addumpdevice. The following two sections show you how to use both methods.

T I P   You'll find it easier, and faster, if you first dump a database or transaction log to a disk-based dump device, then use a backup utility to move the resulting dump file to a tape or other backup media. Having SQL Server place database or log dumps directly on a backup device can be substantially slower as it's not optimized for that type of access.

Using SQL Enterprise Manager to Add a Dump Device   Using SQL Enterprise Manager to add a dump device removes the burden on the DBA to remember the syntax required for the system-stored procedures that must be executed to perform the task.

To add a dump device by using SQL Enterprise Manager, follow these steps:

1. Launch SQL Enterprise Manager from the Microsoft SQL Server 6.5 group. Select the server that is going to be managed. From the Tools menu, choose Database Backup/ Restore. The Database Backup/Restore dialog box appears as shown in Figure 5.12.

FIG. 5.12
The Backup tab is chosen by default when entering this dialog box.

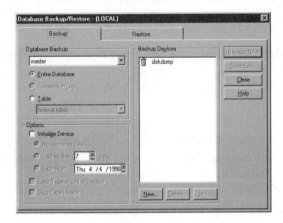

2. Click the New button to create a new dump device. The New Backup Device dialog box is displayed (see Figure 5.13).

FIG. 5.13
SQL Server places all disk-based dump devices in the Backup subdirectory by default.

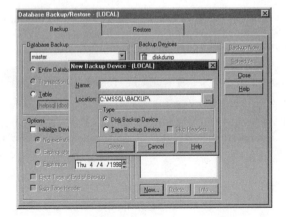

3. Enter a <u>N</u>ame and specify a <u>L</u>ocation for the device.

 TIP Click the . . . button to find a particular directory on the server or network.

4. Specify whether the device is <u>T</u>ape or Dis<u>k</u>, and then click the C<u>r</u>eate button. The device is added to SQL Server and to the list of available devices.

N O T E SQL Server allocates resources for a dump device in the list and in the `sysdevices` system catalog table. It doesn't, however, actually create a file/output item until a backup is actually performed to the device. If you click the dump device to inspect it before you perform a backup, you'll receive error #3201, and SQL Server will say that the device is offline. Don't worry about this error unless you're sure that a backup has been performed to the device. If that's the case, you'll want to rerun your backup to ensure that it completes successfully. ■

Using *sp_addumpdevice*   SQL Server's system-stored procedure `sp_addumpdevice` is used to add dump devices to the system. `sp_addumpdevice` is the only way that you can add a diskette-based device for dumping to the SQL Server. The syntax for `sp_addumpdevice` is as follows:

```
sp_addumpdevice {'disk' ¦ 'diskette' ¦ 'tape'},
      'logical_name',
      'physical_name'
```

N O T E Previous versions of SQL Server had some other parameters for `sp_addumpdevice` that were used to define the characteristics of the media being added. This is no longer necessary because SQL Server now inspects the device to determine its characteristics automatically. ■

The options for the system-stored procedure `sp_addumpdevice` are as follows:

- *logical_name*—This is the logical name of the device that is going to be used for backups/dumps.

- *physical_name*—This is the physical name of the device that is going to be used for the dump. For a `'disk'` or `'diskette'` dump device, specify the full path of the output file that should be created. For a `'tape'` device, reference the locally attached tape device by using Windows NT's Universal Naming Convention, UNC, such as `"\\.\tape0"`.

The following example adds a disk-based dump device to SQL Server:

```
sp_addumpdevice
      'DiskBackup',
      'C:\SQL60\Data\DISKBACKUP.DAT'
```

The following example adds a remote disk-based dump device on the network workstation/server MainFileServer:

```
sp_addumpdevice
      'NetworkBackup',
      '\\MainFileServer\Data\NETBACKUP.DAT'
```

Part

I

Ch

5

The following example adds a tape dump device to SQL Server:

```
sp_addumpdevice
        'TapeBackup',
        '\\.\Tape0'
```

Dropping Devices

There are two ways to drop a device. These are by using SQL Enterprise Manager or by using the system-stored procedure `sp_dropdevice`. Dropping a device frees the disk space associated with that device for other uses by the operating system or server.

If a device is not in use or is not correctly sized, it will be necessary to drop it so that it can be appropriately resized or the disk space given back to the operating system for other uses.

Using SQL Enterprise Manager to Remove Devices   SQL Enterprise Manager provides a simple interface to the removal of database devices and is a convenient tool for managing large enterprises where lots of servers are involved. The DBA no longer has to know all the physical layouts of the server's devices because they are represented graphically by SQL Enterprise Manager.

> **CAUTION**
>
> The drop device feature of SQL Enterprise Manager defaults to not removing the device file physically from the hard drive, nor does it give you an option to tell it to do so. Consequently, using SQL Enterprise Manager to remove a disk device won't actually make any disk space available for use on the server. You must go to a command prompt or to an Explorer Window and manually delete the file.
>
> If you're deleting a device so that the server frees up some allocated disk space, you're probably better off using `sp_dropdevice` and specifying `DELFILE`.

To use SQL Enterprise Manager to remove a database device, follow these steps:

1. In the SQL Enterprise Manager screen, select the server from which you want to remove the device. From the <u>M</u>anage menu, choose De<u>v</u>ices. The Manage Database Devices window appears (see Figure 5.14).

FIG. 5.14
SQL Enterprise Manager's Manage Database Devices window lists all the devices that are available on the server that is being managed.

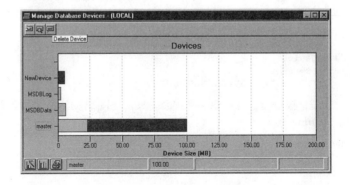

2. Click the device that you want to remove. From the Manage Database Devices window's toolbar, click the Delete Device button. A message box appears that confirms that you want to delete the device, as shown in Figure 5.15.

FIG. 5.15
This is the last chance to abort a device deletion.

If the database device has one or many databases or logs on it, a second warning dialog box appears, asking permission to drop all the databases/logs that reside on it (see Figure 5.16).

FIG. 5.16
This dialog box lists databases that are using the device about to be deleted. You must drop these databases before the device can be deleted.

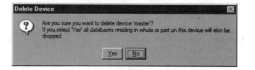

Using *sp_dropdevice* to Remove Devices   The system-stored procedure `sp_dropdevice` is provided for dropping devices from SQL Server. The syntax for `sp_dropdevice` is as follows:

```
sp_dropdevice logical_name[, DELFILE]
```

The options for the system-stored procedure `sp_dropdevice` are as follows:

- *logical_name*—This is the name of the device to be removed.
- *DELFILE*—If DELFILE is included, the physical file that was created on the server is also removed.

An error occurs if this procedure is run against a device that has databases in it. The databases must be dropped before the device can be deleted.

Defining Databases and Transaction Logs

Databases are logical entities in which SQL Server places tables and indexes. A database exists on one or many database devices. Correspondingly, a database device can have one or many databases on it.

Every database has a transaction log associated with it. The transaction log is a place where SQL Server writes all the database transactions before writing them to the database.

There are two types of operations written to the transaction log. The first, as you might guess, is the process of working with transactions in the programming sense. These "open" transactions let your application ensure database consistency based on the process that is going on in your application. In other words, it's a form of checkpoint in your application that lets you make sure you get everything done that you expect for a specific operation.

The other type of information written to the transaction log is the before-and-after picture of information in your database when you perform operations on it. That is, when you update a row, the before-and-after values of the row are stored in the transaction log.

In either event, the transaction log is used to recover the database should an error occur that requires a roll-back or roll-forward of information. It is what SQL Server uses to ensure database consistency relative to both the rules managed by the server, and the processing completed by your applications.

By default, the transaction log is placed on the same database device as the database. You can improve performance, however, by creating two devices, one for the log and one for the database itself. This helps performance because you'll be able to minimize the physical movement of the read-write heads on the disk drive. If you have only one physical drive for both the database and the log, the disk drive read-write operations will need to race back and forth between the database and the log on each operation.

Logs are a sequential type of operation, typically just logging new information to the end of the log. Because this is true, by placing the log on a different drive, you allow it to be fairly optimized, always ready for the next item to log. It won't have to re-seek the end of the log prior to writing the information to disk.

SQL Server can logically maintain up to 32,767 databases on a single server. However, it's more likely that the server will run out of disk, memory, and CPU resources before this limit is ever reached. A database can be up to 1T (Terabyte) in size and can have as many as 32 device *fragments,* which are portions of the database on different devices.

Given that physical disk sizes don't typically support this size of a hard drive, it would seem to be impossible to get a database much bigger than 320G, 10G/drive approximate current maximum disk size, by using SQL Server. However, a database device actually can be mapped to multiple physical devices, provided some form of software- or hardware-based striping is in use.

Striping is highly recommended because it provides substantial performance gains due to multiple physical disk drives being used for a single database device. When used with RAID, striping also provides an extra level of data integrity in case of a media failure.

▶ **See** Appendix B, "Understanding RAID," for more information, **p. 731.**

Creating a Database and Transaction Log

After you've created the device for a database and transaction log, you'll be able to create the database itself. This is the last step that you need to complete prior to creating the tables and other structures on which your system will be based. When you create a new database, SQL Server uses a template database, the *model* database, as the starting point for the database. You can think of the model database as having the default objects that are implemented on your systems databases.

The model database consists of the standard SQL Server objects:

- Groups and users—the only user created in a completely default system is the dbo, or Database Owner, user. The group created is the Public group, of which dbo is a member.
- Tables—no tables are included in the default model database.
- Views—no views are included in the default settings for the model database.
- Stored Procedures—there are no stored procedures included in the model database.
- Rules—Rules are not provided as part of the model database.
- Defaults—If you have defaults you want to impose on all new databases, you'll need to manually add them; there are none provided in the model database.
- User-Defined Datatypes—if you have datatypes that you want available in all databases, be sure to add them here. They'll automatically be included in all subsequent databases.

If you have certain attributes you want installed in any database you create, you can implement them in the model database. Then, when new databases are created, the custom attributes are inherited by the new database. One example of this is the case where you have a series of database administrators that you want to have access to all databases created on the system. By including them in the user list, you can make sure they're included in each database, with appropriate rights, as the databases are created.

You manage the model database as you do any other, and there are no limitations on the objects you can place within the database. You can use SQL Enterprise Manager to work with the different objects in the database.

There are two ways to create a database and transaction log. You can use either SQL Enterprise Manager or the CREATE DATABASE command. Each of these is described next.

N O T E You must either be the System Administrator, or SA, for the SQL Server, or you must have had appropriate rights granted to you by the SA in order to create databases. If you do not have rights, SQL Server will not allow you to create the new database. ∎

Using SQL Enterprise Manager to Create Database and Transaction Logs To create a database using SQL Enterprise Manager, follow these steps:

1. Launch SQL Enterprise Manager from the Microsoft SQL Server 6.5 group. Select the server that is going to be managed. From the Manage menu, choose Databases. The Manage Databases window appears (see Figure 5.17).

Part

I

Ch

5

FIG. 5.17
Each existing database
is shown as a bar on
the graph, with the dark
area representing
unused space in the
database.

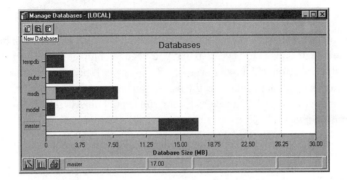

2. Click the New Database toolbar button to create a new database.

3. Enter the details about the database being added, including the name, the devices that the data and logs should be placed on, and how much disk space should be used for each. This is shown in Figure 5.18.

FIG. 5.18
In the SQL Enterprise
Manager's New
Database dialog box,
the required information
is entered to add a
3M database called
NewDatabase on the
NewDevice for data and
logs.

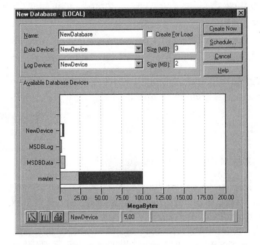

T I P SQL Server 6.0 introduced a new database creation option that stops any users from accessing a database until a load operation is performed. This option is very useful for a database administrator who wants to create a database without having any users connect to it.

Click the Create For Load check box in the New Database dialog box to stop any users from accessing the database until after the load operation has been completed.

4. Click Create Now. After the database is successfully created, the Manage Databases window appears, showing the new database in the graph (see Figure 5.19).

FIG. 5.19
The NewDatabase has been added, based on the model database, and is mostly empty.

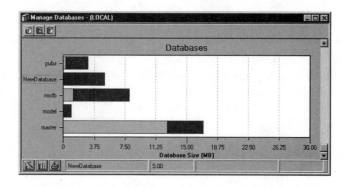

Using the *CREATE DATABASE* Command to Create Database and Transaction Logs The CREATE DATABASE command is the Transact-SQL method for creating a database. The syntax for CREATE DATABASE is as follows:

```
CREATE DATABASE database_name
     [ON {DEFAULT ¦ database_device} [= size]
     [, database_device [= size]]...]
     [LOG ON log_device [= size]
     [,log_device[= size]]...]
     [FOR LOAD]
```

The options for the Transact-SQL command CREATE DATABASE are as listed in Table 5.3.

Table 5.3   *CREATE DATABASE* Parameters

Parameter	Description
database_name	This is the name of the database to be created. The database name must comply with the standard rules for naming objects.
database_device	This is the device or list of devices that this database is to be created on and how much disk space, in megabytes, is to be reserved on each. If DEFAULT is specified, SQL Server chooses the next free default database device to use.
log_device	The LOG ON parameter is where the log device is specified. Like the database device, it's possible to specify more than one device to be used for the logging of the database being created.
FOR LOAD	This parameter denies user access until a LOAD operation has been completed on the database.

Part

I

Ch

5

The following example creates the same database that was created in the preceding section by using SQL Enterprise Manager:

```
CREATE DATABASE NewDatabase
     On NewDevice = 3
     Log On NewDevice = 2
```

TIP Be sure to read the size of the database in the message that SQL Server returns. If the full size of the requested database is not available, SQL Server creates the database as large as possible to fit the device or devices you indicated.

The actual size of the resulting database is returned in the status message from SQL Server. Because no error message is issued if the device selection was not large enough, this is your only indication that the database size differs from what you requested.

Displaying Database Information

When you're working with an existing database, for example, when you want to increase the size, or alter other attributes of the database, it's helpful to determine exactly how the database is set up. As you might imagine by now, you can do this with both the SQL Enterprise Manager and ISQL.

The Manage Databases window in SQL Enterprise Manager provides a graphical display of all the information about a database. You can also right-click the database name in the tree view, then select Edit... from the resulting menu, which enables you to edit the different facets of the database configuration.

You can perform all of the database-centric administration of your SQL Server from the Edit... option for the database.

To view this information in ISQL, use the system-stored procedure sp_helpdb. The syntax for sp_helpdb is

sp_helpdb database_name

If a database_name is supplied, sp_helpdb reports information about that database. If not, it reports information about all the databases on the server. For example, sp_helpdb model results in Listing 5.2:

Listing 5.2 Sample Output from sp_helpdb

```
name                db_size         owner          dbid    created     status
model                  1.00 MB sa                  3       Apr  3 1996 no
options set

device_fragments              size          usage
master                            1.00 MB data and log

device                        segment
master                        default
master                        logsegment
master                        system
```

Listing 5.3 shows the use of sp_helpdb for all the databases on the server. The information provided shows only the total size of the database and any options in effect:

Listing 5.3 Multiple-Database Sample Output from *sp_helpdb*

```
/*---------------------------
sp_helpdb
------------------------*/
name          db_size    owner dbid created     status
----------------------------------------------------------
master        17.00 MB   sa    1    Jun  7 1995 trunc. log on chkpt.
model         1.00 MB    sa    3    Jun  7 1995 no options set
msdb          4.00 MB    sa    5    Nov 23 1995 trunc. log on chkpt.
NewDatabase   5.00 MB    sa    6    Jan  7 1996 no options set
pubs          3.00 MB    sa    7    Jun  7 1995 select into/bulkcopy, trunc.
    log on chkpt., dbo use only
tempdb        7.00 MB    sa    2    Jan  7 1996 select into/bulkcopy, single
    user
```

In Listing 5.4, a database is supplied, and more detailed information, including device fragment information, is returned from SQL Server:

Listing 5.4 Sample Output from *sp_helpdb* for a Specific Database

```
/*---------------------------
sp_helpdb NewDatabase
------------------------*/
name          db_size    owner dbid created     status
----------------------------------------------------------
NewDatabase   5.00 MB    sa    6    Jan  7 1996 no options set

device_fragments                    size          usage
-----------------------------------  -----------  -------------------
NewDevice                            2.00 MB log only
NewDevice                            3.00 MB data only

device                              segment
-----------------------------------  ---------------------------
master                              default
master                              logsegment
master                              system.
```

N O T E The segment information is displayed only if you're executing sp_helpdb from the database that you're inspecting. ■

Part

I

Ch

5

Increasing the Size of the Database and Transaction Log

SQL Server lets you resize the database if its space is consumed by user data. In the same way, transaction logs can be increased in size if they get full too quickly and require excessive dumping.

Using SQL Enterprise Manager   To increase the size of a database or transaction log by using SQL Enterprise Manager, follow these steps:

1. Run SQL Enterprise Manager; select the required server, and from the Manage menu choose Databases. Double-click the database that needs to be adjusted. The Edit Database dialog box appears as shown in Figure 5.20. You can also right-click the database you want to work with and select Edit... from the resulting menu.

FIG. 5.20
SQL Enterprise Manager's Edit Database dialog box enables you to configure options that apply to the currently selected database.

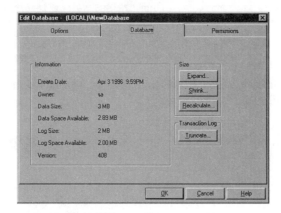

2. Click the Expand button to display the Expand Database dialog box (see Figure 5.21).

FIG. 5.21
At the bottom of the dialog box is a graph showing all the devices on the server and the amount of free space in each.

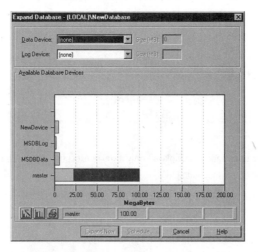

3. If you're expanding the database, select the device that you want to expand the database into from the Data Device drop-down list box. In the Size (MB) text box next to the drop-down box, enter the number of megabytes that are required.

4. If you're expanding the log, select the device that you want to expand the log into from the Log Device drop-down list box. In the Size (MB) text box next to the drop-down box, enter the number of megabytes that are required.

TIP To add a new device for the database or log to grow into, select <new> from either drop-down list box, and the New Database Device dialog box is displayed.

5. Click Expand Now to expand the database/log and return to the Edit Database dialog box. The Edit Database dialog box is updated and reflects the addition of the new log or database devices in the Log Space Available or Database Space Available fields.

N O T E SQL Enterprise Manager also provides an option to shrink a database. This is done by internally calling DBCC SHRINKDB. Note that the SQL Server must be started in single-user mode to perform these operations.

If it's not started in single-user mode, there will be users, system handles such as the CHECKPOINT and MIRROR handlers, that can't be removed from the database and, therefore, prevent the operation from succeeding.

To start SQL Server in single-user mode use the -m keyword and start SQL Server from the command-line. ▓

Using the *ALTER DATABASE* Command to Extend a Database   Transact-SQL provides the ALTER DATABASE command to allow a database to be extended. Transaction logs are also extended by using the ALTER DATABASE command. After the database is extended, the system-stored procedure sp_logdevice is used to specify that the extension to the database is actually for transaction log use.

The syntax for ALTER DATABASE is as follows:

```
ALTER DATABASE database_name
    [ON {DEFAULT ¦ database_device} [= size]
    [, database_device [= size]]...]
    [FOR LOAD]
```

The options for the Transact-SQL command ALTER DATABASE are as listed in Table 5.4.

Table 5.4   *ALTER DATABASE* Parameters

Parameter	Description
database_name	This is the name of the database that is being extended.
database_device	This is one or more database devices and the size, in megabytes, to be allocated to the database.

Part

I

Ch

5

continues

Table 5.4   Continued

Parameter	Description
ON DEFAULT	If DEFAULT is specified, SQL Server allocates the requested space to the first free database device or devices that have enough space to meet the request.
FOR LOAD	If FOR LOAD is specified, SQL Server stops any user processes from connecting to the database until a LOAD has completed. FOR LOAD can be specified only if the database was initially created with the FOR LOAD option.

In this example, NewDatabase is extended by 5M on the NewDevice database device:

```
ALTER DATABASE NewDatabase
    On NewDevice = 5
```

In the following example, NewDatabase is extended by a further 5M, and the logs are placed on the extended portion:

```
ALTER DATABASE NewDatabase
    On NewDevice = 5
Go
sp_logdevice NewDatabase, NewDevice
```

Dropping Databases

Dropping a database frees up any space that it consumed on any database devices and removes any objects that it contained.

Dropping a database isn't something you can easily undo, so be careful. If you do find you need to recover a database that has been dropped, you will be forced to do one of two things. You'll either need to do a restore of the database and its associated transaction logs, or you can sneak around SQL Server.

If you have yet to remove the physical file on your server, you'll still have the .DAT file associated with the device on your hard drive. You can re-use this file by remounting it using the sp_dbinstall command:

```
sp_dbinstall database_name, device_name, disk_file_name.dat, size, type
➥[, location]
```

where the *type* is either "system" or "data" and the *location* is where you want the new device to be located.

CAUTION

Except in cases where you're absolutely certain that you don't need the database information any more, you should always first DUMP the database to disk and back up the resulting file prior to dropping the database.

Having the resulting database dump file available will certainly save you headaches in those cases where a user needs "just one more thing before you delete the database."

N O T E Be sure to remember the difference between dropping a database and dumping one.
Dropping a database drops all the tables and indexes and removes the logical area on the
database device reserved for the database. Dumping a database creates a backup of the database's
data onto a disk, diskette, or other type of media. ■

User accounts that had their default database as the database that is being dropped will have
their default database changed to *master*. Only the SA or the database owner (dbo) can drop a
database. The master, model, and tempdb databases can't be dropped by any user account.
Also, any databases that are participating in replication or have active users can't be dropped
until the replication is suspended or until the users have disconnected from the database.

Using SQL Enterprise Manager to Drop a Database   To use SQL Enterprise Manager to
drop a database, follow these steps:

1. Run SQL Enterprise Manager; select the server that the database resides on, and from
   the Manage, menu choose Databases. The Manage Databases window is displayed (see
   Figure 5.22). You can also right-click the database and select the Delete option from the
   menu.

FIG. 5.22
SQL Enterprise
Manager's Manage
Databases window lists
all the active databases
on the currently
managed server.

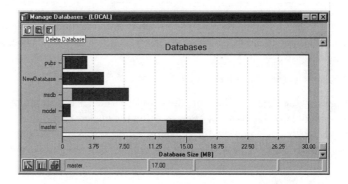

2. Click the database that you want to drop.
3. Click the Delete Database toolbar button. A message box is displayed, asking for
   confirmation to drop the database as shown in Figure 5.23.
4. Click Yes, and the database is dropped.

FIG. 5.23
This message box is the
last chance that you
have to abort a
database drop.

Part
I

Ch
5

Using the *DROP DATABASE* Command to Drop a Database The syntax for the DROP DATABASE command in Transact-SQL is as follows:

```
DROP DATABASE database_name, [database_name...]
```

database_name is the name of the database to be dropped.

Databases in all normal *states*, including Active, Damaged, Suspect, Off-line, or Not recovered, can be dropped by using the DROP DATABASE command. A database that is still in Recovery status must be dropped by using the system-stored procedure sp_dbremove. If you have a database in this mode, it is indicated by an error message when you use the Drop command.

TIP If you have a database that you cannot access in order to drop it, you can use the DBCC command DBREPAIR to remove the database:

```
dbcc dbrepair(database_name, dropdb)
```

This will correct the problem with the database and immediately drop the database. You don't need this command as much with SQL 6.x because the DUMP command drops the database in most cases, but if you're using versions of SQL Server prior to 6.x, you need to use this command to drop damaged databases, or databases that otherwise fail with the standard DROP command.

You can also use a stored procedure approach to dropping databases. The sp_dbremove command enables you to indicate which database to remove, and you can also ask that the device be removed.

```
Sp_dbremove database, [dropdev]
```

If you specify the DROPDEV option, the database's device is also removed, assuming of course that no other active databases or logs reside on the device. One other benefit of the stored procedure approach is that sp_dbremove removes databases in *all* states, whether they be in recovery mode, suspect, or "normal" at the time the command is issued.

Defining Segments

Segments are logical groups of disk devices, or portions of devices, on which database objects are placed. Database segments are created in a database, which in turn can be placed on a particular database disk device. The advantage of segments is that individual objects, such as tables and indexes, can then be explicitly placed in a segment, allowing for greater performance.

Typically, two segments would be created for a database that spans two disk devices. These segments would then be used in such a way that all the tables with non-clustered indexes would be created on one segment, and the non-clustered indexes for these tables would be created on the other segment.

Non-clustered indexes are indexes that are binary search trees of the data. This has a tremendous performance advantage because the reading and writing of the data and index pages can execute concurrently on two physical devices rather than run serially.

▶ **See** Chapter 11, "Managing and Using Indexes and Keys," for more information about creating indexes, **p. 325**.

N O T E   SQL Enterprise Manager doesn't have any user interface to work with data segments, and so all the work has to be done with ISQL. ▓

Segments are also good for allowing the TEXT and IMAGE data, associated with a database table, to be stored on a separate physical device, and for splitting large tables across separate physical devices.

 T I P   Better performance and far easier management are provided by splitting the database devices themselves across multiple disks at the operating system or hardware level by the use of Raid, instead of the use of segments.

Using Default Segments

When a new database is created, three default segments are created for it. The SYSTEM segment houses all the system tables and their indexes. The LOGSEGMENT stores the transaction log for the database. The DEFAULT segment stores any user-created objects, unless they're explicitly moved or placed on a different segment.

Adding Segments

You add segments by using the system-stored procedure `sp_addsegment`. The syntax for `sp_addsegment` is as follows:

```
sp_addsegment segment_name, database_device
```

The options for the system-stored procedure `sp_addsegment` are as follows:

- `segment_name`—The name of the segment that is being added.
- `database_device`—The name of the database device on which this segment should be placed.

The following example creates a segment on the database device NewDevice:

```
sp_addsegment seg_newdevice1, NewDevice
```

Extending Segments

You can extend segments by using the system-stored procedure `sp_extendsegment`. When a segment is extended, it simply allocates more database disk devices to it for the use of any objects placed in the segment. The syntax for `sp_extendsegment` is as follows:

```
sp_extendsegment segment_name, database_device
```

Part

I

Ch

5

The options for the system-stored procedure sp_addsegment are as follows:

- *segment_name*—The name of the segment to be extended.
- *database_device*—The name of the database device on which this segment should be extended.

The following example extends the segment `seg_newdevice1` on to the database device NewDevice2:

```
sp_extendsegment seg_newdevice1, NewDevice2
```

TIP

If you want to extend the DEFAULT segment, you must enclose `default` in quotation marks because `default` is a reserved word. For example,

```
sp_extendsegment 'default', NewDevice
```

Using Segments

After segments are created on a database, you can place an object on those segments in two ways. Both CREATE TABLE and CREATE INDEX have an ON Segment option that lets a table or index be created on a particular segment.

▶ **See** Chapter 6, "Creating Database Tables and Using Datatypes," for more information about creating tables on segments, **p. 131**.

SQL Server also provides a system-stored procedure, `sp_placeobject`, which directs the server to place any new data for a table onto a new segment. You need to use this for tables that you want to partially load on one segment and then switch over to another segment. Executing `sp_placeobject` doesn't move any previously existing data allocations to the new segment. It only causes future allocations to occur on the requested new segment.

The syntax for `sp_placeobject` is as follows:

```
sp_placeobject segment_name, object_name
```

The options for the system-stored procedure `sp_placeobject` are as follows:

- *segment_name*—This is the name of the segment on which the object should be placed.
- *object_name*—This is the object to be moved. The object can be a fully qualified table column if the column's data type is IMAGE or TEXT. Because SQL Server doesn't store IMAGE or TEXT data in the same data pages as the rest of the table data, these column types can be placed on their own segment. This provides substantially better performance. IMAGE or TEXT data should be placed with `sp_placeobject` before table population to ensure that all rows' data is stored in the correct segments.

The following example makes all further data allocations for the table authors on the new segment seg_data2:

```
sp_placeobject seg_data2, authors
```

The following example moves the logo column from the pub_info table to a new segment for image data:

```
sp_placeobject seg_ImageData, 'pub_info.logo'
```

Dropping Segments

Dropping segments removes them from the database devices on which they reside. A segment can't be dropped if it contains any database objects. Those objects need to be dropped first. For information about dropping tables see Chapter 6, "Creating Database Tables and Using Datatypes."

▶ **See** Chapter 11, "Managing and Using Indexes and Keys," for information about dropping indexes, **p. 325**.

Segments are dropped by executing the system-stored procedure sp_dropsegment. The syntax for sp_dropsegment is as follows:

```
sp_dropsegment segment_name[, device_name]
```

- *segment_name*—This is the name of the segment that is to be dropped.

- *device_name*—This is the database device from which the segment should be removed. If no database device is specified, the segment is dropped from all the devices that it spans. If, however, a database device name *is* specified, the segment is removed only from that device.

Using the *Tempdb* Database

Tempdb is a special database that is used by SQL Server to handle any *dynamic* SQL requests from users. Tempdb is a workspace for SQL Server to use when it needs a temporary place for calculations, aggregations, and sorting operations. The sorts of things that Tempdb is used for include the following:

- Creating temporary tables for sorting data.

- Holding temporary tables created by users and stored procedures.

- Storing the data that matches any server cursors that are opened by a user process.

- Holding values for temporary user-created global variables.

One key advantage to using Tempdb is that its activity isn't logged. This means that any data manipulation done on Tempdb temporary tables is much faster than on normal disk devices.

This is a double-edged sword, however, because if SQL Server is brought down at any time, all the information in Tempdb is lost. Take care not to rely on Tempdb without having application code that can restart itself in the event of a server shutdown.

Part
I

Ch
5

Adjusting *Tempdb*'s Size

The default size of `Tempdb`, when SQL Server is installed, is 2M. For most production environments, this size is insufficient. If the environment is highly active with large queries or lots of requests for queries, it's recommended that `Tempdb` be extended.

`Tempdb` is created in the master device by default and can be expanded in that device, or it can be moved so that it spans multiple database devices. Changing the size of `Tempdb` is accomplished in the same way as resizing any other database. To increase the size of `Tempdb`, follow the same steps outlined earlier in the section entitled "Increasing the Size of the Database and Transaction Log."

Placing *Tempdb* in RAM

`Tempdb` is critical to server performance because SQL Server uses it for just about every query/operation that occurs. You have the unique option of being able to place `Tempdb` in RAM. Placing `Tempdb` in RAM dramatically decreases the amount of time required for sorting.

Before placing `Tempdb` in RAM, you must consider how `Tempdb` uses memory now available in the server. All RAM, allocated to SQL Server, is paged based on a least recently used, LRU, algorithm. What this means is that quite often, data in `Tempdb` is in memory anyway as part of a regular page.

You shouldn't place `Tempdb` in RAM unless sufficient RAM is available to the server to handle its normal operations. It's unlikely that you'll perceive any benefit from `Tempdb` being in RAM unless the server has more than 64M of memory due to insufficient resources on the server. With 128M or more of RAM, it's quite likely that you'll achieve performance gains by having `Tempdb` in RAM.

There are no data-integrity considerations with `Tempdb` in RAM, because none of the operations that occur on `Tempdb` are logged. What this means is that `Tempdb` is rebuilt every time the server is restarted, and any data that was in it, whether or not `Tempdb` was in RAM or on a disk device, is lost.

To place `Tempdb` in RAM, you must use the system-stored procedure *sp_configure* and restart the server.

▶ **See** Chapter 16, "Understanding Server, Database, and Design Query Options," for more information on using sp_configure and other configurable options of SQL Server, **p. 463**.

Using Removable Media for Databases

A new feature introduced in SQL Server 6.0 enables databases to be placed on removable media, such as CD-ROMs and magneto-optical, MO, drives. This feature permits the mass distribution of databases in a more friendly form than a backup tape, which the client must restore before using. Also, a CD-ROM-based database is truly read-only and is a great way of securing data integrity.

N O T E SQL Enterprise Manager doesn't have any user interface to allow the creation of removable media, so all the work has to be done with ISQL. It's possible to create a device and database on a removable drive attached to the Windows NT system. This won't, however, be the same as a removable-media-capable database and shouldn't be done. ■

Creating a Removable Database

A removable database has to be created in such a way that three devices are used: one for the system catalog, one for the user data, and one for the transaction log. Only the SA can create removable databases.

SQL Server has a special system-stored procedure, sp_create_removable, that creates a database and devices that are acceptable for use when creating a database for removable media purposes. It's important that you use this stored procedure because it guarantees that the database created is usable on a removable device. The syntax for sp_create_removable is as follows:

```
sp_create_removable database_name, sysdevice_name_,
    'sysdevice_physical', sysdevice_size,
    logdevice_name, 'logdevice_physical', logdevice_size,
    datadevice1_name, 'datadevice1_physical',
    datadevice1_size [... , datadevice16_name,
    'datadevice16_physical', datadevice16_size]
```

The options for the system-stored procedure sp_create_removable are are listed in Table 5.5.

Table 5.5   *Sp_Create* Removable Parameters

Parameter	Description
database_name	The name of the database to be created.
sysdevice_name	The logical name to use for the device that will hold the system catalog tables.
sysdevice_physical	The physical device path and file name that will be used to store the data for the system catalog device.
Syssize	The size, in megabytes, of the device.
logdevice_name	The logical name to use for the device that will hold the transaction log.
logdevice_physical	The physical device path and file name that will be used to store the data for the log device.
Logsize	The size, in megabytes, of the device.
datadeviceN_name	The logical name to use for the device that will hold the user data. There can be up to 16 data devices.

Part

I

Ch

5

Table 5.5 Continued	
Parameter	**Description**
datadeviceN_physical	The physical device path and file name that will be used to store the data for datadevice.
Datasize	The size, in megabytes, of the device.

The following example creates a 1M data, log, and system catalog database and appropriate devices called MyRemovable:

```
/*----------------------------
sp_create_removable MyRemovable, MySys, 'C:\SQL60\DATA\REMOVABLE\MYSYS.DAT', 1,
      MyLog, 'C:\SQL60\DATA\REMOVABLE\MYLOG.DAT', 1,
      MyData, 'C:\SQL60\DATA\REMOVABLE\MYDATA.DAT', 1
----------------------------*/
CREATE DATABASE: allocating 512 pages on disk 'MySys'
Extending database by 512 pages on disk MyData
DBCC execution completed. If DBCC printed error messages, see your System
    Administrator.
Extending database by 512 pages on disk MyLog
DBCC execution completed. If DBCC printed error messages, see your System
    Administrator.
DBCC execution completed. If DBCC printed error messages, see your System
    Administrator.
```

Using the Removable Database

While the database is in development, the following rules should be observed to ensure that the database is usable on removable media:

- Keep the SA as the Database Owner (DBO) of the database

- Don't create any views, or any stored procedures that reference objects that can't be found in the database.

- Don't add any users to the database or change any of the user permissions on the database. You can, however, add groups, and permissions can be assigned to those groups.

- Don't alter any of the database devices created by sp_create_removable.

After database development is completed and you want to test that the database is acceptable for removable media, you should run the system-stored procedure sp_certify_removable. This procedure checks all the conditions required for a removable database and can automatically fix anything that it finds unacceptable. The syntax for sp_certify_removable is as follows:

```
sp_certify_removable database_name[, AUTO]
```

The options for the system-stored procedure sp_certify_removable are as follows:

- *database_name*—This is the name of the database to be certified.

■ AUTO—If AUTO is specified, the stored procedure corrects any problems that it encounters. If you don't specify AUTO, you should correct any problems found using normal SQL Server tools.

> **CAUTION**
>
> If sp_certify_removable reports that it corrected anything when the AUTO flag was specified, it's highly recommended that you retest your application program to make sure that it's still compatible with the database. If no testing occurs, SQL Server could have rendered your application useless without you knowing about it.

As part of its execution, sp_certify_removable also takes all the devices that have been created for use in the removable database off-line and makes them available for copying to the actual physical device. The output from sp_certify_removable is very important because it indicates which database characteristics to use when installing the removable database into a SQL Server.

Listing 5.5 shows the MyRemovable database being certified and brought off-line:

Listing 5.5 Sample Output from Setting Up a *MyRemovable* Device

```
/*---------------------------
sp_certify_removable MyRemovable, AUTO
-------------------------*/
DBCC execution completed. If DBCC printed error messages, see your System
    Administrator.
DBCC execution completed. If DBCC printed error messages, see your System
    Administrator.
DBCC execution completed. If DBCC printed error messages, see your System
    Administrator.
File: 'C:\SQL60\DATA\REMOVABLE\MYLOG.DAT' closed.
Device dropped.
The following devices are ready for removal.  Please note this info. for
    use when installing on a remote system:

Device name   Device type   Sequence    Device frag. used by database
Physical file name
-----------------------------------------------------------------
--------------------
MySys         System + Log 1            1 MB
C:\SQL60\DATA\REMOVABLE\MYSYS.DAT
MyData        Data          2            1 MB
C:\SQL60\DATA\REMOVABLE\MYDATA.DAT

Database is now offline
Closing device 'MyData' and marking it 'deferred'.
Device option set.
Closing device 'MySys' and marking it 'deferred'.
Device option set.
```

Part

I

Ch

5

Installing the Removable Database

After a distribution media/device is made, you must install it on the target SQL Server. Installation is achieved by using the information supplied in the output from sp_certify_removable. This information should be distributed with each CD-ROM or device on which the removable media is placed.

The system-stored procedure sp_dbinstall is used to install a database from removable media. The syntax for sp_dbinstall is as follows:

```
sp_dbinstall database_name, device_name, 'physical_device',
    size, 'device_type'[, 'location']
```

The options for the system-stored procedure sp_dbinstall are listed in Table 5.6.

Table 5.6   sp_dbinstall Parameters

database_name	The name of the database to be installed. This can be any name that is valid for a database and doesn't need to be the same as the original device name.
device_name	The name of the database device that is to be installed.
physical_device	The full path information for the device on the removable media.
Size	The size of the device being created.
device_type	The type of device being created on the target SQL Server. Valid types are 'SYSTEM' and 'DATA'. The 'SYSTEM' device must be created first. If more than one 'DATA' device exists, each should be installed by using sp_dbinstall.
Location	The location to use on the local drive for the device being installed. The system device must be installed locally, but the data devices can be left on the removable media, if necessary.

The following example installs the system device created earlier by the system-stored procedure sp_certify_removable in the section "Using the Removable Database" from a CD-ROM in drive E:

```
sp_dbinstall MyRemovable, MySys, 'e:\MySys.dat', 1,'SYSTEM',
'c:\sql60\data\invsys.dat'
```

After the system device is installed, the data device is installed, but left on the CD-ROM:

```
sp_dbinstall MyRemovable, MyData, 'e:\MyData.dat', 1,'DATA'
```

After all the data devices are installed, you need to place the database on-line so that users can access it. This is achieved by using sp_dboption. The following example shows you how to bring MyRemovable online:

```
sp_dboption MyRemovable, OFFLINE, FALSE
```

Uninstalling a Removable Media Database

If a removable media database is no longer required, you can remove it by using the system-stored procedure sp_dbremove. This procedure removes any entries from the system catalog relating to the database that was installed. The syntax for sp_dbremove is as follows:

```
sp_dbremove database_name[, dropdev]
```

The options for the system-stored procedure sp_dbremove are as follows:

- database_name—This is the name of the database to be removed/dropped.
- dropdev—If the keyword dropdev is supplied, sp_dbremove also removes any references in the system catalog to devices that were created as a result of the removable media database being created.

sp_dbremove doesn't remove the physical data files that were used to store the database devices. This needs to be done manually. See the *Caution* in the previous section for more information about removing device files manually.

From Here...

In this chapter, you learned all about devices, databases, and segments. This chapter provided you with information on how to create all the fundamentals for your server. From here you should consider looking at the following chapters to further develop your SQL Server and application programming knowledge:

- Chapter 6, "Creating Database Tables and Using Datatypes," shows how you can create tables in the databases and segments created in this chapter.
- Chapter 11, "Managing and Using Indexes and Keys," explains how to place the new indexes you create on the new index segments that you created in this chapter.
- Chapter 16, "Understanding Server, Database, and Design Query Options," explains how to further configure your SQL Server and databases for better performance.
- Chapter 19, "SQL Server Administration," tells you how to use the dump devices for backups and restores.

Part

I

Ch

5

CHAPTER 6

Creating Database Tables and Using Datatypes

Data-processing systems involve the storage, processing, and retrieval of information. You must define where data will be stored before it can be processed and retrieved. All units of information, from CHARacters to the logical definition of the entire database, can be defined through SQL Server components.

Create database tables

You learn how to create tables using a Transact-SQL statement or a Windows application.

Define table columns using different datatypes

SQL Server has many datatypes for you to choose from for the storage of your data.

Define a table column to permit or disallow NULL entries

You can choose to leave the value of a table column undefined rather than stored as a value.

Define and use user-defined datatypes

SQL Server permits you to define your own datatypes facilitating the subsequent definition of table columns and other database structures.

Add rows to a table using an INSERT statement

The INSERT statement provides a simple way to store rows in a database table.

Define and use table and column constraints

Version 6 of SQL Server added the ability to define several CHARacteristics of columns when the table is created instead of later using separate statements.

You may recall from prior chapters that the structure of a SQL Server system is:

- Devices equate to the physical file stored on your hard disk. These files typically have an extension of DAT.

- Databases are created on one or more Devices. Databases are the storage mechanism for the information associated with your application, and the databases give you a means of setting up logical boundaries between this application and others. The database is also the starting point for most security relative to your application.

- Transaction logs are also created on one or more devices.

- Tables are sets of related information stored within the database. In older systems, those that do not use this approach to storage, tables are the equivalent of the physical files on disk—one table per file. In dBase for example, the equivalent is a single database file on disk, which relates to one table within a database.

- Columns are individual pieces of information, traditionally referred to as fields. If you think of a table as a spreadsheet, you'll have a good idea of how it is laid out.

- Rows are sets of columns and there is one row per record in more traditional, non-SQL terms. Again, if you think of a spreadsheet metaphor, this makes a good deal of sense.

In this chapter, you find out how to create the tables and the components of the table, the row and column. As with other database systems, each column can have a specific datatype associated with it, and each datatype has certain CHARacteristics. ■

Creating Tables

Data in a relational database such as SQL Server is stored in tables that are two-dimensional arrays. You'll recall from Chapter 1 that you have experience working with tables from everyday life, such as train or bus schedules.

The columns and rows of a table are already familiar to database users. Tables were chosen as the logical structure for storing data because of their familiarity to users and ease of use for retrieving, displaying, and manipulating data.

You can create SQL Server database tables with the CREATE TABLE Transact-SQL statement, or with SQL Enterprise Manager. In the next two sections, you see how to create tables using these two approaches.

You can create up to two billion tables in each database. The major part of the creation of a table is the definition of the datatypes for columns, explained in the remainder of this chapter.

Using Transact-SQL to Create Tables

In Transact-SQL, you can create tables using the Create Table statement. Create Table lets you set up several different options to the table, including where it's located, how the columns are defined, and so on. The syntax for CREATE TABLE is as follows:

```
CREATE TABLE [[database.]owner.]table_name
(column_name datatype [not NULL ¦ NULL] IDENTITY[(seed, increment)][constraint]
[, column_name datatype [not NULL ¦ NULL IDENTITY[(seed, increment)]]].
[constraint]...)
 [ON segment name]
```

> **N O T E** For more information on identity columns, see the "Identity Property" section later in this chapter. ■

Enter the name of the table (*table_name*) following the keywords CREATE TABLE. You can use up to 30 CHARacters to name a database object, such as a table. The column names are entered within parentheses. You define the name and type of the column by entering a column name up to 30 CHARacters long, followed by a Transact-SQL datatype.

> **N O T E** Everything stored in a database is stored as an object. A database object, such as a table, has information kept about it in system tables. For example, a table created by you has the name of the table, the type of data that is stored in its columns, and other CHARacteristics stored in the system table sysobjects. ■

Optionally, you can enter the database in which the table is created, as well as an owner of the table. You'll find it more convenient to define the current database in which you're working first with a USE *database-name* command. After you define your current database with the USE command, all subsequent commands are performed within the database specified with the USE command.

> **N O T E** Your SQL Server account is defined with a current database. The default database that you're directed to should be the one in which you work exclusively or most often. ■

If you don't enter the name of the owner of an object, such as a table, when you create a table, you'll be its owner. Often, tables are created from the SA account, to restrict subsequent access to the tables.

The owner of the database in which the table is defined is automatically granted the CREATE TABLE permission, which allows the creation of tables. The database owner or the SA can grant CREATE TABLE permission to other users so that they can create tables in the database. You don't have to grant permission to create temporary tables in a database.

You can use ON *segment_name* to specify the segment on which the table is created. The segment must have already been created and assigned to a logical device. If you later create a non-clustered index for your table and don't specify a segment, the table and the non-clustered segment are placed in the default segment.

One use you might find for defining specific segments for a table is the separation of the table information from the clustered indexes that support it. You can optimize the system by placing

Part
I

Ch
6

the table on a different segment from its non-clustered indexes. If you specify the creation of a table and its non-clustered index on different segments, SQL Server can perform queries that use the index faster.

 TIP Before using segments, consider carefully whether you can effect the same performance gains by using Windows NT's RAID capabilities. By placing information on different segments, the goal is typically to help lessen the read-write head movement on the disk drive. If you have drives that are striped using the capabilities of NT, you'll have the same results, or at least close enough to them, to warrant consideration of the RAID approach.

Using striped drives can also save you the hassle of working with and remembering segments when you create databases, tables, and indexes.

Queries that use a table's non-clustered index can be performed faster if both are located on different segments, and if the segments are on different logical devices located on different physical disks. Sets of information, such as an index and its associated table, that are stored on different physical disks can be accessed faster than a set stored on a single disk.

Data can be referenced faster because the underlying operating system and disk subsystems can perform a large part of the data transfer from two physical disks simultaneously. Sets of data located on a single physical disk must be accessed separately due to the physical layout of the disk drive.

▶ **See** "Defining Non-Clustered Indexes," **p. 326**.

Using SQL Enterprise Manager to Create Tables

Using SQL Enterprise Manager to create tables gives you the advantage of the graphical interface to specify the different attributes to the table. This includes things like datatypes, column lengths, and so on. To create tables with Enterprise manager, you still need to know the same information as you do when you create the tables with ISQL. The difference is in how the interface takes care of some of the details for you.

To begin working with tables, start Enterprise Manager, and then select the server you want to work with. Next, open the Databases tree, and open the database to which you want to add the new table. When you do, you'll see two different options: Groups/Users and Objects. Select and open the Objects tree and you'll be presented with the following list:

- Tables
- Views
- Stored Procedures
- Rules
- Defaults
- User Defined Datatypes

Right-click the Tables option; you now have two options. You should select New Table. When you do, a dialog box is displayed, allowing you to define a table for your system. See Figure 6.1 for an example with some of the values already entered.

FIG. 6.1
SQL Enterprise Manager will walk you through the options necessary to create a table.

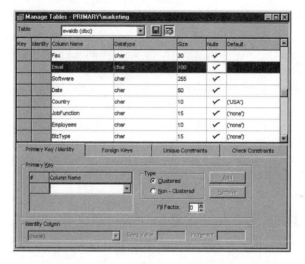

When you create a new column, you're prompted for the different datatypes, including any custom datatypes you've created, with a drop-down list box in the datatype column in the dialog box. This ensures that you select valid data types, and in some cases, the Size attribute is determined for you based on the datatype selection (see Figure 6.2).

FIG. 6.2
You'll be prompted for the datatype, and Enterprise Manager may try to indicate preset sizes for you based on your selection.

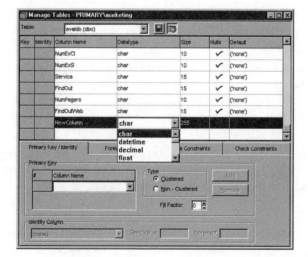

Part

I

Ch

6

When you're satisfied with your table, select the disk button to save the table. In Figure 6.2, you'll notice several different options displayed on the bottom portion of the dialog box. These are the Advanced Options, which you should browse through when you're creating or managing a table. Each of the options presented can be changed after the fact, but changes may require some updating of your table.

Other options, for example, in order to indicate the identity column for your table, must be completed when the table is created. They cannot be added after the fact. One way around this is to create a new table, based on the original but with the modifications you need. Then, using the transfer utility, you can copy the contents of the original table into the newly created table.

Finally, rename the original table, something like "old_*tablename*" and rename the new table to the original name. This step allows any applications you have that reference the table to keep working with the table without modification. Of course, saving the original with the modified name is a safety precaution, and you should extensively test any applications that use the new table prior to dropping the original table.

Understanding Datatypes

The major part of defining a table is specifying the datatypes for the columns of the tables. Transact-SQL lets you define several datatypes, including those for the storage of CHARacters, numbers, and bit patterns. You can also define your own datatypes for use in stored procedures, tables, and other work that you'll be doing with the database tables.

You must define at least one column for a table, and you can define up to 250 columns. You're also limited to a maximum row length of 1,962 bytes.

You can use image or text datatypes to get around the 1,962-byte limit for rows. Columns that are defined by using the image and text datatypes are stored outside the table and can store more than two billion bytes of data.

You should be careful to follow the rules for relational database design, whenever feasible, to ensure the optimum response time and use of your SQL Server engine.

▶ For more information on database design, refer to Chapter 4, "Data Modeling, Database Design, and the Client/Server Model."

Tables are created using a unit of measure called an *extent*. When you create a new table, the allocation of space for the table is initially set at one extent, which is eight pages, each of which is 2K in size. When the table fills the space in the already allocated extents, additional extents are automatically implemented—up to the space allocated to the overall database size.

Use the system procedure sp_spaceused to obtain a report on the space allocated to a table or the graphical display in SQL Enterprise Manager. See Chapter 5, "Creating Devices, Databases, and Transaction Logs," for information on displaying allocated space.

Creating Temporary Tables

Creating a temporary table is a useful technique. You can create two types of temporary tables in SQL Server: local and global. A *local* temporary table is created if the first CHARacter of the table name is a pound sign (#). A local temporary table can be accessed only in the session in which it is created. A local temporary table is automatically dropped when the session in which it is created ends. You can't use more than 20 CHARacters, including the pound sign, to name a local temporary table.

You create a temporary table that can be accessed in any session by defining a table with two pound signs (##) as the first two CHARacters of the table name. Each session can be created by a different user on a different client system. A temporary table that is accessible from multiple sessions is called a *global temporary table* and is automatically dropped when the last session using it ends.

 T I P Constraints can be defined for temporary tables but foreign key constraints are not enforced.

You can use temporary tables to store sets of data that need to be operated on before permanent storage. For example, you can combine *the results of the data from multiple data sets* into a temporary table and then access the combined data in the temporary table throughout your session. Data that has already been combined in a temporary table can be accessed faster than data that must be dynamically accessed from multiple tables. A temporary table that combines the results of two tables is faster to access because SQL Server doesn't need to reference the database tables to retrieve the information.

▶ **See** "Performing Relational Joins," **p. 242**.

> **N O T E** Sessions are established differently depending on how you'll be accessing the server. A session is associated with a live connection to the database. For example, if you query a table and use a Dynaset type of dataset, that is, one that's active and updatable, the session will remain active. If you then connect to the database for another dataset inquiry, a separate and distinct session will be opened. Information in the temporary tables from the first session won't be available to the second session. ■

You might also find it convenient to use a temporary table to make a set of data available to a stored procedure that's invoked from another procedure. You'll find it easier to make data available to another procedure within a temporary table rather than pass data as a set of parameters.

▶ **See** "Managing Stored Procedures and Using Flow-Control Statements," **p. 403**.

Selecting Datatypes

The *datatype* is the first CHARacteristic you define for the column of a table. The datatype of a column controls the type of information that can be stored within the column. Define the

Part

I

Ch

6

datatype by following the column name with a keyword that may also require some parameters. After you define the datatype of a table column, it's stored as a permanent CHARacteristic and can't be changed.

You can also use datatypes to define other data-storage structures, such as parameters and local variables. Parameters and local variables are storage structures defined in RAM instead of on disk. You're limited to a subset of the datatypes for the definitions of parameters and variables.

▶ **See** "Using Parameters with Procedures," **p. 407**, and "Defining and Using Variables," **p. 428**.

The next sections review each of the different system-defined datatypes that you can use in the definition of your SQL Server tables and stored procedures.

Numeric *integer* Datatypes

Numeric integers are the first of several datatypes that you can use to define storage objects. Integer datatypes enable you to store whole numbers. You can directly perform arithmetic operations on integers without using functions. Numbers stored in integer datatypes always occupy the same amount of storage space, regardless of the number of digits within the allowable ranges for each integer datatype.

N O T E The name of a datatype, such as integer, is case-insensitive.

int* or *integer   int (or integer) is the first of three integer datatypes. You can store negative and positive whole numbers within the range of –(2**31) to 2**31—approximately 4.3 billion numbers. The range is –2,147,483,648 to 2,147,483,647. Each value that is stored in an int datatype is stored in four bytes, using 31 bits for the size or magnitude and one bit for the sign.

N O T E A set of two asterisks is used to denote exponentiation. The range of numbers for numeric digits is frequently referenced using a base number raised to a power because it allows the range to be specified precisely and compactly.

smallint   smallint is the second integer datatype. You can store whole numbers within the range –32768 to +32767. Each value that is stored in a smallint datatype occupies two bytes and is stored as 15 bits for the magnitude and one bit for the sign.

tinyint   You can store only whole positive numbers in a storage structure defined as tinyint within the range 0 to 255. Each value stored as a tinyint occupies one byte.

The following example shows the creation of a table with three columns (see Listing 6.1). The columns are defined as the int, smallint, and tinyint datatypes. A single row is inserted into the number_example table with values within the acceptable range for storage of each datatype. Select is subsequently used to retrieve the row.

CAUTION

Database languages and programming languages have keywords. Keywords are the words that force an action to occur in an environment. To avoid confusion and error, avoid using keywords when naming tables, columns, and so on.

Listing 6.1 *create table number_example*

```
create table number_example
(int1 int,int2 smallint,int3 tinyint)
INSERT into number_example
values (400000000,32767,255)
(1 row(s) affected)

select * from number_example
int1        int2    int3
----------- ------- ----
400000000   32767   255
(1 row(s) affected)
```

Enforcing Value Ranges   SQL Server automatically enforces the insertion of values within the range of each datatype. In the following example (see Listing 6.2), values are inserted into columns, defined as `smallint` and `tinyint`, although the values are outside the range of acceptable values.

The column values are specified in the `values` clause of the `INSERT` statement in the same order in which the columns were defined in the table. SQL Server returns an error message that describes the reason for the failed row insertion, such as the attempted insertion of a value that is outside the allowable range for the datatype.

Listing 6.2 *INSERT into number_example*

```
INSERT into number_example
values (1,32768,1)
Msg 220, Level 16, State 1
 Arithmetic overflow error for type smallint, value =  32768.
INSERT into number_example
values (1,1,256)
Msg 220, Level 16, State 2
 Arithmetic overflow error for type tinyint, value =  256.
```

Part

I

Ch

6

TIP   Use a `tinyint` or `smallint` to store integer values in one-quarter or one-half the storage space used for storing integer values in an `int` datatype. These are especially useful as flags, status indicators, and so forth.

Numeric *floating-point* Datatypes

`Floating-point datatypes` are the second group of several numeric datatypes you can use to define storage structures, such as table columns. Unlike the `integer` datatypes, `floating-point` datatypes can store decimal numbers.

Unfortunately, the `floating-point` datatypes are subject to the rounding error. The storage of a value in a `numeric` datatype, which is subject to the rounding error, is accurate only to the number of digits of precision specified. For example, if the number of digits of precision is 15, a number larger than 15 digits can be stored, but the digits beyond 15 may inaccurately represent the initial number inserted into the storage.

Also, the number may inaccurately return results of computations that involve `floating-point` datatypes. The rounding error affects a number's least-significant digits, the ones at the far right. You can accurately store numbers within the number of digits of precision available in `floating-point` datatype.

N O T E Microsoft calls datatypes, such as the `floating-point` datatypes, *approximate numeric datatypes* because values stored in them can be represented only within the limitations of the storage mechanism. You should avoid performing comparisons, such as in a WHERE clause, of data that is stored in approximate datatypes because a loaded value that is larger than the number of digits of precision is altered by the rounding effect during storage. ■

The *REAL* Datatype   The first of the floating-point datatypes is REAL, which is stored in four bytes. You can store positive or negative decimal numbers in the REAL datatype, with up to seven digits of precision. You can store numbers in a column defined as REAL within the range of 3.4E–38 to 3.4E+38.

The range of values and representation is actually platform-dependent. Remember that SQL Server evolved from the original Sybase SQL Server implementation. The REAL datatype stored on each of the several computer systems that a Sybase version was written for varied in the range of allowable CHARacters and the actual representation of CHARacters. For example, the range of decimal numbers stored by OpenVMS on Digital's VAX computers is 0.29E – 38 to 1.7E+38.

The underlying operating system that SQL Server runs on is supported on Intel, MIPS, PowerPC, and Alpha AXP systems. You should consider the previously stated value, the range of 3.4E–38 to 3.4E+38, as approximate and check the range of allowable numbers for the `floating-point` datatype that is stored in four bytes on your Windows NT system.

You should also realize that data stored in `floating-point` datatypes, that is moved between different NT platforms with different processor architectures may require conversion to compensate for different representations and range of values.

floating*[(n)]* Datatypes   The second of the `floating-point` datatypes is `float`, that is stored in eight bytes if a value for *n* is omitted. You can store positive or negative decimal numbers in the `float` datatype with as many as 15 digits of precision. You can store numbers in a column defined as `float` within the range of 1.7E–308 to 1.7E+308.

If you specify a value for *n* within the range of 1 to 7, you're actually defining a `real` datatype. If you specify a value within the range of 8 to 15, the datatype has the identical CHARacteristics as if *n* were omitted.

In the following example (see Listing 6.3), a table is created with two columns defined as `real` and `float`. A single row is added with identical numbers that are subsequently added to each column of the table. The retrieval of the row from the table shows that the number stored in the real column was stored accurately to only 7 digits, the maximum number of digits of precision for a `real` datatype. The same 11-digit number was stored correctly in the column defined with the datatype `float` because `float` allows up to 15 digits to be stored accurately.

Listing 6.3 *create table precision_example*

```
create table precision_example
(num1 real,num2 float)
INSERT into precision_example
values (4000000.1234,4000000.1234)
select * from precision_example
num1                 num2
-------------------  -------------------
4000000.0            4000000.1234
(1 row(s) affected)
```

decimal[(p[, s])] **and** *numeric[(p[, s])]* **Datatypes**   You can use either the name `decimal` or `numeric` to select a datatype that, unlike `float` or `real`, allows the exact storage of decimal numbers. The scale and digits of precision are specified in the arguments *p* and *s*. You can store values within the range $10**38-1$ through $-10**38$ using 2 to 17 bytes for storage.

Use *p* to define the number of digits that can be stored to the left and right of the decimal point. Use *s* to define the number of digits to the right of the decimal point that must be equal to or less than the value of *p*. If you omit a value for *p*, it defaults to 18; the default of *s* is 0. Table 6.1 shows the number of bytes that are allocated for the specified precision (value of *p*).

Table 6.1   Number of Bytes Allocated for Decimal/Numeric Datatypes

Bytes Allocated	Precision
2	1–2
3	3–4
4	5–7
5	8–9
6	10–12
7	13–14

Part

I

Ch

6

continues

Table 6.1 Continued

Bytes Allocated	Precision
8	15–16
9	17–19
10	20–21
11	22–24
12	25–26
13	27–28
14	29–31
15	32–33
16	34–36
17	37–38

Listing 6.4 shows the storage and subsequent retrieval of a single row stored with the columns of a table defined as numeric/decimal datatypes. This example shows the default precision and scale and an explicit precision and scale being displayed.

Listing 6.4 *create table definition_example*

```
create table definition_example
(num1 decimal,num2 numeric(7,6))
INSERT into definition_example
values (123456789123456789,1.123456)
select * from definition_example
num1                     num2
--------------------------------
123456789123456789      1.123456
(1 row(s) affected)
```

N O T E   The maximum precision permitted in the numeric/decimal datatypes is 28 unless you start SQL Server from the command line and change the precision. Use the command sqlservr with the option /p, which has the following syntax:

sqlservr [/dmaster_device_path][/pprecision_level]

For example, the following command starts SQL Server with a maximum precision of 38:

sqlservr /dg:\sql60\data\master.dat /p38

If no value is specified after the precision qualifier /p, the precision for the numeric/decimal datatype is set to the maximum of 38. ■

CHARacter Datatypes

You'll frequently use *CHARacter datatypes* to define table columns or other storage structures. CHARacter datatypes allow the storage of a wider variety of symbols than numeric datatypes. CHARacter datatypes enable you to store letters, numeric symbols, and special CHARacters such as ? and >. You enter CHARacter data in either single or double quotation marks (' or ") when loading it into a storage area, such as the column of a table.

***CHAR* Datatype**   CHAR is the first type of CHARacter datatype. When you store data in a CHAR datatype, each symbol or CHARacter stored uses one byte. The number in parentheses specifies the size of storage for all sets of CHARacters. For example, if you define a table column as the datatype CHAR(15), each value of the column is 15 bytes in size and can store 15 CHARacters. If you enter fewer than 15 CHARacters, SQL Server adds blanks after the last specified CHARacter.

You can define a CHAR(*n*) datatype to contain up to a maximum of 255 CHARacters. Remember, the column value always contains the specified number of CHARacters. SQL Server automatically adds spaces to the end of a CHAR value to fill the defined length of space.

N O T E   If a column is defined CHAR and allowed to be NULL, it will be treated as a varCHAR column. ■

N O T E   Although the default installation of Windows NT uses the ASCII code to store CHARacter datatypes, you can install Windows NT so that UNICODE is used instead of ASCII. UNICODE stores CHARacter symbols in 16 bits, two bytes, rather than ASCII's one byte. If Windows NT is defined to use UNICODE instead of ASCII, you must confirm the size of each CHARacter for CHARacter datatypes in applications, such as SQL Server. ■

***varCHAR* Datatype**   You can use the varCHAR datatype to store a variable-length string of up to 255 CHARacters. Unlike the CHAR datatype, the storage space used varies according to the number of CHARacters stored in each column value of rows of the table.

For example, if you define the table column as varCHAR(15), a maximum of 15 CHARacters can be stored in the corresponding column of each table row. However, spaces aren't added to the end of the column value until the size of each column is 15 bytes. You can use a varCHAR to save space if the values stored in a column are variable in size. You can also specify a varCHAR datatype using the keyword CHAR varying.

Using CHARacter Datatypes   In Listing 6.5, a table is created with two columns defined as CHAR and varCHAR datatypes. The inserted row stores only two CHARacters in each column of the row. The first column is padded with three spaces so that it occupies five bytes of storage. The second column of the row isn't padded and occupies only two bytes of storage to store the two CHARacters. The retrieval of the row in the example displays each column value identically, masking the underlying storage difference.

Listing 6.5 *create table string_example*

```
create table string_example
(CHAR1 CHAR(5),CHAR2 varCHAR(5))
INSERT into string_example
values ('AB','CD')
select * from string_example
CHAR1CHAR2
- - - - - - - - - -
AB    CD
(1 row(s) affected)
```

In the following example (Listing 6.6), a row is inserted into the table that contains column values that are longer by one CHARacter than the maximum length of the datatypes of the table columns. The select statement in the example shows that the column values of the inserted row were truncated, or cut off, and contain only the first five CHARacters of the column values. You don't receive a message that the truncation occurs when a row is inserted.

Listing 6.6 *INSERT into string_example*

```
INSERT into string_example
values ('abcdef','abcdef')
select * from string_example
CHAR1CHAR2
- - - - - - - - - -
AB    CD
abcde abcde
(2 row(s) affected)
```

 TIP Use the text datatype, which allows the storage of more than four billion CHARacters to store sets of CHARacters that are longer than 255 CHARacters.

Here are a few points about text and other CHARacter data types that will help when you begin using them:

- When a table column is defined using the CHAR or varCHAR datatype, the maximum length is specified for all values that are later inserted into the column. SQL Server automatically truncates all CHARacters that are longer than the maximum length that was defined. SQL Server doesn't notify you that the truncation is being performed.

- When you use CHAR datatypes, the fields are padded with extra spaces to fill the entire defined space for the column. If you're referencing these types of columns in reports, the output columns may not line up. If the extra spaces in the field are the problem, either use a trim statement in your query or store the data as a varCHAR.

datetime and *smalldatetime* Datatypes

The datetime and smalldatetime datatypes store a combination of the date and time. You'll find it more convenient to store dates and times in one of the date and time datatypes instead of a datatype, such a CHAR or varCHAR. If you store data in one of these datatypes, you can easily display them because SQL Server automatically formats them in a familiar form. You can also use specialized date and time functions to manipulate values stored in this manner.

If you store date and time in CHAR or varCHAR, or if you store time in numeric datatypes, date and time values aren't automatically formatted in conventional ways when they're displayed.

***datetime* Datatype**   datetime lets you define storage structures, such as table columns. In the datetime datatype, you can store dates and times from 1/1/1753 AD to 12/31/9999 AD.

The total storage of a datetime datatype value is eight bytes. SQL Server uses the first four bytes to store the number of days after or before the base date of January 1, 1900. Values that are stored as negative numbers represent dates before the base date. Positive numbers represent dates since the base date. Time is stored in the second four bytes as the number of milliseconds after midnight.

N O T E   Datetime values are stored to an accuracy of 1/300th of a second (3.33 milliseconds) with values rounded downward. For example, values of 1, 2, and 3 milliseconds are stored as 0 milliseconds; the values of 4 through 6 milliseconds are stored as 3 milliseconds. ▪

When you retrieve values stored in datetime, the default format for display is MMM DD YYYY hh:mmAM/PM, for example, Sep 23 1949 11:14PM. You must enclose datetime values in single quotation marks when they're used in an INSERT or other statement. You can enter either the date or time portion first, because SQL Server can recognize each portion and store the value correctly.

You can use upper- or lowercase CHARacters for the date and one or more spaces between the month, day, and year when you enter datetime values. If you enter time without a date, the default date is January 1, 1900. If you enter the date without the time, the default time is 12:00 A.M. If you omit the date and the time, the default value entered is January 1, 1900 12:00 A.M.

You can enter the date in several ways. Each is recognized and stored correctly by SQL Server. You can enter the date in an alphabetic format, using either an abbreviation for the month or the full name of the month. You can use or omit a comma between the day and year.

If you omit the century part of the year, decades that are less than 50 are represented as 20 and those that are 50 or more are entered as 19. For example, if you insert the year 49, the complete year stored is 2049. If you enter the year as 94, the complete year stored is 1994. You must explicitly enter the century if you want a century other than the default. You must supply the century if the day is omitted from the date value. When you enter a date without a day, the default entry is the first day of the month.

The option set dateformat isn't used if you specify the month of the year in alphabetic format. If you installed SQL Server with the US_English Language option, the default order for the display of datetime values is month, day, and year. You can change the default order for the display of the date portion of a datetime value using the set dateformat command.

▶ **See** "Understanding Server, Database, and Design Query Options," in **p.463**.

You can enter dates several ways, including the following examples:

- Sep 23 1949
- SEP 23 1949
- September 23 1949
- sep 1949 23
- 1949 sep 23
- 1949 23 sep
- 23 sep 1949

The numeric format for datetime values permits the use of slashes (/), hyphens (-), and periods (.) as separators between the different time units. When you use the numeric format with a datetime value, you must specify the month, day, and year of the date portion of the value.

In the numeric format, enter a separator between the month, day, and year entered in the order defined for dateformat. If you enter the values for a datetime datatype that is in the incorrect order, the month, day, or year will be misinterpreted and stored incorrectly. If you enter the information in the incorrect order, you may also receive an error message that tells you the date is out of range.

The following is an example of several entries for the numeric form of the date portion of a datetime datatype value with set dateformat defined as month, day, and year and the language as US_English:

- 6/24/71
- 06/24/71
- 6-24-1971
- 6.24.1971
- 06.24.71

The last of the possible formats for the date portion of a datetime datatype value is an unseparated 4-, 6-, or 8-digit value, or a time value without a date value portion. The dateformat controlled through set dateformat doesn't affect datetime datatype values referenced as the unseparated digit format.

If you enter a 6- or 8-digit unseparated value, it's always interpreted in the order of year, month, day. The month and day are always interpreted as two digits each; four unseparated digit values are interpreted as the year; the century and the month and day default to the first month and the first day of that month. Table 6.2 lists the possible interpretations of unseparated digit datetime datatype values:

Table 6.2 Interpretation of Unseparated Digit Dates for *datetime* Datatypes

Digits	Equivalent Representation in Alphabetic Format
710624	June 24, 1971
19710624	June 24, 1971
1971	January 1, 1971
71	Not valid
"	January 1, 1900 12:00 A.M.

When working with the datetime datatype, keep in mind that if you insert a column with an empty string as a value, and that column is defined as a datetime column, you won't get a NULL entry as you might expect. When two single quotation marks are used with no CHARacters inserted between them as the value for either of the date and time datatypes, the entry January 1, 1900, and 12 midnight is always inserted by SQL Server.

You must enter the time with the time units in the following order: hours, minutes, seconds, and milliseconds. You must have a colon as a separator between multiple time units to allow a set of digits to be recognized as a time rather than a date value. You can use AM or PM, specified in upper- or lowercase, to specify before or after midnight.

You can precede milliseconds with a period or a colon, which affects the interpretation of the millisecond unit. A period followed by a single digit specifies tenths of a second; two digits are interpreted as hundredths of a second; three digits are interpreted as thousandths of a second. A colon specifies that the following digits will be interpreted as thousandths of a second. Table 6.3 shows several possible interpretations of the time portion of a datetime datatype value.

Table 6.3 *datetime* Datatype Values

Time	Interpretation
11:21	11 hours and 21 minutes after midnight
11:21:15:871	11 hours, 21 minutes, 15 seconds, and 871 thousandths of a second A.M.
11:21:15.8	11 hours, 21 minutes, 15 seconds, and eight tenths of a second A.M.
6am	6 A.M.
7 PM	7 P.M.
05:21:15:500 AM	5 hours, 21 minutes, 15 seconds, and 500 milliseconds after midnight

smalldatetime smalldatetime is the second of the date and time datatypes you can use to define storage structures, such as table columns. In the smalldatetime datatype, you can store dates and times from 1/1/1900 AD to 6/6/2079 AD.

The total storage of a smalldatetime datatype value is four bytes. SQL Server uses two bytes to store the number of days after the base date of January 1, 1900. Time is stored in the other two bytes as the number of minutes after midnight. The accuracy of the smalldatetime datatype is one minute. You can use smalldatetime to store values that are within its more limited range and lesser precision when compared to datetime.

TIP   Use the smalldatetime datatype instead of the datetime datatype to store values in half the storage space.

In Listing 6.7, one column is defined using the datetime datatype, and the second column is defined using the smalldatetime datatype. After the table is created, a minimum value is inserted into each column of a single row for the respective datatypes.

Listing 6.7   *create table date_table* Example

```
create table date_table
(date1 datetime,date2 smalldatetime)
INSERT into date_table
values ('Jan 1 1753','Jan 1 1900')
select * from date_table
date1                       date2
----------------------------------------------------
Jan 1 1753 12:00AM          Jan 1 1900 12:00AM
(1 row(s) affected)
```

In the following example, successive INSERT statements insert a date that is beyond both the range of the columns defined using the smalldatetime and the range of datetime datatypes. An error is returned as a result of both INSERT statements.

In the following example, the conversion of CHAR to smalldatetime results in a smalldatetime value out of range:

```
INSERT into date_table
values ('May 19 1994', 'Jun 7 2079')
Msg 296, Level 16, State 3
```

The following example shows a syntax error converting datetime from a CHARacter string.

```
INSERT into date_table
values ('Jan 1 10000','May 19 1994')
Msg 241, Level 16, State 3
```

Specialized Datatypes

Transact-SQL contains a set of specialized datatypes for data storage. Most of the time you'll store data in more conventional datatypes such as integer, floating-point, and CHARacter. You can store dates and times in the datetime or smalldatetime datatypes.

Although you'll probably find that you can use the integer, floating-point, CHARacter, and date/time datatype formats for storing 90 percent of your data, in some cases you'll probably need a more custom solution.

In these cases, you can use one or more of the specialized datatypes. For example, you may need to store only data that can be represented as true or false, yes or no. Because this is a binary condition, you may decide to create a custom datatype. As another example, you may need to store sets of data in a column that is larger than the 255 CHARacter limitation of the conventional CHARacter datatypes. Several additional datatypes are available, so you can choose the best datatype for storing your information.

bit   You can use the bit datatype to store information that can be represented in only two states. A bit datatype is stored in a single bit. As a result, only two possible patterns can be stored—zero(0) or one(1). If you enter any other value than zero or one in a data-storage structure, such as a table column, one is stored. You can't define the bit datatype to allow NULL entries.

 TIP Although it is not explicitly stated in the SQL Server documentation, the bit datatype corresponds to the Boolean datatype in other DBMSes and programming languages.

You can also use a single byte to define up to eight different bit columns of a table using the bit datatype. The amount of space allocated for one or more bits is a single byte, and the bit columns don't have to be contiguous. If you define nine columns of a table using the bit datatype, two bytes are used for the total of nine bit datatypes.

N O T E   SQL Server stores information about columns defined using bit datatypes in the syscolumns system table by storing an offset to the bit column in the status column. You can't define an index that uses a column defined as a bit datatype. ■

timestamp   If you define a column of a table using the timestamp datatype, a counter value is automatically added to the timestamp column whenever you insert a new row or UPDATE an existing row. You can't explicitly enter a value into the column defined as a timestamp. A uniformly increasing counter value can be implicitly inserted only into a timestamp column by SQL Server.

The counter value inserted by SQL Server into a `timestamp` column specifies the sequence of operations that SQL Server has performed. Values entered into a `timestamp` column are stored in a `varbinary(8)` format, not a `datetime` or `smalldatetime` format. NULL values are permitted in a `timestamp` column by default. A `timestamp` value isn't a date and time, but it's always unique within the table and database. You can define only a single column of a table as a `timestamp`.

N O T E   Timestamps are often used to ensure that a row can be uniquely identified. If you're updating columns in a row, it's a common practice to specify the timestamp field in the `where` clause of your UPDATE statement. This ensures that you UPDATE only one row of the table. You can be assured of the uniqueness of the value because the server maintains and UPDATEs it any time you insert or UPDATE a row.

Timestamps are also used, again, as part of the `where` clause, to prevent two people from updating the same row. Because the timestamp is UPDATEd automatically whenever an UPDATE is made to the row, you can be sure that you're not going to overwrite someone else's information. If someone else UPDATEs a row that you're now working on, when he or she saves the UPDATE, the row's timestamp will be *UPDATEd*, no longer matching your copy. When you issue the UPDATE command to save your changes, the `where` clause will fail because it can't find the specific row that you retrieved. Timestamps are excellent, server-maintained ways to make sure that you have a unique row identifier.

If you define a column with the column name timestamp and don't specify a datatype, the column is defined using the `timestamp` datatype. You can display the current `timestamp` value that is applied to the next timestamp column of an UPDATE row, or UPDATEd to a new row added using the global system variable @@dbts.

N O T E   You can use a `select` statement to reference the global variable @@dbts using the following syntax:

`select @@dbts`

For example, the execution of this statement during the preparation of this chapter returned the following current `timestamp` value:

`0x01000000a3d2ae08`

binary(n)   You can use the `binary` datatype to store bit patterns that consist of up to 255 bytes. Use the integer specified in parentheses to define the length of all bit patterns from one to 255 bytes. You must specify the size of a binary column to be at least one byte, but you can store a bit pattern of all zeroes.

You must enter the first binary value preceded with `0x`. You can enter binary data using the CHARacters zero through nine and A through F. For example, enter the value A0 by preceding it with `0x`, in the form `0xA0`. If you enter values greater than the length that you defined, the values are truncated. Values are also padded with zeroes after the least significant digit.

Here's another example (see Listing 6.8). A column defined as `binary(1)` can store up to the maximum value of `ff`. In the following example, a table is defined as having two columns, with the datatypes `binary(1)` and `binary(2)`. Three `INSERT` statements are used to enter successive pairs of values of `0`, `1`, `ff`, and `fff` in both columns.

Listing 6.8 *create table binarytable* **Example**

```
create table binarytable
(x binary(1),y binary(2))
INSERT into binarytable
values (0x0,0x0)
INSERT into binarytable
values (0x1,0x1)
INSERT into binarytable
values (0xff,0xff)
INSERT into binarytable
values (0xfff,0xfff)
select * from binarytable
...
x   y
----------
0x00 0x0000
0x01 0x0100
0xff 0xff00
0x0f 0x0fff
(4 row(s) affected)
```

varbinary(n)   You can use the `varbinary` datatype to store bit patterns that consist of *up to 255 bytes*. You use the integer specified in parentheses to define the maximum length of all bit patterns from one to 255 bytes. You must specify the size of a binary column to be at least one byte, but you can store a bit pattern of all zeroes.

Unlike the `binary` datatype, `varbinary` datatype storage is limited to just enough space for the length of the actual value. Like the `binary` datatype, you must enter the first binary value preceded with `0x`. You can enter binary data using the CHARacters zero through nine and A through F. If you enter values that are greater than the maximum length you defined, the values are truncated.

In Listing 6.9, a table is defined with two columns with the `varbinary(1)` and `varbinary(2)` datatypes. Three `INSERT` statements are used to enter successive pairs of values of `0`, `1`, `ff`, and `fff` in both columns.

Part

I

Ch

6

Listing 6.9   *create table varbinarytable* Example

```
create table varbinarytable
(x varbinary(1),y varbinary(2))
INSERT into varbinarytable
values (0x0,0x0)
INSERT into varbinarytable
values (0x1,0x1)
INSERT into varbinarytable
values (0xff,0xff)
INSERT into varbinarytable
values (0xfff,0xfff)
select * from varbinarytable
...
x    y
----------
0x00 0x00
0x01 0x01
0xff 0xff
0x0f 0x0fff
```

Unlike the values entered into a table in which the columns are defined as binary(1) and bi-nary(2), the values are stored in only the amount of space required. Values are truncated if they're greater than the maximum space defined when the table is created.

text and *image* Datatypes

Use text and image datatypes to store large amounts of CHARacter or binary data. You can store more than two billion data bytes in either a text or image datatype. It's wasteful to pre-allocate space for text or image datatypes to any significant extent, so only a portion of the space is pre-allocated. The remaining space is dynamically allocated.

N O T E   image datatypes are sometimes used for embedded OLE objects that are part of a row. ▪

text   Use a text datatype for storing large amounts of text. The CHARacters stored in a text field are typically CHARacters that can be output directly to a display device, such as a monitor, window, or printer. You can store from one to 2,147,483,647 bytes of data in a text datatype.

N O T E   You can store an entire résumé in a single column value of a table row. ▪

Your data is stored in fixed-length strings of CHARacters in an initially allocated 2K (2,048 bytes) unit. Additional 2K units are dynamically added and are linked together. The 2K data pages are logically, but not necessarily physically, contiguous. If you use an INSERT statement to insert data into a column defined as text, you must enclose the data within single quotation marks.

If you define a column using the text datatype and permit NULLs, using an insert statement to place a NULL value in the column doesn't allocate even a single 2K page, which saves space. However, any UPDATE statement will allocate at least one 2K page for the text column regardless of any value that may or may not be supplied for that column.

image   You can use the image datatype to store large bit patterns from 1 to 2,147,483,647 bytes in length. For example, you can store employee photos, pictures for a catalog, or drawings in a single column value of a table row. Typically, the data stored in an image column isn't directly entered with an INSERT statement.

Your data is stored in fixed-length byte strings in an initially allocated 2K (2,048 bytes) units. Additional 2K units are dynamically added and are linked together like the pages for a text column. The 2K data pages are logically, but not necessarily physically, contiguous.

Using *text* and *image* Datatypes   Values that are stored as either text or image datatypes are displayed just as other columns are when you use a select statement. The number of bytes displayed is limited by the global value @@Textsize, which has a default value of 4K. You can specify the NULL CHARacteristic for text or image columns. A NULL for a text or image column of a table doesn't allocate any 2K pages of storage, unless an UPDATE is performed on a row containing the NULL value.

In Listing 6.10, two table columns are defined using image and text. Values are inserted into each column of a single row using an INSERT statement. The row is then retrieved from the table with a select statement.

Listing 6.10   *create table imagetext_table* **Example**

```
create table imagetext_table
(image1 image,text1 text)
INSERT into imagetext_table
values ('123456789aczx+=\','12345678aczx+=')
select * from imagetext_table
image1                                      text1
--------------------------------------------------------
0x313233343536373839961637a782b3d5c         12345678aczx+=

 (1 row(s) affected)
```

Part

I

Ch

6

Data in a column defined as an image datatype isn't automatically translated from its ASCII representation when it's displayed with a select statement. Data stored in a column defined as the text datatype is automatically translated to ASCII CHARacters when the data is output with a select statement. An image column isn't meant to be direct output. It can be passed on to another program, perhaps running on a client system that processes the data before it's displayed.

Restrictions on *text* and *image* Columns   You'll encounter several restrictions on the use of data stored in text and image datatypes. You can define only table columns using the text or image datatypes. You can't define other storage structures, such as local variables or parameters, as text or image datatypes.

The amount of data that can be stored in a text or image table column makes each datatype unsuitable for use or manipulation in many Transact-SQL statements. This is simply because the amount of data that would have to be manipulated is too great. You can't specify a table column in an ORDER BY, GROUP BY, or compute clause that is a text or image datatype. SQL Server won't try to sort or group a table's rows using a column that can contain more than four billion bytes of data because too much data would have to be moved around and too large a space would have to be allocated in which to order the rows.

Here are some things to keep in mind when you create your query:

- You can't use a text or image column in a UNION unless it's a UNION all.
- You can't use a subquery that returns data values from a text or image datatype.
- You can't use a text or image column in a where or having clause, unless the comparison operator like is used.
- You can't specify distinct followed by a table column defined as a text or image datatype.
- You can't create an index or a primary or foreign key defined using a table column that you've defined as an image or text datatype.

MONEY Datatype

The MONEY datatype stores monetary values. Data values stored in the MONEY datatype are stored as an integer portion and a decimal-fraction portion in two four-byte integers. The range of values that you can store in the MONEY datatype is from –922,337,203,685,477.5808 to 922,337,203,685,477.5807. The accuracy of a value stored in the MONEY datatype is to the ten-thousandth of a monetary unit. Some front-end tools display values stored in the MONEY datatype rounded to the nearest cent.

smallMONEY Datatype

The smallMONEY datatype stores a range of monetary values that is more limited than the MONEY datatype. The values you can store in the smallMONEY datatype ranges from –214,748.3648 to 214,748.3647. Data values stored in the smallMONEY datatype are stored as an integer portion and a decimal-fraction portion in four bytes. Like values stored in a table column defined using the MONEY datatype, some front-end tools display values stored in the smallMONEY datatype rounded to the nearest cent.

 TIP   You can store your monetary values in half the storage space if you choose the datatype smallMONEY instead of the MONEY datatype.

When you add values to a table column defined as MONEY or smallMONEY, you must precede the most significant digit with a dollar sign ($) or a sign of the defined monetary unit.

In Listing 6.11, a table is created with two columns that are defined using the MONEY and smallMONEY datatypes. In the first INSERT statements, values are incorrectly added because they aren't preceded with a dollar sign. A select statement shows that the values displayed are identical to those that were stored.

Listing 6.11 *create table monetary_table* Example

```
create table monetary_table
(MONEY1 MONEY,MONEY2 smallMONEY)
INSERT into monetary_table
values (16051.3455,16051.3455)
select * from monetary_table
MONEY1                          MONEY2
-------------------------------------------------
16,051.35                       16,051.35
(1 row(s) affected)
```

In a continuation of the same example (see Listing 6.12), a three-digit monetary value is added to both table columns, followed by a value that is outside the storage bounds for the datatype on the computer architecture.

```
INSERT into monetary_table
values ($123,$123)
INSERT into monetary_table
values (922337203685477,214748.3647)
Msg 168, Level 15, State 1
```

The integer value 922337203685477 is out of the range of machine representation, which is four bytes.

A large monetary value, which is defined as a MONEY datatype, is added to the first column. It's incorrectly entered because it isn't preceded by a dollar sign ($). The select statements show that the number is stored incorrectly. If you enter a value into a table column defined as MONEY or smallMONEY, it's stored as a floating-point datatype, which makes it subject to the rounding error (see Listing 6.12).

Part

I

Ch

6

Listing 6.12 *INSERT into monetary_table* Example

```
INSERT into monetary_table
values (922337203685476.,0)
MONEY1                          MONEY2
----------------------------------
16,051.35                       16,051.35
123.00                          123.00
922,337,203,685,475.98 0.00
```

In Listing 6.13, the same large number that was previously entered without a dollar sign has been correctly entered with the dollar sign. A subsequent `select` statement shows that the large monetary value was correctly stored.

Listing 6.13 *INSERT into monetary_table* Example

```
INSERT into monetary_table
values ($922337203685476.,0)
select * from monetary_table
MONEY1                         MONEY2
-----------------------------------
16,051.35                      16,051.35
123.00                         123.00
922,337,203,685,475.98 0.00
922,337,203,685,476.00 0.00
```

Added to the table are values that contain four digits to the right of the decimal place. When the values are subsequently displayed with a `select` statement, the values are displayed to two decimal places, to the nearest cent (see Listing 6.14).

Listing 6.14 *INSERT into monetary_table* Example

```
INSERT into monetary_table
values ($922337203685477.5807,$214748.3647)
select * from monetary_table
MONEY1                         MONEY2
-----------------------------------
16,051.35                      16,051.35
123.00                         123.00
922,337,203,685,475.98         0.00
922,337,203,685,476.00         0.00
922,337,203,685,477.58 214,748.36
```

sysname Datatype

The sysname datatype is a user-defined datatype, defined as varCHAR(30), and doesn't allow NULLs. sysname is used for defining columns in system tables. You shouldn't use sysname to define the datatype of columns in your tables. You can use varCHAR(30), or you can define your own user-defined datatypes. See the section titled "Creating User-Defined Datatypes" later in this chapter.

Understanding *NULL* and *not NULL*

Now that you've learned about the additional datatypes that can be defined for Transact-SQL storage structures, such as columns, parameters, and local variables, you should understand a second CHARacteristic that you can define. In addition to specifying the datatype of a table column, you can specify an additional CHARacteristic for each datatype: NULL or not NULL.

The NULL CHARacteristic for a table column lets you omit the entry of a column value in the column. If you define the CHARacteristic for a column as not NULL, SQL Server won't let you omit a value for the column when you insert a row. The NULL CHARacteristic provides a type of validation.

The default CHARacteristic for a column is not NULL, which doesn't allow an undefined column value. A NULL that is defined for a column is stored differently than a space, a zero, or a NULL ASCII CHARacter, which is all zeroes. The interpretation of a NULL entry is undefined or un-available because no explicit or implicit value is assigned to the column when a row is inserted.

If you reference a row that contains a NULL, the entry (NULL) is displayed in place of a column value to indicate that there's no entry in the row for that column.

There are two ways to designate that a column or storage structure contains a NULL:

- If no data is entered in the row for that column and there's no default value for the column or datatype, a NULL is entered automatically. You can define a default value that is inserted automatically into the table column when a column value is omitted. A default value can be added in place of a NULL.

- You can enter a NULL explicitly by using NULL or NULL without quotation marks when a row is inserted into the table. If you enter NULL within quotation marks, it's stored as a literal string rather than a NULL.

In the following example (see Listing 6.15), a table is created that permits a NULL entry for numeric integer datatypes and CHARacter datatypes. A NULL is explicitly inserted into both columns of a single row in the table. A select statement displays (NULL) for both column values of the row.

Listing 6.15 *INSERT create table NULLtable* **Example**

```
create table NULLtable
(x int NULL, y CHAR(10) NULL)
INSERT into NULLtable
values (NULL,NULL)
select * from NULLtable
x          y              1
-------------------
(NULL)       (NULL)
(1 row(s) affected)
```

N O T E   You can specify the keyword NULL in lower- or uppercase when you specify a NULL entry for the column of a row. The default display of a column that contains a NULL entry is "(NULL)."

To continue the example (see Listing 6.16), NULL is entered in the second column (y) because only the x column precedes the values clause. A NULL value is added to the second column y

Part
I

Ch
6

implicitly because no value is specified in the list port, signified by the values within parentheses separated by a comma, of the `values` clause.

Listing 6.16 *INSERT into NULLtable* **Example**

```
INSERT into NULLtable
(x)
values (5)
select * from NULLtable
x                 y
--------------------------
5                 (NULL)
(2 row(s) affected)
```

ANSI Support for *NULLs*

You can change the behavior of SQL Server to automatically permit NULLs on table columns, or user-defined datatypes, if no reference to the NULL CHARacteristic is specified when a column, or user-defined datatype, is defined. You can use a `set` command to change the NULL CHARacteristic for columns or user-defined datatypes defined during a client session. You can also change the NULL CHARacteristic for an entire database using the system procedure `sp_dboption`.

Use the following `set` command to cause NULLs to be permitted automatically in table columns or user-defined datatypes:

SET ANSI_NULL_DFLT_ON

Use the following `sp_dboption` command to cause NULLs to be permitted automatically in table columns or user-defined datatypes:

sp_dboption *database-name*, 'ANSI NULL default', true

ANSI NULLability permits SQL Server not only to conform to a standard form of SQL, but to be tailored to match the SQL dialect of other SQL used with other server databases. You can more easily use SQL Server if you can modify the syntax and behavior of Transact-SQL to match a dialect of SQL that you've used previously. For example, if you change the default NULLability of SQL Server by defining the `sp_dboption` option as true, it automatically permits NULLs in column definitions, like in Gupta's SQLBase database.

N O T E If you've changed the NULL CHARacteristic during a session, or for a database, you can set it back to the default using one of the following commands:

SET ANSI_NULL_DFLT_OFF

sp_dboption *database-name*, 'ANSI NULL default', false ■

NULL Manipulation

When you compare a NULL value to any non-NULL value of a column or other data-storage structure, the result is never logically true. If you compare a NULL value to another NULL value, the result is also never a logical true. NULL values don't match each other because unknown or undefined values aren't assumed to be identical.

However, rows that contain multiple NULL values in a column referenced in an ORDER BY, GROUP BY, or DISTINCT clause of a select statement are treated as identical values. All three clauses group together rows with identical values. ORDER BY is used to sort rows, and, in the case of NULLs, all entries in the same column are sorted together. Columns containing NULLs appear at the beginning of a sequence of rows that are sorted in ascending order.

GROUP BY forms groups using identical values, and all NULLs of a column are placed in a single group. The distinct keyword used in a select clause removes all duplicates from one or more column values and removes multiple NULL values as well. Columns that contain NULLs are considered to be equal when you define an index that uses a NULL column.

▶ **See** "Using an *ORDER BY* Clause," **p. 207**, "Using a *GROUP BY* Clause," **p. 216**, and "Using DISTINCT to Retrieve Unique Column Values," **p. 211**.

If you perform computations with columns or other data structures that contain NULLs, the computations evaluate to NULL. In the following example, the evaluation of the expression x=x+1 evaluates to NULL because the x column contains only a single row with a NULL defined for the x column:

```
select * from NULLtable
where x=x+1
x          y
--------------------
(0 row(s) affected)
```

The following example returns an error because a column defined as not NULL is compared with a NULL expression:

```
select * from employees
where badge=NULL
Msg 221, Level 16, State 1
```

A column of the datatype integer doesn't allow NULLs. It may not be compared with NULL.

Using *ISNULL()*

ISNULL() is a system function that returns a string of CHARacters or numbers in place of (NULL) when a NULL is encountered in a data-storage structure, such as a table column. The syntax of the function is as follows:

```
ISNULL(expression,value)
```

The expression is usually a column name that contains a NULL value. The value specifies a string or number to be displayed when a NULL is found. In the following example, ISNULL() is used to return a number when a NULL is encountered in the value of a row, or return the CHARacter string 'NO ENTRY' when a NULL is encountered.

```
select x,ISNULL(x,531),y, ISNULL(y, 'NO ENTRY')
from NULLtable
x                           y
- - - - - - - - - - - - - - - - - - - - - - - - - - - - - - - - - - - - -
(NULL)      531            (NULL)      NO ENTRY
(1 row(s) affected)
```

N O T E   You may decide that it's easier to avoid using NULL rather than deal with the intricacies of working with NULLs. You can decide to use a specific pattern that is entered for a datatype that has the meaning of no entry or undefined, instead of NULL. ■

identity Property

In addition to defining the datatype of a column to allow or disallow NULLs, you can define a column with the property of identity. When you define a column with the property identity, you can specify both an initial value (seed), which is automatically added in the column for the first row, and a value (increment), which is added to that last value entered for the column. When you add rows to the table, you omit entering a value for the column defined with the identity property. The value for the identity column is automatically entered by adding the increment value to the column value of the last row.

In the following example, the second column is defined with the property identity (see Listing 6.17). After two rows are added to the table, a subsequent retrieval of the table rows shows that the identity column values were generated by the identity mechanism.

Listing 6.17   *create table identity_table* Example

```
create table identity_table
(name CHAR(15),row_number integer identity(1,1))
INSERT into identity_table
(name)
values ('Bob Smith')
INSERT into identity_table
(name)
values ('Mary Jones')
select * from identity_table
name             row_number
- - - - - - - - - - - - - - - - - - - - - - - - -
Bob Smith        1
Mary Jones       2

(2 row(s) affected)
```

You can assign the identity property only to a column that is defined with the datatypes int, smallint, tinyint, decimal(p,0), and numeric(p,0)—but not if the column permits NULLs. If you omit a seed and increment value when specifying the identity property on a table column, they default to one. Also, only a single column of a table can be defined with the property identity. The identity property doesn't guarantee that rows will be unique. You must establish a unique index on the identity column to guarantee unique table rows.

 TIP You can use the keyword identitycol, as well as the name of the column, to reference the column of a table that is defined with the property identity.

Creating and Using Constraints

Constraints are defined to provide data integrity on a table and in individual columns. The create table statement enables you to create primary and foreign keys, define unique columns and rows, and specify check and default constraints.

PRIMARY KEY Constraints

You use PRIMARY KEY constraints for column integrity, as well as referential integrity. The definition of a PRIMARY KEY constraint for a table has several effects. The PRIMARY KEY constraint ensures that all rows of a table are unique by ensuring that one or more columns don't permit duplicate values to be entered.

A PRIMARY KEY constraint also disallows NULL for the column(s) in which the constraint is defined. A PRIMARY KEY constraint creates a unique index on the column(s) defined in the constraint. A secondary effect is that the index can be used for faster retrieval of rows of the table than if no index were defined on the table.

N O T E The definition of a PRIMARY KEY constraint on a single table doesn't by itself permit referential integrity. You must also define corresponding foreign keys in the tables whose rows will be combined with the table in which you define the PRIMARY KEY constraint. ■

The syntax of the PRIMARY KEY constraint is as follows:

```
CONSTRAINT constraint_name PRIMARY KEY CLUSTERED (column_name_1 column_name_n)
```

In the following example, the employees table has a PRIMARY KEY constraint defined on the badge column.

```
Create table employees4
(name CHAR(20),department varCHAR(20),badge integer,
constraint badge_pays2 foreign key (badge) references employees4 (badge))
```

FOREIGN KEY Constraint

A FOREIGN KEY constraint is used along with a previously defined PRIMARY KEY constraint on an associated table. A FOREIGN KEY constraint associates one or more columns of a table with an identical set of columns that have been defined as a PRIMARY KEY constraint in another table. When the column values are UPDATEd in the table in which the PRIMARY KEY constraint is defined, the columns defined in another table as a FOREIGN KEY constraint are automatically UPDATEd.

The PRIMARY KEY and FOREIGN KEY constraints ensure that corresponding rows of associated tables continue to match so that they can be used in subsequent relational joins. The automatic updating of the corresponding columns of different tables after they're defined as PRIMARY KEY and FOREIGN KEY constraints is called *declarative referential integrity*, a feature added to SQL Server in version 6.0.

The syntax of the FOREIGN KEY constraint clause is as follows:

```
CONSTRAINT constraint_name FOREIGN KEY (column_name_1 column_name_n) REFERENCES
_table_name (column_name_1 column_name_n)
```

The table named after the keyword REFERENCES is the table in which the corresponding column(s) are defined as a PRIMARY KEY constraint. In the following example, the badge column in the pays2 table is defined as a FOREIGN KEY constraint that associates, or references, with the badge column in the employees4 table.

```
Create table pays
(hours_worked integer, pay_rate integer,badge integer,
constraint badge_pays2 foreign key (badge) references employees4 (badge))
```

N O T E The corresponding columns that are defined as PRIMARY KEY and FOREIGN KEY constraints don't have to have the same names. However, it's simpler to understand the columns in different tables that are defined as associated PRIMARY KEY and FOREIGN KEY constraints if their names are identical. ■

unique Constraint

You apply the unique constraint to any table column to prevent duplicate values from being entered into the column. A restriction is that the column can't be defined as the primary key or part of the primary key of the table. The unique constraint is enforced through the automatic creation of a unique index for the table that is based on the column. In the following example, a unique constraint is applied to the badge column of the employees2 table:

```
Create table employees2
(name CHAR(20), department varCHAR(20),badge integer,
constraint badge_nodupes unique nonclustered (badge))
```

check Constraint

A check constraint limits the values that can be entered into one or more columns of a database table. You can use a check constraint, for example, to limit the range of values that can be stored in a column defined as numeric datatypes.

The process of associating a check with a table column is called *binding*. You can define and associate multiple checks with a single column. A check can be defined for a column, even though a rule is already defined on the column. In the following example, a check constraint is defined on the column department to restrict subsequent entries to valid departments:

```
Create table employees5
(name CHAR(20), department varCHAR(20),badge integer
check valid_department (department in
[ccc] ('Sales','Field Service','Software','Logistics')))
```

> **N O T E** Check and other constraints can seem as though they duplicate the function of other
> mechanisms in SQL Server. If you've had this perception, it's accurate. In version 6.0 of
> SQL Server, Microsoft changed its version of SQL, Transact-SQL, to conform to a standardized form of
> SQL, ANSI SQL. Although Transact-SQL already had existing ways of performing some operations, such
> as rules and defaults, the addition of ANSI SQL syntax to Transact-SQL added alternate ways of
> performing the same operations.
>
> You can often choose to implement a feature, such as a restriction on the values that can be entered
> into a column, in the way that you feel is the easiest to set up. For example, you can choose to restrict
> the values entered into the columns of a table using a check constraint instead of defining a rule and
> binding it to the column.
>
> However, you should investigate each mechanism, because one may be more appropriate for your use.
> Although a check constraint is quicker and simpler to set up to restrict the column values than a rule,
> a rule is more flexible in one way.; after you define a rule, it can be bound to a column in multiple
> tables. A rule may prove more useful to you if you're going to use it to restrict column values on
> columns that are in multiple tables. ∎

default Constraint

You use a default constraint to have a value automatically added to a table column when no value is entered during an insert. You can define a default constraint to the most frequently occurring value within a table column and thus relieve a user of the need to enter the defined default constraint value when a new row is added to the table. The syntax of the default constraint clause is as follows:

```
DEFAULT default_name value FOR column_name
```

In the following example, a default value is specified for the department column for the employees6 table:

```
Create table employees6
(name CHAR(20),department varCHAR(20),badge integer,
DEFAULT department_default 'Sales' for department)
```

You can also use a default, which you must define and then bind to a table column, to have a value automatically added to a table column. Although Microsoft recommends that you use a default constraint to add a value automatically to a table column, after a default is defined, it can be bound to columns in different tables, instead of in a single table.

▶ **See** "Managing and Using Rules, Constraints, and Defaults," **p. 379**.

Microsoft recommends that you use a default constraint instead of a default when you're defining a default value for a column in a single table because a default constraint is stored with the table, instead of as a separate database object. If you drop a table, the constraint is automatically dropped. When a table is deleted, a default bound to a column of the table isn't deleted.

N O T E   With a default constraint, you can use a set of functions called *niladic functions*. A niladic function inserts a value that is generated by SQL Server.

Niladic functions allow a system-supplied value, such as information about the current user or a timestamp, to be inserted when no value is specified. The ANSI niladic functions that can be used with a default constraint are current_user(), session_user(), system_user(), user(), and current_timestamp(). current_user(), session_user(), and user() return the user name stored in the database of the user issuing an insert or UPDATE. The system_user() function returns the SQL Server logon ID of the user, and the current_timestamp() function returns the date in the same form as that which is returned by the getdate() function. ■

Creating User-Defined Datatypes

You can define your own datatype, which can then be used as a datatype for a storage structure, such as a table column. You always define a user-defined datatype as one of the existing system datatypes. A user-defined datatype enables you to define a datatype that can contain a length specification, if necessary, and a NULL CHARacteristic.

You can use a descriptive name, which describes the type of data that it contains, for the user-defined datatype.

Creating User-Defined Datatypes with *sp_addtype*   You can define a user-defined datatype with the system procedure sp_addtype, which uses the following syntax:

```
sp_addtype user_defined_datatype_name, system_datatype, NULL ¦ NULL
```

After you define a user-defined datatype, you can use it to specify the datatype of a storage structure such as a table column. You can use the system procedure sp_help to display a user-defined datatype. You can create and then bind defaults and rules to user-defined datatypes. You bind rules and defaults to user-defined datatypes with the same procedures used for system datatypes sp_bindefault and sp_bindrule.

An error message is generated if you specify not NULL for a column and don't create a default, or specify a value at insertion. You can also change the NULL or not NULL CHARacteristic for a user-defined datatype when you define a column in a table.

In Listing 6.18, a user-defined datatype is created by using sp_addtype. The CHARacteristics are displayed with sp_help. A new table is created in which the column is defined using the user-defined datatype.

Listing 6.18 *sp_addtype names* **Example**

```
sp_addtype names, 'CHAR(15)', NULL
Type added.
sp_help names
Type_name       Storage_type     Length NULLs Default_name     Rule_name
------------    ---------------   ------ ----- ---------------  ---------
names           CHAR             15      1     (NULL)           (NULL)
create table usertype_table
(CHARstring names)
```

In Listing 6.19, a value is inserted into the table and subsequently retrieved. The insertion of the string results in a truncation of the inserted string to 15 CHARacters. The example also displays the table in which a column is defined by using a user-defined datatype.

Listing 6.19 *INSERT into usertype_table* **Example**

```
INSERT into usertype_table
values ('this is a string')
select * from usertype_table
CHARstring
---------------
this is a strin
(1 row(s) affected)
sp_help usertype_table
Name                              Owner                            Type
----------------------------      ----------------------------     -----------
usertype_table                    dbo                              user table
Data_located_on_segment           When_created
----------------------------      ----------------------------
default                           May 19 1994 12:46PM
Column_name     Type             Length NULLs Default_name     Rule_name
--------------  ---------------  ------ ----- ---------------  -----------
CHARstring      names            15      1     (NULL)           (NULL)
Object does not have any indexes.
No defined keys for this object.
```

Part

I

Ch

6

Creating User-Defined Datatypes with the Enterprise Manager   To define a user-defined datatype using the Enterprise Manager, follow these steps:

1. Expand the databases by clicking the plus (+) box next to the Databases folder. Click a database to select it. Your user-defined datatype will be created in the selected database.

2. Choose User Defined Datatypes from the Manage menu.

3. Enter a name in the New Name field of the Manage User-Defined Datatypes dialog box.

4. Enter a system datatype in the Datatype field. Enter a length for the datatype in the Length field if you choose a datatype such as CHAR or varCHAR. You can also decide to allow NULLs, apply a previously defined rule or default value to the user-defined datatype, or specify an owner.

5. Click OK to complete the creation process. See Figure 6.3 for an example of the dialog box that enables you to work with the datatypes.

FIG. 6.3

You can list the user-defined datatypes from the Manage User-Defined Datatypes dialog box.

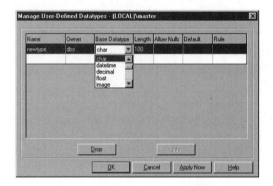

Dropping User-Defined Datatypes   You can use the system procedure sp_droptype to remove a user-defined datatype. The procedure uses the following syntax:

```
sp_droptype typename
```

You can't drop a user-defined datatype if one or more tables have a column, which is defined using it. You can drop the user-defined datatype only if it isn't in use by any tables. In the following example (see Listing 6.20), a user-defined datatype can't be dropped until you first drop the sole table in which a column is defined using the user-defined datatype:

Listing 6.20   *sp_droptype names* Example

```
sp_droptype names
Type is being used. You cannot drop it.
object                  type owner             column               datatype
--------------------    ---- ----------------  -------------------  ----------
usertype_table          U    dbo               CHARstring           names
(1 row(s) affected)
```

```
drop table usertype_table
This command didn't return any data or rows:
sp_droptype names
Type has been dropped.
```

You can also drop a user-defined datatype through the Enterprise Manager. To do so, follow these steps:

1. Expand the databases by clicking the plus (+) box next to the Databases folder. Click a database to select it. Your user-defined datatype will be created in the selected database.

2. Choose User Defined Datatypes from the Manage menu.

3. Select the user-defined datatype.

4. Click Drop.

Working with Datatypes

You can't name objects with names of commands or other reserved words because datatypes are objects in the database. Datatypes are stored in the SysTypes system table along with their coded values. You can use the following select statement (see Listing 6.21) to display the datatypes and their code value in the type column:

Listing 6.21   systypes Example

```
select name,type
from systypes
order by type
name                            type
----------------------------    ----
image                           34
text                            35
timestamp                       37
varbinary                       37
intn                            38
sysname                         39
varCHAR                         39
binary                          45
CHAR                            47
badge_type                      47
tinyint                         48
bit                             50
smallint                        52
int                             56
badge_type2                     56
smalldatetime                   58
real                            59
MONEY                           60
datetime                        61
```

Part

I

Ch

6

continues

Listing 6.21   Continued

```
float                   62
floatn                  109
MONEYn                  110
datetimn               111
smallMONEY             122
(24 row(s) affected)
```

You can use sp_helpsql to display information about the CHARacteristics of system datatypes, as shown in Listing 6.22:

Listing 6.22   Review of Datatypes

```
sp_helpsql 'datatype'
helptext
----------------------------------------------------------------
Datatype
Datatype                 Definition

Binary(n)                Fixed-length binary data. Maximum
                         length=255 bytes.
Bit                      A column that holds either 0 or 1.
CHAR(n)                  CHARacter data. Maximum length=255 bytes.
Datetime                Dates and times with accuracy to milliseconds.
Float                    Floating-point numbers.
Image                    Large amounts of binary data (up to
                         2,147,483,647 CHARacters.)
Int                      Integers between 2,147,483,647 and
                         -2,147,483,648.
MONEY                    Dollar and cent values.
Real                     Floating point numbers with 7-digit precision.
Smalldatetime           Dates and times with accuracy to the minute.
Smallint                 Integers between 32,767 and -32,768.
SmallMONEY              Monetary values between 214,748.3647 and
                         -214,748.3648.
Text                     Large amounts of CHARacter data (up to
                         2,147,483,647 CHARacters).
Timestamp               Automatically UPDATEd when you INSERT or UPDATE a
                         row that has a timestamp
                         column, or use BROWSE mode in a
                         DB-LIBRARY application.
Tinyint                 Whole integers between 0 and 255.
Varbinary(n)            Variable-length binary data. Max
                         length=255 bytes.
VarCHAR(n)              Variable-length CHARacter data. Max
                         length=255 bytes.
```

Creating Tables and Defining Columns Through the Enterprise Manager

In addition to creating a table with the `create table` statement, you can create a table through the Enterprise Manager. To do so, follow these steps:

▶ **See** "SQL Enterprise Manager To Create Tables," **p. 134**.

1. Expand the databases by clicking the plus (+) box next to the Databases folder. Click a database to select it. Your table will be created in the selected database.

2. Choose Tables from the Manage menu.

3. Enter a column name in the Column Name field.

4. Use the mouse or Tab key to move to the Datatype field. Select a datatype from the list that is displayed.

5. If the datatype that you've chosen requires the specification of a length, enter it into the Length field.

6. To allow NULL values, leave the NULLs field selected.

7. If you've previously defined default values, you can choose one in the Default field.

8. Repeat steps 3 through 7 to continue specifying up to 250 columns and their CHARacteristics.

Figure 6.4 shows the Manage Tables window after information for three columns has been entered.

FIG. 6.4
The NULL property is automatically enabled for each column that you enter, though you can deselect it.

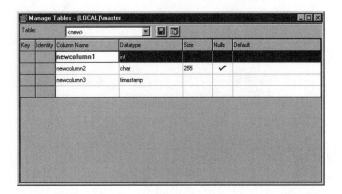

9. Click the Save Table button on the Manage Tables toolbar to bring up the Specify Table Name dialog box.

10. Enter a name for the new table in the Specify Table Name dialog box (see Figure 6.5).

Part
I

Ch
6

FIG. 6.5
To complete the
operation, enter the
name you want to use
to reference the new
table.

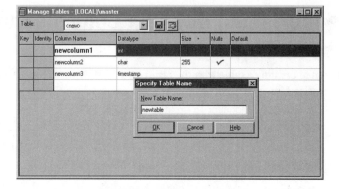

11. Click <u>O</u>K. The new table is displayed as the selected table in the Manage Tables window.

You also can define properties on columns such as an `identity`, `primary key`, or `constraint` by clicking the Advanced Features tool on the toolbar of the Manage Tables window while you're defining the table. For example, in Figure 6.6, a column has been defined as an identity column in the Identity Column combo box of the Manage Tables window after the Advanced Features tool is clicked.

FIG. 6.6
You can specify an
initial value (seed) and
increment for your
identity column.

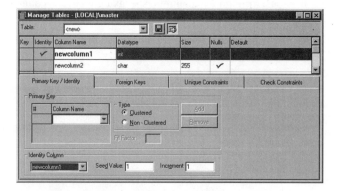

Adding Data to a Table with *INSERT*

After you create a table, you can add data using an `INSERT` statement. Several forms of the `INSERT` statement can be used to add new rows to a table. Each `INSERT` statement can add only a single row to a table. The complete form of the `INSERT` statement uses the following syntax:

```
INSERT INTO table_name
(column_name_1,...,column_name_n)
VALUES ('string_1',...'lstring_')
```

List the table columns to receive values separately, enclosed by parentheses and separated by commas, after the INSERT clause. Enter the values that will be added to the table columns in parentheses in the same order as the column names in the previous line. The list of column values is preceded by the VALUES keyword.

You don't have to list the columns and their values in the same order as they are defined in the table. You must, however, enter the values in the VALUES clause in the correct order as the column names listed in the previous line. If you do not, data values may be inserted into the wrong columns.

In the following example, the columns are listed in the order in which they were defined in the table, but they don't have to follow the same order. The values are entered in the VALUES clause in an order that corresponds to the order of the columns named in the previous line.

```
INSERT into employees
(name, department, badge)
values ('Bob Smith', 'SALES', 1834)
```

If you omit one or more column names, a NULL or default value is entered into the table row. In the following example, the name and badge columns are listed in the INSERT statement. The values clause omits a value for the department.

```
INSERT into employees
(name, badge)
values ('Bob Mariah', 1999)
```

Table 6.4 shows the resulting entry for a table if an explicit value isn't listed in the values list of an INSERT statement.

Table 6.4   Effect of *NULL* and Default Values on Table Column Entries

Column CHARacteristic(s)	User Entry	Resulting Entry
NULL defined	No default value defined	NULL
not NULL defined	No default value defined	Error, no row inserted
NULL defined	Default value defined	Default value
not NULL defined	Default value entered	Default value

N O T E   Use (NULL) within the values list to insert a NULL into a column that has been defined to permit the NULL. ■

Part

I

Ch

6

From Here...

In this chapter, you've learned to create database tables. The process of creating a table involves the selection of the appropriate datatypes for your table columns. In addition, you've learned to add the additional CHARacteristics that can be defined for a table column including the NULL CHARacteristic and the various constraints. You learned to create, drop, and list the CHARacteristics of a table using Transact-SQL syntax and the Enterprise Manager.

For further discussion about topics mentioned in this chapter, see the following chapters:

- Chapter 7, "Retrieving Data with Transact-SQL," teaches you how to use Transact-SQL syntax to retrieve the data that you've stored in table columns.

- Chapter 11, "Managing and Using Indexes and Keys," teaches you how to create and use keys and indexes and how to constrain rows and columns to unique values.

- Chapter 13, "Managing and Using Rules, Constraints, and Defaults," teaches you how to create and bind rules and defaults to user-defined datatypes and table columns.

- Chapter 14, "Managing Stored Procedures and Using Flow-Control Statements," teaches you how to define storage structures, such as parameters and local variables, using system variables. You also learn how to reference global variables.

- Chapter 16, "Understanding Server, Database, and Design Query Options," shows you how to use query options to control the display of data through set command options.

P A R T

II

Up and Running with SQL Server

Retrieving Data with Transact-SQL

You usually don't want to access and display all the data stored in a database in each query or report. You may want some, but not all, of the rows and columns of data. Although you can access all the information, you probably don't need to display all rows and columns because it's too much information to examine at one time.

In previous chapters, you learned that the information stored in a relational database is always accessed as a table. If you reference a printed table of information, you usually don't read all the rows and columns. You probably look at only part of the table to obtain the information you need. The table exists in a printed form only because it's a traditional way of storing information.

If you can reconsider your requests for information from the database, you can start to eliminate the queries that produce unwanted or unneeded results. In these cases, you can produce output that presents exactly what is needed and nothing more. ■

Retrieve data from a table by using a SELECT statement

The SELECT statement is used to choose the data that is be displayed from database tables.

Use comparison, Boolean, and range operators in SELECT statements to specify table rows

You can write queries that specify selected table rows.

Return rows of a table in sorted order by one or more columns and eliminate duplicate rows

You can manipulate the rows of a table, including changing their presentation order.

Use embedded queries to return rows used as the input values to outer queries

By using embedded queries, or subselect statements, you can fine-tune the results returned to your application.

Setting Up a Demonstration Database and Table

The data stored on your database, or the disk of your computer system, is analogous to a set of printed tables. You don't need to retrieve an entire table when you issue queries to display information from the database. You construct a query using a Transact-SQL statement, which returns only the relevant portion of the column or rows of your database tables.

Table 7.1 shows an example table structure and its data, which will be used for several examples in this chapter. For information on creating tables, see Chapter 5, "Creating Devices, Databases, and Transaction Logs" and Chapter 6, "Creating Database Tables and Using Datatypes."

On the CD

You can find a sample script that creates a small database, this table, and inserts the appropriate values in the table on the CD accompanying this book. The file name for the script is `chap6-1.sql`.

Table 7.1   A Table Containing 12 Rows

Name	Department	Badge
Bob Smith	SALES	1834
Fred Sanders	SALES	1051
Stan Humphries	Field Service	3211
Fred Stanhope	Field Service	6732
Sue Sommers	Logistics	4411
Lance Finepoint	Library	5522
Mark McGuire	Field Service	1997
Sally Springer	Sales	9998
Ludmilla Valencia	Software	7773
Barbara Lint	Field Service	8883
Jeffrey Vickers	Mailroom	8005
Jim Walker	Unit Manager	7779

The table is limited to 12 rows to make it easier to work with the examples. The typical size of a table for a production database might have more columns of information and nearly always has more rows of information. The size of the table won't make any difference in showing the operation of Transact-SQL statements. The statements work identically, regardless of the size of the tables operated on. The examples in this chapter are easier to understand if a small number of rows and columns are present in the table used to show SQL operations.

Retrieving Data from a Table with *SELECT*

Your queries of a database are a selection process that narrows the information retrieved from the database to those rows that fit your criteria. As you've seen earlier in this chapter and in Chapter 2, which covered database design, your goal as you work with tables should always be to return only the information needed to fulfill the user's request. If you retrieve any more information, the user is required to wait for a longer period of time than is necessary. Any less information than is needed results in additional queries against the database. This modeling of sets of data is always a balancing act that requires continued refinement.

The SQL SELECT statement is used for the selection process. The various parts of a SELECT statement target the data in the database tables. The complete syntax of the SELECT statement is shown in Listing 7.1.

Listing 7.1 Syntax of the *SELECT* Statement

```
SELECT [ALL | DISTINCT] select_list
       [INTO [new_table_name]]
[FROM {table_name | view_name}[(optimizer_hints)]
       [[, {table_name2 | view_name2}[(optimizer_hints)]
       [..., {table_name16 | view_name16}[(optimizer_hints)]]]]
[WHERE clause]
[GROUP BY clause]
[HAVING clause]
[ORDER BY clause]
[COMPUTE clause]
[FOR BROWSE]
```

A SELECT statement is like a filter superimposed on a database table. Using SQL keywords, the database is narrowed to target the columns and rows that are to be retrieved in a query. In the filter comparison, shown in Figure 7.1, the widest part of the filter selects all the rows and columns of a database for retrieval. The narrowest portion of the filter indicates selection of the smallest cross-section of data that can be retrieved from a table, a single row with only one column.

FIG. 7.1
SELECT queries are used to target specific columns and rows of a database.

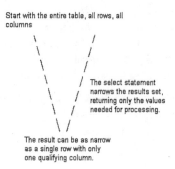

Start with the entire table, all rows, all columns

The select statement narrows the results set, returning only the values needed for processing.

The result can be as narrow as a single row with only one qualifying column.

Part

II

Ch

7

Most SQL queries retrieve rows and columns that are narrower than the entire table, represented by the base of the filter in the figure, but wider than the single row and column, as shown in the point of the triangle opposite the triangle's base. You'll typically need to retrieve more than a single row and column, but less than all the rows and columns of the database.

This is where more complicated SELECT statements are used. As you're going to see in this, and the next few chapters, the numbers and types of operations you can perform on your database tables can range from simple selects to complicated, server-resolved queries that provide precisely the information you need.

As you read through the different things you can do with SQL, keep in mind that you can, and should, try it out using ISQL or ISQL/W against your own tables. That's the quickest way to learn, the fastest way to get started.

Selecting a Query Tool

There are several different ways you can enter queries to be sent to SQL Server. Although it's beyond the scope and intent of this book to discuss development languages at length, it's likely that, during your testing and experimentation with SQL Server, you'll use one of at least three different tools:

- The SQL Enterprise Manager Query Tool
- ISQL for Windows
- ISQL command line version

Initiating the query, sending it to the server, and viewing the results of your query, are all covered in the next sections and these sections serve as the foundation for your use of these tools for the balance of the book.

▶ You can also use Microsoft Query to send queries to, and receive results from, SQL Server. Another alternative is to use Access to work with SQL Server. For more information about this approach, **see** Chapter 26, "Upsizing Microsoft Office 97 Applications to SQL Server," **p. 709**.

Using the Enterprise Manager Query Tool

SQL Enterprise Manager is an obvious choice with which to experiment for many different reasons. The primary benefit of this tool is the fact that you can use the other functions of the Enterprise Manager to help you work with table structures; other servers and other features of SQL Server that might not relate to, or be controllable by, your query.

Running queries in Enterprise Manager is much like working with ISQL for Windows. The dialog box you use is identical and offers the same functionality as ISQL/w. To use the Query tool from SQL Enterprise Manager, follow these steps:

1. Select the server from the list of available, registered servers.

2. Open the Query window by choosing Tools, Query Analyzer, or by clicking the appropriate toolbar button.

3. From the resulting dialog box, select the database with which you want to work. If you had highlighted a database prior to selecting the tool, that database will already be selected. See Figure 7.2 for an example.

FIG. 7.2

Be sure to select the database you want to work with prior to entering your query.

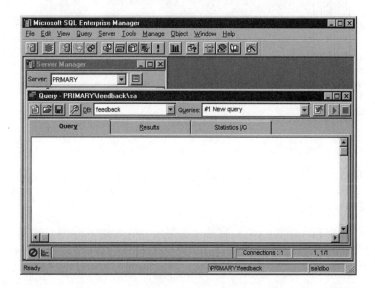

4. You enter your query in the text window portion of the Query tab; then press Ctrl+E, press the green play button, or select Query, Execute from the menu.

5. You'll be automatically taken to the Results tab, where you'll see the incoming results from your query. These results are displayed as they are received, so if your query requires processing time on the server for each row, you're likely to see as little information as a single line as each appropriate result is determined.

N O T E   With ISQL in its command-line version, you must enter a GO statement after each batch you want to process against the server. Although you can enter these in the Query Tool, it's not necessary. When you select Execute, as in the preceding step 4, all of the contents of the query window are sent to SQL Server for processing.

The exception to this is if you have highlighted one or more sections of the query window, only those highlighted portions are sent to SQL Server. This is a good way to test a specific statement out of a batch of statements, and a good tool for debugging your queries. ■

Part
II

Ch
7

Using ISQL for Windows

If you're looking for the convenience of using the Query Tool from Enterprise Manager without having to work through the entire Enterprise Manager environment, then ISQL for Windows is perfect. When you start ISQL/W, you are prompted to sign in to SQL server, provide a user ID, password, and, if needed, a server to use (see Figure 7.3).

FIG. 7.3

Because ISQL/W doesn't store usernames and passwords as Enterprise Manager does when you register a server, you need to sign in each time you access the server for a new session.

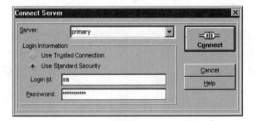

After you sign in, you are presented with the query window with three tabs. These tabs are for the query, results, and statistics. They enable you to profile what it takes for SQL Server to fulfill your request.

Note that you must select the database you want to work with in the <u>D</u>B listbox. If you don't you receive a message, like that shown next, indicating that the object you're looking for does not exist.

```
Msg 208, Level 16, State 1
Invalid object name 'feedback'.
```

Such a message probably means that you don't have the right database selected for your query, or that you don't have the right name for your table. Either way, make sure you're indicating an object that is currently *in scope* for your session.

As with Enterprise Manager, you execute your query after you've entered it by pressing Ctrl+E, pressing the green play button, or by selecting Query, Execute from the menu. When you do, the Results tab is automatically selected and you can see what happens as SQL Server processes your request.

N O T E   With ISQL in its command-line version, you must enter a GO statement after each batch you want to process against the server. Although you can enter these in the Query Tool, it's not necessary. When you select Execute, as in step 4 above, all of the contents of the query window are sent to SQL Server for processing.

The exception to this is if you have highlighted one or more sections of the query window, only the highlighted portions are sent to SQL Server. This is a good way to test a specific statement out of a batch of statements and a good tool for debugging your queries. ■

Using ISQL from the Command-Line

The last, most commonly used query tool for accessing SQL Server from the command-line is ISQL. This type of access is especially helpful in cases where you're running a series of scripts as you can create a batch file and run the entire series unattended. It's also helpful as a low-overhead approach to testing your queries.

The simplest way to start ISQL interactively is:

```
isql -Sservername -Uusername -Ppassword
```

Provide the server, user name, and password that should be used and you'll be presented with the equivalent to the DOS c> prompt, a 1> prompt, indicating that ISQL is ready and waiting on your input.

From here, you can enter the query you want to run, press Enter, enter a GO statement, and then press Enter. Remember, with the ISQL command-line version, you *must* enter the GO statement, or the query statements you enter will not be executed.

When you run the query, you'll see any messages about the processing as it occurs. This can be seen in the example shown next and is how you'll find out about any error messages.

```
1> select * from feedback
2> go
Msq 208, Level 16, State 1, Line 1
Invalid object name 'feedback'
1>
```

Remember, too, you'll need to use the USE statement to select the database you want to access. For example, the following would produce the results desired from the fragment shown above:

```
1> use feedback
2> select * from feedback
3> go
```

N O T E This example assumes you have a database named *feedback* and a table within that database, also named *feedback*. ■

T I P You can use the -i option to run ISQL from the command line and pass in a file that contains the SQL statements you want to run. For example,

```
isql -imysql.sql -Sprimary -Uusername -Ppassword
```

runs the mysql.sql file and the results are displayed to the monitor as they are generated.

Part

II

Ch

7

In the next sections, you learn about all of the different portions of the SELECT statement, starting with the basics.

Specifying the Table with *FROM* (Required Element)

Different parts of the SELECT statement are used to specify the data to be returned from the database. The first part of the selection process occurs when fewer than all the database tables are referenced. You can retrieve data stored in the database separately by referencing some tables, but not others, in a SELECT statement.

A SELECT statement uses the FROM clause to target the tables from which rows and columns are included in a query. The syntax of the FROM clause is as follows:

```
[FROM {table_name ¦ view_name}[(optimizer_hints)]
[[, {table_name2 ¦ view_name2}[(optimizer_hints)]
[..., {table_name16 ¦ view_name16}[(optimizer_hints)]]]]
```

In the following complete SELECT statement, the FROM clause specifies that the returned data should include only data from the employee table:

```
SELECT *
FROM employee
```

N O T E Note that SELECT * will return all columns without the need to specifically call them out in the query statement. ■

N O T E In the examples shown in this chapter, the Transact-SQL keywords used to form clauses are written in uppercase. You can, however, use lowercase keywords.

Remember, however, if you installed Microsoft SQL Server with the default binary sort order, the names of your database objects, including the names of tables and columns, must match in case. ■

You can also specify multiple tables in the FROM clause, as in the following example:

```
FROM table_name_1,...,table_name_n
```

Each table is separated from the names of other tables with a comma. This is a separator used with lists of information in FROM and other Transact-SQL clauses. The list in a FROM clause often specifies multiple tables instead of a single table.

In the following example of a SELECT statement, the FROM clause references the data from two tables:

```
SELECT *
FROM employee,pay
```

The Employee and Pay tables are targeted, and all rows and columns are retrieved from these.

N O T E   As you'll see later in the section "Using a Wildcard in the SELECT Clause," using `Select *` returns all columns from the requested table or tables. This can cause queries that take quite some time to complete. You should avoid using `Select *` if possible because it does not restrict the returned data set at all. ■

N O T E   In a relational database, you must provide instructions within the SELECT statement to match the rows from two or more tables together. To learn how to match, or join rows from multiple tables, see Chapter 8, "Adding, Changing, and Deleting Information in Tables." ■

The SQL query language lets you choose tables from different databases. You can specify the name of the database in which the table is located by inserting the database name to the left of the table name. Next, place a period, the database owner name, and another period, followed by the table you need to work with, as shown in the following example:

```
database_name.owner.table_name
```

In the following example, the employee table in the database company and the owner dbo is specified:

```
SELECT *
FROM company.dbo.employee
```

N O T E   The DBO keyword specifies the database owner. You can refer to the dbo at any time. SQL will know that you're referring to the owner of the specific database. ■

In the previous example, the table was created by using the system administrator's account, so the owner is dbo. If you omit the name of the database and owner when you reference a table, SQL Server looks for the table or tables that you specified in the FROM clause in the current database. You must enter the name of the database in which a table was created, along with its owner, to include the rows and columns from tables in different databases.

Specifying Columns with *SELECT* (Required Element)

As you work with the SELECT statement, keep in mind that you can control the data elements returned in two different manners. First, you can divide the data vertically, limiting the columns that are returned in your results. This is done with the SELECT statement when you indicate the columns you want to have returned.

The other way you can divide your results set is horizontally, controlling which rows qualify for the results set. You use the WHERE clause, shown in coming sections, to divide your tables in this manner.

Part

II

Ch

7

The columns of values returned from database tables are specified as part of the SELECT clause immediately following the SELECT keyword. One or more of the columns are entered as a list. Each column, like the tables in a FROM clause, is separated by a comma:

```
SELECT column_name_1,...column_name_n
FROM table_name_1,...table_name_n
```

In the following code example, the name and badge columns are selected for retrieval. The results are shown in Figure 7.4. This example uses the SQL Windows application utility ISQL/w to perform the retrieval of rows.

```
Select name, badge
from employee
```

FIG. 7.4

SELECT statements, and the different options you can use within them, are the tool you use to limit results sets.

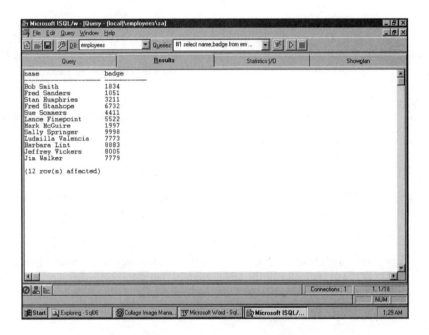

N O T E The code listings are what should be entered into the query page of an ISQL/w session. Figures, such as Figure 7.4, show what the results should look like when the Execute button is pressed. ■

In previous chapters, you learned that one of the basic tenets of a relational database is that operations on database tables always return another table, as a results set. The rows and columns of database tables that are targeted for retrieval are always assembled into a temporary table. In most cases, this table is maintained only until the data is provided to the requesting client.

The new temporary table, shown in Figure 7.4, was constructed from the three-column Employee table. According to the SELECT statement, the temporary table targets all rows of the permanent table's three columns and eliminates the second column, Department. The temporary table is deleted after the rows are provided to the requesting client.

Figure 7.5 shows the query, involving the Employee table, performed with the command-line form of ISQL.

FIG. 7.5

Transact SQL produces the same results from a command-line prompt that it does the GUI environment.

 TIP Use the ED command to edit a long statement to be entered at the command line. This invokes the system editor with the previous command entered. After exiting the system editor, it places the edited statement as the next statement.

You can display table columns in a different order than you originally defined. To change the default order for the display of table columns, simply list the names of the columns in the order in which you want the columns displayed. In the following example, the order of display for the columns of the Employee table is reversed from the order in which they were defined (see Figure 7.6).

```
select badge, department, name
from employee
```

Changing the order of the displayed columns of a database table is consistent with the characteristics of a relational database. You may remember from Chapter 2 that the access of data from a relational database doesn't depend on the manner in which the data is physically stored. You simply specify the names of the columns in the order in which you want them returned in the SELECT clause of the SELECT statement.

 TIP You can display the same column of a table in multiple places if you need to improve the readability of the table, as in a train schedule.

Part
II

Ch
7

FIG. 7.6

The SELECT clause determines the order columns are listed.

Using a Wildcard in the *SELECT* Clause

You can use an asterisk (*) in the SELECT clause to specify all columns for inclusion in the retrieval. The following code shows a query that uses an asterisk to reference all columns of the Employee table with the results shown in Figure 7.7. The name, department, and badge columns are displayed in the query results.

```
Select *
from employee
```

N O T E Although numerous examples throughout this book show SELECT statements with the asterisk (*) in the SELECT clause, you should always use caution in using the asterisk with production databases.

The asterisk is used in the examples because it's convenient to use to reference all of the columns. In many of the sample queries that use the asterisk, it has little effect on the amount of time it takes to perform the query.

You shouldn't use an asterisk with a production database because you probably need to access only some of the table columns in a query instead of all of them. Eliminating some table columns can dramatically reduce the time it takes to retrieve the rows when several rows are retrieved.

You can specify the column names even if all the columns should be retrieved so that the query is more descriptive. If the query is saved and later in need of revision, the columns and rows that the query retrieves will be easy to determine by reviewing the query.

One additional benefit of indicating the column names is that later, if you add columns to the table, the results from the query will remain constant and will not suddenly include new information. ▪

FIG. 7.7

You can use the asterisk wild card character in the SELECT clause of a SELECT statement to return all elements of the table.

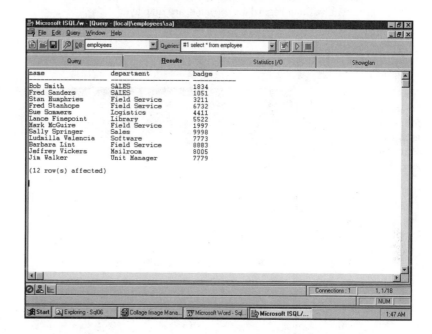

Specifying the Rows of a Table

In the previous examples, all table rows of a database are retrieved. Your goal will often be to retrieve only certain rows. For example, if you have tables that contain millions of rows, you'll probably never execute a query to retrieve all rows from the tables. Every query that you execute specifies a specific results set because it's impractical to retrieve or manipulate all rows in a single query.

The WHERE keyword is used to form a clause that you add to a SELECT statement to specify the rows of a table to be retrieved. A WHERE clause uses the following syntax:

```
SELECT column_name_n,...column_name_n
FROM table_name_1,...table_name_n
WHERE column_name comparison_operator value
```

A WHERE clause forms a row selection expression that specifies, as narrowly as possible, the rows that should be included in the query. A SELECT statement that includes a WHERE clause may return a single row or even no rows if none of the rows matches the criteria specified in the SELECT statement.

Part

II

Ch

7

In the example from the following code, results shown in Figure 7.8, a WHERE clause specifies that only the rows with the sales department are retrieved. All rows that contain the sales department, without regard for the case, are displayed.

```
select *
from employee
where department = "sales"
```

FIG. 7.8

The sort order that you defined during the installation of SQL Server determines case-sensitivity.

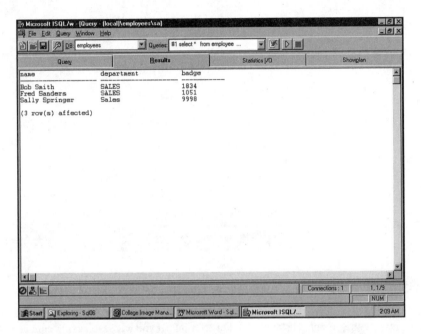

N O T E The default sort order is defined as case-insensitive during installation. If you change this after installation, you'll need to reinstall SQL Server. ■

The following code results, as seen in Figure 7.9, show that the SELECT statement returns a single row because only one row contains the mailroom department:

```
select *
from employee
where department = "mailroom"
```

The query result for a row that contains the personnel department retrieves no rows, as shown in the following code and in Figure 7.10. The count line, which displays the number of rows retrieved, is at the bottom of the output window.

A retrieval in which no rows match the criteria of the SELECT statement doesn't return an error message. Instead, the message (0 row(s) affected) is displayed.

FIG. 7.9

The count message shows "row(s)" but only a single row is included in the results set.

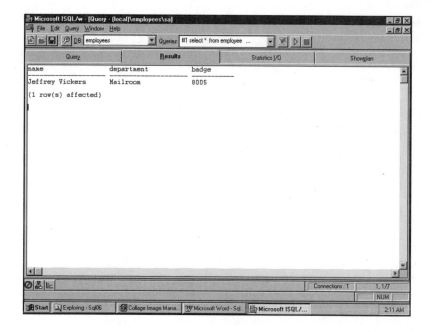

N O T E If you work with query products other than Transact-SQL, you may receive an error message when no rows are retrieved. A query that returns no rows is considered valid by Transact-SQL, SQL 92, as well as other SQL dialects. ▪

```
select *
from employee
where department = "personnel"
```

 You can refer to the @@ERROR system symbol, which is called a global variable, to learn whether the previous operation was successful. SQL Server returns a zero (0) to @@ERROR if the previous operation was successful. After you execute a SELECT query that retrieves zero rows, @@ERROR contains a zero (0), indicating that no error occurred.

```
select @@error
```

A SELECT statement can be used to display the contents of @@ERROR, so the results are returned as rows retrieved from a table. The dashes (–) are displayed underneath the location of where a column header would appear if a column, rather than @@ERROR, was specified. A count message is also displayed for the one value (0) retrieved from the global variable.

Part
II

Ch
7

FIG. 7.10

You can enclose the value in the WHERE clause in single or double quotation marks.

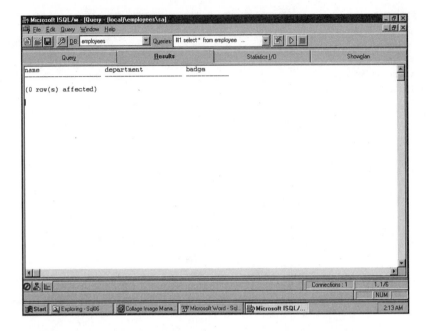

▶ For more information on working with @@ERROR, **see** Chapter 14, "Managing Stored Procedures and Using Flow-Control Statements." **p. 403**.

Using Comparison Operators in a *WHERE* Clause   The syntax for the WHERE clause allows the use of a comparison operator following the name of a table column and before a column value.

In the earlier examples, only the comparison operator = (equal) was used. Additional comparison operators can be used to retrieve different rows. Table 7.2 lists the comparison operators that you can use in the WHERE clause.

Table 7.2   Comparison Operators

Symbol	Meaning
=	Equal
!=	Not equal
<>	Not equal
<	Less than
>	Greater than
<=	Less than or equal to
>=	Greater than or equal to
LIKE	Equal to value fragment

N O T E Table 7.2 lists the LIKE keyword as one of the comparison operators. Although LIKE isn't listed as one of the comparison operator symbols in the Microsoft documentation, LIKE is used exactly as a comparison operator. For more information on this operator, see the later section "Using the Comparison Operator *LIKE*." ■

The syntax for a WHERE clause that uses a comparison operator is as follows:

```
SELECT column_name_1,...column_name_n
FROM table_name_1,...table_name_n
WHERE column_name comparison_operator value
```

N O T E You can optionally use spaces around the comparison operations. Your query will execute correctly with or without spaces around the comparison operators. ■

In addition to the = (equal) comparison operator that was used in the preceding section, you can use the <> (not equal) operator.

You can use the not-equal operator to retrieve all rows except those that contain the value to the right of the <> operator. The following code (see results in Figure 7.11), shows a SELECT statement that contains a WHERE clause for all rows from the Employee table except those that contain the sales department.

```
select *
from employee
where department <> "sales"
```

FIG. 7.11

You can use the comparison operators <> or ! = for "not equal."

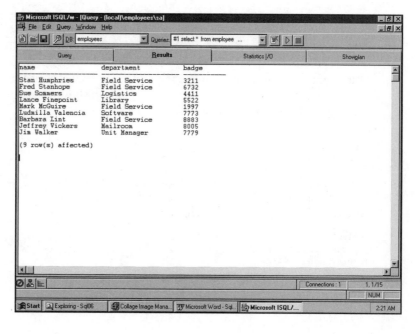

Part
II

Ch
7

The < (less than) comparison operator can be used to retrieve rows that are less than the value specified for the column in the WHERE clause. In the following code, (see results in Figure 7.12), the rows that contain a badge number less than 5000 are retrieved from the employee table.

```
select *
from employee
where badge < 5000
```

FIG. 7.12

The results include rows with badge numbers less than 5000.

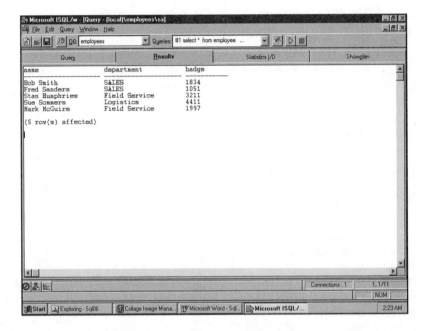

The > (greater than) comparison operator retrieves rows that contain a value greater than the value used in the WHERE clause. In the following code, rows with badge numbers greater than 8000 are retrieved from the employee table (see Figure 7.13).

```
select *
from employee
where badge > 8000
```

The <= (less than or equal to) comparison operator returns rows that have a value equal to or greater than the value in the WHERE statement. The following code returns rows that contain the value less than or equal to badge number 3211 (see Figure 7.14).

```
select *
from employee
where badge <= 3211
```

FIG. 7.13
The results include rows with badge numbers greater than 8000.

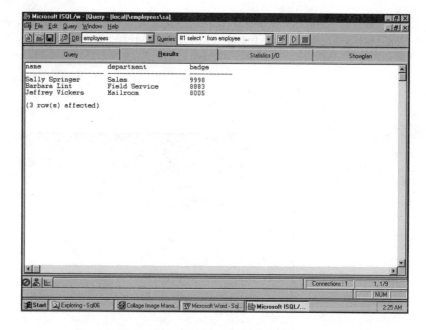

FIG. 7.14
The results include rows with badge numbers less than or equal to 3211.

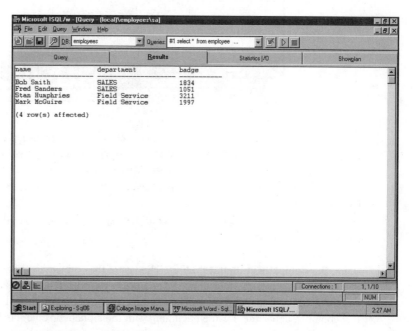

Part
II

Ch

7

The >= (greater than or equal to) comparison operator returns rows that are greater than or equal to the value in the WHERE clause. Comparison operators can be used with columns that contain alphabetic values, as well as numeric values. The following code uses >= in the WHERE clause to retrieve rows that are alphabetically greater than or equal to software for the department column (see Figure 7.15).

```
select *
from employee
where department >= "software"
```

FIG. 7.15

The results include
rows that contain the
software department.

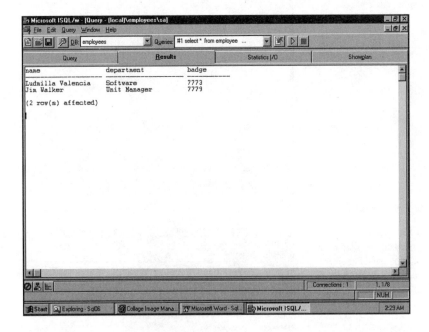

N O T E When you use comparison operations with columns that are defined as datatypes, such as CHAR or VARCHAR, SQL Server uses the binary representation of all characters including alphabetic characters. For example, an uppercase letter A is stored with a lower binary value than an uppercase B. A character value of B is considered greater than the value of an uppercase A using its binary representation.

For values that are more than a single character, each character is successively compared using the binary representation. ■

Using the Comparison Operator _LIKE_ The last of the comparison operators is a keyword, instead of one or two special symbols. The LIKE keyword is followed by a value fragment instead of a complete column value. The example query in the following code retrieves all rows that contain a department name beginning with the alphabetic character S (see Figure 7.16). A wildcard character, such as the percent sign (%), can follow the letter S. This wildcard character is used to match any number of characters up to the size of the column, minus the number of characters that precede the percent sign.

TIP You can also use the % before a value fragment in the WHERE clause of a SELECT statement, such as "%s." You can also use wildcards multiple times. The percentage option tells SQL Server to match anything in these positions.

You can use it to find a word within a complete phrase if needed. For example, "%find this%" could be found within the string "The cow asked where he could find this type of fork on the farm" and would be returned.

CAUTION

Use of the LIKE operator typically results in SQL Server not using the indexes associated with a given table. It tells SQL Server to compare the string you indicate and find any occurrence that matches the wildcard string you provide.

For this reason, it's not recommended that you use this type of search or comparison on large tables. At the very least, be sure to warn users that the wait time may be substantial as the system locates the rows that fit their search criteria.

```
select *
from employee
where department like "s%"
```

FIG. 7.16

The query retrieves only the rows that contain a department starting with the letter s.

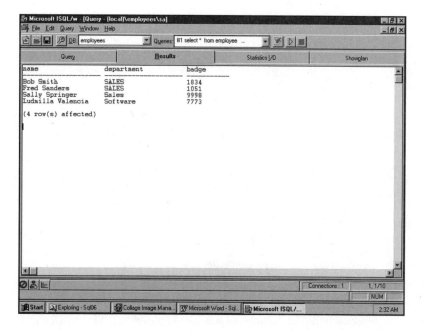

Part II

Ch

7

An underscore (_) is another wildcard that you can use to specify a value fragment. Each underscore used in the specification of a value fragment can match any one character. The example shown in the following code uses four underscores following the S to match any rows containing a column value that begins with an s followed by any four characters (see Figure 7.17). Unlike the example shown in Figure 7.16, the query retrieves only the rows that contain Sales or SALES. It doesn't retrieve the rows that include Software.

```
select *
from employee
where department like "s____"
```

FIG. 7.17

You can use the underscore (_) wildcard along with the percent sign (%) in a WHERE clause.

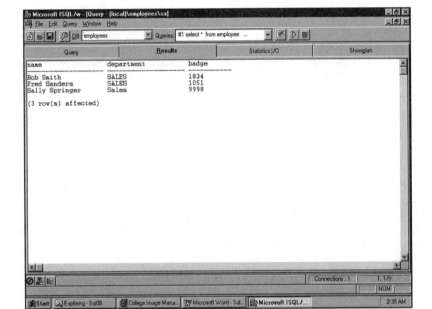

You can use square brackets ([ ]) as wildcards in a WHERE clause that uses the LIKE comparison operator. The square brackets specify a range of values. In the following code, the brackets are used to specify a range of any upper- or lowercase characters as the first character of the department column (see Figure 7.18).

```
select *
from employee
where department like "[a-zA-Z]%"
```

In Figure 7.19, % and [ ] are combined to specify that the rows for retrieval have any upper- or lowercase letter as their first character, as well as any additional characters up to the width of the column. The department column is wide enough to store 20 characters. Figure 7.20 shows that you can combine wildcards to specify a value fragment.

FIG. 7.18

You can use any wildcard combination in the value fragment.

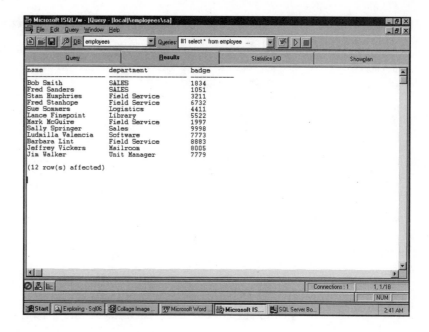

You can also use a caret (^) after the left bracket to specify a range of values to be excluded from the rows retrieved in a SELECT statement. For example, the SELECT statement, shown in the following code, retrieves all rows from the Employee table except those with first characters that fall within the range F through M (see Figure 7.19).

```
select *
from employee
where department like "[^F-M]%"
```

You can use wildcards only in a WHERE clause that uses the LIKE keyword. If you use the asterisk (*), underscore (_), brackets ([ ]), or caret (^) with any of the other comparison-operator symbols, they're treated as literal column values. For example, the following code contains the same query issued in Figure 7.20, but an equal sign (=) has been substituted for the LIKE query (see Figure 7.20). The identical query with an equal comparison operator instead of LIKE doesn't retrieve any rows.

```
select *
from employee
where department = "[^F-M]%"
```

Part
II

Ch
7

FIG. 7.19
A SELECT statement that excludes a range of values from F through M.

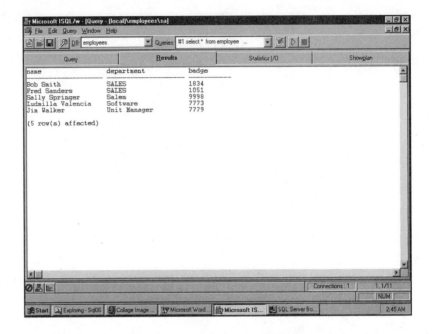

FIG. 7.20
When you use wild cards with comparison operators other than LIKE, they're treated as literal column values.

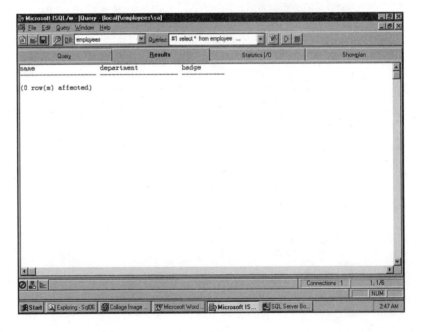

Selecting Columns and Rows with the *WHERE* Clause   You can retrieve a subset of a table's columns and rows in a SELECT statement by combining the use of specific, called-out columns and the use of a restricting WHERE clause. In the following code, only two columns, name and department, are selected, and only for the rows that contain the "Field Service" value in the department column (see Figure 7.21).

```
select name, department
from employee
where department = "Field Service"
```

FIG. 7.21
A SELECT statement
can limit both the rows
and columns retrieved.

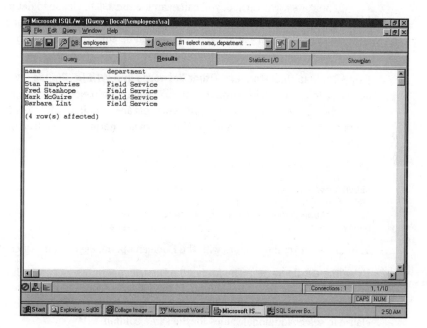

You may remember from Chapter 1 that you can create more than 250 columns in a table and an unlimited number of rows. It's almost always impractical, except for small, simple tables, to retrieve all columns and rows of a table. If you correctly construct your query, you can also reference columns from multiple tables in a single query.

The SELECT clause is descriptive because it invokes a selection operation on a table's rows and columns. Keep in mind the analogy of the data-retrieval triangle introduced earlier in this chapter. The SELECT statement effectively superimposes a triangle over a table to retrieve some, but not all, columns and some, but not all, rows.

Part
II

Ch
7

Keep in mind the following tips:

- SQL Server doesn't return an error for a query that results in no returned rows. Although this is not true of other software products, for example, some programming languages expect an error when no records are retrieved from a file, SQL Server and Transact-SQL consider a query that returns no rows a valid query.

- If you're certain rows exist in the database that match your criteria, try modifying your WHERE clause so only one condition is applied. Run the query with only the first condition. If no rows are returned, you can examine the WHERE clause to determine the problem. If information is returned, add the next portion or portions of the original WHERE clause, running the query after each. You should be able to quickly narrow down which portion of the constricting clause is going awry.

Using Boolean Operators and Other Keywords in a *WHERE* Clause   You can use Boolean operators to retrieve table rows that are based on multiple conditions specified in the WHERE clause. Booleans are used the way conjunctions are used in the English language. Boolean operators are used to form multiple row-retrieval criteria. Use Boolean operators to closely control the rows that are retrieved.

The syntax for the use of a Boolean is as follows:

```
SELECT column_name_1,...column_name_n
FROM table_name_1,...table_name_n
WHERE column_name comparison_operator value
Boolean_operator column_name comparison operator
```

You can use several operators with the Boolean option, each is described in the next sections.

Using the OR _Operator_   The first of the Boolean operators is OR, which you can use to select multiple values for the same column. In the following code, OR is used to form a WHERE clause to retrieve rows containing two column values (see Figure 7.22). Continue to add ORs to the WHERE clause to select additional values for the same column.

```
select *
from employee
where department = "field service"
or department = "logistics"
```

The following query retrieves the rows of the employee table that contain three column values (see Figure 7.23).

```
select *
from employee
where department = "field service"
or department = "logistics"
or department = "software"
```

FIG. 7.22
You can use any number of ORs with different comparison operators in each statement.

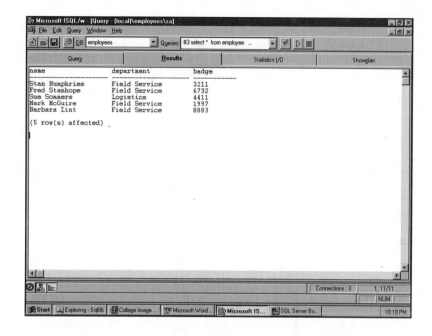

FIG. 7.23
You can use additional ORs to select more than two values from the same column.

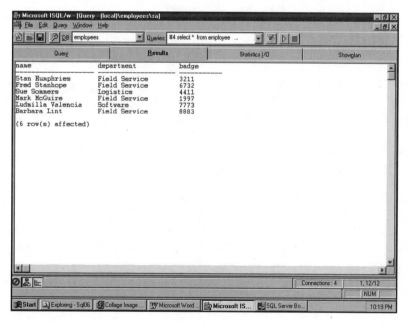

You can specify different columns in the WHERE clause of a SELECT statement that uses an OR. The query in the following code retrieves rows that are either members of the Field Service department with any badge number, or have a badge number that's less than 6000 but are members of any department (see Figure 7.24).

```
select *
from employee
where department = "field service"
or badge < 6000
```

FIG. 7.24

You can use multiple Boolean operators to specify criteria for the rows to be returned by a SELECT statement.

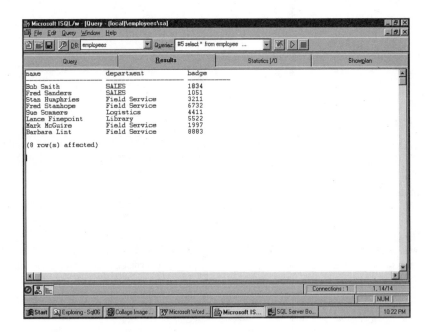

Using the AND Operator   Use the AND Boolean operator if you want the rows returned by the query to meet both comparisons specified in the WHERE clause.

In the following code, a query is used to retrieve a row that contains a specific Name and badge combination (see Figure 7.25). If two rows in the table contained Bob Smith, the Boolean AND is used to specify a criterion that requires the row to also contain the badge value 1834. Multiple rows would be returned only if more than one row contained the values Bob Smith and 1834.

```
select *
from employee
where name = "bob smith"
and badge = 1834
```

FIG. 7.25

You can also use AND and OR together in a WHERE clause.

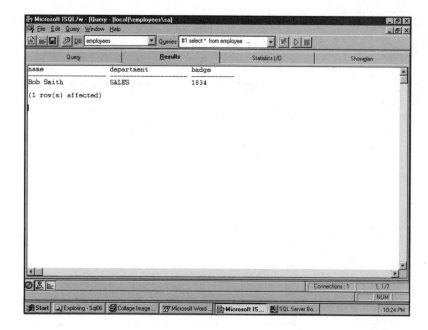

Populating one column of the table with unique values allows individual rows to be retrieved. A unique row is returned if one of the specified columns is the column that contains unique values.

N O T E Defining a column with a unique row or a combination of rows allows individual rows to be retrieved or manipulated. You may remember that SQL Server enables you to store rows that have duplicate values across all table columns. If you allow rows to be individually selected, you establish the capability to reference one table row at a time, if necessary. ▓

▶ **See** the section in Chapter 6 titled "User-Defined Datatypes," **p. 164**.

Using the NOT Operator NOT is an additional Boolean operator that you can use as part of a WHERE clause. Use NOT to specify negation. You use NOT before the columns that will be used in the comparison. For example, if you wanted to select based on a value not equaling another value, you'd use the following statement:

```
select *
from employee
where not department = "field service"
```

This query retrieves all rows of the Employee table that contain any department except Field Service (see Figure 7.26).

Part

II

Ch

7

TIP You can use NOT instead of the not-equal comparison operators != and <>. A WHERE clause that uses NOT for negation is visually easier to understand than one that uses != (not equal).

FIG. 7.26
You can use NOT for negation the same way the not-equal comparison operators (!= and <>) are used.

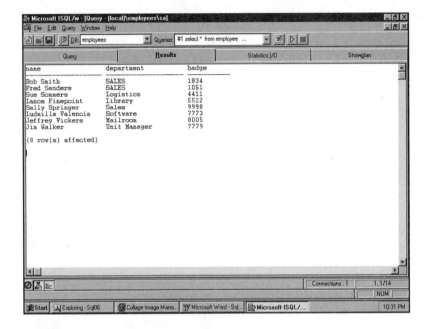

You can also use NOT in a WHERE clause in combination with AND and OR. In the following code, NOT is used to retrieve all rows of the employee table that are members of the Field Service department, except for Mark McGuire (see Figure 7.27).

```
select *
from employee
where department = "field service"
and not name = "mark mcguire"
```

Using *BETWEEN* to Select a Range of Values   Although you can use a number of ORs in a WHERE clause to specify the selection of multiple rows, another construction is available in Transact-SQL. You can use the BETWEEN keyword with AND to specify a range of column values to be retrieved.

In the following code, a WHERE clause that includes BETWEEN is used to specify a range of badge values to be retrieved from the Employee table (see Figure 7.28). Use BETWEEN after the name of the column, followed by one end of the range of values, the AND keyword, and the other end of the range of values.

```
select *
from employee
where badge between 2000 and 7000
```

FIG. 7.27
You can use OR, as well as AND with the NOT Boolean operator.

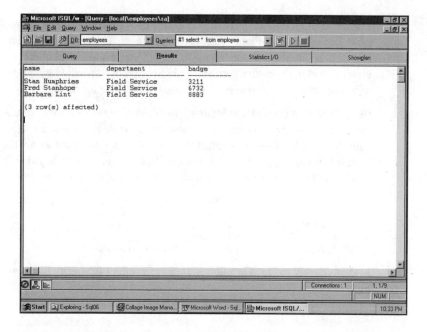

FIG. 7.28
The table doesn't have to contain rows that are identical to the column values used to specify the range of values referenced by BETWEEN.

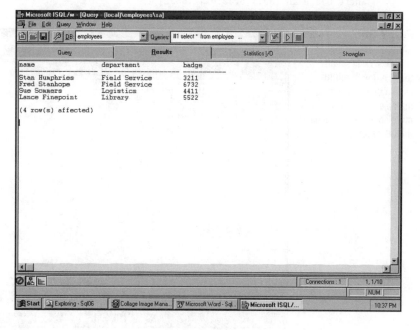

The actual numbers that form the range of values for retrieval don't need to be stored in the table. For example, in Figure 7.28, badge numbers 2000 and 7000 don't have to be stored in the table. Those numbers simply specify a range. Also, a successful query, one that returns an error code of 0, can return zero rows within the range specified by the WHERE clause that contains a BETWEEN. No rows need to be stored in the table for the query to execute correctly.

Using *IN* to Specify a List of Values   You can't always use a WHERE clause with BETWEEN to specify the rows that you want to retrieve from a table in place of a WHERE clause that contains multiple ORs. The rows that contain the column values specified within the range of values will include rows that you don't want. You can, however, use the IN keyword in a WHERE clause to specify multiple rows more easily than if you use multiple ORs with a WHERE clause.

A statement that uses IN uses the following syntax:

```
SELECT column_name_1,...column_name_n
FROM table_name_1,...table_name_n
WHERE column_name IN (value_1, ...value_n)
```

In the following code, IN is followed by a list of values to specify the rows to be retrieved (see Figure 7.29).

```
select *
from employee
where badge in (3211,6732,4411,5522)
```

FIG. 7.29

A WHERE clause that contains IN is simpler to write than a WHERE clause that contains multiple ORs and is more specific than using the BETWEEN operator.

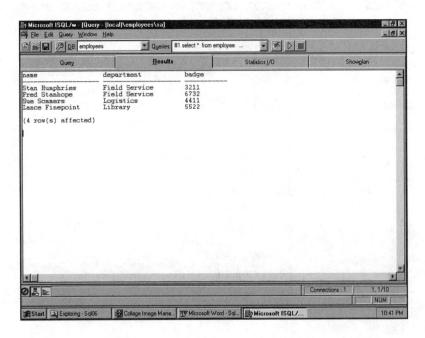

Using an *ORDER BY* Clause

You may remember that the rows of a relational database are unordered. As part of your SELECT statement, you can specify the order in which you want the rows retrieved and displayed. This is done by adding an ORDER BY clause to sort the table rows that are retrieved by a SELECT statement.

> **NOTE** The rows of a SQL Server database are usually retrieved in the order in which you insert the rows into the table. If you create a clustered index for a table, the order of the rows returned by a query is the order of the clustered index. You can't, however, rely on the stored order of rows for two reasons.
>
> - You can create an index for a table that didn't have a clustered index. After the clustered index is created for the table, the rows are retrieved in a different order than before the index is created.
>
> - The clustered index for a table can be deleted at any time, which affects the order in which rows are subsequently retrieved.
>
> If you want to return the table rows in a specific order, you must add an ORDER BY clause to a SELECT statement. ■

The syntax of a SELECT statement that contains an ORDER BY clause is as follows:

```
SELECT column_name_1,...column_name_n
FROM table_name_1,...table_name_n
ORDER BY column_name_1,...column_name_n
```

The following code, shown in Figure 7.30, shows a SELECT statement in which the rows are ordered by department. The rows of the employee table are retrieved in ascending order by default.

```
select *
from employee
order by department
```

If you include the name of a second column after the name of the first column, the second column orders the rows that are duplicates of the first column. In the following code, ORDER BY is used to order the rows of the employee table first by the department and then by the badge column (see Figure 7.31).

```
select *
from employee
order by department, badge desc
```

FIG. 7.30
You can use multiple columns to determine the order of rows retrieved.

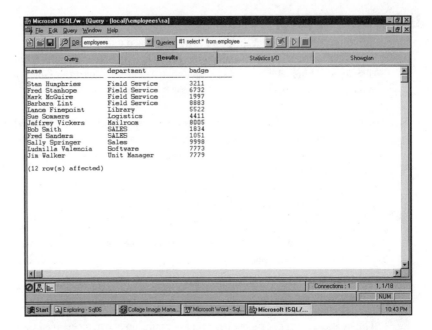

FIG. 7.31
By adding parameters to the ORDER BY, you can increase the fields that are used in the sort.

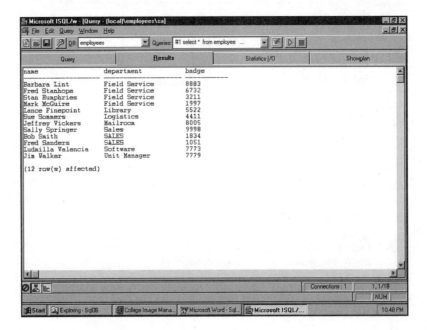

Notice that the DESC keyword is added after the second named column to order the badge numbers in descending badge order. You can also use the keyword ASC to specify explicitly that a column's order in the ORDER BY clause be ascending. It's unnecessary, however, because the order of a column is ascending by default.

When you use ORDER BY in a SELECT statement, you can specify the columns in the ORDER BY clause by their order number in the SELECT clause. In the following code, the department and badge columns from the Employee table are referenced in the ORDER BY clause by their order of occurrence from left to right in the SELECT clause (see Figure 7.32).

```
select department, badge
from employee
order by 1, 2
```

FIG. 7.32

If you use a SELECT statement that references the columns using column numbers instead of names, you'll need to be sure and reference them in the order they are called out in the query.

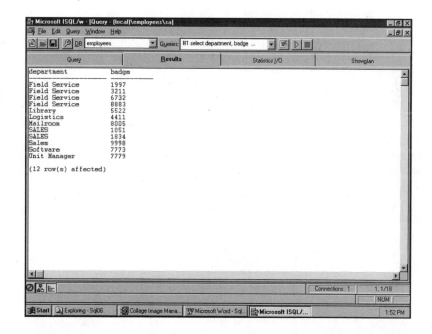

CAUTION

The number of columns referenced by column number in the ORDER BY clause can't be greater than the number of columns in the SELECT clause of a SELECT statement. If you specify a number that's larger than the number of columns in the SELECT clause, you receive an error message saying that you're out of range of the number of items in the select list.

Part

II

Ch

7

SQL Server doesn't use the order of the column defined in a table, such as employee, in the ORDER BY clause. This is because, in a relational database, the syntax of a query language that references database data should be independent of the manner in which the data is stored.

If Transact-SQL used the order of columns as they are defined in the table, the column number would be based as a physical characteristic of the stored data. It's more appropriate to reference the columns using the relative order of the columns in the SELECT clause.

Another problem exists in trying to reference table columns by the order in which the columns are defined in a table. You can specify columns from different tables in the SELECT clause. You can't, for example, reference two columns that are both defined as the third column in two tables, because the column numbers are identical.

You have complete control over specifying columns in the SELECT clause of a SELECT statement. You can reference the same column more than once in a SELECT clause, and the column values will be displayed multiple times. In the following code, the badge column is referenced twice in the SELECT clause (see Figure 7.33).

```
select badge, name, department, badge
from employee
```

FIG. 7.33

Multiple instances of the same column can be used to improve readability.

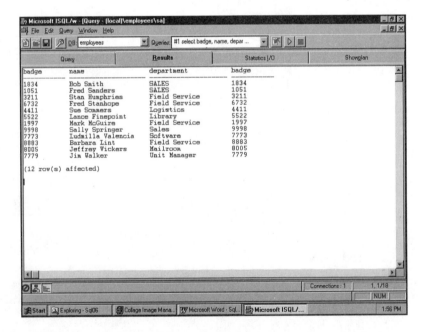

You may not immediately see a reason for displaying the values of a column more than once. If a listing is wide enough, it can be convenient to display a column, often the unique identifier for each row, as the first and last columns of a display, as Figure 7.34 shows. A train schedule is an example of a wide output in which the stations are often displayed in the first, center, and last columns to make the output display easier to read.

Using *DISTINCT* to Retrieve Unique Column Values

You can construct your database table so that you never allow duplicate rows to be stored, or to allow duplicate rows. Unless you define a constraint on your table, such as a unique key, you can store duplicate rows in the table. Although you can disallow duplicate rows in the table, you can allow duplicates for some columns. You may want to find the unique entries that exist in a table column. The DISTINCT keyword is used to return the unique values of a column.

The following code shows the different departments of the employee table (see Figure 7.34).

```
select distinct department
from employee
```

FIG. 7.34

You can use DISTINCT with multiple columns to return the unique values of a column.

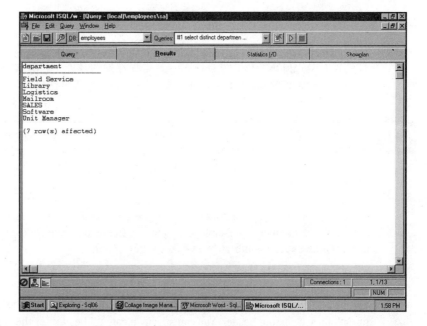

If you use DISTINCT with multiple columns, the rows retrieved are unique by the combination of the columns specified after the DISTINCT keyword. The combination of the values from the Department and badge columns must return all rows. Whenever you combine a column that contains non-duplicate values, such as badge, with a column that contains duplicate values, such as Department, the combination of the two is non-duplicate.

Using Arithmetic Operators

You can use arithmetic operators to form expressions in Transact-SQL. Expressions are evaluated within the statements in which they appear. You need arithmetic operators to manipulate the data retrieved from tables. You can use the arithmetic operators in the SELECT clause to add, subtract, multiply, and divide data from columns that store numeric data.

Part
II

Ch
7

Table 7.3 shows the arithmetic operators you can use in Transact-SQL.

Table 7.3   Transact-SQL Arithmetic Operators

Symbol	Operation
+	Addition
−	Subtraction
*	Multiplication
/	Division
%	Modulo (remainder)

You can form expressions by using arithmetic operators on columns defined with the datatypes TINYINT, SMALLINT, INT, FLOAT, REAL, SMALLMONEY, and MONEY. You can't use the modulo operator (%) on columns defined with the MONEY, SMALLMONEY, FLOAT, or REAL datatypes.

TIP   The modulo operator (%) is used to return an integer remainder that results from the division of two integer values. As a result, it can't be used with datatypes that can contain non-integer values. You receive an error message if you try to use the operator on columns defined as other than integer datatypes, even if the column values are whole numbers.

You can use arithmetic operators to form expressions in the SELECT clause of a SELECT statement with both numeric constants and columns. In the following code, an expression is used to increment the badge numbers by five (see Figure 7.35).

```
select badge, badge + 5
from employee
```

When you use an expression in a SELECT clause, the display for the evaluation of the expression doesn't have a column header. You can specify a column header for the expression by preceding the expression with a text string followed by an equal sign (=). For example, the following code shows the expression preceded by the specified column header in the SELECT clause of the SELECT statement (see Figure 7.36). You can enclose the text string in single or double quotation marks to retain embedded spaces.

N O T E   If you perform an arithmetic operation on a column that contains a NULL, the result is NULL. This means that, if you're developing an application and an operation is returning NULL as a result, you should check to make sure the values you're using in the equation are valid and not-NULL. ■

```
select badge, "badge + 5" = badge + 5
from employee
```

FIG. 7.35
You can use multiple arithmetic operators to operate on column names, constants, or a combination of column names and constants.

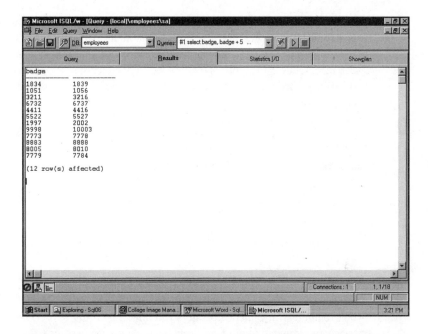

FIG. 7.36
You can also specify an alternate column header for any column without using the column name in an expression.

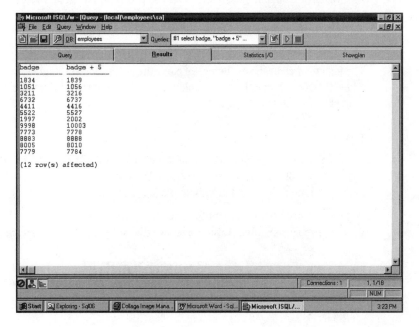

Computed columns are not stored in the database. They may exist in a temporary table that is created during the execution of the SELECT statement. Because the data is not in the database, there is no way to directly verify the results of a computed column. One easy way to compute a value incorrectly is to ignore operator precedence. Arithmetic operators are performed in predetermined order unless parentheses are used. Table 7.4 shows the order in which arithmetic operators are executed.

Table 7.4   Precedence Order of Arithmetic Operators

Operator	Order of Precedence
*	1st
/	1st
%	1st
+	2nd
–	2nd

If you use multiple arithmetic operators with the same order of precedence, the expressions are evaluated from left to right. You can use parentheses to control the order of execution. Expressions in parentheses are evaluated before any other expressions. Use parentheses to evaluate expressions that contain addition and subtraction before the expressions that contain multiplication, division, and modulo operators.

The following code shows the use of parentheses in the SELECT clause. The constant five is added to each value of the badge column. After the constant is added to badge, the sum is multiplied by two (see Figure 7.37).

```
select "badge + 5 * 2" = (badge + 5) * 2
from employee
```

You can perform arithmetic operations on different numeric datatypes in the same expression, a procedure called *mixed mode arithmetic*. The datatype of the result is determined by the rank of the datatype code stored in a column of a system table.

You can use a SELECT statement to retrieve the datatype names and their code numbers from the systypes system table. Table 7.5 shows the codes for the numeric datatypes.

Table 7.5   Type Codes for the Numeric Datatypes

Datatype	Code
TINYINT	48
SMALLINT	52
INT[EGER]	56

Datatype	Code
REAL	59
MONEY	60
FLOAT	62
SMALLMONEY	122

FIG. 7.37
You can use parentheses to make the evaluation order more descriptive, even if the parentheses are unnecessary.

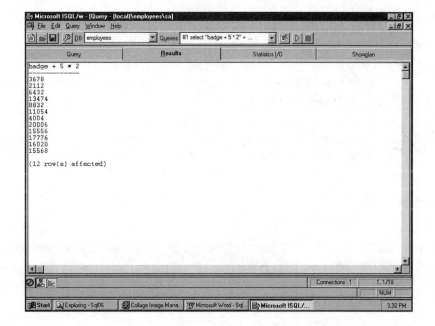

When you write expressions using different datatypes, the results are returned in the datatype of the highest ranked datatype. For example, the values of a column that is defined as either a TINYINT or a SMALLINT datatype is converted to INT if they're evaluated in an expression that contains an INT datatype.

One exception to the datatype code rule applies to expressions that include columns with the FLOAT and MONEY datatypes. The evaluation of an expression that contains FLOAT and Money is returned as the MONEY datatype, even though the code number for MONEY (60) is lower than FLOAT (62). You can retrieve the code numbers for all the Transact-SQL datatypes by using the query in following code.

```
select name, type
from systypes
order by type desc
```

This statement retrieves the names and codes for all Transact-SQL datatypes in order from the highest code numbers.

Part
II

Ch
7

Using a *GROUP BY* Clause

The GROUP BY clause divides a table into groups of rows. The rows in each group have the same value for a specified column. Duplicate values for each different value are placed in the same group. Grouping enables you to perform the same functions on groups of rows.

You can group by any number of columns in a statement. Columns in the select list must be in the GROUP BY clause or have a function used on it. The syntax of a SELECT statement that contains a GROUP BY clause is as follows:

```
SELECT column 1,...column n
FROM tablename
GROUP BY columnname 1, columnname n
```

GROUP BY targets only unique column values after sorting by ascending column value (default). GROUP BY is unlike the ORDER BY clause, which sorts records in ascending order but doesn't remove duplicate column values.

The example query shown in the following code groups the rows by the department column (see Figure 7.38). The departments are first sorted to group them together. The duplicate departments aren't displayed because the purpose of the GROUP BY clause in a SELECT statement is to form groups of rows for subsequent action by other clauses.

```
select department, "headcount" = count(*)
from employee
group by department
```

FIG. 7.38

A SELECT statement containing a GROUP BY clause sorts rows by the columns included.

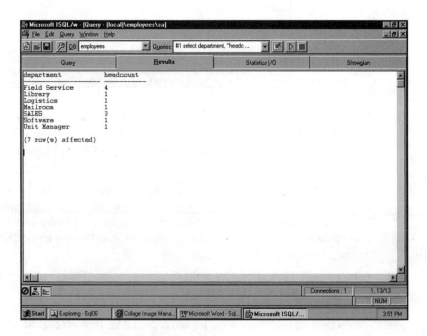

▶ **See** the Chapter 9 section titled "Using COUNT()," **p. 263**, for more information on using the function shown in the previous example.

For example, you can select specific groups with a HAVING clause, which compares some property of the group with a constant value. If a group satisfies the logical expression in the HAVING clause, it's included in the query result. The syntax of a SELECT statement with a HAVING clause is as follows:

```
SELECT column 1,...column n
FROM tablename
GROUP BY columnname
HAVING expression
```

The HAVING clause is used to determine the groups to be displayed in the output of the SELECT statement. The following code shows the use of a HAVING clause (see Figure 7.39).

```
select department, "headcount" = count(*)
from employee
group by department
having count(*) = 1
```

FIG. 7.39

An example SELECT statement containing a HAVING clause that limits the returned rows.

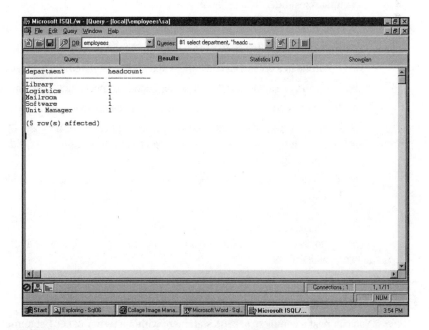

Using a *COMPUTE* Clause in a *SELECT* Statement

You can use a COMPUTE clause in a SELECT statement with functions such as SUM(), AVG(), MIN(), MAX(), and COUNT(). The COMPUTE clause generates summary values that are displayed as additional rows. The COMPUTE clause works like a so-called control break, a mechanism used in applications called *report writers*. You can use the COMPUTE clause to produce summary values for groups, as well as to calculate values using more than one function for the same group.

N O T E   A *report writer* is an application that permits you to retrieve data from a database without using SQL statements. A report writer is designed with a graphical user interface that permits you to point and click buttons and menu commands to retrieve database data. You might find it useful to purchase a report writer to retrieve data from your database as well as using SQL statements.

You can also use report writers that are built in to some applications, like Microsoft Access, and allow these applications to generate the SQL statements and control breaks for you. ■

The general syntax of the COMPUTE clause is as follows:

```
COMPUTE row_aggregate(column name)
[,row_aggregate(column name,...]
[BY column name [,column name...]
```

▶ **See** Chapter 9, "Using Functions," for more information on the aggregate function shown in the previous example. **p. 261**.

Several restrictions apply to the use of a COMPUTE clause in a SELECT statement. The following list summarizes the COMPUTE clause restrictions:

- You can't include text or image datatypes in a COMPUTE or COMPUTE BY clause.
- DISTINCT isn't allowed with row aggregate functions.
- Columns in a COMPUTE clause must appear in the statement's SELECT clause.
- You can't use SELECT INTO in the same statement as a COMPUTE clause.
- If you use COMPUTE BY, you must also use an ORDER BY clause.
- Columns listed after COMPUTE BY must be identical to, or a subset of those in the ORDER BY clause. They must also be in the same order, left to right, start with the same expression, and not skip any expressions.
- You must use a column name or an expression in the ORDER BY clause, not a column heading.

N O T E   You can use a clause that contains the keyword COMPUTE without BY to display grand totals or counts. You can also use both a COMPUTE and a COMPUTE BY clause in a SELECT statement. ■

Using Subqueries

You can nest a complete SELECT statement within another SELECT statement. A SELECT statement that is nested within another SELECT statement is called a *subquery*. The nested or inner SELECT statement is evaluated and the result is available to the outer SELECT statement. To use a subquery, enclose a SELECT statement within parentheses to specify that it should be evaluated before the outer query.

The row, or rows returned by the SELECT statement in parentheses are used by the outer SELECT statement. The rows returned by the inner SELECT statement are used in the position of the value in the WHERE clause of the outer SELECT statement. For example, in the following code, all rows are retrieved for the Employee table, where the department is equal to the same department in which Bob Smith is a member (see Figure 7.40).

```
select *
from employee
where department = (
select department
from employee
where name = "bob smith")
```

FIG. 7.40
You can nest a subquery within the subquery by using an additional set of parentheses around an enclosed SELECT statement.

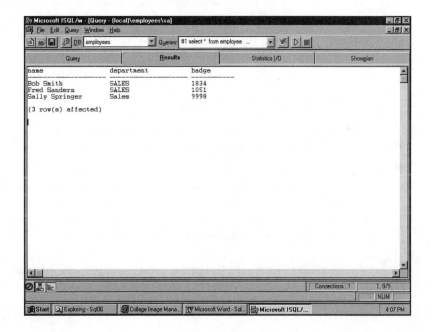

Some restrictions apply to the use of subqueries. The SELECT list of a subquery must return one of two things:

- A single value, as in the last example shown. This example selects a value from the second table and uses that value as a parameter to the outer query.
- A count of rows that satisfy an EXISTS test. EXISTS returns the number of rows in which the test value is found. For example,

  ```
  ...
  if exists select * from mytable where myname="Brennan"
  ...
  ```

  would be valid as a subquery as long as the table contained at least one row with a value of "Brennan."

This would result in the following error if a comparison operator such as = (equal to) were used in the WHERE clause of the outer query:

Part
II

Ch
7

```
Msg 512, Level 16, State 1
Subquery returned more than 1 value. This is illegal when the subquery
follows =, !=, <, <= , >, >=, or when the subquery is used as an expression.
Command has been aborted.
```

N O T E Use a NOT IN to eliminate rows that match the results of a subquery. ■

You're restricted in the choice of datatypes within subqueries. You can't use either the IMAGE or TEXT datatypes in the SELECT clause of the subquery. Also, the datatype of the value(s) returned by the subquery must match the datatype used in the WHERE clause of the outer query.

Here are some key points to keep in mind:

- ■ If you try to use the rows returned by a SELECT statement within another SELECT statement and receive an error, your nested SELECT statement probably returned more than one row value to the WHERE clause of your outer SELECT statement.

- ■ Unless you're sure that the inner SELECT statement will return only a single row value, you should use an IN qualifier in the WHERE clause of the outer SELECT statement.

Using *ANY* and *ALL* You can use ANY and ALL to modify the comparison operators that precede a subquery. In Transact-SQL, ANY and ALL don't have the same meaning that they do in the English language. For example, when > (greater than) is followed by ALL, it's interpreted as greater than all values, including the maximum value returned by a subquery. When > (greater than) is followed by ANY, it's interpreted as greater than at least one, which is the minimum.

 If you have difficulty understanding the results of queries that contain one or more nested queries, you can execute each subquery separately. If you record the result of the execution of an inner query, you can use the values to help you interpret the results of the outer queries.

N O T E The = ANY keyword is evaluated identically to IN. It would be clearer to use an IN instead of = ANY. ■

Specifying Optimizer Hints The optimizer hints clause is somewhat misleading. You use the optimizer clause of the SELECT statement to override the data-retrieval methods that are automatically chosen by the query optimizer. When a query is executed, a portion of SQL Server, called the query optimizer, determines how the retrieval of the data from the database is performed.

For example, although an index may exist on a table that is referenced in a query, the query optimizer may determine that it would be faster to retrieve the rows from the table without using the index. The query optimizer may not use an index because the number of rows requested by the query are few in number, and it would be faster to directly access the data rows instead of both the index rows and then data rows.

If multiple indexes exist on a table, the query optimizer will choose to return the rows of the table using the index that would result in the fastest retrieval of information.

You may, however, want to override the way in which the retrieval of rows will be achieved. For example, if two indexes, one clustered and one non-clustered, exist on a table, the query optimizer may choose to use the non-clustered index for the retrieval of the table rows. You can use the optimizer hints clause in a SELECT statement to force a retrieval using the clustered index. You want the rows to be retrieved by the clustered index because they will automatically be returned in ascending sorted order by the column or columns on which the clustered index was created.

For example, you can use the following optimizer hints clause in a SELECT clause to specify that the rows of a table will be retrieved by the clustered index:

```
select * from employee (index=0)
```

This statement specifies the index name or ID to use for that table. Zero (0) forces the use of a clustered index if one exists. If you use a optimizer hint of one (1), a non-clustered index is used for retrieval of rows targeted in the SELECT statement.

N O T E You can confirm the method that is used to retrieve your rows by using the query option SHOWPLAN. This option returns information about how SQL Server performed your query. For example, if the rows of the query were retrieved without using an index, the method table scan appears in the information returned by SHOWPLAN.

SHOWPLAN also clearly specifies if a clustered or non-clustered index *is used for retrieval in a query*. Click the Query Options button on the toolbar to bring up the Query Options dialog box, then select the Show Query Plan check box to return SHOWPLAN information. ▪

TIP You can also use the syntax *index=index_column_name* as an optimizer hint in a SELECT statement in place of the index number.

You can use a second set of optimizer hints to control the synchronization, or locking of the tables in your SELECT statement. You can use the locking optimizer hints to override the way in which SQL Server normally controls access to data from multiple clients.

Using NOLOCK   You use the NOLOCK optimizer hint to permit you to read rows that SQL Server would normally not permit you to access. For example, if you use NOLOCK in a SELECT statement, you can read uncommitted rows.

Using HOLDLOCK   You use HOLDLOCK to prevent other clients from changing rows that are part of your SELECT clause until your transaction is complete. Normally, other clients can modify the rows when they're displayed. One restriction of HOLDLOCK is that you can't use it in a SELECT clause that also contains a FOR BROWSE clause, discussed later.

Part
II

Ch
7

Using **UPDLOCK** You use an UPDLOCK like HOLDLOCK to prevent other clients from changing rows that are part of your SELECT clause. UPDLOCK releases the rows of your table and the end of the command or next transaction, instead of at the end of the transaction only.

Using **TABLOCK** You use TABLOCK like HOLDLOCK to prevent other clients from changing rows. TABLOCK, unlike HOLDLOCK, acts on the entire table, instead of just on the rows of your table. You can use TABLOCK along with HOLDLOCK to prevent other clients from changing rows of your entire table until your transaction completes.

Using **PAGLOCK** You use PAGLOCK like HOLDLOCK to prevent other clients from changing rows. PAGLOCK prevents other clients from changing rows a table page at a time, instead of the entire table.

Using **TABLOCKx** You use TABLOCKx to prevent other clients from displaying, as well as changing, an entire table referenced in your SELECT clause until your command or transaction is complete.

You might implement this option in cases where you're updating a table and it's imperative that the updated information is always displayed at the client. It's simply a way of locking the information until it's certain that you're able to provide complete, updating information to the client applications that may be accessing it.

Using **FASTFIRSTROW** You use FASTFIRSTROW to retrieve the rows of a table using a non-clustered index. Unlike the index=1 optimizer hint, the first row of the query is returned more quickly through use of optimized read techniques. The total time that it takes to perform the query may be longer than if the non-clustered index were used with the FASTFIRSTROW option. You use FASTFIRSTROW to get better response time by returning the initial results of your query faster.

N O T E The *response time* for a database such as SQL Server is usually defined as time that it takes to display, on a client system monitor, the first row of a query. *Throughput* is the amount of time that it takes to complete an operation, whether or not part of the operation involves the display of information as feedback to a client. ■

Using the *FOR BROWSE* Option

You can use the FOR BROWSE clause in a SELECT statement to read a table within which another client is now adding, deleting, or updating rows. Normally, SQL Server won't permit you to read a table while pending updates, deletes, or inserts are uncommitted. There are restrictions on what other clauses your SELECT statement can contain when you use the FOR BROWSE clause.

To use the FOR BROWSE clause in a SELECT statement, the SELECT statement must contain a table with a timestamp column and a unique index. To use the FOR BROWSE clause in a SELECT statement, the SELECT statement can't contain a UNION clause. FOR BROWSE should be the last clause of a SELECT statement.

Unique indexes and timestamp columns are required attributes of tables to be used with the FOR BROWSE clause. If a table doesn't meet these requirements, a retrieval statement executes as though the FOR BROWSE clause weren't present in the SELECT statement. A SELECT statement that tries to read the rows from a table that's being modified waits for the default query timeout interval of five minutes.

If the modification is completed within that time, the rows are displayed by the waiting query. If the pending modification doesn't complete within the timeout interval, the query fails. The FOR BROWSE clause in a SELECT statement permits you to read rows of a table while they're being changed.

> **CAUTION**
>
> If you use the FOR BROWSE clause in a SELECT statement, remember that you're looking at table rows whose values may not be kept by the user who's modifying the table. You must be willing to take a chance that a change you see in a table using a SELECT statement containing the FOR BROWSE clause may not be kept.

From Here...

In this chapter, you've learned to write queries for the retrieval of data from a database so the results set contains only the required rows or columns. In addition, you've learned to manipulate the returned data, performing arithmetic operations and sorting the rows. Finally, you've learned to use optimization techniques to override the default actions of SQL Server to retrieve data faster or in different ways.

For more information about the topics mentioned in this chapter, see the following chapters:

- Chapter 1, "Introducing Microsoft SQL Server," shows the syntax used for the command-line form of interactive SQL (ISQL).
- Chapter 6, "Creating Database Tables and Using Datatypes," discusses the treatment of NULLs as column values as well as column datatypes.
- Chapter 8, "Adding, Changing, and Deleting Information in Tables," teaches you how to combine rows from multiple tables in the same query.
- Chapter 11, "Managing and Using Indexes and Keys," teaches you how to create and use keys and indexes and how to constrain rows and columns to unique values.
- Chapter 14, "Managing Stored Procedures and Using Flow-Control Statements," teaches you how to use conditional statements and check status in global variables, such as @@ERROR.

Part
II

Ch

7

Adding, Changing, and Deleting Information in Tables

How to change data and characteristics of your database tables

SQL Server permits you to change the column values of tables and add new columns to a table.

Perform typical database operations on your tables

See how to complete standard add, change, and delete operations on your database tables.

Operations made on multiple tables

You'll learn to combine data from multiple tables using relational joins and the UNION statement.

Remove one or more unwanted rows from a table

SQL Server permits you to remove selected rows from a table with the DELETE statement.

Understanding how to retrieve information from your database, as outlined in the last chapter, is only the start of making full use of SQL Server. As you saw in Chapter 4, "Data Modeling, Database Design, and the Client/Server Model," it takes some planning to implement a good database structure. By planning, you introduce some intricacies into how you work with the information in the database. This is because, in many cases, you must work with more than one table to retrieve or update the information for a given transaction.

Information that is stored in multiple tables is often combined in a single query, called a *Join*. A Join lets you combine rows logically across tables, producing a single output table.

The tables must be created with related columns of data, typically by creating a common key between the tables. You must be able to issue queries that not only combine but also eliminate values from multiple tables. This is where the restrictive clauses of the SELECT statement come into play. The goal is always that only the requisite rows appear in the resultant record set.

The typical database operations, add, change, and delete, are accomplished with INSERT, UPDATE and DELETE statements, respectively. These statements can operate on one or more rows in your table and can be directed against a logical view across multiple tables.

In addition to changing the values contained in existing columns within table rows, you'll find that you may need to add additional columns of information to a database table. You use the ALTER TABLE statement to add one or more columns to an already existing table, as well as change other characteristics of the table.

In this chapter, you learn to write queries that retrieve rows of related information from multiple tables. You also learn to update and delete the rows of a database table and to change the characteristics of database tables by adding columns. ■

Adding Rows

Of all the operations you perform on your database tables, the act of adding information to your database is probably the most basic. After all, you have to have the information in the system before you can write a really great client/server application.

To add information to your tables, you use the INSERT statement. The INSERT statement lets you indicate the table and columns you're inserting information into, and the values that are to be inserted. The syntax of the INSERT statement is as follows:

```
INSERT [into] [target] [(columns)] [DEFAULT ¦ values ¦ statement]
```

The into clause is optional, but you might want to consider including it because it makes it a bit easier to read. It's sort of like commenting your code. It doesn't impact performance positively or negatively, so the added clarification on the statement might prove useful at a later time.

The target parameter can refer to one of two things:

> Table—Indicates the name of the table into which you want to insert the values. This can also take the form, as indicated in Chapter 7, "Retrieving Data with Transact-SQL," of specifying the database.owner.tablename you want to insert into. This is probably the option you'll use most often.

> View—You can use views to insert information into the underlying tables. For more information about this technique of updating your tables, see Chapter 10, "Managing and Using Views."

In most cases, you'll be calling out the name of the table you'll be inserting into, but you must indicate one of the two options, or SQL Server won't know where to store the information you're inserting.

Columns tells SQL Server into which columns you'll be inserting. More importantly, however, it specifies two additional items: order of the incoming information, and whether any columns are being excluded from the incoming data.

For example, if you have a table with Name, Address, and Phone as columns, your insert statement might begin as follows:

```
insert into addresses (Name, Phone)...
```

This example would let you insert two values, but would skip the address column.

> **CAUTION**
>
> If you call out the columns in your INSERT statement and do not provide information for a column that does not allow NULLs, the insert fails.
>
> You can work around this by using the DEFAULT option, indicating a value that should be used if a value is not provided in the INSERT statement. The easier approach is to define a Default Constraint on the table. You can find out more about this option in Chapter 6 in the "Default Constraint" section and in Chapter 13, "Managing and Using Rules, Constraints, and Defaults."

The last option gives the values that should be placed in the database to SQL Server. For example, to insert a record with the partial field listing used in the previous code snippet, the statement should look like the following:

```
insert into addresses (Name, Phone) values ("Caitlin Wynkoop", "520-555-1212")
```

This statement results in the single row being inserted with the updated name and phone number . The Address column is null, or populated by the default value assigned to it.

If you want to insert a row that simply contains all of the default values that you've defined as DEFAULT constraints for the table, you can use the DEFAULT VALUES clause on the INSERT statement. When you do, the values for the columns in the table are all set up to contain the defaults or NULL, whichever is defined for the table with which you are working.

The final option for inserting information into your tables is to use a SELECT statement to gather the values to be inserted. This may seem a bit strange at first, but you'll use this often when you consider moving information from one table to another for backup purposes, structure changes, or simply so you can work with the data on a test table, rather than on the production tables.

Here's a simple example of this type of INSERT statement:

```
insert into addresses
    (name, phone, address)
    values (select name, phone, address
    from prod_addresses)
```

In this example, the prod_addresses table contains the source information. Of course, it could also contain other columns, beyond those being pulled as the source for the addresses table, but, in this example, it's only required that you insert the three columns indicated.

What happens is that a single, new row is created in the addresses table for each row in the prod_addresses table. Note that the columns do not need to be specified in the physical order in which they appear on the addresses table.

The same is true of the `prod_addresses` table. The columns are indicated in the order in which they are needed to populate the first table. Keep in mind that the order, although not important in and of itself, *must* match between the tables. If it doesn't, you end up with one of two things happening. First, you have values from the source table showing up in the wrong columns in your target table. This problem can be a difficult one to track down because it generates no error indication from SQL Server.

Second, the insert fails because the data types are not correct from one table to the other. For example, if you try to insert a `CHAR` type from the second table into an `INT` in the target, SQL Server is unable to copy the information into the target.

In the next section, you see how you can use the `UPDATE` statement to make changes to values in your database tables.

Making Changes to Existing Information

An update or change can be performed in SQL Server in two ways. Under certain conditions, changes can be made directly to the rows of database tables. When a direct update of the table row can be made, the operation is done quickly and requires little overhead to perform the operation. An update directly to the rows of a table is referred to as an *update in place*.

A second way that you can change the rows of a table is an *indirect* or *deferred* update. In such an update, the change is made by deleting the row to be modified and then inserting the row as a new row with the new values in place. Although it typically still occurs quickly, a deferred update is slower because two operations are required to make a change in the row of a table: the delete, and the insertion.

The conditions under which a direct update can be performed are primarily determined by restrictions set on the database table. The following conditions must be met for a direct update to be performed on a table:

- The updated column can't be part of a clustered index.
- An update trigger can't be defined on the table.
- The table can't be set up for replication.

Also, a number of conditions must be met for an update in place to be performed on updates that change a single row:

- For a table column, which is defined using a datatype of variable length, such as VARCHAR, the updated row must fit in the same database page. In general, this means that the information you're inserting can't be larger than the information you're replacing.
- If a nonclustered index that allows duplicates is defined for the column, the updated column must be a fixed-size datatype or composed of multiple fixed datatypes.

- If a unique, nonclustered index is defined on the column and the WHERE clause of the UPDATE statement uses an exact match for a unique index, the updated column must be a fixed-size datatype or composed of multiple fixed datatypes. The column in the WHERE clause can be the same column as the updated column.

- The byte size of the updated row value can't be more than 50 percent different from the original row, and the total number of new bytes must be equal to or less than 24.

The following set of conditions must be met for an update in place that changes multiple rows:

- The updated column must be defined as a fixed-length datatype.

- The updated column can't be part of a unique, nonclustered index.

- If a nonunique, nonclustered index is defined on the column and the WHERE clause of the UPDATE statement isn't the same column as the updated column, an updated column must be a fixed-size datatype or composed of multiple fixed datatypes.

- The table can't include a timestamp column.

  ▶ **See** Chapter 12, "Understanding Transactions and Locking," in the section titled "Understanding Locks," **p. 355** for more information.

  ▶ **See** Chapter 11, "Managing and Using Indexes and Keys," in the section "Defining Indexes," **p. 325** for help about creating indexes.

  ▶ **See** Chapter 15, "Creating and Managing Triggers," in the section titled "Using INSERT and UPDATE Triggers," **p. 451** to learn more about other factors that may come into play when you update your tables. For example, triggers can be set up to automatically start a process when you do an update. It is important to understand this functionality as you design your system.

If needed, perhaps because you'll be making many subsequent updates on your database tables, you can plan the table design so that all updates are direct. You can consider all the restrictions for direct updates to ensure that your updates are performed as quickly as possible.

You can use the query option, SHOWPLAN, to determine whether an update was direct or deferred. SHOWPLAN shows you exactly what SQL Server is doing behind the scenes when you execute a query. For example, for a simple query, Listing 8.1 is what SHOWPLAN indicates.

Listing 8.1 Output from *SHOWPLAN* Operation

```
STEP 1
The type of query is SELECT (into a worktable)
GROUP BY
Vector Aggregate
FROM TABLE
wwwlog
Nested iteration
```

continues

Listing 8.1   Continued

```
Table Scan
TO TABLE
Worktable 1
STEP 2
The type of query is SELECT
FROM TABLE
Worktable 1
Nested iteration
```

You turn on SHOWPLAN as a toggle. By issuing a SET SHOWPLAN ON command, all queries for that session with SQL Server will include the information like that shown in the previous listing. Key items of note include Table Scan entries. Table scans are almost never a good thing and can be downright crippling on large tables. What a table scan means is that SQL Server couldn't use any existing index to retrieve the information in the manner you requested. Instead, SQL Server read each and every row in the table to determine how it compared to your criteria. This is a much slower process than that of working an index on a table.

There will be cases where you cannot prevent a table scan, but if you can add an index that makes sense, you should consider doing so. The index will improve your performance, sometimes dramatically and make your users much happier with you.

The Process of Updating Rows

Obviously, it's likely that users will change the information in your database after it's initially entered. You can use an UPDATE statement to modify the existing column values of table rows. The simplified syntax of an UPDATE statement is as follows:

```
UPDATE table_name
SET column_name_1 = value,......column_name_n = value
WHERE column_name comparison operator value
```

The first thing you need to indicate is the table name; this can be specified with the database and owner as prefixes to the table name.

As with the SELECT statement, you use the WHERE clause to identify the rows to be changed. The WHERE clause, used as part of a SELECT statement, narrows the scope of your selection of rows that will be returned or affected by the query. In an UPDATE statement, the WHERE clause is used to identify the rows that are changed, instead of the rows to be displayed.

TIP   You can use the UPDATE statement to change erroneous entries or misspellings for the column values of existing rows of a table.

In the following example, the values for the department and badge columns of the Employees table are changed for the employee Bob Smith. If more than one row has an employee named Bob Smith, the department and badge number of each row is changed.

```
update employees
set department = 'SALES', badge = 1232
where name = 'Bob Smith'
```

N O T E You can also UPDATE views as well as tables with the UPDATE statement. You simply use the name of the View in place of the table name in the UPDATE clause of the UPDATE statement. In many different operations, views are treated the same as tables. For more information on working with Views in this manner, see Chapter 10, "Managing and Using Views." ∎

You can use UPDATE to change multiple rows that match the criteria specified by the WHERE clause. In the following example, all rows that contain the department SALES are changed to MARKETING:

```
update employees
set department = 'MARKETING'
where department = 'SALES'
```

CAUTION

You must be careful to specify only the rows you want changed. If you omit a WHERE clause from an UPDATE statement, the change specified in the SET clause is made to every row of the table. The following example shows a change that is made to all rows of a table:

```
update employees
set wageclass = 'W0'
```

There are usually two reasons why an UPDATE statement doesn't contain a WHERE clause. First, where the WHERE was inadvertently omitted, or, second, because you purposely want to change a column for all rows of a table. For example, when you added a new column to a table with the ALTER TABLE command, you may have assigned a null value for the new column for all existing rows of the table. You can use an UPDATE statement without a WHERE clause to add a non-null value to the new column for all rows.

 T I P You can use a SELECT count(*) statement with the same criteria, specifically, your WHERE clause, that you plan to use in your UPDATE statement to learn the number of rows that will be subsequently changed by your UPDATE statement. By first determining the number of rows that will be affected by your UPDATE, you're more likely to notice any mistakes in your criteria.

▶ **See** the section in Chapter 9 titled "Using COUNT," For more information on using the Count function, **p. 263**

SET Clause Options

You can also use an expression or the keywords DEFAULT and NULL in the SET clause of an UPDATE statement. If you use an expression in a SET clause instead of a constant value, the expression is first evaluated, and its result is assigned to the rows that are specified in the UPDATE statement.

In the following example, a raise in the hourly rate is given to all employees by updating the rate column of the pays table:

```
update pays
set rate=rate+2
```

You can use the keyword, J, to change the column value of the specified rows of a table to nulls. The table column that is to be assigned a null value must have been created with the NULL characteristic originally. In the following example, an employee who has been moved out of his current department, but not yet assigned to another department, has his department changed to a null:

```
update employees
set department=null
where name='Bob Smith'
```

You can also use the UPDATE statement to assign a DEFAULT value if a default value has been associated with the table column. In the following example, the department for an employee is changed to the default value that was previously established and associated with the department column:

```
update employees
set department=default
where name ='Sally Springer'
```

▶ **See** the sections in Chapter 13 titled "Creating Defaults" and "Binding Defaults." For more information on how you can create values that are used as defaults and put into place in your tables automatically by SQL Server **p. 393/394**

N O T E   As indicated in the earlier section on using the Insert statement, if a default doesn't exist for the column and the column permits nulls, the column value is changed to a null. ∎

Deleting Rows

Removing rows from a database table is another operation that you must be able to perform to maintain a database. Use a DELETE FROM statement to remove table rows. The syntax of a DELETE [FROM] statement is as follows:

```
DELETE [FROM] table_name
WHERE column_name = 'value'
```

> **CAUTION**
>
> The DELETE statement is one to be taken seriously and cautiously. It's extremely easy to remove all rows from a table and, before you know it, you'll be looking for your most recent backup to restore your table values. There are few, if any, cases where you'll not want a very explicit WHERE clause with your DELETE statement, and you should always reread your statement prior to pressing the EXECUTE button.

You don't need to use the keyword FROM. It's optional in the DELETE statement. You can delete rows from tables, as well as update tables, through views.

In the following example, the operation of the DELETE statement removes all rows that match the criteria specified in the WHERE clause of the DELETE statement. In this case, we're removing all rows that contain the department "SALES."

```
delete from employees
where department = 'SALES'
```

 TIP You can first use a COUNT function in a SELECT statement that has an identical WHERE clause to your DELETE statement to determine the number of rows that will be subsequently removed.

Keep in mind, when you are using the DELETE statement, that the sort order, which was selected when you installed SQL Server, is very important. If you find that upper- and lower-case specifics as part of the WHERE clause don't seem to have any effect on the criteria, it's likely that the sort order is case-insensitive. If you want all your subsequent DELETE and UPDATE statements to be case-sensitive, you might want to update SQL server. Use SQL setup from the SQL server program group to effectively reinstall SQL Server with a case-sensitive sort order specified.

▶ **See** the section in Chapter 3 titled "Installing Server and Client Software," for more information on setting SQL Server options **p. 59**

You can use a DELETE FROM statement to remove multiple rows and individual rows. However, use the DELETE FROM statement carefully. If you don't use a WHERE clause in a DELETE FROM statement, all table rows are removed, leaving you with an empty table. You'll receive no warning before the DELETE FROM statement is executed. In the following example, all rows of the specified table are deleted:

```
delete from employees
```

N O T E The execution of a DELETE statement without a WHERE clause that removes all rows of a table is most often an accident. If you want to delete all rows of a table, but still keep the table intact, you should use the TRUNCATE statement. The syntax of TRUNCATE table is as follows:

```
Truncate table_name
```

continues

continued

The advantage of using a TRUNCATE TABLE statement is that the removal of rows is faster than with an equivalent DELETE statement. The TRUNCATE statement is faster because it removes pages of information that contain multiple table rows at a time whereas the DELETE statement removes individual rows at a time. However, you can't recover table rows with the TRUNCATE TABLE statement. Unlike the DELETE statement, the TRUNCATE statement does not maintain a copy of the deleted rows even if it's part of a defined transaction.

TRUNCATE TABLE and DELETE TABLE retain the database table. If you want to permanently remove a table, as well as all of the rows that it contains, you can use the DROP TABLE statement, which uses the following syntax:

DROP TABLE *table_name*

After you drop a table, you can't recover the rows that it contained except from a previously made backup copy of the table. ■

TIP Another advantage of the TRUNCATE statement is that it doesn't log the removal of the information in the transaction log. If you have a situation where your transaction log has become full, you can still use the TRUNCATE statement to remove rows and free-up space in the database.

Adding Columns with *ALTER TABLE*

You primarily use the ALTER TABLE command to add more columns to an existing table. You're limited in the operations you can perform on existing columns. For example, you can't delete a column or change the size or datatype of an existing column.

NOTE Using the ALTER TABLE statement you can implement changes to the datatype of existing columns. The ALTER TABLE statement in SQL Server and Transact-SQL, however, doesn't permit datatype changes to existing rows. In Microsoft SQL Server, you must create a new table, and then read the rows out of the old table into the new table to effect such a change. ■

▶ For more information, see the sections titled "Changing the Width of a Table Column" and "Removing a Column from a Table" later in this chapter.

The syntax of the ALTER TABLE statement is as shown in Listing 8.2.

Listing 8.2 *Alter* Table Database Syntax

```
ALTER TABLE [[<database.>]<owner.>]<table_name>
ADD <column_name> <datatype> NULL [constraint],
<column_name> <datatype> NULL...] [constraint]
[WITH NOCHECK]
[DROP [CONSTRAINT]
      constraint_name [..., constraint_name_n]]
```

When ALTER TABLE is executed, it doesn't expand existing rows. It changes only the internal description of the added columns in the system tables. Each time an existing row is read from the disk, SQL Server adds the additional null entry for the new column or columns before it's available to a user.

When a new row is written to the disk, SQL Server creates the new row with the additional column and its value. SQL Server writes the row with the additional column unless no value is specified for the new row and its value remains a null. In Listing 8.3, sp_help is used to display the existing characteristics of a table in which three columns are defined:

Listing 8.3   Database Specifics for the Employees3 Table *sp_help* employees3

Name		Owner		Type
employees3		dbo		user table
Data_located_on_segment		When_created		
default		Jul 5 1994 10:08PM		
Column_name	Type	Length	Nulls	
Default_name	Rule_name			
name	char	30	0	(null)	(null)
department	char	30	0	(null)	(null)
badge	int	4	0	(null)	(null)
Object does not have any indexes.				
No defined keys for this object.				

ALTER TABLE is used to add a new column to the table. You use the sp_help procedure to verify that the new columns have been added to the table. In Listing 8.4, SELECT causes all rows of the new table, including nulls in the new column for all rows, to be displayed:

Listing 8.4   *Alter Table* and *Query Table* Output

```
alter table employees3
add wageclass char(2) null
sp_help employees3
```

Name		Owner		Type
employees3		dbo		user table
Data_located_on_segment		When_created		
default		Jul 5 1994 10:08PM		
Column_name	Type	Length	Nulls	
Default_name	Rule_name			
name	char	30	0	(null)	(null)
department	char	30	0	(null)	(null)
badge	int	4	0	(null)	(null)
wageclass	char	2	1	(null)	(null)

continues

Listing 8.4   Continued

```
Object does not have any indexes.
No defined keys for this object.
select * from employees3
name                          department                       badge  wageclass
----------------------------  -------------------------------  -----  --------
Stan Humphries                Field Service                    3211   (null)
Fred Stanhope                 Field Service                    6732   (null)
Sue Sommers                   Logistics                        4411   (null)
Lance Finepoint               Library                          5522   (null)
Mark McGuire                  Field Service           1997            (null)
Sally Springer                Sales                   9998            (null)
Ludmilla Valencia             Software                7773            (null)
Barbara Lint                  Field Service           8883            (null)
Jeffrey Vickers               Mailroom                8005            (null)
Jim Walker                    Unit Manager            7779            (null)
Bob Smith                     SALES                   1234            (null)
(11 row(s) affected)
```

You can use an UPDATE statement to define values for new columns that are added to a table with ALTER TABLE.

The null values are inserted when a new column is added to the table with the ALTER TABLE statement. In Listing 8.5, all table rows have a new value added to the column that was added with an earlier UPDATE TABLE statement. A subsequent SELECT statement is used to display all rows of the table that include the new column values.

Listing 8.5   Update and Select Output

```
update employees3
set wageclass='w4'
(11 row(s) affected)
select * from employees3
name                    department          badge       wageclass
--------------------    -----------------   ----------  --------
Stan Humphries          Field Service       3211        w4
Fred Stanhope           Field Service       6732        w4
Sue Sommers             Logistics           4411        w4
Lance Finepoint         Library             5522        w4
Mark McGuire            Field Service       1997        w4
Sally Springer          Sales               9998        w4
Ludmilla Valencia       Software            7773        w4
Barbara Lint            Field Service       8883        w4
Jeffrey Vickers         Mailroom            8005        w4
Jim Walker              Unit Manager        7779        w4
Bob Smith               SALES               1234        w4
(11 row(s) affected)
```

You can also define a new column that you've added to a table with the identity characteristic. In Chapter 5 you learned that the identify characteristic permits you to define an initial value for the first row of the table, the seed, and a value that is added to each successive column to automatically generate a new column value, the increment.

N O T E You can't assign the Identity characteristic to an existing column. Only new columns that are added to a table with the ALTER TABLE command can be defined with the identity characteristic. Also, if the value, automatically generated for a new column by the identity mechanism, exceeds the allowable values for the column's datatype, the ALTER TABLE statement fails, and an error is displayed. ■

▶ **See** the section in Chapter 5 titled "identity Property," **p. 91**, for more information on establishing an identity column.

In the following example, an additional column is added to table pays, which is defined with the identity characteristic and can be subsequently used as a row number:

```
Alter table pays
add row_number identity(1,1)
```

You can also add one or more columns to a table using the SQL Enterprise Manager. To add a column to an existing table through the SQL Enterprise Manager, follow these steps:

1. Right-click a selected table to which you want to add a column.
2. Choose Edit from the menu.
3. Enter one or more columns in the Manage Tables dialog box. You enter a column name, choose a datatype and a size for the datatype.
4. Click the Save Table tool on the toolbar to keep the additional columns that you've added to a table. In Figure 8.1, an additional column, wageclass, is added to the employees table.

FIG. 8.1
You can't deselect the null property on a column added to an existing table.

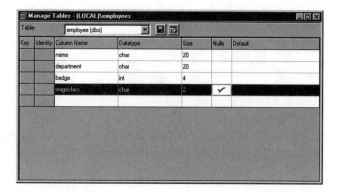

T I P You can also double-click a table to open it and edit its structure.

Changing the Width of a Table Column

Remember, that you can't use ALTER TABLE to change the size of an existing table column or its datatype. You can use ALTER TABLE only to add a new column. You also can't change the size of the column of a table through the SQL Enterprise Manager. You can, however, drop a column or narrow its datatype by creating a new table with smaller, but compatible, datatypes and fewer columns.

In Listing 8.6, a new table is created in which the name and datatype of the first column are identical to the first column in an existing table, but the first column in the new table is smaller in size. In the new table, the second column is defined as VARCHAR instead of CHAR, as it's defined in the second column of the existing table. The new table's third column is defined as SMALLINT instead of INT, as it's defined in the corresponding Badge column in the existing table. The SMALLINT datatype uses half the storage space of INT.

After the new table is created, all rows of the older table are loaded into the new table with an INSERT statement. A SELECT statement is then used to display the rows of the new table.

Listing 8.6   *Create Table* **and** *Select* **Output**

```
create table employees4
(name char(15), department varchar(20),badge smallint)
insert into employees4
select name,department,badge from employees
(11 row(s) affected)
select * from employees4
name             department            badge
-------------- -------------------- ------
Stan Humphries  Field Service        3211
Fred Stanhope   Field Service        6732
Sue Sommers     Logistics            4411
Lance Finepoint Library              5522
Mark McGuire    Field Service        1997
Sally Springer  Sales                9998
L. Valencia     Software             7773
Barbara Lint    Field Service        8883
Jeffrey Vickers Mailroom             8005
Jim Walker      Unit Manager         7779
Bob Smith       SALES                1234
(11 row(s) affected)
```

The sp_help procedure in Listing 8.7 shows the difference between datatypes in the corresponding columns of the two tables used in the example. The example shows only the relevant parts of the display returned by sp_help.

Listing 8.7 Table Details for the Employees Table

```
sp_help employees
Name                                        Owner                              Type
------------------------------   ------------------------------   -------
employees                        dbo                                user table
...
name              char             20      0    (null)            (null)
department        char             20      0    deptdefault       (null)
badge             int              4       0    (null)            (null)
...
sp_help employees4
Name                                        Owner                              Type
------------------------------   ------------------------------   -------
employees4                       dbo                                user table
...
name              char             15      0    (null)            (null)
department        varchar          20      0    (null)            (null)
badge             smallint         2       0    (null)            (null)
...
```

The INSERT table statement successfully completes because the data from the earlier table is compatible with the columns defined for the new table. If the data isn't compatible between the tables, you receive an error message. In Listing 8.8, a new table that defines a column as a character datatype is created. The attempted insertion of the corresponding column from one table results in an error message because the datatypes can't be implicitly converted.

Listing 8.8 Creating the Table and then Selecting the Results from the INSERT Operation

```
create table onecolumn
(badge char(4))
insert into onecolumn
select badge from employees
Msg 257, Level 16, State 1
Implicit conversion from datatype 'int' to 'char' is not allowed.
Use the CONVERT function to run this query.
```

NOTE If you're transferring a large number of rows between tables, you can first set a database option called select into/bulkcopy. If the select into/bulkcopy option is set, your rows are copied into a new table faster because SQL Server keeps less information in its transaction logs about your operation. The lack of complete log information about your operation, which prevents an undo or rollback operation to be done later, is probably not important because you still have the rows in the original table intact should the need arise to undo any operations.

continues

continued

From an ISQL/W command line, the `select into/bulk copy` option can be set on or off by issuing the following command:

`sp_dboption database_name, 'select into/bulkcopy', TRUE¦FALSE`

For example, the following command turns on `select into/bulkcopy` for the database employees:

`sp_dboption database_employees, 'select into/bulkcopy', true` ■

 T I P You can also change a database option using the graphical interface of the SQL Enterprise Manager rather than a command line.

Removing a Column from a Table

Although you can't remove a column from a table with the ALTER TABLE command, you can remove a column from a table through a series of operations. You also can't remove a column from a table with the SQL Enterprise Manager. First, create a new table that you define with all but one of the columns in an existing table. Then use an INSERT statement to copy rows from the original table to the new table, minus the column that you didn't define in the new table.

In the following example, a new table, which contains only two of the three columns defined in an existing table is defined; INSERT is used with a SELECT statement that references only two of the three columns of the original table in the SELECT clause:

```
create table employees5
(name char(20), badge int))
insert into employees5
select name,badge from employees
```

Adding Constraints with *ALTER TABLE*

You can also use the ALTER TABLE command to add, drop, apply, or bypass constraints or checks on existing tables. Constraints are defined to provide data integrity on added columns. The ALTER TABLE statement, like the CREATE TABLE statement, enables you to add a column to a table with primary and foreign key, unique, and check and default constraints. You can add or drop constraints to or from a table without adding a new column. The syntax for constraints is identical to the syntax used for defining constraints in the CREATE TABLE statement.

▶ **See** the section in Chapter 13 titled "Creating and Using Constraints," for more information about defining constraints, **p. 379**

In the following example, a unique CONSTRAINT is added to the badge column for the table employees2:

```
ALTER TABLE employees2
ADD
CONSTRAINT badgeunc UNIQUE NONCLUSTERED (badge)
```

> **N O T E** Microsoft added a number of additional options to the ALTER TABLE statement in version
> 6 of SQL Server. All the additions were characteristics that were made to a table in other
> ways before version 6. You can continue to use the older and more direct ways of changing table
> characteristics. For example, an index, default, or rule can be defined and subsequently associated
> with a table using CREATE INDEX, CREATE RULE, or CREATE DEFAULT commands.
>
> The changes that were made to the ALTER TABLE statement, as well as many other statements, allow
> Transact-SQL to meet the specifications of a standardized specification of SQL, ANSI SQL. The addi-
> tions for ANSI compatibility result in multiple ways of performing the same operations, sometimes
> using different keywords or syntax. ■

You can easily drop a constraint from a table using the DROP CONSTRAINT clause of the ALTER
TABLE statement. You simply specify the name of the constraint to be removed from a table
after the keywords DROP CONSTRAINT. For example, to remove a DEFAULT constraint on the department column for the employees table, enter the following statement:

```
alter table employees
drop constraint department_default
```

Using the *WITH NOCHECK* Clause

You can add a NOCHECK clause to an ALTER TABLE statement to specify that a CHECK or FOREIGN
KEY constraint shouldn't be applied on the existing rows of a table. The constraints added with
the ALTER TABLE statement that contain the WITH NOCHECK clause are in effect only for rows that
are subsequently changed or inserted. You can use a NOCHECK clause in an ALTER TABLE statement when you're certain that the existing data doesn't violate the constraints to speed up the
execution of the ALTER TABLE statement.

You can't use WITH NOCHECK to override the initial checking of PRIMARY KEY and UNIQUE constraints. By default, SQL Server applies the constraints to existing rows in the table, as well as
new rows that are added or changed later. You'll receive an error message and the ALTER TABLE
statement will fail if existing data violates your constraint.

You can also specify that a CHECK constraint, which is added to a table through the ALTER TABLE
statement, isn't applied to the existing rows of a table through the NOT FOR REPLICATION clause.
NOT FOR REPLICATION operates as though the WITH NOCHECK clause were added to the ALTER
TABLE statement. The NOT FOR REPLICATION clause is added to an ALTER TABLE statement for a
different purpose than the WITH NOCHECK clause.

If you set up the automatic copying of a table and table rows from one server system to another, the actual work of ensuring the server system that receives a copy of the data is done by
an intermediate server. The NOT FOR REPLICATION clause is added to an ALTER TABLE statement
to prevent the table copy on the intermediate server from being checked—an unnecessary
operation.

▶ **See** the section in Chapter 17 titled "Setting Up and Managing Replication," for more
information, **p. 501**

Adding Constraints Through the SQL Enterprise Manager

You can add table and column constraints through the SQL Enterprise Manager. To add a constraint to a table or column through the Enterprise Manager, follow these steps:

1. Right-click a selected table to which you want to add a constraint in the main window of the Server Manager.

2. Choose Edit from the menu. You can also double-click the table.

   Click the Advanced Features tool on the toolbar. You can click the Primary Key/Identity, Foreign Keys, Unique Constraints, or Check Constraints tabs to create each type of constraint.

3. Enter the requisite information in the Constraint box that is displayed after you click a tab. For example, in Figure 8.2, a Check Constraint is entered on the department's column for the employees table to prevent any department that isn't one of three department values from being entered and stored.

4. Click the Save Table toolbar button to apply the constraint to the table.

FIG. 8.2

The Not for Replication check box can also be checked when the Check Constraint option is defined.

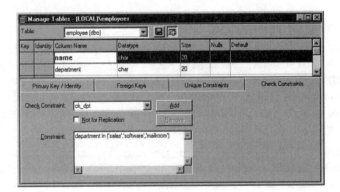

Performing Relational Joins

You can combine and display the rows of different tables and operate on the data by using the same statements used in single tables. The rows of multiple tables can be combined in various ways. The first way is called an *equi-join or natural join.*

You perform a natural join or equi-join by matching equal values for rows in shared columns between multiple tables. You must define one of the two tables so that a column from one of the tables is duplicated in the second table. The column from the original table can be its primary key if it also is a column with values that make the rows of the table unique. The duplicate column that is added to a second table is referred to as a *foreign key.*

You define a foreign key to permit rows from different tables to be related. In a sense, the matching columns are used to form virtual rows that span a database table. Although each table is limited to 250 columns, matching columns to combine rows from multiple tables can result in an almost unlimited number of columns that can be combined across tables.

You use a standard SELECT statement with a WHERE clause to retrieve data from two or more tables. The syntax of a SELECT statement used to join two tables is as follows:

```
SELECT column_name_1,...column_name_n
FROM table_name_1, table_name_2
WHERE primary_key_column=
foreign_key_column
```

The CREATE TABLE and INSERT statements in Listing 8.9 are used to create a new table, to be used for subsequent relational join examples, in the same database. Each row that is added to the pays table matches one row of the employees table.

Listing 8.9 Populating the *pays table*

```
create table pays
(hours_worked int, rate int,badge int)
go
insert into pays
values (40,10,3211);
go
insert into pays
values (40,9,6732);
go
insert into pays
values (52,10,4411);
go
insert into pays
values (39,11,5522);
go
insert into pays
values (51,10,1997);
go
insert into pays
values (40,8,9998);
go
insert into pays
values (55,10,7773);
insert into pays
values (40,9,8883);
go
insert into pays
values (60,7,8005);
go
insert into pays
values (37,11,7779);
go
```

In Listing 8.10, three columns from two tables are displayed after the Badge column is used to combine the rows that have matching Badge numbers:

Listing 8.10   Selecting from the Related Tables

```
select name, department,hours_worked
from employees,pays
where employees.badge=pays.badge
name                 department
hours_worked
------------------   ------------------- --
Stan Humphries       Field Service      40
Fred Stanhope        Field Service      40
Sue Sommers          Logistics          52
Lance Finepoint      Library            39
Mark McGuire         Field Service      51
Sally Springer       Sales              40
Ludmilla Valencia    Software           55
Barbara Lint         Field Service      40
Jeffrey Vickers      Mailroom           60
Jim Walker           Unit Manager       37
(10 row(s) affected)
```

An equi-join doesn't eliminate any of the table columns from the temporary tables that are formed by the joining of tables. You must use a WHERE clause to match the corresponding rows of the tables. You also shouldn't use the asterisk wildcard character to reference all columns of the combined tables. If you use an asterisk, the columns with matching values are displayed twice.

In Listing 8.11, the rows of two tables are accessed without using a WHERE clause. SQL Server forms a cross-product of the rows in both tables. If you don't try to combine the rows using matching columns, each row of the second table in the FROM clause is added to every row of the first table. The Badge column is displayed from both tables because the asterisk wildcard is used in the SELECT clause.

Listing 8.11   Selecting from the Related Tables Without the *WHERE* Clause

```
select *
from employees,pays
name                 department       badge   hours_worked rate   badge
------------------   ---------------  ------  ------------ ------  ----
Stan Humphries       Field Service    3211    40           9       6732
Stan Humphries       Field Service    3211    40           10      3211
Stan Humphries       Field Service    3211    52           10      4411
Stan Humphries       Field Service    3211    39           11      5522
Stan Humphries       Field Service    3211    51           10      1997
Stan Humphries       Field Service    3211    40           8       9998
Stan Humphries       Field Service    3211    55           10      7773
Stan Humphries       Field Service    3211    40           9       8883
Stan Humphries       Field Service    3211    60           7       8005
Stan Humphries       Field Service    3211    37           11      7779
```

```
Fred Stanhope      Field Service   6732    40          9   · 6732
...
(100 row(s) affected)
```

The combination of all rows of the second table with the first table results in a *cross-product*, also called a *Cartesian Product*, of the two tables. In the example, the employees table and the pays table each contain 10 rows, so the resultant cross-product creates 100 rows in the temporary table. However, only 10 of the 100 rows belong together. The badge numbers match in one out of every 10 rows between the two tables.

 TIP The SELECT statement operates on multiple tables whether or not they were designed to be combined with a relational join. It's important to always use a WHERE clause, which eliminates rows that don't have matching column values.

If you don't use a WHERE clause, you receive a temporary table that contains the cross-product of the number of rows in the first table multiplied by the number of rows in the second table. For example, two tables that each contains only 100 rows joined without a WHERE clause return 10,000 rows.

If you reference one of the columns used to match the rows across both tables, you must indicate the table in which the column is defined. Any time you reference a column that has the same name in multiple tables, you must somehow specify which column is from which table to prevent ambiguity. The following example displays an error because SQL Server doesn't know from which table to display the Badge column:

```
select badge
from employees,pays
where employees.badge=pays.badge
Msg 209, Level 16, State 1
Ambiguous column name badge
```

To avoid ambiguity, the table columns used for matching rows are preceded by the table in which they're defined and separated by a period (.). In the following example, the Badge column is displayed from the first table by preceding the name of the Badge column with its table name:

```
select employees.badge
from employees,pays
where employees.badge=pays.badge
badge
----------
3211
6732
4411
5522
1997
9998
7773
8883
8005
7779
(10 row(s) affected)
```

Using Range Variables

In the previous example, the name of the table is used to prevent ambiguity when referencing table columns in a SELECT statement when multiple tables are referenced. In fact, what appears in the examples to be the name of the table preceding the column name is actually a *range variable.*

N O T E Other dialects of SQL refer to a range variable as an alias. ■

Range variables are symbolic references for tables that are specified in the FROM clause of a SELECT statement. You can use a range variable in a preceding clause, such as the SELECT clause, or in a clause that comes after the FROM clause, such as a WHERE clause. Define a range variable by specifying a character constant following the name of a table in the From clause of a SELECT statement, as in the following syntax:

```
...
From table_name_1 range_name_1, ...,table_name_n range_name_n
...
```

You can define a range variable for each table that is specified in the FROM clause. You can use as many as 30 characters, the limit for any permanent or temporary object in Transact-SQL, to define the range variable. A range variable can be defined to provide a shorter reference to a table in a SELECT statement. In Listing 8.12, a range variable is defined for each table. The range variables are used in both the SELECT and WHERE clauses:

Listing 8.12 Selecting Specific Rows from the Related Tables

```
select e.badge,p.id
from employees e,pays p
where e.badge=p.id
badge        id
---------- ----
3211         3211
3211         3211
3211         3211
3211         3211
6732         6732
4411         4411
5522         5522
1997         1997
9998         9998
7773         7773
8883         8883
8005         8005
7779         7779
3211         3211
3211         3211
3211         3211
3211         3211
(17 row(s) affected)
```

Range variables are so named because after they're defined, the symbolic reference applies to, or ranges through, the table. As in the previous example, you can define a range variable to be a single character and use it as a short nickname for a table.

Range variables can be quite handy because several tables with long names can be specified in a SELECT statement. You can combine rows from as many as 16 tables in SQL Server using Transact-SQL. If you don't explicitly define range variables in the FROM clause, they're implicitly created using the complete name of each table.

In the following example, the rows from three tables are combined using the Badge columns that are defined in all the tables. The range variables are implicitly defined to the table names and are used in both the SELECT and WHERE clauses. The WHERE clause first combines the first and second tables. The first and third tables use the AND Boolean operator:

```
select pays.badge, name,department, pay rate
from employees,pays, salaries
where employees.badge = pays.badge
and employees.badge=salaries.badge
```

N O T E   Transact-SQL automatically establishes range variables for use in queries. If you don't specify a range variable for the name of a table in the FROM clause, a range variable is created with the same name as the table, as in the following example:

```
select name
from employees
```

This snippet is internally rewritten as

```
select employees.name
from employees employees
```

Although it seems unnecessary to create range variables when only a single table is named in the query, they are mandatory when you reference tables that contain columns with the same names in the same query. ∎

Using Many-to-One and One-to-Many Joins

You may not have tables that have only one corresponding row in each table. In previous examples, only a single row in the employees table matches the value of a single row in the pays table. It's possible that you'll have to create or work with tables in which more than one entry is a match for the entries in another table.

In the ensuing examples, rows have been added with identical badge numbers in the employees table. Three employees have been added, each with a last name of Smith and each with the same badge number. In the tables referenced in the following examples, badge isn't defined as a primary key; so duplicate badge numbers can be present. Three employees with last names of Humphries have also been added, each with the same badge number as the original employee, Stan Humphries. Listing 8.13 shows the rows of the employees table after the additional seven rows are added.

N O T E Although you usually define a primary and foreign key by using the corresponding columns of tables that you subsequently want to combine rows from for display, you aren't required to define the columns as keys. SQL Server permits you to perform joins on tables that don't have primary or foreign key definitions. You should realize that the assignment of primary and foreign keys to a table isn't required, though it's often desirable, if you combine data from different tables. ■

Listing 8.13   Selecting Rows in a Sorted Order

```
select * from employees
order by badge
name                  department              badge
--------------------  ----------------------  ----
Bob Smith             SALES                   1234
Henry Smith           Logistics               1234
Susan Smith           Executive               1234
Mark McGuire          Field Service           1997
Gertie Humphries      Sales                   3211
Stan Humphries        Field Service           3211
Stan Humphries Jr     Sales                   3211
Winkie Humphries      Mailroom                3211
Sue Sommers           Logistics               4411
Lance Finepoint       Library                 5522
Fred Stanhope         Field Service           6732
Ludmilla Valencia     Software                7773
Jim Walker            Unit Manager            7779
Jeffrey Vickers       Mailroom                8005
Barbara Lint          Field Service           8883
Sally Springer        Sales                   9998
(16 row(s) affected)
```

The pays table is unaltered and contains only the original 10 rows, as shown in Listing 8.14.

Listing 8.14   Selecting Rows from the Pays Table in a Sorted Order

```
select * from pays
order by badge
hours_worked rate        badge
------------ ----------  ----
51           10          1997
40           10          3211
52           10          4411
39           11          5522
40            9          6732
55           10          7773
37           11          7779
60            7          8005
40            9          8883
40            8          9998
(10 row(s) affected)
```

You can combine tables that have an unequal number of matching rows. Listing 8.15 joins the employees table, in which two sets of entries match a single entry for the badge column in the pays table. The join of the employees table with the pays table is called *many-to-one*.

Listing 8.15 Creating the Join Across Tables

```
select name,pays.badge,hours_worked,rate
from employees,pays
where employees.badge=pays.badge
name                    badge       hours_worked    rate
----                    ----        ------------    ----
Fred Stanhope           6732        40              9
Stan Humphries          3211        40              10
Gertie Humphries        3211        40              10
Stan Humphries Jr       3211        40              10
Winkie Humphries        3211        40              10
Sue Sommers             4411        52              10
Lance Finepoint         5522        39              11
Mark McGuire            1997        51              10
Sally Springer          9998        40              8
Ludmilla Valencia       7773        55              10
Barbara Lint            8883        40              9
Jeffrey Vickers         8005        60              7
Jim Walker              7779        37              11
(13 row(s) affected)
```

If you switch the order of the joined tables, it becomes a *one-to-many join*. Listing 8.16 returns the same rows that were returned in the previous example:

Listing 8.16 Creating the Join Across Tables by Employee Badge

```
select name,pays.badge,hours_worked,rate
from pays,employees
where pays.badge=employees.badge
name                    badge       hours_worked    rate
----                    ----        ------------    ----
Fred Stanhope           6732        40              9
Stan Humphries          3211        40              10
Gertie Humphries        3211        40              10
Stan Humphries Jr       3211        40              10
Winkie Humphries        3211        40              10
Sue Sommers             4411        52              10
Lance Finepoint         5522        39              11
Mark McGuire            1997        51              10
Sally Springer          9998        40              8
Ludmilla Valencia       7773        55              10
Barbara Lint            8883        40              9
Jeffrey Vickers         8005        60              7
Jim Walker              7779        37              11
(13 row(s) affected)
```

Using Many-to-Many Joins

You may also want to join tables where more than one row matches more than one row in a second table, which is referred to as a *many-to-many join*. In Listing 8.17, two tables are combined after one row is added to pays with a 3211 badge number, 73 hours_worked, and rate of 31.

Listing 8.17   Showing the New Row Added

```
select name,pays.badge,hours_worked,rate
from employees,pays
where employees.badge=pays.badge
name                     badge        hours_worked   rate
----                     ----         ------------   ----
Fred Stanhope            6732         40             9
Stan Humphries           3211         40             10
Gertie Humphries         3211         40             10
Stan Humphries Jr        3211         40             10
Winkie Humphries         3211         40             10
Sue Sommers              4411         52             10
Lance Finepoint          5522         39             11
Mark McGuire             1997         51             10
Sally Springer           9998         40             8
Ludmilla Valencia        7773         55             10
Barbara Lint             8883         40             9
Jeffrey Vickers          8005         60             7
Jim Walker               7779         37             11
Stan Humphries           3211         73             31
Gertie Humphries         3211         73             31
Stan Humphries Jr        3211         73             31
Winkie Humphries         3211         73             31
(17 row(s) affected)
```

The additional row is added to the displayed temporary table . If the row value is restricted to only the badge number 3211, eight rows are returned.

Many-to-many queries are often not desirable and can produce results that are difficult to follow. In most cases, it's best to implement either a one-to-many or a many-to-one relationship, even if it entails adding an intermediary table (see Listing 8.18).

▶ For more information on database design approaches, **see** Chapter 4, "Data Modeling, Database Design, and the Client/Server Model," **p. 73**

Listing 8.18   Showing the Many-to-Many Relationship

```
select name,pays.badge,hours_worked,rate
from employees,pays
where employees.badge=pays.badge
and pays.badge=3211
name                     badge        hours_worked   rate
----                     ----         ------------   ----
Stan Humphries           3211         40             10
```

```
Gertie Humphries       3211      40          10
Stan Humphries Jr      3211      40          10
Winkie Humphries       3211      40          10
Stan Humphries         3211      73          31
Gertie Humphries       3211      73          31
Stan Humphries Jr      3211      73          31
Winkie Humphries       3211      73          31
(8 row(s) affected)
```

Using Outer Joins

In the previous join examples, *we* excluded the rows in either of the two tables that didn't have corresponding or matching rows.

Previous examples, in which the rows of two tables were joined with a WHERE statement, included all rows of both tables. However, a query that includes all rows from both tables is probably never useful, except to understand the way in which SQL Server combines the rows. You can combine any two or more tables with a WHERE clause and receive a set of rows that were never meant to be combined and thus receive a meaningless result.

In practice, you'll combine only the rows from tables that have been created to be matched together. Tables that are designed to be combined have common columns of information so that a WHERE clause can be included in a query to eliminate the rows that don't belong together, such as those that have identical values.

N O T E   You must ensure that the information used to combine tables— the corresponding values in common columns— remains valid. If a one-to-many relationship exists, and the value in one table is changed, the corresponding identical value, or values, must also be updated in other tables.

Referential integrity involves ensuring that you have valid information in common columns across tables used to join tables. You'll read more about referential integrity in subsequent chapters. Chapter 15, "Creating and Managing Triggers," discusses the mechanism for maintaining referential integrity and Chapter 11, "Managing and Using Indexes and Keys," discusses the common table columns on which joins are based. ▪

Use outer joins to return table rows that have both matching and nonmatching values. You may need to return the rows that don't contain matching values in the common table columns for either one table or the other tables specified in the SELECT statement.

If, for example, you join the employees table with the pays table used in the previous examples, you can specify the return of rows with matching values along with rows without matching values. The specification of the outer join is positional, which means that you use a special symbol that precedes or follows the comparison operator in the WHERE clause of a SELECT statement.

An outer join references one of the two tables joined using the table's position in the WHERE clause. A *left-outer join* specifies the table to the left of a comparison operator, and a *right-outer join* specifies the table to the right of a comparison operator. The following table shows the symbol combination used for outer joins.

Symbol Combination	Join
*=	Left-outer join
=*	Right-outer join

A left-outer join (*=) retains non-matching rows for the table on the left of the symbol combination in a WHERE statement. A right-outer join (=*) retains non-matching rows for the table on the right of the symbol combination.

In Listing 8.19, a SELECT statement specifies a join in the WHERE clause to return only rows that contain matching values in a common column for the two tables:

Listing 8.19   Join Limited by a WHERE Clause SELECT *

```
from employees,pays
where employees.badge=pays.badge
name                   department      badge   hours_worked rate     badge
-------------------    --------------  ------  ------------ --------  ------
Stan Humphries         Field Service   3211    40           10        3211
Gertie Humphries       Sales           3211    40           10        3211
Stan Humphries Jr.     Sales           3211    40           10        3211
Winkie Humphries       Mailroom        3211    40           10        3211
Fred Stanhope          Field Service   6732    40           9         6732
Sue Sommers            Logistics       4411    52           10        4411
Lance Finepoint        Library         5522    39           11        5522
Mark McGuire           Field Service   1997    51           10        1997
Sally Springer         Sales           9998    40           8         9998
Ludmilla Valencia      Software        7773    55           10        7773
Barbara Lint           Field Service   8883    40           9         8883
Jeffrey Vickers        Mailroom        8005    60           7         8005
Jim Walker             Unit Manager    7779    37           11        7779
Stan Humphries         Field Service   3211    73           31        3211
Gertie Humphries       Sales           3211    73           31        3211
Stan Humphries Jr.     Sales           3211    73           31        3211
Winkie Humphries       Mailroom        3211    73           31        3211
(17 row(s) affected)
```

In Listing 8.20, a left-outer join is used in the WHERE clause of a SELECT statement to specify that both rows containing matching values for a common column and the rows from the left table, employees, are included in the rows returned. This join might be useful if you needed to find out what employees don't have a pay rate associated with them.

Before the following query was executed, additional rows were added to the employees table that don't have corresponding values in a common column in the pays table:

Listing 8.20 Left-Outer Join Limited by a *WHERE* Clause

```
select *
from employees,pays
where employees.badge*=pays.badge
name                department     badge   hours_worked rate      badge
----------------    -------------  ------- ------------ --------  ----
Stan Humphries      Field Service  3211    40           10        3211
Stan Humphries      Field Servic   3211    73           31        3211
Fred Stanhope       Field Service  6732    40           9         6732
Sue Sommers         Logistics      4411    52           10        4411
Lance Finepoint     Library        5522    39           11        5522
Mark McGuire        Field Service  1997    51           10        1997
Sally Springer      Sales          9998    40           8         9998
Ludmilla Valencia   Software       7773    55           10        7773
Barbara Lint        Field Service  8883    40           9         8883
Jeffrey Vickers     Mailroom       8005    60           7         8005
Jim Walker          Unit Manager   7779    37           11        7779
Bob Smith           SALES          1234    (null)       (null)    (null)
Bob Jones           Sales          2223    (null)       (null)    (null)
Gertie Humphries    Sales          3211    40           10        3211
Gertie Humphries    Sales          3211    73           31        3211
Stan Humphries Jr.  Sales          3211    40           10        3211
Stan Humphries Jr.  Sales          3211    73           31        3211
Winkie Humphries    Mailroom       3211    40           10        3211
Winkie Humphries    Mailroom       3211    73           31        3211
Susan Smith         Executive      1234    (null)       (null)    (null)
Henry Smith         Logistics      1234    (null)       (null)    (null)
(21 row(s) affected)
```

N O T E Recall that null values don't match, so rows that contain nulls in the primary and foreign
key columns display only with outer joins and not with equi-joins. ■

In Listing 8.21, a right-outer join is used in the WHERE clause of a SELECT statement to specify
that both rows that contain matching values for a common column, and the rows from the right
table, pays, are included in the rows returned. Two additional rows, which don't have corresponding values in a common column in the employees table, are first added to the pays table.

Listing 8.21 Right-Outer Join Limited by a WHERE Clause

```
insert into pays
values (40,10,5555)
insert into pays
values (40,10,5555)
select *
from employees,pays
where employees.badge=*pays.id
name                department     badge   hours_worked rate      id
----------------    -------------  ------- ------------ --------  ----
Stan Humphries      Field Service 3211     40           10        3211
```

continues

Listing 8.21   Continued

```
Gertie Humphries      Sales           3211      40          10          3211
Stan Humphries Jr.    Sales           3211      40          10          3211
Winkie Humphries      Mailroom        3211      40          10          3211
Fred Stanhope         Field Service   6732      40           9          6732
Sue Sommers           Logistics       4411      52          10          4411
Lance Finepoint       Library         5522      39          11          5522
Mark McGuire          Field Service   1997      51          10          1997
Sally Springer        Sales           9998      40           8          9998
Ludmilla Valencia     Software        7773      55          10          7773
Barbara Lint          Field Service   8883      40           9          8883
Jeffrey Vickers       Mailroom        8005      60           7          8005
Jim Walker            Unit Manager    7779      37          11          7779
Stan Humphries        Field Service   3211      73          31          3211
Gertie Humphries      Sales           3211      73          31          3211
Stan Humphries Jr.    Sales           3211      73          31          3211
Winkie Humphries      Mailroom        3211      73          31          3211
(null)                (null)          (null)    40          10          5555
(null)                (null)          (null)    40          10          5555
(19 row(s) affected)
```

 TIP Left- and right-outer joins can be used to show rows that contain nulls that wouldn't have corresponding entries across tables, and would *only* be displayed with other non-matching entries.

Combining Query Results with *UNION*

Use a *UNION* to combine the results of two or more queries. A UNION merges the results of the
first query with the results of a second query. UNION implicitly removes duplicate rows between
the queries. A UNION returns a single results set that consists of all the rows that belong to the
first table, the second table, or both tables.

You should define the queries that contain a UNION clause so that they're compatible. The queries should have the same number of columns and a common column defined for each table.
You can't use a UNION within the definition of a view.

The syntax for queries that include a UNION clause is shown in Listing 8.22.

Listing 8.22   Using the *UNION* Clause

```
SELECT column_name_1, ..., column_name_n
FROM table_name_1, ... , table_name_n
WHERE column_name comparison_operator value
[GROUP BY...]
[HAVING ...
UNION
SELECT column_name_1, ..., column_name_n
FROM table_name_1, ... , table_name_n
WHERE column_name comparison_operator value
```

```
[GROUP BY...]
[HAVING...]
[ORDER BY...]
[COMPUTE...
```

In Listing 8.23, the badge numbers that are common to both tables are displayed using two Select statements that are bound with a UNION clause. The ORDER BY clause is used after the last query to order the final results. The ORDER BY clause appears only after the last SELECT statement. Recall that UNION implicitly removes duplicate rows, as defined by the query.

Listing 8.23 Using the *UNION* Clause with an *Order By* Clause

```
select badge from employees
union
select badge from pays
order by badge
badge
----------
1234
1997
3211
4411
5522
6732
7773
7779
8005
8883
9998
(11 row(s) affected)
```

In Listing 8.24, the same set of queries is used except the ALL keyword is added to the UNION clause. This retains query-defined duplicates, only the Badge column, in the resultant rows. The duplicate rows from both tables are retained.

Listing 8.24 Using the *UNION* Clause

```
select badge from employees
union all
select badge from pays
order by badge
badge
------
1234
1234
1234
1997
1997
3211
```

continues

Listing 8.24 Continued

```
3211
3211
3211
3211
3211
4411
4411
5522
5522
6732
6732
7773
7773
7779
7779
8005
8005
8883
8883
9998
9998
(27 row(s) affected)
```

In Listing 8.25, the datatypes referenced in the query for one of the two columns aren't compatible; the execution of the example returns an error because of this:

Listing 8.25 Data Conversions in the Use of *UNION*

```
select name,badge from employees
union
select hours_worked,badge from pay
Msg 257, Level 16, State 1
Implicit conversion from datatype 'char' to 'int' is not allowed.
 Use the CONVERT function to run this query.
```

You can use a UNION clause with queries to combine the rows from two compatible tables and merge the rows into a new third table. To illustrate this merge, in which the results are kept in a permanent table, a new table is created that has the same datatypes as the existing employees table. Several rows are first inserted into the new table (see Listing 8.26).

Listing 8.26 Inserting Rows into the Test Table

```
create table employees2
(name char(20),department char(20),badge int)
go
insert into employees2
values ('Rod Gilbert','Sales',3339)
go
insert into employees2
```

```
values ('Jean Ratele','Sales',5551)
go
insert into employees2
values ('Eddie Giacomin','Sales',8888)
```

Each table now has rows that contain employees records. If you use a UNION clause to combine the SELECT statements along with INSERT INTO, the resultant rows can be retained in a new table.

The SELECT statement that references the employees table uses WHERE to restrict the rows returned to only those with the Sales department. All three rows of the employees2 table are in the Sales department; so no WHERE clause is necessary (see Listing 8.27).

Listing 8.27   Creating the Work Table Employees3

```
create table employees3
(name char(20),department char(20),badge int))
go
insert into employees3
select * from employees
where department='Sales'
union
select * from employees2
(6 row(s) affected)
select * from employees3
name                    department          badge
----                    ----------          ----
Eddie Giacomin          Sales               8888
Gertie Humphries        Sales               3211
Jean Ratele             Sales               5551
Rod Gilbert             Sales               3339
Sally Springer          Sales               9998
Stan Humphries Jr       Sales               3211
(6 row(s) affected)
```

As in the previous example, you could use UNION to combine multiple tables, or combinations of selected columns and rows from tables, into an existing or new table. You could have tables with identical columns at different office locations in which rows are added throughout the day.

At the end of the work day, you can use a set of SELECT statements with a UNION clause to add the separate collection tables to a master table at a central location. After the rows are copied to the master table, the rows of the collection tables can be removed using a DELETE FROM statement without a WHERE clause, or a TRUNCATE statement as mentioned earlier in this chapter.

You can combine up to 16 SELECT statements by adding additional UNION clauses between each set of SELECT statements. You can use parentheses to control the order of the UNIONs. The SELECT statements within parentheses are performed before those that are outside parentheses. You don't need to use parentheses if all the UNIONs are UNION ALL. You also don't need parentheses if none of the UNIONs are UNION ALL.

In Listing 8.28, three tables are combined by using a UNION clause. IN is used with the first table to specify multiple forms of one department. The second table doesn't use WHERE, and all rows are selected. The third table specifies only a single case-sensitive department name, assuming the sort order is case-sensitive.

You don't need parentheses to control the order of the merges because no UNIONs use ALL. The resultant rows are ordered by Badge and Name using an ORDER BY clause that can appear only after the last SELECT statement.

Listing 8.28   Creating Merged Output

```
select name,badge
from employees
where department in ('SALES','Sales','sales')
union
select name,badge
from employees2
union
select name,badge
from employees3
where department='Sales'
order by badge,name
name                    badge
- - - -                 - - - -
Bob Smith               1234
Gertie Humphries        3211
Stan Humphries Jr       3211
Rod Gilbert             3339
Jean Ratele             5551
Eddie Giacomin          8888
Sally Springer          9998
(7 row(s) affected)
```

Reality Check

There are some techniques you can use to help safeguard your applications against the changes that you'll be implementing using Add, Change, Delete operations as outlined here. For example, you can do the old stand-by; you can back up the table to another table until you're certain all changes are appropriate and no applications have been changed.

You can also use Transactions if you're writing an application to complete these tasks. By putting a transaction around these types of update statements, you can roll back the transaction if you later determine that you don't need to make the changes after all. Of course the scope of the transaction is only good until a COMMIT is reached, but you do have some leeway.

▶ **See** the section in Chapter 12 starting with "Using and Understanding Transactions," for additional information about transactions, **p. 355**

One other thing that happens frequently is that you find out several users are using your database system from applications and systems you might not have been aware of. Remember, the whole point of ODBC and especially SQL Server as an intelligent server engine is to allow open access to your databases. That means that a user could be coming in to your database and using the structures there from Excel, Access, Visual Basic, or other application environments—all in addition to any applications specifically developed to use the database.

When you change the structure of a table, you run the risk of breaking the structures that users need in their tools. One way to avoid this disruption is to provide your users with *Views* on the database. Have them link their applications to these Views and you'll be able to provide a level of abstraction between the user and the underlying database tables. This is a simple way to keep from breaking applications just for making basic database table structure changes.

▶ For more information about using Views, **see** Chapter 10, "Managing and Using Views."

In short, keep a close eye on who is using your database and how. You can do this by locking down the security and requiring logins that you control. You do this not so much because of a need to control, but to better understand user needs when you consider any changes.

From Here...

In this chapter, you learned to add and delete rows from a database table, as well as change the characteristics of a table. You also learned how to perform operations on multiple tables using relational joins and UNION statements. Additional related information can be found in the following chapters:

- Chapter 4, "Data Modeling, Database Design, and the Client/Server Model," teaches you how you can create tables that logically lend themselves to the types of joins we've covered here.
- Chapter 11, "Managing and Using Indexes and Keys," teaches you how to define the common columns in tables that are used to perform joins.
- Chapter 12, " Understanding Transactions and Locking," teaches you how to set up a query so that you can undo it.
- Chapter 15, "Creating and Managing Triggers," teaches you how to maintain referential integrity, which ensures that correct rows are joined between tables.

Using Functions

There are many cases where you need to have an operation performed on the information in your table prior to returning it to a SELECT request or for use in another project. When this happens, you can either write some logic yourself and use it to work with the information coming back, or you can look to SQL Server to provide some of this functionality for you.

An example of letting SQL Server do the work for you is the COUNT() function, probably one of the most used functions provided with SQL Server. COUNT does just what its name indicates. It counts the rows that you indicate in your query. You find out more about this specific function later, but it's important to understand some key elements to functions. First, they execute on the server, saving on bandwidth. Second, they run faster than if they were executing on your local system because they have immediate access to your database information.

Functions execute a section of code that performs an operation, which returns a desired value. For the function to perform its operation, you must usually supply the required data as a list in which each element is called a parameter. You can use functions with columns of data and other storage structures of Transact-SQL. You can also use functions in the SELECT or Where clause of SELECT statements, in expressions, and, for SELECTed functions, such as system and niladic functions, in constraint-defined tables or views. ∎

How to use functions to operate on the data in the database tables

Transact-SQL contains numerous functions to analyze and manipulate table data. From counting rows to performing mathematical analysis, find out how to apply these functions to your systems.

How to use system functions

You can use system functions to return information about your computer system and SQL Server, including who the current user is and more.

How to combine functions

You learn to use the information that is returned from one function within a second function in order to return needed information.

N O T E   Niladic functions are special functions for use with constraints you set up for your tables. Niladic functions return a user or timestamp value and are useful for inserting a default value in the table. ■

Using Basic SQL Functions

A small subset of Transact-SQL functions illustrate how functions are used in Transact-SQL statements. Also, the subset of SQL functions are generic and are typically available in any dialect of SQL.

N O T E   If you've worked with another dialect of SQL, then you're probably familiar with the handful of basic functions. Unfortunately, the set of functions, used across different vendors' dialects of SQL, is extremely small. The remaining functions may be comparable across server database SQL dialects, though they aren't identical. ■

Some of the basic Transact-SQL functions are shown in Table 9.1.

Table 9.1   Basic Transact-SQL Functions

Function	Operation
AVG	Average
SUM	Sum
MIN	Minimum value
MAX	Maximum value
COUNT	Count

These, and other functions in a SELECT clause, are used as if they are column identifiers. They return their results as columns in the resulting data set.

The objects or arguments of a function must be enclosed in parentheses. If the function requires more than a single argument, the arguments are separated by a comma (,).

The syntax for the use of functions in the SELECT clause of a SELECT statement is as follows:

```
SELECT function (column_1 or *),...function (column_n)
FROM table
```

Note that NULL values aren't used for computation of AVERAGE, SUM, MIN, MAX. If all elements of a set are NULL, the function return is NULL. COUNT, when used with an asterisk (*), determines the number of rows in a column, even if it contains NULL values.

Using *AVG*

The AVG function returns the arithmetic average of the column values referenced. In the following example, AVG is used to return the average of the Pay Rate column for all rows of the Pays table.

```
SELECT avg(pay_rate)
from pays
```

Using *COUNT*

The COUNT function returns the numbers of columns that match the SELECTion expression. The asterisk wild card (*) is used as an argument for the COUNT function. If * is used in place of the column name in a SELECT clause, the asterisk specifies all rows that meet the criteria of the SELECT statement. The COUNT function counts all table rows that meet the criteria. The following syntax is used with the COUNT function:

```
SELECT COUNT(column_name)
FROM table_name
```

For example, the following SELECT statement returns the number of rows in the Employees table:

```
SELECT count(*)
from employees
```

If a WHERE clause is used in your SELECT statement, the COUNT function applies to only the rows that match the criteria specified in the WHERE clause. For example, the following COUNT statement returns the number of employees in the Sales Department:

```
SELECT count(*)
from employees
where department='Sales'
```

 TIP You can improve the performance of the COUNT function by specifying a column name to count and making sure that the column you specify is both indexed and not NULL. By doing so, SQL Server can use its optimization techniques to return the count of the rows more quickly.

Using *MAX*

MAX returns the largest value in a column. The syntax of MAX is as follows:

```
SELECT MAX(column_name)
FROM table_name
```

In the following example, MAX is used to return the maximum, or greatest number of hours_worked, for all rows of the Pays table.

```
SELECT max(hours_worked)
from pays
```

Using *MIN*

MIN returns the smallest value in a column. In the following example, MIN is used to return the minimum number of hours_worked for all rows of the Pays table.

```
SELECT min(hours_worked)
from pays
```

In the next example, MIN is used to return the lowest rate of pay for employees in the Field Service department. Both the Pay and Employees tables must be referenced in the SELECT statement because the Department column is in the Employees table, while the Rate column is in the Pays table. The corresponding badge numbers in each table are used to combine the appropriate rows.

```
SELECT min(rate)
from employees,pays
where employees.badge=pays.badge
and department='Field Service'
```

Using *SUM*

SUM returns the summation of such entities as column values. The SUM function returns the total of the non-NULL values in the numeric expression, which is often just a column name, that follows the SUM keyword. The syntax for SUM is as follows:

```
SUM([DISTINCT] <expression>)
```

In the following example, the result would be the sum of the hours_worked for all rows of the Pays table displayed:

```
SELECT sum (hours_worked)
from pays
```

 Rows that contain a NULL value in the column referenced by the SUM function are automatically skipped in the calculation.

You can use multiple functions within a single statement. The following example returns the average, minimum, and maximum of the hours_worked column in the Pays table:

```
SELECT avg(hours_worked), min(hours_worked), max(hours_worked)
from pays
```

In the following, more complicated example, a SELECT statement is used to return the maximum and average rate, minimum hours_worked, and the count of all rows of the Employees table:

```
SELECT max(rate),min(hours_worked),avg(rate),count(*)
from employees,pays
where employees.badge=pays.badge
```

Using *DISTINCT* with *COUNT*

If the COUNT function is used to reference a column name, it returns the number of values. The COUNT function includes duplicates in its count, but it doesn't include NULL values. If you add the keyword DISTINCT, the COUNT function returns the number of each unique value. The following syntax for the COUNT function is used with the keyword DISTINCT in a SELECT statement:

```
SELECT COUNT(DISTINCT column_name)
FROM table_name
```

In the following example, the keyword DISTINCT is used with the COUNT function in a SELECT statement to display the number of different departments in the Employees table:

```
SELECT count(distinct department)
from employees
```

Using *CUBE* and *ROLLUP*

The CUBE and ROLLUP operators were added to SQL Server 6.5 to make it easier to access large amounts of data in a summary fashion. When a SELECT statement is cubed, aggregate functions are transformed into super-aggregate functions that return only the rows necessary to report a summary of the information requested. The rollup operator differs from cube only because it is sensitive to the order of columns in the GROUP BY clause.

> **N O T E** There are several things to be aware of when using the CUBE and ROLLUP operators. First, a GROUP BY column list can be no more than 900 bytes. Second, there is a maximum of 10 columns. Next, columns or expressions must be specified in the GROUP BY clause. GROUP BY ALL can't be used. Finally, these operators are disabled when trace flag 204 is on. ■

Book sales are a perfect example. A query that returns a book title and the number of books ordered for each invoice in a database would return a row for each invoice. If the cube operator were applied to this query, it would only return a row for each title and the total quantity ordered for that title.

Using String Functions

Functions are used to perform various operations on binary data, character strings, or expressions, including string concatenation. String functions are used to return values commonly needed for operations on character data. The following list shows the set of string functions:

ASCII	PATINDEX	SPACE
CHAR	REPLICATE	STR
CHARINDEX	REVERSE	STUFF
DIFFERENCE	RIGHT	SUBSTRING
LOWER	RTRIM	UPPER
LTRIM	RTRIM	+

String functions are usually used on CHAR, VARCHAR, BINARY, and VARBINARY datatypes, as well as datatypes that implicitly convert to CHAR or VARCHAR. For example, you can use the PATINDEX function on CHAR, VARCHAR, and TEXT datatypes.

You can nest string functions so that the results returned by an inner function are available for the operation performed by the outer function. If you use constants with string functions, you should enclose them in quotation marks. String functions are usually used in SELECT or WHERE clauses.

> **CAUTION**
>
> You should ensure that the result returned by a nested function is compatible as input to the function in which it's embedded. In other words, if your function is expecting a string variable, be sure that the nested function returns a string, not a numeric value. Check your functions and datatypes carefully to determine if they're compatible. Otherwise, the set of functions can't work correctly.

Using *ASCII*

ASCII returns the ASCII code value of the leftmost character of a character expression. The syntax of the ASCII function is as follows:

```
ASCII(<char_expr>)
```

> **N O T E**   Remember that ASCII only returns the code associated with the leftmost character. If you need to have the ASCII value associated with the remaining portion of the string, you need to write a function that can walk down the string and return each value in succession. ■

Using *CHAR*

CHAR converts an ASCII code into a character. If you don't enter the ASCII code within the range of values between zero and 255, a NULL is returned. The syntax of the CHAR function is as follows:

```
CHAR(<integer_expr>)
```

In the following example, the ASCII and CHAR functions are used to convert a character to the decimal ASCII value and the decimal ASCII value to a character:

```
SELECT ascii('Able'),char(65)
----------- -
65          A
```

Using *SOUNDEX*

SOUNDEX returns a four-digit, or SOUNDEX, code, which is used when comparing two strings with the DIFFERENCE function. SOUNDEX could be used to search for duplicates with similar spellings in a mailing list. SOUNDEX can also be used in a word processor to return words that are similar to one that is misspelled.

The syntax for use of the SOUNDEX function is as follows:

```
SOUNDEX(<char_expr>)
```

SOUNDEX ignores all vowels unless they're the first letter of a string. In the following example, SOUNDEX is used to return evaluation values for a series of strings.

```
SELECT soundex ('a'),soundex ('aaa'),soundex ('b'),soundex ('red'),
 soundex ('read')
----- ----- ----- ----- -----
A000  A000  B000  R300  R300
SELECT soundex ('right'),soundex ('write')
----- -----
R230  W630
```

Using *DIFFERENCE*

DIFFERENCE returns the difference between the values of two character expressions returned by SOUNDEX. The difference is rated as a value from zero to four, with a value of four as the best match. Define the threshold within the range zero to four and perform subsequent operations defined by your criteria. The syntax of the DIFFERENCE function is as follows:

```
DIFFERENCE(<char_expr1>, <char_expr2>)
```

In the following example, the difference between the and teh is four, a value that is considered a good match. If you were using DIFFERENCE along with SOUNDEX in a program such as a spelling checker, teh can be treated as a misspelling of "the."

```
SELECT difference(soundex('the'),soundex('teh'))
-----------
4
```

N O T E The value that is returned by the DIFFERENCE function is fixed according to the design of the DIFFERENCE function. You must decide how you use the value returned. In the example, a value of four means that the two character strings, the and teh, are as alike as they can be using the soundex scale of values.

If you're looking for a misspelling of a department stored in the Department column of a table such as Employees, a value of three or less may be a different department or a misspelling of a department. ■

Using *LOWER*

LOWER, which converts uppercase strings to lowercase strings, uses the following syntax:

```
LOWER(<char_expr>)
```

Using *UPPER*

UPPER, which converts lowercase strings to uppercase strings, uses the following syntax:

```
UPPER(<char_expr>)
```

In the following example, UPPER and LOWER are used to convert a mixed-case string to all-uppercase and all-lowercase:

```
SELECT upper('Bob Smith1234*&^'),lower('Bob Smith1234*&^')
---------------- ----------------
BOB SMITH1234*&^ bob smith1234*&^
```

Using *LTRIM*

LTRIM removes leading spaces from a string. To save space, you can remove leading spaces from a string before it's stored in the column of a table. The leading spaces can also be removed before you perform additional processing on the string. LTRIM uses the following syntax:

```
LTRIM(<char_expr>)
```

In the following example, LTRIM is used to remove leading spaces from a string:

```
SELECT ltrim('   middle    ')
--------------
middle
```

N O T E In this example, the returned value of ('____middle____') still contains trailing spaces. You need to use the next function, RTRIM, to remove trailing spaces. ■

Using *RTRIM*

RTRIM removes trailing spaces from a string. As with LTRIM, trailing spaces can be removed before you store the string in the column of a table. Like LTRIM, RTRIM can be used to remove trailing spaces before you perform further processing on the string. RTRIM uses the following syntax:

```
RTRIM(<char_expr>)
```

N O T E In many cases, you want to work with the string without any leading or trailing spaces. Remember that you can nest these functions, so you can use the syntax as indicated in the following example:

```
SELECT RTRIM(LTRIM('   middle    ')
```

This example returns only the word "middle", with no spaces surrounding it. ■

Using *CHARINDEX*

CHARINDEX returns the starting position of the specified character expression within a specified string. The first parameter is the character expression, and the second parameter is an expression, usually a column name, in which SQL Server searches for the character expression. CHARINDEX cannot be used with Text and Image datatypes. The syntax of the CHARINDEX function is as follows:

```
CHARINDEX(<'char_expr'>, <expression>)
```

In the following example, CHARINDEX returns the starting character position of the word "Service" in a row of the Department column of the table Employees. An uppercase S, the first letter in Service, is the seventh character in the Field Service department.

```
SELECT charindex('Service',department)
from employees
where name='Stan Humphries'
-----------
7
```

> **N O T E** CHARINDEX can be used with other functions. The value returned by CHARINDEX can be used with other functions to extract parts of strings from within other strings. For example, CHARINDEX could be used within the string expression in the second argument of SUBSTRING. ∎

Using *PATINDEX*

PATINDEX returns the starting position of the first occurrence of substring in a string such as the value of a table column. If the substring isn't found, a zero is returned. You can use a PATINDEX function with data stored as CHAR, VARCHAR, and TEXT datatypes.

Wild card characters can be used in the substring as long as the percent sign (%) precedes and follows the substring. The syntax PATINDEX is as follows:

```
PATINDEX('%substring%', <column_name>)
```

In the following example, PATINDEX returns the character position for the first character of the substring within the string of characters stored in the department for the employee Stan Humphries. Stan Humphries is a member of the Field Service department.

```
SELECT patindex('%erv%',department)
from employees
where name='Stan Humphries'
-----------
8
```

Using *REPLICATE*

REPLICATE returns multiple sets of characters specified in the first argument of the function. The second argument specifies the number of sets to be returned. If the second argument, an integer expression, is a negative number, the function returns a NULL string. The syntax of REPLICATE is as follows:

```
REPLICATE(character_expression, integer_expression)
```

In the following example, REPLICATE returns a string of identical characters and also returns two iterations of the same sequence of two characters:

```
SELECT replicate ('a',5),replicate('12',2)
----- ----
aaaaa 1212
```

Using *REVERSE*

REVERSE returns the reverse order of a string of characters. The character string argument can be a constant, a variable, or a value of a column. The syntax REVERSE is as follows:

```
REVERSE(character_string)
```

In the following example, the example would return the two constant strings that are enclosed in quotation marks, but their contents would be reversed:

```
SELECT reverse('12345678910'),reverse('John Smith')
----------- ----------
01987654321 htimS nhoJ
```

In the following example, the result is a table column displayed without REVERSE. The same column is displayed in a different order using the REVERSE attribute. Finally, the same string that is the name of the column of the Employees table is processed as a constant because it's enclosed in parentheses:

```
SELECT name,reverse(name),reverse('name')
from employees
where name='Bob Smith'
name
-------------------- -------------------- ----
Bob Smith            htimS boB            eman
```

Using *RIGHT*

RIGHT returns part of a character string, starting at the number of characters from the right, as specified in the function argument. If the number of characters in the integer expression argument is negative, perhaps as the result of a nested function, RIGHT returns a NULL string. The syntax of the RIGHT function is as follows:

```
RIGHT (character_expression, integer_expression)
```

The following example shows two identical strings, one that is displayed with a RIGHT function and also without a function. The second parameter of the RIGHT function 4 specifies to return from four characters from the end of the string to the rightmost character of the string.

```
SELECT '12345678', right ('12345678',4)
-------- ----
12345678 5678
(1 row(s) affected)
```

> **CAUTION**
>
> You can't use a function, such as the RIGHT function, on TEXT or IMAGE datatypes. You must use the specialized set of string handling functions with TEXT and IMAGE datatypes. These special functions are discussed later in this chapter in the section titled "Using TEXT and IMAGE Functions."

Using *SPACE*

SPACE returns a string of spaces for the length specified by the argument to the function. If the argument integer value is negative, SPACE returns a NULL string. The SPACE syntax is as follows:

```
SPACE(<integer_expr>)
```

In the following example, SPACE returns multiple spaces between two string constants:

```
SELECT 'begin',space(15),'end'
----- --------------- ---
begin                end
```

Using *STR*

STR converts numeric data to character data. The STR syntax is as follows:

```
STR(<float_expr>[, <length>[, <decimal>]])
```

You should ensure that both the length and decimal arguments are non-negative values. If you don't specify a length, the default length is 10. The value returned is rounded to an integer by default. The specified length should be at least equal to or greater than the part of the number before the decimal point plus the number's sign. If <float_expr> exceeds the specified length, the string returns ** for the specified length.

In the following example, a series of constant numbers is converted to strings. The first number is completely converted because the second argument, the length, specifies the correct size of the resultant string, five numeric digits, the minus sign (–), and the decimal place (.). When the same constant value is converted using a length of six, the least-significant digit is truncated.

The third constant is correctly displayed using a length of six because it's a positive number. The same constant can't be displayed with a length of two, so two asterisks (**) are displayed instead.

```
SELECT str(-165.87,7,2)
go
SELECT str(-165.87,6,2)
go
SELECT str(165.87,6,2)
go
SELECT str(165.87,2,2)
go
-------
-165.87

------
-165.9
------
165.87

--
**
```

Using *STUFF*

STUFF inserts a string into a second string. The length argument specifies the number of characters to delete from the first string, beginning at the starting position. You can't use STUFF with TEXT or IMAGE datatypes. The STUFF syntax is as follows:

```
STUFF(character_string_1,starting_position,length,character_string_2)
```

In the following example, the string abcdef is inserted into the first string, beginning at the second character position. The abcdef string is inserted after the number of characters specified by the length argument are deleted from the first string:

```
SELECT stuff('123456',2,4,'abcdef')
---------
1abcdef56
```

If the starting position, or length, is negative, or if the starting position is larger than the first character_string, STUFF displays a NULL string. In the following example, a NULL is the result of the code shown because the starting position is a negative value:

```
SELECT stuff('wxyz',-2,3,'abcdef')
(null)
```

If the length to delete is longer than the length of the first character string, the first character string is deleted to only the first character. In the following example, only the first character of the first character string remains after the second character string is inserted:

```
SELECT stuff('123',2,3,'abc')
----
1abc
```

Using *SUBSTRING*

You can use SUBSTRING to return a part of a string from a target string. The first argument can be a character or binary string, a column name, or an expression that includes a column name. The second argument specifies the position at which the substring starts. The third argument specifies the number of characters in the substring.

Like several other string-only functions, you can't use SUBSTRING with Text or Image datatypes. The SUBSTRING syntax is as follows:

```
SUBSTRING(character_string, starting_position,length)
```

In the following example, multiple SUBSTRINGs are used along with the SPACE function to separate the first name from the last name, each of which is stored in a single column of the Employees table.

```
SELECT substring(name,1,3),space(4),substring(name,5,5)
from employees
where badge=1234
---------- ---- -----
Bob      Smith
```

Unlike earlier examples, the following example uses a function in several SQL statements.

Multiple functions are often used in stored procedures or other batch objects. See Chapter 14, "Managing Stored Procedures and Using Flow-Control Statements," for more information about the use of local variables and the SELECT statement in the following example. Like the previous example, the first name is separated from the last name with multiple spaces added between the names, all of which is done by using multiple functions.

```
declare @x int
SELECT @x=charindex(' ',(SELECT name from employees where name='Bob Smith'))
SELECT @x=@x-1
    SELECT substring(name,1,@x), right(name,@x+2)
from employees
where badge=1234
-------------------
Bob              Smith
```

Concatenation

The concatenation operator symbol (+) concatenates two or more character or binary strings, column names, or a combination of strings and columns. Concatenation is used to add one string to the end of another string. You should enclose character strings within single quotation marks. The syntax of the concatenation operator is as follows:

```
<expression> + <expression>
```

Conversion Functions

Conversion functions are used to concatenate datatypes that could not be concatenated without a change in datatype. CONVERT is one of the functions that you can use for datatype conversion. In the following example, a string constant is concatenated with the current date returned using the GETDATE date function. GETDATE is nested within CONVERT to convert it to a datatype, in this case VARCHAR, which is compatible with the string constant.

```
SELECT 'The converted date is ' + convert(varchar(12), getdate())
---------------------------------
The converted date is Jul 11 1994
(1 row(s) affected)
```

Using Arithmetic Functions

Arithmetic functions operate on numeric datatypes, such as INTEGER, FLOAT, REAL, MONEY, and SMALLMONEY. The values returned by the arithmetic functions are six decimal places. If you encounter an error while using an arithmetic function, a NULL value is returned and a warning message is displayed.

Two query processing options can be used to control the execution of statements that include arithmetic functions. The keyword for each of the two arithmetic operations is preceded by the SET keyword. You can use the ARITHABORT option to terminate a query when a function finds an error. ARITHIGNORE returns NULL when a function finds an error. If you set both ARITHABORT and ARITHIGNORE, no warning messages are returned.

There are numerous mathematical functions available in Transact-SQL (see Table 9.2).

Table 9.2   Transact-SQL Mathematical Functions

Function	Parameters	Return
ACOS	`(float_expression)`	Angle in radians whose cosine is a FLOAT value.
ASIN	`(float_expression)`	Angle in radians whose sine is a FLOAT value.
ATAN	`(float_expression)`	Angle in radians whose tangent is a FLOAT value.
ATAN2	`(float_expr1,float_expr2)`	Angle in radians whose tangent is `float_expr1/floatexpr2`.
COS	`(float_expression)`	Trigonometric cosine of angle in radians.
COT	`(float_expression)`	Trigonometric cotangent of angle in radians.
SIN	`(float_expression)`	Trigonometric sine of angle in radians.
TAN	`(float_expression)`	Trigonometric tangent of an angle in radians.
DEGREES	`(numeric_expression)`	Degrees converted from radians returned as the same datatype as expression. Datatypes can be INTEGER, MONEY, REAL and FLOAT.
RADIANS	`(numeric_expression)`	Radians converted from degrees returned as the same datatype as expression. Datatypes can be INTEGER, MONEY, REAL, and FLOAT.
CEILING	`(numeric_expression)`	Smallest INTEGER >= expr returned as the same datatype as expression. Datatypes can be INTEGER, MONEY, REAL, and FLOAT.
FLOOR	`(numeric_expression)`	Largest INTEGER <= expr returned as the same datatype as expression. Datatypes can be INTEGER, MONEY, REAL, and FLOAT.
EXP	`(float_expression)`	Exponential value of expression.
LOG	`(float_expression)`	Natural log of expression.
LOG10	`(float_expression)`	Base 10 log of expression.
PI()		Value is 3.1415926535897936.

Function	Parameters	Return
POWER	(*numeric_expression,y*)	Value of expression to power of *y* returned as the same datatype as expression. Datatypes can be INTEGER, MONEY, REAL, and FLOAT.
ABS	(*numeric_expression*)	Absolute value of expression returned as the same datatype as expression. Datatypes can be INTEGER, MONEY, REAL, and FLOAT.
RAND	([*integer_expression*])	Random float number between zero and one using optional int as seed.
ROUND	(*numeric_expr,integer_expr*)	Rounded value to precision of *integer_expr* returned as the same datatype as expression. Datatypes can be INTEGER, MONEY, REAL, and FLOAT.
SIGN	(*numeric_expression*)	One, zero, or –1 returned as the same datatype as expression. Datatypes can be INTEGER, MONEY, REAL, and FLOAT.
SQRT	(*float_expression*)	Square root of expression.

The following example shows the use of ABSOLUTE, RANDOM, SIGN, PI, and RANDOM within an expression:

```
SELECT abs(5*-15),rand(),sign(-51.23),pi(),round((10*rand()),0)
-----  -------------------  ---------  ---------------------  ----
75     0.3434553056428724   -1.0       3.141592653589793       8.0
(1 row(s) affected)
```

In another example of the use of mathematical functions, FLOOR and CEILING are used to return the largest and smallest integer values that are less than or equal to, or greater than or equal to, the specified value.

```
SELECT floor(81),ceiling(81),floor(81.45),
ceiling(81.45),floor($81.45),ceiling(-81.45)
--------  --------  -------------  -------------  -----------  --------
81        81        81.0           82.0           81.00        -81.0
(1 row(s) affected)
```

ROUND always returns a value, even if the length is invalid. If you specify that the length is positive and longer than the digits after the decimal point in ROUND, a zero is added after the least-significant digit in the returned value. If you specify that the length is negative and greater than or equal to the digits before the decimal point, 0.00 is returned by ROUND.

The following example shows the effects of using ROUND functions on various values. In the first example, the decimal number is rounded to two decimal places. The second number is displayed as 0.00 because the length is negative.

```
SELECT round(81.4545,2), round(81.45,-2)
------------------------ ---------------
81.45                    0.0
(1 row(s) affected)
```

In the following example, the first number is rounded down to three decimal places, and the second number is rounded up to a whole number because it's more than half the value of the least-significant digit.

```
SELECT round(81.9994,3),round(81.9996,3)
----------------------- -----------------------
81.999                  82.0
(1 row(s) affected)
```

Using *TEXT* and *IMAGE* Functions

In addition to PATINDEX, you can use several functions for operations on TEXT and IMAGE datatypes. You can also use relevant SET options and global variables with TEXT and IMAGE datatypes.

Using *SET TEXTSIZE*

SET TEXTSIZE specifies the number of bytes that are displayed for data stored as TEXT or IMAGE datatypes with SELECT statements. The SET TEXTSIZE syntax is as follows:

SET TEXTSIZE *n*

Use *n* to specify the number of bytes to be displayed. You must specify the value of *n* in the function SET TEXTSIZE as an INTEGER. If you specify *n* as zero (0), the default length in bytes, up to 4K bytes, is displayed. The current setting for TEXTSIZE is stored in the global variable @@TEXTSIZE.

In the following example, the TEXTSIZE default is first used to display a table column defined as the datatype TEXT. SET TEXTSIZE is defined to two (2), and as a result, only two bytes of the table-column text are displayed. Finally, TEXTSIZE is reset to the default of 4K using a value of zero (0).

Listing 9.1   Reviewing the Content of a *TEXT* Column

```
SELECT * from imagetext_table
image1          ...                                      text1
------------------------- ...  ----------------------------------
0x31323334353637383961637a782b3d5c    ... 12345678aczx+=
(1 row(s) affected)
set textsize 2
go
SELECT text1 from imagetext_table
go
set textsize 0
go
SELECT * from imagetext_table
```

```
go
text1
-------------  ...  --------------------------------------
12
(1 row(s) affected)

image1            ...                                        text1
------------------------   ...   --------------------------------
0x31323334353637383961637a782b3d5c   ... 12345678aczx+=
(1 row(s) affected)
```

Using *TEXTPTR*

TEXTPTR returns a value in VARBINARY format as a 16-character binary string. The value re-turned is a pointer to the first database page of stored text. The text pointer is used by the SQL Server system rather than by you, although the value is accessible by using TEXTPTR.

SQL Server automatically checks if the pointer is valid when the function is used. The system checks that the return value points to the first page of text. The TEXTPTR syntax is as follows:

```
TEXTPTR(column_name)
```

Using *READTEXT*

READTEXT is a statement rather than a function. It is used along with the TEXT and IMAGE func-tions. READTEXT extracts a substring from data stored as a TEXT or IMAGE datatypes. You specify the number of bytes to include in the substring that follow an offset. The READTEXT syntax is as follows:

```
READTEXT [[<database.>]<owner.>]<table_name.><column_name>
 <text_pointer> <offset> <size>
```

In the following example, TEXTPTR retrieves the point to the first page of text for the one-and-only row of the table. The pointer is stored in a local variable @v. READTEXT is then used to ex-tract a substring starting at the third byte, using an offset to skip past the first two bytes and retrieve the specified four bytes.

```
declare @v varbinary(16)
SELECT @v=textptr(text1) from imagetext_table
readtext imagetext_table.text1 @v 2 4
(1 row(s) affected)
text1
-------------------------------------------...--------------------------
3456
```

Using *TEXTVALID*

TEXTVALID returns either zero (0) or one (1), depending on whether a specified text pointer is valid or invalid. You must include the name of the table as part of your reference to the column defined as the datatype TEXT. The TEXTVALID syntax is as follows:

```
TEXTVALID('table_name.column_name', text_pointer)
```

In the following example, TEXTVALID determines the validity of a pointer to a data column stored as the datatype text. Recall that the output of one function can be used as the input to another function, as in the following example:

```
SELECT textvalid('imagetext_table.text1',(SELECT textptr(text1)
from imagetext_table))
go
- - - - - - - - - - -
1
(1 row(s) affected)
```

In the next example, a SELECT statement that contains a WHERE clause returns a table row. As a result, TEXTVALID returns a zero, which is an invalid value because no row column was located.

```
SELECT textvalid('imagetext_table.text1',(SELECT textptr(text1)
from imagetext_table where text1 like '5'))
- - - - - - - - - - -
0
(1 row(s) affected)
```

Using Conversion Functions

You often don't have to explicitly perform conversions because SQL Server automatically performs them. For example, you can directly compare a character datatype or expression with a DATETIME datatype or expression. SQL Server also converts an INTEGER datatype or expression to a SMALLINT datatype or expression when an INTEGER, SMALLINT, or TINYINT is used in an expression.

▶ **See** the Chapter 6 section titled "Numeric integer Datatypes" for more information on datatypes, **p. 138**.

Use a conversion function if you're unsure whether SQL Server will perform implicit conversions for you or if you're using other datatypes that aren't implicitly converted.

Using *CONVERT*

As mentioned earlier, CONVERT performs the explicit conversion of datatypes. CONVERT translates expressions of one datatype to another datatype as well as to a variety of special date formats. If CONVERT can't perform the conversion, you'll receive an error message. For example, if you attempt to convert characters contained in a column defined as a CHAR datatype to an INTEGER datatype, an error is displayed.

The CONVERT syntax is as follows:

```
CONVERT(<datatype> [(<length>)], <expression> [, <style>])
```

You can use CONVERT in SELECT and WHERE clauses or anywhere an expression can be used in a Transact-SQL statement.

Keep the following key concepts in mind when you use the CONVERT function:

■ If you omit a length specification, it defaults to a value of 30.

- Any unrecognized values that appear in DATETIME-to-SMALLDATETIME conversions aren't used.

- Any conversions of BIT datatypes convert non-zero values to one (1) in keeping with the usual storage of BIT datatypes.

- Integer values that you convert to MONEY or SMALLMONEY datatypes are processed as monetary units for the defined country, such as dollars for the United States.

- If you convert CHAR or VARCHAR datatypes to INTEGER datatypes, such as INT or SMALLINT, the values must be numeric digits or a plus (+) or minus (-) sign.

- Conversions that you attempt to make to a datatype of a different size or type can truncate the converted value and display + after the value to denote that truncation has occurred.

- Attempted Conversions to a datatype with a different number of decimal places can also result in truncation.

- Conversions that you specify as TEXT datatypes to CHAR and VARCHAR datatypes can be up to only 255 characters, which is the maximum length for CHAR and VARCHAR datatypes. The default of 30 characters is used if an explicit length is not supplied.

- The conversion of data stored as IMAGE datatypes to BINARY and VARBINARY datatypes can also be up to only 255 characters, with a default of 30 characters.

In the following example, a numeric constant is converted to a CHAR datatype, a decimal constant is converted to an INT datatype, and a decimal constant is converted to a BIT datatype:

```
SELECT convert(char(4),1234),convert(int,12.345),convert(bit,87453.34)
---- ----------- ---
1234 12          1
(1 row(s) affected)
```

In the next example of using CONVERT, several table columns are converted from an INT datatype to a CHAR datatype. The attempted conversion of the same table column to a VARCHAR datatype of an inadequate length results in truncation of each column value.

Listing 9.2   Using the *CONVERT* Statement

```
SELECT badge,convert(char(4),badge),convert(varchar(2),badge)
from employees
badge
----------- ---- --
3211        3211 *
6732        6732 *
4411        4411 *
...
```

You can use the style argument of the CONVERT function to display the date and time in different formats. You can also use the style argument as part of a CONVERT function when you convert dates and times to CHAR or VARCHAR datatypes. Table 9.3 shows the different style numbers that can be used with CONVERT.

Table 9.3 Style Numbers for the *CONVERT* Function

Without Century (yy)	With Century (yyyy)	Standard	Display
-	0 or 100	default	mon dd yyyy hh:miAM(orPM)
1	101	USA	mm/dd/yy
2	102	ANSI	yy.mm.dd
3	103	English/French	dd/mm/yy
4	104	German	dd.mm.yy
5	105	Italian	dd-mm-yy
6	106		dd mon yy
7	107		mon dd, yy
8	108		hh:mi:ss
9	109		mon dd yyyy hh:mi:sssAM (or PM)
10	110	USA	mm-dd-yy
11	111	Japan	yy/mm/dd
12	112	ISO	yymmdd
13	113	Europe	dd mon yyyy hh:mi:ss:mmm (24h)
14	114	-	hh:mi:ss::mmm (24h)

In the following example, the current date and time are implicitly displayed using GETDATE, and GETDATE appears within CONVERT using different style numbers.

```
SELECT getdate(),convert(char(12),getdate(),3),convert(char(24),
getdate(),109)
----------------------------  -----------  ------------------------
Jul 12 1994  1:34PM          12/07/94      Jul 12 1994  1:34:49:440
(1 row(s) affected)
SELECT convert(char(24),getdate(),114),convert(char(24),getdate(),112)
----------------------------  ------------------------
13:36:45:223                  19940712
(1 row(s) affected)
```

Using Date Functions

You can use several functions to perform operations with DATE datatypes. Use date functions to perform arithmetic operations on DATETIME and SMALLDATETIME values. Like other functions, date functions can be used in the SELECT or WHERE clauses, or wherever expressions can be used in Transact-SQL statements.

Using *DATENAME*

DATENAME returns a specified part of a date as a character string. DATENAME uses the following syntax:

DATENAME(<*date part*>, <*date*>)

Using *DATEPART*

DATEPART returns the specified part of a date as an integer value. DATEPART uses the following syntax:

DATEPART(<*date_part*>, <*date*>)

Using *GETDATE*

GETDATE returns the current date and time in SQL Server's default format for DATETIME values. Use a NULL argument with GETDATE. GETDATE uses the following syntax:

GETDATE()

Using *DATEADD*

DATEADD returns the value of the date with an additional date interval added to it. The return value is a DATETIME value that is equal to the date plus the number of the date parts that you specify. DATEADD takes the date part, number, and date arguments in the following syntax:

DATEADD (<*date part*>, <*number*>, <*date*>)

Using *DATEDIFF*

DATEDIFF returns the difference between parts of two specified dates. DATEDIFF takes three arguments, which are the part of the date and the two dates. DATEDIFF returns a signed integer value equal to the second date part, minus the first date part, using the following syntax:

DATEDIFF(<*date part*>, <*date1*>, <*date2*>)

Table 9.4 shows the values used as arguments for the date parts with the date functions.

Table 9.4   Date Parts Used in Date Functions

Date Part	Abbreviation	Values
Year	yy	1753-9999
Quarter	qq	1-4
Month	mm	1-12
Day of Year	dy	1-366
Day	dd	1-31
Week	wk	1-54
Weekday	dw	1-7 (Sun-Sat)
Hour	hh	0-23
Minute	mi	0-59
Second	ss	0-59
Millisecond	ms	0-999

The following examples show the use of several of the date functions. In the first example, the columns of a table that are defined as DATETIME and SMALLDATETIME datatypes are displayed without any functions.

```
SELECT * from date_table
date1                          date2
---------------------------    ---------------------------
Jan 1 1753 12:00AM             Jan 1 1900 12:00AM
(1 row(s) affected)
```

In the following example, the keyword year is used with DATENAME to return the year with the century from a DATETIME value:

```
SELECT datename(year,date1) from date_table

1753
(1 row(s) affected)
```

In the following example, hour is used with DATENAME to return the hour from a DATETIME datatype value:

```
SELECT datename(hour,date1) from date_table
---------------------------
0
(1 row(s) affected)
```

In the following example, month is used with DATENAME to return the number of the month from a DATETIME datatype value:

```
SELECT datepart(month,date1) from date_table
----------
1
(1 row(s) affected)
```

In the following example, GETDATE function is used in a SELECT statement to display the current date and time:

```
SELECT now=getdate()
now
--------------------------
May 19 1994  2:00PM
(1 row(s) affected)
```

In the following example, GETDATE is nested within DATEPART to display only the current day as part of a SELECT statement:

```
SELECT datepart(day,getdate())
----------
19
(1 row(s) affected)
```

In the following example, GETDATE is nested within DATENAME to display only the name of the current month as part of a SELECT statement:

```
SELECT datename(month,getdate())
---------------------------
May
(1 row(s) affected)
```

In Listing 9.3, the current date and the date stored in a DATETIME column are first displayed for reference. DATEDIFF is then used to display the number of days between the two DATETIME values.

Listing 9.3 Using the *DATETIME* Datatypes

```
SELECT getdate()
--------------------------
May 19 1994  2:12PM
(1 row(s) affected)
SELECT date1 from date_table
date1
--------------------------
Jan 1 1753 12:00AM
(1 row(s) affected)
SELECT new=datediff(day,date1,getdate())
from date_table
new
----------
88161
(1 row(s) affected)
```

Using System Functions

You can use systems functions to obtain information about your computer system, user, database, and database objects. The system functions permit you to obtain information, such as the characteristics of database objects within stored procedures and in conjunction with conditional statements you can perform different operations based on the information returned.

You can use a system function, like other functions, in the SELECT and WHERE clauses of a SELECT statement, as well as in expressions. If you omit the optional parameter with some system functions, as shown in Table 9.5, information about your computer system and the current user database is returned.

Table 9.5   System Functions

Function	Parameter(s)	Information Returned
HOST_NAME()		The name of the server computer
HOST_ID()		The ID number of the server computer
SUSER_ID	(['login-name'])	The login number of the user
SUSER_NAME	([server_user_id])	The login name of the user
USER_ID	(['user_name'])	The database ID number of the user
USER_NAME	([user_id])	The database username of the user
DB_NAME	(['database_id'])	The name of the database
DB_ID	(['database_name'])	The ID number of the database
GETANSINULL	(['database_name'])	Returns 1 for ANSI nullability, 0 if ANSI nullability is not defined
OBJECT_ID	('object_name')	The number of a database object
OBJECT_NAME	(object_id)	The name of a database object
INDEX_COL	('table_name', index_id, key_id)	The name of the index column
COL_LENGTH	('table_name', 'column_name')	The defined length of a column
COL_NAME	(table_id, column_id)	The name of the column
DATALENGTH	('expression')	The actual length of an expression of a datatype
IDENT_INCR	('table_or_view')	The increment (returned as numeric(@@MAXPRECISION,0)) for a column with the identity property

Function	Parameter(s)	Information Returned
IDENT_SEED	('table_or_view')	The seed value, returned as numeric(@@MAXPRECISION,0), for a column with the identity property
STATS_DATE	(table_id, index_id)	The date that the statistics for the index, index_id, were last updated
COALESCE	(expression1, expression2, ... expressionN)	Returns the first non-null expression
ISNULL	(expression, value)	Substitutes value for each NULL entry
NULLIF	(expression1, expression2)	Returns a NULL when expression1 is NULL when expression1 is equivalent to expression2

In the following example, the system function HOST_ID is used to return the name of the Windows NT server system to which a user is connected:

```
SELECT host_name ()
----------------------------
NT1

(1 row(s) affected)
```

In the following example, multiple system functions are used to return information about the Windows NT server system, the current database, and the current user:

```
SELECT host_name (),host_id (),db_name (), db_id (), suser_name ()
---------- -------- ---------- -------------------------
NT1        0000005e employees          6       sa

(1 row(s) affected)
```

N O T E You may not have reason to use any of the system functions. You may only need to use the system functions if you're performing some administrative operation with the database. Several of the system functions require that you have access to the system tables in order to return useful information. Access to these depends on the security of your login ID.

You would not usually use the system functions in the SELECT clause of a SELECT statement that displays the information on your monitor. Rather, system functions, like other functions, can be used within other functions, and the information returned is recorded in local variables or a temporary or permanent table. System functions provide information, which is usually used for advanced programming or administrative operations. Administrative operations can be performed within stored procedures, as well as in an interactive session.

For example, the system function STATS_DATE returns the date the last time that statistics were updated for an index on a table. The database administrator must periodically update the statistics for a table so that the query optimizer has valid information to use to decide whether or not to use an

continues

Part

II

Ch

9

continued

index for the retrieval of rows from a table. SQL Server does not automatically update the table statistics used by the query optimizer.

You can use a system function, such as STATS_DATE (as shown in the previous example), to determine if it's time to update the statistics for the indexes of a table so the query optimizer will work properly.

You can also combine the system function STATS_DATE with the functions GETDATE and DATEDIFF to return the update statistics date, the current date, and the difference between the two dates. Using these three functions and a conditional statement in a procedure, you can run the procedure periodically to determine if the statistics for a table index have been updated within some period of time, for example, a week.

If the difference between the STATS_DATE and the GETDATE is more than seven days, an UPDATE STATISTICS command should be issued. Other system functions can also be used to determine if a system operation on the database, or their objects, needs to be performed. ■

For example, in the Listing 9.4, the SELECT statement returns the statistics update date for two indexes on the table company:

Listing 9.4   Retrieving System Statistics

```
SELECT 'Index' = i.name,
       'Statistics Update Date' = stats_date(i.id, i.indid)
           from sysobjects o, sysindexes i
               where o.name = 'company' and o.id = i.id
Index                              Statistics Update Date
-------------------------------    --------------------------
badge_index                        Sep 18 1995  3:24PM
department_index                   Sep 18 1995  3:27PM

(2 row(s) affected)
```

▶ **See** the section titled "Using Date Functions" earlier in this chapter.

▶ **See** Chapter 14, "Managing Stored Procedures and Using Flow-Control Statements," for more information about working with stored procedures, **p. 403**.

Using *ISNULL* and *NULLIF*

ISNULL is a system function that returns a string of characters or numbers in place of (NULL) when a NULL is encountered in a data-storage structure, such as a table column. The syntax of the function is as follows:

```
ISNULL(expression,value)
```

The expression is usually a column name that contains a NULL value. The value specifies a string or number to be displayed when a NULL is found. In the following example, the ISNULL function is used to return the character string 'No entry' when a NULL is encountered:

```
SELECT ISNULL(y, 'No entry') from nulltable
y
```

```
- - - - - - - - - -
     No entry
(1 row(s) affected)
```

The NULLIF function returns a NULL if the two expressions are identical. If they are not, the second expression is returned. The NULLIF function is usually used with the CASE statement. In the following example, a NULL is returned for identical strings while the first parameter is returned when the strings don't match:

```
SELECT nullif ('same','same'),space (2),nullif ('same','different')
---- -- ----
(null)    same
 (1 row(s) affected)
```

> **N O T E** The space function is used in the example of the NULLIF function to provide a visual separation between the values returned by the use of the function twice in the SELECT statement. ■

Using *COALESCE*

The form of the COALESCE function that uses the syntax COALESCE (expression1,expression2) is similar to the NULLIF statement. Unlike the NULLIF statement, the COALESCE statement, with two parameters, returns expression2 when a NULL is returned and returns expression1 if NOT NULL is encountered.

You can also use COALESCE with more than two parameters. COALESCE returns the first non-null expression in the list of parameters when no NULL is used. If no non-null values are present, when COALESCE is used with more than two parameters, the function returns a NULL.

> **N O T E** The COALESCE function is designed for use in a CASE statement, which is discussed in the chapter on stored procedures. Please consult Chapter 14 on stored procedures for additional information on the COALESCE function. ■

▶ **See** the Chapter 14 section titled "Using CASE Expressions," **p.439**.

Using Niladic Functions

Niladic functions return a user or timestamp value, which is automatically placed in the row of a table when the value is omitted from an INSERT or UPDATE statement. Niladic functions are defined as part of a DEFAULT constraint in a CREATE or ALTER TABLE statement. You can use any of the following niladic functions:

USER

CURRENT_USER

SESSION_USER

SYSTEM_USER

```
CURRENT_TIMESTAMP
```

```
APP_NAME
```

The niladic functions USER, CURRENT_USER, and SESSION_USER all return the database username of the user executing an INSERT or UPDATE statement. The function SYSTEM_USER returns the user's login ID. CURRENT_TIMESTAMP returns the current date and time in the same form as the GETDATE function. APP_NAME returns the program name for the current session if one has been set.

Niladic functions cannot be used outside the DEFAULT CONSTRAINT of a CREATE or ALTER TABLE statement. For example, you cannot use the niladic functions in the SELECT clause of a SELECT statement.

▶ **See** the Chapter 13 section titled "Managing and Using Rules, Constraints, and Defaults," for more information on setting up these options, **p. 379**.

Reality Check

Remember, the goal of your implementation needs to be to return the smallest number of rows possible in each query you submit to the server. To that end, the set of SQL functions you use can be very helpful.

In many cases, you'll find that if you're working with information from the database in your application, you can consider carefully how you're using it—what the end-goal is for the information. If you're trying, for example, to analyze a set of numbers and then use the result to show the application user, consider using server-side functions—those outlined in this chapter—to help mold the information as you need it.

When you use these functions, you create a true client-server application, one that allows the server to do the database-information manipulation that it's so good at. You also optimize things for the client. Because the client won't have to manipulate the information returned from the database, response time to the user will be faster.

This directly impacts systems that you convert from older database types. For example, in one project that was completed, the database was converted to SQL Server from Btrieve™. In Btrieve, the data manipulation, relationships, and so on are all managed by the application.

When the database was converted, it was necessary to redesign the system to allow the back-end system a more active role in the manipulation of the information in the system. This meant removing some functionality from the client side and implementing it on the server. Of course this led to code changes in the application, potentially impacting the schedule to cut over the application.

One approach you may want to take with legacy systems is to first convert the database, leaving the processing assignments between the client and server side as they were in the original system. After the system is online, and you've worked out the kinks in the data conversion, you can begin writing the stored procedures to automate the processes on the server.

Because you'll not be impacting the database, only providing a new way to get information from it, the application will still work during the process of creating the stored procedures. Then, when you're ready on the database side, you can go back into the code and make the changes, one by one, to use the stored procedures instead of the client-side processing. As you're doing a controlled cut-over on the client application, you can test each change carefully.

At the same time, you're controlling the risk to the client application by only implementing a single new function at a time.

From Here...

In this chapter you've learned the use of various functions that return information about your system and characteristics of SQL Server. In addition, you learned how to use functions to perform operations on table data. Functions can be used both in an interactive session and in stored procedures.

For information about SELECTed aspects of the topics mentioned in this chapter, review the following chapters:

- Chapter 6, "Creating Database Tables and Using Datatypes," discusses the values that can be stored in various Transact-SQL datatypes.

- Chapter 14, "Managing Stored Procedures and Using Flow-Control Statements," discusses the variables used for the temporary storage of values returned by functions, as well as the global variables used to store information relevant to the use of functions.

- Chapter 16, "Understanding Server, Database, and Design Query Options," shows you how to use SET options to control the display of data through the use of functions used in SELECT statements.

Managing and Using Views

Views are static definitions for the creation of dynamic tables constructed from one or more sets of rows according to predefined selection criteria. Views can be used to define numerous combinations of rows and columns from one or more tables. A defined view of the desired combination of rows and columns uses a simple SELECT statement to specify the rows and columns included in the view. ■

How to create a virtual table

You'll learn how to create stored SELECT statements. You can use the information referenced by these statements like database tables.

How to create views that are defined on multiple tables

You'll learn to create views that perform relational joins between tables in order to combine information from multiple tables.

How to manipulate data in views

You'll learn to add, update, and delete rows in tables by using views.

How to create a view of a view

Learn to create a view that is based on other views rather than tables.

How to manage views

Find out how to edit, list, and delete views through Transact-SQL statements and the SQL Enterprise Manager.

Understanding Views

Simply put, a *view* is a sort of bookmark on your table, or a way of returning to a window of the information. This window is actually a set of instructions that tell SQL Server how you want to see the information in your view. This includes the parameters, formatting, and other information SQL Server uses to query the database and retrieve your information.

Technically, a *view* is a stored definition of a SELECT statement that specifies the rows and columns to be retrieved when the view is later referenced. You can define up to 250 columns of one or more tables in a view. The number of rows that you can define is limited only by the number of rows in the tables referenced.

N O T E If you're familiar with the Access environment, you'll know views as queries. Queries in Access can, depending on their makeup, be manipulated, changed, or updated or have rows deleted from them, just as you would a table. In fact, you can specify a query nearly anywhere you'd indicate a table.

In SQL Server, the queries are called views, but the balance of the information you already know in working with queries is accurate. You can update views, as they're based on simple or complex SELECT statements or functionality, and your application can refer to them in statements just as it would the underlying tables. ■

Views are aptly named because they function as the set of rows and columns that you can see through their definition. After the view is defined, you reference the view as if it were a table. Although a view appears as a permanent set of rows and columns stored on a disk in a database, it's not. A view doesn't create a permanent copy of the selected rows and columns of a database.

A view performs the SELECT statement contained within its definition when the view is later referenced just like a table. The temporary table that is created and returned to the monitor is unavailable after the display of its rows is complete. A view enables you to execute a SELECT statement when you reference the view as a table.

CAUTION

It's easy to be misled and believe that a view is a table. After the view is defined, you always access data through it as if it were a table. Try to remember that the data referenced through a view is always coming from its underlying table. Also, if you add columns to the underlying table that the view is defined on, the new columns don't appear in the view unless the view is first deleted and then redefined.

One thing that you can do to help in this area is to use consistent naming conventions. One example of this might be to add a prefix to all views, perhaps starting each with "vw_". This will let you know immediately when you see the name that the underlying object is a view.

A view can be used to access an entire table, part of a table, or a combination of tables. Because the portion of a table you access is defined within the view, you don't have to repeat the selection statements. You can use views to simplify access to the database. Even if you create complicated views that use multiple clauses, you can perform the SELECT statement in the view just as easily as in a view that contains a simple SELECT statement. For more detailed information about creating and working with SELECT statements, see Chapter 7, "Retrieving Data with Transact-SQL."

You can also use views to provide security in the database. You can grant permissions on a view that are different from the permissions granted on the tables the view is based upon. You can provide access to only the rows and columns referenced through a view, but not provide access to all rows and columns directly through the table.

▶ **See** "SQL Server Security," **p. 575**.

Creating a View

You can create a view either through a command-line ISQL session, an ISQL/w session, or through the SQL Enterprise Manager. A view is stored as a separate object in your database through which you have an alternate way of viewing and, with limitations, modifying a table. You should remember that you can create a view only in the current database. The syntax to create a view in an ISQL or ISQL/w session is as follows:

```
CREATE VIEW view_name [WITH ENCRYPTION] AS
SELECT statement...
FROM table_name ¦ view_name
[WHERE clause] [WITH CHECK OPTION]
```

You can also create a new view through the SQL Enterprise Manager by performing the following steps:

1. Within the current database, select the Views folder.
2. From the Views folder menu click New View. Figure 10.1 shows the Manage Views dialog box for the current database.

FIG. 10.1
You should replace <VIEW NAME> with a name for your view.

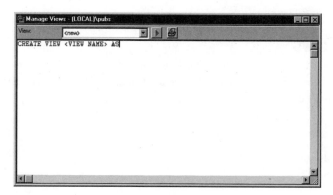

3. Enter the view definition within the Manage Views dialog box. You can also select an existing view and edit it. Figure 10.2 shows a previously designed view.

FIG. 10.2

You can use the View box to select other views for display or subsequent editing.

4. Click the Execute tool button, shown in Figure 10.2, to save the new view definition. You'll receive an error message if your view can't be created. The creation of your view will fail if a view already exists with the same name.

Selective Columns

You can define a view that is made up of some, but not all, of the columns of a table. In the following example, a view is defined as a pseudotable that has two of the three columns of the Employees table:

```
create view twocolumns as
select name, badge
from employees
```

When you've defined the view, you can use a SELECT statement to access it just like a table. For example, the view created in the previous example can be referenced in the following manner to display the name and badge for all rows:

```
select *
from twocolumns
```

Selective Rows

You can also define a view that references some, but not all, of the rows of a table. In the following example, the sales1 view is defined to contain only the rows in which the department is equal to SALES from the Employees table:

```
create view sales1 as
select name, department, badge
from employees
where department='SALES'
```

You can also use one or more Boolean operators in the WHERE clause of a SELECT statement to specify the rows contained in the view. In the following example, a view is defined that contains all columns from the table that are members of the Sales department and that have a badge number greater than 1,000.

```
create view sales2 as
select name, department, badge
from employees
where department='Sales'
and badge>1000
```

For more information about Boolean operators, see Chapter 7, "Retrieving Data with Transact-SQL."

TIP You can use a WHERE clause in the SELECT statement that references a view even though the SELECT statement view within the view definition can include a WHERE clause. The view is treated just like an actual table.

Part
II

Ch
10

Selective Columns and Rows

You can also define a view that comprises a combination of only some columns and rows of a table. In the following example, the view is defined and provides access to only two of the three columns, and only for the rows that contain the Sales department:

```
create view twocolumnsales as
select name,badge
from employees
where department='SALES'
```

You can continue to use a simple SELECT statement to reference the view like a table to retrieve the set of columns and rows defined in the view. For example, to show all rows and columns that are defined in the three previous views, you can use the following three SELECT statements:

```
select *
from twocolumns
select *
from sales1
select *
from twocolumnsales
```

TIP You don't necessarily need to specify all of the columns in the table within the view. You can specify specific columns, calling each as a specific part of the SELECT statement. It's not a requirement to use an asterisk (*) to reference all columns defined in the view.

You can't distinguish a view from a table in the way you use a view. You have to see the view definition to distinguish a view from a table. You can create views for all the combinations of rows and columns that you access together from database tables.

N O T E   You can establish a naming convention for views and tables so that the name of each is self-descriptive as a table or view. For example, the table Employees could be named employees_table, and the view sales could be named sales_view. Remember that you can use up to 30 characters for the name of an object such as a view or table. You can also use a single character within the name of a view or table, such as *v* for a view and *t* for a table, if you run short of characters. ■

CAUTION

If you name views and tables so that each is obviously a table or view, for example, employees_table or sales_view, you may defeat the purpose of a view. A feature of the view is that it is nearly indistinguishable from a table. You work with a view in the same way that you work with a table.

It can be an advantage to permit views and tables to be indistinguishable from one another to database users that needn't perform complicated queries. A complicated query can be defined within the view and the user told to use a simple SELECT statement to access the new "table," which is actually the view.

You can encounter some restrictions when you define a view. You can't define a view on a temporary table. Temporary tables are transitory database structures and exist only until data retrieved from a permanent table is displayed to an output device, such as a monitor.

If you were allowed to define a view based on a temporary table, the data might not be available when you reference it through the view. The temporary table on which the view was defined was automatically deleted.

▶ **See** "Creating Temporary Tables," **p. 137**.

You also can't define a trigger on a view. A trigger can be defined only on a permanent table. It makes sense to define a trigger only on a table because a table is the permanent underlying source of the data for all views. If you were permitted to define a trigger on a view, SQL Server would still have to reference the underlying table to locate the data specified by the trigger. It's simpler to establish triggers that are based directly on tables.

N O T E   A *trigger* is a database object that is automatically executed when a table row is inserted, updated, or deleted. It's primarily designed to maintain referential integrity. See Chapter 15, "Creating and Managing Triggers," for more information. ■

In addition, you can't include ORDER BY in the definition of a view. The rows of a view are unordered like the rows of a database table. If you were permitted to use a SELECT statement that includes an ORDER BY clause in a view, the rows would be ordered and a view would have different characteristics than a database table.

If a view is designed to be used like a permanent table, it must have similar or identical characteristics. You can use an ORDER BY clause when you retrieve rows from a view just as you would retrieve rows from a table. Remember, using views is a two-step process. First, you define the view and save it in the system. This is exactly like creating a table in the system for future use.

Second, you `select` information from the dataset that is created by the view—two steps, two opportunities to manage the return information.

When you work with the view, you can also further restrict the values that are returned. For example, you could have a view that limits the results set of a name and address database to only doctors. When you select from the view, you can further limit the results by indicating that you want only the general practitioners.

Think of views and selecting information from them as coin sorters. You know, those banks that everyone's seen where you drop a coin in the top slot, it rattles around in the bank, and it then comes to rest in the proper location for the denomination in the bank—quarter, dime, nickel, and penny. The bank is your view; it sorts and presents the information.

Now, in this example, you have two options. You can say "give me all the dimes," or you can say "give me all the dimes with a date of 1969." This is the `SELECT` statement against the view. You're deciding which parts of the information represented by the view you're interested in.

▶ **See** "Using an `ORDER BY` Clause," **p. 207**.

You also can't use `COMPUTE` in a view. `COMPUTE` creates a virtual column for the actual columns of a table or view.

▶ **See** "Using a `COMPUTE` Clause in a `SELECT` Statement," **p. 217**.

You can't use `DISTINCT` in the `SELECT` clause in a view. You can however, use `DISTINCT` in a `SELECT` clause of the `SELECT` statement that references a view to return nonduplicate rows. You could also always ensure the rows retrieved through a view are unique by defining a unique key or index on the underlying table that the view references.

▶ **See** "Using `DISTINCT` to Retrieve Unique Column Values," **p. 211**.

In the following example, a view that contains `DISTINCT` in its `SELECT` clause can't be successfully defined.

```
create view departments as
select distinct departments
from employees

Msg 154, Level 15, State 2
A DISTINCT clause is not allowed in a view.
```

You can't use `INTO` as part of a `SELECT` statement within a view. `INTO` redirects rows into another table rather than to a monitor. In Listing 10.1, a view can't be successfully created because it contains an `INTO` clause in its `SELECT` statement.

Listing 10.1   A Failed Attempt to Create a View

```
sp_help two
Name                  Owner                  Type
----------------------------------------------------------------
two                   dbo                    user table
Data_located_on_segment      When_created
----------------------------   ---------------------------
```

continues

Listing 10.1   Continued

```
default                     Oct 2 1994  1:33PM
Column_name    Type     Length Nulls Default_name   Rule_name
-------------- --------------- ------ ----- ---------------
name           char       25     0    (null)         (null)
badge          int         4     0    (null)         (null)
Object does not have any indexes.
No defined keys for this object.
create view selectinto as
select name,badge
into two
from employees
Msg 154, Level 15, State 3
An INTO clause is not allowed in a view.
```

Simple and Complex Views

In understanding views, you may find it helpful to further categorize them. Recall that you can define views that access multiple tables as well as individual tables. *Simple views* are those you define that access any combination of rows and columns from which single tables are called. *Complex views* are those that provide access to the rows and columns of multiple tables.

The syntax for a complex view uses the same syntax in the SELECT statement that is directly used for the retrieval of rows and columns. Use the following syntax to specify the rows and columns from multiple tables of a database:

```
CREATE VIEW view_name AS
SELECT column_1,...column_n
FROM table_1,...table_n
WHERE table_key_1=table_key_2
,...AND table_key_1=table_key_n
```

In the following example, the Name and Department columns are referenced from the Employees table and the Hours_Worked column is selected from the Pays table in the definition of the view. The WHERE clause is used to match the rows from the Employees table with the corresponding rows in the Pays table.

The Badge column is used in each table to match the rows in the same way in which a corresponding column can be used to match rows from a SELECT statement that is used outside a view.

```
create view combo as
select name,department,hours_worked
from employees,pays
where employees.badge=pays.badge
```

You access the rows and columns through a complex view the same way that you access rows and columns in a simple view. For example, you can reference the rows and columns defined in the combo view with the following SELECT statement:

```
select *
from combo
```

 TIP Rather than require a user to perform a complicated SELECT statement, you can place the complex query within the view and have the user reference the view.

Displaying Views

When you create a view, the definition of a view is stored in the syscomments system table. One way that you can display the stored definition of a view from the syscomments table is by using the sp_helptext stored system procedure.

Part II

Ch

10

 TIP You can also use sp_helptext to display the text of a stored procedure, trigger, default, or rule as well as a view. Use sp_help to list the characteristics of a view or other objects.

In Listing 10.2, a simple view is defined that selects all rows of the Sales department. The rows of the Employees table are retrieved through the sales view. The sp_helptext sales procedure is used to display the definition of the view.

Listing 10.2   Creating a Basic View

```
sp_helptext sales1
text
------------------
create view sale1 as
select * from employees
where department='Sales'
(1 row(s) affected)
```

The view definition that is stored in the syscomments table is retrieved by sp_helptext and displays the view definition as the row of a table. The column header is text, the view definition is the row, and the count message specifies the count of the one row retrieved.

 TIP If you find that a view has seemingly vanished when you return to SQL Server at a later date after you've created the view, make sure you're in the right database. Views are, by definition, database specific and won't be visible unless you're using the right database.

You can also display the definition of a view through the SQL Enterprise Manager by performing the following steps:

1. Select the Views folder under the Objects folder in the database in which the view was created. Notice that an icon of a pair of eyeglasses appears to the left of each view to distinguish views from other objects. Figure 10.3 shows the expanded list of views that are currently defined for the pubs database.

FIG. 10.3

You can also double-click the selected view to display it.

2. Click the right mouse button to bring up the Manage Views menu. Open the Manage Views menu and choose Edit or open the Manage menu and choose Views. Figure 10.4 shows the definition of the view titleview displayed through the Enterprise Manager.

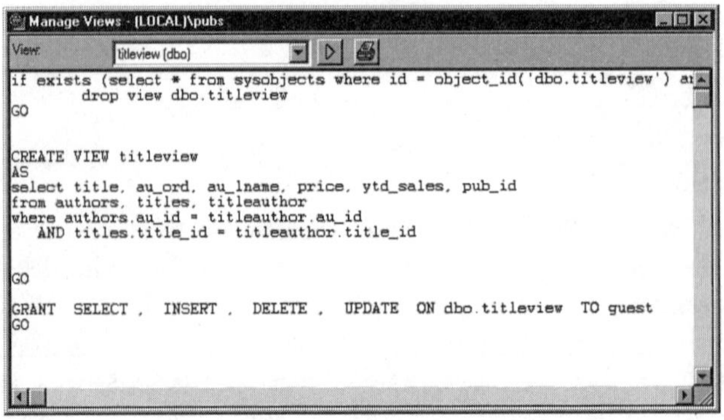

FIG. 10.4

You can edit the view displayed in the Manage Views dialog box of the SQL Enterprise Manager.

Editing Views

You must use the SQL Enterprise Manager to edit an existing view. You cannot edit a view from a command-line ISQL or ISQL/w session. You would edit a view in order to change the columns or rows that are referenced by the view. For example, you'll need to add the name of a column that you inadvertently omitted when you originally defined the view.

To edit a view through the SQL Enterprise Manager, perform the following steps.

1. Select the Views folder under the Objects folder in the database in which the view was created.

2. Click the right mouse button to bring up the Manage Views menu and choose Edit or choose Views from the Manage menu or double-click the left mouse button on the selected view.

3. Make your changes after the keywords CREATE VIEW <view name> AS.

4. Click the Execute button, shown in Figure. 10.5, in the Manage Views dialog box.

Figure 10.5 shows the view titleview after it has been changed. The view now shows only titles with a price greater than 50.

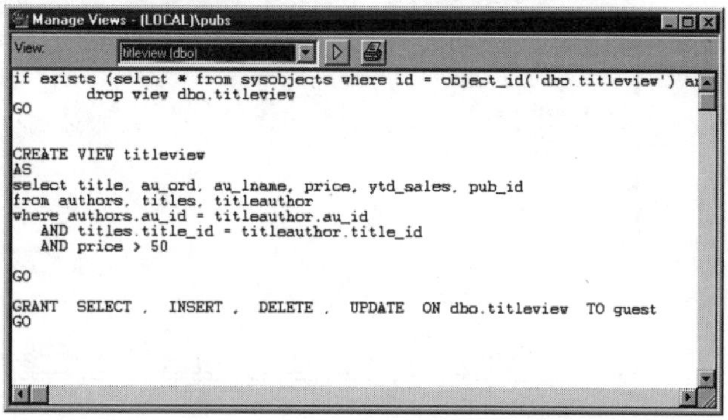

Part

II

Ch

10

FIG. 10.5

You can change the name of the view in the Manage Views dialog box to create a new view.

If you examine the SQL statements within the Manage Views dialog box within which your view is displayed, you'll note a conditional statement that precedes the definition of your view. The conditional statement, which begins with the keyword IF, checks to see if your view is already defined and deletes the view in order to redefine it as if it is a new view.

The deletion of your view is done to satisfy the requirements of SQL Server, which does not permit the direct editing of an existing view. The Manage Views dialog box automatically generates the code to delete the view and re-create it with whatever changes you've made.

You could effectively edit an existing view from ISQL or ISQL/w only by deleting the existing view and creating a new one using the same name as the view that you deleted. You'll find it much easier to change views through the SQL Enterprise Manager.

Adding the *WITH ENCRYPTION* Clause

You may not want users to be able to display the definition of a view from the syscomments table. If you add WITH ENCRYPTION in the CREATE VIEW statement, you can't subsequently list the definition of the view. In Listing 10.3, a view is created whose definition can't be subsequently displayed with the procedure sp_helptext.

Listing 10.3   Creating Protected Views

```
create view test_view_encryption with encryption as
select * from company
go
sp_helptext test_view_encryption
go
The object's comments have been encrypted.
```

You also can't view the definition of an encrypted view from the SQL Enterprise Manager. Figure 10.6 shows the information returned when an encrypted view is displayed.

FIG. 10.6

The owner of an encrypted view can still drop it and create a new view with the name of the dropped view.

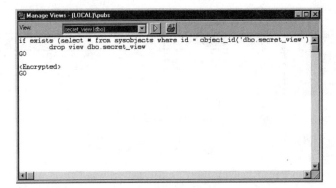

CAUTION

A disadvantage of encrypting view definitions is that views can't be re-created when you upgrade your database or SQL Server. During an upgrade, the definitions of a view are used to re-create the view, which can't be done if the view definition is encrypted. You would also be unable to upgrade a database if you delete the view definition stored as a row in the syscomments table.

N O T E   You can also encrypt procedures and triggers. The reason for encryption is security. You can prevent users from displaying the objects, such as tables or views, that an object, such as a view, references. You can use encryption along with object permissions to control access to objects and object definitions. ■

Displaying View Associations

One way that you can display the tables or views upon which a view is defined is to use the system procedure sp_depends. You may need to display the tables or views that a view references in order to discover and correct problems that you may encounter when you use the view.

In the following example, sp_depends shows that the sales view is defined from the Employees table user.

```
sp_depends sales
Things the object references in the current database.
object                      type              updated selected
------------------------------------------ ----------------
dbo.employees          user table            no        no
(1 row(s) affected)
```

> **NOTE** You can also use sp_depends to display information about tables and views that are dependent upon procedures. sp_depends references the sysdepends system table to locate dependencies. sp_depends shows only references to objects within the current database. ■

You can also display dependencies through the SQL Enterprise Manager. To display the dependencies of a view, click the right mouse button and choose Dependencies from the menu. For example, in Figure 10.7, the dependencies of the view titleview are displayed in the Object Dependencies dialog box. The Object Dependencies dialog box shows that the view is defined based on the four tables.

FIG. 10.7

The same icons used for tables and views in the Server Manager window of the SQL Enterprise Manager are used in the Type column of the Object Dependencies dialog box.

Part
II

Ch
10

Creating Views of Views

You can define a view that references a view rather than a table. You can also create a view that references several views or a combination of views and tables. In Listing 10.4, the first view that is created is based on a table. A second view is created that references the first view. Regardless of the number of views defined, they must all eventually reference a table because it is the permanent source of data.

Listing 10.4   Creating "Virtual" Views

```
create view salesonly as
select name,department,badge
from employees
where department='Sales'
go
This command did not return data, and it did not return any rows
create view salespersons as
select name
from salesonly
This command did not return data, and it did not return any rows
```

In a continuation of the previous example, Listing 10.5 retrieves rows from the permanent table through a view that was defined on a previously created view. sp_depends is used to confirm that the second view was defined based on the first view.

Listing 10.5   Using "Virtual" Views

```
select * from salespersons
name
-------------------
Bob Smith
Mary Jones
John Garr
(3 row(s) affected)
sp_depends salespersons
go
Things the object references in the current database.
object              type          updated selected
------------------------------- ---------------- --
dbo.salesonly       view          no      no
(1 row(s) affected)
```

sp_depends doesn't iterate through views that are defined using other views. If a view references another view rather than a table, sp_depends shows the view rather than the original table. The sp_depends procedure shows only the view or table that the view directly references in the view definition.

> **CAUTION**
>
> Although sp_help shows you the columns included in the rows, it doesn't show you the rows included. Clauses, such as WHERE, aren't displayed by sp_help. You must examine the view definition with sp_helptext.
>
> If you want to see the columns or rows that are included in a view that is defined on one or more views, you'll have to use sp_helptext to display all the view definitions. If a view is defined only on tables, the definition of the view displayed by sp_helptext specifies the rows and columns that are included. It's better to define views directly on tables rather than on other views.

You should use the Object Dependencies dialog box in the SQL Enterprise Manager to display object dependencies. Unlike sp_depends, the listing of object dependencies in the Object Dependencies dialog box shows the multiple level of views and tables that a view is based upon. For example, the Object Dependencies dialog box shows that the view lowtitleview is defined directly based on the view titleview, and indirectly to four tables. In Figure 10.8, this is indicated with the eyeglasses icon in the Type column for sequence number five, and the table icon in the Type column for sequence number four. The sequence numbers are used to illustrate level or depth of objects on which the view is defined.

FIG. 10.8
Object dependencies have levels indicated by the sequence number.

Renaming Columns in Views

You can rename the columns of the base tables in the view. Define the list of alternate column names following the name of the view and preceding the keyword, as in the view definition. Use the following syntax to assign alternate names for the columns referenced in a view:

```
CREATE VIEW view_name [ (view_column_1,...view_column_n) ] AS
SELECT statement...
FROM table_name or view_name
[WHERE clause]
```

In Listing 10.6, alternate names for the columns of the Employees table are specified as part of the view definition. A single letter is used for the alternate column name in the view. After the list of column names for the view is defined, the alternate column names appear as new column headers as well as in other clauses, such as a WHERE clause.

Listing 10.6   Creating Alternative Names for Columns

```
create view view8 (a,b,c)
as
select name,department,badge from employees
(1 row(s) affected)
select * from view8
a                        b                        c
------------------       ------------------       ----------------
Mary Jones               Sales                    5514
Dan Duryea               Shipping                 3321
John Garr                Sales                    2221
Mark Lenard              Sales                    3331
Bob Smith                Sales                    1
Minty Moore              Sales                    7444
(6 row(s) affected)
```

N O T E   You don't have to create a view to rename the column of a table during retrieval. Instead, you can rename a column with a SELECT clause outside a view using the following syntax:

SELECT *column_name=renamed_name*

. . .

A new name that contains embedded spaces can be enclosed within single quotation marks. The new name isn't permanent. It only applies within the SELECT statement. ▪

Renaming Views

You can use sp_rename to rename a view. The system procedure uses the following syntax:

sp_rename *old_name, new_name*

Use a comma (,) between the old_name and the new_name to separate the parameters from the procedure name. In Listing 10.7, the sales view is renamed sales2. After the view is renamed, sp_depends shows that the renamed procedure is still based upon the permanent Employees table.

Listing 10.7   Renaming a View

```
sp_rename sales, sales2
Object name has been changed.
sp_depends sales2
Things the object references in the current database.
object               type               updated selected
-----------------    ---------------    ------- --------
dbo.employees        user table             no      no
(1 row(s) affected)
```

You can also rename a view using the SQL Enterprise Manager. To rename a view through the Enterprise Manager, perform the following steps:

1. Left-click the view to select it.

2. Click the right mouse button. Choose Rename.

3. Enter a new name for the view in the Rename Object dialog box.

4. Click OK.

Part
II
Ch
10

Figure 10.9 shows the Rename Object dialog box. When the Rename Object dialog box is first brought up, the current name of the view is displayed. Edit the existing name, or delete the old name and enter a new name to rename the view.

FIG. 10.9

The same Rename Object dialog box is used to rename other database objects.

TIP   You can use `sp_rename` to rename other database objects, including tables, columns, stored procedures, triggers, indexes, defaults, rules, and user-defined datatypes.

CAUTION

Although you can rename views with the `sp_rename` procedure, SQL Server does not change the name of a table or view in the stored definition of a view in the table syscoments. It warns you of this when you rename a view or similar objects. In Listing 10.8, a warning is displayed when the table Employees is renamed with the procedure `sp_rename`. The procedure `sp_helptext` shows that the old name of the table, employees, is retained in the definition of the view based on the renamed table.

Listing 10.8   Renaming a View with Dependencies

```
sp_rename employees,newname
Warning - Procedures, views or triggers reference this object
and will become invalid.
Object name has been changed.
sp_helptext salesonly
go
text
--------------------------------------------------------
create view salesonly as
select name,department,badge
from employees
where department='Sales'
select * from salesonly
go
name                    department              badge
-------------------     --------------------    ----------
Fred Sanders            SALES                   1051
Bob Smith               SALES                   1834
Sally Springer          Sales                   9998

(3 row(s) affected)
```

CAUTION

However, both the sp_depends procedure and the Object Dependencies dialog box will display the updated name of renamed tables and views. For example, Figure 10.10 shows the object dependencies for the view salespersons, which references the view salesonly while the view salesonly references the table newname, formerly named employees.

You should try not to rename objects unless it's absolutely necessary.

FIG. 10.10

You can display the dependencies for another view or table by selecting its name in the Subject Object list box.

Dropping Views

You can use the DROP VIEW command to remove a view from a database. Dropping a view has no effect on the permanent table that the dropped view is based upon. The definition of the view is simply removed from the database. The DROP VIEW syntax is as follows:

```
DROP VIEW view_name_1, ... view_name_n
```

You can drop multiple views in a single DROP VIEW by using a list of views separated by commas after the DROP VIEW keywords. The following example drops the sales2 view:

```
drop view sales2
This command did not return data, and it did not return any rows.
```

You can also use the SQL Enterprise Manager to drop views by performing the following steps:

1. Left-click the view to select it.
2. Click the right mouse button. Choose Drop.
3. Click the Drop All button.

Figure 10.11 shows the Drop Objects dialog box. The view that was selected in the Server Manager dialog box is automatically selected in the Drop Objects dialog box.

FIG. 10.11
You can use the Show Dependencies button to display the object dependencies before you drop the view.

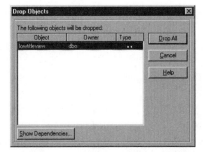

CAUTION

If you drop a view in which another view is defined, the second view returns the following error when you reference it, such as in a SELECT statement.

```
Msg 208, Level 16, State 1
Invalid object name 'name_of_dropped_view'.
Msg 4413, Level 16, State 1
```

View resolution was unsuccessful because the previously mentioned objects, upon which the view directly or indirectly relies, don't currently exist. These objects need to be re-created in order to use the view.

You should consider defining views directly on tables rather than other views. Tables are less likely to be dropped than views because tables are the objects in which rows are actually stored, unlike views, which are simply a different way of looking at the data in a table.

Inserting Rows Through Views

In addition to retrieving rows of data through a view, you can also use the view to add rows to the underlying table on which the view is defined. To easily add a row, reference all table columns in the view. In the example shown next, a new row is added to the permanent Employees table through an INSERT statement that specifies the sales view.

After you've created the view, you reference the view in an INSERT statement to add rows just as if you've referenced a table in the INSERT statement. The rows inserted through the view are added to the underlying table on which the view was defined.

In Listing 10.9, the view definition is first displayed to demonstrate that the view references the underlying table, Employees, and is restricted only to rows that contain the department, Sales. When a new row is inserted through the view, the row is subsequently retrieved from both the view and the table.

Listing 10.9   Showing a View Definition, Then Querying the View

```
sp_helptext sales
go
text
------------------
create view sales as
select * from employees
where department='Sales'
go
insert into sales
values ('Mark Lenard','Sales',3331)
select * from sales
where badge=3331
go
name                    department              badge
------------------      ------------------      -----
Mark Lenard             Sales                   3331
(1 row(s) affected)
go
select * from employees
where badge=3331
name                    department              badge
------------------      ------------------      -----
Mark Lenard             Sales                   3331
(1 row(s) affected)
```

In the previous example, the row that was inserted through the view matched the criteria specified in the WHERE clause of the view, that is, the inserted row contained the department, Sales. Although you may find it odd, SQL Server will permit you to insert a row through a view even though it doesn't match the criteria of WHERE clauses defined within the view.

After a row is inserted through a view that does not match the criteria specified in the WHERE clause of the view, you can't retrieve the row through the view. The criteria for rows defined in WHERE prevents you from retrieving the new row that you've just inserted. For example, in the following INSERT statement, a row is inserted through a view into the Employees table on which the view sales is defined. As you'll recall from the definition of the sales view in the previous example, rows can have only the Sales department.

A subsequent SELECT statement is unable to retrieve the newly inserted row through the view. However, the row was added to the underlying table Employees. A SELECT statement that references the table retrieves the new row that was added through the view. Both examples are shown in Listing 10.10:

Listing 10.10 Testing a View

Part

II

Ch

10

```
insert into sales
values ('Fannie Farmer','Logistics',6689)
go
select * from sales
where badge=6689
name                    department          badge
--------------------    ----------------    ----------
(0 row(s) affected)
go
select * from employees
where badge=6689
go
name                    department          badge
--------------------    ----------------    ----------
Fannie Farmer           Logistics           6689
(1 row(s) affected)
```

You can become confused when you add a row to the underlying table through a view in which the row doesn't match the criteria for inclusion in the view. The row can be inserted through the view, but it cannot be retrieved and subsequently displayed through the same view. The row effectively disappears when retrieved through the view, but it still can be accessed through the table on which the view is based.

Fortunately, you can add the WITH CHECK OPTION clause to your view definition to prevent an operation, such as the insertion of a row through a view, that can't be subsequently displayed through the view.

WITH CHECK OPTION, which is applied to the SELECT statement that is defined within the view, restricts all changes to the data to conform to the row selection criteria defined within the SELECT statement. For example, if a view is defined based on the table, Employees, that contains a WHERE clause that specifies only the department, Sales, only rows that contain the department, Sales, can be inserted in the table, Employees, through the view. WITH CHECK OPTION is illustrated in Listing 10.11:

Listing 10.11   Creating a Restrictive View

```
create view check_with_check as
select * from company
where department='Sales' with check option
go
This command did not return data, and it did not return any rows
insert into check_with_check
values ('Bob Matilda','Field Service',3325,2)
go
Msg 550, Level 16, State 2
The attempted insert or update failed because the target view
either specifies WITH CHECK OPTION or spans a view which specifies
WITH CHECK OPTION and one or more rows resulting from the operation
did not qualify under the CHECK OPTION constraint.
Command has been aborted.
update check_with_check
set department='Hardware Repair' where department='Field Service'
go
(0 row(s) affected)
delete from check_with_check
where department='Field Service'
go
(0 row(s) affected)
```

TIP If you find that after you've added a row to a view the row seems to disappear, you may have added a row that doesn't meet the criteria for the view. Another way this can happen is if the view has changed since you added the row, making the row no longer part of the view's dataset.

TIP You can prevent the first instance of this by using WITH CHECK OPTION, keeping rows from being inserted through the view that don't match the criteria for the view. Of course, this won't help in the second case where the view was changed after the row was inserted, but it's a good measure nonetheless.

In the previous example, a view was created that included all columns of the underlying table on which it was defined. If one or more columns of the underlying tables aren't present in the view, the missing columns must be defined to allow a NULL or have a default value bound to the missing columns. If not, you can't add the row to the table through the view.

In Listing 10.12, a view is created that includes two columns of the Employees table. The insertion of a row through the view is unsuccessful because the Department column was defined with NOT NULL.

Listing 10.12 A View that Fails Due to Not Null Constraints

```
create view namebadge as
select name,badge
from employees
go
insert into namebadge
(name,badge)
values ('Russell Stover',8000)
Msg 233, Level 16, State 2
The column department in table employees may not be null.
```

After a default is defined for the Department column and bound to the column in the Employees table, a new row can be inserted through the namebadge view. The addition of the default for the Department column in the Employees table permits a value to be applied by default when a new row is inserted through the namebadge view. This is shown in Listing 10.13.

Listing 10.13 View Is Successful with a Default Implemented

```
create default deptdefault
as 'Sales'
go
sp_bindefault deptdefault, 'employees.department'
Default bound to column.
go
insert into namebadge
(name,badge)
values ('Russell Stover',8000)
(1 row(s) affected)
```

N O T E A default can be bound to a user-defined datatype or column of a table. A default can't be bound to the column of a view. However, the defaults bound to table columns that are referenced in a view are applied to the columns if a new row is inserted through the view. ■

Listing 10.14 shows that when the row is inserted into the underlying Employees table through the namebadge view, successive SELECT statements are used to retrieve the new row through the view and the table:

Listing 10.14 Using a View to Retrieve Inserted Rows

```
select * from namebadge
where name='Russell Stover'
go
name                    badge
-------------------- -----------
Russell Stover          8000
(1 row(s) affected)
select * from employees
where name='Russell Stover'
go
name                  department            badge
-------------------- -------------------- -----------
Russell Stover        Sales                 8000
(1 row(s) affected)
```

▶ **See** "Defining Defaults," **p. 393**.

▶ **See** "Creating Database Tables and Using Datatypes," **p. 132**.

Using Views to Delete Rows

You can delete rows through views even though all columns are not referenced in the view. In Listing 10.15, a row that was previously added to the Employees table through the namebadge view is deleted by using the namebadge view. A subsequent SELECT statement demonstrates that the row is deleted.

Listing 10.15 Confirming Deletion of a Row

```
delete from namebadge
where name='Russell Stover'
go
(1 row(s) affected)
select * from namebadge
where name='Russell Stover'
go
name                    badge
-------------------- -----------
(0 row(s) affected)
```

You can't delete a row if the criteria specified in the SELECT clause doesn't include the row specified for deletion. It isn't necessary to add WITH CHECK OPTION to the definition of the view to prevent the deletion of rows that don't match the criteria specified by the WHERE clause of the view. In the following example, one or more rows of the Shipping department is specified for deletion through the sales view. Even if multiple rows were stored in the underlying permanent Employees table upon which sales are based, the rows can't be deleted through the sales view.

```
delete from sales
where department='Shipping'
go
(0 row(s) affected)
```

You also can't delete a row from the underlying table of a view if the column that you specify in the WHERE clause of a DELETE statement specifies a column that isn't specified in the view. The following example returns an error because the column specified in the WHERE clause isn't present in the namebadge view used in the DELETE statement:

```
delete from namebadge
where department='Shipping'
go
Msg 207, Level 16, State 2
Invalid column name 'department'.
```

You can, however, delete the row through a view that was defined with a WHERE clause that specifies criteria that include the row or rows specified in the DELETE statement. You can also delete one or more rows directly through the table upon which the view was defined. In the following example, a row is deleted using a DELETE statement that references the table containing the row:

Part

II

Ch

10

```
delete from employees
where department='Shipping'
go
(1 row(s) affected)
```

Using Views to Update Rows

You can use an UPDATE statement to change one or more columns or rows that are referenced through a view. Any changes that you specify through the view are made to the underlying table in which the view is defined. In Listing 10.16, a single row is updated through the sales view:

Listing 10.16   Updating a View

```
select * from sales
go
name                   department             badge
--------------------   --------------------   ----------
Bob Smith              Sales                  1234
Mary Jones             Sales                  5514
John Garr              Sales                  2221
Mark Lenard            Sales                  3331
(4 row(s) affected)
update sales
set badge=0001
where name='Bob Smith'
go
(1 row(s) affected)
```

continues

Listing 10.16   Continued

```
select * from sales
where name='Bob Smith'
name                 department           badge
------------------   ------------------   -----------
Bob Smith            Sales                1
(1 row(s) affected)
```

You can change one or more columns or rows so that they no longer meet the criteria for inclusion in the view. Listing 10.17, a row is updated through a view and a column value is changed so that the row no longer matches the criteria defined in the view:

Listing 10.17   Rows Can Be Inserted that Don't Meet the Criteria for a View and Will Not Show Up in Its Results Set

```
update sales
set department='Field Service'
where name='Bob Smith'
go
(1 row(s) affected)
select * from sales
where name='Bob Smith'
go
name                 department           badge
------------------   ------------------   -----------
(0 row(s) affected)
```

You can also update the underlying table by updating through a view that is defined on a view. In Listing 10.18, the update to the Employees table is performed through a view that is defined using the sales view.

Listing 10.18   You Can Update Against a View, Even if It Works Against Another View

```
select * from onlyname
name
go
-----------------------
Bob Smith
Fred Sanders
(2 row(s) affected)
update onlyname
set name='Bob Orieda'
where name='Bob Smith'
go
(1 row(s) affected)
select * from onlyname
```

```
go
name
-----------------------
Fred Sanders
Bob Orieda
(2 row(s) affected)
select * from employees
where name like 'Bob%'
go
name                       department           badge
-------------------------  -------------------  ------
Bob Orieda                 SALES                1834
(1 row(s) affected)
```

The updated row that was changed through the onlyname view, which was based on the underlying Employees table through the sales view, is displayed through both the nameonly view and the Employees table. The updated row is also displayed through the sales view. The results are shown in Listing 10.19.

Listing 10.19   The Results

```
select * from sales
where name like 'Bob%'
go
name                       department           badge
-------------------------  -------------------  ------
Bob Orieda                 SALES                1834
(1 row(s) affected)
```

Any changes to the data that you make by updates through views are always reflected in the underlying tables. Views permit you to establish virtual tables with data rows organized like tables, though they are dynamically created as the view is referenced. It's convenient to use views as the only access to data. It is best not to allow tables to be directly referenced.

N O T E   Users of older databases, such as hierarchical or network databases, may remember that their databases could be manipulated only through entities equivalent to views. Network databases had to be indirectly accessed through an entity called a *subschema*. A subschema functioned like a view.

The usual definition of a subschema is that it serves as the entity through which a programmer or user views the database. You always had to use a subschema to access a network database. Usually, a default subschema was created for a network database that permitted access to the entire database if necessary. ■

You can update underlying tables through multitable views if the updated columns are part of the same table. Listing 10.20 shows a row that is successfully updated through the multitable combo view.

Listing 10.20 Updating Rows Through Multitable Views

```
create view combo (a,b,c) as
select name,employees.badge,pays.badge
from employees,pays
where employees.badge=pays.badge
go
This command did not return data, and it did not return any rows
update combo
set a='Jim Walker II'
where b=3211
go
(1 row(s) affected)
select * from combo
where b=3211
go
a                              b           c
------------------------------ ----------- -----------
Jim Walker II                  3211        3211
(1 row(s) affected)
```

You can't, however, update the view columns that are used to match rows between the tables because they're part of separate tables. In the next example, the column b and column c views are based on the Badge columns in the Employees and Pays tables. An error is returned that cites an unsuccessful update because the columns are from two tables.

```
update combo
set c=1111, b=1111
where b=8005
go
Msg 4405, Level 16, State 2
View 'combo' is not updatable because the FROM clause names multiple tables.
```

You can update a value in a single column directly through the view, and you can use a trigger to update the corresponding value in a related table. In Listing 10.21, a trigger has been defined to automatically update the Badge column in the Pays table if the Badge column in the Pays table is changed. When the badge is changed through the b column in the combo view, the trigger automatically activates to change the corresponding value in the Pays table.

Listing 10.21 Updating a Row to Test a Trigger

```
update combo
set b=9999
where c=4411
go
(1 row(s) affected)
select * from combo
where b=9999
```

```
go
a                           b           c
. . . . . . . . . . . . . . . . . . . .   . . . . . . . . . . .   . . . . . . . . . . .
Sue Sommers                 9999        9999
(1 row(s) affected)
```

Exploring Other View Characteristics

A view remains defined in the database if you drop the table upon which it's based. However, an error is returned when the view is referenced if its underlying table is undefined. If you create a new table with the same name as the one referenced by the view that was dropped, you can again retrieve data from the underlying new table through the view.

Listing 10.22 drops a table upon which a view is based. As shown in the following example, sp_help confirms that the view remains defined even though you have deleted the table upon which it's based. When the view is used in a SELECT statement, an error is returned because the table doesn't exist. After the table is re-created and rows are loaded from an existing table, the view is used to reference rows for the underlying new table.

Part
II
Ch
10

Listing 10.22   View Objects Are Independent of the Tables on Which They Are Based

```
drop table employees3
go
This command did not return data, and it did not return any rows
sp_help namebadge3
go
Name                      Owner             Type
. . . . . . . . . . . . . . . . . . . . . . . . . . . . .   . . . . . . . . . . . . . . . .
namebadge3                dbo               view
Data_located_on_segment When_created
. . . . . . . . . . . . . . . . . . . . .   . . . . . . . . . . . . . . . . . . . . . . . . .
not applicable            Oct 2 1994 11:45AM
Column_name Type Length Nulls Default_name Rule_name
. . . . . . . . . . . . .   . . . . .   . . . . . . . . . . . . .   . . . . . . . . . . . . .   .
name        char  25     0     (null)       (null)
badge       int   4      0     (null)       (null)
No defined keys for this object.
select * from namebadge3
go
Msg 208, Level 16, State 1
Invalid object name 'employees3'.
Msg 4413, Level 16, State 1
View resolution could not succeed because the previously mentioned
objects, upon which the view directly or indirectly relies, do not
currently exist.  These objects need to be re-created for the view
 to be usable.
create table employees3
```

continues

Listing 10.22   Continued

```
(name char(25),department char(20),badge int)
go
This command did not return data, and it did not return any rows
insert into employees3
select * from employees
go
(12 row(s) affected)
select * from namebadge3
where name='Sally Springer'
go
name                    badge
----------------------- -----------
Sally Springer          9998
(1 row(s) affected)
```

If you use a SELECT clause in a view with an asterisk (*) to specify columns, the new columns added to the table with an ALTER TABLE statement won't be available in the old view. The new table columns are made available only if the view is dropped and re-created.

In Listing 10.23, a view is defined that uses an asterisk (*) in the SELECT clause of a SELECT statement to reference all columns of the Employees table. After an additional column is added to the table with an ALTER TABLE statement, the view doesn't display the NULL entries in the new column that was added to the table. The new Wageclass column is available through the view only after the view is dropped and re-created.

Listing 10.23   Views Are Static in Nature and Take into Account those Columns Available When the View is Initially Created

```
sp_helptext sales3
go
text
------------------
create view sales3
as
select * from employees3
where department='SALES'
go
(1 row(s) affected)
select * from sales3
go
name              department       badge
----------------- ---------------- -----------
Fred Sanders      SALES            1051
Bob Orieda        SALES            1834
(2 row(s) affected)
alter table employees3
add wageclass int null
```

```
go
This command did not return data, and it did not return any rows
select * from sales3
go
name                    department          badge
------------------------ -------------------- -----------
Fred Sanders            SALES               1051
Bob Orieda              SALES               1834
(2 row(s) affected)
select * from employees3
where department='SALES'
go
------------------------ -------------------- -----------
Fred Sanders            SALES               1051        (null)
Bob Orieda              SALES               1834        (null)
(2 row(s) affected)
drop view sales3
go
This command did not return data, and it did not return any rows
create view sales3 as
select * from employees3
where department='SALES'
go
This command did not return data, and it did not return any rows
select * from sales3
go
name                    department          badge   wageclass
------------------------ ------------------- ----------- -----------
Fred Sanders            SALES               1051    (null)
Bob Orieda              SALES               1834    (null)
(2 row(s) affected)
```

Understanding the Advanced Use of Views

After you've worked through views for a bit, you should consider some additional helpful, though perhaps less obvious, uses for them. Views are a powerful component of SQL Server, and they offer the capability for you to leverage your SQL Server implementation by enhancing everything from the user experience to security on the system.

In the next sections, you'll see how you can implement views to achieve more advanced cuts at your information, and how you can use them to enhance the security of the information on your system.

Security Management with Views

It might not seem like security comes into play too much with views, but indeed it's one of the most frequent uses you'll have for them. Whether your intent is to protect the data from users or users from themselves, you'll do well to look into implementing a solid array of views and supporting functions.

The first approach to SQL Server security is, of course, the setting of permissions at the user and group level. This allows you to lock down specific tables and columns, giving you a great deal of protection for the system. One of the drawbacks to this method is that users accessing your database with other than your expected applications may run into trouble. This results in error messages when you've protected a table's columns.

When you're just starting the information analysis of a table, you'll often find that you issue a `SELECT * FROM tablename` statement. This statement will typically retrieve all rows and all columns from the table so you can determine how to lay out and request the information you need from the table.

If you issue this type of statement against a table that has permissions denied on a given column or columns, you'll receive an error message and no information will be returned.

`SELECT permission denied on column...`

This can be frustrating for the users if they receive this message and are not aware of the columns that are in the table. If they don't know the columns, they'll be forced to refer to your documentation, or they'll need to talk with support staff to determine the columns available and the correct statement to retrieve them.

You can avoid all of this by creating views and letting users gain access to information using the views, rather than directly querying the underlying tables. As you've seen throughout this chapter, the views have the added advantage of being able to hide database relationship complexities from the user as well.

When you create a view, and select only the columns that accurately reflect the users privilege level to the information, they will be able to use the `SELECT *` approach. This will eliminate the error message and will keep your database information most accessible to the user.

You can further lock down the information by mixing a series of views and stored procedures. By creating views as read-only, you can then force users to do updates and new record insertions using stored procedures. Since they're using stored procedures, you can control how records are modified, perform checks on the incoming information, and more.

▶ **See** Chapter 14, "Managing Stored Procedures and Using Flow-Control Statements," for additional information about creating and managing stored procedures, **p.403**.

For extreme situations, you can actually create stored procedures that act as views on your tables. These stored procedures are simple and take the form of your `SELECT` statement as the content of the stored procedure. When you do this, you can even remove the `SELECT` permissions on the table. Users will need only to have execute permissions for the stored procedures. This is the ultimate lock-down approach for your tables, but it doesn't come without a price.

For example, you'll have to create stored procedures to do all operations that relate to the tables in your system. This means even the simple things like standard insert operations and allowable browsing of the tables will have to be programmed. In most installations, this isn't necessary, but there will undoubtedly be extreme cases where you need absolute control.

One drawback to this is that your users will have a much more difficult time just browsing the tables from other applications. For example, from Excel, without some alternative approaches, the user won't be able to use the powerful features that are built into the application that enable browsing of ODBC databases. The same may be true of other third-party applications.

> **TIP**
>
> When you're creating a tightly managed, secure system, if you need to test user rights you can use the SETUSER statement to impersonate another user. By doing so, you can "pretend" you're that user, test access points, and then return to your typical developer role and fine tune the process.
>
> In order to use this statement, you must be the SA or the DBO.
>
> The SETUSER statement has the syntax:
>
> SETUSER *username* [with noreset]
>
> When you execute this statement, the rights associated with the *username* you specify will become your rights. You can create objects, test your access levels, and so on. Anything this user can or cannot do, you'll be able to mimic.
>
> The statement remains in effect until you issue a SETUSER statement for either a different user or with no parameters, or until you USE a different database, whichever comes first.

Reality Check

Views are a powerful component available to you for use in many different circumstances. Views are an inexpensive resource as they don't store information other than the statements that control the content represented by the view. At IKON, we use views daily in our applications as a way of removing the requirement to do a join at the application level. Since we can use the view to accomplish the join, it saves coding in the application, and your application can be consistent in how it works with the database tables.

One of the key applications in which we've implemented views includes the timekeeping system. This system uses SQL Server as the backend database engine, and it has both Visual Basic and Access components on the client side. The client applications are used to enter timeslips and query the user's database of past slips. The Access application uses different views in presenting users the information in the system at the administrative level. The view makes it possible to use relatively simple applications on the user side without regard for the underlying relationships between the tables.

Additionally, new views have been created to make it easier to query the database with other applications. From Excel to custom-built Visual Basic applications, the view ensures that the database information is selected in the most expeditious manner and that it uses all available indexes. There are some drawbacks to views; for example, if they contain columns not required for the calling routines, they can bog down the processing unnecessarily.

In one instance, a view was taking a substantial amount of time to produce the desired dataset. When a new view was created with a smaller target dataset, it was found that the original dataset contained several columns that were not needed. By removing the columns, it also removed the requirement for joins to support the columns, speeding up the query and results-return process.

In short, and within reason, don't hesitate to create a new view to support a specific program or query process. The overhead is low, the performance payback is potentially high, and you can always drop the view later without impacting your data.

From Here...

In this chapter you've learned to create virtual tables that use a stored SELECT statement to create a subset of the rows and columns, or a combination of the rows and columns, of one or more database tables. You've also learned to change previously defined views using the SQL Enterprise Manager and display and remove views when they're no longer needed. Finally, you learned to add, update, and delete rows through views, applying the changes to the underlying tables from which the views are defined.

For specific information about the topics mentioned in this chapter, see the following chapters:

- Chapter 6, "Creating Database Tables and Using Datatypes," discusses the treatment of NULLs as column values, as well as the column datatypes.

- Chapter 8, "Adding, Changing, and Deleting Information in Tables," teaches you how to combine rows from multiple tables in the same query, including the use of COMPUTE and COMPUTE BY.

- Chapter 11, "Managing and Using Indexes and Keys," teaches you how to create and use keys and indexes and how to constrain rows and columns to unique values.

- Chapter 15, "Creating and Managing Triggers," teaches you how to create and use triggers to maintain referential integrity in the database.

Managing and Using Indexes and Keys

One of the most important responsibilities of a database designer is to correctly define a database table for optimal performance. SQL Server's basic design of a table doesn't define how data is to be accessed or stored physically, beyond the data-type constraints and any referential constraint placed on a column or columns designated as PRIMARY KEY. Instead, SQL Server provides a mechanism of indexes or keys to a table that help SQL Server optimize responses to queries.

Without an index, SQL Server must *table scan*, or read every row in a table, before it can know the answer to any given query. In large tables this is obviously an expensive option for the server to take. Indexes provide a way for SQL Server to organize pointers to the data required. An index in a database works the same way as an index in a reference book. Like an index in a book, an index in a database is a list of "important" values that have references to pages in the database table containing the information that matches the index value. This allows the database to read from a typically smaller list of index pages that will, in turn, point to the data to answer any given request. ∎

What indexes are for and how to create them

Indexes are used to make it easier and faster to retrieve data. They can be created at the same time a table is created, or they can be added to the table at a later time.

The different kinds of indexes that can be created

There are several types of indexes. Each index tracks data and stores that tracking information in different ways. Some indexes also affect the way the data is physically stored in the database.

What keys are for and how to create them

Rows of data contain unique values that can be used to identify each individual row. The columns that contain these unique values are called key columns. For key columns to be guaranteed unique, they must be declared when creating a table. Key column definitions can also be added or modified after a table is created.

Defining Indexes

Indexes are SQL Server's internal method of organizing the data in a table in such a way that it can be retrieved optimally. Optimal, in this case, refers to the quickest way. Indexes are collections of unique values in a given table and their corresponding list of pointers to the pages of data where those values are physically represented in a table.

At a high level, indexes are a shorthand way of the database recording information that it's storing in tables. Indexes are just another kind of object in the database and have storage needs like tables. Just as tables require pages of data to store their rows in, indexes require pages to store their summary data in. The advantage of an index is that, generally, it reduces the number of I/Os required to reach any given piece of data in a table.

When you create an index in SQL Server, you tell the database to scan the table, gather the discrete values in the particular column(s) being indexed, and then write a list of data pages and row identifiers to the index page that match the value being indexed. This allows the server to scan a list of index pages before choosing to scan the whole table, looking for matching data.

Understanding General Index Guidelines

Working with Indexes is a test and test again proposition. You're faced with many different variables that you'll need to weigh against one another in terms of performance and the end-user experience. For example, the indexes you create will generally be driven by the data-retrieval habits of the applications on the system. These approaches to gathering information from your tables will certainly be a key factor in which columns you index.

Optimizing Indexes Based on Usage Patterns

Just when you thought this might be easy, along comes the problem of analyzing only the retrieval situations you'll be supporting. Not only must you consider retrieval but also insertion and update processes. This might seem strange at first, but when you think about what's happening behind the scenes, you'll see that the difference between a query, update, and insert application and an application that is query-only is night and day.

When indexes are updated, that's when the work happens. This is a simple, but very important, rule of thumb. Therefore, if you have a system where you're doing a lot of inserts, you'll do well to limit the indexes that are active on the database tables. When records are inserted or updated, the indexes must be updated as well. In fact, when you update a record in SQL Server, you have the same amount of overhead associated with the transaction as you do with an insert. In general, the magic number on these types of systems is five indexes. As you exceed this number, the performance hit you'll take can be excessive.

On the other hand, if you have a query-centric system, one where few inserts are happening and the focus is more on the analysis of existing information, you can implement all the indexes you need to improve query performance. Your limiting factor in this case becomes disk space, since each index will require additional database space.

Keys to a Successful Index

If you take the time to create an index, make sure you also take the time to determine what you are targeting with the index. This means that you should understand what types of queries will be made to the database. Specifically, this means understanding what columns will be in the WHERE clauses of the SELECT statements.

As you'll see later, when you create an index, it's created by indicating what fields you want to include in the index. The key is that when SQL Server considers an index, one of the field qualifiers to the SELECT statement *must* be the first column in the index. If not, the index will simply not be used.

For example, if you have an index on the ZIP code and state fields of your database, in that order, and you query the database for a record based on state, the index will not be used. SQL Server will have to work out a different means of retrieving the row(s) that meet your request. Depending on a number of factors, this can mean a table scan, the enemy of performance.

On the other hand, if your SELECT statement queries only on ZIP code, it can use the index. This is regardless of the fact that the index also includes the state. SQL Server will ignore that component of the index and work on without it. Your application will still benefit greatly from the index.

Part
II

Ch
11

N O T E   SQL Server manages the decision about what indexes to use to fulfill a given query in a series of pages that summarize the distribution of information in the table. This summary information is how SQL Server determines whether a table scan or an indexed query will be the fastest and best way to satisfy a query.

If you create your table *with* data, this summary information is automatically established for you. If, on the other hand, you create the table and then add data to the table, the summary page will not be updated. In this case, and any case where you're adding, changing, or deleting 10-20% of the information in a given table, you need to update the summary information. You do this by issuing an UPDATE STATISTICS command. The syntax is

Update statistics *table* [,*index*]

where table is the name of the table you want to base the updated summary information on, and index is an optional argument indicating the specific index you want to update statistics for.

This command is never a destructive step and can help performance significantly by allowing SQL Server to learn from the real data in your database. ■

Choosing a Good Index Candidate

First, it's important to understand that you cannot create an index on a column with a datatype of BIT, TEXT, or IMAGE. That said, what general things are helpful to look for in determining what columns to index?

There are some good general rules to follow in looking for good index candidates. (See Table 11.1)

Table 11.1 Good Index Candidates

Description	Notes
Foreign keys	Tables with foreign keys are prime candidates for indexes. There are very few cases where you should *not* have an index on a primary key. It helps the lookup times immensely.
Large results-set queries	For the queries that will be returning a large dataset, you should index whenever possible. Note that this typically breaks the rules of good client/server methodology. You want to always be looking for ways to decrease the size of the results set, not support large datasets. Nonetheless, the requirement will undoubtedly arise and you'll want to support it well with an index.
Order by and group support	Columns that are referenced in these clauses will benefit greatly from an index.

Creating Indexes

SQL Server has two methods of creating indexes. There is a graphical method provided in SQL Enterprise Manager and a Transact-SQL interface using the CREATE INDEX statement. Only the table's owner can create an index on a table.

N O T E SQL Enterprise Manager has a limitation when you create indexes through it that you can't specify a data segment on which to create the index. Moving indexes on to different data segments can significantly improve performance on nonclustered indexes because multiple I/O threads can be used to read the data from the index and data pages concurrently. Use the CREATE INDEX statement in ISQL/w to create an index if you need to specify a segment for the index data. ■

Creating an Index with SQL Enterprise Manager To create an index using SQL Enterprise Manager, follow these steps:

1. Run SQL Enterprise Manager from the Microsoft SQL Server 6.5 group. Figure 11.1 shows the main screen shortly after the startup of SQL Enterprise Manager.
2. Select the server, database, and table that you want to work on. See Figure 11.2.

FIG. 11.1

SQL Enterprise Manager's Explorer view after having just been started. Note that no server is selected.

FIG. 11.2

You use the Explorer-type view from within the Enterprise Manager to select the table objects you want to work with.

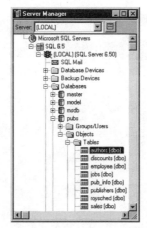

3. From the <u>M</u>anage menu choose <u>I</u>ndexes. The Manage Indexes dialog box, shown in Figure 11.3, appears.

4. Select the New Index from the <u>I</u>ndex combo box. This clears the Index combo box, enabling you to enter the new index name. The Columns In Inde<u>x</u> list is also cleared.

5. Enter `fk_au_id` as the index name, highlight the au_id column, and click the <u>A</u>dd button. Select the check boxes Unique <u>K</u>eys and Ig<u>n</u>ore Duplicate Keys. See Figure 11.4.

FIG. 11.3

The authors table is selected in the top-left combo box, and the aunmind index is selected in the top-right combo box.

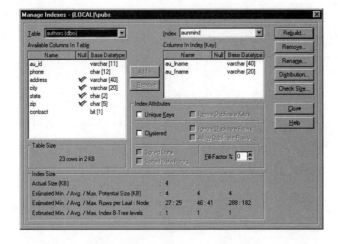

FIG. 11.4

The Manage Indexes dialog box is ready to build a new index.

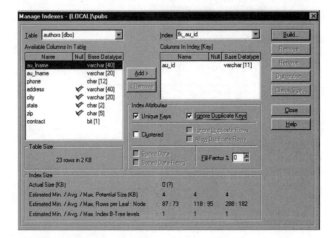

 TIP Prefacing index names with *pk* for primary key or *fk* for foreign key makes it easier to identify the index type without having to inspect its properties.

6. Click the Build button to build the index. A message box appears, asking whether the index should be built now or scheduled as a task to run later. See Figure 11.5. Choose the option that's appropriate for your environment.

Creating an Index with *CREATE INDEX* The Transact-SQL command CREATE INDEX is used by SQL Enterprise Manager to perform the index creation when the Build button is clicked in the Manage Indexes dialog box. The syntax for CREATE INDEX is shown in Listing 11.1.

FIG. 11.5

The Index Build message box seeks confirmation of whether the index should be built immediately or scheduled as a task.

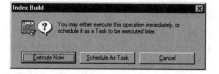

Listing 11.1 Syntax Listing for CREATE INDEX

```
CREATE [UNIQUE] [CLUSTERED ¦ NONCLUSTERED] INDEX index_name
      ON [[database.]owner.]table_name (column_name [, column_name]...)
[WITH
      [FILLFACTOR = x]
      [[,] IGNORE_DUP_KEY]
      [[,] {SORTED_DATA ¦ SORTED_DATA_REORG}]
      [[,] {IGNORE_DUP_ROW ¦ ALLOW_DUP_ROW}]]
[ON segment_name]
```

The options for the Transact-SQL command CREATE INDEX are covered in the following sections.

UNIQUE If an index is created as UNIQUE, SQL Server disallows duplicate values in the index and, therefore, stops a client from inserting a record into the base table. This is the most common use of an index to enforce integrity on a table. Unique indexes can't be created on tables that have duplicate values in the columns being indexed; the duplicate data must be removed first. If enabled, the IGNORE_DUP_KEY option, described below, allows UPDATE or INSERT statements, affecting several rows, that modify index keys to complete, even if the new index key values become duplicates. The duplicate values will be rolled back and the transaction will continue. No error will be generated.

N O T E If you define an index as being unique, and you're declaring it on a column that allows NULL values, you'll run into problems as the table becomes populated. This is because SQL Server will allow a single NULL value in the column during indexing, but when the second NULL column value is inserted it will fail. This is because the column will allow only one value (UNIQUE), and in this case, NULLs are consider a distinct and unique value, of which there can be only one.

In short, if you're defining a UNIQUE key, be sure that none of the columns that are included in the key allow NULLs. ■

CLUSTERED A *clustered index* is a special index that forces SQL Server to store the table data in the exact order of the index. Using a clustered index, to physically store the data in the table in a particular way, can greatly improve access performance to the table. Data requested from tables that are scanned repeatedly, by the index key value for an individual record or set of records in a range, can be found very quickly because SQL Server knows that the data for the index page is right next to it. Any further values are guaranteed to be in the following data pages.

You should always have an index on the table defined as CLUSTERED. This will greatly improve performance by keeping the database in a managed state, but, moreover, it allows you to reuse space from deleted rows. This is because a clustered index will reclaim space in the index and data pages as new rows are inserted.

If CLUSTERED isn't specified in the CREATE INDEX statement, the index is assumed to be NONCLUSTERED.

There can be only one clustered index per table because the data can be in only one physical order.

CAUTION

When you create a clustered index, since the information in the table is physically moved, the entire table is locked, preventing access from any client application. If you're indexing a production table, consider using the Scheduled Index Build option and run the creation of the index after hours.

CAUTION

Specifying a segment for a clustered index to be placed on will actually move the table data too. Be careful using the ON *segment_name* keyword when creating a clustered index. You must have approximately 1.2 times the space required for the entire table available on the target segment for the clustered index and data. If you do not, the segment free space will be filled and a new segment will need to be created. SQL Server won't warn you before index creation that the segment space is inadequate because it has no way of knowing or accurately estimating the size required for the index.

NONCLUSTERED This is the default index type and means that SQL Server will create an index whose pages of index data contain pointers to the actual pages of table data in the database. You can create up to 249 nonclustered indexes in a table.

index_name An index name must be unique by table. This means that the same index name can be given to two indexes, provided that they're indexing different base tables in the database. Index names must follow standard SQL Server naming conventions for objects.

table_name *table_name* is the table that's going to be indexed.

column_name This is the column that's being indexed. If more than one column is placed here, a composite or compound index is created. Multiple columns should be separated by spaces. You can specify up to 16 columns to create a composite key, but the maximum width of the data types being combined can't exceed 256 bytes.

FILLFACTOR = x Specifying a FILLFACTOR on an index tells SQL Server how to "pack" the index data into the index data pages. FILLFACTOR tells SQL Server to preserve space on the index data page for other similar rows that are expected for the same index keys or similar index key values.

CAUTION

The FILLFACTOR should rarely be used. It is included solely for fine-tuning purposes. Even for fine-tuning, it should be used only if future changes in the data can be made with accuracy.

Specifying a FILLFACTOR for frequently inserted database tables can improve performance because SQL Server won't have to split data onto separate data pages when the index information is too big to fit on a single page. Page splitting is a costly operation in terms of I/O and should be avoided if possible.

The number of the FILLFACTOR refers to the percentage of free space that should be preserved on each index page.

A small FILLFACTOR is useful for creating indexes for tables that don't yet contain their complete dataset. For example, if you know that a table is going to have many more values than it does now and you want SQL Server to preallocate space in the index pages for those values so that it won't need to *page split*, specify a low FILLFACTOR of about 10. A page split occurs when the index fills up so that no further values will fit in the current 2K data page. Consequently, SQL Server "splits" the page in two and puts references to the newly created page in the original page.

A high FILLFACTOR will force more frequent page splits because SQL Server will have no room on the index page to add any additional values that may be necessary if a record is inserted into the table. A FILLFACTOR of 100 will force SQL Server to completely fill the index pages. This option is good for highly concurrent, read-only tables. It's inadvisable, however, for tables that are inserted or updated frequently. Every insert will cause a page split, and many of the updates, if key values are updated, will also cause page splits.

If no FILLFACTOR is specified, the server default, usually 0, is used. To change the server default, use the system-stored procedure sp_configure.

▶ **See** "Displaying and Setting Server Options," **p. 379**

Be careful when specifying a FILLFACTOR for a clustered index. It will directly affect the amount of space required for the storage of the table data. Because a clustered index is bound to a table, as the physical order of the table data is mapped to the order of the clustered index, a FILLFACTOR on the index will space each data page of the table apart from the others according to the value requested. This can consume substantial amounts of disk space if the FILLFACTOR is sparse.

N O T E Specifying a FILLFACTOR when creating an index on a table without data has no effect because SQL Server has no way of placing the data in the index correctly. For tables that have dynamic datasets that need to be indexed with an index specifying a FILLFACTOR, you should rebuild indexes periodically to make sure that SQL Server is actually populating the index pages correctly. ■

Part

II

Ch

11

IGNORE_DUP_KEY When SQL is executed, this option controls SQL Server's behavior that causes duplicate records to exist in a table with a unique index defined on it. By default, SQL Server will always reject a duplicate record and return an error. This option allows you to get SQL Server to continue processing as though this isn't an error condition.

This configuration option can be useful in highly accessed tables where the general trend of the data is more important than the actual specifics. It shouldn't be used for tables where each individual record is important, however, unless application code is providing appropriate referential constraints to the data. If multiple records are affected by an update or insert statement, and the statement causes some records to create duplicates, the statement will be allowed to continue. Those records that created duplicates will be rolled back with no error returned.

> **CAUTION**
>
> When enabling `IGNORE_DUP_KEY`, be careful that you don't lose required data due to unwanted updates occurring. If `IGNORE_DUP_KEY` is enabled for a unique index and an update is done to data that causes duplicate records to exist, not only will the duplicates be rejected by the update but the original records will also be removed. This is because SQL Server performs updates by deleting the record and then reinserting it. The reinsertion will fail, due to the duplicity of the record, so neither the original record nor the updated record will exist.

SORTED_DATA SQL Server uses the `SORTED_DATA` keyword to speed up index creation for clustered indexes. By specifying `SORTED_DATA`, you're telling SQL Server that the data to be indexed is already physically sorted in the order of the index. SQL Server will verify that the order is indeed correct during index creation by checking that each indexed item is greater than the previous item. If any item isn't found to be sorted, SQL Server will report an error and abort index creation. If this option isn't specified, SQL Server will sort the data for you as it would do normally.

Using the `SORTED_DATA` keyword greatly reduces the amount of time and space required to create a clustered index. The time is reduced because SQL Server doesn't spend any time ordering the data. The required space is reduced because SQL Server no longer needs to create a temporary workspace in which to place the sorted values before creating the index.

SORTED_DATA_REORG `SORTED_DATA_REORG` is similar to `SORTED_DATA` in that it helps SQL Server's overall performance by making the data physically reside in the database table in the order of the index. The `SORTED_DATA_REORG` keyword tells SQL Server to physically reorder the data in the order of the index. This can be especially useful on nonclustered indexed tables on which you want to reduce the number of page splits due to data no longer being in adjacent data pages. This will help the data be physically adjacent in the database and will reduce the number of nonsequential physical I/Os required to fetch data, which in turn improves performance.

IGNORE_DUP_ROW This option is for creating a nonunique clustered index. If enabled at index creation time on a table with duplicate data in it, SQL Server will:

- Create the index
- Delete the duplicate values
- Return an error message to the calling process indicating the failure. At this point, the calling process should initiate a ROLLBACK to restore the data.

If data is inserted into or updated in the table after the index is created, SQL Server will:

- Accept any nonduplicate values
- Delete the duplicate values, and possibly the original record, if a duplicate occurs during an update
- Return an error message to the calling process indicating the failure. At this point, the calling process should initiate a ROLLBACK to restore the data.

▶ **See** the section titled *"ROLLBACK TRAN,"* in Chapter 12 For more information on rolling back transactions, **p. 355**

N O T E   This option has no effect on nonclustered indexes. SQL Server internally assigns identifiers to the records being indexed and doesn't have to manage the physical order of the data according to the clustering. ▪

ALLOW_DUP_ROW   This option can't be set on an index that's allowed to IGNORE_DUP_ROW. It controls behavior for inserting or updating records in a nonunique clustered index. If ALLOW_DUP_ROW is enabled, no errors are returned and no data is affected if multiple duplicate records are created in a clustered index.

ON segment_name   Specifying a segment for the index to reside on allows the placement of an index on a different segment of the data. This will improve performance of nonclustered indexes because multiple I/O handlers can be used to read and write from the index and data segments concurrently.

Clustered indexes that have a segment name specified will move the data that's being indexed, as well as the index, to the indicated segment.

Understanding Statistics

The value of an index for helping SQL Server resolve a query largely depends on how accurately the index's data reflects the actual data in the database. SQL Server maintains heuristical, or trend, statistics on the data that the index contains to help it choose the appropriate index that will yield the least number of I/Os to get to the actual table data. Clustered indexes, when available, will almost always be chosen as a valid key over nonclustered indexes. Clustered indexes are favored because there is no physical I/O after the data is found in the index since it's on the same page.

SQL Server's statistics-gathering engine is on an as-needed basis, in that the statistics are maintained only when an index is built or the statistics on those indexes are forced to be updated by the UPDATE STATISTICS statement. SQL Server doesn't maintain statistics on the fly

Part

II

Ch

11

purely for performance reasons. The additional overhead of maintaining the statistics dynamically generally isn't considered advantageous to fetching the data because it will consume on average more resources than would have been saved by the additional data. SQL Server's statistics indicate trends in the data and don't necessarily represent every key data element. These trends are what SQL Server uses to determine the best index to use.

The exception to when dynamic index statistics management would be beneficial is when an index is created on a table with no data in it. SQL Server has no way of knowing what the trends in the data are and, as a result, makes very basic assumptions of normal distribution. These assumptions are often very wrong after a number of records are added to the table. This results in SQL Server doing a table scan even though there's an appropriate index. In this situation, perform an UPDATE STATISTICS on the table, and the index's distribution information will be updated.

To determine the last time statistics information was updated on a given index, the DBCC command SHOW_STATISTICS can be used. An example of its use as shown in Listing 11.2:

Listing 11.2 DBCC SHOW STATISTICS Results

```
/*-------------------------------
dbcc show_statistics( authors, fk_au_id )
---------------------------*/
Updated              Rows         Steps         Density
------------------   ----------   ----------   ---------
Dec 10 1995  2:20PM  23           22            0.0434783

(1 row(s) affected)

All density              Columns
----------------------   -------
0.0434783                au_id

(1 row(s) affected)

Steps
----------
172-32-1176
213-46-8915
238-95-7766
267-41-2394
274-80-9391
341-22-1782
409-56-7008
427-17-2319
472-27-2349
486-29-1786
527-72-3246
648-92-1872
672-71-3249
712-45-1867
722-51-5454
724-08-9931
```

```
724-80-9391
756-30-7391
807-91-6654
846-92-7186
893-72-1158
899-46-2035

(22 row(s) affected)

DBCC execution completed. If DBCC printed error messages, see your
System Administrator.
```

In the output from the DBCC SHOW STATISTICS command, you can see that the statistics have been kept up-to-date as of December 10th. In the second example, shown in Listing 11.3, the authors2 table is re-created with the same structures as authors, and the data is copied to it.

On the CD

Listing 11.3   11_03.SQL—Creating the Table authors2 and Its Indexes

```
CREATE TABLE authors2
(
      au_id id NOT NULL ,
      au_lname varchar (40) NOT NULL ,
      au_fname varchar (20) NOT NULL ,
      phone char (12) NOT NULL ,
      address varchar (40) NULL ,
      city varchar (20) NULL ,
      state char (2) NULL ,
      zip char (5) NULL ,
      contract bit NOT NULL
)
GO

 CREATE  INDEX aunmind ON dbo.authors2(au_lname, au_fname)
 WITH  FILLFACTOR = 5
GO

 CREATE  UNIQUE  INDEX barny ON dbo.authors2(au_id) WITH  IGNORE_DUP_KEY
GO

 CREATE  UNIQUE  INDEX fk_au_id ON dbo.authors2(au_id) WITH  IGNORE_DUP_KEY
GO

insert into authors2 select * from authors
GO
```

The previous listing was generated by doing a SQL script generation using Microsoft SQL Enterprise Manager and then changing the table name from authors to authors2. The same DBCC command reports very different results, because the STATISTICS are out of date as shown in Listing 11.4 :

Part
II

Ch
11

Listing 11.4   DBCC Statistics Output Listing Example

```
/*----------------------------
dbcc show_statistics( authors2, fk_au_id )
----------------------------*/
Updated                 Rows        Steps        Density
-------------------- ----------- ----------- -------
                NULL 23          0            0.0

(1 row(s) affected)

All density             Columns
----------------------- -------
0.0                     au_id

(1 row(s) affected)

Steps
----------

(0 row(s) affected)

DBCC execution completed. If DBCC printed error messages, see your
System Administrator.
```

Performing an UPDATE STATISTICS on the authors2 table and then doing the DBCC command yields the identical results to the initial DBCC on the authors table, shown in Listing 11.5:

Listing 11.5   Update Statistics Output Listing Example

```
/*----------------------------
update statistics authors2
go
dbcc show_statistics( authors2, fk_au_id )
----------------------------*/
Updated                 Rows        Steps        Density
-------------------- ----------- ----------- ---------
Dec 11 1995 12:08PM  23          22           0.0434783

(1 row(s) affected)

All density             Columns
----------------------- -------
0.0434783               au_id

(1 row(s) affected)

Steps
----------
172-32-1176
213-46-8915
238-95-7766
267-41-2394
```

```
274-80-9391
341-22-1782
409-56-7008
427-17-2319
472-27-2349
486-29-1786
527-72-3246
648-92-1872
672-71-3249
712-45-1867
722-51-5454
724-08-9931
724-80-9391
756-30-7391
807-91-6654
846-92-7186
893-72-1158
899-46-2035

(22 row(s) affected)

DBCC execution completed. If DBCC printed error messages, see your
System Administrator.
```

Updating Statistics   SQL Server has two ways of updating the statistics that relate to a table. The graphical way can be performed using SQL Enterprise Manager. The Transact-SQL command is UPDATE STATISTICS.

Using SQL Enterprise Manager to Update Statistics   To use SQL Enterprise Manager to update statistics on a table, follow these steps:

1. Launch SQL Enterprise Manager from the Microsoft SQL Server 6.5 group.

2. Select the server, database, and table that you want to work on.

3. From the Manage menu choose Indexes. The Manage Indexes dialog box, shown in Figure 11.6, appears.

FIG. 11.6
The authors table is selected in the Table box, and the aunmind index is selected in the Index box.

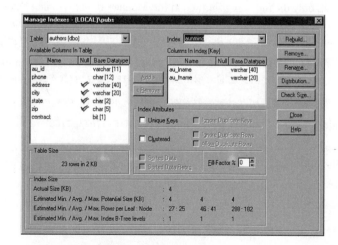

4. Click the Distribution button to view the Index Distribution Statistics dialog box. See Figure 11.7.

FIG. 11.7

This dialog box uses the output of DBCC *SHOW_STATISTICS* to display the information.

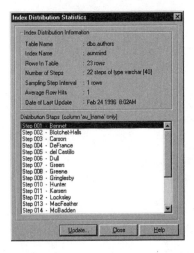

5. Click the Update button to update the statistics. A message box appears, asking whether the statistics should be updated now or scheduled as a task to run later. See Figure 11.8. Choose the option that's appropriate for your environment.

FIG. 11.8

The Update Distribution Statistics message box confirms whether the index statistics should be updated immediately or scheduled as a task.

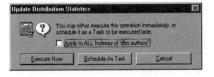

By default, only the index highlighted in the Manage Indexes dialog box will have its statistics updated. If you want to update all of the indexes on the table selected, check the option Apply to ALL Indexes Of check box before either scheduling the task or executing it.

Using UPDATE STATISTICS   The UPDATE STATISTICS statement is used to update the index statistics on a table or index. The syntax for UPDATE STATISTICS is as follows:

UPDATE STATISTICS [[*database.*]*owner.*]*table_name* [*index_name*]

The options for the Transact-SQL command UPDATE STATISTICS are as follows:

- *table_name*—The name of the table that the index resides on. If no index is specified, all the indexes on the table are updated at the same time.
- *index_name*—The name of the index that's to have its statistics updated.

NOTE Performing an UPDATE STATISTICS on a database table can affect the plan that a stored procedure has generated for accessing data. Because stored procedures are compiled and stored in the procedure cache when they're first executed, they can store invalid access paths to data based on the index statistics at the time the procedure was first run. To force a stored procedure to refresh its access path, use the system-stored procedure sp_recompile and pass the table that was updated as a parameter. For example, sp_recompile authors will force all the procedures that use the authors table to be recompiled the next time they're executed. ■

Forcing the Use of a Particular Index   If SQL Server fails to pick an index that you know should provide better performance than the index it chose, you can force the use of an index by specifying it in the FROM clause. To force an index, use the *optimizer hints* or (INDEX = ...) section of the SELECT statement's syntax. In simplified syntax, here's a SELECT statement:

```
SELECT ...
FROM table_name (INDEX = n) /* optimizer hints are placed after the table */
...
```

▶ **See** Chapter 7, "Retrieving Data with Transact-SQL," for more information on the syntax of SELECT statements, **p. 175**

The INDEX keyword tells SQL Server to use the index specified by the numeric *n*. If *n* equals zero (0), SQL Server will table scan. If *n* equals one (1), SQL Server will use the clustered index if one is in the table. The other values of *n* are determined by the number of indexes on the table.

Part
II
Ch
11

TIP An index name can also be used in the optimizer hint instead of an identifying id number.

Listing 11.6 shows SQL Server using the optimizer hints when selecting from the authors table.

Listing 11.6   11_02.SQL—The Same SELECT Statement Performed Four Times to Demonstrate the Use of a Forced Index

```
/* Turn on statistics IO, so that the results can be seen */
set statistics io on
go

/* Basic Select with no hints to show the optimizer
   choosing the clustered index */
Select      AU_ID, AU_FNAME
From  AUTHORS
Where AU_ID between '172-32-1176' and '238-95-7766'
Order By AU_ID
go

/* Force a table scan */
Select      AU_ID, AU_FNAME
From  AUTHORS (INDEX = 0)
Where AU_ID between '172-32-1176' and '238-95-7766'
```

continues

Listing 11.6   Continued

```
Order By AU_ID
go

/* Force the clustered index */
Select      AU_ID, AU_FNAME
From  AUTHORS (INDEX = 1)
Where AU_ID between '172-32-1176' and '238-95-7766'
Order By AU_ID
go

/* Force the first alternate index */
Select      AU_ID, AU_FNAME
From  AUTHORS (INDEX = 2)
Where AU_ID between '172-32-1176' and '238-95-7766'
Order By AU_ID
go
The output is as follows:
AU_ID        AU_FNAME
----------- --------------------
172-32-1176 Johnson
213-46-8915 Marjorie
238-95-7766 Cheryl

(3 row(s) affected)

Table: authors  scan count 1,  logical reads: 1,  physical reads: 0
AU_ID        AU_FNAME
----------- --------------------
172-32-1176 Johnson
213-46-8915 Marjorie
238-95-7766 Cheryl

(3 row(s) affected)

Table: authors  scan count 1,  logical reads: 1,  physical reads: 0
Table: Worktable  scan count 0,  logical reads: 4,  physical reads: 0
AU_ID        AU_FNAME
----------- --------------------
172-32-1176 Johnson
213-46-8915 Marjorie
238-95-7766 Cheryl

(3 row(s) affected)

Table: authors  scan count 1,  logical reads: 2,  physical reads: 0
AU_ID        AU_FNAME
----------- --------------------
172-32-1176 Johnson
213-46-8915 Marjorie
238-95-7766 Cheryl
```

```
(3 row(s) affected)

Table: authors   scan count 1,   logical reads: 29,   physical reads: 0
Table: Worktable   scan count 0,   logical reads: 4,   physical reads: 0
```

> **CAUTION**
>
> The effects of forcing an index are clearly shown in these examples. The last example shows an extremely expensive option being forced on the server. You can cause major performance problems by forcing index use, so it's generally not recommended that you update the indexes.
>
> Forcing index selection in a query is also dangerous if the application code is left unchanged and the indexes are changed or rebuilt. Changing the indexes may cause severe performance degradation due to the forcing of indexes that no longer provide optimal performance.

Displaying Index Information

SQL Server has two ways to show information about indexes. The graphical method is via SQL Enterprise Manager's Index Manager. The command-line method is via the system-stored procedure sp_helpindex and the ODBC stored procedure sp_statistics.

SQL Enterprise Manager's Index Manager has been discussed in detail in previous sections in this chapter. Please refer to the section "Using SQL Enterprise Manager to Update Statistics" for instructions on how to view the statistics associated with an index.

sp_helpindex The system-stored procedure sp_helpindex has been provided to get information about indexes. The syntax for the procedure's use is

```
sp_helpindex table_name
```

table_name should be replaced with an unqualified table name. If the table you want to inquire on isn't in the active database, you must change to the required database before executing this procedure.

sp_helpindex will return the first eight indexes that are found on a database table. In Listing 11.7, sp_helpindex shows all the indexes on the authors table:

Listing 11.7   Reviewing Information About Your Indexes

```
/*--------------------------
sp_helpindex authors
--------------------------*/
index_name              index_description
index_keys
-------------------------------------
UPKCL_auidind           clustered, unique, primary key located on default
au_id
aunmind                 nonclustered located on default
```

continues

Part
II
Ch
11

Listing 11.7 Continued

```
au_lname, au_fname
barny                    nonclustered, ignore duplicate key, unique located on
default au_id
fk_au_id                 nonclustered, ignore duplicate key, unique located on
default au_id

(1 row(s) affected)
```

sp_statistics   sp_statistics is a special stored procedure that has been created to help Microsoft "publish" information for the ODBC interface to the database. Microsoft created this stored procedure so that an ODBC driver could retrieve all the relevant information about an index from a single call to the database. The information returned can be gathered in a number of other ways, but it's often convenient to use sp_statistics to summarize all the relevant information on a table. The syntax for sp_statistics is as follows:

```
sp_statistics table_name [, table_owner] [, table_qualifier]
     [, index_name] [, is_unique]
```

The options for the system-stored procedure sp_statistics are as follows:

- *table_name*—This is the name of the table that you require the index information on.
- *table_owner*—This is the owner of the table.
- *table_qualifier*—This is the name of the database in which the table resides.
- *index_name*—This is the specific index that's being requested.
- *is_unique*—If this parameter is set to 'Y', SQL Server will return only unique indexes on the table.

TIP   Many stored procedures have many parameters. To save time, rather than specify all the parameters, you can indicate a particular one by placing an @ sign in front of the parameter name. An example is
```
sp_statistics authors, @is_unique = 'Y'
```

Dropping Indexes

SQL Server has two ways of dropping indexes on a table. The graphical way can be performed by using SQL Enterprise Manager. The command-line way is by using the SQL statement DROP INDEX.

Using SQL Enterprise Manager to Drop an Index   To use SQL Enterprise Manager to drop an index, follow these steps:

1. Launch SQL Enterprise Manager from the Microsoft SQL Server 6.5 group.
2. Select the server, database, and table that you want to work on.

3. From the Manage menu choose Indexes. The Manage Indexes dialog box appears.

4. Click the Remove button to drop the index required. A message box appears, shown in Figure. 11.9, asking whether the index should be removed now or scheduled as a task to run later. Choose the option that's appropriate for your environment.

FIG. 11.9

The Index Removal message box confirms whether you want the index removed immediately or scheduled as a task.

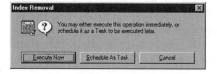

Using the *DROP INDEX* Command   To remove an index using Transact-SQL, use the DROP INDEX statement. The syntax for DROP INDEX is as follows:

```
DROP INDEX [owner.]table_name.index_name
[, [owner.]table_name.index_name...]
```

The options for the Transact-SQL command DROP INDEX are as follows:

- *table_name*—The name of the table that the index resides on. If the user running DROP INDEX is the DBO or SA and the table isn't owned by that user, *table_name* can be prefaced with the *owner* of the table.

- *index_name*—The name of the index to be removed. You can remove multiple indexes by indicating them in the same statement, separated by commas.

The following example drops the barny index on the authors table:

```
Drop Index authors.barny
```

No output is generated after executing this command.

Defining Keys

Keys and indexes are often synonymous in databases, but in SQL Server a slight difference exists between them. In SQL Server, keys can be defined on tables and then used as referential integrity constraints in the same way as the ANSI standard for SQL.

A *primary key* is a unique column or set of columns that defines the rows in the database table. In this sense, a primary key performs the same integrity role as a unique index on a table. Keep in mind, though, that SQL Server allows only one primary key to be defined for a table. On the other hand, there can be many unique indexes. Primary keys enforce uniqueness by creating a unique index on the table on which they're placed.

Foreign keys are columns in a table that correspond to primary keys in other tables. The relationship of a primary key to a foreign key defines the domain of values permissible in the foreign key. The domain of values is equivalent to a distinct list of values in the corresponding primary key. This foreign key domain integrity is a useful way of enforcing referential integrity between associated sets of columns. Foreign keys don't create indexes on the table when the key is created.

Starting in Version 6.0, primary and foreign keys in SQL Server offer much of the functionality that previously had to be coded with triggers in prior versions of SQL Server. In prior versions of SQL Server, primary and foreign keys weren't much more than documentation and were useful to third-party programs that needed to know key information about a table. Keys provide needed functionality and should be used as a referential integrity enforcer.

Adding Primary and Foreign Keys

In SQL Server you can add primary and foreign keys in two ways. The graphical method is performed by using SQL Enterprise Manager. The command-line method is done by using Transact-SQL commands ALTER TABLE...ADD CONSTRAINT, or by specifying PRIMARY/FOREIGN KEY in the CREATE TABLE statement.

Using SQL Enterprise Manager to Add Primary and Foreign Keys   To use SQL Enterprise Manager to add a primary key, follow these steps:

1. Launch SQL Enterprise Manager from the Microsoft SQL Server 6.5 group.

2. Select the server, database, and table that you want to work on.

3. From the Manage menu choose Tables. The Manage Tables screen, shown in Figure 11.10, appears.

FIG. 11.10

The authors table is selected in the top combo box, and a key icon is in the Key column of the au_id row.

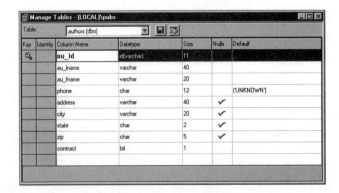

4. Click the Advanced Features toolbar button, with a green plus sign on it, to show the advanced options at the bottom of the window. See Figure 11.11.

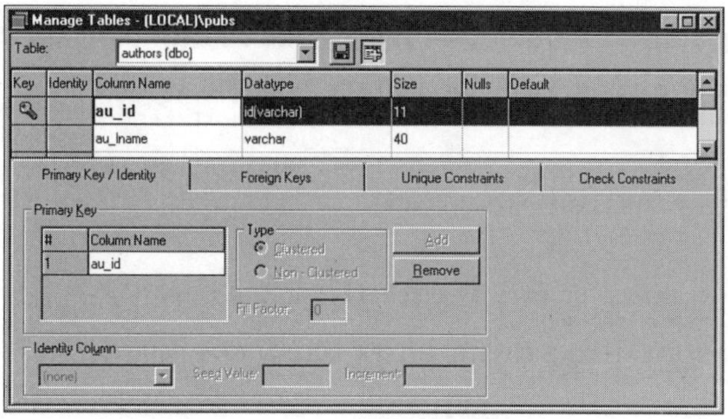

FIG. 11.11

This figure shows SQL Enterprise Manager's Manage Tables window with the Advanced Features visible and the Primary Key/Identity tab active.

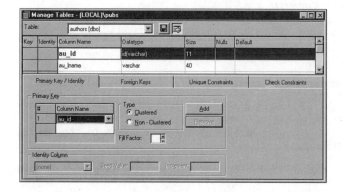

5. Remove the existing primary key by clicking the Remove button and then re-enter the information. See Figure 11.12.

FIG. 11.12

The Primary Key has been reentered and the Add button is now enabled to allow you to create the Primary Key on the table.

Part

II

Ch

11

6. Click the Add button to add the primary key. No message will be shown, but the key icon will return to the table.

7. Click the Save button to save the changes to the table. For the purposes of this exercise, you'll get an error because a foreign key was defined referencing this table. Ignore the error and close the window without saving changes.

Using CREATE TABLE...PRIMARY KEY   The CREATE TABLE syntax has a place for adding a PRIMARY KEY or a FOREIGN KEY in the CONSTRAINT section. A simplified syntax of the CREATE TABLE is shown as follows:

```
CREATE TABLE table_name
( column_name data_type CONSTRAINT ...,...)
```

In Listing 11.8, you'll see tables created in different styles with different types of CONSTRAINTs.

Listing 11.8 11_08.SQL—Creating Tables with Different *CONSTRAINTs*

```
/* create a table where the primary key name is not
   specified, and the database will assign it */

Create TABLE TABLE_A
( COLUMN_A smallint PRIMARY KEY)
go

/* Now create a primary key specifying the name */
Create TABLE TABLE_B
( COLUMN_B smallint CONSTRAINT PK_COLUMN_B PRIMARY KEY)
go

/* Now create a foreign key referencing TABLE_A */
Create TABLE TABLE_C
( COLUMN_C smallint FOREIGN KEY (COLUMN_C) REFERENCES TABLE_A(COLUMN_A))
go

/* Now Create a multi-column primary key */
Create TABLE TABLE_D
( COLUMN_D1 smallint CONSTRAINT PK_D_COLUMNS PRIMARY KEY
(COLUMN_D1, COLUMN_D2), COLUMN_D2 smallint)

go

/* now create a foreign key referencing the multi-column
   primary key */
Create TABLE TABLE_E
( COLUMN_E1 smallint FOREIGN KEY (COLUMN_E1, COLUMN_E2)
                REFERENCES TABLE_D( COLUMN_D1, COLUMN_D2),
   COLUMN_E2 smallint)
go
```

N O T E   When you add a PRIMARY KEY to a table with the ALTER TABLE...ADD CONSTRAINT syntax or in the CREATE TABLE statement, if you don't indicate any parameters for the key, a clustered, unique index is created on the table. To specify a nonclustered index, add NONCLUSTERED immediately after PRIMARY KEY to the statement. ■

Using *ALTER TABLE...ADD CONSTRAINT*   The ALTER TABLE...ADD CONSTRAINT syntax is very similar to the CREATE TABLE logic. In Listing 11.9, the same tables are created, but the ALTER TABLE syntax is used to add the keys.

Listing 11.9 11_09.SQL—Altering Tables to Add Primary and Foreign Keys

```
/* create the table */
Create TABLE TABLE_A
( COLUMN_A smallint)
go
```

```
/* add the basic primary key without specifying the name */
Alter Table TABLE_A ADD PRIMARY KEY (COLUMN_A)
go

/* create the table */
Create TABLE TABLE_B
( COLUMN_B smallint)
go

/* add the primary key specifying the name */
Alter Table TABLE_B ADD CONSTRAINT PK_COLUMN_B PRIMARY KEY (COLUMN_B)
go

/* create the table */
Create TABLE TABLE_C
( COLUMN_C smallint)
go

/* Now create a foreign key referencing TABLE_A */
Alter Table TABLE_C ADD FOREIGN KEY (COLUMN_C) REFERENCES TABLE_A(COLUMN_A)
go

/* create the table */
Create TABLE TABLE_D
( COLUMN_D1 smallint,
  COLUMN_D2 smallint)
go

/* Now add the multi-column primary key */
Alter Table TABLE_D ADD CONSTRAINT PK_D_COLUMNS PRIMARY KEY
(COLUMN_D1, COLUMN_D2)
go

/* create the table */
Create TABLE TABLE_E
( COLUMN_E1 smallint,
  COLUMN_E2 smallint)
go

/* now add the foreign key referencing the multi-column
   primary key */
Alter Table TABLE_E ADD CONSTRAINT FK_E_COLUMNS FOREIGN KEY
(COLUMN_E1, COLUMN_E2)
REFERENCES TABLE_D( COLUMN_D1, COLUMN_D2)
go
```

Part

II

Ch

11

N O T E Microsoft SQL Server 6.5 adds two new options to the ALTER TABLE...ADD CONSTRAINT syntax. These are WITH CHECK ¦ NOCHECK, and NOT FOR REPLICATION. The WITH NOCHECK option is provided so that a constraint can be added without checking the existing data for referential integrity constraints.

Microsoft added the NOT FOR REPLICATION option to allow replication to occur without requiring constraints to be dropped and re-added after the replication took place. ■

▶ **See** "Creating and Using Constraints," for more information on constraints, **p. 161**

Displaying Key Information

SQL Server has two ways to show information about keys. The graphical method is via SQL Enterprise Manager's Table Manager. The command-line method is via the system-stored procedures sp_help and sp_helpconstraints, and the ODBC stored procedures sp_pkeys and sp_fkeys.

SQL Enterprise Manager's Table Manager has been discussed in detail in previous sections in this chapter. Please refer to the section titled "Using SQL Enterprise Manager To Add Primary And Foreign Keys" for information on how to view the constraints on a table.

sp_helpconstraint   SQL Server's primary way of displaying information about keys is through the system-stored procedure sp_helpconstraint. Its syntax is as follows:

sp_helpconstraint *table_name*

sp_help   sp_help is a generic system-stored procedure that returns information about database tables. Part of the output from sp_help is information on keys on a table. The syntax for sp_help is

sp_help *table_name*

sp_pkeys and sp_fkeys   SQL Server provides two system-stored procedures, sp_pkeys and sp_fkeys, that can be used to view key information stored in the database. sp_pkeys and sp_fkeys are procedures that have been created to help ODBC implementers access SQL Server's system catalog tables easily.

The syntax for the two procedures is identical and is as follows:

sp_pkeys ¦ sp_fkeys *table_name*

table_name is the table for which the keys need to be found.

Examples of Using System-Stored Procedures to View Primary and Foreign Keys   Listing 11.10 shows some examples of the output from sp_pkeys, sp_fkeys, and sp_help:

Listing 11.10   Sample Output from the System Stored Procedures

```
/*----------------------------
sp_helpconstraint TABLE_D
----------------------------*/
Object Name
------------------------
TABLE_D

constraint_type          constraint_name       constraint_keys
----------------------   ----------------      -------------------
PRIMARY KEY (clustered)  PK_D_COLUMNS          COLUMN_D1, COLUMN_D2

Table is referenced by
----------------------------------------------------------------
```

```
pubs.dbo.TABLE_E: FK_COLUMNS
/*----------------------------
sp_help table_d
----------------------------*/
Name            Owner          Type        When_created
----------------------------------------------------------------
TABLE_D         dbo            user table Dec 11 1995  7:42PM

Data_located_on_segment
-----------------------------
default

Column_name   Type                        Length Prec Scale Nullable
----------------------------------------------------------------------
COLUMN_D1     smallint                       2     5    0    no
COLUMN_D2     smallint                       2     5    0    no

Identity     Seed     Increment
-----------------------------
No identity column defined.     (null)  (null)

index_name    index_description      index_keys
-----------------------------------------------
PK_D_COLUMNS clustered, unique, primary key located on default
        COLUMN_D1, COLUMN_D2

constraint_type     constraint_name      constraint_keys
--------------------------------------------------------
PRIMARY KEY (clustered)    PK_D_COLUMNS  COLUMN_D1, COLUMN_D2

Table is referenced by
----------------------
pubs.dbo.TABLE_E: FK_COLUMNS
/*----------------------------
sp_pkeys table_d
----------------------------*/
table_qualifier  table_owner   table_name   column_name     key_seq
pk_name
----------------------------------------------------------------------
pubs             dbo           TABLE_D      COLUMN_D1       1
PK_D_COLUMNS
pubs             dbo           TABLE_D      COLUMN_D2       2
PK_D_COLUMNS

(2 row(s) affected)
/*----------------------------
sp_fkeys table_d
----------------------------*/
pktable_qualifier    pktable_owner     pktable_name       pkcolumn_name
fktable_qualifier    fktable_owner     fktable_name       fkcolumn_name

key_seq update_rule delete_rule fk_name                    pk_name
--------------------------------------------------------------------
pubs                 dbo               TABLE_D            COLUMN_D1
pubs                 dbo               TABLE_E            COLUMN_E1
```

continues

Listing 11.10	Continued				
1	1	1	FK_COLUMNS		PK_D_COLUMNS
pubs		dbo		TABLE_D	COLUMN_D2
pubs		dbo		TABLE_E	COLUMN_E2
2	1	1	FK_COLUMNS		PK_D_COLUMNS

Dropping Keys

SQL Server has two methods for dropping primary and foreign keys. The graphical method is performed by using SQL Enterprise Manager. The command-line method is done by using the Transact-SQL command ALTER TABLE...DROP CONSTRAINT.

Using SQL Enterprise Manager   To use SQL Enterprise Manager to drop a key, follow these steps:

1. Launch SQL Enterprise Manager from the Microsoft SQL Server 6.5 group.
2. Select the server, database, and table that you want to work on.
3. From the Manage menu choose Tables. The Manage Tables dialog box appears.
4. Click the Advanced Features toolbar button, with a green plus sign on it, to show the advanced options at the bottom of the window. Refer to Figure 11.11 for a picture of the Manage Tables dialog box.
5. Remove the existing primary key by clicking the Remove button, or click the Foreign Keys tab and remove the required foreign key.
6. Click the Save button, which looks like a diskette, to save the changes to the table. If you get any referential constraint errors, you'll need to go to those tables and remove the primary/foreign keys that are causing the problem.

Using ALTER TABLE...DROP CONSTRAINT   To drop a foreign key using SQL, use the ALTER TABLE...DROP CONSTRAINT statement. The syntax for this SQL statement is as follows:

```
ALTER TABLE table_name DROP CONSTRAINT constraint_name
```

The table_name is the name of the table that the constraint applies to. The constraint_name is the name of the constraint.

N O T E   You can't drop a primary key if other tables reference it as a foreign key. You must drop those foreign keys first. ■

Reality Check

If ever there was a list of double-edged swords, indexes are likely to be very close to the top of the list relating to SQL Server configuration and management. The typical system cycle appears to be that of creating an index to individually satisfy each and every select statement, then realizing that performance is taking a serious hit from the indexing. From that point on, the discussion, and often heated debate, about indexes comes around to the fewer the better, but make the ones implemented count.

One thing to keep an eye on is the use of the update statistics option. In the first part of this chapter, this option was covered and it was explained that the statistics managed by SQL Server are only as good as the data loading at the time the index is created. When you implement a system, you'll typically do so with either empty database tables or a sample database set. Then, as the system is accepted, the databases grow significantly in size.

The model data you had in the system for testing may, in actuality, bear little resemblance to the real-life data in the system. From the pattern of information entered, to the values in the columns, there's nothing like real-life use to determine real-life data patterns. After you've had the system up for a bit, make *sure* you update statistics. This is critical. In many systems we've done in our integration work, this step alone boosts performance dramatically. Consider making the update process a scheduled process, perhaps once every six months at sites where data distribution is relatively stable, more often at sites where the mix of information is more dynamic.

If you're creating a system that is built to support more query options, consider indexing every column on which you allow queries. Now, before a bunch of e-mail is sent out, be sure that systems you consider this option for are query-only type systems, not update systems. As indicated earlier, query-related systems don't suffer from too many different indexes. Don't do this on tables where you are inserting information as well as updating it.

From Here...

In this chapter, you learned how to create, view, and manage indexes on your data tables. This information is very important to help you create an optimized database that won't be bogged down by user queries that force table scans.

From here, you should look at the following chapters for more information:

- Chapter 7, "Retrieving Data with Transact-SQL," shows how you can examine your queries to make sure that they're hitting the indexes defined on the tables.
- Chapter 16, "Understanding Server, Database, and Design Query Options," explains how to make changes to your global server, database, and query configurations to further optimize your queries.

Part II
Ch 11

Understanding Transactions and Locking

A good understanding of transactions and locking is essential if you want to write database applications for more than one user. Even single-user applications require some understanding of locking, although the impact of locking yourself is not nearly as drastic as that of locking an enterprise network of hundreds of users.

SQL Server offers the programmer several different styles of locking. This chapter provides you with the information that you need to accurately assess what your application requires in terms of transaction control and locking.

As a programmer, you should always concentrate on minimizing the amount of locking that occurs so that you decrease the chances of users interfering with each other.

Table 12.1 outlines the basics of a transaction, whether imposed implicitly by SQL Server or explicitly by your application.

What transactions are and how to use them

SQL Server uses groups of statements and operations, called transactions, to manage its workload. Unless specifically stated, transactions are not actually written to the database until SQL Server reaches processing checkpoints.

What types of isolation levels are at your disposal

Depending on the isolation level that you are using, a SELECT statement might return information that changes during your query's life.

How to interpret and avoid locks

You can place locks on pages, tables, and now even rows. The type of lock that you use can avoid or cause deadlocks between users.

Table 12.1   The ACID Requirements for Transactions

*A*tomicity	A transaction is assumed to be complete or not. Although this requirement seems obvious, it's important to understand that either all or none of the transaction becomes final. For example, if you're posting a transfer of funds from one account to another, the funds are deposited into the target account *and* they are removed from the original account, as in a commit, or nothing happens at all, as in an abort.
*C*onsistency	A transaction should "leave things as it found them." In other words, when a transaction starts, the system is in a known state. When a transaction commits, the system must once again be in a known, consistent state. You cannot leave anything hanging from a transaction; it must be a full and complete operation. Of course, by definition, an aborted transaction also fulfills these requirements because it reverts to the state of the system prior to opening the transaction.
*I*solation	Transactions must stand alone and have no effect or dependence on other transactions. Dependence on another transaction causes deadlocks, resulting in rollback operations. This attribute is also known as *serializability.*
*D*urability	Once completed, the transaction's objective has been met and there is no further reason for the operation to be undone. In other words, after a transaction is completed, it stays completed even if something happens to the system. This typically is the reason for wrapping an important operation in one large transaction, ensuring that all or nothing applies to the database tables.

A transaction does not enforce these rules in and of itself. Instead, you, as the developer, must keep these requirements in mind. You should strive to meet each of these objectives for each transaction that you create, without exception. If an operation doesn't measure up to the ACID test, don't continue coding until the operation meets the requirements. You won't be sorry later. ■

Defining Transactions

A *transaction* is a logical unit of work that you want the SQL Server to perform for you. That unit of work can include one or many SQL statements, if you appropriately define the unit of work to the server by delineating which statements within a batch are part of a transaction.

In ISQL, you can execute single-statement transactions by entering their text and typing **go**. Single-statement transactions are ideal if the required results are simple and self-contained. For example, the following statement returns a list of tables from the database currently being used:

```
Select       *
From  SYSOBJECTS
```

```
Where TYPE = 'U'   /* user-defined tables */
Order By NAME
```

You can find the text for this statement in 12_01.SQL on the companion CD-ROM.

In some instances, however, you must do more than one thing in a transaction and condition-ally undo it if something goes wrong. In such cases, multistatement transactions come into play. Such transactions enable you to combine two or more SQL statements and send them to the server for processing. You can also define an event that undoes any work submitted. List-ing 12.1 shows an example of a multistatement transaction. You can find the text for this state-ment in 12_02.SQL on the companion CD-ROM.

Listing 12.1   12_02.SQL—An Example of a Multistatement Transaction

```
Create Table TABLE_A(
      X       smallint null,
      Y       smallint null)
Go
Create Table TABLE_B(
      Z       smallint null)
Go

Begin Tran
      Update        TABLE_A
      Set   X = X + 1
      Where         Y = 100

      Update TABLE_B
      Set   Z = Z + 1

      If @@rowcount = 0 or @@error !=0 /* no rows were hit by our update */
      Begin
            Rollback Tran
            Print 'Error occurred, no rows were updated'
            Return
      End
Commit Tran
```

TIP   To make your scripts and stored procedures easier to read, format them with indented sections within transaction blocks.

You can also set up SQL Server to start transactions automatically when certain operations are performed. You shouldn't use this technique in a production environment, because in such environments it is better to have your application declare explicit transactions. However, the IMPLICIT_TRANSACTIONS option can be helpful in a development or testing environment. You set this option with the SET statement as follows:

```
set IMPLICIT_TRANSACTIONS ON ¦ OFF
```

Part

II

Ch

12

> **CAUTION**
>
> If you set this option, you still must issue corresponding COMMIT statements. Otherwise, the transactions remain open and can bog down, if not lock up, your system. You should not use this option in a production environment. Instead, set your transactions explicitly in your routines.

After you set up SQL Server, the following operations automatically begin transactions:

- ALTER TABLE
- CREATE
- DELETE
- DROP
- FETCH
- GRANT
- INSERT
- OPEN
- REVOKE
- SELECT
- TRUNCATE TABLE
- UPDATE

Limitations on Transactions

Within a transaction, you cannot perform certain actions. These are general actions that you cannot undo, at least not without significant repercussions to major components of the system. Keep in mind that transactions are meant to protect groups of processing statements, not so much to back up the management of your system. If you want to protect yourself from a potential system-damaging change, consider dumping the database and transaction log prior to the operation that you want to perform.

The following actions are not allowed within a transaction:

- Altering a database
- Creating a database
- Creating an index
- Creating a procedure
- Creating a table
- Creating a view
- Initializing a disk
- Dropping

- Dumping a transaction
- Granting
- Loading a database
- Loading a transaction
- Reconfiguring
- Revoking
- SELECTing into
- Truncating a table
- Updating statistics
- Performing `sp_dboption` or other procedures that modify the master database

N O T E A new type of transaction enables you to distribute transactions. The Distributed Transaction Coordinator controls such transactions. This type of transaction is quite useful for transactions that occur at remote locations but affect centralized inventory levels.

For more information on the Distributed Transaction Coordinator, see Chapter 18, "Using the Distributed Transaction Coordinator."

Optimistic Versus Pessimistic Locking

When you write multiuser database applications, you can take one of two approaches to transaction control: optimistic or pessimistic locking. *Optimistic locking* assumes that your application code does nothing to explicitly enforce locks on records while you work on them. Instead, you rely on the database to manage this enforcement on its own while you concentrate on application logic. *Pessimistic locking* assumes that the application code attempts to enforce some type of locking mechanism.

To implement optimistic locking in your application without having it grind to a halt under excessive locks on the server, you must carefully observe some simple rules:

- Minimize the amount of time that a transaction is held open by limiting the amount of SQL code that occurs within a BEGIN TRAN...COMMIT TRAN section.
- Rely on application code to guarantee that updates are hitting the right record instead of holding locks while a user browses data.
- Ensure that all application codes update and select from tables in the same order. This prevents any deadlocks from occurring.

If you assume that SQL Server will manage locking and that you have nothing to worry about, you are taking a *very* optimistic locking approach. Unfortunately, such an approach isn't very pragmatic because it assumes that a programmer or user can do nothing to explicitly cause locking. In fact, many situations can cause a large amount of locking to occur on a server, potentially disabling it for the enterprise that it supports.

Background Information on Locking

This section provides some background on the basics of locking as they pertain to, and are implemented by, SQL Server. This background should give you a basic understanding of some of the more detailed items discussed in the sections that follow. Specifically, this section focuses on the following two key aspects of locking:

■ Page sizes and granularity of data

■ Types of locks

Page Sizes and Granularity of Data   SQL Server's internal basic unit of work is a 2K data page. Therefore, any activity that the server executes must do work on at least 2K of data. Further, a table has several pages of data associated with it; the number of pages depends on the number and size of rows that the table contains. SQL Server can reference data in a table only one page at a time. If an update hits a single record in a table and a lock is held for some period of time, probably more than one row is in fact being locked.

How does this affect a database application? One of the most important considerations when writing a multiuser application is that you must provide a way for multiple users to work independently of one another. For example, two users must be able to update customer records simultaneously while answering phone calls from customers. The greater the capability to manipulate data in the same table without affecting other users by locks, the greater the concurrency of an application and the greater the chance of being able to support many users.

A highly accessed table, such as a table of unique values for the rest of the system, should be made as concurrent as possible. To do so, force as few rows of data as possible onto the same data page, thereby limiting the number of coincidental rows locked as the result of a user action. Additionally, you should keep users' transactions to a minimum duration when hitting these tables.

Two other types of locks can occur that lock data at a higher level than a single data page: table and extent.

Table locks occur when a user issues a query to update a table without including a WHERE clause, which implies that the user wants to update every row. In addition, table locks can occur when the number of data pages locked exceeds the Lock Escalation Threshold defined for the particular table or database.

Extent locks occur when SQL Server must create a new database extent—eight pages of data—to respond to a user query. Unfortunately, MS SQL offers no controls for handling extent locks, so you simply should know that they occur and what they mean.

▶ **See** the section titled "LE Thresholds" later in this chapter, for more information on extent locks.

Types of Locks   SQL Server can place several types of locks on database pages and tables. The possible page locks are SHARED, EXCLUSIVE, and UPDATE. SHARED and EXCLUSIVE locks are reasonably self-explanatory; SHARED locks allow another process to acquire a lock on the same page, and EXCLUSIVE locks don't.

Multiple processes can have SHARED locks on the same data page. These locks usually are acquired when data is being read. It is important, however, that no other process can take an EXCLUSIVE lock to perform statements within the Data Manipulation Language (DML) until all SHARED locks have been released.

EXCLUSIVE locks of table pages are given to a process that is updating a record on a page, inserting a new record at the end of a page, or deleting a record from a page. These locks disallow any other process from accessing the page.

The UPDATE lock type is somewhere between a SHARED and EXCLUSIVE lock. It allows a process to acquire a SHARED lock on the page until an update has occurred on it. UPDATE locks are acquired when a CURSOR is being built in the server. UPDATE locks are automatically promoted to EXCLUSIVE locks when an update occurs on one of the pages associated with the cursor.

At the table level, SQL Server has SHARED and EXCLUSIVE locks that work the same way as they do at the page level. SQL Server also has INTENT locks. INTENT locks indicate that a table has several pages on it that SQL Server *intends* to lock at the page level in response to a user process. Such might be the case as SQL Server reads a table, but your specific query is ahead of the query that is locking pages in the table.

SQL Server 6.5 adds *insert row-level locking*. This new lock allows multiple users to insert records into the same page. This lock was added because of a large amount of contention with inserts at the end of tables. The reason for the contention is that when you insert new rows into a table—unless the table has a clustered index—all new rows go to the table's last page. If multiple users are inserting to the same page, the time to insert the row, commit the implicit transaction, and move on takes a performance hit in heavy processing environments.

▶ **See** Chapter 24, "Creating and Using Cursors," for additional information on cursors, **p. 677**.

Defining Isolation Levels

SQL Server provides several ways to cause locks to be held or released while querying the database. One of those ways is by setting a transaction's isolation level. As its name implies, an *isolation level* specifies to the database how "protected" to keep the data that other users and requesters of data on the server are currently working with.

SQL Server has three different types of isolation levels: Read Committed, Read Uncommitted, and Repeatable Read. The following three sections document each.

N O T E Transaction isolation levels are set for the entire time that a session is connected to the database. If you change isolation levels for a specific part of your application, do not forget to change back to the default so that other parts of the application are not adversely affected.

To achieve the same effects as isolation levels for a single SELECT statement, refer to the section "Holding a Lock Explicitly," for more information. ■

The *Read Committed* Level Read Committed is the default method of operation for SQL Server. It does not allow you to retrieve "dirty" or uncommitted data from the database. Read Committed acquires SHARE locks on all the pages it passes over inside a transaction. If another user performing a deletion or insertion that is committed or rolled back during the life of your query, you might receive some data pages that are not rereadable or that might contain values that exist in the database only temporarily.

If you need to ensure that other users cannot affect the query's results during the life of a particular transaction, make sure that you use the Repeatable Read isolation level.

To set your isolation level to Read Committed, perform the following SQL statement:

```
Set Transaction Isolation Level Read Committed
Go
```

For more information, refer to Table 12.2 and the sections following it. These explain the other types of locks and how they relate to each other.

The *Read Uncommitted* Level   Read Uncommitted is the same as the NOLOCK keyword on an individual SELECT statement. No SHARED locks are placed on any data that you pass over in the query. Additionally, no locks held by other users are observed. For example, if another user has deleted a whole table from which you are about to select, but that user has yet to commit a transaction, you still can read the data from it and not receive any error conditions.

> **CAUTION**
>
> You shouldn't use the Read Uncommitted transaction isolation level for any applications that require data integrity, because you have no guarantee that the data you are working with is the same or, indeed, in the database at all. Use Read Uncommitted sparingly in your applications and possibly only for such procedures as reporting applications on tables that are statistically unaffected by the average transactions that post against your server.

To set your isolation level to Read Uncommitted, perform the following SQL transaction:

```
Set Transaction Isolation Level Read Uncommitted
Go
```

The *Repeatable Read* (Serializable) Level   Repeatable Read is the most *exclusive* type of locking that you can force SQL Server to maintain. Repeatable Read guarantees that the data you are reading remains unaffected by other transactions issued from other users during the life of a given transaction that you are working on. Because of Repeatable Read's explicit locking of data from other users, Repeatable Read reduces the database's concurrency, and reduces the number of different users who can access data at the same time without affecting each other. Take care that you do not use Repeatable Read unwisely in your application. Not many places actually require it.

To set your isolation level to Repeatable Read, perform the following SQL transaction:

```
Set Transaction Isolation Level Repeatable Read
Go
```

Creating and Working with Transactions

In the "Defining Transactions" section earlier in this chapter, you saw how to delineate a transaction using BEGIN, COMMIT, and ROLLBACK. This section describes SQL Server's keywords or Transact-SQL statements required for transaction control.

> **CAUTION**
>
> At some point in your code, you must follow each BEGIN TRAN with a matching COMMIT TRAN or ROLLBACK TRAN. Transactions *must* begin and end in pairs; otherwise, the server continues holding locks until the client is disconnected.

The *BEGIN TRAN* Keyword When you issue a BEGIN TRAN to the database, SQL Server marks in the database's transaction logs the point to return to in the event of a ROLLBACK TRAN. BEGIN TRAN explicitly tells SQL Server to treat all the following work, until a COMMIT or ROLLBACK is encountered, as one logical unit. The work can contain many operations.

You can issue operations that affect a database without a BEGIN TRAN statement. You cannot, however, conditionally undo work that you send to the server that you do not precede with a BEGIN TRAN so that SQL Server knows the state to which it must return the database.

> **N O T E** SQL Server's transaction logs monitor transactions contained within BEGIN and COMMIT statements. If a media failure occurs before data physically changes on the database, SQL Server recovers or ensures that it applies those changes by "rolling forward" those unapplied transactions to the database the next time the server is brought back online. ▪

The *COMMIT TRAN* Keyword Issuing a COMMIT TRAN to the database signals SQL Server that the work succeeded and that you no longer want to group any additional work inside the transaction.

By definition, a COMMIT TRAN also implies that you've fulfilled the requirements of the ACID test presented in Table 12.1.

The *ROLLBACK TRAN* Keyword ROLLBACK TRAN is SQL Server's equivalent of your favorite word processor's Edit, Undo menu option. Sending a ROLLBACK to the database server causes it to undo all the work to the most recent BEGIN TRAN statement. Typically, a ROLLBACK TRAN is issued during a long transaction if any particular part of it encounters any SQL error.

> **CAUTION**
>
> SQL Server enables you to call *remote* stored procedures within a transaction. Because of the nature of the *Remote Procedure Call* (RPC) interface with the other server on which the RPC executed, however, SQL Server cannot roll back any such calls. When writing applications that require RPCs, make sure that you include additional RPCs to undo your previous work programmatically.

Understanding DDL and Database Statements

A new feature to SQL Server 6.5, *DDL* (Data Definition Language), and database modification statements are now allowed inside a transaction. The following statements can appear in transactions:

ALTER TABLE	CREATE TRIGGER	DROP TABLE
CREATE DEFAULT	CREATE VIEW	DROP TRIGGER
CREATE INDEX	DROP DEFAULT	DROP VIEW
CREATE PROCEDURE	DROP INDEX	GRANT & REVOKE
CREATE RULE	DROP PROCEDURE	SELECT INTO
CREATE TABLE	DROP RULE	TRUNCATE TABLE

These statements are important because they allow SQL Server 6.5's new database schema management features to function. Many of these statements modify the table structures on the system or create new ways to access the information.

 TIP SQL Server does not provide a direct way to drop a table column, but you can work around this omission. Create a new table with the required schema, minus the column, and use the SELECT INTO Transact-SQL command to copy the data.

Using Named Transactions and SavePoints

When you examine large, stored procedures and applications with large bodies of SQL code, the code is inevitably pretty unreadable. Such code is text-based and relies heavily on the premise that all programmers work with the same style of format and layout. For this reason, when transactional programming is involved, it becomes even more important to use good indenting to mark blocks of code clearly.

However, even the most careful programmer will find that it becomes a bit of a nightmare to remember how many indents to roll back out of in the event of an error condition or some programmatic constraint. Named transactions and SavePoints are used for just this purpose. They provide a way to roll back work to a given *named* or *saved* portion of the code that has been executing, even if the portion of code is at a higher nesting level.

Using Named Transactions   Named transactions provide a convenient way to attach an identifier to a whole body of work. Use named transactions to make it easier to undo large portions of code. To create a named transaction, add the name of the transaction to the BEGIN TRAN statement, as shown in Listing 12.2. You can find the text for this statement in 12_05.SQL on the companion CD-ROM.

Listing 12.2   12_05.SQL—Demonstrating How to Add the Transaction's Name to a *BEGIN TRAN* Statement

```
/* Open outer transaction */
Begin Tran UPDATE_AUTHORS
     Update AUTHORS
     Set    CONTRACT = 1
     Where  AU_ID = '341-22-1782'

     /* Open inner transaction */
     Begin Tran UPDATE_TITLEAUTHOR
          Update TITLEAUTHOR
          Set    ROYALTYPER = ROYALTYPER + 25
          Where  AU_ID = '341-22-1782'
          If @@error != 0
          Begin
               Rollback Tran UPDATE_TITLEAUTHOR
               Print 'Failed to update Royalties'
               Return
          End
     Commit Tran UPDATE_TITLEAUTHOR
Commit Tran UPDATE_AUTHORS
```

N O T E   If you omit the transaction's identifier or name when committing or rolling back a transaction, SQL Server simply undoes the work to the most recent BEGIN TRAN, regardless of the transaction's name. When using named transactions, be careful to code all your work consistently, either using names or not, throughout your work. If you do not use a consistent style, programmers might step on each other's transactions inadvertently. ■

Using SavePoints   SavePoints are simply another way to perform a named transaction. They provide a method of marking a place in the code at which you can use a ROLLBACK to undo work. To create a SavePoint, issue the following SQL command:

```
SAVE TRANSACTION <TRAN_NAME>
```

You then use only the identifier, *<TRAN_NAME>*, when performing your ROLLBACK, as shown in Listing 12.3. You can find the text for this statement in 12_06.SQL on the companion CD-ROM.

Listing 12.3   12_06.SQL—A Statement for Performing a *ROLLBACK* with a SavePoint

```
Begin Tran
     Update AUTHORS
     Set    CONTRACT = 1
     Where  AU_ID = '341-22-1782'

     /* save our work to this point */
     Save Transaction AuthorDone
```

continues

Part

II

Ch

12

Listing 12.3 Continued

```
        Update TITLEAUTHOR
                Set    ROYALTYPER = ROYALTYPER + 25
                Where  AU_ID = '341-22-1782'
        If @@error != 0 Or @@RowCount > 1
        Begin
                /* rollback and exit */
                Rollback Tran AuthorDone
                Print 'Error occurred when updating TitleAuthor'
                Return
        End
Commit Tran
Print 'Transaction Committed'
```

CAUTION

Although the transaction in Listing 12.3 rolls back the UPDATE on TITLEAUTHOR, SQL Server holds locks on the TITLEAUTHOR table until either COMMIT or ROLLBACK completes the entire transaction. This side effect of using a SavePoint can cause an application to lock unexpectedly.

TIP

If your application seems to hold locks continuously after the first transaction executes, you probably have issued more BEGIN TRANs than you have corresponding COMMIT TRANs or ROLLBACK TRANs.

Remember that you must enclose transactions in pairs of BEGIN and COMMIT or ROLLBACK. If you fail to do so, you tell SQL Server that you want to keep the transaction open longer.

To help identify your code problems, walk through your application and monitor error conditions carefully. Probably an error condition is occurring and some code is returning control before closing an open transaction. Also, check the value of the system variable @@trancount, which indicates how deeply nested in transactions you are.

Using Serialized Columns Without *IDENTITY*

SQL Server 6.0 introduced a *serial* datatype called the IDENTITY. In this datatype, SQL Server automatically assigns the next sequential value to a column in a table. IDENTITYs are valuable in applications that have a high transaction volume and must identify each record uniquely.

For some applications that must support multiple database back ends and for those applications that require SQL Server 4.x compatibility, you can implement the same kind of feature as an IDENTITY column by performing the following steps:

On the CD

1. Create a table with columns in it to store a table name and the current value. You can find the text for all the following statements in 12_07.SQL on the CD-ROM.

```
/* create the table */
Create Table Record_IDs(
    Table_Name  varchar(30),
```

```
        Current_ID   int)
Go

/* add a primary clustered index */
Create        Unique Clustered Index PK_Record_IDs
        on Record_IDs( Table_Name ) with FILLFACTOR = 1
Go
```

2. Insert into the table some records that correspond to tables in the target database:

```
Insert Record_IDs
        Select    Name,        1
        From    Sysobjects
        Where   Type = 'U' /* user-defined tables */
```

3. Create a stored procedure that has a consistent access interface to the table and locks the table so that no other users can modify the data while a given process is accessing it:

```
Create Procedure up_GetID                       /* up = user procedure */
        @psTableName        varchar(30),              /* p = parameter */
        @rnNewID     int OUTPUT          /* r = receive or output parameter */
As
Declare
        @nSQLError int,
        @nRowCount int

Begin Tran
        /* First update the record to acquire the exclusive lock on the page
*/

        Update Record_IDs
        Set     Current_ID = Current_ID + 1
        Where   Table_Name = @psTableName

        /* Check for errors */
        Select      @nSQLError = @@error,
            @nRowCount = @@rowcount
        If @nSQLError != 0 OR @nRowCount != 1
        Begin
            Rollback Tran
            Return -999 /* failed to update the record correctly */
        End

        /* Select back the value from the table that we've already locked */
        Select      @rnNewID = Current_ID
        From    Record_IDs
        Where   Table_Name = @psTableName

        /* Check for errors */
        Select      @nSQLError = @@error,
            @nRowCount = @@rowcount
        If @nSQLError != 0 OR @nRowCount != 1
        Begin
            Rollback Tran
            Return -998 /* failed to select record correctly */
        End
```

```
                  Commit Tran
                  Return 0
                         Go
```

4. Test the new procedure:

```
Declare
        @nRecordID   int,
        @nRC         int,
        @sMsg        varchar(255)

/* Fetch a record ID for use in inserting the new record */
Exec @nRC = up_GetID 'table_A', @nRecordID OUTPUT

If @nRC != 0
        Print 'An error occurred fetching new Record ID'
Else
Begin
        Select @sMsg = 'New Record value is ' + Convert( varchar(4),
@nRecordID )
        Print @sMsg
End
Go
```

 TIP To create identifying columns, always use the new IDENTITY column rather than the TIMESTAMP datatype. The IDENTITY column is much easier to reference and use in application code and can impose less data overhead if you use a small datatype for it, such as TINYINT or SMALLINT.

Understanding Locks

In addition to understanding the background information provided earlier in this chapter, you need to know how to handle locking when it occurs in your database.

Displaying Lock Information

There are two ways to review information about locks held in the database: by using the SQL Enterprise Manager or by executing the system stored procedure sp_lock. (Actually, SQL Enterprise Manager calls sp_lock to display the information.)

Using SQL Enterprise Manager To use the SQL Enterprise Manager to view locked information, perform the following steps:

1. Run SQL Enterprise Manager from the Microsoft SQL Server 6.5 group (see Figure 12.1).

2. Select the server on which you want to work. In Figure 12.2, for example, the user is selecting (LOCAL) (SQL Server 6.50).

3. Choose Server, Current Activity, and click the Object Locks tab. The Object Locks page displays as shown in Figure 12.3.

FIG. 12.1

When initially started, SQL Enterprise Manager shows that no server is selected.

FIG. 12.2

By clicking the plus sign next to the server, you expand its tree of devices, databases, and logins.

Part
II

Ch
12

FIG. 12.3

The Object Locks page of the Current Activity dialog box displays the currently locked objects.

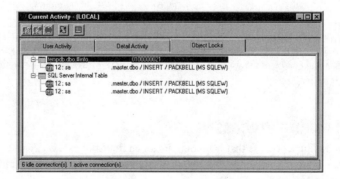

To get more information about the individual statement that is causing locking, you can either double-click the process that is in the Object Locks page or click the View Details toolbar button shown in Figure 12.3. You then see the Process Details dialog box shown in Figure 12.4.

FIG. 12.4

The Process Details dialog box shows additional information about the SQL statement that is causing locks.

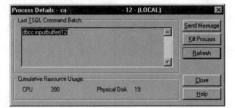

Using _sp_lock_ The `sp_lock` system stored procedure returns a list of processes and the types of locks that they are holding on the system. To get the locks that a particular process is holding, add the process ID to the command, as follows:

```
sp_lock spid
```

Note the following example code:

```
Begin Tran
     Update authors
     set au_id = au_id
go
sp_lock
go
rollback tran
go
```

The output of the sp_lock follows:

spid	locktype	table_id	page	dbname
10	Sh_intent	640005311	0	master
10	Ex_table	16003088	0	pubs
10	Sh_table	288004057	0	pubs
10	Ex_extent	0	320	tempdb

TIP Many system procedures return an OBJECT_ID column to identify a database object. To get the object's name quickly, use the system function OBJECT_NAME(). For example, SELECT OBJECT_NAME(1232324).

Killing a Locking Process

Before killing a process that is holding locks on the database, verify with the sp_who and sp_lock system procedures that the spid (server process ID) you are targeting to kill in fact belongs to the user holding the locks.

When reviewing the output from sp_who, examine the blk spid column to identify a blocked user. Trace the tree of the blocks back to the parent spid and kill that user process. To kill a user process, you can either use SQL Enterprise Manager or execute the Kill command.

You can also use DBCC to check the status of transactions open against a given database. Using the OPENTRAN statement for DBCC, you can determine which transactions are open and when they were started. The syntax for the command is as follows:

```
dbcc opentran [(database ¦ databaseID)] [WITH TABLERESULTS]
```

If you don't specify the database name or ID, the command runs against the current database, listing open transactions. If you specify the WITH TABLERESULTS option, you receive a listing of the same results, but with output formatted a bit more to enable you to save it for use in a workbook or in another table. This listing can be a big help if you're troubleshooting a problem and want to look for trends that are occurring for the transactions.

Using SQL Enterprise Manager   When you use SQL Enterprise Manager to kill a process, you first must find the process that is causing locking. How you kill a process was outlined previously in the section "Using sp_lock."

After you find a process that you need to kill, you can click the toolbar's Kill Process button in the Current Activity dialog box (see Figure 12.5).

FIG. 12.5
The toolbar's Kill Process button enables you to halt an activity.

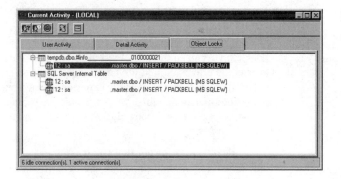

Part
II

Ch
12

A warning dialog box appears so that you can change your mind and undo your action (see Figure 12.6).

FIG. 12.6
The warning dialog box enables you to confirm that you want to kill a process.

Using _KILL_   After identifying the user process (spid) that you want to kill, execute the following SQL statement to kill it:

```
KILL spid
```

This statement kills most processes that exist on the server. In certain circumstances, some processes can't be killed. Usually such a process is in an Extent or Resource lock waiting for the underlying operating system to complete a task. Monitor the process with sp_who until it leaves this condition, and then execute the KILL command.

Holding a Lock Explicitly

If you have application code that must explicitly hold locks on particular sets of data, SQL Server provides extensions to the basic SELECT statement that have this functionality. SQL Server enables you to add *optimizer hints* or keywords to your SELECT statements that tell it how to process the data that matches your results. You can place several kinds of hints on a set of data that a SELECT statement affects: NOLOCK, HOLDLOCK, UPDLOCK, TABLOCK, PAGLOCK, and TABLOCKX.

Table 12.2 explains the two most obscure options, and the next series of sections explains the others.

Table 12.2   Explicit Lock Conditions

Option	Description
UPDLOCK	Locks the values in the table for a future update, but enables other users to read the information in the table. This condition can help prevent delays that users might typically experience when simply browsing or reviewing the data in tables while updates are occurring. If you use this option, users still can review the database contents, but they can't update the locked rows.
PAGLOCK	Explicitly tells SQL Server that you want to use shared page locks. The only time that you might use this option is when issuing a TABLOCKX lock on a table, preventing all other reads. See the coming sections for additional information about TABLOCKX locks. By default, this option is on.

The _NOLOCK_ Option   The NOLOCK option enables a query to read from dirty data. *Dirty* data is data that other users' updates and deletions might have affected. If you select records from a table with the NOLOCK keyword, any other user's EXCLUSIVE locks are ignored. Such a lock indicates that a user updated a record, but does not lock the data itself.

NOLOCK is a useful option when you are writing applications that use a small sample of records with fluctuating values that do not affect the data statistically—that is, for applications in which trends of data are more important than the actual values themselves. Be careful to differentiate clearly between data fetched with the NOLOCK keyword and data that is legitimately accurate according to the known condition of the database as a whole.

CAUTION

When selecting data with the NOLOCK keyword, keep in mind that during the time that you are reading from the data page in which the data resides, another user's actions might affect your data in such a way that makes it invalid. For example, another user might delete a record that you are reading, and while you are reading it, the user's COMMIT is processed and the record is removed.

If you are reading data that is no longer available, you receive error messages 605, 606, 624, or 625. You should process these errors the same way that you process a deadlock condition: by informing the users that an error has occurred and asking them to retry their operations. Advanced applications might automatically retry initially to avoid confusing users unnecessarily.

The *HOLDLOCK* Command   A normal SELECT on tables acquires a SHARED lock on a page while the SELECT is passing through the data. A SHARED lock does not prohibit another user from updating a record or attempting to gain an EXCLUSIVE lock on the data page that the SELECT currently is processing. In addition, the SHARED lock expires on a data page as the next page is being read. If you want to maintain data integrity for the life of the SELECT, because you might need to scroll backward and forward through the result set, use the HOLDLOCK command to force SQL Server to hold the SHARED lock until the transaction is complete.

The *TABLOCK* and *TABLOCKX* Commands   As its name implies, TABLOCK forces a SELECT statement to lock the entire table or tables affected by the SELECT for the duration of the statement. TABLOCKX forces an exclusive table lock for the life of the transaction, denying any other user access to the table until the transaction has been completed.

Do not place a table lock (TABLOCK) on a table unless you have a good programmatic reason. TABLOCKs often create unnecessary overhead and undue locking in the server. Instead, rely on Lock Escalation (LE) thresholds to manage TABLOCKs for you.

Part

II

Ch

12

Using Lock Escalation Options

SQL Server locks data at the page level. Any query that you execute on the server holds locks on at least one full page. If you start updating or locking multiple pages on a table, SQL Server starts consuming resources to manage your requests. At a certain point, based on a percentage of pages locked per table, the database can lock the entire table more efficiently than it can keep managing the individual pages that a given transaction is locking.

Fortunately, SQL Server enables you to configure the way it *escalates* locks from page level to table level. You set these options at the server level using the server stored procedure sp_configure.

LE Thresholds   Using sp_configure, you can set three different types of lock escalation (LE) thresholds: LE threshold maximum, LE threshold minimum, and LE threshold percent.

The server uses the threshold maximum to determine when to escalate a set of page locks to a table lock. The default for the server is 200 pages. To change this value, use the statement shown in Listing 12.4. You can find this statement's text in 12_08.SQL on the companion CD-ROM.

On the CD

Listing 12.4   12_08.SQL—A Statement that Changes the Default Threshold Maximum Value

```
Use Master
Go
sp_configure 'LE threshold Maximum', NNN   /* where NNN is the new number
                                              of pages */
Go
Reconfigure
Go
```

You use the threshold minimum with the threshold percent to stop a table lock escalation from occurring on a table with few rows. Suppose that you set the LE threshold percent at 50 percent. This setting tells SQL Server that if more than half the data pages are being locked, you want to lock the whole table. This setting is reasonable unless you have a small table with only a few pages. The threshold minimum that defaults to 20 pages stops the threshold percentage from escalating page locks to table locks unless its minimum number of pages has been locked.

Using the threshold percentage, you can set a generic level at which you want to escalate a set of page locks to a single table lock relative to the number of rows in the table. This configuration option's default value is zero, which tells SQL Server to use the LE threshold maximum to determine escalation.

TIP

Despite the LE thresholds, you can force locking on pages and tables by using the HOLDLOCK and TABLOCK keywords when issuing a SELECT statement to the server.

Reality Check

After you start working with transactions, the transaction log can quickly become your mortal enemy. Over time, you issue many transactions and leave many open. You might recall that when you truncate a transaction log, the log dumps its contents but only to include all committed transactions. If you have many uncommitted transactions, you won't free up the log much at all.

You can solve this problem by using the DBCC OPENTRAN approach mentioned earlier. You still have to troubleshoot your code to determine what went wrong, but at least you can start to free up the processes that have filled the transaction log.

In one especially interesting case, a developer opened a transaction, performed operations, and verified that the code performed correctly. When the transaction never showed up in the database table itself, the developer decided a server restart was in order. When SQL Server came back up, had finished recovering the database, and allowed the developer back in to the system, the data was unchanged, even though the routine had apparently executed correctly.

In this case, of course, the developer left the transaction open. When the server restarted, it rolled back the operations performed within the transaction, restoring the database to the state that it was before the developer ran the routine. The stored procedure's code didn't have any syntax errors, only a missing COMMIT statement at the termination of the processing.

When in doubt, check for open, pending processes. Also, be sure to review open or pending locks. You can save a lot of trouble by installing a small bit of error control and referencing the @@trancount intrinsic SQL Server variable to confirm that, as you leave a stored procedure, the relevant transactions have been completed and committed.

From Here...

In this chapter, you learned about the fundamentals of locking and transactions and how they affect your application. In addition, you learned about the internals of SQL Server and how it manages many users hitting the same table.

To develop your SQL Server and application programming knowledge further, see the following chapters:

- Chapter 6, "Creating Database Tables and Using Datatypes," tells you how you can redefine some of your tables to enable better concurrency.
- Chapter 11, "Managing and Using Indexes and Keys," shows you how you can optimize table access by creating a clustered index with a sparse FILL FACTOR.
- Chapter 16, "Understanding Server, Database, and Design Query Options," provides an understanding of how the options that you set up for the server affect database applications and transaction locks.

Part
II

Ch
12

Server-Side Logic and Capabilities

Managing and Using Rules, Constraints, and Defaults

How to use rules and defaults

Rules are used to enforce value restrictions on columns. Defaults suggest column values or provide a value when a column is inserted into a view that does not include that column.

What associates rules and defaults with columns

Rules and defaults can be defined and stored in the database but are still not enforced on any columns. They must be bound to a column to enforce the rule or default.

How to display information about rules and defaults

Rules and defaults can be bound to multiple columns. It might be necessary to periodically review the use of rules and defaults.

You'll recall from previous chapters that maintaining referential integrity in your database tables is one of the biggest benefits of using SQL Server. It has the ability to manage the information flow into and out of the system by enforcing your criteria on the database side, rather than expecting the application to control this type of information. This leads to data independence from applications, making an open database system possible.

To make this possible, SQL Server implements several tools that help you manage the information in your system. In this chapter, you'll find out about three of these tools: rules, constraints, and defaults. In addition, you can use triggers to manage information as it flows through your system, and you should be sure to read up on and understand triggers as you design your system. ■

▶ **See** Chapter 15, "Creating and Managing Triggers," for more information about Triggers, **p. 447**

Table 13.1 gives you an overview of what these terms mean and how you use them in your systems.

Table 13.1   Understanding Rules, Constraints, and Defaults

Type of Control	Description
Rule	Rules control the values that can be stored within table columns and within user-defined datatypes. Rules use expressions that are applied to columns or user-defined datatypes to restrict the allowable values that can be entered. A rule is stored as a separate database object. With this independence comes the ability to apply a rule not only to columns of a table but also to user-defined datatypes. Also, because a rule is stored separately from the table on which it's imposed, if a table on which a rule is applied is dropped, the rule remains available to be applied against other tables. A column can have only one rule.
Constraints	Constraints are defined on a table column when the column is defined in a CREATE TABLE statement. Microsoft considers constraints preferable to rules as a mechanism for restricting the allowable values that can be entered into a table column because you can define multiple constraints on a column, but you can only define a single rule for a column. The type of constraint that is comparable to a rule is a CHECK constraint. When a table is dropped, its CHECK constraints are no longer available. A table can have more than one constraint applied to it.
Default	Defaults supply a value for an inserted row when users do not supply one with their information to be inserted.

N O T E   You should consider the advantages of using constraints and rules. For example, a table column can have a rule, but only one, and several CHECK constraints defined on it. A table column is restricted by the combination of a rule and one or more CHECK constraints that apply to the column. ▪

▶ **See** "Creating and Using Constraints," for more information on constraints, **p. 161**

Defining Rules

A rule provides a defined restriction on the values for a table column or a user-defined datatype. Any data that you attempt to enter into either a column or a user-defined datatype must meet the criteria defined for the user-defined datatype or column. You should use rules to implement business-related restrictions or limits.

Rules enable you to specify which tests should be performed in one of several ways. First, you can use a function to perform a test on the information. Functions are used to return a comparison value that you can use to validate the value in the column.

In addition, you can use comparison operators like BETWEEN, LIKE, and IN to complete the test on the value in the new data. Once again, your point is to test the new value and make sure it falls within the bounds you've set for it.

For example, you can use a rule to limit the values in a department column to only valid, allowable departments. If there are only four departments in which an employee can be a member, you can define a rule to limit the values entered into the department column to only the four department names. Use a rule to specify the range of allowable values for a column of user-defined datatype.

N O T E SQL Server provides an automatic validation for datatypes. You'll receive an error message if you enter a value that is outside the range of allowable values for the datatype and if you enter a value that is incompatible with the datatype. For example, you can't enter alphabetic or special characters, such as an asterisk (*) and question mark (?), in an int integer datatype.

You should keep this in mind when you define a column or user-defined datatype. If you choose a correct datatype for a column or user-defined datatype, it may make the definition of the rule simpler or even unnecessary. ■

Remember, you can use a user-defined datatype to define a new datatype based on one of the system datatypes, such as CHAR and int, or specialized datatypes. You'll find that user-defined datatypes for table columns must be identically defined across tables. In addition, you can't define a rule for a system datatype, only for a user-defined datatype.

For example, instead of redefining a column, such as badge number, that is defined in multiple tables to be used for relational joins, you can define a user-defined datatype and use it as the datatype of badge in each table that it's defined. If the range of values can be identical for the badge number columns, you can define a rule for a user-defined datatype called badge and use it as the datatype for all badge number columns across tables.

Creating Rules

Remember, rules are a separate object in your database. Because of this, you have to first create the rule and then bind it to a column. You create a rule with a CREATE RULE statement. The syntax of the CREATE RULE statement is as follows:

```
CREATE RULE rule_name
AS condition_expression
```

If you create a rule in the current database, it applies to only columns or user-defined datatypes within the database in which it is defined. You can use any expression in a rule that is valid in a WHERE clause, and your rule can include comparison or arithmetic operators.

The conditional expression you use in a rule must be prefaced with the @ symbol. Use @ to specify a parameter that refers to the value later entered into a table column with either an UPDATE or INSERT statement.

N O T E When you create a rule, be sure to pay close attention to the datatypes you use within it for the comparison. SQL Server does no datatype checking against the values that are using the rule, so you must ensure that the datatype is compatible with the values you'll be checking. Errors that result from datatype mismatches will not be evident until the rule runs for the first time, at which time you'll receive an error message. ■

In the following example, CREATE RULE is used to create a list of values using an IN keyword to form a condition expression. Although the parameter used in the condition expression is descriptively identical to the column name in the table to which it's later bound, the parameter can be defined using any set of alphanumeric characters.

```
create rule department_values
as @department in ('Sales','Field Service','Logistics','Software')
```

N O T E If you add a rule and other database objects to the database Model, the rule is automatically available in any database that is created subsequently. When you create a new database, it's created using the Model database as a template. Any objects that are in the Model database are automatically duplicated in new database.

If you create a set of rules that can and should be used throughout all your databases, create the rules first in the Model database by using the database administrator's account (**sa**) for access before you create your databases. ■

The rule must restrict values to those that are compatible with the column datatype. You can't use constants, within a condition expression, that aren't compatible with the column or user-defined datatype to which the rule is subsequently applied. You can define the name of the rule so that it includes the name of the column or user-defined datatype to which it will be bound to make it descriptive.

You can also create a rule through the SQL Enterprise Manager by performing the following steps:

1. After you start the SQL Enterprise Manager, select the server and the database in which the rule is to be defined.

2. Expand the Objects folder and select Rules.

3. Click the right mouse button and select New Rule to bring up the Manage Rules dialog box. Alternatively, you can choose Rules from the Manage menu to bring up the Manage Rules dialog box.

4. Enter the description of the rule in the Description list box and a name for the rule in the Rule drop-down list box.

5. Click Add to create the new rule.

6. Click Close to close the Manage Rules dialog box.

Figure 13.1 shows the Manage Rules dialog box for the creation of the rule, department_values, through the SQL Enterprise Manager.

FIG. 13.1

The Rules page of this dialog box creates the rule but does not bind it to a column or user-defined datatype.

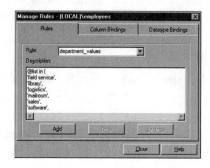

Binding Rules

The definition of a rule doesn't include the specification that applies the rule to either a table column or user-defined datatype. If you only define a rule, it's never in effect; it's only created as an object in the database.

After you define a rule, you must bind it to a column or user-defined datatypes. A rule bound to a column or user-defined datatype specifies that the rule is in effect for the column or user-defined datatype. All values that you enter into a column or user-defined datatype must satisfy the criteria defined by the rule.

You use sp_bindrule to bind a rule to a column or user-defined datatype. sp_bindrule uses the following syntax:

```
sp_bindrule rulename, table_name.column_name, [futureonly]
```

After you bind a rule to a column or user-defined datatype, information about the rule is entered into system tables. A unique rule ID number is stored in the syscolumns and systypes system tables. A rule has a row in syscolumns if it is bound to a column and in systypes if it is bound to a user-defined datatype.

The first parameter of sp_bindrule specifies the name of the rule. You can use as many as 30 characters for the name of the rule. If you wish, you can include the name of the table column or user-defined datatype within the name of the rule.

Enter the name of either the table column or the user-defined datatype to which the rule will be applied. You must enter the name of the table column preceded by the name of the table in which it's defined, enclosed in single quotation marks. If you enter only the name of an object, it is interpreted by SQL Server as the name of a user-defined datatype. When you enter a column name use a period to separate the table name from the column name to which the rule is to be bound. A rule that is bound to a datatype restricts the values that can be added to the table column defined with the user-defined datatype.

Part

III

Ch

13

The third parameter, `futureonly`, is used only for the management of user-defined datatypes. `futureonly` prevents the rule from being applied to table columns that are already defined using the user-defined datatype. Use `futureonly` to specify that the rule only applies to columns that are subsequently created using the user-defined datatype to which the rule is bound.

You can also bind a rule to a table column or user-defined datatype using the SQL Enterprise Manager by performing the following steps:

1. After you start the SQL Enterprise Manager, select the server and the database in which the rule is defined.

2. Expand the Objects folder and select Rules.

3. Select the rule to be bound. Click the right mouse button and select Edit. Alternatively, you can choose Rules from the Manage menu to bring up the Manage Rules dialog box.

4. Click the Column Bindings or Datatype Bindings tab.

5. For a column binding, select the name of the table in the Table field, the column in the Column field, and the rule in the Bindings field. For a datatype binding, switch to the Datatype Bindings page. Select the user-defined datatype in the User-Defined Datatype field and the rule in the Binding column.

6. Click Bind.

7. Click Close to close the Manage Rules dialog box.

Figure 13.2 shows the Manage Rules dialog box for the binding of the `department_values` rule to the department column in the Employee table.

FIG. 13.2
You can bind a rule to the columns of multiple tables.

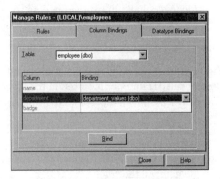

 TIP You can double-click a selected rule to bring up the Manage Rules dialog box.

Figure 13.3 shows the Manage Rules dialog box for the binding of rules to a user-defined datatype.

FIG. 13.3

You can bind a rule to a user-defined datatype when you create the datatype through the SQL Enterprise Manager.

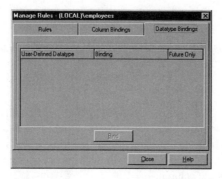

You may have already realized that conflicts can occur with rules and some precedence conventions that are used to resolve the conflicts. You might encounter a situation in which you have a table column that is defined using a user-defined datatype and both the datatype and column have rules that are bound to them. The following list includes three precedence rules that apply to rule binding:

- Rules that you bind to columns take precedence over rules you bind to datatypes. If rules are bound to both a table column and the user-defined datatype with which the column is defined, the rule that is bound to the table columns is used. If you bind a new rule to a table column, it also overrides a rule bound to the user-defined datatype to which the column is defined.

- If you bind a new rule to a column or datatype, the new rule replaces the old one. You can have only a single rule bound to a column or user-defined datatype.

- If you bind a rule to a user-defined datatype, it doesn't replace a rule bound to a column of that datatype. Table 13.2 summarizes rule precedence.

Table 13.2   Rule Precedence

New Rule Bound to...	Old Rule Bound to User-Defined Datatype	Old Rule Bound to Column
User-defined datatype	Replaces old rule	No change
Column	Replaces old rule	Replaces old rule

Part
III

Ch
13

Rules don't apply to the data that has already been entered in the table. Values that are currently in tables don't have to meet the criteria specified by rules. If you want a rule to constrain the values entered in the table, define a rule directly or indirectly, through a user-defined datatype, before data is entered into a table.

> **CAUTION**
>
> When you copy information into your database using the BCP utility, rules are not enforced. This is because the BCP utility is meant to complete changes in a bulk fashion as quickly as possible. If you are concerned
>
> *continues*

continued

about the integrity of incoming information, consider importing the information into a working table and then writing an application that will insert each row into your production table, leaving the rules in force for the insertions.

In Listing 13.1, the procedure, `sp_bindrule`, is used to bind the rule, `department_values`, to a the column department in the table, Employees. A subsequent INSERT statement fails its attempt to enter a value in the table column that doesn't meet the criteria defined by the rule. SQL Server returns a descriptive error message that specifies that the attempted INSERT violates the rule bound on the table column.

Listing 13.1   Output Showing Details for a Rule

```
sp_bindrule department_values, 'employees.department'
go
Rule bound to table column.
insert into employees
values ('Dan Duryea','Shipping',3321)
go
Msg 513, Level 16, State 1
A column insert or update conflicts with a rule imposed by a previous
CREATE RULE command. The command was aborted. The conflict occurred in
database 'master', table 'employees', column 'department'
Command has been aborted.
```

Listing 13.2 defines a new user-defined datatype and rule that is later bound to the datatype:

Listing 13.2   Output Showing Details for a Rule and Datatype

```
sp_addtype badge_type2, int, 'not null'
go
Type added.
create rule badgerule2
as @badge_type2 >000 and @badge_type2 <9999
go
This command did not return data, and it did not return any rows
sp_bindrule badgerule2, badge_type2
Rule bound to datatype.
```

 TIP You can restrict the range of allowable values by using the appropriate system datatype—for example, `smallint` instead of integer.

N O T E Microsoft says that there are three types of rules that you can define: rules with a range, a list, or a pattern. The two previous examples use a range (`...@badge_type2 >000` and `@badge_type2 <9999`) and a list (`...@department in ('Sales','Field Service', 'Logistics')`) to restrict values for the rule. The following example shows the third type of rule, which is a rule that uses a pattern to restrict values. The example restricts values to any number of characters that end with "S" through "U."

```
Create rule pattern_rule
@p like '%[S-U]'
```

You may find it easier to define and use rules if you understand the types of rules that you can create. ▨

Displaying Rule Bindings

You can use the system procedure, sp_help, to display information about the user-defined datatypes or table columns that have rules bound to them. In the following example, information displayed about the user-defined datatype created in an earlier example includes the rule that is bound to the datatype:

```
sp_help badge_type2
Type_name  Storage_type  Length Nulls  Default_name Rule_name
-------------  ---------------  ------ -----  ---------------
badge_type2  int              4      0      (null)       badgerule2
```

You can also display rule binding information by clicking Bindings in the Manage Rules dialog box. In Figure 13.4, the Manage Rule Info dialog box shows a rule bound to a table column.

FIG. 13.4

You can also unbind a rule from the Manage Rule Info dialog box.

Displaying Rules

sp_help displays information about a database object, such as a user-defined datatype or column, including the name of a rule that is bound to the datatype or column. sp_help doesn't show the rule itself when information about the object to which it's bound is shown.

You can use sp_help to display information about a rule. It doesn't, however, return much information about a rule. In the following example, sp_help returns information about the rule, badgerule2 and shows only its owner, the type of object, a defined segment on which it's located, and the date and time it was created:

```
sp_help badgerule2
Name                          Owner           Type
------------------------------- ---------------
badgerule2                    dbo             rule
```

Part III
Ch
13

```
Data_located_on_segment      When_created
----------------------- --------------------
not applicable          Oct 24 1994 10:40AM
```

You'll probably be more interested in displaying the rule itself instead of the characteristics of the rule as an object. To display the definition of a rule itself, use sp_helptext. The definition of a rule is saved as the row of a system table, so the definition of a rule is returned as the row of a table. The following example shows the rule that is used to constrain the range of allowable badge numbers defined in previous examples:

```
sp_helptext badgerule2
text
---------------------------
create rule badgerule2
as @badge_type2 >000 and @badge_type2 <9999
(1 row(s) affected)
```

You can also use the SQL Enterprise Manager to display rules. A rule definition is shown in the Description field of the Manage Rules dialog box. Double-click a selected rule or right-click and select Edit to bring up the description of a rule in the Manage Rules dialog box. Refer to Figure 13.1 to see the Manage Rules dialog box with the description of the rule within the Description field.

Finally, keep in mind that rules are defined within a set of system tables, which is local to each database. The rules defined within one database aren't available within another database. You can select the rule definition within an ISQL/w session, store it as a file, and then open the file to recover the rule. You can define the rule after you use a USE command to position yourself to the database in which the rule will be applied.

Unbinding Rules

At some point, you may no longer want the values that are entered into a column or user-defined datatype to be constrained by a rule. You can unbind a rule using sp_unbindrule, which removes the constraint from a bound column or user-defined datatype. Unbinding a rule makes it non-applicable to a column or user-defined datatype. The sp_unbindrule syntax is as follows:

sp_unbindrule *table_name.column* or *user_datatype* [, futureonly]

Like sp_bindrule, if the first parameter of sp_unbindrule is a column, it must be preceded by the name of the table in which it's defined and entered in single quotation marks. Otherwise, the first parameter is interpreted as the name of a user-defined datatype.

Use futureonly, the optional third parameter, only with rules that are bound to user-defined datatypes. Table columns that are already defined using the user-defined datatype have the rule applied to the columns unless the futureonly optional parameter is present. The futureonly option prevents existing columns from inheriting the rule. Only new columns that are defined using the user-defined datatype are affected by the rule.

You can also use the SQL Enterprise Manager to unbind a rule from a table column or user-defined datatype by clicking Unbind after selecting the rule in the Manage Rule Info dialog box (see Figure 13.5).

FIG. 13.5
The name of the rule is removed from the Bound Columns field of the Manage Rule Info dialog box.

In Listing 13.3, `sp_help` displays the Employees table, which has a rule that is defined on the department column. `sp_unbindrule` unbinds the rule from the department column of the Employees table. A subsequent display of the Employees table shows that the rule has been unbound from the table column.

Listing 13.3   Output Showing a Table and the Process of Removing a Rule from the Table

```
sp_help employees
go
Name            Owner                   Type
------------------------------- ------------
employees       dbo                     user table
Data_located_on_segment         When_created
------------------------------- ------------
default                 May 12 1994 10:15AM
Column_name Type Length Nulls Default_name  Rule_name
-------------- --------------- ------- ----- -------
name    CHAR    20      0      (null)        (null)
department CHAR 20      0      (null) department_values
badge      int  4       0      (null)        (null)
Object does not have any indexes.
No defined keys for this object.
sp_unbindrule 'employees.department'
go
Rule unbound from table column.
sp_help employees
go
Name            Owner                   Type
------------------------------- ------------
employees       dbo                     user table
Data_located_on_segment         When_created
------------------------------- ------------
default                 May 12 1994 10:15AM
Column_name  Type Length Nulls Default_name Rule_name
-------------- --------------- ------- ----- --------
```

Part
III

Ch
13

continues

Listing 13.3 Continued

```
name         CHAR    20     0     (null)      (null)
department   CHAR    20     0     (null)      (null)
badge        int      4     0     (null)      (null)
Object does not have any indexes.
No defined keys for this object.
```

You can also unbind a rule by replacing the current rule with a new one. sp_bindrule binds a new rule to that column or datatype. The old rule is automatically unbound from the user-defined datatype or table column.

In Listing 13.4, the attempted redefinition of the existing department_values rule is unsuccessful because a rule can't be replaced by one with the same name. A new rule is created, and it's bound to the same column to which the department_values rule is bound. The new rule replaces the old department_values rule.

Listing 13.4 You Cannot Create a Rule with the Same Name as Another in the Database

```
create rule department_values
as @department in ('Sales','Field Service','Logistics','Shipping')
go
Msg 2714, Level 16, State 1
There is already an object named 'department_values' in the database.
create rule depart2
as @department in ('Sales','Field Service','Logistics','Shipping')
go
This command did not return data, and it did not return any rows
sp_bindrule depart2, 'employees.department'
go
Rule bound to table column.
```

In Listing 13.5, which is a continuation of the previous example, an INSERT into the Employees table demonstrates that the new rule has been bound to the department column. The old rule for department would have disallowed the addition of a row that contains the shipping department. A SELECT statement shows that the new row was added to the table. Finally, sp_help shows that the new depart2 rule is bound to the department column of the Employees table and replaces the old department_values rule.

Listing 13.5 Output Showing Table Definition

```
insert into employees
values ('Dan Duryea','Shipping',3321)
go
(1 row(s) affected)
select * from employees
go
name                 department           badge
```

```
.................... .................... ............
Bob Smith           Sales                1234
Mary Jones          Sales                5514
Dan Duryea          Shipping             3321
(3 row(s) affected)
sp_help employees
go
Name                              Owner                      Type
..........................        ......................     ............
employees                         dbo                        user table
Data_located_on_segment          When_created
..............................    ..........................
default                           May 12 1994 10:15AM
Column_name    Type           Length Nulls Default_name   Rule_name
.............  .............  ......  ....  .............  .............
name           CHAR            20     0     (null)         (null)
department     CHAR            20     0     (null)         depart2
badge          int             4      0     (null)         (null)
Object does not have any indexes.
No defined keys for this object.
```

Renaming Rules

You can rename rules, like other objects, using sp_rename. You can also use sp_rename to rename other user objects, such as tables, views, columns, stored procedures, triggers, and defaults. The sp_rename syntax is as follows:

sp_rename *object_name*, *new_name*

In Listing 13.6, an existing rule is renamed. After the rule is renamed, a display of the Employees table shows that the new name of the rule is in effect for the department column.

Listing 13.6 Renaming Objects

```
sp_rename depart2, depart3
go
Object name has been changed.
sp_help employees
go
Name                              Owner                      Type
..........................        ......................     ............
employees                         dbo                        user table
Data_located_on_segment          When_created
..............................    ..........................
default                           May 12 1994 10:15AM
Column_name    Type           Length Nulls Default_name   Rule_name
.............  .............  ......  ....  .............  .............
name           CHAR            20     0     (null)         (null)
department     CHAR            20     0     (null)         depart3
badge          int             4      0     (null)         (null)
Object does not have any indexes.
No defined keys for this object.
```

Part

III

Ch

13

You can also rename a rule by using the SQL Enterprise Manager with the Rename Object dialog box. Right-click a selected rule and select Rename. In the Rename Object dialog box, enter a new name in the New Name field. Click OK. Figure 13.6 shows the Rename Object dialog box.

FIG. 13.6

The new rule name immediately replaces the old name in the Server Manager dialog box of the SQL Enterprise Manager.

Dropping Rules

You can use the DROP RULE statement to permanently remove a rule from a database. The rule is immediately removed if it's not bound to any columns or user-defined datatypes. If the rule is bound to a column or a datatype, you must first unbind the rule from all columns and user-defined datatypes to be able to drop the rule. You can drop multiple rules with a single DROP RULE statement. The DROP RULE syntax is as follows:

```
DROP RULE rule_name_1[,...rule_name_n]
```

In Listing 13.7, an initial attempt to remove a rule is unsuccessful because the rule is bound to a table column. After the rule is unbound from the table column, it's successfully removed. Sp_helptext demonstrates that the object is gone.

Listing 13.7   Removing a Rule

```
drop rule depart3
go
Msg 3716, Level 16, State 1
The rule 'depart3' cannot be dropped because it is bound to one or more column.
sp_unbindrule 'employees.department'
go
Rule unbound from table column.
drop rule depart3
go
This command did not return data, and it did not return any rows
sp_helptext depart3
go
No such object in the current database.
```

You can also drop rules through the SQL Enterprise Manager. Select the name of the rule in the Rule field of the Manage Rules dialog box (refer to Figure 13.1). Click Drop to remove the rule. Click Close to close the Manage Rules dialog box.

TIP Keep in mind that you can only have a single rule bound to either a user-defined datatype or a table column. If you have a rule defined and then bind a new rule to the same column as the first, the first rule will be replaced.

In addition, if you bind a rule to a user-defined datatype without using `futureonly`, it effectively replaces the rule for all table columns defined from the user-defined datatype.

Defining Defaults

You can use defaults to define a value, which is automatically added to a column, if no value is explicitly entered. You bind a default to a column or user-defined datatype using `sp_binddefault`. You must define a default value that is compatible with the column datatype. A default can't violate a rule that is associated with a table column.

Default definitions, like rule definitions, are stored in the syscomments table. Also like rules, if you bind a new default to a column, it automatically overrides an old rule. A default bound to the column takes precedence over a default bound to the user-defined datatype.

Creating Defaults

You can define a default using the CREATE DEFAULT statement. The name used in the second parameter of the `sp_bindefault` is interpreted as a user-defined datatype unless it's preceded with the table name. It must be preceded by the name of a table to be interpreted as a column of a table. The CREATE DEFAULT syntax is as follows:

```
CREATE DEFAULT default_name AS constant value
```

> **CAUTION**
>
> If you define a default with a value that is longer than the table column to which it's subsequently bound, the default value entered into the column is truncated. Make sure the datatype and size of your column matches that of the default you're trying to establish.

You can also create a default using the SQL Enterprise Manager by performing the following steps:

1. After you start the SQL Enterprise Manager, select the server and the database in which the default is to be created.
2. Expand the Objects folder and select Defaults.
3. Click the right mouse button and select New Default to bring up the Manage Defaults dialog box. Alternatively, you can choose Defaults from the Manage menu to bring up the Manage Defaults dialog box.
4. Enter a value for the default in the Description field and a name for the default in the Default field.

Part
III

Ch
13

5. Click Add to create the new default.

6. Click Close to close the Manage Defaults dialog box.

Figure 13.7 shows the Manage Defaults dialog box for the creation of the default department_rule through the SQL Enterprise Manager.

FIG. 13.7
You can also manage existing defaults using the Manage Defaults dialog box.

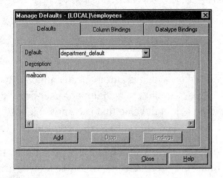

Binding Defaults

You can use the system procedure, sp_bindefault, to bind a default to a user-defined datatype or table column. The second parameter can be the name of a table column or a user-defined datatype. Use the third parameter to specify that the default value should only be applied to new columns of tables that are defined, not to existing columns of tables. The sp_bindefault syntax is as follows:

```
sp_bindefault default_name, table_name.column_name, [futureonly]
```

In Listing 13.8, a default is defined and bound to the department column of the Employees table. A row is inserted into the table that omits a value for the department column in the list of values. A subsequent SELECT statement demonstrates that the default value was added to the department column for the newly inserted row.

Listing 13.8   Defining a Default

```
create default Department_default as 'Sales'
go
sp_bindefault Department_default, 'employees.department'
go
Default bound to column.
insert into employees
(name, badge)
values ('John Garr',2221)
go
(1 row(s) affected)
select * from employees
```

```
where badge=2221
go
name                      department              badge
--------------------      -----------------       -----------
John Garr                 Sales                   2221
(1 row(s) affected)
```

In the following example, a default is defined and bound to a user-defined datatype. The second parameter of sp_bindefault is interpreted as a user-defined datatype because no table name precedes the object name. The third parameter isn't specified, so the default value is applied to any table columns that are defined using the user-defined datatype.

```
create default badge_default
as 9999
sp_bindefault badge_default, badge_type2
Default bound to datatype.
```

N O T E When you define a table column that permits NULL values, a NULL is added to a row when the column isn't referenced at the time a row is inserted into the table. A NULL entry is automatically inserted, just as a default value is automatically inserted. The definition of a NULL remains the same. It's meaning, however, is still undefined, which is different from the automatic insertion of an actual value. ▪

▶ **See** "Understanding *NULL* and *NOT NULL*" **p. 156**

You can use the SQL Enterprise Manager to bind a default to a table column or user-defined datatype by performing the following steps:

1. After you start the SQL Enterprise Manager, select the server and the database in which the default is defined.

2. Expand the Objects folder and select Defaults.

3. Select the default to be bound. Click the right mouse button and select Edit. Alternatively, you can choose Defaults from the Manage menu to bring up the Manage Defaults dialog box.

4. Click the Column Bindings or Datatype Bindings tab.

5. For a column binding, select the name of the table in the Table field, the column in the Column field, and the default in the Binding field. For a datatype binding, switch to the Datatype Bindings page. Select the user-defined datatype in the User-Defined Datatype field and the default in the Binding column.

6. Click Bind.

7. Click Close to close the Manage Defaults dialog box.

Figure 13.8 shows the Manage Defaults dialog box for the binding of the department_default default to the department column in the Employee table.

FIG. 13.8

You can bind a default to the columns of multiple tables.

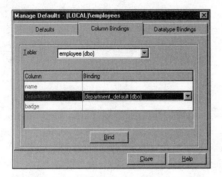

You can only bind a single default value to a given column. If you try to bind a default to a column on which one already exists, you receive an error message from SQL Server. You need to use the `sp_unbindefault` statement to remove the existing default and then apply the new default to the column.

Unlike rules, Defaults are applied during bulk copy operations. If you have both a default and a rule on a given column, the default is applied first and then the rule is checked. This helps keep your rule from having to be aware of NULL values because the default will have already updated the value appropriately.

In the next section you find out how to determine what defaults are already in place for a given column.

Displaying Bindings

You can use `sp_help` to display the defaults bound to either table columns or user-defined datatypes. In Listing 13.9, `sp_help` displays the default bound to the badge column:

Listing 13.9   Showing Defaults Bound to a Table

```
sp_help employees
go
Name                             Owner                            Type
-------------------------------  -------------------------------  ----------
employees                        dbo                              user table
Data_located_on_segment          When_created
-------------------------------  -------------------------------
default                          Oct 18 1994 12:52PM
Column_name    Type          Length Nulls Default_name      Rule_name
-------------  ------------   ------ ----- ----------------  --------
name           CHAR            20      0    (null)            (null)
department     CHAR            20      0    (null)            (null)
badge          int             4       0    badge_default     (null)
Object does not have any indexes.
No defined keys for this object.
```

You can also display default bindings using the SQL Enterprise Manager. One way in which you can display default bindings through the SQL Enterprise Manager is from the Manage Default Info dialog box. Click Bindings to display default bindings in the Manage Default Info dialog box (see Figure 13.9).

FIG. 13.9
You can bind a default to both a user-defined datatype and a table column.

 TIP A default bound to a table column is also displayed in the Default file of the Manage Table dialog box in the SQL Enterprise Manager.

Displaying Defaults

You can use the procedure `sp_helptext` to display the value defined for a default. The definitions of defaults are stored as rows in the syscomments system table. The display of a default definition is shown as the row of a table. In the following example, the default for a table column is shown using `sp_helptext`:

```
sp_helptext Department_default
go
text-----------------------------------------
create default Department_default as 'Sales'
(1 row(s) affected)
```

You can also use the SQL Enterprise Manager to display a default. A default definition is shown in the Description field of the Manage Defaults dialog box. Double-click a selected rule or right-click and select Edit to bring up the description of a default in the Manage Defaults dialog box. Refer to Figure 13.7 to see the Manage Defaults dialog box with the default values.

Unbinding Defaults

When you no longer want the default value automatically entered into a column or user-defined datatype, you must unbind the default by using `sp_unbindefault`, which removes the default from a bound column or user-defined datatype. Unbinding a default makes it non-applicable to a column or user-defined datatype. The `sp_unbindefault` syntax is as follows:

```
sp_unbindefault table_name.column_name [,futureonly]
```

Part
III

Ch
13

Use the third parameter, which is optional, to specify that only new columns defined using the user-defined datatype aren't bound using the default. You only use the third parameter for user-defined datatypes. You don't use it for table columns. In Listing 13.10, a default is unbound from a table column. sp_help is first used to verify that the default is bound to the table column. Thereafter, sp_help is used after the default is unbound to verify that the default was unbound from the table column.

Listing 13.10 Verifying the Removal of a Default

```
sp_help employees
go
Name                          Owner                          Type
----------------------------  -----------------------------  ------------------
employees                     dbo                            user table
Data_located_on_segment       When_created
----------------------------  -----------------------------
default                       Oct 18 1994 12:52PM
Column_name    Type          Length Nulls Default_name      Rule_name
-------------  -----------    ------ ----- ---------------   ----------
name           CHAR            20     0    (null)            (null)
department     CHAR            20     0    (null)            (null)
badge          int             4      0    badge_default     (null)
Object does not have any indexes.
No defined keys for this object.
sp_unbindefault 'employees.badge'
go
Default unbound from table column.
sp_help employees
go
Name                          Owner                          Type
----------------------------  -----------------------------  ----------
employees                     dbo                            user table
Data_located_on_segment       When_created
----------------------------  -----------------------------
default                       Oct 18 1994 12:52PM
Column_name    Type          Length Nulls Default_name      Rule_name
-------------  -----------    ------ ----- ---------------   ----------
name           CHAR            20     0    (null)            (null)
department     CHAR            20     0    (null)            (null)
badge          int             4      0    (null)            (null)
Object does not have any indexes.
No defined keys for this object.
```

You can also use the SQL Enterprise Manager to unbind a default from a table column or user-defined datatype by clicking Unbind after selecting the default in the Manage Defaults Info dialog box. Figure 13.10 shows the Manage Default Info dialog box after the department_default default has been unbound from the user-defined datatype department.

FIG. 13.10

The name of the default is immediately removed from the Bound Columns or Bound Datatypes field of the Manage Default Info dialog box.

Renaming Defaults

You can use system procedure, sp_rename, to rename a default. In Listing 13.11, a default is renamed using sp_rename. After the default is renamed, the table in which the default is bound to a column is displayed using sp_help to confirm that the default was renamed.

Listing 13.11   Renaming a Default

```
sp_rename Department_default, dept_default
go
Object name has been changed.
sp_help employees
go
Name                            Owner                         Type
------------------------------  ----------------------------  ----------
employees                       dbo                           user table
Data_located_on_segment         When_created
------------------------------  ----------------------------  ----------
default                         May 12 1994 10:15AM
Column_name     Type           Length Nulls Default_name    Rule_name
-------------   ------------   ------ ----- -------------   --------
name            CHAR             20     0    (null)          (null)
department      CHAR             20     0    dept_default    (null)
badge           int              4      0    (null)          (null)
Object does not have any indexes.
No defined keys for this object.
```

You can also rename a default using the SQL Enterprise Manager with the Rename Object dialog box by right-clicking a selected default and selecting Rename. In the Rename Object dialog box (refer to Figure 13.6), enter a new name in the New Name field. Click OK.

N O T E   All database objects can be renamed using the sp_rename system procedure of the Rename Object dialog box in the SQL Enterprise Manager. ▪

Part
III

Ch
13

Dropping Defaults

You can permanently remove a default with the DROP DEFAULT statement. The default is immediately removed if it's not bound to any columns or user-defined datatypes. If the default is
bound to a column or a datatype, you must first unbind the default from all columns and user
datatypes before you can drop the default. You can drop multiple defaults with a single
DROP DEFAULT statement. The DROP DEFAULT syntax is as follows:

DROP DEFAULT *default_name_1* [*,...default_name_n*]

In the following example, an attempt to drop a default is unsuccessful because the default is
bound to a table column. After the column is unbound from a table column, the default can be
successfully dropped.

```
drop default dept_default
go
Msg 3716, Level 16, State 1
The default 'dept_default' cannot be dropped because it is bound to one or
more columns.
sp_unbindefault 'employees.department'
go
Default unbound from table column.
drop default dept_default
go
This command did not return data, and it did not return any rows
sp_helptext dept_default
No such object in the current database.
```

You can also drop defaults through the SQL Enterprise Manager. Select the name of the default
in the Default field of the Manage Defaults dialog box (refer to Figure 13.7). Click Drop to
remove the default. Click Close to close the Manage Defaults dialog box.

Reality Check

ODBC is both a blessing and a curse. With ODBC, you can query and work with databases
from nearly any Microsoft Office application, Web sites, and more. This is now especially true
with Office 97's capability to connect directly to database sources from within each of the applications. This is great for the user but can be disastrous for the developers because they no
longer control the client-side application used to manipulate the database.

This is where rules, defaults, and constraints are useful. By implementing this low-level check
on the database side of the equation where the information is ultimately stored, you remove
the dependence on the client application. You also make your database strong enough that it
can guarantee the relationships between tables.

In large-scale applications, rules and these types of server-side constraints play another, just as
important, role. You should consider having a person or team of people that is responsible for
the database engine and the implementation of the rules you're defining here. By centralizing
the responsibility for these control mechanisms, you'll save a lot of heartache, especially compared to having this function distributed among departments.

In large development teams, it's difficult to make sure all of the developers know all of the different rules that pertain to the database on which they're working. Because you can implement these rules separately from the development work they're doing, you'll still be assured of a well-mannered application in the database sense, even if many different developers had their hand at writing the code to access the database. By placing the management of the database with a central person or team, you can be sure that no duplication will occur, and you'll be able to optimize the database to reflect the requirements of the team as a whole.

From Here...

Rules are very powerful tools used to enforce limitations on column and user-defined datatype values. After a rule is created, it must then be bound to columns or datatypes. Rules and datatypes can be bound to multiple table columns or user-defined datatypes. Defaults provide a way to provide an initial value to columns. Initial values can be used as suggestions or as a way to allow users, with a limited view of a table, to insert rows that contain data in columns to which they do not have access.

For information about the type of restrictions that are provided by constraints, see the following chapters:

- Chapter 6, "Creating Database Tables and Using Datatypes," teaches you how to define data columns and user-defined datatypes. You'll also learn the allowable range of values for each system datatype.

- Chapter 15, "Creating and Managing Triggers," shows how you can add more control to the database back-end, reacting programmatically to data changes in your tables.

Part
III

Ch
13

Managing Stored Procedures and Using Flow-Control Statements

As your systems become more complex, you'll need to spend more time carefully integrating SQL code with your host application code. In this chapter, you review the logic and flow control statements that you have available to you in your SQL code.

At a high-level, Stored Procedures are a way that you can create routines and procedures that are run on the server, by server processes. These routines can be started by an application calling them, or called by data integrity rules or triggers.

The benefit of Stored Procedures comes from the fact that they run within the SQL Server environment on the server. Although at first this might not seem to be any obvious advantage, it goes to the heart of the client-server model. Remember the rule of thumb that the system doing the work to satisfy a given situation should be the system most suited for that work? Since SQL Server manages the databases in your system, it makes sense that it would be the best place to run the stored procedures against that data.

What flow-control statements are available and how to use them

Programming languages were built around flow control, but databases were built around data. Flow-control statements were added to databases to facilitate the writing of stored procedures.

How to work with a host language, returning information about the success or failure of your routine

Return codes or visual output to the user can increase the effectiveness of a stored procedure.

How to work with variables within your procedures

Variables must be assigned a data type and a scope. Find out how you declare your variables and control how they are used within your stored procedures.

Stored procedures can return values, modify values, and can be used to compare a user-supplied value against the pre-requisites for information in the system. They run quickly, with the added horsepower of the average SQL Server hardware, and they are database-aware and able to take advantage of SQL Server's optimizer for best performance at runtime.

You can also pass values to a stored procedure, and it can return values that are not necessarily part of an underlying table, but are, instead, calculated during the running of the stored procedure.

The benefits of stored procedures on a grand scale include:

- Performance—Because stored procedures run on the server, typically a more powerful machine, the execution time is generally much less than at the workstation. In addition, because the database information is readily at hand and on the same system physically, there is no wait for records to pass over the network for processing. Instead, the stored procedure has immediate, ready access to the database, which makes working with the information extremely fast.

- Client/server development benefits—By breaking apart the client and server development tasks, you can sometimes help to decrease the time needed to bring your projects to completion. You can develop the server-side pieces separately from the client-side, and you can re-use the server-side components between client-side applications.

- Security—As mentioned earlier in the chapter on Views, you can use stored procedures as a tool to really clamp down on security. You can create stored procedures for all add, change, delete, and list operations and make it so you can programmatically control each of these aspects of information access.

- Server-side enforcement of data-oriented rules—This is ultimately one of the most important reasons for using an intelligent database engine; the stored procedures let you put into place the rules and other logic that help control the information put into your system.

N O T E   It's important to keep the client/server model in mind when you're building your systems. Remember, data management belongs on the server, and data presentation and display manipulation for reports and inquiries should reside on the client in the ideal model. As you build systems, be on the lookout for those items that can be moved to the different ends of the model to optimize the user's experience with your application. ■

Although SQL is defined as a non-procedural language, SQL Server permits the use of flow-control keywords. You use the flow-control keywords to create a procedure that you can store for subsequent execution. You can use these stored procedures to perform operations with an SQL Server database and its tables instead of writing programs using conventional programming language, such as C or Visual Basic.

Some of the advantages that Stored Procedures offer over dynamic SQL Statements are:

- Stored procedures are compiled the first time that they're run and are stored in a system table of the current database. When they are compiled, they are optimized to select the best path to access information in the tables. This optimization takes into account the actual data patterns in the table, indexes that are available, table loading, and more. These compiled stored procedures can greatly enhance the performance of your system.

- Another benefit is that you can execute a stored procedure on either a local or remote SQL Server. This enables you to run processes on other machines and work with information across servers, not just *local* databases.

- An application program written in a language, such as C or Visual Basic, can also execute stored procedures, providing an optimum solution between the client-side software and SQL Server. ■

Defining Stored Procedures

You use the CREATE PROC[EDURE] statement to create a stored procedure. Permission to execute the procedure that you create is set by default to the owner of the database. An owner of the database can change the permissions to allow other users to execute the procedure. The maximum stored procedure name length is 30 characters. The syntax that you use to define a new procedure is as follows:

```
CREATE PROCEDURE [owner,] procedure_name [;number]
[@parameter_name datatype [=default] [OUTput]
...
[@parameter_name datatype [=default] [OUTput]
[FOR REPLICATION] ¦ [WITH RECOMPILE] , ENCRYPTION
AS sql_statements
```

> **CAUTION**
>
> Be sure you reload your stored procedures again after information has been saved in the database tables that represents, both in volume and content, the information that your application can expect to see. Because stored procedures are compiled and optimized based on the tables, indexes, and data loading, your query can show significant improvement just by reloading it after "real" information has been placed in the system.

In Listing 14.1, a simple procedure is created that contains a SELECT statement to display all rows of a table. After the procedure is created, its name is entered on a line to execute the procedure. If you precede the name of a stored procedure with other statements, you use the EXEC[UTE] procedure name statement to execute the procedure.

Part
III

Ch
14

Listing 14.1 Creating and Running a Stored Procedure

```
create procedure all_employees
as select * from employees

exec all_employees

name                  department            badge
------------------    ------------------    ----------
Bob Smith             Sales                 1234
Mary Jones            Sales                 5514
( 2 row(s) affected)
```

T I P If your call to the stored procedure is the first in your batch of commands, you don't have to specify the EXEC[UTE] portion of the statement. You can simply call the procedure by name, and it will be executed automatically.

N O T E As mentioned earlier, naming conventions for SQL objects are an important part of your implementation plan. In a production system, you will often have hundreds of stored procedures, many tables, and many more supporting objects. You should consider coming up with a naming convention for your stored procedures that will make it easy to identify them as procedures and will make it easier to document them. In many installations, a common prefix for the stored procedure name is sp_. ▪

You can create a new procedure in the current database only. If you're working in ISQL or ISQL/W, you can execute the USE statement followed by the name of the database to set the current database to the database in which the procedure should be created. You can use any Transact-SQL statement in a stored procedure with the exception of CREATE statements.

When you submit a stored procedure to the system, SQL Server compiles and verifies the routines within it. If any problems are found, the procedure is rejected and you'll need to determine what the problem is prior to re-submitting the routine. If your stored procedure references another, as yet unimplemented stored procedure, you'll receive a warning message, but the routine will still be installed.

If you leave the system with the stored procedure that you previously referred to uninstalled, the user will receive an error message at runtime.

N O T E Stored procedures are treated like all other objects in the database. They are, therefore, subject to all of the same naming conventions and other limitations. For example, the name of a stored procedure cannot contain spaces, and it can be accessed using the database <object> convention. ▪

Using Parameters with Procedures

Stored procedures are very powerful, but to be most effective, the procedure must be somewhat dynamic, which enables you, the developer, to pass in values to be considered during the functioning of the stored procedure. Here are some general guidelines for using parameters with stored procedures:

- You can define one or more parameters in a procedure.
- You use parameters as named storage locations just like you would use the parameters as variables in conventional programming languages, such as C and Visual Basic.
- You precede the name of a parameter with an *at* symbol (@) to designate it as a parameter.
- Parameter names are local to the procedure in which they're defined.

You can use parameters to pass information into a procedure from the line that executes the parameter. You place the parameters after the name of the procedure on a command line, with commas to separate the list of parameters if there is more than one. You use system datatypes to define the type of information to be expected as a parameter.

In Listing 14.2, the procedure is defined with three input parameters. The defined input parameters appear within the procedure in the position of values in the VALUE clause of an INSERT statement. When the procedure is executed, three literal values are passed into the INSERT statement within the procedure as a parameter list. A SELECT statement is executed after the stored procedure is executed to verify that a new row was added through the procedure.

N O T E When a procedure executes as the first statement in a series of statements, the procedure does not have to be preceded by the keyword EXECUTE. The name of the procedure to be executed is simply placed as the first keyword on the line. ▪

 T I P Be sure to check the documentation for the host language you are using with SQL Server to determine the correct calling sequence for the host language. Actual calling syntax varies from language to language.

Listing 14.2 Creating a Stored Procedure with Input Parameters

```
create procedure proc4 (@p1 char(15), @p2 char(20), @p3 int) as
insert into Workers
values (@p1, @p2, @p3)

proc4 'Bob Lint',Sales,3333

select * from Workers
where Badge=3333
```

continues

Part
III

Ch

14

Listing 14.2 Continued

```
Name                            Department      Badge
------------------------------  --------------  -----------
Bob Lint                        Sales           3333

(1 row(s) affected)
```

The semicolon and integer after the name of a procedure enables you to create multiple versions of a procedure with the same name. In Listing 14.3, two procedures with the same name are created as versions one and two. When the procedure is executed, the version number can be specified to control the version of the procedure that is executed. If no version number is specified, the first version of the procedure is executed. This option is not shown in the example above, but is available if needed by your application. Both procedures use a PRINT statement to return a message that identifies the procedure version.

Listing 14.3 Using Versions of Stored Procedures

```
create procedure proc3;1 as
print 'version 1'

create procedure proc3;2 as
print 'version 2'

proc3;1

version 1

proc3;2

version 2

proc3

version 1
```

In the previous example, proc3 is executed without preceding it with the keyword EXECUTE because it is executed as the first statement on a line.

TIP You can use the SET NOEXEC ON command the first time that you execute a procedure to check it for errors. This prevents you from executing it when errors may cause it to fail.

You can create a new stored procedure through the SQL Enterprise Manager, as well as in ISQL or ISQL/W. Perform the following steps to create a new stored procedure through the SQL Enterprise Manager:

1. Select Stored Procedures under the Objects of the selected database in the Server Manager window.

2. Right-click Stored Procedures and select New Stored Procedures from the menu. You can also select Stored Procedures from the Manage menu to bring up the Manage Stored Procedures dialog box. You can enter Transact-SQL statements in the dialog box. The Manage Stored Procedures dialog box is brought up with the keys that are used to define a stored procedure. Figure 14.1 shows the Manage Stored Procedures dialog box before any statements are typed into the dialog box.

FIG. 14.1
You can also edit an existing stored procedure in the Manage Stored Procedures dialog box.

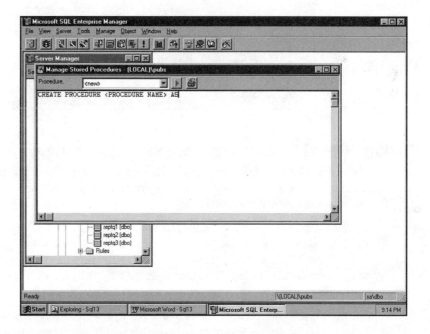

3. You must overwrite <PROCEDURE NAME> in the Manage Stored Procedures dialog box with the name of your new procedure.

4. Click the Execute button to create and store your procedure. Figure 14.2 shows a simple Transact-SQL statement and a new procedure name entered in the Manage Stored Procedures dialog box.

Part III
Ch 14

FIG. 14.2
Click the Procedures list box to display a list of the procedures in the selected database.

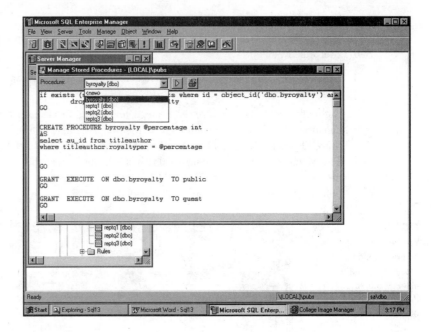

Calling Stored Procedures from Your Application

When you call stored procedures from other applications environments, there are a few useful tricks that you should know about. For starters, when your stored procedures take parameters, you have a couple of different options.

First, you can always provide all parameters in the order in which they are declared. Although this is easy to develop for, consider carefully whether this makes sense in the long run. There will probably be cases where you want to make a multipurpose stored procedure that calls for more parameters than would be required, on the whole, for any given call. In those cases, you're *expecting* to have some parameters that are not specified in each call.

You use a test for null on a parameter to determine whether it was provided. This means you can test directly against Null, or you can use the IsNull comparison operator.

▶ **See** Chapter 9, "Using Functions," in the section titled "Using ISNULL and NULLIF," for more information about ISNULL **p. 286**

On the application side, it can be quite cumbersome to have to specify each value on every call to the stored procedure, even in cases where the value is NULL. In those cases, the calling application can use *named arguments* to pass information to SQL Server and the stored procedure. For example, if your stored procedure allows up to three different arguments, name, address, and phone, you can call the routine as follows:

```
Exec sp_routine @name="blah"
```

When you provide the name of the argument being passed, SQL Server can map it to its corresponding parameter. This is, typically, the best way to pass information to SQL Server, and it also helps make the code more readable because you can tell which parameters are being passed.

Displaying and Editing Procedures

You use the system procedure `sp_helptext` to list the definition of a procedure, and `sp_help` to display control information about a procedure. The system procedures `sp_helptext` and `sp_help` are used to list information about other database objects, such as tables, rules, and defaults, as well as stored procedures.

Procedures with the same name, regardless of version number, are displayed together and dropped together. In Listing 14.4, the definition of procedures `proc3`, version one and two, are both displayed when the procedure is specified with the `sp_helptext` system procedure.

Listing 14.4   Viewing Different Versions of Stored Procedures

```
sp_helptext proc3

text
---------------------------------------------
create procedure proc3;1 as
print 'version 1'
create procedure proc3;2 as
print 'version 2'

(1 row(s) affected)
```

In Listing 14.5, the system procedure `sp_help` is used to display information about the procedure `proc3`. If the version number is used with the `sp_help` system procedure, an error is returned.

Listing 14.5   *sp_help* Only Shows the Most Current Version

```
sp_help proc3

Name                            Owner                                    Type
----------------------------    -----------------------------------     -----------------
proc3                           dbo                                      stored procedure
Data_located_on_segment When_created
----------------------- -------------------------
not applicable          Dec 7 1994  1:50PM
```

Part

III

Ch

14

You can use an additional system procedure just to return information about stored procedures. The system procedure sp_stored_procedures is used to list information about stored procedures. In the following example, the procedure sp_stored_procedures is used to display information about a previously stored procedure.

```
sp_stored_procedures procall

procedure_qualifier  procedure_owner  procedure_name
➥ num_input_params num_output_params num_result_sets remarks
➥ ---------------------------
master  dbo  procall;1  -1  -1 -1  (null)

(1 row(s) affected)
```

> **TIP** You can use the command SET SHOWPLAN ON before you execute a procedure to see how SQL Server will perform the necessary reads and writes to the database tables when the statements in your procedure are executed. You can use this information to help determine whether additional indexes or different data layout would be beneficial to the query.

You use the SQL Enterprise Manager to list and edit existing procedures. Double-click the procedure to be edited in the list of stored procedures in the main window of the server Manager. The selected procedure is displayed and can be changed in the Manage Stored Procedures dialog box that is displayed.

You can't directly edit stored procedures. You'll notice in the Manage Stored Procedures dialog box (refer to Figures 14.1 and 14.2) an existing procedures has additional Transact-SQL statements added prior to the procedure definition. The conditional IF statement is used to check whether the procedure is already defined and delete the procedure. The old procedure definition must be removed and a new procedure, with the name you specify, is substituted for the old procedure.

Making Changes and Dropping Stored Procedures

Two closely related tasks that you'll, no doubt, have to perform are making changes to existing stored procedures and removing no longer used stored procedures. In the next two sections, you see exactly how you accomplish both of these tasks and understand why they are so closely related.

Changing an Existing Stored Procedure   Stored procedures cannot be modified in place, so you're forced to first drop the procedure, then create it again. Unfortunately, there is no ALTER statement that can be used to modify the contents of an existing procedure. This stems largely from the query plan that is created and the from fact that stored procedures are compiled after they are initiated.

Because the routines are compiled, and the query plan relies on the compiled information, SQL Server uses a binary version of the stored procedure when it is executed. It would be difficult or impossible to convert from the binary representation of the stored procedure back to English to allow for edits. For this reason, it's imperative that you maintain a copy of your stored procedures in a location other than SQL Server. Although SQL Server can produce the code that was used to create the stored procedure, you should always maintain a backup copy.

You can pull the text associated with a stored procedure by using the sp_helptext system stored procedure. The syntax of sp_helptext is as follows:

```
Sp_helptext procedure name
```

For example, pulling the text associated with the all_employees stored procedure results in the display shown in Figure 14.3.

FIG. 14.3

You can review the text associated with a stored procedure with the sp_helptext statement.

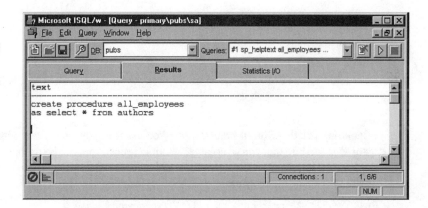

Alternatively, if you want to review the stored procedure in the Enterprise Manager, you can do so by selecting the Database, Objects, Stored procedures and then double-clicking the stored procedure you want to view. The result, shown in Figure 14.4, is not only a listing of the stored procedure, but also the proper statement to drop it and insert a new copy, should you so desire.

After you have the text, you can recreate the routine with the changes you need.

Part

III

Ch

14

FIG. 14.4

The Enterprise Manager sets up the syntax to drop and then recreate the stored procedure, if needed.

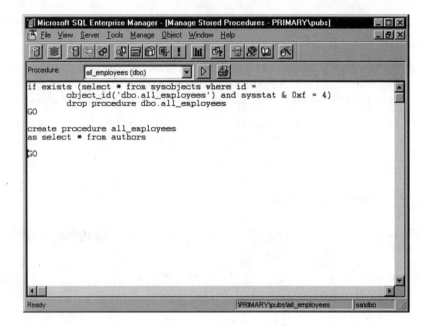

Removing Existing Stored Procedures   You use the DROP PROCEDURE statement to drop a stored procedure that you've created. Multiple procedures can be dropped with a single DROP PROCEDURE statement by listing multiple procedures separated by commas after the keywords DROP PROCEDURE in the syntax:

```
DROP PROCEDURE procedure_name_1, ...,procedure_name_n
```

Multiple versions of a procedure can't be selectively dropped. All versions of a procedure with the same name must be dropped at the same time by using the DROP PROCEDURE statement that specifies the procedure without a version number.

In the following example, the two versions of the procedures proc3 are dropped:

```
drop procedure proc3
This command did not return data, and it did not return any rows
```

You can also drop a selected procedure in the SQL Enterprise Manager. Right-click the selected procedure, and choose Drop from the menu that is displayed.

Understanding Procedure Resolution and Compilation

The benefit of using a stored procedure for the execution of a set of Transact-SQL statements is that it is compiled the first time that it's run. During compilation, the Transact-SQL statements in the procedure are converted from their original character representation into an executable form. During compilation, any objects that are referenced in procedures are also converted to alternate representations. For example, table names are converted to their object IDs and column names to their column IDs.

An execution plan is also created just as it would be for the execution of even a single Transact-SQL statement. The execution plan contains, for example, the indexes to be used to retrieve rows from tables that are referenced by the procedure. The execution plan is kept in a cache and is used to perform the queries of the procedure each time it's subsequently executed.

 TIP You can define the size of the procedure cache so that it is large enough to contain most or all the available procedures for execution and save the time that it would take to regenerate the execution plan for procedures.

Automatic Recompilation

Normally, the procedure's execution plan is run from the memory cache of procedures that permits it to execute rapidly. A procedure, however, is automatically recompiled under the following circumstances:

- A procedure is always recompiled when SQL Server is started, usually after a reboot of the underlying operating system, and when the procedure is first executed after it has been created.

- A procedure's execution plan is also automatically recompiled whenever an index on a table referenced in the procedure is dropped. A new execution plan must be compiled because the current one references an object, the index, for the retrieval of the rows of a table that doesn't exist. The execution plan must be redone to permit the queries of the procedure to be performed.

- Compilation of the execution plan is also re-initialized if the execution plan in the cache is currently in use by another user. A second copy of the execution plan is created for the second user. If the first copy of the execution plan weren't in use, it could have been used rather than a new execution plan being created. When a user finishes executing a procedure, the execution plan is available in the cache for reuse by another user with appropriate permissions.

- A procedure is also automatically recompiled if the procedure is dropped and re-created. All copies of the execution plan in the cache are removed because the new procedure may be substantially different from the older version and a new execution plan is necessary.

N O T E It's often the case that SQL Server remains up and running on the server system continuously. As a database server, it must be available whenever users on client PC workstations must access the SQL Server databases. The server computer and SQL Server need never be stopped and restarted unless a major error occurs, hardware malfunctions, or an update to a new version of SQL Server or Windows NT is in process. The recompilation of stored procedures would not be done frequently on systems that run non-stop. ■

Part
III

Ch
14

T I P When SQL Server is installed, you can specify that it should automatically restart when the server system is rebooted.

Note that because SQL server attempts to optimize stored procedures by caching the most recently used routines, it is still possible that an older execution plan, one previously loaded in cache, may be used in place of the new execution plan.

To prevent this problem, you must both drop and recreate the procedure or stop and restart SQL Server to flush the procedure cache and ensure that the new procedure is the only one that will be used when the procedure is executed.

You can also create the procedure using a WITH RECOMPILE option so that the procedure is automatically recompiled each time that it's executed. You should do this if the tables accessed by the queries in a procedure are very dynamic. Tables that are very dynamic have rows added, deleted, and updated frequently, which results in frequent changes to the indexes that are defined for the tables.

In other cases, you may want to force a recompilation of a procedure when it would not be done automatically. For example, if the statistics used to determine whether an index should be used for a query are updated, or an entire index is created for a table, recompilation is not automatic. You can use the WITH RECOMPILE clause on the EXECUTE statement when you execute the procedure to do a recompilation. The syntax of the EXECUTE statement with a recompile clause is:

```
EXECUTE procedure_name AS
.Transact-SQL statement(s)
...
WITH RECOMPILE
```

If the procedure you're working with uses parameters and these parameters control the functionality of the routine, you may want to use the RECOMPILE option. This is because, within the stored procedure, if the routine's parameters may determine the best execution path, it may be beneficial to have the execution plan determined at runtime, rather than determining it once and then using this plan for all accesses to the stored procedure.

N O T E It may be difficult to determine whether a procedure should be created with the WITH RECOMPILE option. If in doubt, you'll probably be better served by not creating the procedure with the RECOMPILE option. This is because, if you create a procedure with the RECOMPILE option, the procedure is recompiled each time the procedure is executed, and you may waste valuable CPU time to perform these compiles. You can still add the WITH RECOMPILE clause to force a recompilation when you execute the procedure. ■

You can't use the WITH RECOMPILE option in a CREATE PROCEDURE statement that contains the FOR REPLICATION option. You use the FOR REPLICATION option to create a procedure that is executed during replication.

▶ **See** the Chapter 17 section titled "Setting Up and Managing Replication," **p. 501** for more information about replication.

You can add the ENCRYPTION option to a CREATE PROCEDURE statement to encrypt the definition of the stored procedure that is added to the system table syscomments. You use the ENCRYPTION option to prevent other users from displaying the definition of your procedure and learning what objects it references and what Transact-SQL statements it contains.

> **CAUTION**
>
> Unless you absolutely must encrypt procedures for security reasons, you should leave procedures unencrypted. When you upgrade your database for a version change or to rebuild it, your procedures can only be recreated if the entries in syscomments are not encrypted.

Defining Procedure Auto Execution

You can use the system stored procedure, sp_makestartup, to define a procedure to execute automatically at the startup of SQL Server. You can mark any number of procedures to execute automatically at startup. The syntax sp_makestartup is as follows:

sp_makestartup procedure_name

The procedures that are defined to execute automatically at startup execute after the last database has been automatically started and recovered at startup of SQL Server. You can use the system procedure sp_helpstartup to list the procedures that are defined to execute at startup. You use the system procedure, sp_unmakestartup, to prevent a procedure from executing automatically.

In Listing 14.5, a new procedure is created that is marked for the automatic execution when SQL Server is started. In addition, the list startup procedures are also listed before and after the procedures are removed from automatic execution at startup.

Listing 14.5 Creating an Automatic Execute Stored Procedure

```
create procedure test_startup as
print 'test procedure executed at startup'
go
sp_makestartup test_startup
go
Procedure has been marked as 'startup'.
sp_helpstartup
go
Startup stored procedures:
-----------------------------
test_startup

(1 row(s) affected)
sp_unmakestartup test_startup
go
Procedure is no longer marked as 'startup'.
sp_helpstartup

Startup stored procedures:
```

Part
III

Ch

14

Understanding Procedure and Batch Restrictions

Sets of Transact-SQL statements are referred to as batches and include stored procedures. The rules or syntax for the use of Transact-SQL statements in batch apply to the following list of objects:

- Procedures
- Rules
- Defaults
- Triggers
- Views

The syntax is primarily a set of restrictions that limit the types of statements that can be used in batch. Most of the restrictions are the statements that create objects, change the database, or query environment, and don't take effect within the current batch.

For example, although rules and defaults can be defined and bound to a column or user-defined datatype within a batch, the defaults and rules are in effect until after the completion of the batch. You can't drop an object and reference or recreate it in the same batch.

Some additional Set options that are defined with a batch don't apply to queries contained in the batch. For example, the Set option SET NOCOUNT ON will affect all queries that follow it within a stored procedure, and suppress the count line for the execution of SELECT statements. The SET SHOWPLAN ON option does not affect the queries used within a stored procedure, and a query plan isn't displayed for the queries in the procedure.

Understanding the End-of-Batch Signal *GO*

As you've seen throughout this book, if you use the command line ISQL for the execution of a set of Transact-SQL statements, the GO command is used to specify the end of the set of statements. GO is used on a line by itself. The GO command is required if you interactively use a set of statements or read in statements from an input file to ISQL.

The GO command is not required to execute a set of Transact-SQL statements that are used in the Windows GUI application form of ISQL, ISQL/W. GO is also not required in a series of Transact-SQL statements that are executed within batch objects, such as stored procedures, rules, defaults, triggers, or views. In Listing 14.6, the GO command is used first to cause the execution of the USE command and then to signal the end of the second batch, which contains two SELECT statements.

Listing 14.6   Working with a Batch Job in ISQL

```
C:>isql/U sa
Password:
1>use employees
2>go
```

```
1>select * from Workers
2>select count(*) from Workers
3>go

Name                              Department        Badge
-----------------------------     ---------------   -----------
Bob Smith                         Sales             1234
Sue Simmons                       Sales             3241
Mary Watkins                      Field Service     6532
Linda Lovely                      Library           7888

(4 row(s) affected)
----------


----------
4

(1 row(s) affected)
```

In the following example, the GO command is used with the file query1.sql, which contains the following commands:

```
use employees
go
select * from Workers
select max(Rownum) from Rownumber
go
```

The Transact-SQL statements within the file are executed with the invocation of ISQL, which returns the display shown in Listing 14.7:

Listing 14.7 Results of Running the Batch in *query1.sql*

```
isql /U /i query1.sql /n /P ''
Name                              Department              Badge
-----------------------------     ----------------------  -----------
Bob Smith                         Sales                   1234
Sue Simmons                       Sales                   3241
Mary Watkins                      Field Service           6532
Linda Lovely                      Library                 7888

(4 rows affected)

--------------
          19

(1 row affected)
```

Part
III

Ch
14

TIP You can also use a /o file-spec to direct the output of the execution of ISQL to a file instead of to your monitor and to *capture* the output of any statements executed during the ISQL session.

Using Flow-Control Statements

Transact-SQL contains several statements that are used to change the order of execution of statements within a set of statements, such as a stored procedure. The use of such flow-control statements permits you to organize statements in stored procedures to provide the capabilities of a conventional programming language, such a C or COBOL. You may find that some of the retrieval, update, deletion, addition, and manipulation of the rows of database tables can more easily be performed through the use of flow-control statements in objects, such as stored procedures.

Using *IF...ELSE*

You can use the keywords IF and ELSE to control conditional execution within a batch, such as a stored procedure. The IF and ELSE keywords enable you to test a condition and execute either the statements that are part of the IF branch or the statements that are part of the ELSE branch. You define the condition for testing as an expression following the keyword IF. The syntax of an IF...ELSE statement is as follows:

```
IF expression
     statement
[ELSE]
     [IF expression]
     statement]
```

N O T E It's impossible to show examples of the use of conditional statements that can be formed with the keywords IF and ELSE without using other keywords. The examples shown next use the keywords PRINT and EXISTS. In the subsequent examples, the keyword PRINT is used to display a string of characters. ■

The keyword EXISTS is usually followed by a statement within parentheses when used in an IF statement. The EXISTS statement is evaluated to either True or False, depending on whether the statement within the parentheses returns one or more rows, or no rows, respectively.

You needn't use an ELSE clause as part of an IF statement. The simplest form of an IF statement is constructed without an ELSE clause. In the following example, a PRINT statement is used to display a confirmation message that a row exists in a database table. If the row doesn't exist in the table, the message, No entry, is displayed. Unfortunately, the message is also displayed after the verification message is displayed because you're not using the ELSE option.

```
if exists (select * from Workers
where Badge=1234)
    print 'entry available'
print 'No entry'
```

```
entry available
No entry
```

In the following example, the row isn't found in the table so only the PRINT statement that follows the IF statement is executed:

```
if exists (select * from Workers
where Badge=1235)
    print 'entry available'
print 'No entry'
```

```
No entry
```

The previous two examples show the problem of using an IF statement that doesn't contain an ELSE clause. In the examples, it's impossible to prevent the message, No entry, from appearing. You add an ELSE clause to the IF statement to print the No entry message, if a row isn't found and the condition after the IF isn't True.

In the following example, our previous examples are rewritten to use IF and ELSE clauses. If a row that is tested for in the IF clause is in the table, only the message, employee present, is displayed. If the row isn't found in the table, only the message, employee not found, is displayed:

```
if exists (select * from employees
where name='Bob Smith')
    print 'employee present'
else print 'employee not found'
```

> **CAUTION**
>
> Unlike some programming languages you may have used, when used alone, the Transact-SQL IF statement can have only one statement associated with it. As a result, there is no need for a keyword, such as END-IF, to define the end of the IF statement. See Using BEGIN...END in the next section for information on grouping statements and associating them with an IF...ELSE condition.

Using *BEGIN...END*

You use the keywords BEGIN and END to designate a set of Transact-SQL statements to be executed as a unit. You use the keyword BEGIN to define the start of a block of Transact-SQL statements. You use the keyword END after the last Transact-SQL statement that is part of the same block of statements. BEGIN...END uses the following syntax:

```
BEGIN
    statements
END
```

Part

III

Ch

14

You often use BEGIN and END with a conditional statement such as an IF statement. BEGIN and END are used in an IF or ELSE clause to permit multiple Transact-SQL statements to be executed if the expression following the IF or ELSE clause is True. As mentioned earlier, without a BEGIN and END block enclosing multiple statements, only a single Transact-SQL statement can be executed if the expression in the IF or ELSE clause is True.

In Listing 14.8, BEGIN and END are used with an IF statement to define the execution of multiple statements if the condition tested is True. The IF statement contains only an IF clause; no ELSE clause is part of the statement.

Listing 14.8   Controlling Flow with the *IF* Statement

```
if exists (select * from employees
where badge=1234)
    begin
        print 'entry available'
        select name,department from employees
        where badge=1234
    end

entry available
name                    department
------------------- --------------------
Bob Smith           Sales

(1 row(s) affected)
```

In Listing 14.9, an ELSE clause is added to the IF statement to display a message if the row isn't found:

Listing 14.9   Using *ELSE* with an *IF* Statement

```
if exists (select * from employees
where department='Sales')
    begin
        print 'row(s) found'
        select name, department from employees
        where department='Sales'
    end
else print 'No entry'

row(s) found
name                    department
------------------- --------------------
Bob Smith           Sales
Mary Jones          Sales

(2 row(s) affected)
```

Listing 14.10 returns the message that follows the ELSE clause because no row is found:

Listing 14.10   Output When the *ELSE* Option is Executed

```
if exists (select * from employees
where department='Nonexistent')
    begin
        print 'row(s) found'
        select name, department from employees
        where department='Nonexistent'
    end
else print 'No entry'

No entry
```

Using *WHILE*

You use the keyword WHILE to define a condition that executes one or more Transact-SQL statements when the condition tested evaluates to True. The statement that follows the expression of the WHILE statement continues to execute as long as the condition tested is True. The syntax of the WHILE statement is as follows:

```
WHILE
    <boolean_expression>
    <sql_statement>
```

> **N O T E**   As with the IF...ELSE statements, you can only execute a single SQL statement with the WHILE clause. If you need to include more than one statement in the routine, use the BEGIN...END construct as described above. ∎

In Listing 14.11, a WHILE statement is used to execute a SELECT statement that displays a numeric value until the value reaches a limit of five. The example uses a variable that is like a parameter in that a variable is a named storage location. You define the datatype of a variable using a DECLARE statement to control the way information is represented in the variable. A variable is always referenced preceded by an *at* sign (@) like a parameter.

In the example, the value stored in the variable is initialized to one and subsequently incremented. The statements associated with the WHILE execute until the variable *x* reaches a value of five:

Listing 14.11   Using a Variable to Control Execution

```
declare @x int
select @x=1
while @x<5
begin
```

continues

Listing 14.11   Continued

```
print 'x still less than 5'
select @x=@x+1
end
go
(1 row(s) affected)
x still less than 5
(1 row(s) affected)
x still less than 5
(1 row(s) affected)
x still less than 5
(1 row(s) affected)
x still less than 5
(1 row(s) affected)
```

A more meaningful example of the use of a WHILE statement can be shown after two additional Transact-SQL keywords are introduced and explained. An example using WHILE along with the keywords BREAK and CONTINUE will be shown a little later in this section.

Using *BREAK*

You use the keyword BREAK within a block of Transact-SQL statements that is within a conditional WHILE statement to end the execution of the statements. The execution of a BREAK results in the first statement following the end of block to begin executing. The syntax of a BREAK clause is as follows:

```
WHILE
   <boolean_expression>
   <sql_statement>
BREAK
   <sql_statement>
```

In Listing 14.12, the BREAK within the WHILE statement causes the statement within the WHILE to terminate. The PRINT statement executes once because the PRINT statement is located before the BREAK. After the BREAK is encountered, the statements in the WHILE clause aren't executed again.

Listing 14.12   Example of Using a Variable to Control Execution

```
declare @x int
select @x=1
while @x<5
begin
    print 'x still less than 5'
    select @x=@x+1
    break
end

(1 row(s) affected)
x still less than 5
(1 row(s) affected)
```

Using *CONTINUE*

You use a CONTINUE keyword to form a clause within a conditional statement, such as a WHILE statement, to explicitly continue the set of statements that are contained within the conditional statement. The syntax of the CONTINUE clause is as follows:

```
WHILE
 <boolean_expression>
 <statement>
BREAK
 <statement>
CONTINUE
```

In Listing 14.13, a CONTINUE is used within a WHILE statement to explicitly define that execution of the statements within the WHILE statement should continue as long as the condition specified in the expression that follows WHILE is True. The use of CONTINUE in the following example skips the final PRINT statement:

Listing 14.13   Controlling Flow with *CONTINUE*

```
declare @x int
select @x=1
while @x<5
begin
    print 'x still less than 5'
    select @x=@x+1
    continue
    print 'this statement will not execute'
end

(1 row(s) affected)
x still less than 5
(1 row(s) affected)
x still less than 5
(1 row(s) affected)
x still less than 5
(1 row(s) affected)
x still less than 5
(1 row(s) affected)
```

Examples of Using *WHILE*, *BREAK*, and *CONTINUE*

Although the two previous examples use BREAK and CONTINUE alone, you don't typically use either CONTINUE or BREAK within a WHILE statement alone. Both BREAK and CONTINUE are often used following an IF or ELSE that are defined within a WHILE statement, so an additional condition can be used to break out of the WHILE loop. If two or more loops are nested, BREAK exits to the next outermost loop.

Part
III

Ch
14

In Listing 14.14, a BREAK is used with an IF statement, both of which are within a WHILE statement. The BREAK is used to terminate the statements associated with the WHILE if the condition specified by the IF statement is True. The IF condition is True if the value of the local variable, @y, is True:

Listing 14.14   Controlling Flow with *CONTINUE*

```
declare @x int
declare @y tinyint
select @x=1, @y=1
while @x<5
begin
     print 'x still less than 5'
     select @x=@x+1
     select @y=@y+1
     if @y=2
     begin
          print 'y is 2 so break out of loop'
          break
     end
end
print 'out of while loop'

(1 row(s) affected)
x still less than 5
(1 row(s) affected)
(1 row(s) affected)
y is 2 so break out of loop
out of while loop
```

In Listing 14.15, a WHILE statement is used to permit only the rows of a table that match the criteria defined within the expression of the WHILE statement to have their values changed:

Listing 14.15   Using *WHILE* to Control Program Flow

```
begin tran
while (select avg(price)from titles) < $30
begin
     select title_id, price
     from titles
     where price >$20
     update titles set price=price * 2
end

(0 row(s) affected)

title_id price
-------- -------------------------
```

```
PC1035    22.95
PS1372    21.59
TC3218    20.95

(3 row(s) affected)
(18 row(s) affected)
(0 row(s) affected)

title_id price
-------- ------------------------
BU1032    39.98
BU1111    23.90
BU7832    39.98
MC2222    39.98
PC1035    45.90
PC8888    40.00
PS1372    43.18
PS2091    21.90
PS3333    39.98
TC3218    41.90
TC4203    23.90
TC7777    29.98

(12 row(s) affected)
(18 row(s) affected)
(0 row(s) affected)
```

You must be careful when defining the WHILE statement and its associated statements. As shown in the following example, if the condition specified with the WHILE expression continues to be True, the WHILE loop executes indefinitely.

```
while exists (select hours_worked from pays)
print 'hours worked is less than 55'

(0 row(s) affected)
hours worked is less than 55
(0 row(s) affected)
...
```

If the evaluation of the expression following the WHILE returns multiple values, you should use an EXISTS instead of any comparison operators. In the following example, the error message that is returned is descriptive of the problem:

```
while (select hours_worked from pays) > 55
print 'hours worked is less than 55'

Msg 512, Level 16, State 1
Subquery returned more than 1 value.  This is illegal when the subquery follows
➡ =, !=, <, <= , >, >=, or when the subquery is used as an expression.
Command has been aborted.
```

In this case, you'll want to use EXISTS to determine the comparison value.

Defining and Using Variables

You may recall that earlier in this chapter variables were described as similar to parameters in that they are named storage locations. Variables in Transact-SQL can be either local or global. You define local variables by using a DECLARE statement and assigning the variable a datatype. You assign an initial value to local variables with a SELECT statement.

You must declare, assign a value, and use a local variable within the same batch or stored procedure. The variable is only available for use within the same batch or procedure, hence the name local variable.

You can use local variables in batch or stored procedures for such things as counters and temporary holding locations for other variables. Recall that local variables are always referenced with an @ preceding their names. You can define the datatype of a local variable as a user-defined datatype, as well as a system datatype. One restriction that applies to local variables is that you can't define a local variable as a text or image datatype.

The syntax of a local variable is as follows:

```
DECLARE @variable_name datatype [,variable_name datatype...]
```

The SELECT statement is used to assign values to local variables, as shown in the following syntax:

```
SELECT @variable_name = expression ¦select statement
[,@variable_name = expression select statement]
[FROM list of tables] [WHERE expression]
[GROUP BY...]
[HAVING ...]
[ORDER BY...]
```

If the SELECT statement returns more than a single value, the variable is assigned to the last value returned. In Listing 14.16, two local variables are defined and used to return the number of rows in the table. The CONVERT function must be used to convert the numeric format of the number of rows to a text datatype for the PRINT statement. The message that is displayed by the PRINT statement is first built and assigned to a local variable because the concatenation can't be done within the PRINT statement:

Listing 14.16 Storing Values into Variables

```
declare @mynum int
select @mynum = count(*)from Workers
declare @mychar char(2)
select @mychar = convert(char(2),@mynum)
declare @mess char(40)
select @mess ='There are ' + @mychar + 'rows in the table Workers'
print @mess

(1 row(s) affected)

(4 row(s) affected)
```

```
(1 row(s) affected)

There are 4 rows in the table Workers
```

Each SELECT statement returns a count message in the previous example. If you want the count message suppressed, you must first execute the SET NOCOUNT statement. In Listing 14.17, the same statements that were executed in the previous example are re-executed with the count turned off:

Listing 14.17   Storing Values into Variables (Example with *SET NOCOUNT* in Force)

```
declare @mynum int
select @mynum = count(*)from Workers
declare @mychar char(2)
select @mychar = convert(char(2),@mynum)
declare @mess char(40)
select @mess ='There are ' + @mychar + 'rows in the table Workers'
print @mess

There are 4 rows in the table Workers
```

Using *PRINT* with Variables

You'll recall that in examples shown earlier in this chapter, PRINT was used to display a message to the assigned output device. You use the keyword PRINT to display ASCII text or variables up to 255 characters in length. You can't use PRINT to output datatypes other than CHAR, VARCHAR, or the global variable @@VERSION.

Recall that you can't concatenate string data in a PRINT statement directly. You must concatenate text or variables into a single variable and output the results with the PRINT statement. The syntax of the PRINT statement is as follows:

```
PRINT 'text' ¦@local_variable ¦ @@global_variable
```

Using Global Variables

Although your stored procedure parameters are limited in scope to the procedure in which they are defined, SQL Server has several intrinsic global variables. These variables, defined and maintained by the system, are available at any time within your stored procedures. Keep the following guidelines in mind when you work with global variables:

- Global variables are not defined by your routines, they are defined at the server level.
- You can only use the pre-declared and defined global variables.
- You always reference a global variable by preceding with two *at* signs (@@).
- You shouldn't define local variable with the same name as system variables because you may receive unexpected results in your application.

Part

III

Ch

14

You reference a global variable to access server information or information about your operations. Table 14.1 lists the names of all Microsoft SQL Server global variables and a brief description of the information that is contained within them.

Table 14.1   Global Variables for Microsoft SQL Server

Global Variable	Description
@@CONNECTIONS	total logons or attempted logins
@@CPU_BUSY	cumulative CPU Server time in ticks
@@DBTS	value of unique timestamp for database
@@ERROR	last system error number, 0 if successful
@@FETCH_STATUS	status of the last FETCH statement
@@IDENTITY	the last inserted identity value
@@IDLE	cumulative CPU Server idle time
@@IO_BUSY	cumulative Server I/O time
@@LANGID	current language ID
@@LANGUAGE	current language name
@@MAX_CONNECTIONS	max simultaneous connections
@@MAX_PRECISION	precision level for decimal and numeric datatypes
@@MICROSOFTVERSION	internal version number of SQL Server
@@NESTLEVEL	current nested level of calling routines from 0 to 16
@@PACK_RECEIVED	number of input packets read
@@PACKET_SENT	number of output packets written
@@PACKET_ERRORS	number of read and write packet errors
@@PROCID	current stored procedure ID
@@ROWCOUNT	number of rows affected by last query
@@SERVERNAME	name of local server
@@SERVICENAME	name of the running service
@@SPID	current process server ID

Global Variable	Description
@@TEXTSIZE	current of max text or image data with default of 4K
@@TIMETICKS	number of microseconds per tick-machine independent. tick is 31.25 milliseconds/1/32 sec.
@@TOTAL_ERRORS	number of errors during reads or writes
@@TOTAL_READ	number of disk reads (not cache)
@@TOTAL_WRITE	number of disk writes
@@TRANCOUNT	current user total active transactions
@@VERSION	date and version of SQL Server

In Listing 14.18, a global variable is used to retrieve the version of SQL Server, which is concatenated with a string literal and the contents of a second global variable:

Listing 14.18 Using Global Variables

```
PRINT @@VERSION
declare @mess1 char(21)
select @mess1 = 'Server name is ' + @@servername
PRINT @mess1

Microsoft SQL Server  6.50 - 6.50.201 (Intel X86)
Apr  3 1996 02:55:53
Copyright  1988-1996 Microsoft Corporation

(1 row(s) affected)

Server name is Primary
```

Using Additional Procedure and Batch Keywords

Several additional keywords can be used within stored procedures or batches of Transact-SQL commands. These additional keywords don't fall into a single descriptive category of similar function. Some of these keywords are GOTO, RETURN, RAISERROR, WAITFOR, and CASE.

Using GOTO

You use a GOTO to perform a transfer from a statement to another statement that contains a user-defined label. A GOTO statement used alone is unconditional. The statement that contains the destination label name follows rules for identifiers and is followed by a colon (:).

Part

III

Ch

14

You only use the label name without the colon on the GOTO line. The syntax of the GOTO statement is as follows:

```
label:
```

```
GOTO label
```

Listing 14.19 shows the use of the GOTO statement that transfers control to a statement that displays the word *yes* until the value of a variable reaches a specified value. The COUNT was turned off prior to execution of the statements in the example:

Listing 14.19 Using the *GOTO* Statement

```
declare @count smallint
select @count =1
restart:
print 'yes'
select @count =@count + 1
while @count <= 4
goto restart

yes
yes
yes
yes
```

Using *RETURN*

You use the RETURN statement to formally exit from a query or procedure and optionally provide a value to the calling routine. A RETURN is often used when one procedure is executed from within another. The RETURN statement, when used alone, is unconditional, though you can use the RETURN within a conditional IF or WHILE statement. The syntax of the RETURN statement is as follows:

```
RETURN [integer]
```

You can use a RETURN statement at any point in a batch or procedure. Any statements that follow the RETURN are not executed. A RETURN is similar to a BREAK with one difference. A RETURN, unlike a BREAK, can be used to return an integer value to the procedure that invoked the procedure that contains the RETURN. Execution of statements continue at the statement following the statement that executed the procedure originally.

To understand the use of the RETURN statement, you must first understand the action performed by SQL Server when a procedure completes execution. SQL Server always makes an integer value available when a procedure ends. A value of zero indicates that the procedure executed successfully. Negative values from –1 to –99 indicate reasons for the failure of statements within the procedure. These integer values are always returned at the termination of a procedure even if a RETURN statement isn't present in a procedure.

You can optionally use an integer value that follows the RETURN statement to replace the SQL Server value with your own user-defined value. You should use non-zero integer values so that your return status values don't conflict with the SQL Server status values. If no user-defined return value is provided, the SQL Server value is used. If more than one error occurs, the status with the highest absolute value is returned. You can't return a NULL value with a RETURN statement. Table 14.2 shows several of the return status values that are reserved by SQL Server.

Table 14.2   Selected Microsoft SQL Server Status Values

Return Value	Meaning
0	successful execution
−1	missing object
−2	datatype error
−3	process was chosen as a deadlock victim
−4	permission error
−5	syntax error
−6	miscellaneous user error
−7	resource error, such as out of space
−8	nonfatal internal problem
−9	system limit was reached
−10	fatal internal inconsistency
−11	fatal internal inconsistency
−12	table or index is corrupt
−13	database is corrupt
−14	hardware error

You must provide a local variable that receives the returned status in the EXECUTE statement, which invokes the procedure that returns status. The syntax to specify a local variable for the returned status value is the following:

```
EXEC[ute] @return_status=procedure_name
```

Listing 14.20 shows a return value from a called procedure that executes successfully and returns zero (0). The example shows the definition of the called procedure proc1. This stored procedure is executed from a set of Transact-SQL statements entered interactively.

N O T E When a set of Transact-SQL statements execute together, whether the statements are part of a procedure or not, the rules for batch operations apply. This is true even if the set of statements are typed in interactively. ■

N O T E A procedure that is invoked within another procedure with an EXECUTE statement is most often referred to as a *called procedure*. Call refers to an equivalent operation used in some programming languages. The keyword used in these languages to invoke the equivalent of a section of code from a program is CALL. This is the same as running a subroutine or function in these other languages. ■

Although the called procedure doesn't contain a RETURN statement, SQL Server returns an integer status value to the procedure that called proc1.

Listing 14.20   Showing the Results from a Stored Procedure Call When No Explicit Return Value is Defined

```
create procedure proc1 as
select * from employees

declare @status int
execute @status = proc1
select status = @status

name                     department            badge
--------------------     -----------------     ----------
Bob Smith                Sales                 1234
Mary Jones               Sales                 5514

(2 row(s) affected)

status
----------
0

(1 row(s) affected)
```

In Listing 14.21, proc2 is identical to the procedure proc1 that was used in the previous example except that proc2 contains a RETURN statement with a user-defined positive integer value. A SELECT statement is to display the returned status value from proc2 to confirm that the specified value on the RETURN statement in proc2 is returned to the next statement after the statement that executed proc2.

Listing 14.21 Returning a Status from the Stored Procedure

```
create procedure proc2 as
select * from employees
return 5

declare @status int
execute @status = proc2
select status = @status


name                    department              badge
-------------------     -------------------     ----------
Bob Smith               Sales                   1234
Mary Jones              Sales                   5514

(1 row(s) affected)

status
----------
5

(1 row(s) affected)
```

In Listing 14.22, the returned value is checked as part of a conditional statement. A message is displayed if the procedure executed successfully. This third example of Transact-SQL return statements is more typical of the usage of return status in a production environment.

Listing 14.22 Linking Stored Procedures Based on Return Values

```
declare @status int
execute @status = proc1
if (@status = 0)
begin
     print ''
     print 'proc1 executed successfully'
end

name                    department              badge
-------------------     -------------------     ----------
Bob Smith               Sales                   1234
Mary Jones              Sales                   5514

proc2 executed successfully
```

TIP You can nest procedures within other procedures up to 16 levels in `Transact-SQL`.

Using *RAISERROR*

You use the `RAISERROR` statement to return a user-specified message in the same form that SQL Server returns errors. The `RAISERROR` also sets a system flag to record that an error has occurred. The syntax of the `RAISERROR` statement is as follows:

```
RAISERROR (<integer_expression>¦<'text of message'>, [severity] [, state]
➥ [, argument1] [, argument2] )
[WITH LOG]
```

The `integer_expression` is a user-specified error or message number and must be in the range 50,000 to 2,147,483,647. The `integer_expression` is placed in the global variable, `@@ERROR`, which stores the last error number returned. An error message can be specified as a string literal or through a local variable. The text of the message can be up to 255 characters and is used to specify a user-specified error message. A local variable that contains an error message can be used in place of the text of the message. `RAISERROR` always sets a default severity level of 16 for the returned error message.

In Listing 14.23, a local variable is defined as a character datatype that is large enough to receive the error number specified in the `RAISERROR` statement after the error number is converted from the global variable, `@@ERROR`. The `RAISERROR` statement first displays the message level, state number, and the error message, `Guru meditation error`. The error number 99999 is then displayed separately using a `PRINT` statement.

Listing 14.23 Working with Errors in the Stored Procedure

```
declare @err char(5)
raiserror 99999 'Guru meditation error'
select @err=convert(char(5),@@ERROR)
print @err
go
Msg 99999, Level 16, State 1
Guru meditation error

(1 row(s) affected)

99999
```

You can also add your message text and an associated message number to the system table sysmessages. You use the system stored procedure, `sp_addmessage`, to add a message with a message identification number within the range 50,001 and 2,147,483,647. The syntax of the `sp_addmessage` system procedure is as follows:

```
sp_addmessage message_id, severity, message text' [, language [, {true ¦ false}
[, REPLACE]]]
```

> **CAUTION**
>
> If you enter a user-specified error number that has not been added to the sysmessages table and do not explicitly specify the message text, you'll receive an error that the message can't be located in the system table as shown in the following example:
>
> ```
> raiserror (99999,7,2)
> go
> Msg 2758, Level 16, State 1
> RAISERROR could not locate entry for error 99999 in Sysmessages.
> ```

User-defined error messages generated with a RAISERROR statement, but without a number in the sysmessages table return a message identification number of 50,000.

The severity level is used to indicate the degree or extent of the error condition encountered. Although severity levels can be assigned in the range of one through 25, you should usually assign your system message a severity level value from 11–16.

Severity levels of 11–16 are designed to be assigned through the sp_addmessages statement, and you can't assign a severity level of from 19–25 unless you're logged in as the administrator. Severity levels 17–19 are more severe software or hardware errors, which may not permit your subsequent statements to execute correctly.

Severity levels of 20–25 are severe errors and won't permit subsequent Transact-SQL statements to execute. System messages that have severity levels over nineteen can be problems, such as connection problems between a client system and the database server system or corrupted data in the database.

N O T E Microsoft suggests that severe errors, those that have a severity level of nineteen or higher, should also notify the database administrator. The database administrator needs to know of these problems because such problems are likely to impact many different users and should be attended to as soon as possible. ▪

When specifying messages, you enter an error message within single quotes of up to 255 characters. The remaining parameters of the sp_addmessage procedure are optional. The language parameter specifies one of the languages SQL Server was installed with. U.S. English is the default language if the parameter is omitted.

The next parameter, either True or False, controls whether the system message is automatically written to the Windows NT application event log. Use True to have the system message written to the event log. In addition, True results in the message being written to the SQL Server error log file.

The last parameter, REPLACE, is used to specify that you want to replace an existing user-defined message in the sysmessages table with a new entry.

Listing 14.24 shows the use of the sp_addmessage system stored procedure that adds a system message with an associated identification number and severity. A subsequent SELECT statement retrieves the message from the system table sysmessages. Finally, the RAISERROR statement is used to return the user-defined system message.

Listing 14.24   Using *sp_addmessage*

```
sp_addmessage 99999,13,'Guru meditation error'
go
select * from sysmessages where error=99999
go
raiserror (99999, 13,-1)
go
New message added.
error          severity dlevel description          languid
-----------    -------- ------ ------------------    ------
99999          13       0      Guru meditation error   0

(1 row(s) affected)

Msg 99999, Level 13, State 1
Guru meditation error
```

You can use the system-stored procedure, sp_dropmessage, to remove a user-defined message from the system table sysmessages when it is no longer needed. The syntax of the sp_dropmessage is as follows:

```
sp_dropmessage [message_id [, language ¦ 'all']]
```

You're only required to enter the message number to drop the message. The two additional optional parameters permit you to specify the language from which the message should be dropped. You can use the keyword all to drop the user-defined message from all languages.

In the following example, a user-defined message in the default language of U.S. English is removed from the system table, sysmessages:

```
sp_dropmessage 99999
go
Message dropped.
```

Using *WAITFOR*

You use a WAITFOR statement to specify a time, a time interval, or an event for executing a statement, statement block, stored procedure, or transaction. The syntax of the WAITFOR statement is as follows:

```
WAITFOR {DELAY <'time'> ¦ TIME <'time'> ¦ ERROREXIT ¦ PROCESSEXIT ¦  MIRROREXIT}
```

The meaning of each of the keywords that follow the WAITFOR keyword is shown in the following list:

- DELAY—Specifies an interval or time to elapse
- TIME—A specified time, no date portion, of up to 24 hours
- ERROREXIT—Until a process terminates abnormally
- PROCESSEXIT—Until a process terminates normally or abnormally
- MIRROREXIT—Until a mirrored device fails

In the following example of a WAITFOR statement, a DELAY is used to specify that a pause of forty seconds is taken before the subsequent SELECT statement is executed:

```
waitfor delay '00:00:40'
select * from employees
```

In the second WAITFOR example, a TIME is used to wait until 3:10:51 PM of the current day until the subsequent SELECT statement is executed.

```
waitfor time '15:10:51'
select * from employees
```

Using *CASE* Expressions

You can use a CASE expression to make an execution decision based on multiple options. Using the CASE construct, you can create a table that will be used to lookup the results you are testing and apply them to determine what course of action should be taken. The syntax of the CASE expression is as follows:

```
CASE [expression]
WHEN simple expression1¦Boolean expression1 THEN expression1
[[WHEN simple expression2¦Boolean expression2 THEN expression2] [...]]
    [ELSE expressionN]
END
```

If you use a comparison operator in an expression directly after the CASE keyword, the CASE expression is called a *searched expression* rather than a *simple* CASE expression. You can also use a Boolean operator in a searched CASE expression.

In a simple CASE expression, the expression directly after the CASE keyword always exactly matches a value after the WHEN keyword. In Listing 14.25, a CASE expression is used to substitute alternate values for the column department in the table company. In the following example, a CASE expression is used to return a corresponding set of alternate values for three department values of the table company.

Listing 14.25   Using *CASE* Expressions and Tests

```
select name,division=
case department
     when "Sales" then "Sales & Marketing"
     when "Field Service" then "Support Group"
     when "Logistics" then "Parts"
     else "Other department"
end,
badge
from company
go
name                 division           badge
-------------------  -----------------  ----------
Fred Sanders         Sales & Marketing  1051
Bob Smith            Sales & Marketing  1834
Mark McGuire         Support Group      1997
Stan Humphries       Support Group      3211
Sue Sommers          Parts              4411
Lance Finepoint      Other department   5522
Fred Stanhope        Support Group      6732
Ludmilla Valencia    Other department   7773
Jim Walker           Other department   7779
Jeffrey Vickers      Other department   8005
Barbara Lint         Support Group      8883
Sally Springer       Sales & Marketing  9998

(12 row(s) affected)
```

If you don't use an ELSE as part of the CASE expression, a NULL is returned for each non-matching entry, as shown in Listing 14.26:

Listing 14.26   Output from a Sample *CASE* Test

```
select name,division=
case department
when "Sales" then "Sales & Marketing"
when "Field Service" then "Support Group"
when "Logistics" then "Parts"
end,
badge
from company
go
name                 division           badge
------------------------------------------------
Fred Sanders         Sales & Marketing  1051
Bob Smith            Sales & Marketing  1834
Mark McGuire         Support Group      1997
Stan Humphries       Support Group      3211
Sue Sommers          Parts              4411
```

```
Lance Finepoint        (null)            5522
Fred Stanhope          Support Group     6732
Ludmilla Valencia      (null)            7773
Jim Walker             (null)            7779
Jeffrey Vickers        (null)            8005
Barbara Lint           Support Group     8883
Sally Springer         Sales & Marketing 9998

(12 row(s) affected)
```

You'll recall that a searched CASE expression can include comparison operators and the use of AND as well as OR between each Boolean expression to permit an alternate value to be returned for multiple values of the column of a table. Unlike a simple CASE expression, each WHEN clause is not restricted to exact matches of the values contained in the table column.

In Listing 14.27, comparison values are used in each WHEN clause to specify a range of values that are substituted by a single alternative value:

Listing 14.27   Using the *WHEN* Clause with *CASE* Statements

```
select "Hours Worked" =
case
when hours_worked < 40 then "Worked Insufficient Hours"
when hours_worked = 40 then "Worked Sufficient Hours"
when hours_worked > 60 then "Overworked"
else "Outside Range of Permissible Work"
end
from pays
go
Hours Worked
---------------------------------
Worked Sufficient Hours
Worked Sufficient Hours
Overworked
Worked Insufficient Hours
Overworked
Worked Sufficient Hours
Overworked
Worked Sufficient Hours
Outside Range of Permissible Work
Worked Insufficient Hours
Worked Sufficient Hours
Worked Sufficient Hours

(12 row(s) affected)
```

N O T E   When a CASE construct is executed, only the first matching solution is executed. ■

Part

III

Ch

14

> **CAUTION**
>
> You must use compatible datatypes for the replacement expression of the THEN clause. If the replacement expression of a THEN clause is a datatype that is incompatible with the original expression, an error message is returned.
>
> For example, a combination of original and replacement datatypes is compatible if the one is a variable length character datatype (VARCHAR) with a maximum length equal to the length of a fixed length character datatype (CHAR). In addition, if the two datatypes in the WHEN and THEN clauses are integer and decimal, the resultant datatype returned will be decimal in order to accommodate the whole and fractional portion of the numeric value.

You can also use both the COALESCE and NULLIF functions in a CASE expression. You use the COALESCE function to return a replacement value for any NULL or NOT NULL values that are present in, for example, the column of a database table. The syntax of one form of the COALESCE function is:

```
COALESCE (expression1, expression2)
```

In Listing 14.28, the COALESCE function is used to display either the product of hours_worked times rate or a zero if the columns hours_worked and rate are NULL:

Listing 14.28   Using the *COALESCE* Function

```
select badge, "Weekly Pay in Dollars"=coalesce(hours_worked*rate,0)
from pays2
go
badge       Weekly Pay in Dollars
----------- ---------------------
3211        400
6732        360
4411        520
5522        429
1997        510
9998        320
7773        550
8883        360
8005        420
7779        407
1834        400
1051        360
3467        0
3555        0
7774        0

(15 row(s) affected)
```

N O T E A COALESCE function is equivalent to a searched CASE expression where a NOT NULL expression1 returns expression1 and a NULL expression1 returns expression2. An equivalent CASE expression to a COALESCE function is as follows:

```
CASE
    WHEN expression1 IS NOT NULL THEN expression1
    ELSE expression2
END
```

You can use a COALESCE function as part of a SELECT statement as an alternative way of returning an identical display or because you find the COALESCE function simpler to use. ■

You can also use a NULLIF function with or in place of a CASE expression. The NULLIF function uses the following syntax:

```
NULLIF (expression1, expression2)
```

In Listing 14.29, a simple SELECT statement is first used to display the table without using a NULLIF function to show all column values for all rows. A second SELECT statement is used to operate on the columns, badge, and old_badge.

Listing 14.29   Using the *NULLIF* Function

```
select * from company2
go
name                    department          badge       old_badge
--------------------    ----------------    ---------   -----------
Mark McGuire            Field Service       1997        (null)
Stan Humphries          Field Service       3211        (null)
Sue Sommers             Logistics           4411        (null)
Fred Stanhope           Field Service       6732        (null)
Ludmilla Valencia       Software            7773        (null)
Jim Walker              Unit Manager        7779        (null)
Jeffrey Vickers         Mailroom            8005        (null)
Fred Sanders            SALES               1051        1051
Bob Smith               SALES               1834        1834
Sally Springer          Sales               9998        9998
Barbara Lint            Field Service       8883        12
Lance Finepoint         Library             5522        13

(12 row(s) affected)

select name,nullif(old_badge,badge)
from company2
go
name
--------------------    ----------
Mark McGuire            (null)
Stan Humphries          (null)
Sue Sommers             (null)
Fred Stanhope           (null)
Ludmilla Valencia       (null)
```

continues

Listing 14.29   Continued

```
Jim Walker            (null)
Jeffrey Vickers       (null)
Fred Sanders          (null)
Bob Smith             (null)
Sally Springer        (null)
Barbara Lint          12
Lance Finepoint       13

(12 row(s) affected)
```

The example only returns non-null values for rows that contain old_badge values that are different than new column values. In addition, a NULL is returned if no old column values were present. You can combine the use of the NULLIF and COALESCE functions to display the returned information in a more organized way.

Listing 14.30 combines a COALESCE and NULLIF function to return an old badge number only if it was different than the current badge number or if it was defined. If not, a new badge number is displayed.

Listing 14.30   Combining the *COALESCE* and *NULLIF* Functions

```
select name,badge=coalesce(nullif(old_badge,badge),badge)
from company2
go
name                  badge
-------------------   ----------
Mark McGuire          1997
Stan Humphries        3211
Sue Sommers           4411
Fred Stanhope         6732
Ludmilla Valencia     7773
Jim Walker            7779
Jeffrey Vickers       8005
Fred Sanders          1051
Bob Smith             1834
Sally Springer        9998
Barbara Lint          12
Lance Finepoint       13

(12 row(s) affected)
```

Reality Check

Stored procedures are nearly always the backbone of your system. You'll find that they make a good scaling point to move functionality from the client to the server. In cases where you find that you're repeating an SQL Server access over and over, consider moving it to a stored procedure and calling it from the application.

Perhaps one of the biggest benefits, of using stored procedures, for a software development house is the division of work between the development of the client application and the development of the server-side components. This was especially true in one case where an application was developed for an insurance company. Both the user interface and the database management were a challenge to implement.

By breaking development between the database and the client-side UI, it was possible to bring the project in on time, but still maintain experts in the development of the respective sides. The only thing, for example, that the UI development team knew about the database was the set of calls they needed to make (stored procedures) to get access to the information they needed. They didn't worry about the complicated search algorithms, the database management, or the rules implementations that were necessary behind the scenes.

On the other hand, the only thing the database team had to know about the user interaction with the application was the required response time and what the incoming information would look like. They didn't need to worry about what the dialog boxes looked like, or how the user set up the application.

If you think about it, you're breaking the development cycle into components as you do your application: client and server. You should use client-development experts for the tasks at which they are best—designing the interface, developing reports, and working with the users. Use the server-side developers for what they are best at—developing a solid database plan, implementing the server-side enforced rules, and so on. It provides you with real leverage on the personnel and project development cycles.

From Here...

In this chapter, you've seen how you can use Transact-SQL to control the flow of your SQL Server-based application. Remembering to use these techniques to manipulate information on the server can significantly improve performance of your application.

Here are some other areas of interest relating to the materials covered here:

- Chapter 5, "Creating Devices, Databases, and Transaction Logs," teaches you how to create and use user-defined datatypes.
- Chapter 13, "Managing and Using Rules, Constraints, and Defaults," teaches you how to create and use rules and defaults.
- Chapter 15, "Creating and Managing Triggers," teaches you how to use triggers to maintain referential integrity in the database.
- Chapter 21, "Optimizing Performance," teaches you ways to optimize the operation of SQL Server, including the correct sizing of the procedure cache.

Part
III

Ch
14

Creating and Managing Triggers

Use triggers to enforce data integrity

SQL Server's triggers enable you to enforce very customized referential integrity.

Find information about triggers

SQL Server provides several system-stored procedures that you can use to view information on triggers.

Explore trigger examples and tips on writing your own triggers

This chapter presents practical examples of how to write triggers that, for example, send e-mail.

Triggers are methods that SQL Server provides to the application programmer and database analyst to ensure data integrity. These methods are quite useful for those databases that will be accessed from a multitude of different applications, because they enable the database to enforce business rules instead of relying on the application software. ■

Understanding SQL Server Triggers

SQL Server's capability to manage your information effectively stems from its capability to help you control the data in your system as it flows through the tables and application logic that you build into your application. You've seen how stored procedures enable you to execute logic on the server, and you've seen how you can implement rules and defaults to help further manage the information in the database.

SQL Server considers rules and defaults *before* information is written to the database. They are a sort of "prefilter" for information and can prevent an action against the data item based on their role in controlling the database activity.

Triggers, on the other hand, are "postfilters" that execute after the data update passes and SQL Server has considered the rules, defaults, and so on.

A trigger is a special type of stored procedure that SQL Server executes when an insert, modify, or delete operation is performed against a given table. Because triggers run after the operation would take effect, they represent the "final word" on the modification. If the trigger causes a request to fail, SQL Server refuses the information update and returns an error message to the application attempting the transaction.

The most common use of a trigger is to enforce business rules in the database. Triggers are used when the standard constraints or table-based *Declarative Referential Integrity (DRI)* are inadequate.

N O T E Triggers run after the application of rules and other referential integrity checks. Therefore, if an operation fails these other checks, the trigger does not run. An operation must have otherwise succeeded before SQL Server will consider or execute a trigger's conditions or operations. ■

Triggers don't affect the server's performance significantly, and are often used to enhance applications that must perform many cascading operations on other tables and rows.

In SQL Server 6.x, Microsoft added ANSI-compliant DRI statements that you can use in the CREATE TABLE statement. The types of rules that these DRI statements can enforce are relatively complex. When these DRI statements are used in a CREATE TABLE statement, understanding exactly how SQL Server created the table can be quite difficult.

Besides the inability to perform complex business rule analysis based on values supplied when a trigger executes, DRI has one important limitation: The current implementation does not permit referencing values in other databases. Although this problem might seem relatively insignificant, it has a substantial impact on programmers attempting to write distributed applications that might need to check data constraints or values on other databases and servers.

Creating Triggers

When you create a trigger, you must be the database's owner. This requirement might seem odd at first, but if you consider what's happening, it really makes a lot of sense. When you add a trigger to a column, row, or table, you're changing how the table can be accessed, how other objects can relate to it, and so on. Therefore, you're actually changing the database schema. Of course, this type of operation is reserved for the database owner, protecting against someone inadvertently modifying your system's layout.

Creating a trigger is much like declaring a stored procedure, and it has a similar syntax:

```
CREATE TRIGGER [owner.]trigger_name
ON [owner.]table_name
FOR {INSERT, UPDATE, DELETE}
[WITH ENCRYPTION]
AS sql_statements
```

The following are options for the Transact-SQL command CREATE TRIGGER:

- *trigger_name*. The name of the trigger must conform to standard SQL Server naming conventions.

- INSERT, UPDATE, and DELETE. These keywords define the trigger's scope, determining the actions that initiate the trigger.

- WITH ENCRYPTION. This option enables developers to prevent users in their environment from reading the trigger's text after it has been loaded onto the server. The option is convenient for third-party application developers who embed SQL Server into their products and do not want to enable their customers to disassemble and modify the code.

  SQL Server stores the text of a trigger in the system catalog table syscomments. Use the WITH ENCRYPTION option carefully, because if the original trigger text is lost, you cannot restore the encrypted text from syscomments.

- *sql_statements*. A trigger can contain any number of SQL statements in Transact-SQL, if you enclose them in valid BEGIN and END delimiters. The next section describes limitations on the SQL permitted in a trigger.

CAUTION

SQL Server uses the unencrypted text of a trigger stored in syscomments when a database is upgraded to a newer version. If the text is encrypted, you cannot update and restore the trigger to the new database. Make sure that the original text is available to upgrade the database when necessary.

N O T E To provide a good level of recovery for your applications, you should always maintain an offline copy of your stored procedures, triggers, table definitions, and the overall structure of your SQL Server application's server side. You can use this information to reload the server if any problems occur. ▪

N O T E When a trigger executes, SQL Server creates a special table into which it places the data that caused the trigger to execute. The table is either inserted for insert and update operations or deleted for delete and update operations. Because triggers execute after an operation, the rows in the inserted table always duplicate one or more records in the trigger's base table. Make sure that a correct join identifies all the record's characteristics being affected in the trigger table so that the trigger does not accidentally modify the data itself. ■

Examining Limitations of Triggers

SQL Server limits the types of SQL statements that you can execute while performing a trigger's actions. Most of these limitations derive from the fact that you cannot roll back the SQL, which you might need to do if the update, insert, or delete causing the trigger to execute in the first place is also rolled back.

The following is a list of Transact-SQL statements that you cannot use in a trigger's body text. SQL Server rejects the compilation and storing of a trigger with these statements:

- All database- and object-creation statements: CREATE DATABASE, TABLE, INDEX, PROCEDURE, DEFAULT, RULE, TRIGGER, and VIEW
- All DROP statements
- Database object modification statements: ALTER TABLE and ALTER DATABASE
- TRUNCATE TABLE

N O T E DELETE triggers do not execute when a TRUNCATE operation is initiated on a table. Because the TRUNCATE operation is not logged, the trigger has no chance to run. Only the table owner and the *sa* are permitted to perform a TRUNCATE, and this permission cannot be transferred. ■

- Object permissions: GRANT and REVOKE
- UPDATE STATISTICS
- RECONFIGURE
- Database load operations: LOAD DATABASE and LOAD TRANSACTION
- All physical disk modification statements: DISK
- Temporary table creation: either implicit through CREATE TABLE or explicit through SELECT INTO

Additionally, you need to understand the following limitations clearly:

- You cannot create a trigger on a view, but only on the base table or tables on which you created the view.
- Any SET operations that change the environment, while valid, are in effect only for the life of the trigger. All values return to their previous states after the trigger finishes executing.

- You cannot execute a trigger by manipulating binary large object (BLOB) columns of datatype TEXT or IMAGE, whether logged or not by the database.
- You should not use SELECT operations that return result sets from a trigger because of the special handling of result sets required by the client application code, whether in a stored procedure or not. Carefully ensure that all SELECT operations read their values into locally defined variables available in the trigger.

Using Triggers

This section presents examples of the creation of several types of triggers. These examples aren't very sophisticated but should give you ideas on how you might implement triggers in your own environment.

Triggers *fire* or *execute* whenever a particular event occurs. The following subsections demonstrate the different events that can cause a trigger to execute and should give you some ideas of what you might have your trigger do when such events occur.

Using *INSERT* and *UPDATE* Triggers

INSERT and UPDATE triggers are particularly useful because they can enforce referential integrity constraints and ensure that your data is valid before it enters the table. Typically, INSERT and UPDATE triggers are used to update timestamp columns or to verify that the data on the columns that the trigger is monitoring meets the criteria required. Use INSERT and UPDATE triggers when the criteria for verification are more complex than a declarative referential integrity constraint can represent.

In Listing 15.1, the trigger executes whenever a record is modified or inserted into the SALES table. If the order date is not during the first 15 days of the month, the record is rejected.

On the CD

Listing 15.1   15_1.SQL—A *SALES* Trigger Disallowing Specified Records

```
Create Trigger Tri_Ins_Sales
On      SALES
For     INSERT, UPDATE
As
/* declare local variables needed */
Declare     @nDayOfMonth      tinyint
/* Find the information about the record inserted */
Select      @nDayOfMonth = DatePart( Day, I.ORD_DATE )
From  SALES S, INSERTED I
Where S.STOR_ID = I.STOR_ID
And   S.ORD_NUM = I.ORD_NUM
And   S.TITLE_ID = I.TITLE_ID
/* Now test rejection criteria and return an error if necessary */
If @nDayOfMonth > 15
Begin
      /* Note: Always Rollback first. You can never be sure what
      kind of error processing a client may do that may force locks
      to be held for unnecessary amounts of time */
```

continues

Listing 15.1   Continued

```
ROLLBACK TRAN
RAISERROR ( 'Orders must be placed before the 15th of
              the month', 16, 10 )
End
Go
```

N O T E   Notice how the previous join refers to the inserted table. SQL Server specially creates this *logical* table to enable you to reference information in the record that you are modifying. By using the alias I as shown, you can easily reference the table in the join criteria specified in the Where clause. ■

Notice that the code segment references a new table. If you review the list of tables, you'll notice that the database doesn't include the table. In this case, the inserted table contains a copy of every row that would be added if the transaction is allowed to complete. You use the inserted table's values to feed the information to any comparisons that you want to make to validate the transaction.

The columns in the inserted table exactly match those in the table with which you're working. You can perform comparisons on the columns, as in the example, which compares the columns against the sales database to verify that the sales date is valid.

You can also create triggers that can do their work only if a given column is updated. You can use the If Update statement in your trigger to determine whether the trigger processing should continue:

```
if update(au_lname)
    and (@@rowcount=1)
    begin
    ...
end
```

In this case, the only time that the code within the segment executes is if the specific column, au_lname, is updated. Keep in mind that although a column is being updated, it isn't necessarily being *changed*. Many applications, including most proprietary systems, simply update the entire record if any change is made.

Before taking further action in the trigger, you might find it helpful to compare the new value against the old value (with the inserted table stores) to see whether the value has indeed changed.

Using *DELETE* Triggers

DELETE triggers are typically used for two reasons. The first reason is to prevent deletion of records that will cause data integrity problems if they indeed are deleted. An example of such records are those used as foreign keys to other tables.

The second reason for using a DELETE trigger is to perform a cascading delete operation that deletes children records of a master record. You might use such a trigger to delete all the order items from a master sales record.

TIP

When you create a trigger, remember that it can affect more than one row. You must consider this possibility in any procedure that the trigger runs. Be sure you check the @@rowcount global variable to see exactly what is happening before you begin working with the information.

Triggers take into account the sum total of all rows that the requested operation affects, so they must be capable of considering the different combinations of information in the table and respond according to what you need. For example, if you issue a DELETE * from Authors statement, the trigger must accommodate the fact that the statement will delete all records from the AUTHORS table.

In the example in Listing 15.2, the @@rowcount variable prevents the deletion of more than one row at a time.

In Listing 15.2, the trigger executes whenever a user attempts to delete a record from the STORES table. If the store has sales, the trigger denies the request.

On the CD

Listing 15.2   15_2.SQL—The *STORES* Trigger Disallows Removal of More than One Store

```
Create Trigger Tri_Del_Stores
On     STORES
For    DELETE
As
/* First check the number of rows modified and disallow
anybody from deleting more than one store at a time */
If @@RowCount > 1
Begin
      ROLLBACK TRAN
      RAISERROR ( 'You can delete only one store at a time.', 16, 10 )
End
/* declare a temp var to store the store
that is being deleted */
Declare      @sStorID char(4)
/* now get the value of the store being nuked */
Select       @sStorID = D.STOR_ID
From   STORES S, DELETED D
Where S.STOR_ID = D.STOR_ID
If exists (Select *
           From    SALES
           Where   STOR_ID = @sStorID )
Begin
      ROLLBACK TRAN
      RAISERROR ( 'This store cannot be deleted because there are
                  still sales valid in the SALES table.', 16, 10 )
End
Go
```

TIP Using RAISERROR is an easy way to send the calling process or user detailed, specific information about the error to the calling process or user. RAISERROR enables you to specify error text, severity levels, and state information, all of which combine for more descriptive error messages for the user. RAISERROR also makes it easy to write generic error handlers in your client applications.

Listing 15.2 shows several transaction-management statements that enable you to stop the operation. For more information about transactions, see Chapter 12, "Understanding Transactions and Locking."

Notice that the code segment references a new table. If you review the list of tables present, you'll notice that the database doesn't list this new table. In this case, the deleted table contains a copy of every row that would be deleted if the transaction were allowed to complete. You use the deleted table's values to feed the information to any comparisons that you want to make to validate the transaction.

The columns in the deleted table exactly match those in the table with which you're working. You can perform comparisons on them, as in Listing 15.2, in which they're compared against the sales database to verify that the store has no sales outstanding.

Using Special Transaction Management with Rollback Triggers

If you are working with triggers and transactions, you might want to consider working with a special trigger option, the rollback trigger:

```
Rollback trigger   [with raiserror errornumber [message]]
```

The rollback trigger option is, in essence, an abort-all statement. When a rollback is encountered, the trigger's processing stops and the data modification that caused the trigger to execute in the first place is not disallowed.

When you use the rollback trigger statement, you have the option—even the responsibility—to indicate an error number and optional message. Except in very rare situations, you should use the RAISERROR option, because it tells the calling routines that you have stopped the action from occurring. The rollback trigger statement doesn't stop processing for a batch of updates; instead, the trigger fails only the current item. Therefore, the code that you develop to update the database must check the return state of the update to ensure that it succeeded.

When the routine returns from the update operation, always check the @@error global variable to ensure that the updates happened as planned.

Using Triggers that Send E-Mail

One of the better features of SQL Server is its capability to invoke behavior directly from the operating system. You must predefine such behavior through SQL Server's extended procedures, but they enable you to create incredibly powerful trigger operations. SQL Server is relatively unique in its capability to support features specific to the operating system. SQL

Server can offer this support because it runs only on Windows NT, which has a very standardized programming interface across all its supported hardware platforms, such as Intel, MIPS, Alpha, and PowerPC.

Triggers can call any of the extended procedures (xp_*) available to the server and any external procedures that you add to the server with the sp_addextendedproc command. In Listing 15.3, the trigger demonstrates how to send e-mail when a record is deleted from the underlying AUTHORS table.

On the CD

Listing 15.3   15_3.SQL—A Trigger Sending E-Mail to ChiefPublisher, Indicating that an Author Has Been Deleted from the System

```
Create Trigger Tri_Del_Authors_Mail
On     AUTHORS
For    DELETE
As
/* declare some variables to store the author's name */
Declare     @sLName varchar(40),
       @sFName varchar(20),
       @sAuthor varchar(60)
/* now get the value of the author being removed */
Select      @sLName = D.AU_LNAME,
       @sFName = D.AU_FNAME
From   AUTHORS A, DELETED D
Where A.AU_ID = D.AU_ID
/* Send mail message */
Select @sAuthor = @sLName + ', ' + @sFName
exec master.dbo.xp_sendmail @recipient = 'ChiefPublisher',
@message = 'deleted ' + @sAuthor
Go
```

Using Nested Triggers

You can nest triggers up to 16 layers deep. If nested trigger operations are not desirable, however, you can configure SQL Server to disallow them. To toggle this option, use the nested trigger option sp_configure.

▶ **See** "Displaying and Setting Server Options," **p. 464**

Triggers become nested when the execution of one trigger modifies another table that includes another trigger, which therefore executes.

TIP   You can check your nesting level at any time by inspecting the value in @@NestLevel. The value is between zero (0) and 16.

SQL Server cannot detect nesting that causes an infinite loop during the creation of a trigger until the situation occurs at execution time. A trigger can cause an infinite loop. For example, suppose that TABLE_A includes TRIGGER_A, which executes when TABLE_A is updated. When executed, TRIGGER_A causes an update on TABLE_B. TABLE_B has a similar trigger, TRIGGER_B, that executes when TABLE_B is updated and causes an update of TABLE_A. Thus, if a user updates either table, the two triggers continue executing each other indefinitely. On detecting such an occurrence, SQL Server shuts down or cancels the trigger.

N O T E If a trigger causes an additional modification of the table from which it executes, the trigger does not cause itself to execute recursively. The current version of SQL Server has no support for *reentrant* or *recursive* stored procedures or triggers. ■

As another example, suppose that the SALES table includes one trigger, and the STORES table includes another. Listing 15.4 defines both triggers.

On the CD

Listing 15.4   15_4.SQL—Two Nested Triggers that Execute If a *DELETE* Occurs on the *SALES* Table

```
/* First trigger deletes stores if the sales are deleted */
Create  Trigger Tri_Del_Sales
On      SALES
For     DELETE
As
/* Announce the trigger being executed */
Print "Delete trigger on the sales table is executing..."
/* declare a temp var to store the store
that is being deleted */
Declare @sStorID char(4),
        @sMsg    varchar(40)
/* now get the value of the store being deleted */
Select  @sStorID = STOR_ID
From    DELETED          /* DELETED is a fake table created
                            by SQL Server to hold the values of
                            records deleted */
Group By STOR_ID
/* Now delete the store record */
Select @sMsg = "Deleting store " + @sStorID
Print @sMsg
Delete      STORES
Where       STOR_ID = @sStorID
Go
/* Second trigger deletes discounts if a store is deleted */
Create  Trigger Tri_Del_Stores
On      STORES
For     DELETE
As
/* Announce the trigger being executed */
Print "Delete trigger on the Stores table is executing..."
```

```
/* Declare a temp var to store the store
  that is being deleted */
Declare @sStorID char(4),
        @sMsg    varchar(40)
/* now get the value of the store being deleted */
Select  @sStorID = sTOR_ID
From    DELETED              /* DELETED is a fake table created
                               by SQL Server to hold the values of
                               records deleted */
Group By STOR_ID
If @@rowcount = 0
Begin
        Print "No rows affected on the stores table"
        Return
End
/* Now delete the store record */
Select @sMsg = "Deleting discounts for store " + @sStorID
Print @sMsg
Delete  DISCOUNTS
Where   STOR_ID = @sStorID
Go
```

If a DELETE executes on the SALES table, as shown in Listing 15.5, the trigger executes on the SALES table, which in turn causes a trigger to execute on the STORES table.

Listing 15.5   Results of Executing a *DELETE* on the *SALES* Table

```
/*-------------------------
Delete from sales where stor_id = '8042'
-------------------------*/
Delete trigger on the sales table is executing...
Deleting store 8042
Delete trigger on the Stores table is executing...
Deleting discounts for store 8042
```

 Triggers and DRI usually don't work well together. For example, in Listing 15.5, you must first drop the Foreign Key constraint on the DISCOUNTS table before it can actually complete the DELETE. Wherever possible, you should implement either triggers or DRI for integrity constraints.

Displaying Trigger Information

If you want to view the behavior that a trigger is enforcing on a table, you must display the information that describes any triggers that the table owns. There are several ways to obtain information about a trigger on any given table. This section demonstrates the two most common ways: SQL Enterprise Manager (SQL EM) and the system procedures sp_help and sp_depends.

Using SQL Enterprise Manager

To use the SQL Enterprise Manager to view information about a trigger, perform the following steps:

1. Run SQL Enterprise Manager from the SQL Server 6.5 group.

2. Select the server on which you want to work.

3. Select the table on which you want to work (see Figure 15.1).

FIG. 15.1

After highlighting a table, you can right-click and use the quick menu to perform common operations that are also available from the Manage menu.

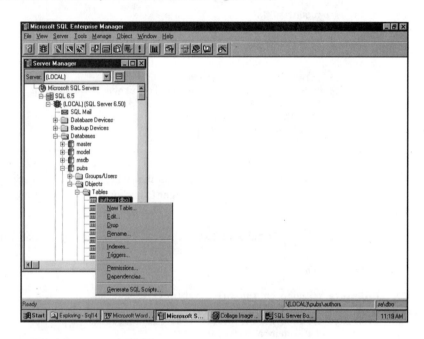

4. Choose Manage, Triggers. The SQL Enterprise Manager's Manage Triggers dialog box appears as shown in Figure 15.2.

FIG. 15.2

In the SQL Enterprise Manager's Manage Triggers dialog box, the toolbar's second combo box lists the triggers that are active on the table in the first combo box.

Using *sp_help*, *sp_depends*, and *sp_helptext*

The system procedures sp_help, sp_depends, and sp_helptext provide valuable information for determining whether a trigger exists, what it references, and what its actual text or source code looks like. (These procedures work only if you did not use the ENCRYPTION option when creating the trigger.)

Using *sp_help*   sp_help is a generic system procedure that reports information about any object in the database. The procedure requires the following syntax:

```
sp_help [object_name]
```

If you omit object_name, SQL Server reports information on all user objects found in the sysobjects system catalog table.

sp_help is useful for determining who created a trigger and when he or she created it. Listing 15.6 is an example of the output from sp_help when used on the trigger Tri_Del_Authors.

Listing 15.6   Using *sp_help* to View Information About *Tri_Del_Authors*

```
/*---------------------------
sp_help Tri_Del_Authors
---------------------------*/
Name                 Owner         Type                When_created
-----------------    -----------   ----------------    --------------
Tri_Del_Authors      dbo           trigger             Nov 26 1995  4:37PM
Data_located_on_segment
---------------------
not applicable
```

Listing 15.7 shows a more advanced trigger that will be used in the following sections.

Listing 15.7   15_5.SQL—An Advanced Trigger Demonstrating Information Returned from *sp_helptext*

```
/* create a basic trigger to stop anyone deleting an
author that still has records titleauthor table */
Create Trigger Tri_Del_Authors
On    AUTHORS
For   DELETE
As
/* First check the number of rows modified and disallow
anybody from removing more than one author at a time */
If @@RowCount > 1
Begin
      ROLLBACK TRAN
      RAISERROR ( 'You can delete only one author at a time.', 16, 10 )
End
/* declare a temp var to store the author
that is being deleted */
Declare      @nAuID id
```

continues

Listing 15.7 Continued

```
/* now get the value of the author being deleted */
Select      @nAuID = D.AU_ID
From   AUTHORS A, DELETED D    /* DELETED is a fake table created
                                  by SQL Server to hold the values of
                                  records deleted */
Where A.AU_ID = D.AU_ID
If exists (Select      *
           From  TITLEAUTHOR
           Where AU_ID = @nAuID )
Begin
     ROLLBACK TRAN
     RAISERROR ( 'This author cannot be deleted because he/
                 she still has valid titles.', 16, 10 )
End
Go
```

Using *sp_depends*   sp_depends is a useful system-stored procedure that returns a database object's dependencies, such as tables, views, and stored procedures. The syntax is as follows:

```
sp_depends object_name
```

After you add the trigger shown in Listing 15.7, sp_depends produces the output shown in Listing 15.8 when run on the AUTHORS table.

Listing 15.8   Using *sp_depends* to View Dependency Information on the *AUTHORS* Table

```
/*---------------------------
sp_depends authors
--------------------------*/
In the current database, the specified object is referenced by the following:
name                                    type
--------------------------------------  -----------------
dbo.reptq2                              stored procedure
dbo.titleview                           view
dbo.Tri_Del_Authors                     trigger
```

Using *sp_helptext*   User-defined objects—such as rules, defaults, views, stored procedures, and triggers—store their text in the system catalog table syscomments. This table is difficult to read, but you can use the sp_helptext procedure to make the table more accessible.

The syntax for sp_helptext is as follows:

```
sp_helptext object_name
```

If you cannot read the text returned, the trigger was probably stored as ENCRYPTED. In this format, you cannot read the trigger's associated commands. You'll have to contact the trigger's original author and request the procedure's text file.

Dropping Triggers

For several reasons, you might want to remove triggers from a table or tables. You might, for example, be moving into a production environment and want to remove any triggers that you put in place to ensure good quality but which were hurting performance. You might also want to drop a trigger simply to replace it with a newer version.

To drop a trigger, use the following syntax:

```
DROP TRIGGER [owner.]trigger_name[,[owner.]trigger_name...]
```

Dropping a trigger is not necessary if a new trigger is to be created to replace the existing one. When you drop a table, you also drop all its child-related objects, including triggers.

The following example drops the trigger created for `Tri_Del_Authors`:

```
Drop Trigger Tri_Del_Authors
```

Reality Check

Triggers and referential integrity in general present some interesting challenges when you create the SQL Server application from scratch, never mind the times when you're upsizing an application from a different platform. As you'll see in Chapter 26, "Upsizing Microsoft Office 97 Applications to SQL Server," there are several ways you can move your tables and queries to SQL Server. From that point, however, you'll need to know and understand triggers if you're to maintain the referential integrity that you've implemented in Access on the SQL Server side of things.

Perhaps one of the most frequently created triggers is the trigger that controls a deletion on a given record. A major component of many referential integrity scenarios is that of preventing the removal of a record if child, or related, records exist. While simple to implement (see earlier in this chapter for specific examples), be sure to include it on your list of items to check after a conversion.

Referential integrity is a bit of a ghost-feature. You don't see it until you either run into it by breaking a rule, or by looking specifically to see what's in force. It's much less evident than typical objects like tables, stored procedures, and so on. Make sure you use `sp_help` against each table you convert. This will save you the aggravation of finding out you had a trigger that was unknown to you on the original table.

From Here...

In this chapter, you learned about the values of triggers and how you can apply them to enforce referential integrity in your application. In addition, you learned that you can nest triggers and use them to provide more complex business rule validation than constraints that you can define when creating tables.

For more information that might be useful in helping you write effective triggers, see the following chapters:

- Chapter 11, "Managing and Using Indexes and Keys," discusses how to enforce integrity constraints through table-based declarative referential integrity and unique indexes.

- Chapter 13, "Managing and Using Rules, Constraints, and Defaults," shows a different way to enforce integrity constraints on table columns through rules and bound table defaults.

- Chapter 14, "Managing Stored Procedures and Using Flow-Control Statements," provides information on creating stored procedures that you can execute as triggers.

Understanding Server, Database, and Design Query Options

The configuration options for SQL Server 6.5 are grouped into three major areas:

- **Server Options.** These global options affect all operations on the currently active server. These options apply to all logons on the server and to all databases and other objects that the server owns. Server options are generally used for performance tuning and capacity or object-handling management.

- **Database Options.** These global options affect all operations on the currently active database. Database options are generally used to limit access to the database and to enable high-speed Bulk Copy (BCP) operations.

- **Query Options.** These local options affect only the query that is executing. Query options enable you to tune and monitor the activities of individual queries and display additional statistical information about the query's execution. ■

How to configure your server, database, and query with the available options

This chapter will show you how to configure options in SQL Server. These options include logon parameters and Bulk Copy operations specifications.

The purpose of each server, database, and query option

SQL Server has numerous options that can be configured. This chapter will help you understand the impact that they have on the operation and performance of your system.

How to recover a server that won't start

Recovering SQL Server in Minimal Configuration Mode is quite difficult. This chapter will walk you through the steps involved.

Defining Server Options

SQL Server provides configuration options for many different types of server installations. With these options, you can customize the way SQL Server's resources are managed. Specifically, the configuration options deal with the following management issues:

- Memory management
- User and logon handling
- Object size
- Network and physical I/O handling
- Disk, procedure, and read-ahead cache management
- Symmetric Multi-Processing (SMP) management

N O T E   Symmetric Multi-Processing (SMP) computers are computers that conform to a published standard for incorporating more than one CPU in the system unit. SMP computers typically offer substantial performance improvements over single-CPU boxes because they can distribute the processing workload to as many CPUs as are available. Windows NT has been shown to provide near-linear performance improvements on computers with as many as four CPUs. What this statement means is that for every processor you add to the server, you can expect to see a 100 percent performance increase. ■

SQL Server has two sets of server configuration options available. The default or basic server options deal with common server management issues. The advanced server options deal with components of the server that you normally don't have to adjust. Unless you have been advised by a technical support center to specifically configure one of the advanced options, you should not change any of the advanced options.

> **CAUTION**
>
> Sometimes you may not be able to restart a server after you change its configuration. One reason for this problem may be that you overcommitted memory as a result of your configuration changes. To restart a server in this situation, you may need to start the server in minimal configuration mode, which enables you to bring up the server without it attempting to apply the configuration that you set. For more information on starting the server in minimal configuration mode, see the section called "Starting SQL Server in Minimal Configuration Mode from the Command Line," later in this chapter.

Displaying and Setting Server Options

SQL Server provides two ways to display and set configuration options for the server. The graphical method is to use SQL Server Enterprise Manager. The Transact-SQL method uses the system-stored procedure, sp_configure.

Using SQL Enterprise Manager   SQL Enterprise Manager is a very convenient tool to use to change server options. The user interface makes it unnecessary to remember the syntax required for sp_configure or to know all the different options.

To use the SQL Enterprise Manager to display and set server options, perform the following steps:

1. Run SQL Enterprise Manager from the Microsoft SQL Server 6.5 group. The screen should look like Figure 16.1.

FIG. 16.1
After being started, SQL Enterprise Manager shows that no server is selected.

2. Select the server that you want to work on. SQL Enterprise Server shows the items in Figure 16.2.

FIG. 16.2
After you select a particular server, SQL Enterprise Manager shows all of its properties and object folders.

3. From the Server menu, choose SQL Server Configure. When the Server Configuration/ Options dialog box is displayed, click the Configuration page, as shown in Figure 16.3.

4. To change any of the settings for the server, type the required value in the Current column and then click Apply Now. Clicking this button makes the change but leaves the dialog box displayed. If you want to apply the changes and return to the main SQL Enterprise Manager window, click OK instead.

FIG. 16.3

SQL Enterprise
Manager's Server
Configuration/Options
dialog box shows the
Configuration page.

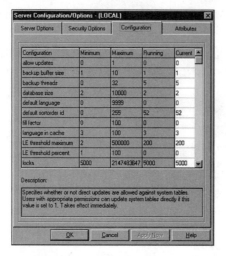

Configuration	Minimum	Maximum	Running	Current
allow updates	0	1	0	0
backup buffer size	1	10	1	1
backup threads	0	32	5	5
database size	2	10000	2	2
default language	0	9999	0	0
default sortorder id	0	255	52	52
fill factor	0	100	0	0
language in cache	3	100	3	3
LE threshold maximum	2	500000	200	200
LE threshold percent	1	100	0	0
locks	5000	2147483647	5000	5000

Description:

Specifies whether or not direct updates are allowed against system tables.
Users with appropriate permissions can update system tables directly if this
value is set to 1. Takes effect immediately.

TIP Press the F1 key on any SQL Enterprise Manager dialog box to display context-sensitive help that
explains the available objects/options.

Using *sp_configure*   Another way of changing server settings is to use sp_configure, a
system-stored procedure. The sp_configure procedure is useful for writing automated
scripts that update the server without user intervention.

The syntax for this procedure is as follows:

```
sp_configure [configuration option, [configuration value]]
```

The configuration option is text that describes the option that needs to change in the server.
SQL Server uses a LIKE operator on the text that is supplied so that you can use any unique set
of characters in the description instead of the full text description. Note that SQL Server requires that any text with spaces or other formatting in the configuration option parameter be
enclosed in quotation marks. Listing 16.1 shows several slightly different sp_configure statements that perform the same function because they are resolved using this "closest match"
approach.

**Listing 16.1   *sp_configure* Requires Only that the Option Being Changed
Is Uniquely Identified**

```
sp_configure "nested Triggers", 0
go
sp_confi— re "nested", 1
go
sp_configure "triggers", 0
go
sp_configure "trig", 0
go
```

NOTE If you don't give parameters to sp_configure, the resulting output is the current status of the server. Listing 16.2 shows an example of the results returned when sp_con- gure is used without a parameter.

The sp_configure information produced in Listing 16.2 includes the advanced options. Notice that the run value for show advanced option is 1. ▩

Listing 16.2 Executing *sp_configure* Without Any Options Returns the Current Server Configuration

```
/*---------------------------
sp_configure
--------------------------*/
name                    minimum     maximum      config_value run_value
--------------------    ----------  ----------   ------------ ----------
allow updates           0           1            0            0
backup buffer size      1           10           1            1
backup threads          0           32           5            5
cursor threshold        -1          2147483647   -1           -1
database size           1           10000        2            2
default language        0           9999         0            0
default sortorder id    0           255          52           52
fill factor             0           100          0            0
free buffers            20          524288       409          409
hash buckets            4999        265003       7993         7993
language in cache       3           100          3            3
LE threshold maximum    2           500000       10           10
LE threshold minimum    2           500000       20           10
LE threshold percent    1           100          0            0
locks                   5000        2147483647   5000         5000
logwrite sleep (ms)     -1          500          0            0
max async IO            1           255          8            8
max lazywrite IO        1           255          8            8
max worker threads      10          1024         255          255
media retention         0           365          0            0
memory                  1000        1048576      8192         8192
nested triggers         0           1            1            1
network packet size     512         32767        4096         4096
open databases          5           32767        20           20
open objects            100         2147483647   500          500
priority boost          0           1            0            0
procedure cache         1           99           30           30
RA cache hit limit      1           255          4            4
RA cache miss limit     1           255          3            3
RA delay                0           500          15           15
RA prefetches           1           1000         3            3
RA slots per thread     1           255          5            5
RA worker threads       0           255          3            3
recovery flags          0           1            0            0
recovery interval       1           32767        5            5
remote access           0           1            1            1
```

continues

Listing 16.2 Continued

```
remote logon timeout 0      2147483647  5       5
remote query timeout 0      2147483647  0       0
resource timeout     5      2147483647  10      10
set working set size 0      1           0       0
show advanced option 0      1           1       1
SMP concurrency      -1     64          0       1
sort pages           64     511         128     128
spin counter         1      2147483647  10000   0
tempdb in ram (MB)   0      2044        0       0
user connections     5      32767       20      20
(1 row(s) affected)
```

If you're having problems using sp_configure and are getting the following error message:

```
Msg 15125, Level 16, State 1
Only the System Administrator (SA) may change configuration parameters.
```

you're not logged into the database as the server administrator (SA). Only the SA can change a server configuration. Log off from ISQL/W or the database tool that you are using and reconnect to the database as the SA user.

Understanding the *RECONFIGURE* Command   After executing sp_configure, the server may return the following:

```
Configuration option changed. Run the RECONFIGURE command to install.
```

This message means that the server has changed the internal value of the configuration, but has not yet applied it. The output in Listing 16.3 shows that the configuration is changed in the config_value column, but the run_value column remains unchanged.

Listing 16.3 Some *sp_configure* Options Require Reconfiguration of the Server

```
/*---------------------------
sp_configure "nested"
go
sp_configure "nested", 0
---------------------------*/
name                 minimum    maximum    config_value run_value
-------------------- ---------- ---------- ------------ ----------
nested triggers      0          1          1            1
Configuration option changed. Run the RECONFIGURE command to install.
name                 minimum    maximum    config_value run_value
-------------------- ---------- ---------- ------------ ----------
nested triggers      0          1          0            1
```

Executing the RECONFIGURE command applies the change to the server as shown in Listing 16.4.

Listing 16.4 *RECONFIGURE* **Forces SQL Server to Adjust the Run Value of a Server Option**

```
/*---------------------------
reconfigure
go
sp_configure "nested"
---------------------------*/
name                  minimum    maximum    config_value run_value
--------------------- ---------- ---------- ------------ ----------
nested triggers       0          1          0            0
```

The RECONFIGURE command is available only to dynamic configuration options. These options can be changed without shutting down and restarting the server. The following is a list of the dynamic options that can be set with sp_configure and then applied dynamically with RECONFIGURE:

allow updates	RA cache hit limit
backup buffer size	RA cache miss limit
free buffers	RA delay
LE threshold maximum	RA prefetches
LE threshold minimum	recovery interval
LE threshold percent	remote logon timeout
logwrite sleep (ms)	remote query timeout
max lazywrite IO	resource timeout
max worker threads	show advanced option
nested triggers	sort pages
network packet size	spin counter

Server Options Explained

The following is a comprehensive list of all the available server options. If the word *advanced* appears in parentheses to the right of the keyword, then this option is only available if you have turned on the Show Advanced Options configuration value. If the word *dynamic* appears in parentheses to the right of the keyword, then you can change this option without shutting down and restarting the server. See the preceding section on the RECONFIGURE command for more information.

Each of the following sections indicates the minimum, maximum, and default values for the option it describes. These values indicate the range of values that the item can have and the default value to which SQL Server is configured when it is first installed.

affinity mask

Minimum: 0

Maximum: 0x7fffffff

Default: 0

On SMP machines, `affinity mask` allows a thread to be associated with a processor. This association is done by using a bit mask. The processors on which the processes run are represented by each bit. You can use either decimal or hexadecimal values to specify values for this setting.

allow updates (Dynamic)

Minimum: 0

Maximum: 1

Default: 0

The `allow updates` configuration option determines whether the system catalog can be updated. If the value is set to 1, the system catalog can be updated. Stored procedures created while the system catalog is updateable will be able to update the system catalog even when this value is returned to 0.

> **CAUTION**
>
> Allowing updates on the system catalog is an extremely dangerous decision. If you decide to allow updates, do so only under very controlled conditions. You also should put the server in single-user mode to prevent other users from accidentally damaging the system catalog. To start the server in single-user mode, execute `sqlservr -m` from the Win32 command prompt.

Because this option can cause so much harm, you must use an additional keyword, WITH OVERRIDE, when executing the RECONFIGURE command. The following is the syntax to enable allow updates:

```
sp_configure "allow updates", 1
go
reconfigure with override
go
```

backup buffer size (Dynamic)

Minimum: 1

Maximum: 10

Default: 1

With this configuration option, you can control backups by increasing or decreasing the amount of memory available to the SQL Server for holding backup data. The numeric value corresponds to 32 2K pages. If you set the value to 4, for example, the server allocates 256K

$(4 \times 32 \times 2K)$ for backups. A larger value helps reduce backup times but also reduces available memory for the server.

backup threads

> Minimum: 0
>
> Maximum: 32
>
> Default: 5

The backup threads configuration option controls how many NT service threads are allocated to striped backup and load operations. When you use multiple CPUs, you may want to increase this value from the default of 5 to improve backup and load times.

cursor threshold (Dynamic, Advanced)

> Minimum: –1
>
> Maximum: 2147483647
>
> Default: 100

The cursor threshold configuration option controls how SQL Server decides to build the results to answer a request for a cursor by a client. The value corresponds to the number of rows expected in the cursor's result set. The accuracy of the cursor threshold is largely based on the currency of the INDEX statistics in the tables for which a cursor is being built. To ensure more accurate picking of the synchronous/asynchronous cursor build, make sure that the statistics on the base tables are up-to-date.

If this option is set to –1, SQL Server will always build the cursor results synchronously, meaning that the server will attempt to build the cursor immediately upon receiving the OPEN CURSOR command. Synchronous cursor generation is usually faster for small result sets.

If this option is set to 0, SQL Server will always build the cursor results asynchronously, meaning that the server will spawn an additional thread to answer the client and it will return control to the client while processing other client requests. For large result sets, this option is preferred because it will stop the server from being bogged down answering a single client's request for a large cursor result.

database   size

> Minimum: 1
>
> Maximum: 10000
>
> Default: 2

The database size option controls the default number of megabytes to reserve for new databases. If the majority of the databases that are being created on a given server are greater than 2M, you should change this value. Also, if the model database grows to be greater than 2M, you will need to adjust this value.

TIP Because the minimum database size is 1M, SQL Server databases can exist on floppy disks. See the Chapter 5, "Creating Devices, Databases, and Transaction Logs" section titled "Using Removable Media for Databases" for more information on this option.

default language

Minimum: 0

Maximum: 9999

Default: 0

The `default language` option controls the default language ID to be used for the server. U.S. English is the default and is always 0. If other languages are added to the server, they will be assigned different language IDs.

default sortorder id (Advanced)

Minimum: 0

Maximum: 255

Default: 52

The `default sortorder id` option controls the sort order that the server uses. The sort order controls the way SQL Server sorts data and returns it to the client. The default is 52, which is the identification number for the dictionary, case-insensitive sort order. Table 16.1 shows the other sort orders that are available.

Table 16.1   Sort Order IDs

ID	Name
30	Binary order
31	Dictionary order, case-sensitive
32	Dictionary order, case-insensitive
33	Dictionary order, case-insensitive, uppercase preference
34	Dictionary order, case-insensitive, accent-insensitive
40	Binary order
41	Dictionary order, case-sensitive
42	Dictionary order, case-insensitive
43	Dictionary order, case-insensitive, uppercase preference
44	Dictionary order, case-insensitive, accent-insensitive

ID	Name
49	Strict compatibility with Version 1.*x* case-insensitive databases
50	Binary order
51	Dictionary order, case-sensitive
52	Dictionary order, case-insensitive
53	Dictionary order, case-insensitive, uppercase preference
54	Dictionary order, case-insensitive, accent-insensitive
55	Alternate dictionary order, case-sensitive
56	Alternate dictionary order, case-insensitive, uppercase preference
57	Alternate dictionary order, case-insensitive, accent-insensitive
58	Scandinavian dictionary order, case-insensitive, uppercase preference
59	Scandinavian dictionary order, case-sensitive
61	Alternate dictionary order, case-insensitive

Part
III

Ch
16

CAUTION

Do not use sp_configure to change the sortorder option. Instead, use the SQL Server setup program if you want to change this value. Changing sortorder requires you to unload and reload the database because the data will need to be stored in a different format.

fill factor

> Minimum: 0
>
> Maximum: 100
>
> Default: 0

The fill factor configuration option controls the default fill factor to use when creating indexes. The *fill factor* refers to how much space SQL Server will reserve in an index page for the potential growth of key values in the index. This option is overridden if you specify a fill factor with the CREATE INDEX command.

A fill factor of 100 forces SQL Server to fill the index pages completely and should only be used for extremely static tables whose key values never change. Smaller fill factor values force SQL Server to reserve space on the index page for new values that may be added to the table or index after the initial table load. The default value of 0 is basically the same as a value of 100, with the exception being that the index pages are not filled to capacity before they are split.

▶ **See** the Chapter 11 section entitled "Creating an Index with CREATE INDEX," **p. 325**

free buffers (Dynamic, Advanced)

> Minimum: 20
>
> Maximum: 524288
>
> Default: 204

The `free buffers` configuration option controls the amount of memory that SQL Server must maintain when lazywriting to disk. Lazywriting increases throughput because values are "written" to memory instead of disk. If this threshold is hit, the lazy writer forces information to disk to ensure that memory pages are kept available.

If you make a change to the `memory` configuration option, the `free buffers` option is automatically adjusted to five percent of the `memory` value. After you restart the server after changing the `memory` option, you can modify the `free buffers` value manually to any value within the range specified.

hash buckets (Advanced)

> Minimum: 4999
>
> Maximum: 265003
>
> Default: 7993

The `hash buckets` configuration option controls the amount of buckets that SQL Server reserves for hashing, or indexing, pages of data to memory. A *bucket* is a logical storage area or counter that SQL Server uses to hold values that it needs to identify memory pages. SQL Server's hashing algorithm requires that a prime number of buckets be made available for use. If you specify a non-prime value, SQL Server will pick the closest prime number.

You probably won't need to change this value unless your server has more than 160M of RAM (8000 × 2K). Note that the default of 7993 value really refers to the closest prime to 8000.

language in cache

> Minimum: 3
>
> Maximum: 100
>
> Default: 3

The `language in cache` configuration option controls the number of languages that SQL Server can store in the language cache simultaneously.

LE threshold maximum (Dynamic)

> Minimum: 2
>
> Maximum: 500000
>
> Default: 200

The `LE threshold maximum` option controls the maximum number of page locks that SQL Server allows a single query to have before escalating a set of page locks on a table to a full table lock. If the number of page locks is exceeded, SQL Server will force a table lock, regardless of the LE threshold percentage configured for the table. This action improves server performance because it prevents memory being allocated unnecessarily to manage the individual page locks.

LE threshold minimum (Dynamic)

> Minimum: 2
>
> Maximum: 500000
>
> Default: 20

The LE threshold minimum option controls the minimum number of page locks that a single query must acquire before SQL Server will escalate a set of page locks on a table to a full table lock. This configuration option is provided so that the LE threshold percentage will not hit on tables that have few pages of data.

LE threshold percentage (Dynamic)

> Minimum: 1
>
> Maximum: 100
>
> Default: 0

The LE threshold percent option controls the percentage of page locks to pages of data in a table that needs to be acquired before SQL Server will escalate the lock to a full table lock. A value of 0, the default, stops SQL Server from performing lock escalation unless the lock escalation threshold maximum is reached.

locks

> Minimum: 5000
>
> Maximum: 2147483647
>
> Default: 5000

The locks option controls the number of locks that SQL Server can maintain at any time. Each lock consumes 32 bytes of RAM, so increasing this value to a large number will most likely require you to make more RAM available to the server. For example, setting this value to 20,000 will result in the lock manager or consuming 625K of RAM (20,000 × 32 bytes = 640,000 bytes).

logwrite sleep (ms) (Dynamic, Advanced)

> Minimum: –1
>
> Maximum: 500
>
> Default: 0

The logwrite sleep option controls the number of milliseconds that SQL Server will wait to write a log entry to disk if the buffer is not full. Increasing this option's value can can have dramatic performance gains on highly DML-active databases because it will force SQL Server to write larger blocks of memory to the log at one time, rather than requiring it to write less than full blocks to disk.

Part

III

Ch

16

A value of –1 is provided to force SQL Server to always write to disk. This value should only be used on systems that are extremely concerned about media failure and are not concerned with I/O throughput performance. A value of 0 forces SQL Server to delay writes to disk if, and only if, other users on the system are in the execute phase of their requests to the server.

max async io

> Minimum: 1
>
> Maximum: 255
>
> Default: 8

The `max async IO` option controls the maximum number of asynchronous I/O requests that SQL Server can make to hardware devices. This value should only be changed from the default on systems that have more than eight physical disks with database devices on them or on systems that are using disk striping to improve performance.

max lazywrite IO (Dynamic, Advanced)

> Minimum: 1
>
> Maximum: 255
>
> Default: 8

With the `max lazywrite IO` option, you can tune the writes from the lazywriter to the real I/O subsystem. This value is dynamically configurable, but it can only be configured up to the value of the `max async io` option. This option is not typically something you would modify on your system.

max worker threads (Dynamic)

> Minimum: 10
>
> Maximum: 1024
>
> Default: 255

The `max worker threads` option controls the maximum number of threads that SQL Server will spawn to handle database operations. By default, SQL Server spawns at least one thread for each listener service that is installed. In addition, threads are spawned for database checkpointing, lazywriting, and for the read ahead manager. The checkpointing process is a process or server operation that writes dirty, or changed, pages of data that are currently cached from memory directly to disk. The lazywriting process manages cached writes to disk and allows transactions to be batched together for a single I/O to disk containing multiple items instead of writing every transaction to disk as it occurs.

The rest of the available threads are allocated for user processes that are making requests. If the number of users is greater than the number of available threads allocated by the server (determined by the amount set in this option), SQL Server uses the available threads in a pooling fashion. The next user process request that the server receives is assigned to the first thread that becomes available after it has completed its assigned task.

media retention

> Minimum: 0
>
> Maximum: 365
>
> Default: 0

The media retention option controls the number of days that a given backup is expected to be retained before it can be reused. If this value is other than 0, SQL Server warns the user that he or she is performing a backup over an existing backup that has not gone past its number of retention days.

This option is useful for SQL servers that are in remote areas where a full-time administrator is not available to manage the environment and where it is likely that the user may incorrectly reuse backup tapes that should be kept for a prescribed period. A good setting is 7, which will stop the tape from being used more than once a week.

memory

> Minimum: 1000
>
> Maximum: 1048576
>
> Default: 4096

The memory configuration option controls the maximum number of 2K pages of memory that SQL Server will consume at startup. To fully optimize your server for use as a database server, you should allocate all available memory to the server after subtracting the minimums required by Windows NT.

> **CAUTION**
>
> If you overcommit the amount of available memory, SQL Server will not start. See the section later in this chapter entitled "Starting SQL Server in Minimal Configuration Mode from the Command Line" to learn how to fix a server that is no longer starting because memory was overcommitted.

To help tune the amount of memory being consumed by SQL Server, you can use the DBCC MEMUSAGE command, which reports the way that memory has been allocated on the server and also shows the top 20 data pages and stored procedures that have been executed. Listing 16.5 shows an example of the output that is displayed without the data page top 20 or the stored procedure top 20.

Listing 16.5   Using *DBCC MEMUSAGE* to Display Information About Memory in Use on the Server

```
/*----------------------------
dbcc memusage
--------------------------*/
```

continues

Listing 16.5   Continued

```
Memory Usage:
                          Meg.      2K Blks  Bytes
    Configured Memory: 16.0000       8192    16777216
           Code size:  1.7166        879     1800000
    Static Structures:  0.2473       127      259328
               Locks:  0.2480        127      260000
        Open Objects:  0.1068         55      112000
      Open Databases:  0.0031          2        3220
   User Context Areas:  0.8248       423      864824
          Page Cache:  8.8951       4555     9327184
        Proc Headers:  0.2143        110      224724
      Proc Cache Bufs:  3.5996      1843     3774464
```

nested triggers (Dynamic)

> Minimum: 0
>
> Maximum: 1
>
> Default: 1

The nested triggers option controls whether triggers will nest or cascade when executed. If this option is set to 0, SQL Server will only execute the first trigger that fires when an update or delete action occurs.

▶ **See** Chapter 15, "Creating and Managing Triggers," **p. 447**

network packet size (Dynamic)

> Minimum: 512
>
> Maximum: 32767
>
> Default: 4096

The network packet size option controls the server-wide maximum network packet size that a client can request. If the client requests a size less than the value specified in the current value, SQL Server will accept it. Greater values than the current value are negotiated to the maximum value specified in this option, however.

This option can improve performance on networks whose base topology supports wider or larger packets than TCP/IP's default of 4096 bytes. This option is especially useful if you are running over a satellite service and want to batch large packets of data to send through the satellite packet service.

You should adjust this option to a higher value for reporting databases that are not acquiring any locks on the datasets because it will allow larger batches of data to be sent to the client at one time, improving network throughput.

CAUTION

Setting the packet size too high can cause locking problems on databases with many transactions. SQL Server will hold locks for an unnecessarily long time in order to fill up a network packet to send to the client. Take care when adjusting this value and perform statistical analysis to prove that the values you have chosen are benefiting you.

open databases

> Minimum: 5
>
> Maximum: 32767
>
> Default: 20

The `open database` option controls the maximum number of databases that SQL Server can maintain in an open condition at any one time. This option should not be arbitrarily set to a high value because each open database does consume some server memory.

If people are unable to connect to a database that you've just created, check to see whether you have exceeded the maximum number of open databases on the server. If you have, use `sp_configure` to increase the number of open databases available on the server and then try to connect to the database again.

open objects

> Minimum: 100
>
> Maximum: 2147483647
>
> Default: 500

The `open objects` option controls the maximum number of objects that SQL Server can hold in memory at one time. An object can be a table page, a stored procedure that is executing, or any other object in the database. Increase this value if the server reports that the maximum number of objects has been exceeded. Take care when assigning values to this option, however. Increasing its value may mean that you have to allocate more memory to the server.

priority boost (Advanced)

> Minimum: 0
>
> Maximum: 1
>
> Default: 0

The `priority boost` option controls the priority SQL Server will run at under Windows NT. The default is 0, meaning that SQL Server will run at a normally high priority, but will allow other tasks to request high threading priority as well. If this option is set to 1, SQL Server will run at the highest priority under the Windows NT scheduler. This value should be set to 1 on systems that are dedicating Windows NT to run SQL Server.

procedure cache

> Minimum: 1
>
> Maximum: 99
>
> Default: 30

The procedure cache option controls the proportion of memory that SQL Server allocates to store the stored procedures that have most recently been executed. For systems that have large amounts of stored procedures, you may need to set this value higher than 30 percent if the total amount of memory available to SQL Server is relatively low. On systems with more than 512M of RAM, you should reduce this value to 10 percent or less. It is extremely unlikely that the amount of stored procedures in memory cache will exceed 50M.

N O T E SQL Server has a stored procedure cache because it does not store the desired query plan/execution plan of the procedure in the database until it is first executed. As a result, procedures take more time to run the first time they are executed because SQL Server has to pull the tokenized procedure text out of private tables, evaluate the text, and determine the correct execution path. This execution path is what is stored in the procedure cache. ■

RA cache hit limit (Dynamic, Advanced)

> Minimum: 1
>
> Maximum: 255
>
> Default: 4

The RA cache hit limit option sets the number of hits in the data page cache that the Read Ahead Manager makes before canceling itself and allowing the query to fetch data from the data page cache instead. You probably won't need to change this option.

RA cache miss limit (Dynamic, Advanced)

> Minimum: 1
>
> Maximum: 255
>
> Default: 3

The RA cache miss limit option controls the number of data page cache misses that are acceptable to the SQL Server before the Read Ahead Manager is started. Setting this value to 1 means the Read Ahead Manager will be fired for every access of a data page. This setting will cause terrible performance and a lot of unnecessary disk thrashing. In most cases, you should leave this option set to the default.

RA delay (Dynamic, Advanced)

> Minimum: 0
>
> Maximum: 500
>
> Default: 15

The RA delay option controls the number of milliseconds that the Read Ahead Manager waits before executing a request.

RA prefetches (Dynamic, Advanced)

> Minimum: 1
>
> Maximum: 1000
>
> Default: 3

The RA prefetches option controls the number of extents (8 × 2K pages) that the Read Ahead Manager will read ahead of the currently scanning execution position.

RA slots per thread (Advanced)

> Minimum: 1
>
> Maximum: 255
>
> Default: 5

The RA slots per thread option controls the number of slots per thread that SQL Server will reserve for Read Ahead processes. The number of slots multiplied by the number of allocated worker threads is the total number of concurrent Read Ahead activities that can be executing.

RA worker threads

> Minimum: 0
>
> Maximum: 255
>
> Default: 3

The RA worker threads option controls the number of Windows NT threads that SQL Server allocates to the Read Ahead Manager. You should configure this value to the maximum number of concurrent users expected on the system. With the option configured in this way, SQL Server will have a Read Ahead thread available to handle each user process.

recovery flags

> Minimum: 0
>
> Maximum: 1
>
> Default: 0

The recovery flags option controls the information that is displayed during the SQL Server startup process. If this option is set to 0, the default, then SQL Server will only report that the database is being recovered/restored by name. If this option is set to 1, then SQL Server will report, in detail, the status of every transaction that was pending at the time the server was shut down and what action SQL Server took to resolve it.

TIP To view the information captured in the error log, choose the Error Log command from the Server menu in SQL Enterprise Manager.

recovery interval (Dynamic)

> Minimum: 1
>
> Maximum: 32767
>
> Default: 5

The `recovery interval` option controls the number of minutes SQL Server requires to re-cover a database in the event that a system failure occurs. This option, combined with the amount of activity that is occurring on the server, controls the amount of time between data-base CHECKPOINTs.

A database CHECKPOINT forces all the changes to dirty data pages from the transaction log information to be written to disk instead of residing in the transaction log buffers or lazywriter buffers. A CHECKPOINT can take considerable time if there has been a lot of activity on the server, but frequent checkpointing will reduce the amount of time required to restart the server because it will not have to ROLLFORWARD as much work from the transaction log.

remote access

> Minimum: 0
>
> Maximum: 1
>
> Default: 1

The `remote access` option controls whether remote SQL Servers are allowed logon access to the server. If this option is set to 0, SQL Server will deny access to remote SQL Servers.

remote conn timeout

> Minimum: –1
>
> Maximum: 32767
>
> Default: 60

The value for `remote conn timeout` represents the number of minutes that may pass without activity for a server-to-server connection. If the value is exceeded, the non-active session is terminated. The only exception to this is when the connection is involved in a DTC-coordinated distribution transaction.

remote logon timeout (Dynamic, Advanced)

> Minimum: 0
>
> Maximum: 2147483647
>
> Default: 5

The `remote logon timeout` option controls the amount of time, in seconds, that SQL Server waits before returning an error to the client process which was requesting the logon to a re-mote server. Setting this option to 0 causes the SQL Server to wait indefinitely.

remote proc trans

Minimum: 0 (FALSE)

Maximum: 1 (TRUE)

Default: 0 (FALSE)

The remote proc trans option allows users to protect the actions of a server-to-server procedure through a DTC-coordinated distributed transaction. When set to True, it provides a DTC transaction that protects certain properties of transactions. After this option is set, new sessions will inherit the configuration setting as their default.

remote query timeout (Dynamic, Advanced)

Minimum: 0

Maximum: 2147483647

Default: 0

The remote query timeout option controls the amount of time, in seconds, that SQL Server waits before returning an error to the client process which was requesting the execution of a query on a remote server. Setting this option to 0 causes the SQL Server to wait indefinitely.

resource timeout (Dynamic, Advanced)

Minimum: 5

Maximum: 2147483647

Default: 10

The resource timeout option controls the amount of time, in seconds, that SQL Server waits before returning an error to the client process which required a server resource. A server resource could be access to a memory buffer, a disk I/O request, a network I/O request, or a log I/O request. Increase the value of this option if a large number of logwait or bufwait timeout warnings are in the SQL Server error log.

set working set size (Advanced)

Minimum: 0

Maximum: 1

Default: 0

The set working set size option controls whether SQL Server requests Windows NT to physically allocate and lock memory to SQL Server. The amount allocated will be equal to the number of pages in the memory configuration option multiplied by 2K, plus the amount of memory requested for tempdb in the tempdb in RAM configuration option.

▶ **See** Chapter 5, "Creating Devices, Databases, and Transaction Logs" in the section "Placing tempdb in RAM," for information about having your tempdb in RAM, **p. 124**

Part

III

Ch

16

show advanced option (Dynamic)

Minimum: 0

Maximum: 1

Default: 1

The show advanced option configuration option controls whether SQL Server displays advanced options and allows you to configure advanced options through sp_configure. If this option is set to 0, SQL Server will respond that an option does not exist if you attempt to change an advanced option. Remember, you must make sure that you have enabled the show advanced option using sp_configure before you'll be allowed to configure advanced options.

SMP concurrency (Advanced)

Minimum: –1

Maximum: 64

Default: 0

The SMP concurrency option controls how SQL Server will operate on a Symmetric Multi-Processing server. The default configuration for a single CPU computer is 0, which means auto-configuration mode. In auto-configuration mode, SQL Server allocates N–1 CPUs to SQL Server from the Windows NT service scheduler, where N is the number of CPUs detected in the server when SQL Server starts.

If SQL Server is installed with Dedicated SMP Support chosen, SQL Server sets this value to –1, which means that all CPUs will be dedicated to SQL Server. If the Windows NT server is not dedicated to running SQL Server and this value is configured to the maximum number of CPUs in the computer, tasks other than SQL Server that are executing on the computer will have poor performance.

sort pages (Dynamic, Advanced)

Minimum: 64

Maximum: 511

Default: 128

The sort pages option controls the number of pages that SQL Server reserves per user for sorting and resolving queries. This value should be closely tuned to the user requirements of the system that is executing on the SQL Server. A higher value will generally result in better performance for systems that do a lot of queries requiring data to be sorted in memory. Setting this value high will cause each user to consume larger amounts of available memory and require you to dedicate more memory to SQL Server.

spin counter (Dynamic, Advanced)

Minimum: 1

Maximum: 2147483647

Default: 10000

The spin counter option sets the maximum number of attempts SQL Server will make to acquire a resource from the SQL Server service manager. This advanced option should not be altered except in extreme situations, such as when you're working with a support center to troubleshoot your system.

tempdb in ram (MB)

> Minimum: 0
>
> Maximum: 2044
>
> Default: 0

The tempdb in ram option controls the amount of memory that SQL Server will reserve for tempdb in RAM. If this option is set to 0, tempdb resides on a physical disk device, which is the default for MASTER's device. If this option is set to any value other than 0, tempdb is placed in a memory chunk. This memory chunk will be contiguously allocated.

If tempdb is resized through the ALTER command while it resides in memory, additional contiguous chunks of memory corresponding to the required ALTER size will be allocated to it. These contiguous chunks may not, however, necessarily be next to the chunks previously allocated. You should shut down and restart the server if the size of tempdb is altered.

user connections

> Minimum: 5
>
> Maximum: 32767
>
> Default: 20

The user connections option controls the maximum number of user processes that can connect to the server at one time. The logical limit is 32767, but the practical limits of server hardware will probably be exceeded before this limit is ever achieved.

The minimum fixed overhead for each user connection is about 40K. If the user connections option is set to a large value, you may have to allocate more memory to the SQL Server.

If users are reporting that they cannot connect, your user connections value may be set too low. Use sp_configure to increase the number of user connections to a higher value so that more concurrent users are permitted.

user options

> Minimum: 0
>
> Maximum: 4095
>
> Default: 0

The user options setting establishes global defaults for users logging on to the system. After a change is made, all new logins will be affected, but existing logons will not change. Users can override these values by using the SET statement.

SYSCONFIGURES and *SYSCURCONFIGS*: System Catalog Tables

SYSCONFIGURES and SYSCURCONFIGS are system catalog tables that SQL Server uses to store information about configuration options that the server is using. These tables are stored in the Master database.

SYSCONFIGURES has information from the server about the available options and their defaults. The sp_configure option, in contrast, comes from the spt_values table in the Master database. Rather than relying on the formatted results returned from sp_configure, you may need to be able to process the configurations on the server in a result set. The query in Listing 16.6 shows the defaults for all the configurable options in the server.

On the CD

Listing 16.6 16_01.SQL—Querying the *SYSCONFIGURES* Table to Review the Defaults

```
/*--------------------------
Select V.NAME,   COMMENT = substring( C.COMMENT, 1, 60 ),
       "DEFAULT" = c.value
From    MASTER.DBO.SPT_VALUES V,
        MASTER.DBO.SYSCONFIGURES C
Where   V.NUMBER = C.CONFIG
And     V.NAME is not null
Order by V.NAME
--------------------------*/
```

NAME	COMMENT	DEFAULT
allow updates	Allow updates to system tables	0
backup buffer size	backup buffer size	1
backup threads	backup threads	5
cursor threshold	cursor threshold	-1
database size	Default database size in megabytes	2
default language	default language	0
default sortorder id	default sortorder ID	52
fill factor	Default fill factor percentage	0
free buffers	Free buffers	409
hash buckets	Hash buckets	7993
language in cache	language cache	3
LE threshold maximum	LE threshold maximum	10
LE threshold minimum	LE threshold minimum	20
LE threshold percent	LE threshold percent	0
locks	Number of locks for all users	5000
logwrite sleep (ms)	logwrite sleep (ms)	0
max async IO	Maximum outstanding async IOs	8
max lazywrite IO	Maximum lazywrite IO	8
max worker threads	Maximum worker threads	255
media retention	Tape retention period in days	0
memory	Size of avbl phys memory in 2k pages	8192
nested triggers	Allow triggers to invoke triggers	0
network packet size	Default network packet size	4096
open databases	# of open dbs allowed for all users	20
open objects	Number of open database objects	500
priority boost	Priority boost	0
procedure cache	% of memory used for procedure cache	30

```
RA cache hit limit    RA cache hit limit                        4
RA cache miss limit   RA cache miss limit                       3
RA delay              RA delay                                  15
RA prefetches         RA prefetches                             3
RA slots per thread   RA slots per thread                       5
RA worker threads     RA worker threads                         3
recovery flags        Recovery flags                            0
recovery interval     Maximum recovery interval in minutes      5
remote access         Allow remote access                       1
remote logon timeout  remote logon timeout                      5
remote query timeout  remote query timeout                      0
resource timeout      resource timeout                          10
set working set size  set working set size                      0
show advanced option  show advanced options                     1
SMP concurrency       SMP concurrency                           0
sort pages            Number of sort pages                      128
spin counter          spin counter                              10000
tempdb in ram (MB)    TempDB in RAM option                      0
user connections      Number of user connections allowed        20
(46 row(s) affected)
```

T I P   In the query in Listing 16.6, the reserved SQL Server keyword DEFAULT was used as a column title. To use any reserved words as text in a column title, enclose them in quotation marks.

SYSCURCONFIGS stores the currently configured values that the server is using. The query in Listing 16.7 shows how to get the current values for each of the configurable options in the server. Using SYSCONFIGURES and SYSCURCONFIGS together, you can write your own programs to dynamically set options and report options on the server.

On the CD

Listing 16.7   16_02.SQL—Querying the *SYSCURCONFIGS* Table to Review the Current Server Configurations

```
/*----------------------------
Select V.NAME,   COMMENT = substring( C.COMMENT, 1, 60 ),
       "CURRENT VALUE" = c.value
From    MASTER.DBO.SPT_VALUES V,
        MASTER.DBO.SYSCURCONFIGS C
Where   V.NUMBER = C.CONFIG
And     V.NAME is not null
Order by V.NAME
---------------------------*/
NAME                  COMMENT                               CURRENT VALUE
-------------------   ----------------------------------    -------------
allow updates         Allow updates to system tables        0
backup buffer size    backup buffer size                    1
backup threads        backup threads                        5
cursor threshold      cursor threshold                      -1
database size         Default database size in megabytes    2
default language      Default language                      0
default sortorder id  Default sortorder ID                  52
```

continues

Listing 16.7   Continued

```
fill factor          Default fill factor percentage       0
free buffers         Free buffers                         409
hash buckets         Hash buckets                         7993
language in cache    # of language information in cache   3
LE threshold maximum Lock Escalation threshold maximum    10
LE threshold minimum Lock Escalation threshold minimum    10
LE threshold percent Lock Escalation threshold percent    0
locks                Number of locks for all users        5000
logwrite sleep (ms)  logwrite sleep (ms)                  0
max async IO         Maximum outstanding async IOs        8
max lazywrite IO     Maximum lazywrite IO                 8
max worker threads   Maximum worker threads               255
media retention      Media retention period in days       0
memory               Size of avbl phys memory in 2k pages 8192
nested triggers      Allow triggers to invoke triggers    0
network packet size  Default network packet size          4096
open databases       # of open dbs allowed for all users  20
open objects         Number of open database objects      500
priority boost       Priority boost                       0
procedure cache      % of memory used for procedure cache 30
RA cache hit limit   RA cache hit limit                   4
RA cache miss limit  RA cache miss limit                  3
RA delay             RA delay                             15
RA prefetches        RA prefetches                        3
RA slots per thread  RA slots per thread                  5
RA worker threads    RA worker threads                    3
recovery flags       Recovery flags                       0
recovery interval    Maximum recovery interval in minutes 5
remote access        Allow remote access                  1
remote logon timeout remote logon timeout                 5
remote query timeout remote query timeout                 0
resource timeout     Resource timeout                     10
set working set size set working set size      .          0
show advanced option Show advanced options                1
SMP concurrency      SMP concurrency                      1
sort pages           Number of sort pages                 128
spin counter         Spin counter                         0
tempdb in ram (MB)   Size of TempDB in RAM (MB)           0
user connections     Number of user connections allowed   20
(46 row(s) affected)
```

> **N O T E**   The queries in Listing 16.6 and Listing 16.7 are joined to the SQL Server system table spt_values. SQL Server uses this table to display value/configuration data. ∎

Defining Database Options

SQL Server has several options available at the database level that enable the database administrator (DBA) to configure how different databases act on a given server.

NOTE In versions prior to SQL Server 6.0, it was necessary to do a CHECKPOINT command in the modified database after performing a change to a database option. In SQL Server 6.0, Microsoft added the dynamic interpretation of procedural logic to stored procedures, making it possible for them to update the sp_dboption system-stored procedure to automatically do the CHECKPOINT for you. ■

Displaying and Setting Database Options

SQL Server provides two ways to display and set configuration options for the database. The graphical method involves using SQL Server Enterprise Manager. The command-line method uses the sp_dboption system-stored procedure.

Using SQL Enterprise Manager   To configure a database using SQL Enterprise Manager, follow these steps:

1. Run SQL Enterprise Manager from the Microsoft SQL Server 6.5 group.

2. Select the server and database that you want to work on.

3. Either double-click the database you want to edit or click the right-mouse button and choose Edit from the menu. When the Edit Database dialog box is displayed, click the Options page (see Figure 16.4).

FIG. 16.4
SQL Enterprise Manager's Edit Database dialog box shows the Options page.

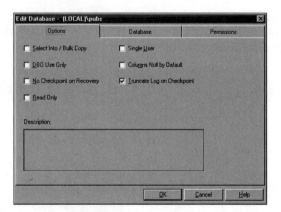

4. To change any of the settings for the database, select the required options and then click OK to apply the changes and return to the main SQL Enterprise Manager window.

Using sp_dboption   You can use the system-stored procedure sp_dboption instead of the SQL Enterprise Manager to set options for the database. The syntax for sp_dboption is as follows:

```
sp_dboption [database name, database option, database value]
```

The database name is the name of the database that is being viewed or changed.

The database option is the name of the option being viewed or changed. Place quotation marks around the option being set if it contains any embedded spaces.

The database value is the new value for the option.

If you don't give sp_dboption any parameters, it will return the available parameters that can be set for any current database. Listing 16.8 shows the result of sp_dboption being executed without parameters.

Listing 16.8   Using *sp_dboption* to Report All the Configurable Database Options

```
/*----------------------------
sp_dboption
-------------------------*/
Settable database options:
-------------------------
ANSI null default
dbo use only
no chkpt on recovery
offline
published
read only
select into/bulkcopy
single user
subscribed
trunc. log on chkpt.
```

If a database is supplied as a parameter, but no database option is supplied, sp_dboption returns the currently active configuration options for the specified database. Listing 16.9 shows an example of this procedure.

Listing 16.9   Seeing Options on a Database Using *sp_dboption*

```
/*-------------------------
sp_dboption pubs
-------------------------*/
The following options are set:
-------------------------
select into/bulkcopy
trunc. log on chkpt.
```

The sp_dboption procedure is similar to the sp_configure procedure in that, for the option being set, it performs a wildcard-style search on the passed-in option parameter so that *dbo*, *dbo use*, and *dbo use only* can all specify the same parameter.

Database Options Explained

The following is a list of all the available user database configuration options. In parentheses following the option name is the equivalent name that SQL Enterprise Manager uses for the option. Options without equivalent commands in SQL Enterprise Manager must be set with sp_dboption.

NOTE The only option that is user-configurable for the Master database is the Truncate Log on Checkpoint option. SQL Server requires that all other configurations be left in their default setups for the Master database to operate correctly. ■

***ANSI null default* (Columns Null by Default)**   The ANSI null default database option controls the way the SQL interpreter parses the CREATE TABLE statement when defining columns. By default, if the NULL keyword is omitted in SQL Server, the SQL interpreter assumes that the column is supposed to be NOT NULL. The ANSI standard specifies the reverse, however; unless otherwise specified, a column is NULL. If, when you define a table, you specify whether a given column is NULL or NOT NULL, your indication will override this setting.

If the database scripts you are using to create a table or set of tables have been created for an ANSI-compatible database, you must turn on this option so that the tables behave the same way they would on another ANSI-compatible database.

***DBO use only* (DBO Use Only)**   The DBO use only database option controls the user access to the database. If this option is set to True, then the only user that may access the database is the database owner, DBO. If this option is turned on while other users are connected to the database, their connections will not be killed. The users will be allowed to stay on the database until they disconnect voluntarily.

***no chkpt on recovery* (No Checkpoint on Recovery)**   The no chkpt on recovery database option controls behavior during the recovery of a database. The default is False, meaning that after a recovery of database or transaction log, a CHECKPOINT operation will occur.

If multiple databases are being used in a primary and secondary fashion and transaction logs are being rolled forward from one database to another, this option should be set to True in order to stop the database from rejecting further transaction logs being applied.

offline   The offline database option, if enabled, will bring a database down into an offline condition. This option is most often used with databases based on removable media, such as a disk or CD-ROM, that need to be swapped out at any given time. Databases that have currently connected or active users cannot be placed offline until those users disconnect. An offline database is not recovered when the server is restarted.

published   The published database option controls whether a database is available for publishing- and subscribing-based replication. If this option is enabled, a repl_subscriber user is added to the database, and the transaction log is monitored for transactions that need to be replicated to other databases.

NOTE The fact that you enable the published option does not cause the database to be replicated. For information about replication and setting up the publisher/subscriber relationship between databases, see Chapter 17, "Setting Up and Managing Replication." ■

***read only* (Read Only)**   The read only database option, if enabled, places a database in read-only mode, making it impossible to insert, update, or delete anything from the database. This is a useful option to turn on for reporting databases. For example, if you are writing an application that simply does a lot of reports for your users, the read only flag will guarantee that the data does not change.

N O T E   If you use this option, don't forget to reverse it in your applications that populate the tables in the database. You must have a way to get information into the database before you can mark it read-only, so your routines that place this information online must disable and then re-enable the option during processing. ▓

***select into/bulkcopy* (Select Into/Bulk Copy)**   The select into/bulkcopy database option controls whether non-logged database operations are permitted in the current database. A non-logged operation, such as the SELECT INTO command, is highly optimized and does not write any entries to the database transaction log, making it unrecoverable.

> **CAUTION**
>
> If you set the select into/bulkcopy option to True, you won't be able to use the transaction log for recovery of a problem database. Be certain you set this option to False to ensure your ability to use the transaction dump and restore capabilities of SQL Server if that will be your backup approach.

This option must be enabled if Bulk Copy (BCP) operations are to be executed against a database table without indexes. However, if a table has indexes, SQL Server will always use the slow load algorithm so that it has a chance to update the indexes.

***single user* (Single User)**   The single user database option limits database access to a single user. If this option is enabled and a user connects, then that user may stay connected, but any other user will be denied access.

If single user mode is turned on, trunc. Log on chkpt. will be disabled because it requires an additional user connection to the database to act as a monitor. The DBO or SA cannot override the single user option. If another user is logged on to a given database, the DBO or SA will not even be able to access the database.

subscribed   The subscribed database option controls whether the database can be part of a subscription-based replication. If this option is set to True, a private account, repl_publisher, is given access as a DBO to the database, and the replication services are activated.

***trunc. log on chkpt.* (Truncate Log on Checkpoint)**   The trunc. log on chkpt. database option controls whether the database logs are truncated when a checkpoint activity occurs. By default, this option is off and it should always be off in situations when it may be necessary to use the transaction logs for replication, backup, or recovery.

If you find that you're executing the checkpoint frequently but still fill up your transaction logs, you need to do one of three things: perform more frequent manual dumping of the transaction logs, enlarge your logs, or use Performance Monitor to run a batch file to dump the logs when they are nearly full.

▶ **See** Chapter 21, "Optimizing Performance," for information on Performance Monitor, **p. 593**

Note that if you have this option enabled, or set it to True, you cannot dump the transaction log. It only exists between checkpoints, so you'll receive an error message indicating that the transaction log cannot be dumped.

One important consideration when using this option is the fact that you cannot use the transaction log as part of your backup approach. Because you cannot dump the transaction log, you can't back it up. Instead, you need to do complete database backups to ensure the safety of the information in your database.

Understanding Query Options

SQL Server has a number of individual options that you can set while querying the database. These options control the behavior of queries when they are executed. These options are also useful statistical and informational gatherers. They can be helpful in diagnosing query problems, such as queries that run slowly for no apparent reason.

Displaying and Setting Database Query Options

SQL Server provides two ways to display and set configuration options for a query. The graphical method is to use ISQL/w or the Query Analyzer of SQL Server Enterprise Manager. The command-line method is to use the system keyword SET.

Using ISQL/w   To use ISQL/w to set or view query options, perform the following steps:

1. Run ISQL/w from the Microsoft SQL Server 6.5 group, and log on to the required server, as shown in Figure 16.5.

FIG. 16.5
After ISQL/w is started, the pubs database is selected.

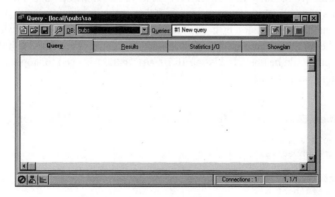

2. From the Query menu, choose Set Options to display the Query Options dialog box, shown in Figure 16.6.

FIG. 16.6
ISQL/w's Query Options
dialog box shows the
Query Flags page.

3. To change any of the settings for the query, select the required options and then click OK to apply the changes and return to the main ISQL/w window.

SET   SQL Server provides an SQL keyword, the SET statement, that you can use to set any query option. If used in a stored procedure, the SET statement is in effect for the life of the procedure and overrides any previous settings. The syntax for the SET statement is as follows:

```
SET Option On ¦ Off
```

Option is any valid SQL Server query option.

Query Options Explained

The following is a list of all the query options that are configurable and what they do. In parentheses following the SET option is its equivalent in ISQL/w.

Arithabort (Abort on Arithmetic Error)   The ARITHABORT option controls what SQL Server will do when an arithmetic error occurs. If this option is set to True, SQL Server aborts any query that causes division by zero or numeric overflow (in which the value is greater than the defined data type) to occur. You can't capture this error at runtime, so if this option is not set, the output could be NULL. In Listing 16.10, ARITHABORT is used to stop a command batch from continuing with invalid data.

On the CD

Listing 16.10   16_03.SQL—Using the *ARITHABORT* Option

```
/* Declare working variables */
Declare @nDecimal Decimal( 8, 2 ),
        @nInteger Integer
/* ensure that the error does not cause an abort */
Set ArithAbort off
/* do a division that is going to cause an error
note that the print statement doesn't
get executed because this is a special error
    condition that SQL Server doesn't "publish"
    for handling */
Select @nDecimal = 8 / 0
If @@error != 0
```

```
        Print 'Error'
/* abort processing if the error occurs again */
Set ArithAbort on
/* This time the division will cause an error and
   the SQL command batch will be terminated, note
that the termination stops any further activity
and the print statement again is ignored */
Select @nDecimal = 8 / 0
If @@error != 0
        Print 'Error'
```

The output is as follows:

```
Divide by zero occurred.
(1 row(s) affected)
Msg 8134, Level 16, State 1
Divide by zero error encountered
```

Arithignore (Ignore Arithmetic Error)   ARITHIGNORE is the opposite of ARITHABORT because it stops the SQL Server from reporting an error condition if an arithmetic error occurs. Listing 16.11 demonstrates how ARITHIGNORE is used and shows that SQL Server does not report any error conditions.

On the CD

Listing 16.11   16_04.SQL—Using *ARITHIGNORE* to Ignore Arithmetic Overflows

```
/* Declare working variables */
Declare @nDecimal Decimal( 8, 2 ),
        @nInteger Integer
/* ensure that the error does not cause an abort */
Set Arithignore on
/* do a division that is going to cause an error
note that the print statement doesn't
   get executed because this is a special error
   condition that SQL Server doesn't "publish"
   for handling */
Select @nDecimal = 8 / 0
If @@error != 0
        Print 'Error'
/* do a print so that we know we are through the
first part of the query */
Print 'Second Query'
/* abort processing if the error occurs again */
Set ArithIgnore off
/* This time the division will cause an error and
the SQL command batch will be terminated, note
   that the termination stops any further activity
and the print statement again is ignored */
Select @nDecimal = 8 / 0
If @@error != 0
        Print 'Error'
```

The output is as follows:

```
(1 row(s) affected)
Second Query
Divide by zero occurred.
(1 row(s) affected)
```

NOCOUNT (No Count Display)   The NOCOUNT option disables the display of the number of rows processed by any SQL statement. The @@ROWCOUNT global variable is still maintained, however. The output in Listing 16.12 shows the effect of NOCOUNT.

On the CD

Listing 16.12   16_5.SQL—Using *NOCOUNT* to Stop the Reporting of Rows Affected by SQL

```
/* Make sure that NoCount is Off (the default) */
Set NoCount Off
/* Do some SQL */
Select  "# Authors" = Count(*)
From    AUTHORS
/* Now turn on NoCount */
Set NoCount On
/* Do the same SQL and observe the different results */
Select  "# Authors" = Count(*)
From    AUTHORS
```

The output is as follows:

```
# Authors
----------
23
(1 row(s) affected)
# Authors
----------
23
```

NOEXEC (No Execute)   The NOEXEC option controls whether SQL Server executes an SQL statement. If you turn on this option, SQL Server will not execute the query, but will perform only the work to determine how the query would have been answered. This option is most commonly used when viewing the SHOWPLAN that a query generates without fetching the data.

N O T E   SQL Server processes queries in two phases: compilation and execution. In the compilation phase, SQL Server validates that the query is OK, checks that all the objects exist and are readable, and generates the query plan or best path to the actual data. In the execution phase, SQL Server starts performing the query, which could include updating the records, fetching the data, and so on. ■

PARSEONLY (Parse Query Only)   The PARSEONLY option is like NOEXEC except that SQL Server does not compile the query or generate the access path to the data. All SQL Server does is check that the query is syntactically accurate.

SHOWPLAN (Show Query Plan)   The SHOWPLAN option shows the query plan that SQL Server generated to answer a query. The query plan can be interpreted by ISQL/w or by SQL Enterprise Manager; a graphical representation is also displayed, as shown in Figure 16.7. For a complete and detailed discussion on interpreting the SHOWPLAN output, refer to Chapter 23, "Understanding *SHOWPLAN* Output," in Microsoft's *SQL Server Administrator's Companion*.

FIG. 16.7

ISQL/w's graphical
SHOWPLAN output can
help you understand
how a query is being
performed.

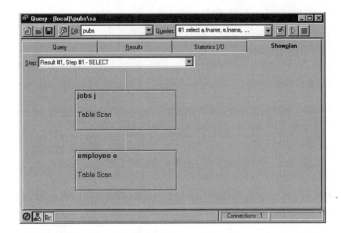

STATISTICS TIME (Show Stats Time)   The STATISTICS TIME option shows the amount of time the server spent in different areas of parsing, compiling, executing, and answering a query. This information can be very useful when you are adjusting queries. The data, however, can be skewed because of server caching.

STATISTICS IO (Show Stats I/O)   The STATISTICS IO option shows the number of logical and physical reads the server did to answer a query. Logical reads are reads that come from cache pages. Physical reads cause the database to go to disk. The number returned is the number of 2K pages read.

Starting the Server in Minimal Configuration Mode

Minimal Configuration mode is a last resort that should only be used when the server fails to start because of an invalid configuration specified with sp_configure. Minimal configuration mode starts the minimum number of services to allow the reconfiguration of the server. Minimal Configuration mode is provided in SQL Server 6.x in place of SQL Server 4.2's and Sybase's bldmaster executable. Prior to version 6.x of SQL Server, the configuration options were written to the bldmaster file. If you couldn't start the server, you had to edit this file manually.

CAUTION

This chapter applies only to SQL Server 6.x. The instructions here are not effective for prior releases. See the Microsoft SQL Server documentation on bldmaster to restart a server prior to SQL Server 6.x.

A server started in minimal configuration mode has the following limitations:

■ All configuration values that affect memory, database, and server are set to their minimums as shown in sp_configure.

■ The stored procedure cache is set to 50 percent of available memory as configured in the minimums of sp_configure. Memory, therefore, is set to 1000 2K pages, or 2M, and procedure cache is 500 pages, or 1M.

■ SQL Server is started in single-user mode at the server level, which is equivalent to the -m command-line option of SQL Server. Because the server is in single-user mode, the CHECKPOINT service is not started. This service is required to guarantee that transactions are written to disk.

 T I P The CHECKPOINT service behaves like a user in the system and is assigned spid 3. You can check that the service is running by executing an sp_who command in ISQL.

■ Remote Access is disabled because the Remote Access service that acts as a user is not able to connect to the server due to single-user limitations.

■ Read Ahead paging is disabled because the Read Ahead service that acts as a user is not able to connect to the server due to single-user limitations.

■ You can't use SQL Enterprise Manager because it requires more than one connection to the server and consumes more resources than are available during minimal configuration mode. You must use ISQL to fix the configuration option that is causing the server startup problems.

■ No autoexec procedures are run on server startup. Again, these procedures rely on being able to connect to the database, and this connection is reserved for the user to correct the server configuration problem through ISQL.

■ tempdb is moved into RAM with 2M designated for its use.

Starting SQL Server in Minimal Configuration Mode from the Command Line

To start the server in Minimal Configuration mode from the command line, perform the following steps:

1. Start the command prompt from the Start menu.
2. Type **start sqlservr –f**.

 T I P The start command launches a separate process thread in which SQL Server is executed. This thread allows you to continue using the same command prompt to do other things. You can start any Windows NT task.

N O T E   To start SQL Server independently of the Windows NT Service Control Manager, use the –c
command line switch. A server started in this fashion starts more quickly and can be fixed
more rapidly in an emergency situation. ▓

Starting SQL Server in Minimal Configuration Mode with the Services Application in Control Panel

To start the server in minimal configuration mode by using the Services application in Control
Panel, perform the following steps:

1. Start Control Panel by double-clicking the Control Panel icon in the Main group of
   Program Manager.
2. Start the Services application by double-clicking the Services icon in the Control Panel
   window.
3. Type **start sqlservr –f**.

Repairing a Server Started in Minimal Configuration Mode

There may be several things you will need to do to repair a server that you had to start in Minimal Configuration mode. If you started your server in Minimal Configuration mode to reset a
configuration, do the following:

1. Start the server in Minimal Configuration mode.
2. Run ISQL.
3. Execute SP_CONFIGURE to change the offending configuration value.
4. Execute RECONFIGURE to change the server value.
5. Execute SHUTDOWN with NOWAIT to shut down the server.
6. Restart the server as you normally would, and confirm that it starts okay. If the server
   still does not start, follow these guidelines again and adjust another configuration value.

If you started your server in Minimal Configuration mode because the server ran out of disk
space, this is what you should do:

1. Start the server in Minimal Configuration mode.
2. Run ISQL.
3. Execute DISK RESIZE to extend a disk device or DISK INIT to create another disk device.
4. Execute ALTER DATABASE to extend the database onto, or to add the database to, a new
   device.
5. Execute shutdown with nowait to shut down the server.
6. Restart the server as you normally would, and confirm that it starts okay. If the server
   still does not start, follow these guidelines again and modify the devices as appropriate.

From Here...

In this chapter, you learned how to configure your server, database, and queries to get optimal performance and to maximize your use of the server. Take a look at the following chapters for more information:

■ See Chapter 7, "Retrieving Data with Transact-SQL," to take advantage of some of the configuration options discussed in this chapter and improve the performance of your SELECT commands.

■ See Chapter 14, "Managing Stored Procedures and Using Flow-Control Statements," to take advantage of the new options to help you stop your stored procedures from getting error conditions and aborting.

Setting Up and Managing Replication

In this chapter, you learn the fundamentals of replication, including how to install and use replication and how it might be a good fit for your projects. Replication is an intricate feature of SQL Server. The boundaries of it have not been defined yet, and there are innovative projects coming that will stretch these boundaries.

Replication is a broad term, and to understand how to install and use it, you first need to understand what it is and what it is not. To help with this, you'll first be introduced to some of the terms that Microsoft uses, how these terms implement the replication capabilities, and what they mean to your system. ■

How to set up replication publications

SQL's capabilities to make information available to other servers add new, distributed capabilities to your systems.

How to set up a SQL Server to receive information that is being replicated

After information is available to your system, there are many different ways you can incorporate it into your database.

The different ways you can distribute information in your system to provide more meaningful data to your users

You can divide information to limit access to only certain elements of a database table.

Understanding the Basics

Replication with SQL Server provides you with the ability to duplicate information between servers. This brings with it the ability to synchronize information sources for multiple domains, even in cases where they are physically separated by distance and possibly poor communications links. Replication, at its most fundamental level, recognizes changes made to information in a database and sends these changes to the remote system or systems for their use.

Microsoft has employed what is called *loose integration* in its replication model. You might have heard of the phrase *real-enough time* in systems implementation. Loose integration follows the real-enough time model. This means that information will flow across the system of servers not in real-time and not necessarily in batch mode, but *as quickly as it can*. The phrase real-enough time was first introduced when information was being distributed by e-mail to remote locations. It was certainly not real-time, as no live connection was maintained between sites.

Using e-mail didn't implement a batch approach, as transactions were often still addressed on a transaction-by-transaction basis. With the e-mail system, you're certain that your transactions are going to make it to the destination when a connection is completed between the remote system and yours.

SQL Server synchronizes the database tables, almost immediately in many cases, but not concurrently with the transaction that made the original change that is to be replicated.

Certainly there are pros and cons to this approach. On the positive side, the user of the system will not be waiting for a remote server to respond before the application can continue. This alone can be a big time-saver. Another benefit is that the system can manage some fault-tolerance in the queue of things to be done.

If you have a transaction that is going to a remote server and the remote system is down, the transaction can be queued for later processing. The server engine on the local side, the distribution engine, can retry the connection to, and update of, the remote server at regular intervals and make sure the transaction happens as soon as possible.

A positive side effect of this approach is to consider that, in reality, wide area networks might need to be connected over slow links. Transactions can be handled as quickly as the connection allows, without bogging down applications that might be using the database tables that are to be replicated.

On the negative side, it's possible to have information in two databases using this schema that is out-of-date or different on different sides of the replication equation. With true replication as implemented in SQL Server at this time, out-of-date schemas is a situation you cannot control, but might have to address if this presents a problem. Remember, there are limited situations where this might occur, such as if a scheduled connection is unavailable or a server goes down. In either case, as soon as the connection is available, the databases are re-synchronized at the next communication with each other.

N O T E If you have multiple databases, tables, or other entities that must be absolutely in sync, you need to work with the two-phase commit capabilities of SQL Server. This entails custom development on your part using the C API and working with DB-Library. Be sure to review Chapters 22 "Communicating with SQL Server," and 23, "Understanding SQL Server and the Internet," for more information about developing applications for use with SQL Server. ▪

There are three different key physical layer components to the SQL replication model: Subscriber, Publisher, and Distributor. Each of these components must be in place to have a functioning replication model.

Understanding the Difference Between Distributed or Replicated Information

There is a distinct implementation difference between *distributing* your information and *replicating* it. In many installations, you'll probably find that you have both scenarios. When you decide to implement a system based on multiple SQL Servers, you need to be very careful to define what information will reside on which SQL Servers. This sounds obvious, but you need to take it to the next step, which is beyond just determining functional requirements.

In many systems that are disbursed, the requirement to implement replication comes from the desire to have information available at a central location. This requirement, combined with the information to be centralized having a remote starting location, provides the foundation for a replication scenario.

This is certainly a system that can be automated using the replication capabilities of SQL Server. The primary requirement is that you put a SQL Server at each location and initiate the replication from the remote locations to the central location. Another alternative might be available if you reverse the flow of information shown in Figure 17.1.

FIG. 17.1
Basic replication model shows information flowing between different points in your system.

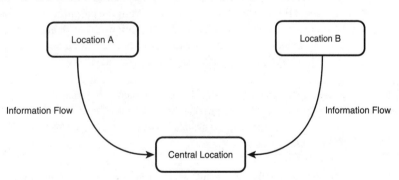

Adding a distributed approach to this scenario might be helpful to enhance your application's performance. Distributed systems, or components of systems, lend themselves to situations that include some or all of the following attributes:

■ The information required at each individual location is different and distinct.

■ The information from one location does not need to be available, in its most up-to-date form, at other locations. Somewhat aged information, if it's needed at all, must suffice at the alternate locations.

■ There is an intelligent agent running at the remote locations, and that agent must be able to respond to basic data request and manipulation requirements, such as copying working sets to a temporary database, and so on.

A good example of a distributed system is a *point-of-sale (POS) system*. In a POS system, you often have sales information at each individual location, but other locations do not have to have that sales information until it has been posted to a central location, if at all (see Figure 17.2).

FIG. 17.2
A typical WAN point-of-sale system lends itself to a mixed distribution- and replication-based system.

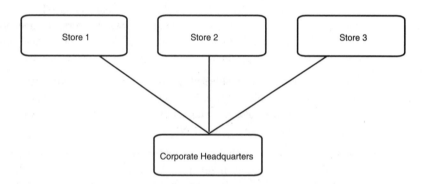

In this configuration, you can see that information flow between the store locations is minimal, and, when it does occur, it's likely to come from the corporate headquarters. Systems like this lend themselves to both a distributed information approach and a replicated scenario. First, you need to understand that replicated information is read-only at the recipient location. You can use the fact that things are read-only to your advantage.

TIP SQL Server's replicated tables are read-only on the subscribing system. If needed, you have to either create triggers on the incoming table that insert the replicated information into a working table, or you need to modify your system to use the tables differently, allowing for the read-only nature of the replicated tables.

In the POS example, you can use replication to send all inventory information, including pricing, store inventory levels, and other stores' sales information, to the different remote locations. Because this information is reasonably static, you can use a scheduled exchange of this information rather than a continuous update. You might want to keep this in mind as the process of setting up replication is discussed in the upcoming sections.

Distributed information can be maintained at the stores. This information includes sales information, customer update information about purchases, credit payments, and so on. You can refer to this as *distributed* because the stores operate on this information separately from the corporate headquarters. They can create, update, delete, and otherwise manage this information on their own.

 TIP Using SQL Server to manage distributed information at the remote locations is not a requirement. You can consider using less expensive options if needed. Other databases that use ODBC are key candidates for the remote locations, as they are able to connect most easily to SQL Server later to update the main database systems.

In short, you should use a distributed environment to provide a fault-tolerant, independent system. The information produced under these routines, and the routines designed to create the distributed information, might or might not be required at the central location. Replicated systems are ideal for information that doesn't change very frequently at the recipients' location. Keep this in mind as you review the different replication and installation options throughout this chapter.

Part
III

Ch
17

N O T E The processes that make up the replication model are all managed by the SQL Executive service. If you experience problems with replication, one of the things you might want to check out is whether the USERID and PASSWORD used by the SQL Executive are still available and have not been changed. You specified these values during the installation process. ■

SQL Server Replication Fundamentals

SQL Server's replication features follow a magazine-type analogy to relate the different roles that are parts of the equation. The model follows an *I'll Publish—You Subscribe* approach that's easy to follow and implement. In the next sections, setting up the different options for replication on both sides of the equation is covered.

N O T E SQL Server 6.5 has added the ability to replicate to ODBC subscribers, such as Access and Oracle. As stated in the SQL Server documentation, the ODBC subscriber must meet the following criteria:

- Must be ODBC Level 1-compliant.
- Must be 32-bit, thread safe, and for the processor architecture—for example, Intel, PPC, MIPS, Alpha—that the distribution process runs on.
- Must be transaction-capable.
- Must support the Data Definition Language (DDL).
- Cannot be read-only. ■

One last consideration that you might want to be aware of concerns the replication between a SQL Server version 6.5 environment and one running version 6.0 of SQL Server. If you'll be working in a mixed environment such as this, you might want to make sure that the Publisher and Distributor components are running on the 6.5 Server.

In addition, you have to treat the 6.0 Server as if it were a standard ODBC data source. This means you need to set up an ODBC configuration in the Control Panel. The positive side is that you'll be working around the limitations of the 6.0 replication, and you can use all of the features outlined in this chapter against the downlevel server. This is the same approach you use if you want to replicate to any other non-SQL Server database.

The final step in getting the downlevel server ready is to install the sqlole65.sql script. This script makes the replication possible, and it makes it possible to use Enterprise Manager from 6.5 against the 6.0 Server. This script is found in the \<platform> subdirectory on your SQL Server 6.5 CD.

TIP If you need to install the ODBC driver pack, it's included on your SQL Server CD in the \<platform>\odbc directory. In addition, for the Intel platform, there are additional driver sets in the \i386\odbcrepl directory.

Before You Start—Test the Connection

Before you go much further, you need to test your connection to remote servers to make sure you can connect to them appropriately. Microsoft provides a utility, located in your BINN subdirectory on the server, that helps you test the ODBC connection between your server and the remote system.

TIP Even if you're not using an ODBC connection directly to work with the other server, as would be the case with a remote SQL Server 6.5 system, it's still a good idea to check your connection with this fast test. It removes a variable should you encounter any problems later.

As you can test a TCP/IP connection with the PING utility, you can test an ODBC connection with the ODBCPING utility. ODBCPING has the following syntax:

```
odbcping [-s servername] [-d dsn] [-u username] [-p password]
```

Though the utility is a command-line, DOS window utility, it provides a solid test of the connection between your servers.

When you run the utility, you can check a direct login by specifying the server name, or test a DSN that you've set up by indicating the DSN. Either way, provide the *username* and *password* for the connection.

When the utility runs, you should receive a message similar to the following:

```
CONNECTED TO SQL SERVER
ODBC SQL Server Driver Version: 02.65.0213
SQL Server Version: Microsoft SQL Server  6.50 - 6.50.201 (Intel X86)
        Apr  3 1996 02:55:53
        Copyright  1988-1996 Microsoft Corporation
```

If you cannot connect successfully, you receive an error message that resembles the following:

```
COULD NOT CONNECT TO SQL SERVER
SQLState: 08001   Native Error: 6
Info. Message: [Microsoft][ODBC SQL Server Driver][dbnmpntw]Specified SQL server
not found.
SQLState: 01000   Native Error: 53
Info. Message: [Microsoft][ODBC SQL Server Driver][dbnmpntw]ConnectionOpen
(CreateFile()).
```

If you cannot connect successfully, check the following:

- Confirm that the remote server is available.
- Make sure the DSN you've defined for the ODBC connection is a *System DSN*. This means that you should not be able to see it when you first start up the ODBC Manager from the Control Panel.
- Make sure you've indicated the right server name on the command line for the ODBCPING command.
- Make sure the user name you provided exists on the remote server, not just the local server, and that it has permissions to log into the server.

If all else fails, consider re-creating the connection in ODBC and try connecting to the server using standard network drive mapping conventions. Chances are good that the server is unavailable or the SQL Server process on the remote server has not yet been started.

Publishing: Providing Information to Other Systems

When you decide you're going to be using replication to provide information to other systems, you, in effect, become a publisher. You publish your information for other systems to receive. At the highest level, the information you provide to other systems is called a *publication*. Publications consist of *articles,* which are the items that are provided to the other systems. Articles are discrete pieces of information that range from the entire contents of a database to a single row or the result of a query. As you'll see later in the chapter, there are several different ways to dissect the information you'll provide via replication, as follows:

- Entire databases
- Entire tables
- Horizontal partitions of information
- Vertical partitions of information
- Custom views of information

Each of these has its advantages and disadvantages. Which you use depends entirely on what types of information you're replicating and how that information will be used by the remote system.

Part
III

Ch
17

N O T E   Any table you want to replicate must have a unique index defined for it. If you don't have one defined, it will not show up in the list of available tables when you define the publication. ▪

If, after you've installed and configured the necessary components of replication, you have problems, consider the following troubleshooting tips:

- Replication might have been established on a scheduled basis. It might be that you set up the replication to occur, at least for synchronization tasks, during the night or some other off-peak time. Check the publication setup options on the publication server to verify when you expect table synchronization tasks to be performed.

- It's possible that enough time hasn't passed since the publication and subscription were set up. By default, synchronization occurs every five minutes. If your table is large, it can take some time to physically transfer the information to the subscription system, or it might be that the initial five minutes has not yet passed.

- The connection might be down between the two servers. Check to see that you can otherwise connect to the servers and make sure that they are up, running, and allowing logons. You should also check utilization on the servers. Microsoft recommends 32M of RAM on the publication system. With less RAM, it's possible that you're running into memory constraint issues and that the server is swapping more information than it should have to while performing the operations demanded of it with replication.

Entire Databases   When you provide entire database articles to the remote system, you are asking SQL Server to monitor all activity for that database and update the users of the information with any changes that occur. This is probably the simplest form of replication to administer, as you're telling SQL Server to send everything.

Keep in mind the basic covenant of replicated tables: The information is read-only at the recipient. It might be that this would be too restrictive on your system to implement this type of full-blown replication.

N O T E   If you're creating a *data warehousing* application—one in which you simply provide snapshot type information to other locations—this just might be the ticket. In these types of applications, you want to provide a picture of the information at a given time. You can create a database of queriable information, provide it to these remote users, and need not worry about the information being changed. You also can be assured of the most recent and updated information at these locations, as SQL Server will monitor it for you and initiate updates on the schedule you designate. ▪

The replication of tables and specific partitions of tables is often the way to go when you have a modifiable, production environment that you're exporting information to.

Entire Tables   When you replicate entire tables, you specify a table that is monitored and sent out by the replication engine whenever changes are made. This table is kept up-to-date based on the export timing and criteria you establish in setting up the publication article.

N O T E You can establish more than one article for a given table. This might be helpful if you want to provide all information to a production, administrative server, but only limited information to a reports-only server that is used by non-administrative personnel. Be aware, though, that each publication you establish requires resources on the server to process the replication event. If possible, consider publishing the table once. After this, you can create a view or other protected viewing mechanism on the receiving server as it works with the client-side software. ■

Horizontal and Vertical Partitions of Information, Custom Views   When you publish horizontal partitions, you're using a SELECT statement that provides all columns of information, but is selective on the rows of information that will be considered. For example, consider the following simple SELECT statement:

```
Select * from Authors where au_lname like "W%"
```

This selects only those authors whose last name starts with a W. These are the authors that are included in published information.

On the other hand, you might want to only publish certain columns of information to the remote system. For example, the Authors table in the Pubs database installed by default with SQL Server includes a Contract field indicating whether the author is under contract. If you're replicating a list of authors to a remote location, the users might not need to know whether you've established a contract with the author. In that case, you can select all fields except the Contract field to be included in the replication article.

You also can export a combination of a vertical and horizontal partition, or you can replicate the results of a view. The selective replication capabilities of SQL Server are the power behind the tool that really begins to broaden the appeal of replication.

Subscribing: The Recipients of Information

After you've set up what information you'll be publishing with the articles and other information covered earlier, you need to move to the subscription system and let it know where to find the information that it will receive. The recipient is called the *subscriber* in the replication scenario. The subscriber sets up a connection to the distribution server and receives the information at the intervals you established when you created the article to be replicated.

Subscriptions include the capability to designate where the information will go, which enables you to control who has access to it by using the standard NT and SQL security capabilities.

The Log Reader Process

There are two silent partners in the replication process that are always running and performing their tasks, but are much less visible when compared to the subscriber and publisher roles. These are the *log reader process* and the *distribution database*.

Replication in SQL Server is transaction log-based. As changes are made to articles that are declared for replication, they show up in the transaction log. The log reader process, an automatic background task on the server, detects these changes and logs them to the distribution server's distribution database.

Part
III

Ch
17

After a transaction has been processed for replication and put in the distribution database, the replication engine publishes it and makes it available to the other servers that need it. You can see the log reader process if you look at the running processes in SQL Server. You can see the process in the list of active connections.

N O T E   If there are any synchronization jobs pending, you also can see those jobs listed in the pending tasks area of the running tasks list. ■

Distribution Server: The Source of Information

The distribution server and database serve as the go-between for the publication server and the subscription server. When you set up the system, as you'll see when you go through the installation process, you have the option to set up a local distribution server or a remote system.

While the distribution database is separate from the other databases in your SQL Server system, it can still be on the same physical server. When you set up a local distribution database on the publication server, SQL Server uses this new database as the mechanism to keep track of the different items that need to be provided to the subscription servers on the network.

The distribution database is also the storage location for the different stored procedures that make up the replication engine. These stored procedures are automatically called when you use replication and are used to automate the different processes that happen under the covers when replication is running.

If you choose to use a remote system as your distribution database, the database is created or referenced on a different server from the publication server. This can be beneficial on a system where you might have high transaction volumes or might otherwise have a server that is bogged down just in the normal processing of transactions or network requests. In these situations, it can be beneficial to have this other system—the distribution database hosting system—manage the replication of information to the subscription servers.

> **CAUTION**
>
> You must have 32M of RAM on the server that will be the distribution system if you combine the distribution and publication operations on a single server. In addition, you might need to install additional memory if a given distribution server is to be used by more than one publication server. It might also be beneficial to implement a multi-processor server in cases where workload on the server is substantial.

You generally won't work directly with the log reader processes or the distribution database, but it's important to understand their functions to correctly set up your system.

Different Server Configurations for Replication

When you establish replication, if you take time now to figure out exactly the best way to lay out your system, you save yourself time later. As with database definitions and ERDs discussed in Chapter 4, "Data Modeling, Database Design, and the Client/Server Model," planning early in the development process really pays off when it comes time to move your system into production.

The configuration options for replication, at least on a physical implementation level, boil down to three different approaches, although there are certainly variations on these that can work well for some situations. The following are the basic three topologies:

- Combined single publisher/distribution, single subscribers
- Single publisher, distribution system, subscribers
- Single publisher, subscriber, publisher, subscribers (data warehousing)

Combined Single Publisher/Distribution, Single Subscribers   The most basic type of installation is the combined publisher/distribution server and a single subscriber system. This enables you to configure a server where the transactions for your system take place and the information is replicated to the subscribing server. Figure 17.3 shows a simple replication configuration.

FIG. 17.3
This is a simple system using a single server as the publication and distribution system and a single subscriber.

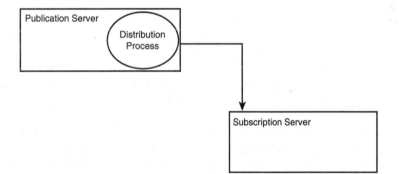

N O T E   The figures and examples indicate a one-way flow of information. You also can install replication's publication features on a subscribing server and effectively replicate other information back to the original publication server. To put it another way, because a system can be both a publication and a subscription server, information can flow in both directions. In this case, you just need to establish appropriate articles for publication. ■

It's likely that many systems that are not extremely high-volume fall into this category, as it's the most straightforward to set up and maintain. Be sure, however, to consider moving the distribution processes if your transaction volume begins to cause the server to become bogged down in processing both application and replication requests.

Single Publisher, Distribution System, Subscribers   By splitting the publication and distribution model, you can begin to address specific performance bottlenecks that can be apparent in your system. If you implement a model of this type, you'll be able to add processors, memory, or other resources to systems as they become overused. As you can see in Figure 17.4, it can be helpful to distribute the configuration of your servers.

FIG. 17.4
Moving the distribution processes enables you to optimize system configurations for optimum performance.

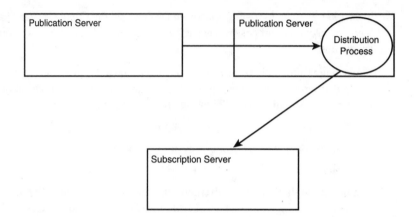

This system topology is also the first step toward a data warehousing system. By copying the information to the intermediary server, if you implement multiple subscription servers using this information, you can ensure that accurate, timely information is distributed without an overwhelming impact on the initial publication system.

In systems where you are publishing to multiple subscribers—especially in cases where the publications might be going out over a slow or remote link—a separate distribution server should be carefully considered. In each of these situations, more server attention, which translates into CPU cycles, is required to complete the replication and is best handled by a separate system.

N O T E   If you do implement this type of scenario, each system—the publication server, the distribution server, and each of the subscribers—is required to obtain separate SQL Server licenses. This cost needs to be part of the analysis when you are considering using a distribution server in this manner. ■

Single Publisher, Subscriber, Publisher, Subscribers   A big topic in the database world right now is *data warehousing*. As mentioned in the last section, replication lends itself well to data warehousing implementations, as it provides you with an automated way to provide read-only access to users of your system. You know the information will be correct and as up-to-date as you need, and because no intervention will be required, SQL Server's replication engine can be set up to update the remote systems at intervals required by your application.

In this scenario, you are publishing the information to an intermediary server that is responsible for secondary replication to subscribers. This is an excellent way to leverage your servers for their distribution to the users of your information. As you can see in Figure 17.5, one approach is to link servers to further distribute information.

This type of installation is also a good candidate for a separate distribution server if there are other operations to be required of the initial subscription and re-publication server. It's also important to keep in mind that memory requirements can increase on the re-publication server to work with the increased number of subscribers.

FIG. 17.5
Re-publishing information leverages your resources and can be helpful in mass distribution or slow-link to multiple subscriber installations.

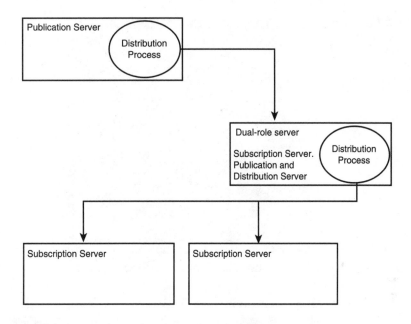

Installing the SQL Server Replication Services

The first step to installing replication is registering the remote server in the Enterprise Manager. There is nothing unique that you need to do to accomplish this, but you must have the server predefined prior to beginning the installation of the replication and subscription services.

> **N O T E** When you define servers in the Enterprise Manager, it's important that you select the correct type of security to be installed at each server. Selecting the Trusted Connection indicates that Integrated Security is in use. If you select the standard logon connection, you need to be sure to specify someone who is a valid user on the remote system and who has sufficient rights to work with the database tables you are replicating. If you do not, you'll receive errors when the replication service tries to connect to the remote server. ■

When you start the replication installation process, one of the first things SQL Server does is verifies that you've declared enough memory for SQL Server processes. The minimum required memory allocated to SQL Server is 8,196K, or almost 8M. You set this option in the Server Configuration dialog box, selected from the Server menu's Configurations option. An example of this is seen in Figure 17.6.

 It's generally recommended that you allocate as much RAM as possible to SQL Server. A good guideline is that you should allocate all RAM except approximately 24M to the SQL Server process. For example, in a 64M system, you should allocate approximately 40M to SQL Server. The 24M handles the network operating system and other base operating requirements of the system.

FIG. 17.6
You must have a minimum of nearly 8M allocated to the SQL Server replication features of your system.

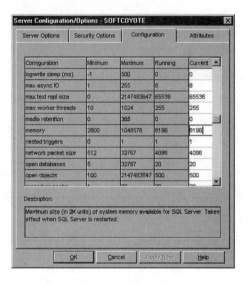

N O T E After you establish the memory configuration, you need to restart SQL Server. You can do this from the Enterprise Manager by selecting the server and then right-clicking it. Select Stop from the menu. After the server has been stopped, as indicated by the red traffic light, restart it. This institutes the changes to the memory configuration you just made. ∎

The next step starts the process of installing replication as a publishing server on your system. Prior to setting up the distribution database, you need to have established both database and log devices. These must have sufficient disk space allocated to support the database that you'll be replicating. These are the devices that you'll place the distribution database and logs onto. The recommended minimum size for these items is 30M, but your size depends significantly on several different factors, as follows:

- What is the size of the databases you'll be replicating? Remember, for each subscriber, there is an initial synchronization that must take place. This means that your distribution database should be at least as large as the combined maximum table size for each table that will be replicated. This size represents the size to support a single article. If you will be publishing multiple articles, you need to figure out a total size based on all articles combined.

- What will the traffic on your system be? More transactions mean more staging of information as it's passed along to the subscribing servers. This effects the database size requirements, and, therefore, the device size requirements.

- How many different articles will you be publishing? Try to avoid using several different articles against a single information source. If you have a table that you need to provide to multiple subscribers, it's worth the effort to try to use only one publication/article combination to fulfill their needs. This is a better use of disk resources, processing resources, and general processing bandwidth at the server.

Select Replication Configuration from the Server menu, and then select Install Publishing from the submenu. This begins the process of setting up the distribution database and other options that govern the server's operation for replication. Figure 17.7 shows the dialog box that you use to set up replication options.

FIG. 17.7
Set the options for the distribution database and processes for replication, including device sizes and naming.

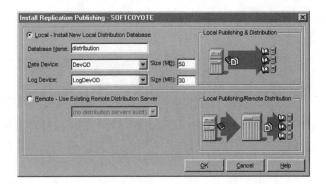

This dialog box enables you to define whether the distribution process will be local or located on a remote system. If you select local, you need to indicate where the distribution database will be installed. If you indicate a remote server, you need to know the server name and the SQL Server process must be already running on that system.

When you click OK, the new database is added to the system, and you are ready to start setting up specific options to enable publishing on your system. If all goes well, you receive a prompt, as shown in Figure 17.8, that enables you to go directly to set up publications on your system.

FIG. 17.8
After the distribution database is created, you can go directly to the definition of your publications and subscriptions.

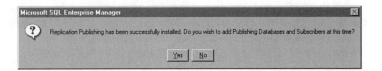

N O T E   If the installation of the distribution database fails for any reason, you need to address the problem before you can continue. A possible reason for experiencing a problem here is if you've registered a server with a user that is nonexistent or has insufficient rights on the remote system. If this is the problem you experience, make sure you create an appropriate user prior to continuing.

After you address any system problems that are presented, you might be faced with needing to completely uninstall replication before you can continue. For more information, see the "Uninstalling Replication" section at the end of this chapter. ■

Part
III

Ch
17

Enabling Publishing

The first step to creating your own publications is to, in essence, turn on publication services, designate a frequency for the services, and indicate which databases are candidates for replication. You can get to the configuration options, shown in Figure 17.9, from the Yes/No dialog box after defining the distribution database, or you can select the Publishing option from the Server, Replication Configuration menu.

FIG. 17.9
With the configuration dialog box, you indicate frequency of updates and which databases are available for replication.

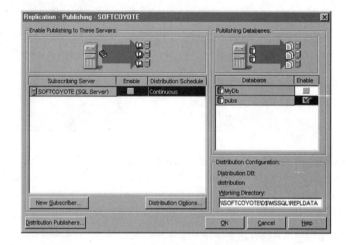

For each server you have registered to the Enterprise Manager, you can indicate whether it is allowed to subscribe to this server by selecting or deselecting the Enable option from the Enable Publishing grid. For each server you allow to subscribe, you can indicate at what frequency you'll be replicating information to the server. The default is to replicate information continuously starting at 12:00 AM and continuing throughout the day.

If you are using a remote link or are only providing snapshot information to the subscription servers, you might want to change this value to a time when the system is generally under less load. This can help decrease the impact on network traffic that will be incurred when the replication process kicks off. Of course, this places your data into a batch-type mode and might not be acceptable at the end user's application.

Selecting or deselecting databases controls which databases you will have to select from when you define publications. If you have a secure database that you want to control, this is the ultimate protection. By not making the database available to the replication process, you can be assured that it will not be included in publications.

You might notice the working directory option shown in the dialog box just below the designation of the distribution database. This directory is where information is kept and staged as it is sent out to the subscription servers. You can change this directory if needed. When SQL replicates a database, it is using a method somewhat like a BCP to copy the data from one system to another. This directory is where the data files are built.

N O T E It might be desirable to indicate a secured location for this directory if you have concerns
about other users modifying or reviewing this information when it's staged. The information
is not readily discernible, but should be protected nonetheless. ▪

If you want to create a custom distribution schedule or control how often information is sent
based on transaction volume, you can click the Distribution Options button. As shown in Figure 17.10, this option also enables you to indicate how long information is maintained at the
distribution server after it has been sent to the remote system.

If you do opt to establish a custom distribution schedule, a separate dialog box enables you to
change a number of options. As shown in Figure 17.11, you can set up on a macro level how
often the replication takes place. This option allows values that range from daily to monthly. As
you select this highest level interval, the balance of the options change to reflect values that
enable you further to define how you would like to have the replication carried out.

FIG. 17.10
You can create custom
distribution schedules
on a server-by-server
basis. This can be
helpful to take into
account time zone
changes and other
loading factors.

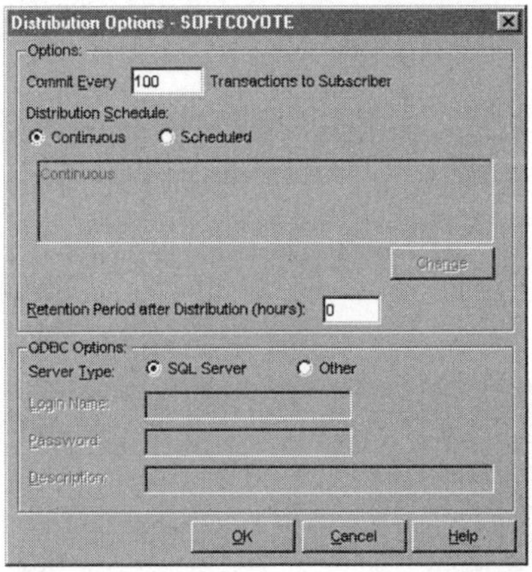

FIG. 17.11
Custom timing for
replication can be
defined for a number
of time intervals.

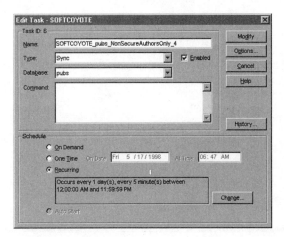

At this point, you're ready to set up the specific publications and articles that you'll make available to other systems. You've defined the servers that have access to the information and the frequency at which it will be provided, and you've indicated where the information will come from in your system. The next step is to create the publications that will be replicated.

TIP If you find that you're having trouble getting information to the subscribing systems, make sure the replication users, `repl_publisher` and `repl_subscriber`, are still defined on the systems that are taking part in the replication.

Publishing Databases: How to Replicate Entire Databases

You might recall that you have two different options when it comes to replicating information on your system. You can either publish the entire database, or you can select specific information in the database to replicate. In this section, setting up replication for an entire database is covered. In the coming sections, setting up targeted articles is discussed. To begin, go into the Replication management options (see Figure 17.12).

NOTE Remembering which option to use from the menus or the topology dialog box can be confusing. It helps to keep in mind that you don't generally use the options on the Server menu after you've installed and set up the basic configuration for replication on your system. All aspects that deal with the specific publications and subscriptions are controlled from the Manage menu. ▪

FIG. 17.12
Use the Manage menu to control all aspects of the replication process after you complete the initial setup.

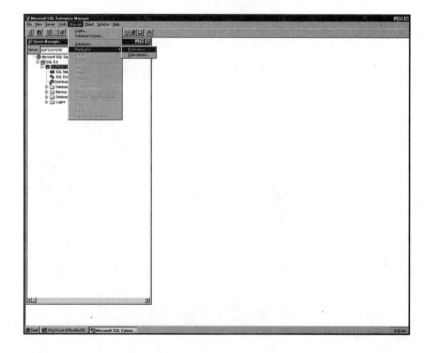

Select Manage, Replication, Publications from the menus to begin working with the different publications that are on your system (see Figure 17.13). This takes you to the dialog boxes that enable you to define and configure the publications and articles that you will be offering.

FIG. 17.13
The initial Manage Publications dialog box shows the databases you've selected to allow for replication.

The dialog box shows each database for which you've enabled replication during the setup phase. Of course, there are no publications listed initially because you've not defined them yet. You use the New, Change, and Remove buttons to manage the different replications in your system. The tree display expands under each database, showing the different publications that are available after they are defined. Under each publication, you can see the articles that have been created. From this display, you can manage all active publications.

Selecting the Tables to Be Published   In the first example, an AllPubs publication is set up to replicate all eligible tables in the PUBS database. Remember, you must have a primary key defined for each table that you need to replicate. You can use the ALTER TABLE command to institute a primary key if needed.

When you select New, you're presented with the dialog box that enables you to set up the publication and indicate the information that should be replicated. Figure 17.14 shows the dialog box that lists the different tables that are available and enables you to set up the specifics of the article.

First, you need to name the article that you're defining. When you do, make sure you do not include spaces or wild-card characters, such as an asterisk, in the name. If you do, when you click Add to save the publication, you are prompted to change the name.

N O T E   You might want to create a naming convention for your publications to make it easier to know what information they provide. This is completely optional, but if you're publishing numerous articles, this information tells the subscription systems to determine which publications they need to be working with. ■

As this article publishes all eligible tables from the PUBS database, simply selecting the <all tables> option will suffice for the definition. Each table is copied to the Articles in Publication pane, and you can tell that they're included by the shared icon that you're familiar with in Explorer and File Manager.

Part
III

Ch
17

FIG. 17.14
Setting up the article
to publish an entire
database only entails
selecting <all tables>
for the article definition.

Establishing Table Synchronization When you establish a publication, you are guaranteed that the subscribing system's tables will be initialized to contain the same information as the replicated table. To do this, there is an initial synchronization step that is completed. You can control how and when this step occurs by selecting the Synchronization tab from the Edit Publications dialog box shown in Figure 17.15.

FIG. 17.15
You can defer synchroni-
zation to a time that
suits your system requirements better, possibly
saving money if remote
connections are used.

If you are replicating information between SQL Servers, you want to make sure you leave the default copy method, using Native Format data files, selected. This enables SQL Server to save the information in as optimized a format as possible when it creates the export file used to initialize the subscriber's database tables. The other option, Character format, saves the exported information in a format that you can use if you are importing to the receiving database using other utilities, or if you're using the information produced by the initial synchronization in a third-party system.

TIP If the transaction log fills up and you're forced to dump and truncate it, you should first unsubscribe any replication servers. After you have done this, dump and truncate the log, then re-subscribe the servers. When you do, they automatically re-synchronize with the publishing server.

You can also set up the schedule of times that controls when the synchronization occurs by clicking the Change button. Establishing these times is very similar to the time frames you set up during the initial configuration of the replication services.

Controlling the Recipients of Subscriptions A key feature and concern regarding replication of databases is security. You've seen when you set up your system for replication that you can determine what subscribing systems will have overall access to your replication services. This presents a possible challenge, though, when you need to provide access to some, but not all, publications that reside on your replication server.

SQL Server enables you to indicate, on a case-by-case basis, what servers have access to any given publication. By default, when you set up a new subscription, SQL Server makes it available to any server with overall access to the replication system of your server. To change this, as indicated in Figure 17.16, select the Security tab of the Edit Publications dialog box.

Part
III

Ch
17

FIG. 17.16
You can easily prevent access to specific publications depending on what servers are requesting the information.

When servers look to your system to select available publications, if their system has not be authorized to use a given publication, it does not show up in the list of available items. You can change this option later to allow or disallow access to a publication by selecting Security from the initial Publications dialog box.

Making Changes to Publications After you've set up publications, you can review them from the Manage Publications window. In Figure 17.17, you can see that each database shows its related publications and articles as they've been defined on the server.

FIG. 17.17
You can use the tree
view of the replication
system to select a
publication or article
to review or modify.

If you want to make a change to a publication, simply highlight it and select Change. You are
presented with the same dialog box that enabled you to define the publication in the first place.
You can modify the tables that are included, how the information is synchronized, and the
security aspects of the publication.

Publishing Partial Databases and/or Tables

Now that you understand how to publish entire databases, this section reviews how to selectively publish information from your replication server. As you might imagine, publishing select information can be quite complicated, although it depends a great deal on how you're
trying to limit the information being replicated and how you go about defining that information.

Limiting Publications to a Single Table   The first and most basic selective publication is
limiting the publication to a single table. You might have noticed that each table available for
replication is listed when you define a given publication. In the first example, the entire database was published by selecting the <all tables> option at the top of the list of tables. The alternative is to select the individual tables that you want to include in the subscription from the
Database Tables list. After you've highlighted the different tables you want to include, click the
Add button, and they are copied to the Articles list (see Figure 17.18).

FIG. 17.18
You can select one or
more individual tables
to be included in the
publication.

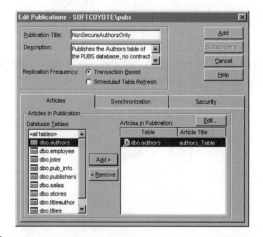

If you do nothing more for this publication, the entire table will be monitored and replicated as part of this publication. You have the same options for managing how the publication will be synchronized and what servers will have access to it as you do when setting up a full-database replication.

The alternative to publishing the entire database table is to partition it. You might recall from earlier sections in this chapter on "Publishing Partial Databases and/or Tables" that you can partition a table in one of two ways: horizontally or vertically. The next section shows how you can control this functionality with your publication.

Partitioning Information to Be Included in a Publication

The two partitioning options, horizontal and vertical, correspond to looking at views of your information based on selectively retrieving rows (horizontal) or columns (vertical) from your database tables. Of course, you can combine these two techniques to provide a concise view of the information in the table if needed.

To establish a partition of information to be used in the article, click the Edit button on the Edit Publications dialog box's Articles tab. This calls up the Manage Articles dialog box that shows two new tabs, Filters and Scripts (see Figure 17.19).

FIG. 17.19
You can select which columns you want to be included in the replication process.

In the example, as discussed earlier in this section, the Contract column information shouldn't be included in the replicated information that is provided to other sites with this publication. By scrolling down the list of columns, you can select and deselect the different columns that you want to include. When you've completed the selection, you will have vertically partitioned the database if you've deselected any columns because the publication will include only those fields that you allowed.

Normally, the SQL Server replication process manages insert, delete, and update operations automatically. This can be a problem if you're inserting information and need to have another process be kicked off by the action of inserting a new row, for example. In these cases, you can

Part
III

Ch
17

click the Advanced button and specify the Insert, Update, and Delete scripts that you'd like to run when records are modified with these operations.

In addition, if you need to do so, you can provide a table-creation script that you need to use in initializing tables. This script is run instead of the standard table script generated by SQL Server based on the source table's definition. This can be helpful if you're defining tables that will receive replicated data, but perhaps not all columns that need to be in a table.

By default, when the table is created, it is created with columns to match the article's definition. This means that, in the example of not copying the Contract column, the column would not exist at all in the recipients' databases. You can modify the creation script here and make sure all appropriate information and columns are included. Figure 17.20 shows how you can modify these values.

FIG. 17.20
You can override SQL's default methods that are used to implement changes to the underlying database tables.

CAUTION

Unless you are very comfortable with modifying these types of SQL scripts, you should consider alternative means of making the changes you need. For example, perhaps you could create a series of triggers on the subscriber that would institute changes needed in the storage of the information so that only certain columns were reused in the end user's system. Remember that changes made here will affect all subscribing systems, and you should ensure that this will not cause unforeseen problems on systems that might vary in their implementation of database structures and table layouts.

You also have the option of controlling the synchronization scripts that will be run by SQL Server. Clicking the Advanced button lets you edit what actions will be taken on synchronization of tables between the publication and subscription systems. The dialog box is shown in Figure 17.21.

FIG. 17.21
You have full control over how indexes and existing tables will be managed during the synchronization process.

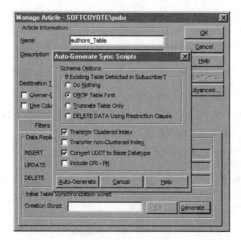

 TIP If there is a chance that the table might already exist on the user's system, be sure to check the DROP Table First option. If you don't, you might have a database table in an unknown state.

If you want to see or edit the actual script that will be created when the table is synchronized, you can click the Auto-Generate button. You are presented with the listing that will be used to create the table when it's initialized.

After you've completed your changes, click OK from the Manage Article dialog box, then Add from the Manage Publications dialog box. The publication is added to the list of available publications, and you're ready to allow other users to start accessing the publications on your system.

You might notice in Figure 17.22 that the AllPubs publication shows a secure publication, which is one with additional limits on who can see and use the information. The key that is showing over the book icon next to the publication name indicates this. On the NonSecureAuthorsOnly publication, there is no key, indicating that the publication is open to subscription by any subscription server with access and overall replication authority on your server.

FIG. 17.22
The new publication and articles are added to the list of active publications, ready for a subscriber to begin receiving the replicated information.

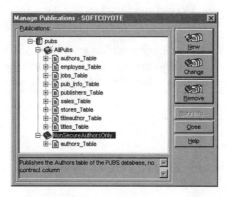

In the next section, setting up subscriptions on the recipient side of the equation is discussed. Now that you've set up the publications, it's a straightforward process to indicate which publications any given subscription server needs to begin receiving replication updates for.

Enabling Subscribing

After the publications have been set up on the publication server, it's a simple task to set up the subscription server to begin receiving the information. Before you can subscribe to a given article, you must follow the same installation steps outlined earlier in this chapter. These steps set up the distribution database and prepare your system to begin working with the replicated information. The only difference is that, when it comes to specifying which databases are visible to the replication process, you'll specify which ones can be the *recipients* of information rather than the source of the information.

▶ **See** "Installing SQL Server's Replication Services," **p. 513**.

When you're ready to initiate subscriptions, select Manage, Replication, Subscriptions from the menu in Enterprise Manager. As shown in Figure 17.23, this brings up a dialog box very similar to the Manage Publications dialog box used to define and create publications.

FIG. 17.23
Select the publication that you want to subscribe to from the list of available items for the server and database in which you are interested.

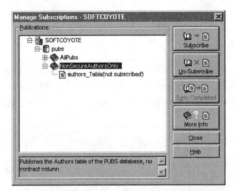

You can drill down into any given publication to see what articles are available and whether you're already subscribed to them. After you've found the publication you want to subscribe to, highlight it and select Subscribe. You can specify where you want the information to go on your local system after it begins arriving from the replication server (see Figure 17.24).

You might notice that there are three different options available to you for synchronization of the database. The last option is to turn off the synchronization altogether. This means that you know for a fact that the database and the concerned tables are in sync with the master system by some other means.

FIG. 17.24
When you select a publication, you need to indicate where you want to store the incoming information on your server.

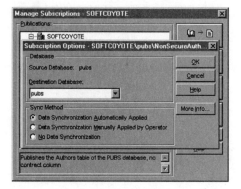

CAUTION

If you are unsure at all about the validity of the information in the database, it's best to allow the system to perform an initial synchronization on the database.

The first option enables you to let the system do the work for you and do the synchronization of information over the standard network connection between this system and the publication server. If you're on a locally attached LAN or a fast connection that is reliable, this is the best option to select and is the default.

If you're on a slower link, it might be that you've opted to bring the update to the system by another means. This includes copying the initial synchronization files from the publication server to tape or disk and then physically bringing them to the subscription system. If you have a slow link and initially populated tables, this might be a good option, as it avoids the initial rush of information across an already slow connection between the two systems.

 Remember, you can schedule the time at which synchronization takes place. Moving it to off-hours can ease network loading significantly.

After you've set up the subscription to the publication server, you might notice that the display of subscriptions is updated to show the active subscription. You can see in Figure 17.25 that, although the subscription is active, it has not yet been synchronized with the publication server.

FIG. 17.25
The list of subscriptions changes to indicate that you're now subscribed to the publication. It also indicates the destination database.

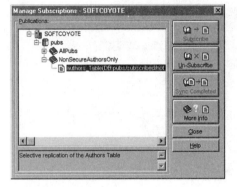

Uninstalling Replication

There might be times when you need to uninstall replication, either on a server-specific basis or on an overall basis. Examples include a server changing physical locations and no longer needing access to sensitive information, or when you've installed several test scenarios and simply want to start over.

The next two sections show how you can cover both of these types of situations using facilities within SQL Server.

Disallowing Specific Servers

If you find that you need to remove a server from the list of servers that are eligible to receive information from your publication server, you need to determine whether you need to restrict only individual publications or if you need to revoke access altogether. If your intent is to re-move access completely, you simply remove the server from the list of eligible candidates that can see the publications on this server.

From the Server menu, select Replication, Publishing. You can indicate which servers are able to subscribe to your server. Figure 17.26 shows the server selection dialog box that appears.

You are presented with a list of subscriptions that are about to be removed and asked to con-firm that you want to remove the server from the list of eligible systems. After you confirm, the server still shows up on the list, but the server will not be able to select publications on the publication server.

FIG. 17.26
Deselect any servers
you no longer want to
make publications
available to.

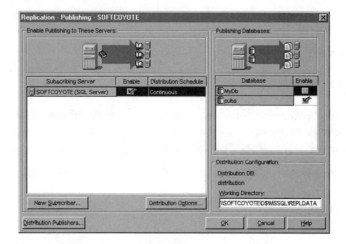

Uninstalling Replication Completely

Carefully consider all options before you opt to remove replication entirely from the system. This operation shuts down *all* replication to *all* subscribing servers, and it does so in a somewhat brute force manner by removing the replication option from the server and deleting the distribution database.

There are three steps for uninstalling replication in SQL Server, as follows:

1. Discontinue all replication services, all publication and subscription services, between this system and other servers with which it is working.
2. Turn off the replication option at the server engine level.
3. Drop the distribution database.

You need to follow these steps to restore your system to its state prior to installing replication. Removing connections to other servers is covered in the section immediately preceding this one: "Disallowing Specific Servers." If you're removing replication from a subscription server, select Server, Replication, Subscriptions instead of Publications; the operations of removing references to foreign servers are the same.

The next step requires issuing an interactive SQL command, so you need to use ISQL/W or another utility to enter the command. Enter the following stored procedure call to turn off the replication option on your system:

```
sp_ServerOption "<servername>", "dist", false
```

N O T E You must be logged in as SA to complete this option. ▪

Part
III

Ch
17

Replace *<servername>* with the name of your server. In our example, because our server name is PLUTO, the command would be:

```
sp_ServerOption "pluto", "dist", false
```

N O T E No results are returned from the call.

This removes the distribution option from your system, which disables replication. The distribution database you established when you first installed replication still remains in the system. Dropping this database is the final step in removing replication from your system.

From the Enterprise Manager, right-click the table that you specified.

CAUTION

Be sure you're selecting the *distribution* database you specified, *not* your databases that contain active, important production information. If you have any doubt about which database to select, you can review the stored procedures for the database, and you can see the replication stored procedures there.

If you select an incorrect database, you permanently drop production information, and your only recourse is to restore from a backup.

From the menu, select Drop Database and confirm that you want to drop the database. If all has gone well, you can make a quick check by selecting Server, Replication from the menus. You should have the Install Replication option available once again.

Reality Check

Probably one of the most often encountered problems with a replication installation is that, when SQL Server was installed, the administrator account was used for the Executive service. Later, when the password is changed on the Administrator account, the replication services stop working, seemingly without cause.

The fact that the SQL Executive must be able to log in, and that it's set up with the Administrator account when you run Setup, makes it easy to forget that the account and the process are linked. You can change the account used by the process by accessing the Control Panel and selecting Services (see Figure 17.27).

Select the SQL Executive Service and select Setup. When you do, you can establish the various startup options that are used when the NT Server is started. You should consider either assigning an account specific to the SQL Executive service, or you can set up the process to use a system account, preventing future problems with user names and passwords. See Figure 17.28 for an example.

By setting up the Executive in this manner, you are preventing the password change problems in the future. Also, make sure you set up the account with the Password Never Expires option.

FIG. 17.27
To update the account used by the SQL Executive service, select the service and choose SETUP.

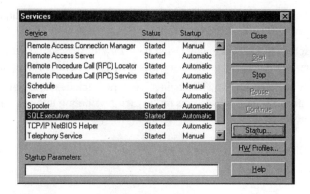

FIG. 17.28
It's a good idea to establish an NT account specifically for the job of supporting the SQL Executive process.

One performance area that has helped in implementations has been to use stored procedures in the replication process. Remember, you can indicate the SQL statement that is used to divide up the information that you work with in the replication process by using a stored procedure in place of the SQL statement. You can take advantage of the fact that SQL Server compiles stored procedures making them faster and more efficient.

From Here...

Replication is a powerful tool, especially in distributed environments. By putting replication into your systems, you can provide an excellent level of usability for applications, a great security layer for the underlying database tables, and better overall data availability.

For additional information about the topics covered in this chapter, please refer to the following chapters:

- Chapter 5, "Creating Devices, Databases, and Transaction Logs," provides additional information about creating the databases that you'll use in the replication process. It also includes information about the management of the transaction log for your applications.

■ For information on managing databases and creating databases and tables, see Chapter 6, "Creating Database Tables and Using Datatypes."

■ In Chapter 11, "Managing and Using Indexes and Keys," information about defining primary keys is provided. You need this information to enable replication for your tables.

■ Chapter 15, "Creating and Managing Triggers," includes information that can help you automatically create subsystems for further distributing information that has been replicated.

Using the Distributed Transaction Coordinator

With SQL Server 6.5, Microsoft began supporting distributed transactions, which are transactions that span more than one server. There are many times when you need to update more than one source of information and you need to apply transaction technologies to the update to ensure that all or none of the changes are made against the database tables. The DTC is the tool that will provide this functionality, as well as utility functions that help you manage the process. ■

Learn how to establish remote server references for your SQL Server

Your server can work with other servers in completing remote transactions. Find out how to provide the connection information to those servers.

See how distributed transactions work

Distributed transactions are an extension of traditional transactions. By allowing transactions to span servers, you can make sure the proper updates are carried out on all database objects.

Find out how to debug transactions

If you should encounter any problems with distributed transactions, you'll want to know how you can trace the cause of the problem and what to do about it. You will find out more about the tools you have available to you to help track down problems.

Understanding Distributed Transactions

As with standard transactions, distributed transactions must follow the ACID rules. For more information on this, be sure to read Chapter 12, "Understanding Transactions and Locking." In short, the transaction must be self-contained and must be *autonomous*, or able to be reversed without affecting other processes. As you might imagine, distributed transactions add a whole new layer of variables to the development and deployment process.

With a typical system, you don't have to work with server-to-server issues, network problems, or other issues that can become a part of the transaction process. You may remember that transactions must be completely self-contained and able to be completed without intervention. With a distributed transaction, you may face issues with hardware failures, server availability, or different loading and performance patterns between the participating servers. As you configure DTC, you'll need to keep these in mind and make sure you set appropriate time-out and latency options.

You can think of the DTC as an extension of standard transactions. The DTC simply allows you to build transactions across servers, rather than contain them within a given server.

DTC is broken up into two different components. The first, the Transaction Manager, is responsible for overall coordination of the transactions. The Transaction Manager is responsible for enforcing the ACID rules and for making sure the transaction objects are complete and that they are addressed as needed to complete the transaction.

The other component, the Resource Manager, has the role of setting up the transaction and making it happen. The Resource Manager's role is to carry out the statements that make up the transaction and make sure the updates happen as requested. More on these components is covered in the next two sections.

Resource Manager

The *Resource Manager* has the task of carrying out the distributed transaction's mission. This means that the commands requested are performed by the Resource Manager against the different tables as needed.

The application doesn't work directly with the Resource Manager, but the transaction objects are submitted to the Transaction Manager. The Transaction Manager sets up the transaction and works with the Resource Manager to make it happen. All of this is transparent to the application, which must only issue the appropriate begin and end transaction statements to ensure a complete distributed transaction.

The Resource Manager is also responsible for making sure that the transaction can be recovered, even in cases of power failure during the resolution of the transaction.

Transaction Manager

The *Transaction Manager* responds when a new distributed transaction is begun. With the transaction begin statement, the Transaction Manager sets up the transaction object and works through two distinct phases of the transaction. These are the PREPARE phase, and the COMMIT phase. This commit is referred to as a two-phase commit, which is something SQL Server could not do before the implementation of the Transaction Manager and the DTC overall.

In the PREPARE phase, the Transaction Manager works with the Resource Manager to complete the operations, but not commit them to the databases involved. You'll recall that with a standard transaction, you open a transaction, perform the actions you need, then commit the transaction, saving the changes to the tables. With distributed transactions, you do basically the same thing. First, you begin the distributed transaction, perform the actions you need to perform, and then commit the changes to the respective database tables.

The Transaction Manager is responsible for making sure that, each step along the way, the proper logging is done, and that the Resource Manager is able to obtain the information and responses it needs to be able to ultimately fulfill the request. The Transaction Manager logs all activity to the msdtc.log file, which is used to roll back transactions if needed.

The Transaction Manager steps in when a BEGIN DISTRIBUTED TRANSACTION request is issued. This statement tells the Transaction Manager to set up a new transaction object and get ready to work through the distributed transaction as needed. The Transaction Manager enlists the proper Resource Managers on the different servers that will be needed to complete the transaction.

When completed, the application issues a COMMIT TRANSACTION or a ROLLBACK TRANSACTION, and the Transaction Manager works with the Resource Manager to complete or abort the task.

Part

III

Ch

18

Building Distributed Transactions

As with a typical transaction, you bracket distributed transactions between BEGIN and COMMIT or ROLLBACK transaction statements. The SQL statements between the two are carried out, then committed or rolled back as a whole depending on the completion of the series of statements.

Configuring Remote Servers for Use with the DTC

When you start a distributed transaction, you indicate the name of the remote server in the transaction's execute statements where you call the stored procedures on the remote system. You need to define those server names before you can reference them in the execute statements. If you don't, SQL Server won't be able to resolve where to look for the stored procedure you're executing.

You set up the server in the Manage Remote Servers dialog box. You access this dialog from the Server menu by selecting the Remote Server option. See Figure 18.1 for an example.

FIG. 18.1

You must define the servers that will be accessed by the DTC by providing the server name and selecting the RPC check box.

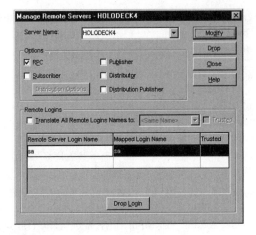

Provide the name of the server and be sure to select the RPC check box. *Remote Procedure Calls, RPC*, is the method that is used by the DTC to communicate with the remote servers. If you don't check this option, the DTC will not be able to work with the other servers.

You'll also need to provide the login information, though the easiest and most direct route is to select the Translate All Remote Logins Names To check box and leave <Same Name> selected. This will use the current user's name as the login on the remote system. Keep in mind that the user must be a valid user on the remote system as well as the local system.

Once these are defined, select the Add button to save the update. Be sure to complete this information for each server that will be working with DTC.

N O T E   If you have any trouble connecting over RPCs, check the network protocols on the server and make sure the RPC service is loaded and available. If it's not, you'll need to add it to the server and will likely have to reboot your system to have the changes take effect. ■

Installing and Configuring the DTC

There are two pieces to setting up the DTC component of SQL Server. First, you need to set up the server-side components. Those components make the DTC available to your applications.

The second piece of software you need to set up is the client interface to the server, allowing you to work with the server-based DTC and specifying the protocol that is used to work with the server.

In the next sections, you'll see how to set up these components on your network.

Setting Up the Server Components of the DTC

When you install SQL Server, it automatically installs the DTC. It's not an automatically started option, though, so you won't see it in the Enterprise Manager until you start it. To start the service, from the Control Panel, select Services and then find the MSDTC service. (See Figure 18.2).

FIG. 18.2
By default, the service does not start automatically when the server is started.

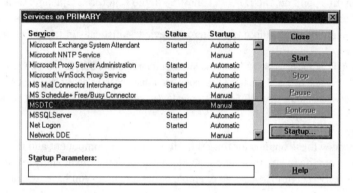

If you'll be using the service regularly, you'll want to set it up to start automatically when your server is started. To set this up, click the Startup button. The service dialog box, shown in Figure 18.3, lets you provide information about several of the options of the DTC server component startup. The two key items are as follows:

- *Startup Type*. Select Automatic to have the service start automatically each time the server is restarted. If you leave the setting at Manual, you can still use the DTC, but you'll have to start the service either from the Service Manager or from the Enterprise Manager each time you need to use the DTC.

FIG. 18.3
You should select automatic start and log on as a system account for the most trouble-free installation.

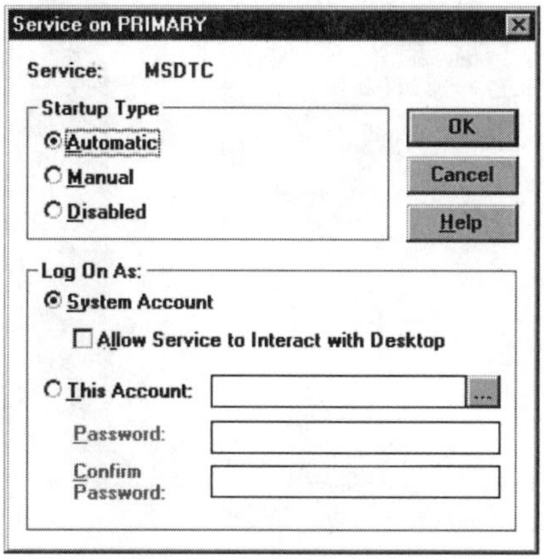

Part III
Ch
18

■ *Log On As*. Indicate the account that should be used by the service when it starts. Remember, if you set up the service to use a non-system account, you'll need to make sure you assign the "Log on as a service" right to the account you select.

Once you've set up the service, be sure you start it manually the first time. If you do not, the DTC won't start until the next time you reboot your server.

From this point on, the DTC will show up in the Enterprise Manager as a new component for the server on which it's running. The link in the tree-view list lets you set additional options for the component, including trace options, review statistical summaries on usage, and so on.

N O T E   If you're using the Enterprise Manager from Windows 95, you won't be able to administer the DTC, and you won't see the option listed under the server. You must be using Windows NT Workstation or Windows NT Server in order to remotely administer the DTC components using Enterprise Manager. ■

To modify these options for the DTC, right-click, the component and then select the option you need from the menu. In addition, you have the option of manually starting or stopping the service. See Figure 18.4 for an example of the functions you have available for the DTC.

These options are covered in the next five sections.

FIG. 18.4

You can work with many of the options associated with the DTC from within Enterprise Manager.

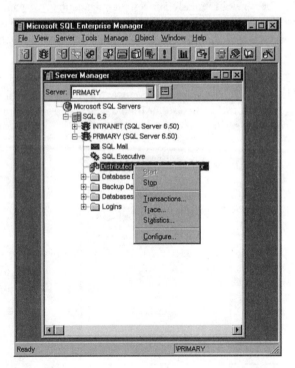

Start/Stop the Service   As the name indicates, this option allows you to start and stop the service from the Enterprise Manager. You cannot, however, set up the service for automatic startup when NT Server starts. To set this up, you'll need to see the earlier section "Setting Up the Server Components of the DTC."

Transactions   The Transactions option brings up a dialog box that shows any open transactions at the time you request the option. Each transaction is listed in a table, and the DTC shows trace information for each transaction so you can track it down should the need arise.

Trace   As with SQL Trace, you can set up filters on DTC transactions. These traces can help you determine where a transaction has gone wrong and how to track it down to correct the situation. The Trace dialog box shows a table of the transactions that you're monitoring and provides the information you'll need to work with them.

When you're running the DTC, it logs its messages to the Windows NT Server's event logs, as well as any trace facilities you may have implemented. You should always review the event logs as well as the trace facilities if you're experiencing trouble with a distributed transaction.

Tracing produces messages with four different severity levels:

- *Error.* This indicates that a fatal error has occurred in the DTC. This may point to other problems in your SQL Server. Be sure to check the errorlog. file in the LOG directory, and also be sure to restart the DTC service. In addition, if you have transactions open at the time you receive this error, be sure you *don't* remove the msdtc.log file, as it will contain the information needed by the DTC to reconstruct the data in your system.

- *Information.* This is like the information notices in the event log. The information presented won't take down the server, but it may be of use to you in debugging or tracing a transaction. This includes starting and stopping the DTC services.

- *Trace.* Information produced as part of the trace process.

- *Warning.* These items are either possibly going to happen or have happened and are bad, but not enough so that the DTC went down. Be sure to review all warning messages and make sure you understand what happened to cause them. You should not put into production any system that generates warning messages.

In addition, the Trace display shows one of several different status states for each transaction:

- *Aborted.* The transaction has been aborted to the best ability of the DTC in the current system state. This means that the DTC has notified, or attempted to notify, each participating system that the transaction should be aborted. This is a final state and only shown as the transaction is flushed from the trace display. Once in this state, the transaction state cannot be changed.

- *Aborting.* The transaction is in the process of aborting. During this time, the Resource Manager is notifying all participating DTCs that the transaction should be aborted. During this time, you cannot change the state of the transaction.

- *Active*. The Resource Manager is actively working the transaction, but it is not yet committed.

- *Committed*. The transaction completed successfully.

- *Forced Commit, Forced Abort*. These states are the result of a forced transaction that had previously been marked In-Doubt.

- *In-Doubt*. Once the DTC on a system other than the coordinating system has been notified that all other systems are prepared, it goes to work to complete the transaction. If it determines that the coordinating system becomes unavailable, the transaction state changes to In-Doubt. You can force a transaction in this state to complete, and it will do so based on the information for that specific system. If the transaction fails, the transaction is marked as Forced Abort, or if it succeeds, it will be marked Forced Commit. Remember, if you commit a transaction in this manner, other participating systems may or may not be up-to-date with the system on which you force the transaction.

- *Notifying Committed*. The coordinating DTC is notifying the different participating systems that the transaction should be committed. Between the time that the DTC is notifying those other systems and the time when they respond with success, this state is in effect. You cannot manually change the state of a transaction when this status is displayed.

- *Only Fail Remain to Notify*. For some reason, one or more participating servers have failed to notify the coordinating system that they've properly committed the transaction as requested during Notifying Committed state. At this point, you can wait to allow the transaction to clear, or you can force the issue, taking into account that those remote unavailable systems will not be updated unless you force each of them to commit as mentioned earlier under the "In-Doubt" status.

- *Prepared*. All participating systems have acknowledged that they are ready and able to commit the transaction.

- *Preparing*. The DTC has been told to commit the transaction and is now checking with each of the other participating systems to ensure that all involved in the transaction are ready and able to commit the transaction.

Three different subsystems generate messages to the logs and the trace facility. These are CM for the Connection Manager and its related activities, LOG for the logging mechanisms, and SVC for the overall DTC service.

Statistics   The Statistics dialog box will show you the volume and types of transactions you're processing through the DTC. The dialog box shows the current and overall total, or aggregate, values for your distributed transactions. See Figure 18.5 for an example.

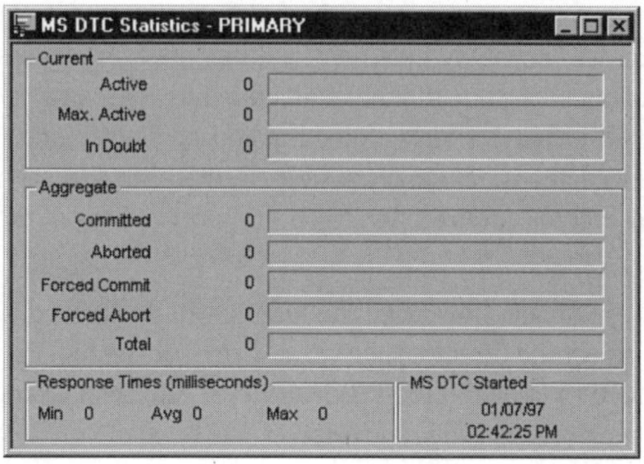

FIG. 18.5
If you think distributed transaction performance may not be up to par, be sure to review the statistics on each of the servers involved in the distributed transactions on your system.

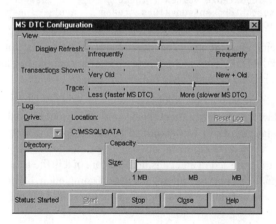

A key value to watch is the Response Times frame. These values represent a good view on how your DTC is doing in working through transactions. If you start to see these values jump, you'll need to review activity on the servers involved in the transactions, and you'll want to make sure the transactions aren't reliant on some factor that creates a bottleneck for the transactions to complete.

Remember, the response times listed are overall response times. To find out about specific transactions, you'll need to use the trace facility.

Configure   There are several different options you can set up for the DTC on the server to help in the monitoring of the server. If you are tracing transactions, though, and you find that performance has been significantly affected, be sure you've set the Trace settings to the Faster MS DTC side of the equation. You set this value by selecting the Configure option from the menu. See Figure 18.6 for an example of the Configuration dialog box.

FIG. 18.6
Be careful not to make the trace frequency too small, as it can affect overall DTC performance on the server.

The display refresh values range from one to 20 seconds. This is another item that can affect the server performance, but it's likely you'll want to set this rather low to see transactions more readily if you're debugging a known issue.

Part
III

Ch
18

Transaction aging runs from one second to five minutes. This controls the age of transactions that are shown. Transactions falling outside this range are still processed, just not displayed. In the normal course of business, it's unlikely you'll need to see transactions that are only a few seconds old. On the other hand, transactions that approach even one minute are surely suspect and need to be reviewed and modified if possible. Remember that the user of your application won't want to sit and wait for a transaction to commit, regardless of the technology happening behind the scenes.

The Log options let you dictate how large the log file will be allowed to get and where it should be located. You can select the directory, drive, and size for the file. To make changes to the log file settings, you'll need to first stop the DTC services. After you've completed your changes, you can restart the services, and the new settings will be in effect.

The Reset Log option will clear the log file and let you start anew. As with the other log file options, you'll need to have the DTC stopped prior to using this option.

Defining Distributed Transactions

As mentioned in the opening section of this chapter, distributed transactions are extensions to the standard transactions that you found out about in Chapter 12, "Understanding Transactions and Locking." Distributed transactions add the DISTRIBUTED keyword to the BEGIN TRANSACTION statement and allow you to indicate different server names on the execute instructions, but otherwise are identical to more typical transactions.

For example, if you have two servers, SQL1 and SQL2, you can create a distributed transaction with the following code snippet:

```
BEGIN DISTRIBUTED TRANSACTION
    insert into localtable values ("These", "are", "inserted", "locally")
    exec sql2.testdb.dbo.sp_addvalues "these", "are", "inserted", "remotely"
COMMIT TRANSACTION
```

The two SQL statements doing the value insertions are nothing that you can't accomplish without the use of the DTC. The catch, of course, is what context they are executed within and the amount of control you have should a problem occur.

Without the DTC, these statements would be executed as two separate and distinct requests. If one failed, it would not necessarily affect the second. This would even be true if you had enclosed the two statements in the standard BEGIN TRANSACTION and COMMIT statements. Because they are running on different servers, the only thing that would be seen by the transaction and considered a part of it is the actual execution of the INSERT statement and the execution, but not successful completion, of the stored procedure call. Regardless of success or failure programmatically of the stored procedure, the transaction would succeed.

With the DTC, the problem of the remote operation is handled, and you'll know for sure the operation succeeded. The DTC effectively extends the reach of the transaction to the second system. With the DTC in effect by using the DISTRIBUTED keyword when you declare the transaction, you'll be able to ensure that all aspects of the transaction succeed, not just the local portions of it.

Debugging Distributed Transactions

If you find that you have transactions remaining on your SQL Server in a pending state, you have a few options available to you that will help to track down the problem area. In general, you can review the statistics that are gathered by the DTC and see how long transactions are taking overall, and you can start to see trends between your servers.

If transactions are slow to complete one of the first areas to look at is the connectivity between your local server and the remote system. If the connection speed is slow, or if either of the servers is being heavily used, it will help explain the execution time of the transactions.

You can also force a transaction to commit by pulling it up in the trace facility, right-clicking the transaction, and selecting the Resolve option. You'll be able to Commit, Abort, or Forget the transaction. See Figure 18.7 for an example.

FIG. 18.7
Once you manually force an outcome for a given transaction, be sure to track down what happened and what caused the transaction to fail to complete on its own.

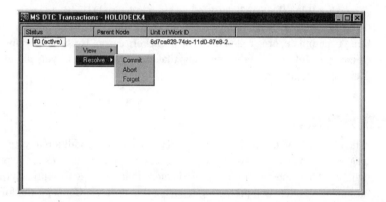

If you have a transaction that is runaway, don't forget that you can run the different components of the logic through ISQL and watch a little more carefully, considering each value and logic step along the way. In the worst-case scenario, consider adding logic to your stored procedures that call the DTC and have them drop values for your variables into a working table along the way, along with checkpoint notations so you will know where in your code you are when the value is written. In psuedo-code:

```
Start procedure
    Write initial value to work table, along with "start of routine"
    Statement 1
    Write state values to work table, along with "before DTC call"
    ...call the DTC participants and start your transaction
```

This admittedly goes back to the debugging days of using msgbox's to show information to the developer during the execution of code. The difference, of course, is that you don't have the luxury of the msgbox when working in this environment.

If you use this approach, be sure you don't put your debugging code inside the transaction. If you do, when the transaction rolls back, you'll also lose your debugging information in the work table as it is reversed out of the system.

Reality Check

In the systems that have been completed by using the DTC, the biggest stumbling block is the lack of ability to really see what's going on, and how to determine what you need to do to fix any problems that arise. This is where the debugging "droppings" mentioned in the last section come into play and can save you many hours of test time. Keep in mind that you can have each of your participating servers log information to work tables, providing you with an overall picture of what's happening on your system.

The other thing that you'll want to keep in mind with DTC-based applications is that you'll need to be sure you test what happens in your application if a distributed transaction either takes too long to complete, or is rolled back for whatever reason. Be sure your application is able to recover gracefully from the situations that are sure to arise as you add more variables to your development picture.

From Here...

The DTC capabilities of SQL Server can be an excellent addition to your system, especially in cases where you're involving several servers with different roles in the processing picture. As with most development issues, there is more than one way to approach moving information around the system and protecting it during that process. Consider the following additional areas of information as you design your system:

- Chapter 12, "Understanding Transactions and Locking," details how you work with transactions, what the ACID properties of a valid transaction are, and how you use them in your applications.
- Chapter 17, "Setting Up and Managing Replication," will give you one alternative to moving information between servers: replication. With replication, you can make sure copies of data are up-to-date at the publisher and subscriber systems for the information. Different capabilities exist with replication when compared with the DTC approach, so be sure to consider both for your application.

SQL Server Administration Topics

SQL Server Administration

This chapter presents several issues to keep in mind as you administer your SQL Server system. For the day-to-day management of SQL Server, you need to know about many different concepts, routines, and ideas.

The everyday operation of SQL Server requires that you spend some time managing the database engine so that the system operates at its fullest potential. By staying on top of the system, you can ensure the optimum response times for users, and you can prevent some common problems with the system altogether.

Some of the concepts in this chapter relate to strictly administrative tasks, and some relate more to management of performance and system tuning. Understanding these topics and the correct definition of your system can ensure that your SQL Server installation succeeds. ∎

Understand and perform checkpoints

SQL Server uses checkpoints to maintain database integrity. This chapter explains how they work and how they affect your SQL Server implementation.

Use the Database Consistency Checker

The Database Consistency Checker provides valuable information about the state of your database and tables, including the capability to repair any inconsistencies that the checker finds in your tables.

Back up SQL Server

To keep any production system reliable, you must back it up. This chapter explains how to use the different tools that SQL Server provides to back up your system.

Transfer information to and from SQL Server

Whether you're bringing up a system based on information from another previously existing system or making changes to other types of existing data sources, you need to know how to transfer information to and from SQL Server.

Understanding and Performing Checkpoints

Checkpoints are a function that SQL Server incorporates to commit changes to a database or configuration option at a known, good point in time. When you configure or modify the server setup, you have to restart it, so you might want to initiate the checkpoint process manually.

When a checkpoint is issued, whether by a manual intervention process or by naturally occurring server-based processes, all dirty pages are saved to disk. A *dirty page* is one containing updates not yet applied to the database's disk image. Checkpoints normally occur approximately every 60 seconds unless you intervene. The actual time interval depends on server loading, recovery options that you've set, and general performance tuning that SQL Server handles. However, the interval should always be quite close to 60 seconds.

After your SQL Server shuts down unexpectedly, it can take longer to start up the next time. This is because SQL Server rolls back and rolls forward transactions to the last checkpoint. As it does so, SQL Server restores the database to the last known good state—the state recorded when the last checkpoint was issued and successfully executed.

N O T E You can also shut down the server manually by issuing the SHUTDOWN command. By issuing CHECKPOINT followed by a SHUTDOWN, you can ensure that SQL Server saves all transaction information appropriately. ▪

When shutting down the server, you can avoid longer startup times by manually issuing the CHECKPOINT command. Manually issuing this command has the same effect as letting the server issue the command automatically. The system saves all information to disk, and can simply start up and "turn on" the databases for access by your client applications. Manually issuing CHECKPOINT is helpful if you're shutting down a server quickly, such as when a power failure occurs and the UPS sustaining the server is nearing its life cycle.

N O T E The CHECKPOINT command is issued at a database level and applied against the current database. If your system has more than one database, you must issue the command against each database. To issue the CHECKPOINT command, you must be the database owner. ▪

Another helpful option is Truncate Log on Checkpoint, which automatically truncates the transaction log whenever a checkpoint is reached. To set this option, select and right-click the database in the SQL Enterprise Manager. Choose Edit and click the Options tab. Figure 19.1 shows the available options.

N O T E If you select the Truncate Log on Checkpoint option, you cannot back up the transaction log during the course of standard backups. This limitation might not present a problem in your installation, because you can still back up databases. However, you should consider your overall backup plan before selecting this option. See the sections later in this chapter for more information on backup and restore operations. ▪

FIG. 19.1
In the SQL Enterprise Manager's Options page, you can control the interval at which SQL Server truncates the transaction log.

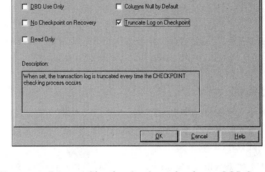

If you enable Truncate Log on Checkpoint for a database, SQL Server truncates the transaction log up to the point of the last successfully committed transaction, unless you are using replication. If you are using replication, SQL Server truncates the log up to the last successfully replicated transaction and successfully committed transaction. Replication requires the use of the transaction log, so you cannot truncate the log if replication has not been propagated to the subscribers for a given publication. Chapter 17, "Setting Up and Managing Replication," presents more information about replication.

Using the Database Consistency Checker

The Database Consistency Checker (DBCC) is a tool that you use to generate detailed information about the database objects that SQL Server manages. Because there are so many different facets to the SQL Server system and its handling of tables, objects, rules, triggers, stored procedures, and more, it is helpful to be able to go into the server and run a "sanity check" to make sure that all is well. The DBCC statement provides this functionality.

Part
IV
Ch
19

Setting Up to Ensure the Best Results: Single-User Mode

Before getting into the use and utility of DBCC, you need to understand two different conditions that are usually in effect whenever you want to use the DBCC statement. First, you should try to ensure that as little activity as possible is affecting SQL Server. If users are accessing the server to make updates or changes, you might receive errors when DBCC runs. Such errors are due to the nature of the calls that DBCC performs. They are very low-level and often require nearly exclusive use of the database.

Second, you often must ensure exclusive access to the database. To do so, use the sp_dboption statement to set the database to single-user mode. The following is the statement's syntax:

```
sp_dboption <database name>, 'single user', True
```

For example, to run some checks on the Pubs database, you use the following statement:

```
sp_dboption 'pubs', 'single user', True
```

This statement prevents other users from using the system while you perform your checks.

> **N O T E** Before updating the system's options, you must be in the Master database. Make sure that you issue a Use Master before attempting to set options using sp_dboption. ∎

After turning on single-user mode, you can perform the checks that you need to ensure that the database is running in top shape. After completing your work with DBCC, you can set the database back to multiuser mode by changing True to False in the sp_dboption command, as in the following example:

```
sp_dboption 'pubs', 'single user', False.
```

Using the DBCC Options

DBCC supports many different options. The next few sections discuss the most frequently used options and how they can assist you in administrating your SQL Server implementation.

Using *DBCC NEWALLOC*   NEWALLOC replaces CHECKALLOC. With CHECKALLOC, the system process stopped if DBCC found an error, sometimes obscuring other problems with the database. NEWALLOC doesn't stop when DBCC finds an error, but continues and reports all errors that it finds in the database structures. The option has the following syntax:

```
DBCC NEWALLOC <database name>
```

If you omit the `<database name>` parameter, SQL Server checks the current database.

When NEWALLOC runs, it returns detailed information about your system and its database objects. You can use this information to direct you toward any problems that might be occurring on the system. Listing 19.1 shows a portion of a report run against the standard Pubs database. This sample indicates the type of information that you can expect to receive from the NEWALLOC option.

Listing 19.1 Sample Output from the *NEWALLOC* Statement

```
Checking pubs
***************************************************************
TABLE: sysobjects          OBJID = 1
INDID=1      FIRST=1       ROOT=8       DPAGES=4      SORT=0
     Data level: 1. 4 Data  Pages in 1 extents.
     Indid       : 1. 1 Index Pages in 1 extents.
INDID=2     FIRST=40       ROOT=41       DPAGES=1     SORT=1
     Indid       : 2. 3 Index Pages in 1 extents.
TOTAL # of extents = 3
***************************************************************
TABLE: sysindexes          OBJID = 2
INDID=1      FIRST=24      ROOT=32       DPAGES=4      SORT=0
     Data level: 1. 4 Data  Pages in 1 extents.
     Indid       : 1. 1 Index Pages in 1 extents.
TOTAL # of extents = 2
...
```

```
...
*******************************************************************
TABLE: pub_info          OBJID = 864006109
INDID=1       FIRST=568       ROOT=584       DPAGES=1       SORT=0
    Data level: 1. 1 Data  Pages in 1 extents.
    Indid      : 1. 2 Index Pages in 1 extents.
INDID=255       FIRST=560       ROOT=608       DPAGES=0       SORT=0
TOTAL # of extents = 2
*******************************************************************
Processed 49 entries in the Sysindexes for dbid 4.
Alloc page 0 (# of extent=32 used pages=57 ref pages=57)
Alloc page 256 (# of extent=25 used pages=34 ref pages=34)
Alloc page 512 (# of extent=15 used pages=39 ref pages=39)
Alloc page 768 (# of extent=1 used pages=1 ref pages=1)
Alloc page 1024 (# of extent=1 used pages=1 ref pages=1)
Alloc page 1280 (# of extent=1 used pages=1 ref pages=1)
...
...
Alloc page 31744 (# of extent=1 used pages=1 ref pages=1)
Alloc page 32000 (# of extent=1 used pages=1 ref pages=1)
Total (# of extent=196 used pages=261 ref pages=254) in this database
DBCC execution completed. If DBCC printed error messages, see your
    System Administrator.
```

As you can see, NEWALLOC returns a great deal of information. Usually, you must examine the returned report and search only for the problems. Focus on the problems reported, if any, and work with them. The balance of the information confirms database table structures, page allocations, and so on. If you receive an error message, you should also receive specific instructions on what you must do to correct the problem.

> **N O T E** If removable devices have objects, NEWALLOC might return warning message 2558. You can ignore this warning. It results from a necessary setting for objects residing on removable devices. ■

Using *DBCC CHECKDB*   When you run CHECKDB, DBCC validates each table and its associated data pages, indexes, and pointers. DBCC tests each to ensure that it properly links to the related information. CHECKDB has the following syntax:

```
DBCC CHECKDB <database name>
```

If you omit the <database name> parameter, SQL Server checks the current database.

Listing 19.2 consists of excerpts of output generated by the CHECKDB option.

Listing 19.2   Sample Output from the *CHECKDB* Statement

```
Checking pubs
Checking 1
The total number of data pages in this table is 4.
Table has 70 data rows.
```

continues

Part
IV
Ch
19

Listing 19.2   Continued

```
Checking 2
The total number of data pages in this table is 4.
Table has 49 data rows.
Checking 3
The total number of data pages in this table is 10.
Table has 283 data rows.
Checking 4
The total number of data pages in this table is 1.
Table has 29 data rows.
Checking 5
The total number of data pages in this table is 23.
Table has 165 data rows.
...

...
Checking 592005140
The total number of data pages in this table is 1.
Table has 14 data rows.
Checking 688005482
The total number of data pages in this table is 2.
Table has 43 data rows.
Checking 864006109
The total number of data pages in this table is 1.
The total number of TEXT/IMAGE pages in this table is 73.
Table has 8 data rows.
DBCC execution completed. If DBCC printed error messages, see your
     System Administrator.
```

Notice that the CHECKDB option also checks system tables. When you run the command, it checks all tables in all aspects of the database that you specify in the command.

 TIP

If you find that checking the entire database takes too long, you can use the CheckTable option. You simply specify CHECKDB as the DBCC option and then list the table name that you want to check. The command examines only the specified table and thus can save you significant time on the analysis steps.

Using *DBCC SHRINKDB*   When you create a database, you often predict a greater disk volume than you actually need to support the database table. After putting the database into production, you can tell how big the database really needs to be. If you've determined that you can make the database smaller and thus free up space for other databases on your system, you can use the SHRINKDB option. Keep in mind that the SHRINKDB option works in pages. Therefore, you have to determine the database's size and divide that size by 2,048 (the size of the database pages) to get the value to specify for this command. The following is the syntax for SHRINKDB:

```
DBCC SHRINKDB <database name>, <new size>
```

Shrinking the Master database is a bad idea, however, because this database contains all information about your system. If you find that shrinking this database is necessary, make sure that you back it up first. If you shrink the Master database, you are modifying the database that manages the different recovery mechanisms for the system. If a system failure occurs while shrinking the Master database, you might not be able to recover the database without a backup.

TIP If you issue the SHRINKDB statement, as shown in the following listing, without a *<new size>* parameter, SQL Server returns the size of the smallest possible database. You can use this value to determine your database's new size.

```
Current Size of Database    Size Database Can be Shrunk To
-----------------------     ------------------------------
32256                       17152

(1 row(s) affected)

Objects pvnt further shrink    Index
-----------------------        -----
syslogs                        data

(1 row(s) affected)

DBCC execution completed. If DBCC printed error messages, see your
        System Administrator.
```

N O T E   You cannot shrink a database to a size that is less than that of the model database. ■

If you request the smallest possible size, SQL Server shows how far you can shrink the database. In addition, an indicator informs you if you can do something to shrink the database further. In the code example shown in the preceding tip, you can reduce the database in its current configuration to 17,152 pages (about 35M). If you can manipulate the other listed items that prevent further shrinking, you can make the database even smaller.

N O T E   You should rarely use the absolute minimum value when shrinking a database, because any active database is bound to grow over time and with use. If you've decreased the database's size so severely that you limit growth for a given application, this size is at cross-purposes with the design goals of your client/server SQL Server-based application. ■

Understanding and Using *update statistics* and *recompile*

SQL Server gains much of its performance from intelligent processing of data stored in the tables. This analysis comes in different forms, but the most significant is the examination of real data in the system to determine the optimal path for retrieving the information.

For example, consider the route to your home. You've likely figured out the best, fastest way to get to your home from your office. After finding the best route, you are of course more likely to take that route, even if someone suggests that you select a different route, because you've taken the time to consider the different roads available and selected the best one possible.

For you to consider seriously a new route home, a new road would have to offer a better route to your home, or there would have to be construction on the existing road that makes it an inefficient route home.

With SQL Server, this analogy holds true. When you implement a stored procedure, SQL Server reviews the SELECT logic of the stored procedure, along with any other data-affecting events. The server determines the best route to take in fulfilling the stored procedure's function. After selecting this route, SQL Server remembers this information so that the next time you run the stored procedure, it's optimized for the data that it affects. SQL Server's "roads" consist of the indexes on the data in the system. The server considers these paths when analyzing the best way to retrieve a given value set.

If you add to the table several rows comprising, for example, more than 20 percent of the table's original size, you should consider updating the statistics associated with the table. The syntax for updating a table is as follows:

```
update statistics <table name>[.index name]
```

Consider the following example:

```
update statistics authors
```

N O T E In this syntax, you do not include quotation marks around the table name that you want to update.

You can specify that only a given index be updated or that the information concerning the entire table be updated. If you specify the index, you must specify it as shown in the syntax, indicating the table in which the index can be found.

The final step to implement these updated indexes and make the stored procedures aware of them is to indicate to SQL Server that it should reconsider the route to take when retrieving the information from the database. To do so, you must recompile the different stored procedures affected by the update statistics that you just ran.

Usually, stored procedures are compiled the first time that they're called after you start SQL Server. Stored procedures are automatically recompiled in other instances, but simply issuing update statistics doesn't cause an automatic recompile. An example of the automatic recompile is when you drop an index that is the basis for a stored procedure. You might have noticed that the first time you call a particular stored procedure, it executes a bit slowly, but that subsequent calls to the stored procedure are often noticeably faster. This is because the optimizer is compiling the stored procedure based on the current statistics of the database tables and any relevant indexes.

You recompile a stored procedure by setting a flag on a table which essentially invalidates any copies of stored procedures that are in procedure cache. This causes SQL Server to reload and recompile the affected stored procedures the next time they are accessed if they reference the table you flagged. To set the flag, use the following command:

```
sp_recompile <table name>
```

where `<table_name>` is the table to be marked for all referencing stored procedures to be recompiled. If successful, the command returns a simple acknowledgment message indicating that the stored procedures will be reloaded and recompiled as shown in the following example:

```
sp_recompile "authors"
go
Each stored procedure and trigger that uses table authors
will be recompiled the next time it is executed.
```

 TIP If you don't recompile the stored procedures that update statistics affects, you won't notice any performance gain until after you stop and restart the server, because that will be the next time that SQL Server reloads and compiles the procedures.

You can't hurt anything by starting the update statistics and recompile operations, but you should run them when the fewest users are on the system, particularly if your database sizes are substantial. The time that it takes to update these parameters can take quite a hit on system performance for your system's users. You should make updating statistics part of your regular, ongoing maintenance, perhaps running the process on each of your high-use tables approximately once a month during high database throughput. When you first bring up a system and are adding information at a high rate, you might want to consider frequent calls to this procedure, perhaps as often as once per day of heavy, new data input.

Backing Up and Restoring Databases and Transaction Logs

Part
IV
Ch
19

One of the most dreaded questions when you call for help with your application is, "When was your last backup?" Getting caught without a backup can be quite painful.

With SQL Server, backing up is often much more important than it is on a stand-alone system. If you support a database with many users, keeping those users' confidence in the system's information is very important. Data loss might incur costs across departments and might dictate significant data reentry.

SQL Server provides a couple of different ways to protect from data loss, or at least minimize it, should the worst happen. These techniques range from physical duplication of the information to backing up the databases and transaction logs at specific intervals during the course of business.

The upcoming sections explain how to back up the system and the trade-offs to consider in determining your optimum backup scenario.

Determining How Often to Back Up

One of the first questions that a new SQL Server customer ponders is how often he or she needs to back up. The answer is simple, but seems sarcastic when first given: Quite simply, how much data can you afford to lose?

The initial answer is usually "none." This answer is fine, but then you must determine what the effect will be on the system plan to incur no loss of data if a catastrophic system failure occurs. Typically, such a plan involves mirroring databases, which costs money to implement. For more information on mirroring a database on your system, see the section "Understanding and Using Mirroring" later in this chapter.

Because the cost of mirroring a system can be quite steep, the next step is to determine the amount of data that can truly be at risk at any given time. To determine this amount, you must first understand that you have to back up two different components to the system. As you've seen throughout this book, the database contains the different tables and all other objects associated with the database. The transaction log contains an incremental log of the things that happen to a database and change it. Essentially, the transaction log contains a "before and after" picture of the data that changes with each block of work the server performs.

Keep in mind that the database backup is a snapshot in time, and the transaction logs contain all the changes since you took that snapshot. At a minimum, you'll want to back up the database weekly and the transaction log daily.

The best plan is a system of rotating backups. Such a system is the safest way to ensure that you have the correct fault tolerance for any system failures that you might experience. All computer professionals agree on one thing: Any system will fail; it's only a question of when. You should have complete, concise, and accurate backups. They are the only lifeline you have in times of hardware failure.

Table 19.1 shows a suggested backup schedule. If you're backing up to tape, this approach requires 29 tapes over the course of a year. The weekly backup of your system requires 14 tapes, and maintaining the monthly archives requires 13. You use the remaining two tapes as working transaction log backups, and as an initial, baseline backup of the database. Remember, this schedule is to maintain backups, not to retain historical data on the system. You should not count on backups for retention and research on historical information. For those purposes, you must rely on alternative backups. Number the tapes sequentially on a permanent label on each tape cassette.

NOTE If your database is large, you might need more than one tape per day, week, or month. In such cases, consider the tape-numbering scheme to be a *tape set* numbering approach. ▨

This backup schedule gives you a full two weeks of backups to fall back on if a problem arises. You should implement a two-week backup cycle because you might not immediately recognize when a problem has arisen. For example, a program change or other system event might cause a problem that isn't detected for a few days. By keeping the two weeks of backups, the odds are good that you will have a clean copy of the information in the recent archives.

Table 19.1   Suggested Backup Approach

Tape Number	Used for	Comments
1	Monday backup	Backup for the first Monday of a two-week cycle
2	Tuesday backup	
3	Wednesday backup	
4	Thursday backup	
5	Friday backup	
6	Saturday backup	
7	Sunday backup*	
8	Monday backup	Backup for the second Monday of cycle
9	Tuesday backup	
10	Wednesday backup	
11	Thursday backup	
12	Friday backup	
13	Saturday backup	
14	Sunday backup*	

You should remove these tapes from the physical site and place them in a separate location.

Backing Up and Restoring Databases

When you back up your databases and transaction logs, you do so by dumping the information in your system to a *dump device,* which SQL Server recognizes as a repository for information and can be either a disk file or a tape device. If you dump information to a disk-based device, for example, the file that SQL Server creates can be backed up to tape, another server, or some other location where you will manage the backup files.

The best way to manage the backup of information is with the SQL Enterprise Manager. Choose Tools, Database Backup/Restore to start working with the backup subsystem. The main Database Backup/Restore dialog box then displays (see Figure 19.2).

Part

IV

Ch

19

FIG. 19.2

The main control panel for backup and restore operations enables you to select and create devices and set scheduling options.

Setting Up Backup Devices   You first must establish the backup devices to use as the destination for information dumped from the working databases and tables. The Database Backup/Restore dialog box's Backup Devices window lists the devices already known to the system. You can accept one of these devices or create your own.

To create a device, choose the New button below the Backup Devices window. The SQL Enterprise Manager then displays the New Backup Device dialog box, shown in Figure 19.3 and prompts you to name the device.

FIG. 19.3

You can create new devices that identify a tape or disk destination for backups.

Notice that as you type the name for the device, the location is updated to include the name that you use.

TIP You can specify a path that points to another physical system when you indicate the backup devices you want to use. By doing so, you can provide good backup coverage without the need for additional storage media.

Consider creating a new device for each day in the 14-day cycle mentioned previously. Then, when you create a scheduled backup, you don't necessarily have to use a tape to store the information if you point to the device on the remote system and use it as a backup destination. If you set up the system to back up to the devices without the append flag, each of the devices you create will be only as big as needed for a single copy of the database you're backing up.

Also, because both your core SQL Server system and the remote system are very unlikely to experience downtimes simultaneously, you are assured of solid backups for your system.

This approach also has the following disadvantages:

- The remote system must always be accessible to the backup and restore process.
- The remote system must have enough disk space to support the dump devices.
- If both systems are in the same building and that building suffers catastrophic damage such as a fire, you'll lose your backup system. This is a major reason for using offsite tape or other media backups.

Keeping these rules in mind, you can see a solution that offers the best of both worlds combines remote system backups and offsite storage for tape backups made slightly less frequently.

N O T E Be sure to note the file name if you're backing up to a file on disk rather than tape. When you copy the backup file from the system for storage, you need to use this file name to back up to tape or elsewhere on the system. ◼

After indicating the name of the device that you want to create, simply choose Create. SQL Server then creates the new device and lists it in the Backup Devices window of the Database Backup/Restore dialog box. You're all set to start creating the backups that you'll need to support your SQL Server. Figure 19.4 shows a database with 14 backup devices, one for each day of a two-week backup cycle.

FIG. 19.4

The Master database now has a backup device for each day of a two-week backup cycle.

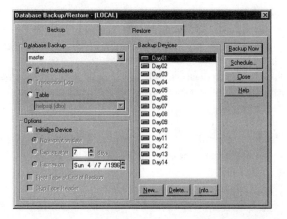

Part

IV

Ch

19

  The Master database does not have an explicit transaction log because it always has the Truncate Log on Checkpoint option set. For this reason, when you back up this database, you cannot do a transaction log backup. You must do a database dump and backup.

The next sections describe in detail what's involved in setting up the backups on the system.

Running the Backup   After creating the devices that you need to support the backups, you must perform the actual backup. You have two options available. The first option is to run backups on demand. Although this option works fine, it requires manual intervention each time you want to back up the system. This approach is more prone than an automated solution to forgetfulness, unexpected meetings, and similar mishaps. The second option is to implement a scheduled backup series and have the system complete the database dumps for you automatically.

The following are some general points to keep in mind as you determine your backup strategy:

- Be sure to back up the transaction logs between backups of the databases. Backing up the transaction log is no different than backing up a database. It's simply an option that you select while defining the backup.

- Make sure you back up each database that you need to protect. No command backs up the entire system, so you must create backup processes for all databases that you are concerned with.

- Be sure to back up the Master database. Because this database includes all information about the other database objects in the system, having this information is very important in case you have to restore the entire system and rebuild from scratch.

You must select the type of backup, either manual or scheduled/automatic, that best fits the systems you are supporting.

Completing Manual Backups   Manual backups are quite straightforward and are a good way to get a feel for how the system works, the time that it takes to back up, and how much impact a database backup will have on your system if other users are on the system when a backup starts.

N O T E   When you first back up, you must initialize the device. To do so, select the Initialize Device check box in the Options panel of the Database Backup/Restore dialog box's Backup page. If you attempt a backup without initializing the device, the SQL Enterprise Manager displays a warning that the device is either offline or uninitialized. ■

To complete the backup, select the device that you want to back up to and choose <u>B</u>ackup Now. The Backup Volume Labels dialog box appears (see Figure 19.5).

FIG. 19.5
If you select a device that has already had a backup completed, the Backup Volume Labels dialog box prompts you to pick the label to which to append information.

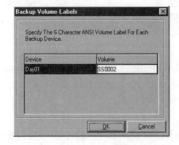

After you select the device and choose <u>O</u>K, the SQL Enterprise Manager completes the backup. A status indicator shows the backup's progress. Finally, a dialog box confirms that the backup succeeded.

Here are a couple of items to keep in mind as you run your backups of the system:

- If you experience difficulty completing a backup, examine the free space on the dump device that you've created. Make sure that you have enough free space for the device to grow to accommodate the information you're saving. Remember also that if you have selected the Append option, the information you save is added to the prior information each time you back up. This option will eventually lead to some very sizable dump devices. By using the rotating tapes as noted previously, you can safely back up to separate dump devices each time you back up because you'll have the prior backup's information stored safely away.

- If you set the Truncate Log on Checkpoint option, you cannot back up the transaction log. From the earlier section "Understanding and Performing Checkpoints," you might recall that one way to help manage transaction log size is to turn on the Truncate Log on Checkpoint option. Another way to manage the size of the log is to dump the transaction log to a backup device. By default, SQL Server also truncates the log after a successful backup. Because both operations take control over truncating the log, they are mutually exclusive. You must turn off the Truncate Log on Checkpoint option before you can successfully back up the transaction log.

Scheduling Automated Backups   The safest bet, especially for incremental backups, is a regularly scheduled, automated backup. To set up automated backups, indicate the database and the device to which you want to back up and then choose the Schedule button in the Database Backup/Restore dialog box. The Schedule Backup dialog box appears (see Figure 19.6).

FIG. 19.6
Scheduled backups are a way to avoid relying on human intervention for the completion of this critical job.

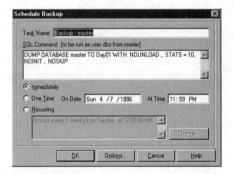

Part
IV

Ch
19

If you're doing append-type backups, the SQL Enterprise Manager prompts you to indicate the volume to which you want to append. After indicating the volume, the Task Schedule dialog box appears as shown in Figure 19.7, enabling you to indicate the details for the scheduled backup.

N O T E   For future reference, take note of the SQL Command text box, shown in Figure 19.6. This text box lists the commands you can run from ISQL that will complete the backup manually. You should keep up with the commands that you can enter manually, because you might want to implement them in your own application later. ■

FIG. 19.7

You have complete flexibility in setting the times for your backups, the recurring intervals, and more. In this example, the user is setting up Monday, Wednesday, and Friday backups.

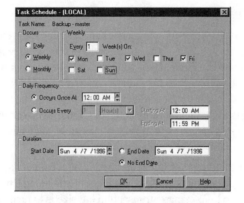

The dialog box's first two options (refer to Figure 19.6), Immediately and One Time, enable you to do a single backup at some predetermined time. These are good first steps. Your first backups should be scheduled *attended* backups so you can ensure that all is working well, the files are created correctly, and your backup process works in general.

After determining that the backup process has succeeded, you can change the allotted times, create recurring backups, and more. To change the times at which the backup occurs, first choose the Recurring option button, then choose Change, as shown in Figure 19.6. The Task Schedule dialog box then appears as shown in Figure 19.7. This dialog box indicates the different options that you have for determining the times at which your backups are to run.

The final step is to set up any options you want to enable. To do so, choose the Options button in the Schedule Backup dialog box. The TSQL Task Options dialog box then appears, presenting several options (see Figure 19.8). The option that you are most likely to select is Write to Windows NT Application Event Log. You should select both the On Success and On Failure options to record to the log successes as well as failures. Together, these options give you a definitive mechanism for checking whether the backup succeeded or failed. Figure 19.8 shows these options set. You can use the TSQL Task Options dialog box's remaining options for e-mail notification if you're using SQL Server's mail services, and for establishing retry parameters. If you are experiencing failures because of network traffic to a remote server that maintains your device, you might want to increase the number of retries.

> **CAUTION**
>
> If you need to modify your system's retry parameters to address a problem, you probably should investigate the cause of the problem before you implement retries. If you have a less reliable connection to the server containing the device that you use for backup, consider moving the device. Backups are too important to leave open to possible problems, such as network traffic, that force you to modify the retry parameters.

Then you choose OK to close the dialog boxes that enable you to define the backup schedule, and you return to the Database Backup/Restore dialog box. You won't immediately notice any indication that the system has just created a successful backup. This is a bit disconcerting, but take heart. The information about the backup is now part of a scheduled background task. For this reason, you must review it from the task-scheduling portion of SQL Enterprise Manager rather than the backup and restore utility dialog boxes. Choose Server, Scheduled Tasks. The Manage Scheduling Tasks dialog box appears as shown in Figure 19.9, listing your backup job as one of the first items in the list of things to do.

FIG. 19.8
Be sure to check the option to log on to the event log for successes as well as failures. This mechanism is useful for following up on your automated processes.

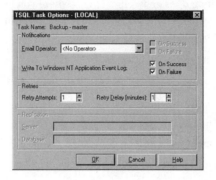

> **CAUTION**
>
> If you are at all uncertain about which tasks you have created to handle the backup job, make sure that you determine which backup jobs you need before you start working with tasks. Because all background activity is managed through the Manage Scheduled Tasks dialog box's Tasks List page, removing or modifying an incorrect item can damage processes that control replication, general cleanup, and many other system jobs.

FIG. 19.9
SQL Enterprise Manager creates scheduled backups as background tasks that you can manage from the SQL Enterprise Manager's Tasks utility.

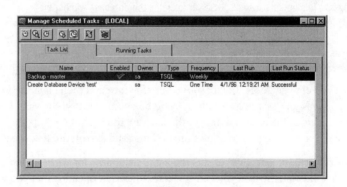

You can also use the Task List page to check the status of backups, which is another way to check whether any problems are occurring. To determine the cause of any problems that you might encounter during the backup process, you should use a combination of the Task List page and the Windows NT event log.

Don't forget that you must be absolutely certain you've backed up all the following:

■ The Master database

■ All databases that you would be sorry to lose

■ All transaction logs for each database that you have in production or that is undergoing significant testing

Using and Understanding Information Restoration from Backups

After creating the backups and continuing to back up your database faithfully, how do you recover the database if something does go wrong? This is where you'll be glad that you put into place a formal backup plan, because such a plan will guide you toward restoring your system to full functionality as quickly as possible.

The following are the steps for restoring your system:

1. Install SQL Server if needed.
2. Restore the Master database if needed.
3. Re-create the devices if needed.
4. Restore the last full database backups you completed.
5. Restore the transaction logs you have backed up since backing up the database.

After completing these steps, you'll have a fully functional system that is up-to-date as of the last transaction log backup.

You've already learned about installing SQL Server and creating devices, but if you want more information on this topic, see Chapter 5, "Creating Devices, Databases, and Transaction Logs," and Appendix H, "What's on the CD?"

 When creating a new database, use the Create for Load option, available on the Create Database dialog box. This option causes SQL Server to create the database without the initial sets of pointers in the database. You already load this information from the backup anyway, so you have no reason to have the work done twice. The time saved in creating the new database can be nearly 50 percent of the time required to create an entirely new database with the option deselected.

When you choose Tools, Database Backup/Restore and then click the Restore tab, the SQL Enterprise Manager first presents a dialog box containing all the valid backups available. This listing includes the date and time of the backup, the type of backup, the database or transaction log, and so on. Figure 19.10 shows the options available on the Restore page.

SQL Server automatically presents the list of databases for which a database backup has been completed. From this list, you can select the different backups that you want to apply to the database you designate in the drop-down list box.

If you know the information on a given backup is good until a certain time, you can indicate that time in the Until Time text box. Note that any transactions pending at the specified time are rolled back and it will appear as though they never occurred. In most cases, you must restore the database and transaction logs in their entirety, so you can accept the default options.

Choose Restore Now to restore the database and transaction logs.

FIG. 19.10

The Restore page's options enable you to designate the source and destination for restoration efforts.

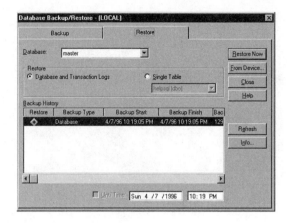

If you created the new database with the Create for Load option, you must update the database options before anyone else can use the database. Until you do so, you'll notice that the Enterprise Manager's display flags the database with which you're working as (loading). During this time, no user except the DBO can use the database. To update the options and give other users access to the database, choose Manage, Databases. The Manage Databases dialog box then appears as shown in Figure 19.11.

FIG. 19.11

You must remember to update the options for any database created explicitly for loading. Otherwise, users cannot access the database.

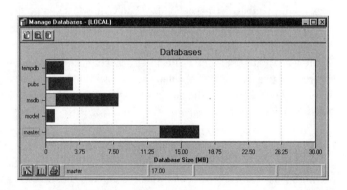

In the Manage Databases dialog box, double-click the bar representing the database you need to update. The familiar Edit Database dialog box appears. Click the Options tab and deselect the DBO Use Only check box (see Figure 19.12).

After completing this step, you're restored to the point of the most recent transaction log backup and should be ready to begin some quick testing to see whether everything restored correctly (and to boost your confidence in the process). At this point, the data and all objects in the database are restored. Users should not notice any change in operation.

FIG. 19.12

By selecting the DBO Use Only check box, you indicate that the database is being loaded and is not ready for production use. Deselect the option to "turn on" the database for other users.

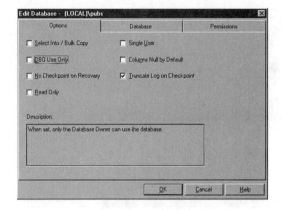

When you are recovering from a system failure, practice will certainly play a key role. As a test of this process, consider using the Pubs database as a Guinea pig. Follow these steps:

1. Perform a database backup of the Pubs database.

2. Make a change to one of the authors in the Authors table. The specifics of the change don't matter. You can add a row, change a name, or make any other change that you will be able to recognize easily later.

3. Back up the database's transaction log. You've now backed up the basic database, and you've also backed up the change that you made as a sort of "delta," or difference, backup.

4. Create a new database, such as RestoreTest. The name does not matter as long as its size is sufficient to support the Pubs database. Make the database size 33M and the transaction log size 30M. Restore the database *only* to your system. You'll have to deselect the transaction log restoration option.

5. Go into ISQL/W and select the rows from the Authors table. They should all be represented correctly, because they existed before your change. Your changes won't appear yet, however, because they occurred after you backed up the database. In a traditional backup scenario, this type of somewhat incomplete backup was as good as it got for recovery.

6. Restore the transaction log only now. Requery the Authors table, which now reflects your changes. This test proves that you correctly logged the transaction log changes against the database table.

You can and should experiment with different scenarios using the test database approach. Then, when you have to restore your database in an actual crisis, you can rest assured that all will go smoothly. Think of these tests as the fire drill for database recovery.

Understanding and Using Mirroring

In addition to the backup and restore techniques covered in the previous sections, SQL Server also supports an additional fault-tolerant option: mirroring. Because hard drives are the most likely suspect for a system failure that affects data, you might want to consider this option to protect your databases.

N O T E Windows NT also supports several fault-tolerant options that are enforced at the operating-system level. For more information, refer to Que's *Special Edition Using Microsoft Windows NT Server* and see the information regarding striped disk storage. ▪

Mirroring takes place at the device level and is transparent to your applications. When you create a device and indicate that it should be mirrored, you simply tell SQL Server where you want to locate the mirror. Be careful when selecting the mirror's location. You do yourself little or no good if you place the mirror device on the same physical drive as the source device. If you do, and the drive fails, you will lose both the source device and the mirror.

Mirroring is done when SQL Server writes changes to a device to two locations at once. The primary location is your standard device. This is the database that you normally use and have incorporated in your system's applications. Because both devices are identical, if a switch is required from the main device to the secondary device, no data loss occurs and your system's users are not interrupted as they use the system.

If SQL Server is using a device and can no longer access the main device, the server automatically switches to the mirror device, making all future changes to the mirror. When you've recovered the drives containing the problem device, you can move the information back to the original device and restart SQL Server using the corrected devices as the default once again.

Setting Up Mirroring

While you create a device or after you create it, if you edit the device, you'll notice an option to establish mirroring. Figure 19.13 shows the options that enable you to work with a device.

Part
IV

Ch
19

FIG. 19.13
Select the Mirroring option to set up mirroring parameters.

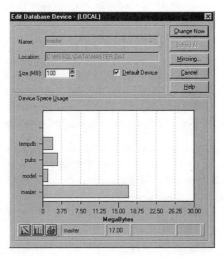

Choose Mirroring to display the Mirror Database Device dialog box, which enables you to indicate the mirror file's location (see Figure 19.14). If you're working from a workstation, keep in mind that the paths you designate are relative to the server. You can select a location that is either on the current server or on a fully qualified network path.

FIG. 19.14

When you select the mirror file's location, SQL Server mirrors the requested database.

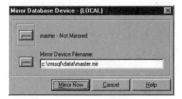

After the process is complete, SQL Server mirrors the device and takes care of the rest. Thereafter, the mirror device reflects any informational changes to the primary device.

CAUTION

If you implement mirroring for a device, make sure that you also mirror the Master database. This database is responsible for maintaining the system information necessary to continue processing if mirroring becomes necessary for any device. By mirroring the Master database, you can enable SQL Server to recover to the mirrored devices that have failed.

If you do not mirror the Master database, you might find that you cannot utilize the mirrors for other devices. The Master database maintains information about the mirrored devices that SQL Server manages, and that information could be lost.

The final step is to tell SQL Server about the mirrored device, especially true in the case of the Master database. Because the Master database helps start the server, you need to indicate to the server where it can find the mirror if necessary. Other devices are managed automatically, so this step is required only for the Master database.

When SQL Server starts up, two required parameters control the Master database's mirrored state: -r and -d. Choose Server, SQL Server, Configure to open the SQL Server Configuration/ Options dialog box shown in Figure 19.15. Choose the Parameters button on the Server Options page and then add the startup parameters. The Server Parameters dialog box then appears as shown in Figure 19.16. In this dialog box, you can indicate the startup options.

Add a new parameter, -r<mirror location>, to indicate the location of the master device's mirror. Even after SQL switches to the mirror device during normal use, when you restart the system, it still must first try the primary Master device. Therefore, you must leave the -d specification that is showing the location of the "normal" Master device. When you add the -r option, you're specifying the fallback position that SQL should use when it has determined that the master device has become unusable.

Choose the Add button to create a new parameter. Be sure to specify the entire path and file name to the mirror device file when you create the -r parameter.

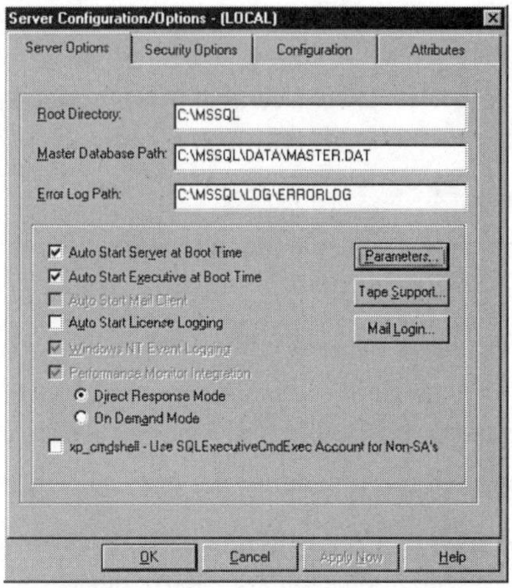

FIG. 19.15
In the SQL Server
configuration sub-
system, you can set
startup options that
enable you to mirror
the Master database.

FIG. 19.16
Be sure to specify both
-r and -d options for
the Master device.
Unless you specify
both, the mirroring will
not work correctly.

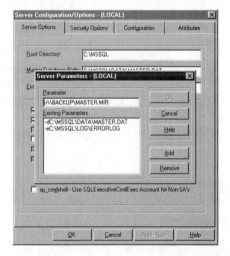

What to Do When Mirroring Is in Force

When SQL Server has switched to a mirror, it automatically suspends mirroring with the original device. This frees up the device to be replaced or otherwise corrected. When the mirroring is active, your system's users will not notice any difference in the functioning of their applications. They can continue working just as they did before the problem was found with the original device.

After replacing the original device or otherwise correcting the detected problem, you can remirror the active device back to the primary device. Remirroring is identical to the original job of mirroring a device. You simply specify the file name to contain the mirror, and SQL Server takes care of the rest.

If you want to switch from a current device to the mirror, as might be the case if you've just brought online a replacement for a failed device, follow these steps, from the creation of the original mirror, to failure of the device, to replacement of the device, to remirroring to return the device to its original state:

1. Mirror the original device.

2. The device fails. SQL Server switches to the mirror device and continues processing.

3. Replace or correct the original device.

4. Remirror the active device back to the original.

5. From the Mirror option on the right-click mirror for the device, you can Unmirror the device. Select the option to Switch to Mirror Device—Replace option.

6. Mirror the device—now the replacement for the original—back to the backup device.

At this point, you're back where you started with the original device being the active device and the mirror standing by as needed to back up the active device.

Mirroring your devices can provide powerful backup capabilities to your key production systems. For more information about backups, be sure to review the backup and restore options presented earlier in this chapter.

Transferring Information to and from SQL Server

The SQL Transfer Object utility provides an excellent way to move information between your system and databases. To start the Transfer Object utility, select the source database. Next, choose Object, Transfer, or right-click the database. Figure 19.17 shows the initial Transfer Objects dialog box.

FIG. 19.17

Select the options carefully when you use the Transfer Object utility. They control the objects that are copied to the new database.

By default, copying an entire database to a new location is as simple as selecting the source and destination database and choosing the Start Transfer button shown in Figure 19.17. SQL Server copies all the different objects to the new database and sets it up to match the source database.

You can also initiate the copy process at a scheduled time, such as when server traffic is lighter and the copy process will not affect the system's users quite as adversely. By choosing Schedule, you can indicate the time at which you want the copy to occur. As shown in Figure 19.18, the scheduling capabilities offered by the Schedule Transfer dialog box are nearly identical to those that you use to set up backups for your server.

FIG. 19.18

You can use the Transfer Object utility to make periodic copies of key information in your system.

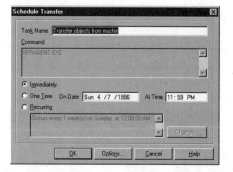

If necessary, you can even use the Transfer Object utility to make rudimentary backups of your system by copying databases to backup devices and databases possibly located on a different server altogether. You should, however, avoid using the Transfer Object Utility as a production solution of backing up your system. The process isn't meant to be a total solution to your system's backup needs and will not support the same level of logging or critical processing checks as the backup process affords. The process, for example, provides no way to transfer only a transaction log for a given database.

If you deselect the Transfer All Objects check box in the Transfer Objects dialog box, as shown in Figure 19.19, you can specify exactly which objects to include in the copy by choosing the Choose Objects button. The Choose Objects to Be Transferred dialog box appears as shown in Figure 19.20. The dialog box lists the different objects available with a typical copy.

You can also indicate the different options that are transferred as part of the scripting process. While putting information from your source database into the destination system, the Transfer Object utility scripts the creation of tables, logon IDs, and other such items that are related to structure or configuration, not based on information or content. You can control these items by deselecting the Use Default Scripting Options check box in the Transfer Objects dialog box and choosing the Scripting Options button. The Transfer Scripting Options dialog box appears as shown in Figure 19.21.

Part
IV
Ch
19

FIG. 19.19

You can select several options that control how objects are transferred during this process.

FIG. 19.20

You can selectively copy specific objects or attributes for your database. You can use this feature to update another system to keep it in sync.

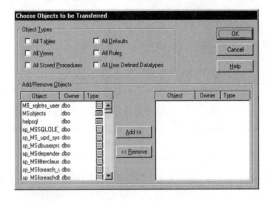

FIG. 19.21

You have complete control over the objects and configurations to include in the transfer. You can deselect logons if you've already set up security on the destination device, for example.

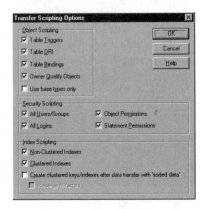

The Transfer Object utility is a good companion to the backup and mirroring features that you've seen earlier in this chapter. By putting these features to use in your installation, you can ensure a maximum amount of uptime for your system's users. Use the Transfer Object utility to make copies of critical system components, then use mirroring and backups for ongoing protection against catastrophic system failures.

Reality Check

In real life, you have to weigh the costs involved with running backups, monitoring your system, and providing the best possible performance for your system's users. Not running backups also entails a cost, however. First, recovery from a catastrophic failure will cost you a lot—possibly your job. If you run a large production system and have not planned for recovering it when something in the database breaks, you'll be in hot water.

Second, depending on how you set up your database and the logging associated with it, not backing up your system requires additional disk space. Your transaction log continues to grow and requires additional disk space. You'll have to decide how to balance frequent backups with physical hardware requirements.

It's not a question of *if* but *when* you'll need to restore to address a database problem. Hard drives fail, bugs in software exist, and people want to revert from that latest and greatest change that you installed. Figure out your backup schedule and stick to it. You might add the dump process as a scheduled task, so that the dump file is always available on the system. Afterward, from a workstation designated to perform the backups, you can run consistent, scheduled backups and can always get the dump files for your SQL Server systems by pointing your backup software to your dump files' location.

Put simply, there is no excuse for not having a backup. When your system fails, all that you should have to tell the system's users is the time frame between backups, so that the users know how much information they need to reenter into the system.

One common tendency regarding database sizing is to make the device and associated databases huge, often as large as you can make them. Try to avoid this temptation. Keep in mind that you cannot easily shrink a database, but you can pretty easily extend it to make it larger.

Part

IV

Ch

19

From Here...

This chapter explored some important administrative utilities that provide the support for good, solid, fault-tolerant system design for your users. The time to implement these items is now, not later. If you wait until you need them, it will be too late. Keep in mind the old computer-support adage mentioned earlier: Components will fail, it's only a matter of time. Plan for the failure; be ready for it. Then recovery will be far less painful and difficult.

To learn more about some of the topics covered in this chapter, see the following additional sources that will help you administrate SQL Server:

■ Chapter 3, "Installing and Setting Up the Server and Client Software," explains the details behind the initial setup and configuration of your system. Remember to add the -r option to the startup command line if you are using mirroring.

■ Chapter 5, "Creating Devices, Databases, and Transaction Logs," covers the specifics of setting up the different components for your system.

■ Que's *Special Edition Using Microsoft Windows NT Server* covers more specifics about disk-based recovery and fault-tolerant systems. Be sure to check into striped disk drive configurations and how you can work with backup devices.

SQL Server Security

Just about everyone is concerned with the security of data. If you're not, then you may not have considered how easy it is to get access to sensitive data on your server. One thing to remember is that sometimes too much security can get in the way of productivity. Make sure that you achieve a balance between your need to manage access to data and monitor users and the users' need to *use* the data.

No document can categorically define every possible security option. This chapter's purpose is to illustrate the features that SQL Server offers and to provide suggestions on what you can do to secure your environment from unauthorized access. ▪

Learn the difference between logins and users

SQL Server manages server access through logins and database access through users.

Protect your data from un-scrupulous browsing

This chapter introduces you to views and stored procedures and how to use them to hide data from users.

Secure your environment

This chapter gives suggestions on how to secure not only SQL Server, but also your physical hardware, LAN, WAN, and Internet access.

Understanding the Types of Security

Securing your data from internal and external attacks is an important job for you as a database administrator. It is important that you can control who and how data is accessed on your server. Security in SQL Server will help you manage the access that you give to your users.

Securing your data from internal attacks is probably your primary concern for most corporate environments. This security will involve the monitoring and management of corporate databases at the direction of the managers of your company. Security is often designed to limit the sorts of data that your employees can see and when they can see it.

Securing your data from external attacks, such as over the Internet, is much more complicated and is generally only applicable to those companies that are beginning to have an Internet presence with their SQL Server databases.

This chapter will focus more on internal security. This security will act in a layered approach, starting with logins and user permissions that secure the basic access to the server. The second layer adds views and stored procedures that limit data access. Finally, the third layer is an external security through methods like physical LAN access, firewalls, and so on.

You can implement SQL Server's security system in three ways on any server: standard, integrated, and mixed. These security methods control how SQL Server manages user accounts on the server and how it interacts with Windows NT's own security system.

To configure a database server's security type for standard, integrated, or mixed security, follow these steps:

1. Run SQL Enterprise Manager from the Microsoft SQL Server 6.5 group (see Figure 20.1).

FIG. 20.1

After being started, SQL Enterprise Manager shows that no server is selected.

2. Select the server that is going to be managed and, from the Server menu, select SQL Server, Configure. After doing so, activate the Security Options page shown in Figure 20.2.

FIG. 20.2

To track the successful and unsuccessful login attempts of your users, enable, or check, the options in the Audit Level group box.

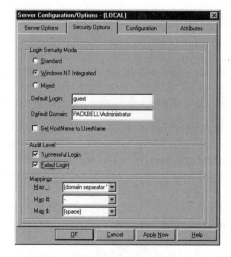

N O T E When you install SQL Server, three users are installed automatically. The system administrator account is set up for the user SA, the system performance monitoring account is set
up for the user PROBE, and the GUEST user is set up for default access to the system.

If you set up your server for use with Replication, two additional users, REPL_PUBLISHER and REPL_
SUBSCRIBER, are installed. These two user IDs manage the communications in the publisher/
subscriber mode. For more information on Replication, see Chapter 17, "Setting Up and Managing
Replication."

As you've seen throughout this book, the SA account is a special account with which you can fully
control the different aspects of your system. For this reason, it is extremely important that you change
the default blank password to one that is more secure. You should never leave a production system
with a blank password. ■

Using Standard Security

In standard security mode, SQL Server is wholly responsible for managing and maintaining
accounts on the server. In this case, SQL Server is responsible for authenticating a user and
for enforcing password/login restrictions. This is the most common way of configuring SQL
Server because it behaves identically to Sybase on any hardware platform and to SQL Server
4.2 on OS/2. The majority of the rest of this chapter will discuss the features of standard security. For more information on Windows NT's integrated security system, refer to Que's *Special
Edition Using Windows NT Server.*

N O T E You should use standard security when no Windows NT servers are being used for file
server duties. In this case, NT's integrated security mechanisms provide no benefit to the
SQL Server. Also, you should use standard security when you expect that several different protocols will
be used to attach to the server. ■

Part
IV

Ch
20

Using Integrated Security

Because SQL Server runs only on Windows NT, Microsoft could take advantage of, and integrate into, Windows NT's excellent security system. When operating in integrated security mode, Windows NT is responsible for managing user connections through its *Access Control List (ACL)*. The advantages of integrated security include single-password access to all resources on a Windows NT domain and password aging and encryption across the network.

A login to the Windows NT server is either granted or denied connection to the SQL Server based on attributes of the user's login account to the NT server. This granting of permission or authentication between client and server creates a trusted login to the server. At this point, NT only validates that the login name is valid for accessing any particular resource available on the network or server.

N O T E   Trusted connections are only available via the *Multi-Protocol NetLibrary (MPNL)* or via Named Pipes communications protocols, so there may be networking reasons that make integrated security infeasible in your environment. MPNL is discussed in the section "Encrypted Multi-Protocol NetLibrary" later in this chapter. For more information on the configuration of other communications protocols for clients, see Chapter 22, "Developing Applications to Work with SQL Server." ■

When a user establishes a trusted connection to the SQL Server, the user is:

- Mapped to an existing SQL Server login if a name match is found.
- Connected as the default login (usually *guest*).
- Connected as SA if the user is the administrator on the NT system.

SQL Server manages all other database-based permissions, such as permissions on tables, views, and other objects, in the same way as a server running in standard security mode. These security permissions are discussed next.

Using Mixed Security

Mixed security, as its name implies, is a combination of both standard and integrated security and means that users can log into the server in either way. When a user connects to a SQL Server in mixed security mode, the server validates the login by first checking whether the login name has already established a trusted connection to the NT server. If no connection is found, SQL Server then performs its own validation of the login name and password supplied. If the requested login is not a known SQL Server login, access is denied.

Creating and Managing User Accounts

SQL Server has two levels of users that are important to understand. The first level of user is a login. A *login* is the ability to attach to the SQL Server itself. SQL Server manages logins on a server-wide basis. All logins are stored in the SYSLOGINS table of the master database. The second level of user is a user. *Users* are SQL Server's way of managing who has permissions to interact with resources, such as tables and stored procedures, in a given database. A user can be in one or many databases. All users are stored in the SYSUSERS table of each database for which they have permission to access.

SQL Server uses these distinctions so that a single user can have different levels of access based on the database to which they are connecting and yet retain the same password. To support this, a user has a login or connection permission to the server. It is this login to which SQL Server associates a password. Without a valid login to the server, a user will not have access to any of the server's databases, with the possible exception of remote systems using remote stored procedures.

Once a login is created, it is then necessary to create a user of a database on that server. This process is very similar to creating an SQL Server system login and is described in the following sections.

Using SQL Enterprise Manager to Create a Login

The SQL Enterprise Manager provides a simple way of creating a login to the database. Perform the following steps:

1. Run SQL Enterprise Manager from the SQL Server 6.5 group.
2. Select the Server to which you want to add a login then select Manage, Logins. This is shown in Figure 20.3.

FIG. 20.3

With the Manage Logins dialog box, you can grant access to all the databases on the server by selecting the required access level in the table at the bottom of the dialog box.

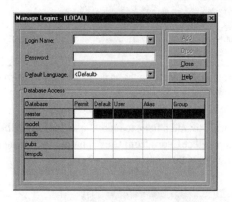

Part
IV

Ch
20

3. Enter the information for the new login and, optionally, indicate the databases that the login will be allowed to access (see Figure 20.4).
4. Click Add to verify that the information is correct and to create the login. Enter the password and verify the password assigned to the user to ensure that the information was entered correctly. This screen is shown in Figure 20.5.

FIG. 20.4

The Manage Logins dialog box shows a new login being created with user access to the PUBS and MASTER databases.

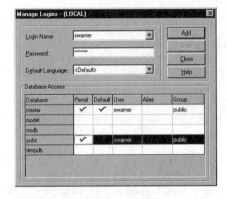

FIG. 20.5

In the Confirm Password dialog box, you must verify password information.

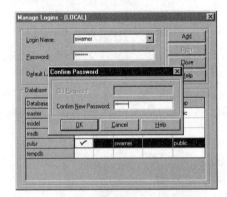

 TIP When you create a new login, set the password to be the same as the login name so that it is easy to remember.

If, at a later time, it is necessary to add a user to a database, highlight the database in the SQL Enterprise Manager and then select Users from the Manage menu. The Manage Users dialog box will appear, as shown in Figure 20.6.

FIG. 20.6

The Manage Users dialog box shows a new user being created.

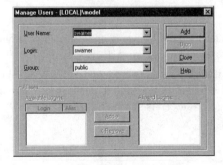

Select the user to be added to the database from the Login drop-down list box and enter the name by which it is to be identified. You should not change the name if you do not want to create an alias. Finally, click Add.

N O T E Use the Aliases group of the Manage Users dialog box to specify that other server logins can also use the currently selected database. When those logins connect to the server, if they use the currently selected database, they will not be governed by their own name but instead will be known and managed by the system under the alias name. Note that the only logins available for selection in the Aliases group will be those logins that have not already been created as a user of the currently selected database. ▦

Dropping Logins and Users with SQL Enterprise Manager

SQL Enterprise Manager's Manage Logins and Manage Users dialog boxes both provide a Drop button. Click this button to drop any user or login that you no longer want to have access to the database or server.

N O T E SQL Server Enterprise Manager is *right-click aware*, which means that you can right-click just about anything in the tree and bring up a context-sensitive menu about the object. To quickly drop a user or login, find the user or login in the tree and right-click it. Click Delete to remove the user or login. ▦

Using *sp_addlogin* to Add Logins to a Server

The sp_addlogin stored procedure is provided to add a login to the server using Transact-SQL statements. The syntax for sp_addlogin is as follows:

```
sp_addlogin login_id [, password [, defaultdb [, defaultlanguage]]]
```

The elements of the statement are:

- *login_id* is the name of the login being added. A login follows standard SQL Server naming conventions.
- *password* is the password to be assigned the login. Passwords are optional but are highly recommended as the most basic of security measures.
- *defaultdb* is the default database in which the SQL Server should place the login after connecting to the database. If left NULL, SQL Server leaves the login in the master database. You should always assign a default database for your users, and you should avoid making it the MASTER database to make sure that objects are not inadvertently created in the MASTER database.
- *defaultlanguage* is the default language that you should assign to the login. If left NULL, SQL Server assigns the default language for the server.

Part IV
Ch
20

TIP The user can change his or her password at any time using the sp_password stored procedure. For example, sp_password 'Agent99', 'MaxwellSmart' changes the currently connected user's password from Agent99 to MaxwellSmart. It's a good idea for the user to change his or her password after the first login and regularly thereafter.

The following is an example of creating a login to the server with the default database of pubs and a password of Allen:

sp_addlogin 'Ronald', 'Allen', pubs

N O T E   SQL Server 6.5 has a new variation of the sp_addlogin stored procedure with which a user can be added to a database while adding that user to the master.dbo.syslogins table. This new procedure takes an additional parameter that identifies the login ID. Only system administrators may use this feature. ■

Using *sp_adduser* to Add New Users to Databases

sp_adduser is similar in style to the sp_addlogin procedure in that it takes an existing login and adds it to the currently active database. Note that you must issue a use command and be in the required database to add a user to before running the sp_adduser stored procedure.

sp_adduser login_id [, username [, grpname]]

The elements of the statement are:

- *login_id* is the name of the login being added as a user to the database. Invalid logins will not be added to the database.
- *username* is provided to enable logins to be "aliased" in a database. This allows the same login to connect to different databases on the same server and have different names in each database.
- *grpname* enables the specification of a user group to which the user will belong. Using groups simplifies security because instead of granting permissions to individual users, the permissions can be granted to the group and then all members of the group receive them.

Following is an example of adding a user to the currently active database. Because no user name is supplied, the login_id is assumed for the user name.

sp_adduser 'Ronald'

sp_droplogin and *sp_dropuser*

To remove a login or user from the server or database, execute the system procedures sp_droplogin or sp_dropuser. Their syntax is very similar, especially when the user name chosen for a given login to a database is the same as the login_id:

```
sp_droplogin login_id
```

and

```
sp_dropuser username
```

Creating and Using Groups

SQLServer provides the ability to create groups of users so that security permissions granted to all members are the same. This is simpler to use and is a more practical approach to security than granting individual users specific permissions on any particular set of tables.

When SQL Server is installed, it installs with PUBLIC, a single group. All users that are created in your system will belong to the PUBLIC group and it will drive the default permissions sets of your users.

Users can belong to one, and only one, additional group on your system so that you can associate custom rights with their account. You'll want to carefully create your groups to encompass the different functionality "classes" of users on your system.

Also, remember that groups are defined on a database-by-database basis, which means that when you define a group in one database, it's not available in others. You'll need to create the group anew in each database as needed. To get around this, you can use the MODEL database. Create the groups you need in that database, then again when it's used as the template for new databases.

Using SQL Enterprise Manager to Add Groups

SQL Enterprise Manager provides an easy method for adding groups to the database. Perform the following steps:

1. Start SQL Enterprise Manager and highlight the database in the server tree for which you want to create a group (see Figure 20.7).

FIG. 20.7
The SQL Enterprise Manager shows the PUBS database highlighted.

2. From the <u>M</u>anage menu, select Gr<u>o</u>ups and enter the information/name of the new group. Select any users that are required members of the group, as shown in Figure 20.8.

FIG. 20.8
In the Manage Groups dialog box, a new group (grp_me) is created with swarner as its only member.

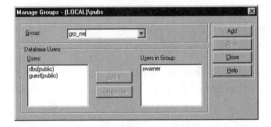

3. Click A<u>d</u>d to add the group to the database.

Dropping Groups with SQL Enterprise Manager

Dropping security groups with SQL Enterprise Manager involves performing the same steps as creating them. You can use the Manage Groups dialog box, shown previously in Figure 20.8, to drop any unneeded groups from the server. Removing a group will not remove any users associated with those groups. Any permissions granted to users because they were members of the groups will be revoked.

Using Permissions and SQL Server

Permissions are the rights to access an object, such as a table, in the database. Permissions are granted to a user or group so that user or group can perform functions such as select data, insert new rows, and update data.

Permissions are implicitly granted to the owner or creator of an object. The owner can then decide to grant permissions to other users or groups as that user sees fit. Several permissions exist on objects in the database:

■ The database owner (dbo) has full permissions on all objects in the database that he owns.

■ The system administrator (SA) has full permissions on all objects in all databases on the server.

SQL Server provides the GRANT and REVOKE commands to give or take away permission from a user. SQL Enterprise Manager also provides an easy way to add and remove permissions. These commands are discussed in the following sections.

Object Permissions

Object permissions are the permissions to act on tables and other objects, such as stored procedures and views, in the database.

The following is a list of permissions available on tables and their descriptions:

- SELECT enables a user to select or read data from a table or view. Note that a SELECT permission can be granted to individual columns within a table or view, not just the entire table.

- INSERT enables a user to add new data to a table or view.

- UPDATE enables a user to change data in a table or view. Note that an UPDATE permission can be granted to individual columns within a table or view, not just the entire table.

- DELETE enables a user to remove data from a table or view.

- EXECUTE enables a user to execute a stored procedure.

- DRI/REFERENCES enables a user to add foreign key constraints on a table.

- DDL/Data Definition Language enables a user to create, alter, or drop objects in the database. Examples are CREATE TABLE, DROP DATABASE, and ALTER TABLE.

- ALL gives the user full permissions on the object. Note that only the SA can use ALL when DDL statements are being used.

Using SQL Enterprise Manager to Manage Permissions

SQL Enterprise Manager provides an easy way of managing permissions for users and groups in a database. Perform the following steps:

1. Start SQL Enterprise Manager and highlight the database in the server tree for which you want to manage permissions (refer to Figure 20.7).

2. From the Object menu, select Permissions and choose either the By User page or the By Object page. This is shown in Figure 20.9.

FIG. 20.9
Changing permissions by checking any of the columns does not take effect until you click the Set button.

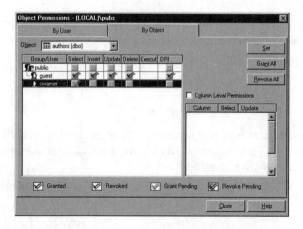

Part
IV

Ch
20

3. Use the Object Permissions dialog box to specify the permissions required for the user, and then click Set to apply the changes (see Figure 20.10).

FIG. 20.10
Use the Object Filters options to limit the types of objects that are displayed in the table at the lower-left part of the dialog box.

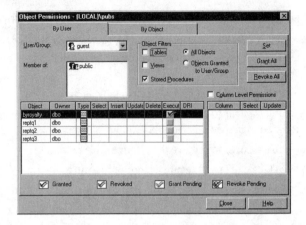

 Use the Grant All and Revoke All buttons to grant or revoke all the permissions on a given table or view to save time.

Using *GRANT* and *REVOKE*

SQL Server's Transact-SQL interface to permissions is through the GRANT and REVOKE statements. The GRANT Transact-SQL command is used to give a permission or permissions to a user or group in SQL Server. Granting a permission enables the user or group to perform the granted permission. The syntax for using GRANT follows:

```
GRANT permission_list
ON object_name
TO name_list
```

Use REVOKE to revoke permissions from a user. The opposite of GRANT, REVOKE is designed to undo or remove any permissions granted from a user or group. The syntax for REVOKE follows:

```
REVOKE permission_list
ON object_name
FROM name_list
```

The parameters for the REVOKE command are:

- permission_list is a list of permissions being granted or revoked. Use a comma to separate multiple permissions. If ALL is specified, all permissions that the grantor has will be granted to the grantee.

- object_name is a table, view, or stored procedure for which permissions are being granted or revoked.

■ name_list is a list of user names or groups for which permissions are being granted or revoked. Use commas to separate multiple names. Specify PUBLIC to include all users.

N O T E If WITH GRANT OPTION is appended to a grant statement, the grantee will be able also to grant his rights to other users. This is a nice option, but it should be used very sparingly. It probably is best if it is used only by the system administrator because of security reasons. ■

The following example grants SELECT and UPDATE permissions on the AUTHORS table:

```
Grant   SELECT, UPDATE
On      AUTHORS
To      PUBLIC
Go
```

The following example revokes DELETE permissions on the EMPLOYEE table:

```
Revoke  DELETE
On      EMPLOYEE
From    PUBLIC
Go
```

Using Views to Enhance Security

Views provide a great way to enhance security because they limit the data that is available to a user. For example, you can have a group of users in grp_junior_emp that is not allowed to view any of the authors who receive more than 50 percent royalties because this amount is only available to the senior managers or other employees within the company. In Listing 20.1, the Transact-SQL shows how you can achieve this.

▶ **See** Chapter 10, "Managing and Using Views," to learn more about creating views with SQL Server, **p. 291**

On the CD

Listing 20.1   20_01.SQL—Using Groups and Views to Create a Well-Secured Environment

```
/* First add the group */
sp_addgroup grp_junior_emp
go
/* now revoke select on the base tables from the public group */
Revoke Select on TitleAuthor from public
go
Revoke Select on Authors from public
go
/* now create the view that limits access */
Create View Vie_Authors
As
      Select       *
      From  AUTHORS
      Where AU_ID in (Select AU_ID
```

Part
IV

Ch
20

continues

Listing 20.1   Continued

```
                         From TITLEAUTHOR
                         Where ROYALTYPER <= 50)
Go
/* grant select on the view to the members of the group */
grant select on Vie_Authors to grp_junior_emp
go
```

Using Stored Procedures to Conceal Objects and Business Rules

You can use stored procedures in a very similar fashion to using views to provide a level of security on the data that completely conceals the data available to a user or the business processes involved in manipulating the data.

In Listing 20.2, you can see the same data concealment as demonstrated in using the view in Listing 20.1 except that it is achieved through using a stored procedure.

On the CD

Listing 20.2   20_02.SQL—Using Groups and Stored Procedures to Conceal Data Structures on the Server

```
/* First add the group */
sp_addgroup grp_junior_emp
go
/* now revoke select on the base tables from the public group */
Revoke Select on TitleAuthor from public
go
Revoke Select on Authors from public
go
/* now create the stored procedure that limits access */
Create Procedure up_SelectAuthors
As
      Select        *
      From   AUTHORS
      Where AU_ID in (Select AU_ID
                      From TITLEAUTHOR
                      Where ROYALTYPER <= 50)
Go
/* grant execute on the view to the members of the group */
grant execute on up_SelectAuthors to grp_junior_emp
go
```

In Listing 20.3, the junior employees are allowed to update the contract flag on the AUTHORS table without having permission to update anything else on the table. This is the sort of procedure that enables you to hide data manipulation from the users while still giving them limited power to work on the data available to them in the server.

On the CD

Listing 20.3 20_03.SQL—Stored Procedure that Enables Users to Update the *AUTHORS* Table

```
/* First add the group */
sp_addgroup grp_junior_emp
go
/* now revoke select on the base table from the public group */
Revoke Update, Delete, Insert on Authors from public
go
/* now create the stored procedure that limits access */
Create Procedure up_SetContractForAuthor
      @nAu_Id id,
      @bContract bit
As
      Update      AUTHORS
      Set   CONTRACT = @bContract
      Where AU_ID = @nAu_Id
      Print "Author's contract flag set."
Go
/* grant execute on the view to the members of the group */
grant execute on up_SetContractForAuthor to grp_junior_emp
go
```

Using Security Beyond SQL Server

You can take a number of steps to provide a more secured environment in which SQL Server will operate. Some of the following sections may seem obvious but are worth thinking about. It is recommended that you designate a person to be responsible for system security at your workplace. This person will live, breathe, and eat security and should be clearly empowered to implement any of the steps outlined in the following sections. *System Security Officers (SSO)* are becoming more and more common within organizations due to the highly accessible nature of public access networks, such as the Internet. Their roles are that of company custodians.

Physical Security

Often overlooked when the security of a system is being designed is the *physical security* of the server itself. Granted, it is unlikely that the average hacker will spend all day sitting on the system console hacking into a server, trying various passwords without being noticed. If the server can be removed physically from its location, however, many unscrupulous users will be prepared to spend more time in the comfort of their homes. This would also include its mass data storage devices, such as tapes and hard drives.

Ensure that physical access to the server is limited. Provide locked doors, preferably with electronic locks, that secure the server, and optionally bolt the server to the structure on which it resides. Remember that in these days of smaller hardware, the server can be a laptop or similarly small device, which makes it easier to steal.

Because Windows NT provides excellent remote administration capabilities, you can remove monitors and keyboards from servers that must be placed in high-access areas. Doing so will prevent an idle person from walking by and examining the server. As an alternative, plenty of hardware manufacturers provide secure casings for server boxes that you can use to provide better security for your server.

It is assumed that you will apply the same level of physical security to the SQL Server as to the following:

- The network file servers
- The network hubs and routers
- Any other shared network device, such as bridges and remote WAN linkup devices

Local Area Network (LAN) Access

A common mistake on LANs is to have unmonitored network nodes that allow access. Ensure that all nodes on the network that do not have computers actually attached to them have been disconnected from the hub so that no one can bring in a laptop and access the LAN at a physical level.

For highly secure environments, provide all users with SecureID cards or similar devices. These devices generate passwords that are authenticated by the network file server and change constantly. This will stop users without valid identification cards from having access to the LAN, even if they have physical access to a node.

At a LAN software level, ensure that all the features of the LAN's software are being used. Most network operating systems provide at least government-approved C2 level of security, but only if you turn it on. Unlike the B2 standard of security, C2 provides the features but does not enforce their use. Windows NT, NetWare 4.1, and some versions of UNIX support C2 security. Make sure that you are doing all the basics of good user management on your LAN, as follows:

- Enforce password aging with a maximum life of 30 days.
- Require unique passwords.
- Require long, eight-character passwords that are validated against a list of invalids. Third-party applications exist to ensure that a client is using good passwords.
- Enforce security blockouts on logins that fail due to invalid passwords.

Remote or Wide Area Network Access

It's much harder to control WAN or remote access to a network than the local access provided through the LAN. Some steps that you can take include:

- Assign IP addresses to all external users and do not allow them to connect with their own addresses. Doing so will enable you to closely monitor all remote connections to your LAN.

- Implement a software- or hardware-based firewall that physically limits external packet traffic on the server's network.
- Enforce routine password changing per the file server guidelines outlined previously in this chapter.
- Audit all remote transactions/IP traffic and scan it for invalid requests.
- Implement secure WAN protocol transport by using hardware-based compression on either end of WAN bridges.

Application Security

You can take a number of steps to make your applications independently secure of the security applied at the SQL Server level. Some ideas to consider are:

- Implement *permission trees* that allow users access to Windows within your application program. You may want to break down access into three levels: view, new, and edit.
- Use application-based audit trails to track the changes of fields and the amount of time spent on any given window in the system.
- Place application-based limits on the amount of money that can be posted for financial systems.

Remember that if the security of your database is important to you, you should always ensure that the database itself is secure with or without application programs. You must do so because sophisticated users on your network and on the Internet, if you are connected, will always be able to use a different application to work with your data if they want, bypassing any application-only security that was being enforced.

Encrypted Multi-Protocol NetLibrary

If security is a serious concern in the environment in which SQL Server is being used, then it is possible to implement the *SQL Server Multi-Protocol NetLibrary (MPNL)*. This feature is available in versions 6.0 and higher. MPNL provides a Remote Procedure Call (RPC)-based interface from clients to the SQL Server. MPNL requires adding the protocol as a listener service to the engine, though MPNL is not actually a listener because it is RPC-based.

One key advantage of MPNL is that it can be encrypted. The encryption algorithm used can be enabled for individual clients. The server, however, must be enabled for encrypted traffic. Support for clients varies. Check your SQL Server documentation for the client support available in your version.

Server enumeration via the `dbserverenum` call in NetLibrary is not supported on servers that are MPNL-enabled. Clients must know the name of servers that are operating in this mode.

Part IV

Ch 20

Reality Check

Security is one of those things that changes from installation to installation. What works best for you may not be the best thing for others, so you'll have to carefully consider before you select integrated, mixed, or standard security for your SQL Server installation. The most common installation choice is mixed security, which gives you the most flexibility but still enables you to use the features of the NT user base as the foundation for your SQL Server users.

Leaving the SA user with no password is, by far, the most common mistake system administrators make. Take the time immediately after installation to put a password on this account. Never allow your developers to use the account for standard maintenance; they can use a permission-based account in the database or databases as they need to make necessary changes to their project databases. No matter how small your shop is, it's just not a good idea to use the SA account for anything other than administration.

SQL Server security is a complex matrix of options. You have the ability to control database access on many different levels. Remember that you can control access to information with views as well as security implemented as outlined in this chapter. Combine the different techniques to make the system as secure, or as open, as you need. When you're designing your system, keep in mind what types of access are possible, even when they're not probable. This means that if your server resides on a system that is also connected to the Internet, be sure to take into account that you should enhance security to prevent unknown users from accessing the system. Your security should be extremely tight if your system is available to the Internet or other outside sources in any way.

From Here...

Having discovered the many facets of SQL Server security, it is most likely that you will spend the next few months trying to fill the holes that you now know exist. If you are lucky enough to be reading this book before you implement SQL Server in your environment, take advantage of what you have learned and apply as many security features as necessary to provide the appropriate control needed.

Take a look at the following chapters for more information that may be useful in creating a secure environment:

- See Chapter 10, "Managing and Using Views," to learn how to hide underlying data tables with views that limit data sets available to users.
- See Chapter 14, "Managing Stored Procedures and Using Flow-Control Statements," to learn how to create stored procedures to provide users with access to data without giving them access to the actual tables.

Optimizing Performance

Performance tuning in the client/server world is something of a magical art. A combination of so many factors can make an application perform well, and knowing where to focus your time is what's most important.

The most critical part of optimizing performance is good documentation. Document statistically how the system works or performs before even starting any performance tuning. As the performance tuning cycle begins, you should monitor and document the effects of all changes so that it's easy to determine which changes were positive and which were negative. Never assume that all changes made for one application automatically apply to another application. Remember, you're ultimately tuning a product that a user is using, not just a database that is being accessed by some unknown client. ■

How to approximately size a database and how to estimate the amount of disk space required

Sizing an SQL Server database can make a difference when you choose the hardware to buy for your server.

How to size the procedure cache for optimal performance

An optimally sized procedure cache substantially improves performance because frequently accessed procedures do not need to be recompiled.

How to use Windows NT's Performance Monitor with SQL Server

Windows NT's Performance Monitor provides complete and up-to-date statistics to help you manage and monitor the performance of SQL Server.

Deciding the Best Way to Create Devices

As you'll see in the balance of this chapter, you need to first determine the database and transaction log sizes, then you can create the devices that will hold them. In creating the device, you'll be presented with a fundamental choice. Will you create a very large device and then place all databases on the single device, or will you create several smaller devices to support the individual databases?

At first glance, it's easier to create a single device, make it very large, and then place your different databases on the device. This may be easiest to implement, but it's not in your best interest in the long run. This is because, in order to restore a device that has become a problem, you'll be faced with taking down *all* production systems, rather than just the affected database and its respective device.

If you can, try to create a device per database and transaction log combination. This enables you to effectively work with each database separately and perform any tuning, updates, backup, and restore work, and so on, that needs to be performed, in many cases, without impacting the other systems.

Sizing a Database

Estimating the size of an SQL Server database is relatively straightforward and can be done with a good level of accuracy. The principle of space calculation is that all the bytes of data per table should be added together along with the associated overhead per row and page of data.

After you have this information calculated, you use it to determine the different sizing aspects of your database, including page fill percentages, table sizes, and ultimately, the size of the devices that you need to have on your system.

You use these values as a divisor to the page size (2K) to determine how many rows of data will fit in a page. The actual available space of a page is 2,016 bytes because 32 bytes are reserved for fixed overhead to manage the rows on the page. In general terms, these calculations are affected by the placement and use FILL FACTOR on indexes and also are affected by whether a clustered index is on the table. FILL FACTOR is discussed later in the chapter in the section, "Effects of FILL FACTOR."

 TIP When it comes to sizing your device to support the database, don't forget to add an allotment for the transaction log and space to grow. Your transaction log should be from 10 percent to 25 percent of the size of your resulting production database. If you leave an extra 10 percent of space available on the device after your projected maximum database and transaction log totals, you'll have the space to extend the databases should the need arise, giving you time to create new devices onto which to extend the database.

After you've created your initial database, you can use the stored procedure sp_spaceused to monitor the size of your database and tables. The syntax of sp_spaceused is:

```
sp_spaceused object [, @updateusage = 'TRUE¦FALSE'
```

For example, if you wanted to check both the entire Publishers (PUBs) database and the Authors table, you could submit the following query:

```
sp_spaceused
go
sp_spaceused authors
```

N O T E The go is required to separate the two queries when they are submitted to SQL Server. ■

When you submit this query, you get the results shown in Listing 21.1, which indicate the space used and the space remaining for each of the respective objects.

Listing 21.1   Output from the *sp_spaceused* Query

database_name	database_size	unallocated space
pubs	3.00 MB	1.77 MB

reserved	data	index_size	
→ unused			
			..........1262 KB
192 KB	108 KB	962 KB	

name	rows	reserved	data
→ index_size	unused		
→			
authors	23	64 KB	2 KB
→ 8 KB	54 KB		

Using this information, you can determine where you stand on utilization of existing database space.

You can also use sp_helpdb to get information about the size, owner, ID, date of creation, and current status for databases in the system. Listing 21.2 shows sample output from calling sp_helpdb.

Listing 21.2   Output from the *sp_helpdb* Query

name	db_size	owner	dbid	created
status				
..........feedback			10.00 MB sa	9
Sep 17 1996 no options set				
ipms	5.00 MB sa		7	Aug 2
➥1996 no options set				
logging	50.00 MB sa		8	Aug 2
➥1996 trunc. log on chkpt.				
marketing	15.00 MB sa		6	Aug 2
➥1996 no options set				

continues

Listing 21.2   Continued

```
master                    17.00 MB sa                1    Apr  3
1996 trunc. log on chkpt.
model                      1.00 MB sa                3    Apr  3
➥1996 no options set
msdb                       8.00 MB sa                5    Aug  2
➥1996 trunc. log on chkpt.
pubs                       3.00 MB sa                4    Apr  3
1996 trunc. log on chkpt.
tempdb                     2.00 MB sa                2    Dec 11
➥1996 select into/bulkcopy
```

In the sections that follow, you'll see how to project how much space your tables will require in hopes of preventing errors if the database grows beyond its current confines.

Datatype Sizes

Each SQL Server datatype consumes a certain number of bytes based on the storage of the data. Table 21.1 defines the amount of storage that each datatype uses.

Table 21.1   Datatype Sizes

Datatype	Size
Char/Binary	The size indicated in the definition
VarChar/VarBinary	The actual data size; use an average estimate
Int	4 bytes
SmallInt	2 bytes
TinyInt	1 byte
Float	8 bytes
Float(b)	4 bytes (numbers with precision of 1–7 digits)
Float(b)	8 bytes (numbers with precision of 8–15 digits)
Double Precision	8 bytes
Real	4 bytes
Money	8 bytes
SmallMoney	4 bytes
Datetime	8 bytes
SmallDatetime	4 bytes
Bit	1 byte
Decimal/Numeric	2–17 bytes depending on the precision

Datatype	Size
Text/Image	16 bytes per table row plus at least one 2K page per NOT NULL column
Timestamp	8 bytes

SQL Server internally defines any NULLABLE column as a VAR datatype. So a CHAR(12) NULL column is actually a VARCHAR(12) column. Therefore, for any columns that permit NULL values, the average expected column size should be used.

Decimal and numeric precision affects the amount of storage required for these datatypes. Table 21.2 indicates the number of bytes required for each range of precision.

Table 21.2 Sizes Based on Numeric Precision

Numeric Precision	Size
0–2	2 bytes
3–4	3 bytes
5–7	4 bytes
8–9	5 bytes
10–12	6 bytes
13–14	7 bytes
15–16	8 bytes
17–19	9 bytes
20–21	10 bytes
22–24	11 bytes
25–26	12 bytes
27–28	13 bytes
29–31	14 bytes
32–33	15 bytes
34–36	16 bytes
37–38	17 bytes

Calculating Space Requirements for Tables

The method of calculating a table's space requirements differs based on whether the table has a clustered index or not. Both calculation methods are shown here, and examples will be drawn from the Pubs database to illustrate their use.

Part
IV
Ch
21

Some things to be aware of when calculating table and index sizes are:

- Performing UPDATE STATISTICS on an index adds an extra page for that index to store the distribution statistics of the data that it contains. Performing UPDATE STATISTICS on the table adds one data distribution page per index on the table.

- For tables with variable-length columns, you should try to average the length of the row by estimating the anticipated average size of the columns on the table.

- SQL Server won't store more than 256 rows per page, even if the row is very short. So if your row is 7 bytes or less in size, the number of data pages required for N rows of data is calculated by N/256 = number of data pages required.

- Text and image data take up a minimum of 2K, or one page, unless, when a row is inserted, the value for the column is specified as NULL.

Tables with Clustered Indexes   The Publishers table has a clustered index. This example estimates the space required for 5,000,000 rows, and assumes that the average length of the VarChar columns is 60 percent of the defined length:

1. Calculate the row length. If the row contains only fixed-length, NOT NULL columns, the formula is

   ```
   2 + (Sum of column sizes in bytes) = Row size
   ```

   If the row contains mixed variable-length fields and/or NULL columns, the formula is

   ```
   2 + (Sum of fixed-length column sizes in bytes) + (Sum of average
      ➥ of variable-length columns) = Subtotal
   Subtotal * (( Subtotal / 256) _+ 1) + (Number of variable-length
      ➥ columns +_ 1) + 2 = Row Size
   ```

   For the Publishers table, the second formula is required:

   ```
   2 + 4 + (60% of 92) = 55.2
   55.2 * ((55.2/256) + 1) + 5 + 2 = 75
   ```

2. Calculate the number of rows that fit on a page. The formula is

   ```
   2016 / (Row Size) = Number of rows per page
   ```

   In this case,

   ```
   2016 / 75 = 27
   ```

 For more accurate calculations, round *down* any calculations for number of rows per page.

3. Calculate the number of pages required to accomodate the number of rows you have. The formula is
   Number Of Rows Required/Number of rows per page = Number of 2K data pages

   In this case,

   ```
   5,000,000 / 27 =  18519
   ```

 For more accurate calculations, round up any calculations for number of pages required.

4. Next, calculate the space required for the clustered index. The size of the clustered index depends on whether the key columns are variable or fixed-length. For fixed-length keys, use this formula:

```
5 + (Sum of column sizes in bytes) = Clustered index size
```

For variable-length keys, use this formula:

```
5 + (Sum of fixed-length column sizes in bytes) + (Sum of average
   ➥ of variable-length columns) = Subtotal
Subtotal * (( Subtotal / 256) _+ 1) + (Number of variable-length
   ➥ columns +_ 1) + 2 = Clustered index size
```

For the Publishers database, the key is a single fixed-length column, so the formula is

```
5 + 4 = 9
```

5. Calculate the number of clustered index rows that will fit on a page. The formula is

```
(2016 / (Clustered index size)) - 2 = Number of rows per page
```

In this case

```
(2016 / 9) - 2 = 222
```

6. Next, calculate the number of index pages by using the following formula:

```
(Number of data pages) / (Number of clustered index rows per page) = Number
of index pages
→ at index level N
```

For this example

```
18519 / 222 = 84
```

Index pages are at multiple levels. To compute all the levels of the index, continue to divide the resulting number of index pages by the number of clustered rows per page until the result is one (1) or less. In this case

```
84 / 222 = 1
```

means that one index page is at the top of the index and all the other pages are actual pointers to data pages.

7. Compute the total number of 2K pages required for the database table:

Data pages: 18,519

Index pages (level 1): 1

Index pages (level 0): 83

Total number of 2K pages: 19,403 (or about 38M)

Tables with Non-Clustered Indexes Tables with non-clustered indexes are calculated in size the same way as a clustered index table, except for the sizing of the index itself. In this example, assume that a non-clustered index has been added to the Roysched table on the title_id column, and that 7,000,000 rows are in the table. The following steps will help you size a non-clustered index:

Part
IV

Ch
21

1. The first step is to calculate the length of the leaf row in the index. A *leaf row* is the bottom row of an index tree and points to the data page. The leaf row's size is the size of the index's columns summed together and is affected by variable or fixed-length columns. Use the following formula if you have only fixed-length columns in the index:

   ```
   7 + (Sum of fixed-length keys) = Size of index row
   ```

   Use the following formula if you used fixed- and variable-length columns in the index:

   ```
   9 + (Sum of length of fixed-length keys) + (Sum of length of
   ➡ variable-length keys) + (Number of variable-length keys)
   ➡ + 1 = Subtotal
    (Subtotal) + ((Subtotal / 256) + 1) = (Size of leaf index row)
   ```

   In the Roysched table, the primary key is fixed-length and isn't NULL, so the formula is as follows:

   ```
   7 + 6 = 13
   ```

2. Next, calculate the number of leaf pages that will be required by using the following formula:

   ```
   2016 / (Size of leaf index row) = Number of leaf rows per page
   ```

   In this case

   ```
   2016 / 13 = 155
   (Number of rows in table) / (Number of leaf rows per page) =
      ➡ Number of leaf pages
   ```

   In this case

   ```
   e.g.: 7,000,000 / 155 = 45,162
   ```

3. Next, calculate the size of the non-leaf row and calculate the number of non-leaf pages. The size of the non-leaf row is calculated according to this formula:

   ```
   (Size of leaf index row) + 4 = Size of nonleaf row
   ```

   In this case, it would be 13+4=**17**, resulting in:

   ```
   (2016 / Size of nonleaf row) - 2 = Number of nonleaf index rows
   ➡ per page
   ```

   In this example, (2016/17)–2=**116**

   ```
   (Number of leaf pages / Number of nonleaf index rows per page)
   ➡ = Number of index pages at Level N
   ```

   In this case, 45,162/117=**386** pages at level 1

   Like the clustered index, result division determines the levels of the index until the result is one (1) or less:

   386 / 117 = **4** pages at level 2.

   4 / 117 = **1** page at level 3.

4. Finally, compute the size of the index by adding the number of pages at the various levels of the index:

   Leaf Pages: 45,162

   Level 1 Pages: 386

Level 2 Pages: 4

Level 3 Pages: 1

Total number of 2K pages: 45553, or about 89M

Effects of *FILL FACTOR*

FILL FACTOR alters the number of rows that SQL Server places on a page. The most likely configuration of FILL FACTOR is to assume that the table never changes its dataset and, therefore, you set FILL FACTOR to 100% to maximize the use of data pages. This affects the calculations by increasing the number of rows that can fit on a page by two (2).

If you're sizing an index with a FILL FACTOR of 100%, don't subtract two (2) from the result of the number of rows per page because SQL Server doesn't pre-allocate these rows for page growth but, instead, puts user data there.

Any other value of FILL FACTOR alters the size of the page itself. For example, a FILL FACTOR of 70% reduces the amount of available space on the page from 2,016 bytes to 1,412 bytes.

Sizing the Procedure Cache

Sizing the Procedure Cache in SQL Server is basically a case of trial and error. Microsoft documents an approximation based on the following formula:

*Procedure Cache = (Maximum Concurrent Users) * (Size of Largest Plan) * 1.25*

To determine the size of a plan in memory, the DBCC MEMUSAGE command should be issued in ISQL. Listing 21.3 illustrates the output from DBCC MEMUSAGE.

Listing 21.3 Output from *DBCC MEMUSAGE*

```
/*----------------------------
dbcc memusage
----------------------------*/
Memory Usage:
...
Buffer Cache, Top 20:
...
Procedure Cache, Top 12:
...
Procedure Name: sp_help
Database Id: 1
Object Id: 1888009757
Version: 1
Uid: 1
Type: stored procedure
Number of trees: 0
Size of trees: 0.000000 Mb, 0.000000 bytes, 0 pages
Number of plans: 1
Size of plans: 0.051249 Mb, 53738.000000 bytes, 27 pages
```

Assuming that sp_help was the largest procedure to be run on a server and that there were to be 150 concurrent users, the following formula should be used:

```
150 * 27 * 2 * 1.25 = 10125K
```

N O T E Memory in the procedure cache is managed as a set of 2K pages. The number of pages reported by DBCC MEMUSAGE, therefore, is multiplied by 2K to derive the amount of memory that the plan actually consumes. ■

An alternative sizing can be estimated based on the need to stop SQL Server from recompiling procedures that fall out of the cache frequently. The procedure cache, like the data cache, works on a Least Recently Used (LRU) algorithm and procedures that are used infrequently are pushed out of the cache if there's no more room to compile a procedure that is requested by a user process.

You should compile a list of the number of critical procedures, or procedures that are most frequently accessed. Execute each one, analyzing the memory used, as reported by DBCC MEMUSAGE. Based on the total memory calculated, the size of the procedure cache can be determined.

Ultimately, the only true judge of an accurate size of procedure cache is to test, test, and test an application and monitor the effects of altering the amount of cache available.

It's possible to run out of procedure cache if the number of active procedures in use and their combined plan sizes are greater than the cache available. In this case, you'll receive error 701, and the calling process that was trying to execute a procedure will be rolled back. If you receive this error message 701, you should resize the procedure cache to a higher percentage of available memory.

Using the Windows NT Performance Monitor

Windows NT's Performance Monitor is an advanced tool that provides statistics about the operation of the NT environment. One of the unique properties of the Performance Monitor is its capability to install performance heuristics and callbacks from other executables in the Windows NT system and report their statistics.

SQL Server's Performance Monitor is just a set of hooks for the core Windows NT Performance Monitor to call. SQL Server groups the statistics that can be displayed into *objects*. These objects group the logical similar statistics.

SQL Server gathers statistics in one of two different modes:

■ In *Direct Response* mode, the Performance Monitor waits for SQL Server to gather statistics and place them in statistics tables. These tables are available at any time for browsing, but they refer to the last period that the server gathered information and, therefore, may not necessarily accurately reflect the current server operating level. However, they can be useful in researching historical problems.

- In *On Demand* mode, the Performance Monitor forces SQL Server to gather statistics and return them when a period elapses in the Performance Monitor. You should take care not to saturate SQL Server with requests for statistics because this is a relatively costly operation and may, in turn, skew the results of the statistics themselves.

To configure either Direct Response or On Demand mode, follow these steps:

1. First run SQL Enterprise Manager from the Microsoft SQL Server 6.5 group and select the server to be configured (see Figure 21.1).

FIG. 21.1
The first thing you need to do is select the server you want to work with.

2. From the menu, choose Server, SQL Server, Configure (see Figure 21.2).

FIG. 21.2
The SQL Enterprise Manager's Server Configuration/Options dialog box lets you set up the modes you want to use.

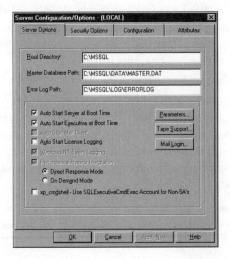

3. Select Direct Response Mode or On Demand Mode and click OK.

SQL Server Statistics Objects

A list of the objects that SQL Server Performance Monitor can report on appears in the following sections. Some of the counters within the objects can be applied to particular instances of activity on the server. For example, the Users object's Physical I/O counter can be applied to each user connected to the system. This process of configuring instances to the particular counter enables you to customize the statistics that you want to monitor.

SQL Server Object   The SQL Server object is the master object and provides a wide variety of statistics. The items that are monitored here are the high-level statistics that are very important to everyday management of your server. Normal monitoring of SQL Server typically watches the I/O and cache statistics to make sure that the physical I/O and memory subsystems aren't being flooded with requests.

The statistics are grouped as follows:

- *Cache Statistics*—The cache options enable you to monitor the performance of both the lazywriter and the amount of free data pages available in the data cache. Also, the cache hit rate can be monitored. The cache hit rate is a useful statistic because it tells you how frequently physical I/O has to be performed to meet a user process request.

- *I/O Statistics*— These statistics report the amount of work being performed by the physical I/O subsystems of SQL Server. They can provide useful information and enable you to monitor saturation on the I/O devices if the Outstanding Reads/Writes gets high. Careful analysis of the I/O statistics can yield an excellent set of data that will help diagnose disk problems in your environment.

- *NET Statistics*— These statistics report the number of reads and writes that SQL Server is placing out on Windows NT's network processing queues. These NET statistics are relatively unimportant and NT's statistics should be monitored instead.

- *RA Manager Statistics*— The Read Ahead Manager provides a number of system statistics that enable the monitoring of the RA's performance. Generally this information will help you tune the server using sp_configure.

- *User Connections*— This provides you with the number of currently connected users to the server.

SQL Server Replication-Published DB Object   The Replication-Published DB object enables you to monitor the publication of transaction log information from a source or publishing database. It is highly recommended that you monitor the performance of this object if you are using replication in your environment. The following statistics help you decide how efficiently your server is publishing data:

- *Replicated Transactions*— These statistics list the number of transactions which are in the transaction log of the primary database that have yet to be placed in the distribution database but have been marked for replication.

- *Replicated Transactions/sec*— These statistics give you the relative performance, which is presented in transactions per second, of the rate of reading out of the published database's transaction log. As the items are read, they are placed in the distribution database for replication.

- *Replication Latency (sec)*—These statistics list the average number of milliseconds that elapse between the time that a transaction is placed in the transaction log and the time it's placed in the distribution database.

SQL Server Replication-Subscriber Object   The Replication-Subscriber object enables monitoring of the replication that is updating tables on the subscribing server/database. Like the Published object (in the preceding section) careful monitoring of this object is essential to the management of effective replication.

The following statistics are provided:

- *Delivered Transactions*— These provide you with the number of transactions that have been executed on the destination database.

- *Delivered Transactions/sec*— These give you the relative performance, which is indicated in transactions per second of delivery of data.

- *Delivered Latency (sec)*—These tell you the time, in seconds, that it takes for a transaction to be executed after it's placed in the distribution database.

- *Undelivered Transactions*— These give you the number of transactions sitting in the distribution databases that have yet to be executed on the subscribing databases.

SQL Server Locks Object   The Locks object is provided to enable the central management of locks in the database. The counters provided in this object detail the totals of the different types of locks: Extent, Intent, Page, and Table. Additional counters are provided to indicate the number of blocking locks.

▶ **See** "Understanding Transactions and Locking," for more information about locks **p. 355**

SQL Server Log Object   The Log object is provided so that alerts can be placed on the size of the transaction log associated with a database in addition to the available free space on it. This enables you to dump the logs at required intervals:

- *Log Size*— The size in megabytes of the transaction log

- *Space Free*— The percentage of the log that is free and available for transactions

SQL Server Users Object   The Users object has the following counters available that track the statistics about user activity on the server:

- *CPU Time*— The amount of CPU consumed by a particular user

- *Locks Held*—The current number of open locks held by a particular user

- *Memory (in 2K Pages)*—The amount of memory, including memory allocated to resolve queries, that a particular user is consuming on the server

- *Physical I/O*— The amount of physical reads and writes of data pages that have occurred as a result of the user's most recent query

Creating and Using Chart Views

Chart views are often the easiest statistical viewing mechanism for a database administrator. With a chart you can track periodic performance in a number of criteria and see prior history in the same view.

To use the SQL Performance Monitor to chart statistics for view, follow these steps:

1. First run SQL Performance Monitor from the Microsoft SQL Server 6.5 group (see Figure 21.3).

FIG. 21.3

Windows NT's Performance Monitor running the SQL Server control file (SQLCTRS.PMC) with the default objects being monitored.

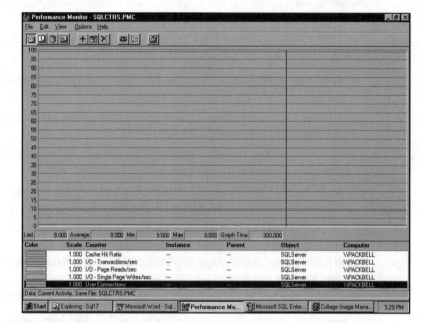

2. From the View menu, select Chart.
3. From the Edit menu, select Add To Chart. This opens the Add To Chart dialog box shown in Figure 21.4.

FIG. 21.4

You use the Add to Chart dialog box to select the counters you want to have displayed in Performance Monitor.

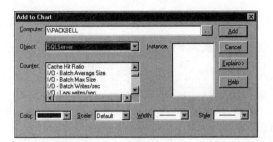

 T I P Click the Explain button to get a short explanation of each counter as you select it.

4. Select the Object from which you want to monitor a counter.

5. Select one or many counters from the Counter list box and, if necessary, specify the instances that you want to apply the counters on, in the Instance list box.

6. Specify the required line attributes for the item(s) being added. Some of these might be color, line style, and so on.

7. Click Add to add the items to the current Performance Monitor Chart (see Figure 21.5).

FIG. 21.5

The Add to Chart dialog box is ready to add SQL Server-Log counters for the Master and Pubs databases.

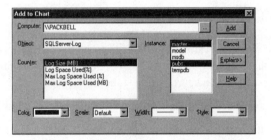

8. Add any other statistics that you want to chart, and then click Done to close the dialog box. The Cancel button changes to a Done button after you add the first item to the chart.

Creating and Using Reports

Performance Monitor can create basic reports of data that are being gathered. These reports show the current, or most recent, values gathered from the statistics of the selected counters.

To use the SQL Performance Monitor to create a report of system statistics, follow these steps:

1. Run SQL Performance Monitor from the Microsoft SQL Server 6.5 group.

2. From the View menu, choose Report.

3. From the Edit menu, select Add To Report (see Figure 21.6).

FIG. 21.6

The Add to Report dialog box has the SQL Server Replication-Published DB object selected as well as all the counters to be added to the report.

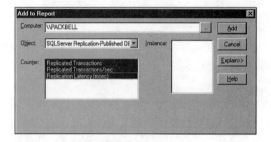

4. Select the Object from which you want to report a counter.

5. Select one or many counters from the Counter list box and, if necessary, go to Instance and specify the number of instances on which you want to apply the counters.

6. Click Add to add the items to the current Performance Monitor report.

7. Add any other statistics that you want to report on and click Done to close the dialog box. The Cancel button changes to a Done button after you add the first item to the chart.

Creating and Using Alerts

Alerts are one of the most useful features of Performance Monitor. Performance Monitor can not only gather statistics from various system objects, but it can also monitor the values of those statistics. If they reach predetermined levels, Performance Monitor can execute a program that can, for example, dial a pager or alert the DBA in some other fashion.

To use the SQL Performance Monitor to create a statistical alert, follow these steps:

1. Run SQL Performance Monitor from the Microsoft SQL Server 6.5 group.

2. From the View menu, select Alert.

FIG. 21.7

The Add to Alert dialog box is ready to add an alert that will send a mail message to the DBA if the used log space on the Pubs database exceeds 75%.

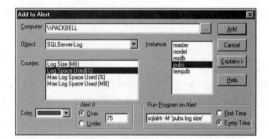

3. From the Edit menu, select Add To Alert (see Figure 21.7).

4. Select the Object from which you want to add an alert counter.

5. Select one or many counters from the Counter list box. If necessary, go to Instance and specify the instances on which you want to apply the counters.

6. Click Add to add the items to the current Performance Monitor Alert list.

7. Add any other statistics for which you want to create alerts and click Done to close the dialog box. The Cancel button changes to a Done button after you add the first item to the chart.

Reality Check

Sizing your database, and understanding how you come up with the different table sizes, is one of the most important ongoing aspects of managing your server. You'll want to manage this aspect of your system closely because if you don't, and the database or transaction logs fill up, your system will come to a grinding halt.

Be sure you do regular backups of the transaction log because this enables you to dump the log and manage the space used by it. You can also use the truncate log on checkpoint option to manage the transaction log, but it's even more imperative that you do regular backups if you use this option.

On the CD accompanying this book you'll find an Excel workbook that will help in your sizing efforts. This workbook lets you indicate the columns, their associated data type, and the indexes that you're defining against a table. If you complete one worksheet for each table in your database, you can easily add together the resulting sizes and have a good idea of the sizing requirements for your database.

If you have a dedicated server, as it's likely you will in a production environment, you should consider running the performance monitor at all times, though with an infrequent timing interval. A good interval might be in the five to ten minute range. In actual use, consider also monitoring the counter for swap file usage. Using this counter, along with the other counters outlined here that are specific to SQL Server, you can see trends in system usage that might indicate a change in usage patterns that would adversely impact your system.

From Here...

In this chapter you learned how to identify and manage statistics that will help you determine the performance characteristics of your server. You also learned how to size a database and how to size the procedure cache.

Consider looking at the following chapters to further develop your SQL Server knowledge:

- Chapter 16, "Understanding Server, Database, and Design Query Options," teaches you to further tune the server after analyzing the information provided by the SQL Performance Monitor.

- Chapter 25, "Accessing SQL Server Databases Through Front-End Products," teaches you to examine how clients connect to the database, and perhaps tune the ODBC interface on the client.

Part
IV

Ch
21

P A R T

V

Developing Applications and Solutions

22

Developing Applications to Work with SQL Server

Developing applications for SQL Server can take many different forms. As you've seen throughout this book, queries executed by the server are at the heart of the system. The queries you've worked with thus far are all based in the SQL language and are generally entered or executed from the ISQL or ISQL/W utilities.

This approach doesn't prove very useful, however, when you're developing an application to work with SQL Server information. The client application—that portion of the program responsible for information formatting, presentation, and other user interaction—is where the power of SQL Server is presented to the average user. The way your application interfaces with the SQL Server can be just as important as all of the hard work you've done behind the scenes in defining the tables, creating the stored procedures, and optimizing the system to work at its peak.

In this chapter, we review a few of the top methods of working with SQL Server from an application development perspective. Each of these technologies is a comprehensive environment for working with SQL Server, and each warrants far more coverage than is afforded here.

Different approaches for developing with SQL Server

You have several options for the specifics of how you'll communicate with SQL Server, making the versatility of the platform a good tool at your disposal.

Cross-platform development capabilities

All of the major development platforms from Microsoft and Borland are SQL-ready.

Exposed object model for SQL administration

You can create administrative modules for your SQL Server using new object-oriented techniques.

This information is provided so you have a starting point of knowledge for selecting the method that is right for you.

The most common methods of working with SQL Server are:

- DB-Library
- ODBC and the Data Access Objects, or DAO
- SQL OLE

The coming sections review the basics of each of these options and explain how they can be useful in your work with SQL Server. ■

Understanding the DB-Library Interface

DB-Library, or DB-LIB, is an API for both C and VB that allows you to work directly with SQL Server. The API provides you with the different tools you need for sending queries to and receiving information from SQL Server. It also provides the means for working with that information by allowing you to extract information from the results sets returned from your queries.

Required Components for DB-LIB

To use DB-LIB, you need to include several different supplemental files with your project. Table 22.1 shows the different files you need in the VB and C environments.

> **N O T E**   Some of the files listed in the following tables might not have been included with your version of SQL Server. If this is the case and the files are necessary, they can be obtained through the SQL Server SDK from Microsoft. ■

Table 22.1   Required Components for DB-LIB

C	Visual Basic
SQLDB.H	VBSQL.OCX
SQLFRONT.H	VBSQL.BAS

Table 22.2 shows the different components that you'll work with as you develop applications with Borland's developer tools. Be sure to use the memory model that matches your application development environment.

Table 22.2   Borland DB-LIB Components

Component File	Description
BLDBLIB.LIB	Large memory model static library
BMDBLIB.LIB	Medium memory model static library

You use slightly different components when developing with Microsoft environments. Table 22.3 shows the required elements in this environment.

Table 22.3 Microsoft-Oriented Components

Element	Description
MSDBLIB3.LIB	Windows: Import library
NTWDBLIB.LIB	Win32: Import library
RLDBLIB.LIB	DOS: Large memory model library
RMDBLIB.LIB	DOS: Medium memory model library

Concepts and Characteristics

Working with DB-LIB typically follows a standard cycle of calls. Two structures are used to establish your connection to the server. Both `dbproc` and `login` are used to establish and continue communications between your application and the SQL Server.

You use the `DBOpen` API call to initiate the connection to the server. `DBOpen` initializes the `DBProcess` structure, giving you the information you need to continue working over the same connection to the server. Table 22.4 shows the different ways you accomplish these steps in the VB or C languages.

Table 22.4 Basic Components for SQL Server Communications with DB-LIB

Description	Visual Basic	C
Initialize new `loginrec` structure	SqlLogin%	dblogin
Set user name for login	SqlSetLUser	DBSTLUSER
Set user password for login	SqlSetLPwd	DBSTLPWD
Set client application descriptive name	SqlSetLApp	DBSTLAPP
Open the connection to SQL Server	SqlOpen%	dbopen
Close the connection to SQL Server	SqlClose	dbclose
Close all connections	SqlExit	dbexit

Using these statements, you create a new login structure and populate the required fields. There are other properties of the login structure, but the user name and password are the only required items.

N O T E   If you are using integrated security, these fields are required, but the server ignores them when the connection is made. The server uses the user's credentials from the currently logged-on user. In this situation, if you know ahead of time that integrated security is used, you might want to pass in arbitrary information in these fields. For example, a user name and password of "blah" will suffice. Because the users are authenticated by their network sign on, the user ID and password are not needed. The sign-on presents the user with an additional dialog box. ▪

The descriptive name is not required, but it is strongly recommended. The reason for supplying this information is simple. If you have a system administrator working with the SQL Server and reviewing the open connections, the name you provide here is shown in the connection listing. By providing meaningful information, the administrator knows who is on the server at any given point. Because of that, you should avoid the temptation to just sign in all users on an application as the application name. If you can provide the application name and the station ID or user ID, you add some key identifying elements that the administrator can use. ▪

Using the login structure and the server name, the call to open the connection is made, and the server connection is opened. When you issue the Open command, a structure is established and returned by the call. In future calls to the server, you'll use this structure pointer whenever you issue a command to the server.

T I P   SQL Server login and logout operations are among the most costly transactions in terms of performance. If you log in each time you need to make a call or series of calls and then log out, you'll find that your application can be slower than you'd expect.

To remedy this, consider using a separate connection for each major classification of work that is to be done. For example, if you have a point-of-sale system, at the front counter you might want to develop a system to maintain the connection open to the Inventory table and the Accounts Receivable and Cash Drawer tables to help performance.

By doing so, you can take the time up front, during the loading of the application, to create your connections to SQL Server. Later, because the connections already exist, the amount of time to access the separate tables is minimized, and the user will have a much easier time using your application.

One consideration in this scenario can be the number of licensed connections you have to SQL Server. You need to make sure you end up running the number of licenses you have purchased for your SQL Server. If you use more, you might have to rethink your application, purchase additional licenses, or do both to have an optimal price-performance installation.

Sending Commands to SQL Server

When you send statements to SQL Server, you first build them in the SQL command buffer. Putting the commands into the buffer is done by calling SqlCmd with the parameters you need to place in the buffer.

N O T E The examples provided here are largely VB-related. Though the actual statement varies in C, the calling conventions are similar and require many of the same approaches as apply to VB. ■

The syntax for `SqlCmd()` in VB is:

```
Status% = SqlCmd(MyConnection%, "<statement>")
```

Each statement is appended to the previous statement, if any, that is currently in the `SqlCmd` structure. Be careful building your statement if it requires more than one line. Remember that the string you specify is simply concatenated with any prior information in the buffer. Consider the following code sample:

```
...
Status% = SqlCmd(MyConnection%,"Select * from pubs")
Status% = SqlCmd(MyConnection%,"where author like 'A%'")
...
```

Why will this statement provide a syntax error and fail? There would not be any resulting spaces between `pubs` and `where` in the example. Be sure to provide spaces in these situations, or you'll generate syntax errors as shown.

After you've created the buffered statement, you need to send it to SQL Server to be executed. You use the `SqlExec` statement to accomplish this:

```
Status% = SqlExec(MyConnection%)
```

Because you've queued up the commands and associated them with the particular connection, `SqlExec` knows exactly what you're executing. It sends the buffered statement to SQL Server and allows SQL to translate and run your request. In this example, the entire command that would be sent to SQL Server would be `Select * from pubs where author like 'A%'` (adding in the required spaces as indicated earlier).

N O T E If you want to call a stored procedure, you can create your command and preface it with `Execute`. For example:

```
...
Status% = SqlCmd(MyConnection%,"Execute GetAuthors 'A%'")
...
```

In this case, you'd be executing a stored procedure called `GetAuthors` and passing a parameter, `'A%'` to the stored procedure, presumably to be used as a search value. Executing the call and processing the results occur the same as if you had issued a select statement. ■

Working with Results Sets

After you've sent your request to SQL Server, you need to be able to work with the information returned from the query. To do so, you need to use two constants to monitor your work with the data sets. These constants are defined in the .BAS files, which are required to develop with the DB-LIB libraries. They are:

- SUCCEED

- NOMOREROWS

When you process returned results sets from SQL Server, you're walking down the rows returned until you receive NOMOREROWS, indicating that all rows that were returned have been accessed by your application. You can retrieve the current status of the record set by using the SqlResults% function. This function returns either SUCCEED or NOMOREROWS, and your application can determine what to do next based on this information.

```
Status% = SqlResults%(MyConnection%)
```

You should call SqlResults before launching into any processing loops. This ensures that you're not working with an empty data set. If you have successfully returned information from your query, you can loop through the results by using SqlNextRow%. SqlNextRow, as the name suggests, works down through the rows in your results, one at a time. The results are placed into the working buffer so you can work with them. When SqlNextRow hits the end of the data set, it returns NOMOREROWS, allowing your application to stop processing the data set.

N O T E Results returned from DB-LIB's functions are enumerated, rather than named, properties. As you work with columns returned, you indicate the column by number, not name. You need to keep in mind the order in which you specify the columns in your select statement or stored procedure. If you do not, the information column you requested might not return what you expect, as it would be returning a different column's information. ■

The final step in working with the information is to retrieve it from the buffer. SqlData and SqlDatLen are the functions that are regularly used to work with this information. Listing 22.1 shows how a sample processing loop would be implemented, allowing you to print the author name.

Listing 22.1 Sample Processing Loop

```
...
Status% = SqlCmd(MyConnection%,"Select au_lname from authors")
Status% = SqlExec(MyConnection%)
While SqlNextRow%(MyConnection%) <> NOMOREROWS
     Print SqlData$(MyConnection%,1)
Wend
Print "No more information to present."
...
```

Closing the SQL Connection

After you've finished working with a given connection, be sure to close the connection, freeing up the memory associated with it and releasing the connection to the server. The SqlClose function closes an associated connection for just this purpose:

```
Status% = SqlClose%(MyConnection%)
```

You need to close each connection you open for access to the server. Alternatively, you might want to call SqlExit, which closes all currently open connections to the server. If your application has completed and is exiting, it might be easier to use the SqlExit statement to ensure that all connections are closed properly.

Client Configuration

Aside from distributing the OCX with your client application, no other modules are required with the client application. The functionality of the DB-LIB add-in is provided in the OCX and .BAS files.

In the C environment, you need to include the appropriate DLLs with your application and network environment. The DLLs will vary depending on the LIBs you employ, as mentioned previously. Please refer to Tables 22.2 and 22.3 for more information.

Advantages and Disadvantages of Using DB-Library

DB-LIB is an SQL Server-specific interface layer. Of the three options presented here, this is the least "portable" between back-end database servers, but is one of the faster ways to access information. This is due not only to the fact that it's an optimized interface, but also that you're developing directly in the host language. The other options, ODBC and SQL OLE, offer similar services but also impose an abstraction layer between your application and the calls to SQL Server.

One thing you might notice is that DB-LIB is very manual in how it is implemented. This is because you create and issue the Select statements, you create and issue the Update statements, and so on. There is no concept of bound, or automatically updating, values. This can be good in that you can control the interface to the server, optimizing the connections and making sure that all data meets your criteria. In addition, you have complete control over the error trapping associated with the transactions.

DB-LIB is an excellent API-level interface to SQL Server. Keep in mind that this is not the method you use to work with SQL Server through more user-oriented tools like Access and Excel. These types of tools use an abstraction layer, Open Database Connectivity (ODBC), to make working with the database less developer-intensive.

Understanding Open Database Connectivity (ODBC)

If you've been working in the personal computer industry for any length of time, you know that there are a significant number of database applications that different people have installed to address different needs. Gone are the days when you could count on a specific database type at the installation site. This is especially true if you're developing a utility program, such as one that is expected to query a database, regardless of where that database came from, who designed it, and so on.

ODBC attempts to rectify this; although, as you'll see, there are some costs involved with this approach. Your best-case solution depends on a number of factors, including how diverse the database types are in the location or locations where you plan to deploy any given solution.

Where Do SQL-DMO Objects Fit In?

With the introduction of Visual Basic 4, Microsoft also introduced the new SQL Data Management Objects, or SQL-DMO. These make it easier to work with the different objects associated with a database, including the database, table, rules, and so on.

SQL-DMO is created by working with OBJECTS in Visual Basic. If you're not familiar with objects, make sure you understand the concept of creating new objects, working with properties in general, working with collections, and so on.

You also need to understand how to set up the references from within Visual Basic to point to the SQL object. You set up the object type by using the following statement:

```
Dim objSQLServer as New SQLOLE.SQLServer
```

After this is established, you can work with the different objects associated with SQL Server by referencing them as you would other properties, methods, and collections associated with other objects. For example, to work with Tables in a given database, you can reference them as shown in Listing 22.2:

Listing 22.2 Working With Tables

```
Dim objSQLServer as NEW SQLOLE.SQLServer
dim objDatabase as SQLOle.Database
objSQLServer.Connect "sqlserver1", "dbdev", "devpw"
For Each objDatabase in objSQLServer.Databases
     Msgbox "Database name: " & objDatabase.Name
Next
Set oSQLServer = Nothing
```

You can see several things at work here. First, the declaration of the SQL Server object makes the connection to the server possible. Next, using the Connect method, the connection to the server is established. The server name in this example is SQLSERVER1 and the user ID and password are DBDEV and DEVPW, respectively.

N O T E If you leave out the reference to the user name and password, you are prompted for them when the application runs. ■

Next, during the for...next loop, the database object's NAME property is displayed in the message box, showing each database available on the server.

Finally, the connection to SQL Server is dropped when the object is set to NOTHING. This releases the connection and the objects associated with it on the client system.

The balance of the objects you'll work with are objects, collections, properties, and methods on the SQL-DMO object. You can access them as you do any other automated object. In addition, you can send commands to SQL Server using the ExecuteImmediate and ExecuteWithResults methods. These allow you to send SQL Statements directly to the server.

Where Do the Data Access Objects (DAO) Fit In?

The Data Access Objects, or DAO, are objects, methods, and properties that make it easier to work with your database. While they still use the ODBC access layers for the transactions with SQL Server, they add an abstract layer between you, the developer, and the ODBC calls needed to accomplish your requests.

The DAO is also the preferred method of accessing your information for use with the Internet Information Server's Active Server Pages and will become more prevalent in the future as more of the tools used to generate Web pages become standardized.

With the DAO, you use collections of objects to work with databases, tables, views, and so on. It's much simpler to refer to an .ADD method on an object to add a new table than it is to use the standard ODBC approach and reference stored procedures. As another example, most collections will have standard property sets. In the following code, the .COUNT property shows the number of TableDefs, or table definitions, in the current database:

```
'Determine how many tables there are and then print
'the results.
i = db.TableDefs.Count
Debug.Print "There are " & Str$(i) & " table(s) in this database."
```

Using these standardized approaches to working with the database, you can help leverage your knowledge to work with just about any datasource accessible by ODBC. In addition, these work in other languages and other environments. For example, the DAO is accessible in Visual Basic for all versions currently available and will be supported into the future.

The examples in the balance of this chapter often reference the DAO form of accessing the feature covered. This helps outline how you use the different properties and methods to work with SQL Server.

Concepts and Characteristics

To address the concern of connectivity to and between database systems, Microsoft developed the ODBC approach. ODBC is a layer of abstraction between the application and the underlying database system. This layer allows you to issue one Select statement and have that statement run against any supported database, including some cases where the databases do not directly support the SQL language.

ODBC serves as the access layer to the operating system and database files. ODBC is responsible for taking your request for information and changing it into the language the database engine will understand and use for retrieving the information in the database.

ODBC presents a common interface to your application. This allows you to develop to a common set of calls and methodologies without having to worry about the subtleties of the underlying database. You can see an excellent example of this in Microsoft Access. In Access, you can choose to link or attach a table to a database. When you do, Access prompts you for the type of database table you want to work with. You have the option of selecting from several formats that Access works with directly, or you can simply select ODBC. When you do, you are presented with the different ODBC configurations you've established. Thus, you are able to select any one of them without regard to database engine.

Access can attach the table to the database because it doesn't know or care about the database. It only knows that it can use the database table with standardized SQL statements, which is the key to ODBC.

Because the main purpose of ODBC is to abstract the conversation with the underlying database engine, the use of ODBC is somewhat transparent after you're connected. This is different when compared with DB-LIB reviewed earlier. DB-LIB required special syntax to buffer statements and work directly with the server. ODBC, on the other hand, requires only that you create the standardized SQL statement and then pass that statement to ODBC.

Understanding ODBC Sessions

When you work with ODBC in your application, you are working with a data source and the database engine it references. As you'll see under the "Client Configuration" section, when you install ODBC, you should install not only the overall ODBC subsystem but also driver-to-database combinations. These combinations are given names and then used in your connection request when you want to access the database they refer to. These database and driver combinations are called *Data Source Names*, or *DSNs*. When you open an ODBC connection and don't otherwise specify this information, ODBC steps in and prompts you for it.

In most languages, when you specify the connect string for ODBC, you have a couple of options. First, you can specify only that it's an ODBC connection you want to open, in which case ODBC steps in and prompts you for the DSN to use.

```
Set db = OpenDatabase("",,"odbc;")
```

In this case, the information provided by the user determines the database that is opened. You can also specify the connection to use by indicating the DSN, UserID, and Password for the connection, as applicable.

```
Set db = OpenDatabase("",,"odbc;<DSN Info>")
```

CAUTION

If you allow your user to specify the ODBC connection to use, you might end up working against a database that you have not planned to interact with. In nearly all cases, your application should provide the DSN information that allows ODBC to connect to the database, ensuring that you know the database schema for the information sources you're accessing.

Your second option is to indicate the details for the connection in the connection string itself. In this type of connection, <DSN Info> represents any of the different items you can specify as part of the DSN. Some of the more commonly used items are shown in Table 22.5.

Table 22.5 Common DSN Elements

Element	Description
DSN	The DSN name you have configured in the ODBC settings
UID	The userID to use to log in to the database
PWD	The password to use for the login

For example, consider the following sample VBA statement:

```
Set db = OpenDatabase("",,"odbc;DSN=MyDSN;UID=MyUserName;PWD=MyPassword")
```

This connects to the ODBC data source using the MyDSN configuration. It also uses the user and password indicated in the parameters. Using this command, the user is not prompted for ODBC DSN information, but is connected automatically.

N O T E   In this example, the db variable represents a VB variable declared as a Database object type. In this example, the db variable will be the reference point for future actions against the database. ■

In this example, we're using some of the DAO to access the ODBC data source. Using this access method, you can work through the tables, fields, and information stored in the database system by using common objects and object browsing methodologies. For a simple example, consider Listing 22.3.

Listing 22.3 Example of Connecting to ODBC with DAO

```
Sub DAOExample()
    'set up the variables
    Dim db As DATABASE
    Dim i As Integer

    'connect to the database
    Set db = OpenDatabase("", , "odbc;DSN=BILLING;UID=SA;PWD=;")

    'Determine how many tables there are and then print
    'the results.
    i = db.TableDefs.Count
    Debug.Print "There are " & Str$(i) & " table(s) in this database."

    'Close the connection
    db.Close
End Sub
```

The output from this routine is a statement indicating the number of tables in the database. By using the object-oriented nature of DAO, it's easy to work quickly with the database connection after it's been established.

The final step to working with SQL is to close the connection. The specifics of how you close it can vary between host languages, but in VB or VBA, you can simply use the .Close method. This closes the connection to the database and frees up the memory structures associated with the connection.

Client Configuration

ODBC drivers are installed when you install SQL Server client utilities. They are also installed or updated when you install several Microsoft products such as Office 95 and Access 95. The drivers are installed on your system, but you still need to create the specific DSNs that you'll be referencing when you open a connection to the database.

The ODBC Administrator is located on the Control Panel, shown in Figure 22.1.

FIG. 22.1

The ODBC Administrator is used to manage new and existing ODBC DSNs.

The Administrator allows you to select from the known ODBC connections so you can make any necessary changes. You can also add new DSNs to your system. Figure 22.2 shows the initial ODBC DSN listing and the different options you can access to manage the DSNs.

FIG. 22.2

The DSN names listed are the names you specify in the ODBC connection string.

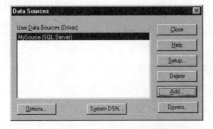

In the next section, you'll see how you can work with new and existing DSNs as well as set up your system so you can take advantage of ODBC in your applications.

Working with ODBC DSNs

From the ODBC Data Sources dialog box, you have two options that relate to managing ODBC connections. The Setup and New options let you specify the different characteristics of the DSNs you establish. Figure 22.3 shows a sample dialog box of options for setting up a SQL Server connection. Note that the dialog box is the same for both setting up a new connection and making changes to an existing connection.

FIG. 22.3

When you set up ODBC connections, you should indicate as much information as possible to make connecting easier for the user of your applications.

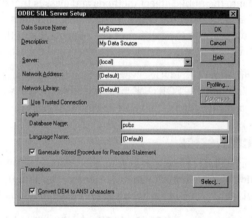

The figure shows the Options portion of the dialog box extended, allowing access to the default database and other less-often used options. The following are key options that you should always set up:

- Data Source Name
- Description
- Server

You should always try to establish the Database Name, as well. Doing so helps ensure that, when the connection is made, it is to the correct database and does not rely on the default database assigned to the user that is logging in.

Advantages and Disadvantages of Using ODBC

Because ODBC provides the abstract access to just about any popular database format available, it brings a fair amount of leverage to your development effort. A key element in the ODBC framework is the capability for your DSN name to refer to any database. This allows you to develop against an Access database and implement your system in production against an SQL Server just by changing the drivers used by the DSN you've defined for the application.

The abstraction of the calls to the database engine is not without cost. The biggest downside to ODBC is that it must be able to support the capability to translate the calls. This means that additional processing overhead can slow the data access a bit. With ODBC, you can gain a significant speed advantage with a true client/server implementation. By taking the processing away from the client and into the server within SQL Server, you can eliminate much of the scrolling of information that is one of the primary slowing points for ODBC.

Consider using stored procedures as the basis for your ODBC calls when database engine processing is required. This saves processing time on both ends of the spectrum.

Understanding the SQL OLE Interface

As you already might be aware, the vast majority of development in emerging technologies is going on in object-oriented development. Microsoft, and other software tool builders, has a major push to bring out into the public object methods and classes that can be reused by third-party developers. This can be seen in the Office 97 suite of applications in their consistent use of Objects and Classes to work with their different components. Everything from sheets in Excel to TableDefs in Access is now accessible with objects and collection.

This accessibility is no different with SQL Server. In one of the newest developments for developers of SQL-based applications, the SQL OLE interface allows you to work with SQL Server using objects, methods, and collections that relate to your database.

Concepts and Characteristics

By including Type Library (TLB) references in your application environment, you can begin using the OLE automation objects to work with SQL Server. The TLB that you need for Visual Basic applications is SQLOLE32.TLB. This library exposes the methods you'll be using.

In short, you use the .Connect method for attaching to SQL Server to begin working with the database. You then are able to use the different objects and collections to perform the administrative tasks associated with SQL Server. It might be easiest to review the SQL Enterprise Manager for examples of how these containers and objects relate to one another.

You work with the SQL OLE objects by first setting up the object variables that refer to the SQL OLE objects. The first step is to set up the reference to the TLB for SQL OLE.

After you've established the references, you can create the routines you need to work with the objects. Listing 22.4 shows setting up a reference to the Database object, followed by printing the tables in the collection to the debug window.

Listing 22.4 Using SQL OLE in Visual Basic Code

```
Sub SQL OLEDemo()
    'declare the variables
    Dim objSQLServer As New SQL OLE.SQLServer
    Dim objDatabase As New SQL OLE.DATABASE
    Dim objTable As New SQL OLE.TABLE

    'connect to the server
    objSQLServer.Connect "pluto", "sa", ""

    'get the PUBS database
```

Part
V

Ch
22

```
Set objDatabase = objSQLServer("pubs")

'iterate through the tables
For Each objTable In objDatabase
    Debug.Print objTable
Next

'disconnect from the server
Set objSQLServer = Nothing

End Sub
```

As you can see, by using the objects and collections in the SQL OLE suite, you can easily navigate the SQL Server you are administering. This gives you the added benefit of providing a concise set of capabilities to your users, possibly limiting access to certain features while granting ready access to others.

Advantages and Disadvantages of Using SQL OLE

SQL OLE requires a good working knowledge of the architecture of SQL Server. If you haven't spent much time in the Enterprise Manager, it might be difficult to picture the object model and work within it. This can be a hindrance for people developing their first application to manage SQL Server. It's probably not a good idea to use SQL OLE and building administrative applications as your first work with SQL Server. SQL OLE will be more meaningful and more useful to you after you've had a chance to become used to the object-oriented nature of managing SQL Server using the native tools available.

On the plus side, the SQL OLE objects provide you with easy, comprehensive, and ready access to the objects that make up the SQL Server's core functionality. By knowing these objects inside and out, you can provide more comprehensive administration of the system, simply because you know and understand the relationships between objects. Also, as mentioned previously, if you have people that are responsible for administering certain aspects of the system, but you need to limit their overall access to high-level tasks, a custom administrative application can be just the ticket. Also, there is no easier way to work with the SQL objects than using the SQL OLE suite of capabilities.

Reality Check

Your choice of how you develop applications to work with SQL Server will depend on a number of factors. At the top of that list is likely the budget, both in dollars and in time, that you have allocated to the project.

With a system that you need to bring on-line quickly, it's typically been found that using the ODBC approach to working with the database is often most practical. As you move through the options, from ODBC to DAO to DB-Lib and so on, performance will increase, but the developer's time will also increase. In addition, you'll find that the application becomes more and more specific to the solution you're trying to provide. This can be an issue if you're trying to create a utility for general use, as compared to a utility to fulfill a specific need.

In solutions developed at customer locations, I've found that reporting and querying applications are best served by the ODBC approach in nearly every case. DB Lib (or other developer library-type approaches) is the tool of choice when developing a complete application that will be used to add, change, delete, and query database tables.

From Here...

You've had a whirlwind tour of the different techniques and technologies that are available to you for working with and administering your SQL Server system and its databases. By combining these technologies with the comprehensive coverage throughout this book on the SQL language and the capabilities of SQL Server, you can develop comprehensive applications for working with SQL Server.

From here, consider reviewing the following related materials:

- Chapter 5, "Creating Devices, Databases, and Transaction Logs," and Chapter 6, "Creating Database Tables and Using Datatypes," detail the different objects in SQL Server and how you can create and manage them. Knowing the relationships between these objects is helpful should you need to develop your own administrative applications using SQL OLE.

- Chapter 7, "Retrieving Data with Transact-SQL," reviews the syntax for the SQL language and how you use it to work with the tables in SQL Server.

Understanding SQL Server and the Internet

Corporate database systems are built on making information widely available to qualified users. The information in these situations comes from many sources, ranging from discussion groups to proprietary systems. Probably the biggest repository of "mass" information is the database. If you've ever just browsed a database without specifying meaningful criteria, you know what is meant by "mass" information. There is often so much information represented that it actually makes it less useful.

By making databases available on your site, you can help users make sense of this information and, at the same time, you'll be able to provide access and presentation without the need for any special software to begin using the database effectively. In short, you have a new avenue to provide this access to the information that is probably already stored on your network.

Database access with the IIS system is provided by giving you ODBC connectivity to the HTML pages that execute on the server when the user makes a request of the system. In this chapter, you'll see how to set up pages, what types of information you can provide, and how you can enhance the presentation of the information to make it the most meaningful to the people who request it. ∎

Find out how to database-enable your site

You'll see how to use the Internet Database Connector to add dynamic Web pages to your site.

Learn how to use the SQL Web Page Wizard

SQL Server's Web Page Wizard helps you create pages that can call stored procedures, run scheduled queries, and much more.

Learn key settings to make logging access to databases work for you

Without some key entries in your system configuration, you may have a difficult time getting valuable logging information from your system. Find out the key ingredients for successful access to your database.

Find out how Active Server pages and new Internet Components work

There are strong efforts being made to build database access into Web sites. These efforts include creating database components that give you DAO-like access to databases from within your HTML pages.

CAUTION

Be aware that the database connector files are likely to contain and convey sensitive and sometimes very confidential information. For example, they'll contain query information that calls out column names, table names, and database sources that map to your ODBC configurations on the server.

In addition, when users click a link to a database connector file, they'll be able to see where you're keeping your scripts and other programs, because it will show up in the URL that is displayed to them.

It is extremely important that your programs, scripts, and supporting files reside in the scripts subdirectory structure and that you provide Execute Only privileges on that directory. Be sure you do not provide Read privileges. This will open your system to unneeded possibilities for trouble, because people would be able to browse and review the applications that are the core of your system.

Setting Up the Internet Database Connector

The Internet Information Server provides access to the ODBC layer with the use of the Internet Database Connector, or IDC. The IDC acts as a go-between for your system, providing the interaction between what is seen in the viewer in terms of HTML and how the information is queried at the database level. The overall access layer map is shown in Figure 23.1.

FIG. 23.1
The IDC provides for access to any ODBC data source.

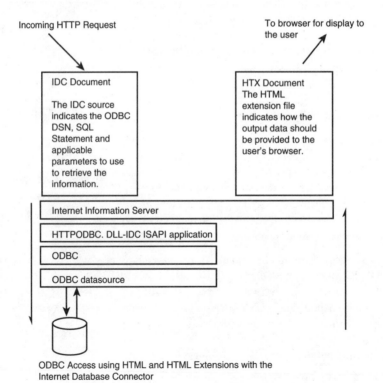

ODBC Access using HTML and HTML Extensions with the Internet Database Connector

When users specify the IDC file in the URL from the browser, they are asking the IIS system to use the IDC file and its statements to query the database and return the results. The IDC is specified in the URL, but the HTX file, or HTML Extension file, is what is actually returned to the user. The HTX file, still a standard HTML file, indicates how the resulting data is displayed, what lines constitute the detail lines of information, and more.

From Figure 23.1, you can see that the engine that is doing the database work with ODBC is HTTPODBC.DLL. This DLL, included when you install the IIS system, is an Internet Server API, or ISAPI, application that runs as an extension to the server software. This extension is database-aware and is able to use the two source files, the IDC and HTX files, required to give the information back to the user.

Part
V
Ch
23

If you did not install the ODBC component of IIS, you'll need to do so to use the IDC. This not only installs the ODBC portions of the environment, but it also configures the server to be aware of the IDC files you'll be using. If you do not install the ODBC components, when users click the IDC link on their Web page, they'll see a prompt to download the IDC file, rather than view the results of the query. See Figure 23.2 for an example of this prompt.

FIG. 23.2
If the server does not recognize the database connector, it will try to download the IDC page to the requesting user, rather than processing it and returning the results.

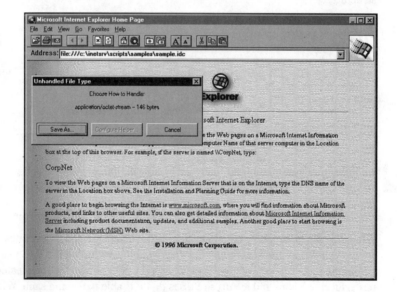

When you install IIS, the ODBC option must be selected. Though it may not indicate disk space requirements if you have already installed ODBC from other applications, it will still be necessary to install it to activate the IDC capabilities. See Figure 23.3.

FIG. 23.3
It's a good rule of thumb to select ODBC for all installations—the setup program is also careful not to overwrite any newer versions of the drivers you may have installed on your system.

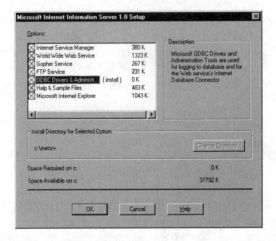

Listing 23.1 shows a sample IDC file taken from the samples included with the server. The sample installs into the \SCRIPTS\SAMPLES subdirectory on your system in the IIS directory structure.

Listing 23.1   A Simple IDC Source File

```
Data source: web sql
Username: sa
Template: sample.htx
SQLStatement:
+SELECT au_lname, ytd_sales from pubs.dbo.titleview
➥where ytd_sales>5000
```

TIP You can indicate more than one SQL statement by using the IDC parameter more than once in the IDC file. Start each SQL statement with the SqlStatement: heading. You'll be able to access both results sets in the HTX file.

When this file is loaded by IIS, IIS examines the extension and determines what application should be used for the source file. For certain items, including the IDC extension, the server comes pre-installed, knowing what to do with the source when it's requested. One of the very powerful capabilities and features of IIS is that it is able to use the same Windows-based extension resolution to determine what to do with a given request. Files with a .GIF extension, for example, are known to be graphic images, and files with an .IDC extension are database connector "applets." You set up custom keys in the Registry. Associations are set up in the tree location shown next.

> **CAUTION**
>
> Any time you work with the Registry you should use extreme caution. Making entries in incorrect locations or with incorrect syntax can render your system inoperable.

You'll use the Regedt32 application to modify the registry. When you start it, look for the following key:

```
location:HKEY_LOCAL_MACHINE
        SYSTEM
             CurrentControlSet
                  Services
                            W3SVC
                                  Parameters
                                       ScriptMap
```

If you add a new entry, make it of the type REG_SZ and indicate the extension to associate. You'll need to include the period before the extension—for example, .IDC—to correctly map the association. For the value, indicate the path and file name that should be executed when the specified extension is loaded. Remember to provide the path from the root and start the path with a backslash, because this will ensure that IIS will be able to locate the application, regardless of the current working directory.

If you are indicating parameters to the call, you can use %s on the key value where you indicate the application to run. For example, suppose that you have a DLL that you want to run whenever a request is received to open a file with a .FUN extension. Your entry would be as follows:

```
.fun = c:\inetsrv\scripts\test\fundll.dll %s %s
```

When you use this option, the first time you use the %s, you'll receive the application to run that was passed to the URL. For example, if your FUNDLL is an application that processes a text file and searches it for a given value, you would expect the user to be passing in the text file and the value to search for. When you provide the URL at the browser level, you first indicate the location of the file you want to run. A question mark is next, followed by any applicable parameters to the call.

For the examples here, the URL that would be used would be something like the following:

```
http://holodeck3/scripts/search.fun?text+to+find
```

The resulting command line would be

```
c:\inetsrv\scripts\test\fundll.dll search.fun text+to+find
```

where each of the two items specified, the source file and search text, is passed as a parameter.

N O T E Because parameters are passed as a single string to your application, as in the previous example with the text+to+find string, your application must be able to parse out the plus signs and rebuild the string, most likely in a buffer that can be used by your application to search the database or text file, as needed. ▪

The results-formatting file, or HTX file, is where things can get a little tricky. As you'll see throughout this chapter, the real power and capability of your system is exposed with the HTX file. Until the information is provided to the template, it's of no use to the requester as he or she will not yet have seen the information. You can have one of the best, most comprehensive databases around, but if the presentation of the data is not what your audience needs, the information might as well be under lock and key.

Listing 23.2 shows a simple HTX template, provided in the samples with the IIS product, that displays the results of a query.

Listing 23.2   HTX Source Files Provide Template Information for the Display of Results from Database Queries

```
<HTML>
<HEAD><TITLE>Authors and YTD Sales</TITLE></HEAD>
<BODY BACKGROUND="/samples/images/backgrnd.gif">
<BODY BGCOLOR="FFFFFF">
<TABLE>
<TR>
<TD><IMG SRC="/samples/images/SPACE.gif" ALIGN="top" ALT=" "></TD>
<TD><A HREF="/samples/IMAGES/db_mh.map"><IMG SRC="/SAMPLES/images/db_mh.gif"
➥ismap BORDER=0 ALIGN="top" ALT=" "></A></TD>
</TR>
<tr>
<TD></TD>
<TD>
<hr>
<font size=2>
<CENTER>
<%if idc.sales eq ""%>
<H2>Authors with sales greater than <I>5000</I></H2>
<%else%>
<H2>Authors with sales greater than <I><%idc.sales%></I></H2>
<%endif%>
<P>
<TABLE BORDER>
<%begindetail%>
<%if CurrentRecord EQ 0 %>
<caption>Query results:</caption>
<TR>
<TH><B>Author</B></TH><TH><B>YTD Sales<BR>(in dollars)</B></TH>
</TR>
<%endif%>
<TR><TD><%au_lname%></TD><TD align="right">$<%ytd_sales%></TD></TR>
<%enddetail%>
<P>
</TABLE>
</center>
<P>
<%if CurrentRecord EQ 0 %>
<I><B>Sorry, no authors had YTD sales greater than </I><%idc.sales%>.</B>
```

```
<P>
<%else%>
<HR>
<I>
The web page you see here was created by merging the results
of the SQL query with the template file SAMPLE.HTX.
<P>
The merge was done by the Microsoft Internet Database Connector and the results
 were returned to this web browser by the Microsoft Internet Information Server.
</I>
<%endif%>
</font>
</td>
</tr>
</table>
</BODY>
</HTML>
```

You'll probably notice several different things right away with this file. First, it's a standard HTML document. There is no strange formatting to speak of, and certainly many of the tags will be familiar if you've developed HTML before. Some of the real fun begins in the new capabilities offered by the HTX file. These new functions, above and beyond standard HTML, enable you to have the resulting Web page react to and change depending on the information that is, or is not, returned from the query. For example, in the section of code noted in the following, you'll see the introduction of conditional testing, examining for an empty set:

```
<%if idc.sales eq ""%>
      <H2>Authors with sales greater than <I>5000</I></H2>
<%else%>
      <H2>Authors with sales greater than <I><%idc.sales%></I></H2>
<%endif%>
```

Several operators are available when you design your pages. Throughout this chapter, you'll learn more about how to use these new database-oriented features.

As mentioned earlier, the IDC source file indicates the ODBC data source that is used to access the database on your system. From the IDC file listing, notice the Data source item. This item indicates that the web sql data source will be used. Before this sample will work on your system, you must have installed and configured the data source for that name using the ODBC control panel applet.

In the next couple of sections, you'll see how to set up the ODBC data sources for both SQL Server and Microsoft Access. You can use any 32-bit ODBC data source with your IIS application, and changes between setting up other data sources should be minimal; therefore, if you use the information presented here, you'll find that the IDC can work with nearly any database installation you may need to use.

Building ODBC Data Sources for SQL Server Databases

One of the most common reasons for problems with the database connector is the setup of the ODBC data source. This is true across database sources not specific to SQL Server, so it's important to understand the details of setting up the driver for access by IIS.

You may recall that IIS is running as a service. This means that while it's running, it's not logged in as you, the administrator; instead, it's running in the background, logging in when needed as either the anonymous user you've set up or as the validated user that's been authenticated by the NT security subsystem. Because you want to give this service access to a database, and because you don't know whom the service will be logging in as, you need to set up the database source a bit differently than you may be accustomed to.

Microsoft has added a new option to the ODBC configurations to support a System DSN. These special data sources give you a way to set up a globally available data source. Because users who log on may be set up to have different access to your system and resources, you need to use the System DSN to make sure they have access to the right databases, regardless of where they log in or who they log in as. Figure 23.4 shows the ODBC setup dialog box, started from the Control Panel.

 TIP If you find that you receive errors trying to access an ODBC data source from your Web pages, one of the first things you should check is that the data source you're referencing is set up as a system data source.

When you start the ODBC manager utility, if the data source is listed in the initial dialog box, it's defined as a user-based data source, not a System DSN. Remove the user-based DSN and redefine it as a System DSN, and you'll be able to see the database.

Remember that the only data sources that the Database Connector can use are the System-level data sources.

FIG. 23.4
ODBC setup for IIS requires that you select the System DSN to configure the driver.

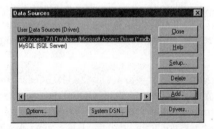

After you select System DSN, you'll be able to use essentially the same options to set up the drivers. Note, too, that you can have more than one driver set up at the system level. This allows you to set up drivers for the different applications you'll be running on the Web. Figure 23.5 shows the Data Sources set up dialog box.

FIG. 23.5
Setting up a system-level ODBC driver configuration is much the same as establishing a new ODBC configuration. You'll need to indicate the driver, database, and other information required to connect to your database engine.

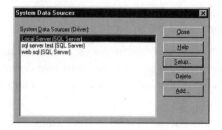

The Data Source Name you provide is what you'll be using in the IDC file as the data source, so be sure to make note of the database configuration names you set up.

In most cases, you'll want the configuration to be as specific as possible. If it's possible to indicate a default database or table, be sure to do so. It will take some of the variables out of the Web page design you'll be doing. By specifying as much information as possible, you'll help ensure that the information is accessible.

Building ODBC Database Sources for Microsoft Access Databases

Microsoft Access database data sources are established the same way as they are for SQL Server. You must set up each data source as a System DSN, making it available to the IDC as it logs in to NT's security subsystem.

Of course, there will likely be changes in the SQLStatement options you indicate in the IDC file. These differences relate to how Access interprets the SQL language elements. However, the statements should be nearly identical, especially in those cases where you're issuing SQL statements that are basically SELECT statements, rather than calling stored procedures, which are not supported by Access.

When you create the DSN, you'll be prompted to select the database with which ODBC should connect. Be sure to provide this information because, even though you can indicate it in code, you can make the connection to the database far more bulletproof with this option turned on. The system won't have to guess where to go to get the information.

User Rights and Security Concerns

Database access using the IDC provides a wide-open query system to your database. You should not allow users to have system administrator-level access to your databases just because it provides a way for someone to gain unwanted administrative access to your system. Instead, consider one of two options. First, if you're allowing anonymous connections to your site, be sure the user you have indicated as the anonymous user (usually IUSR_<machine name>) has appropriate rights to the databases that will be needed.

The way the login process works is to first validate the user using the anonymous login if it's enabled. If enabled and the user indicated as the anonymous user does not have sufficient rights, he'll receive an error message that indicates the fact that he may not have rights to the object(s) requested.

If anonymous login is disabled, the IDC will use the current user's name and password to log on to the database. If this login fails to gain access, the request is denied, and the user is prevented from accessing the database requested.

In short, if you want anonymous users gaining access to your system, you'll need to create the user account you want to access the information. Next, assign the user to the database and objects, allowing access to the systems needed.

The second option you have is to use NT's integrated security with SQL Server. Using this method, the currently logged-in user will be logged on to SQL Server, and the same rights will be in force.

Building Dynamic Web Pages

Dynamic Web pages, those that build themselves on-the-fly to provide up-to-date information, are going to quickly become the mainstay of the intranet and Internet. This is because with a dynamic Web page, you can always count on getting the latest and greatest information. With the IDC, you can create these dynamic Web pages and have them work against a database to retrieve the information you need to let the user review.

There are three components to this type of page:

- Initial source HTML document often containing form fields or other options
- The IDC file for making and carrying out the database commands and data acquisition
- The HTX file for presenting the information returned

While it's not the intent of this book to teach all aspects of HTML, it's important to keep in mind that the samples provided are just that—samples. You'll need to take these samples and adapt them to your organization's way of doing business on the Internet. In short, the HTML code that may be required consists of the field, listbox, and checkbox options provided by HTML. By using these options and the ODBC connectivity, you enable the user to search the possibilities for making a meaningful interface for the user.

When you create a form that you'll be using to prompt the user for information, you create fields and other controls much as you do when creating an application. You'll name the fields and then pass the name and its value to the IDC to be used in your database query, if you desire. In the next sections, you'll see how to create these files and what makes them drive the output pages with the information from the database.

Building Initial Forms to Prompt for Values

Generally speaking, you'll start the process of working with a database by presenting the users with a form, allowing them to select what information they need. As will often be the case, you have the ability to create forms that allow input that can be used to form the SQL statements you'll be passing to the data source. In the cases where you're creating a form, you'll see two basic HTML tags: the <INPUT> and <FORM> tags that allow you to designate actions to take and information to accept on behalf of the user. Listing 23.3 shows a simple form that prompts for an author name to be searched for in the author's table.

Listing 23.3   Simple HTML Form to Initiate a Database Query— (*queform.htm*)

```
<HTML>
<HEAD>
<TITLE>
Que Publishing's Very Simple Demonstration Form
</TITLE>
</HEAD>
<h1>Sample Form for Database Access</h1>
<FORM METHOD="POST" ACTION="/scripts/que/QueForm1.idc">
Enter Name to Find in the Pubs Database: <INPUT NAME="au_lname">
<p>
<INPUT TYPE="SUBMIT" VALUE="Run Query">
</FORM>
</BODY>
</HTML>
```

The key elements are the "POST" instructions and the text box presented to the user. The <FORM> tag indicates what should happen when the form is executed. In this case, the form will send information to the server, hence the POST method. The <ACTION> tag calls out the program or procedure that is run on the server to work with the information sent in. In the example, the QUEFORM1.IDC is called and passed the parameters.

N O T E   The letter case is not significant when you're specifying HTML tags. "INPUT" is the same as indicating "input" and will not cause any different results when it's processed by IIS. ■

It's not immediately apparent what those parameters might be, but if you examine the one or more INPUT fields, you can see that they are named. The following syntax is the basic, required element if you need to pass information back to the host in a forms-based environment:

```
<INPUT NAME="<variable name>">
```

The <variable name> is the name you'll use to reference the value provided by the user. Much as you define a variable in Visual Basic by dimensioning it, you must define and declare the different variables and other controls that are used by your HTML. There are other tags that can be used with the <INPUT NAME> tag, including <VALUE>, which allows you to set the initial value of the item you're declaring. For example, the following line declares a new variable, MyName, and assigns an initial value of "Wynkoop" to it:

```
<INPUT NAME="MyName" VALUE="Wynkoop">
```

For the preceding example, the intention is to create a very simple form that allows the user to type in a name, or portion of the name, that can be used to search the Author's table in the Pubs database. When the HTML is loaded as shown in the preceding, Figure 23.6 is the result.

FIG. 23.6
Allowing the user to indicate values to pass to the database engine adds polished, functional benefits to your application.

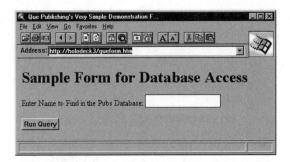

As you can see, the text box size is automatically determined for you as a default. There are <MAXLENGTH> and <SIZE> tags you can place in the INPUT NAME directive if you need to increase the size of the text box. You'll also notice that if you press Enter while you're using this form, the form will automatically be submitted to the server just as if you'd pressed the Submit button. Because there is only a single button on this form, the browser interprets this as a type of "There is only one thing for me to do, so I'll just do it automatically" situation.

What happens in this example from Listing 23.3 is that the browser opens a new URL on the server with the specification

```
http://holodeck3/scripts/que/QueForm1.idc?au_lname=<name>
```

N O T E If you watch your Web browser, it may indicate only that it's loading the URL that is included up to the ? in these examples. The protocol is still passing the parameters to the host; they are simply not shown during the transfer by some browsers. ■

The <NAME> is the name you indicate in the text box prior to pressing Enter or clicking the Submit button. The next step in the process is to run the query against the database engine and see what results are returned.

Building Server Query Source Files

The query source files reside in files in your SCRIPTS area and have a file name extension of .IDC by convention. When the URL is accessed, the server will run the indicated IDC file. As mentioned earlier in this chapter, the IDC file contains the SQL statements and directives necessary to carry out the commands as needed. For this example, Listing 23.4 shows the source for querying the database.

Part
V
Ch
23

> **CAUTION**
>
> To reiterate the note earlier about security, be sure you place your IDC files in directories that have been set up with Execute, but not Read, privileges. This is important because if users can review your source files, they can see column names, table names, SQL login names and passwords, and so on. This is information you want to make sure is private.

Listing 23.4   The IDC File Called by QUEForm.HTM—(*queform1.idc*)

```
Datasource: web sql
Username: sa
Template: queform1.htx
SQLStatement:
+SELECT au_lname, phone, address, city, state, zip
+ from authors
+ where au_lname like '%au_lname%%'
```

The output from this specific file is really nothing. The user will never see this file or output from it directly. This seems a bit strange, but the entire intent of the IDC is to define and perform the query against the data source indicated. After the information is retrieved, the IDC calls the Template indicated and passes in the results to be returned as a Web page.

N O T E   In the example in Listing 23.4, notice that the Where clause specifies like and that there is an extra percent sign in the comparison field. This is standard SQL syntax that allows you to search for wildcarded strings. You specify the part you know, and the IDC will append an extra % character at the end. Because the percent sign is the wildcard for SQL Server, you'll be able to return all items that start with B, for example. ■

Before working down through it, some basics about this source file are important to understand to explain how it works. First, to reference a variable, place it between percentages, as is the case with '%au_lname%' in Listing 23.4. Note that the single quotes are required because the field is a text-based type.

You can reference variables anywhere in the script. This means that even for the items that are seemingly hard-coded, like parameters, you can allow the user to specify them and then call them dynamically from the IDC file.

Second, in cases where your line length is shorter than your actual line, you can call out the item you want to work on, begin specifying the values, and continue indicating the expanding values as long as you place the + in the first column of the file. The plus sign acts as a line-continuation character for these source files.

The data source indicated in the IDC relates to the ODBC data source you establish with the ODBC manager in the control panel. Remember that the data source you use with the IDC must be a system DSN. If it's not, the call to the database will fail.

The Username, and optionally the Password, will override any settings you may have established in ODBC, and they'll override the current user name as well as how it relates to the execution of the query. Other parameters that may be of interest or use in your integration of the IDC file into your installation are shown in Table 23.1.

Table 23.1   IDC Optional Parameters

`RequiredParameters`	By naming the parameters that you must have represented from the form filled out by the user, you can make sure the user didn't just press Enter or otherwise ignore a field. Name the fields you want to assure information from, and IIS will kick back a message if the field is left blank for any reason. When you specify the fields, do not use percent signs but simply name the field. To indicate more than one field, separate each field in the list with a comma.
`DefaultParameters`	You can set up defaults for the fields you are expecting in from the user. Name each field, followed by an equal sign and the value you want it to have. When the field is retrieved from the form, if it's a blank or nonspecified field, the value you indicate will be filled in. Note that `DefaultParameters` are applied prior to `RequiredParameters` being checked, effectively making the use of `RequiredParameters` unneeded if you can indicate an acceptable default. Keep in mind that your page should indicate what the default will be, because the user will not see the substitution that is made in the IDC file when it's processed.
`Expires`	If you submit a query over and over again, you may find that you're retrieving a cached copy of the information rather than an updated database query. This can be especially problematic when developing applications because you'll be continually testing the system, resubmitting queries, and so on. By setting the `<EXPIRES>` tag, established in seconds, to a value that represents a timeframe that should have passed before the query is retried, you will avoid this problem. In other words, how long will it be before the information should be considered "stale" or in need of being refreshed for viewing?
`MaxRecords`	If you are connected over a slower-speed connection, there are few things more frustrating than receiving a huge data file, then realizing that you needed only certain bits of information. For example, you may need to return only the first 100 rows of a table because they will provide the most current, meaningful data to your sales effort. By limiting the `MaxRecords`, you can indicate this in the IDC file, limiting traffic and database interaction with the new option.

You can call SQL Server's stored procedures from an IDC file if you want to specify it in the SQL statement portion of the file. To do so, use the following syntax:

```
EXEC MySP_Name Param1[, Param2...]
```

Include the name of your stored procedure in place of MySP_Name.

In the stored procedure, be sure you're returning results sets, even if they represent only a status value indicating success or failure on the operation. Remember, as with other ODBC data sources, the stored procedure will be passed to the server, and the client will await the response. If your stored procedure does not return a value to the calling routine, you may give the user the impression that you've caused the browser to become frozen.

Part
V
Ch
23

From here, after you've retrieved the values you want to display, you can move on to the results set source files. These files do the work of formatting and displaying information to the user and are explained next.

Building Results Source Files

The results files are where the fun begins in working with the data that comes back from the query. The HTML extension files, with file name extensions of .HTX, are referenced in the Template entry in the IDC. These files dictate how the information is presented, what the user will see, whether items that are returned actually represent links to other items, and so on.

Listing 23.5 shows the sample HTX file for the example you've been reviewing throughout this chapter. You can see that it has a few extra, not-yet-standard items that make the display of information from the database possible.

Listing 23.5   A Sample HTX File—(QueForm1.htx)

```
<!-- Section 1>
<HTML>
<HEAD>
<TITLE>Authors Details</TITLE>
</HEAD>
<TABLE>
<tr>
<TD>
<hr>
<P>
<TABLE BORDER>
 <caption>Query results:</caption>
 <TR>
 <TH><B>Author</B></TH>
 <TH><B>Phone</B></TH>
 <TH><B>Address</B></TH>
 <TH><B>City</B></TH>
 <TH><B>State</B></TH>
 <TH><B>Zip</B></TH>
 </TR>
```

continues

Listing 23.5 Continued

```
<!-- Section 2>
<%begindetail%>
 <TR>
 <TH><B><%au_lname%></B></TH>
 <TH><B><%phone%></B></TH>
 <TH><B><%address%></B></TH>
 <TH><B><%city%></B></TH>
 <TH><B><%state%></B></TH>
 <TH><B><%zip%></B></TH>
 </TR>
<%enddetail%>

<!-- Section 3>
<P>
</TABLE>
<%if CurrentRecord EQ 0%>
  <H2>Sorry, no authors match your search criteria (<%idc.au_lname%>).</H2>
<%else%>
  <H2>Authors with names like "<I><%idc.au_lname%></I>"</H2>
<%endif%>
</center>
</td>
</tr>
</table>
</BODY>
</HTML>
```

When the URL is accessed, the server is going to run the indicated IDC file. As mentioned earlier in this chapter, the IDC file contains the SQL statements and directives necessary to carry out the commands as needed. For this example, Listing 23.4 shows the source for querying the database.

N O T E The lines starting with "`<!--`" are comments and are not interpreted by the HTML client. ■

When you design data-oriented pages, you'll want to make sure you take advantage of HTML's start- and end-tag metaphor. To put it simply, for many of the different items in HTML, when you establish a tag, for instance <HEAD>, until the reciprocal argument, </HEAD>, is encountered, the feature you enabled with the first instance of the keyword is in force.

As you can see in Figure 23.7, the sample file turns on the H1 heading style and then doesn't turn it off, resulting in the entire page using oversized fonts.

In the sample HTML in Listing 23.5, you'll notice that there are three sections called out. These sections are inserted only to make reading and explaining the HTML a bit easier. They aren't necessary for the functioning of the document.

FIG. 23.7
Because HTML tags are evaluated in pairs, missing the closing tag can make a style run through the balance of your HTML document.

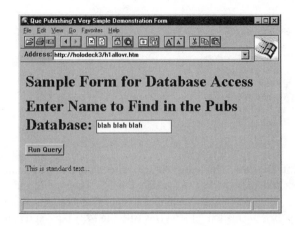

In Section 1, the entire purpose is to set up the page. You'll need to establish fonts, set up background images, do any initial formatting, and so on. You'll also need to start any tables that you want to use. Because you initiate a table, add the rows to it, then turn off the table, tables represent an excellent way to present data that will include an unknown number of rows.

For example, as in Figure 23.8, though two rows are shown, there could just as easily have been 20. The other advantage of using tables to display your database information is that the table will size to the user's visible browser area automatically. You won't need to worry about column widths and other formatting issues.

FIG. 23.8
If you can use tables to display data to the user, you'll be keeping with an already familiar metaphor for the presentation. People are used to table-based data represented in a columnar fashion.

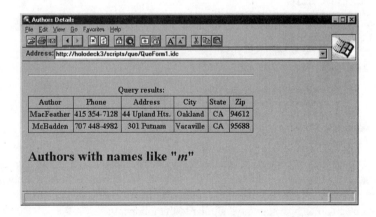

Section 2 is where you'll work with the detail lines that are returned as part of the data set. Notice that this section is bracketed with a <%begindetail%> and <%enddetail%> tags. Everything between these two tags will repeat once for every row returned in the data set. In the preceding example, section 2 consists largely of building the table that will display the information that was returned.

```
<! Section 2>
<%begindetail%>
 <TR>
 <TH><B><%au_lname%></B></TH>
 <TH><B><%phone%></B></TH>
 <TH><B><%address%></B></TH>
 <TH><B><%city%></B></TH>
 <TH><B><%state%></B></TH>
 <TH><B><%zip%></B></TH>
 </TR>
<%enddetail%>
```

When you indicate the data to include, you refer directly to the column names that are in the table or view that is referenced by the IDC file. Place a "<%" before, and "%>" after each column name. In English, the preceding code snippet is reserving a row to put new data into with the <TR> tag, placing the information into the row with the <TH> tags, and ending the row with the closing </TR> tag.

You can do comparisons in your file, as well. For example, if you want to check to make sure that the State was returned as AZ, you could do so in one of two ways. Obviously, the preferred method would be to change your Where clause in the IDC to reflect the fact that you want to filter out non-Arizona states.

Alternatively, you could indicate here that you want to test. Consider the following code sample:

```
<! Section 2>
<%begindetail%>
<%if <%state%> eq "AZ"%>
      <TR>
      <TH><B><%au_lname%></B></TH>
      <TH><B><%phone%></B></TH>
      <TH><B><%address%></B></TH>
      <TH><B><%city%></B></TH>
      <TH><B><%state%></B></TH>
      <TH><B><%zip%></B></TH>
      </TR>
<%endif%>
<%enddetail%>
```

By using the If construct, you can test values and conditions in the data set. You can reference variables that come from the IDC file, as well. To reference these, simply prefix the variable name with IDC. So, if you want to reference the incoming variable from the original HTML form, you can do so by a statement similar to the following:

```
<%if <%idc.au_lname%> eq "Wynkoop">
      <TH><B>Building series…</B></TH>
<%endif%>
```

In this case, the query would go back to the IDC and pull the value for the au_lname variable, make the comparison, and either execute or ignore the statements in the loop following the test. There are three different tests that you can perform. Each is described in Table 23.2.

N O T E You can also use `<%else%>` in your `If...else...endif` loop. ■

Table 23.2   Comparison Operators for Use in HTX Files

EQ   Indicates an equivalent test. "Is item A equal to item B?"

GT   Tests for a condition where one item is greater than the other.

LT   Tests for the condition where one item is less than the other.

In addition, there are two different data set-related variables. `CurrentRecord` allows you to reference the number of times the Detail section has executed. If, after the detail loop has run, you want to determine whether there are records in the data set, you can test this variable to see if it's 0. If it is, no information was returned, and you should display a meaningful message to that effect:

```
<%if CurrentRecord EQ 0>
  <H2>Sorry, no authors match your search crit...
<%else%>
  <H2>Authors with names like "<I><%idc.au_lname%>...
<%endif%>
```

The other tag that corresponds directly to database-oriented actions is the `MaxRecords` option. `MaxRecords` relates to the `MaxRecords` IDC variable. Using this value, you can determine the total number of records that the IDC file will allow.

You use both `CurrentRecord` and `MaxRecords` in conjunction with `<%if%>` statements. They are implemented as controlling variables that help in your structuring of the logical flow of the HTX file. Just keep in mind that, after the processing of the detail section has completed, if `CurrentRecord EQ 0`, there were no results returned from the call.

The final section of the HTX file is used largely to close different HTML tags that were used to set up the display of information on the resulting page. Remember, HTML expects most tags in pairs, so it's a good idea to close each item properly.

```
<!-- Section 3>
<P>
</TABLE>
<%if CurrentRecord EQ 0%>
  <H2>Sorry, no authors match your search criteria (<%idc.au_lname%>).</H2>
<%else%>
  <H2>Authors with names like "<I><%idc.au_lname%></I>"</H2>
<%endif%>
</center>
</td>
</tr>
</table>
</BODY>
</HTML>
```

Notice, too, that the CurrentRecord variable is used to determine the message that is displayed to the user. There either will be a message indicating no matches, or one explaining what was searched for is shown. You can also see that by referencing the "<%idc.au_lname%>" variable, you can pull the user-specified value from the form.

The results of a successful search are shown in Figure 23.9.

FIG. 23.9
A successful match will show the hits on the PUBS database table, and will then show the message indicating what was searched for.

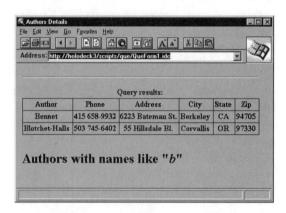

If the search of the database tables is not fruitful, the HTX will display a different message indicating the failure of the process. Figure 23.10 shows this dialog box.

FIG. 23.10
If matches for information are not found, you should code a branch of logic to indicate the problem to the user.

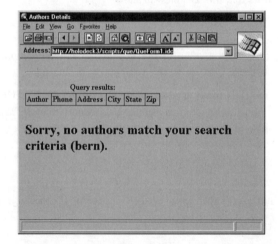

Internet Database Connector: A Summary and Example

To recap how the IDC works overall, first you will code a form or other HTML document that calls the IDC file on the server. The IDC file is located in the protected /SCRIPTS directory and contains the information necessary to open the ODBC connection and submit a query to the database engine. As the results are returned, they are merged into another document, the HTX or HTML extension document. This HTX file includes the information needed to work with both the detail records and the header/footer information for the page.

The result to the user is the display of the requested information in an HTML document style. Of course, the resulting document, based on the HTX file, can include further links to queries or drill-down information if needed. By using this technique, you can allow a user to select high-level values and then narrow the scope, but increase the detail level provided, for the information because the user is able to narrow the parameters for the operation.

An excellent example of the drill-down technique is provided in Microsoft's samples in the GuestBook application. As you query the guestbook, you are returned high-level detail about the names found. Here's a look at the HTX file's Detail section to see what exactly is done to display the information from the database.

```
<%begindetail%>
Name: <a href="/scripts/samples/details.idc?FName=<%FirstName%>&
➥ LName=<%LastName%>"><b><%FirstName%> <%LastName%></b></a>
<p>
<%enddetail%>
```

So, for each name returned by the original query, the result will be to show the first and last names. This HTML sets up the names as links to their own details. The code indicates the <A HREF> tag and references the IDC that retrieves the detail information, DETAILS.IDC. As a result, when the users click this in their browsers, they'll immediately be executing the IDC file and retrieving the next level of detail. Figure 23.11 shows what this initial screen of details looks like when the items are first retrieved.

FIG. 23.11
The initial display of the guestbook contents allows the user to select a name and drill down into the details for that name.

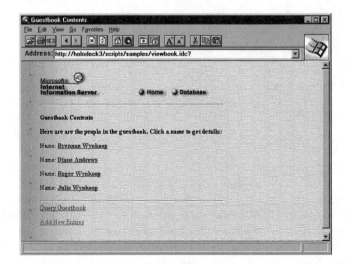

When you click a name to get the details, the IDC is called that retrieves the details from the Guests table on your system. If you take a look at the IDC, you'll see that it's quite simple, returning only a few columns of information based on the name selected from the previous query:

```
Datasource: Web SQL
Username: sa
Template: details.htx
SQLStatement:
+SELECT FirstName, LastName, Email, Homepage, Comment, WebUse
+FROM Guests
+WHERE FirstName = '%FName%' and LastName = '%LName%'
```

The final step is to show the information to the requester. The DETAILS.HTX template is called out in the IDC file, and it shows the detail information for the user as requested. The detail section simply displays the user information that has been provided. The HTX file makes heavy use of the <%if%> operator and the comparison of the contents of a given field to ensure that the only information provided to the user are those fields that are non-blank. See Listing 23.6.

Listing 23.6   The Detail Section from the DETAILS.HTX File

```
<%begindetail%>
<h2>Here are details for <%FirstName%> <%LastName%>:</h2>
<p>
<b><%FirstName%> <%LastName%></b><br>
<p>

<%if Email EQ " "%>
<%else%>
Email Address: <%Email%> <br>
<%endif%>
<%if Homepage EQ " "%>
<%else%>
Homepage: <%Homepage%>
<%endif%>
<p>
Primary Web Role: <%WebUse%>
<p>
<%if Comment EQ " "%>
<%else%>
Comments: <%Comment%>
<%endif%>
<p>
<%enddetail%>
```

Providing this type of increasing detail based on a user's selection is good for all parties concerned. It's good for your system because it can provide only the information needed to determine the direction to go to for the next level of detail. In addition, it's good for the users because it can mean less content to shuffle through to get to the information they really need. Because they will be determining what information is delved into, they'll be able to control how deep they want to go into a given item.

This technique is really great for supplying company information. You can provide overview-type items at the highest level on everything from marketing materials to personnel manuals. Letting people select their research path also relieves you of the responsibility of second-guessing exactly what the user is expecting of the system.

Using SQL Server's Web Page Wizard

As you're sure to have noticed, the race to bring content to your Internet site and make all different types of information available to the user base has been fast and furious. One of the recent advances is the capability to have the database engine automatically generate Web pages for you based on content in the database.

With SQL Server 6.5, you have the ability to schedule a task in the system to automatically create these HTML documents at time intervals ranging from a one-time run to many times per day. You can use this capability for a number of things, including reporting on your server's activity levels to you as an administrator.

In this section, you'll see how to set up these automatically generating pages and what the results of the process are. It's not possible to go into great detail on how to use SQL Server, form good database table design, and other administrative issues regarding SQL Server, because they warrant a much more comprehensive discussion than a single group of sections here.

Prerequisites for SQL Server

Before you can successfully use the Web Page Wizard and the processes it will create, you'll have to have set up your server to allow for this type of access. Specifically, the Web Page Wizard relies on the task manager and SQLExecutive service. You must have the SQLExecutive service set up to automatically start on startup of your server.

To confirm that the service is set to automatically start, select Services from the Control Panel. Scroll down the list of services installed until you see the SQLExecutive service (see Figure 23.12).

FIG. 23.12
Make sure the SQLExecutive service is listed with a Status of Started and that Startup is listed as Automatic.

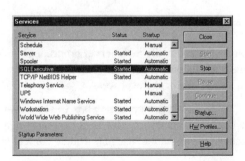

If the service is not already started, click the service and select Sta_rtup. You'll be able to set the options that govern when the service is active and, most importantly, when it will be started by the operating system. You'll want to make sure you indicate a valid user account that will be used to log in to SQL Server. This account must exist in both SQL Server and the User database for your domain if you are not using Integrated security, and the user name and password must be the same in both SQL Server and the domain.

If you're using integrated security, selecting a user from the domain user's list will also provide the name to be logged in to the SQL Server.

N O T E It's a requirement that the information you provide as it relates to the user and password is valid in SQL Server. You will also need to ensure that the account you indicate has access to the database you're reporting against and the MSDB database, because these are key to the creation of the page (see Figure 23.13).

If you do not set up the SQLExecutive to automatically start, the services required to generate the Web content you are setting up will not be available, and the page will not be generated.

If this is the first time you're setting these options, and the SQLExecutive was not previously started, when you select OK to save the user ID and startup option changes, you'll need to reselect the SQLExecutive service and then select _Start. ■

FIG. 23.13
The account you indicate for logon for the service must have access to the different objects in your database(s).

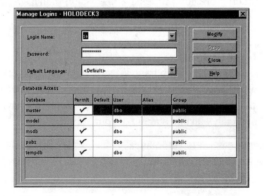

Using the Wizard

The SQL Web Page Wizard is located in the SQL Server program group on your system. You can run the Wizard from a workstation or the server. In either case, it will generate the pages for you in a directory you'll specify later in the process.

Figure 23.14 shows the initial SQL Server login dialog box you're presented with from the Wizard. From this dialog box, you'll need to provide an appropriate login that will allow you access to all tables and databases you want to use in providing content for your page.

FIG. 23.14
Logon to SQL Server is the first step to using the Wizard.

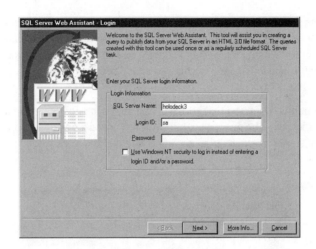

The option to use Windows NT Security to log on assumes you're using integrated security. If you are, selecting this item means that you don't have to provide separate login account and password information prompted for earlier in the dialog box and that the users will be logged on with their own security rights intact for SQL Server. Their NT logon name is used as their SQL Server logon name.

Selecting the Content for the Page   When you select Next >, you'll have three initial options. The first option, Build a query from a database hierarchy, allows you to use the point-and-click interface and indicate the tables and other items you want to include in your query that will be used to generate the page. Figure 23.15 shows an example of what the tree-based architecture will look like if you select this option.

FIG. 23.15
The easiest interface is the Database Hierarchy option because it allows you to select from the listing of objects on your server when deciding which items to provide for a report.

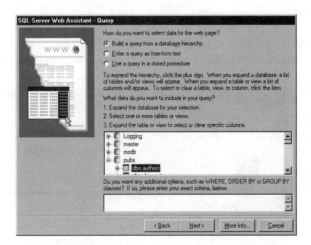

If you select the Free Form query option, you'll be able to create any SQL statement you need to fulfill the requirements for your software. Be sure to select the database you need to work against from the "Which database do you want to query?" list box, or you may end up querying the wrong table, and you'll need to come back and rewrite the query or queries on which you based the page.

Using this option also means that you're taking all responsibility for the formation of SQL Server-specific calls. The query you enter will be passed along and executed by the server. Figure 23.16 shows an example of how the dialog options work when working with the Wizard in this scenario.

FIG. 23.16
Entering the query manually can be powerful and painful all at once. If you're not sure of the syntax, use the more automated features of the Wizard for a few instances of information you want to publish.

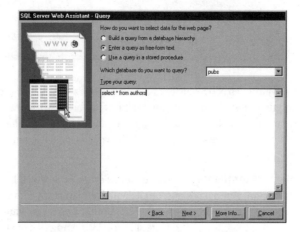

The final option you have in setting up the source of information for your page is to call a stored procedure. When you select the Use a query in a stored procedure button, you'll be able to provide information on the database and stored procedure you want to use. You'll also notice that the text of the stored procedure is shown in the dialog box. You can use this information to verify that you have selected the correct stored procedure (see Figure 23.17).

FIG. 23.17
Calling a stored procedure can be a good way to share coding you've done for an application and put it to use on your Internet server.

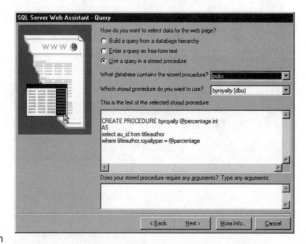

Stored procedures are a powerful mechanism for optimizing your server and providing good database query tuning. You can also take advantage of the fact that if you have another system based on SQL Server, and you're using a stored procedure to produce the results for a printed report, you may be able to reference the same stored procedure in the dialog box and create the report in HTML, making it available at any time.

The text box showing your stored procedure is provided as reference only; you cannot make changes to the code here. If you need to make changes to the code, you'll need to do so by updating the stored procedure in SQL Server. This can be done with ISQL/W, the SQL Enterprise Manager, or any other utility you may be using to manage your stored procedures.

Setting the Update Interval   The next dialog box will prompt you for the frequency at which you'd like to have the page rebuilt. Because the database is the source of information for the page, this item may take some work. The reason is that you'll need to talk with all of the users of the application that creates the data in the database and determine how frequently it is changed.

A frequency set to be too small will cause additional overhead on the server as it handles the request. The impact on performance should be minimal, but if there are many, many requests for data pages such as this, it may begin to show on the access times to the server. For an example (see Figure 23.18).

Your time-frame options and their associated parameters are

- Now, No parameters.
- Later, specify date and time that the page should be created (once only).
- When data changes, select data tables and indicate anticipated change that should be monitored as a trigger to update the HTML code.
- On certain days of the week, indicate day of week and time of day.
- On a regular basis, specify number of hours, days, or weeks that should pass before the item is regenerated.

FIG. 23.18
Be sure to select a useful time interval: Too frequent will force the server to rebuild the page without reason; too infrequent an update process makes the information a bit less useful because it may go out of date.

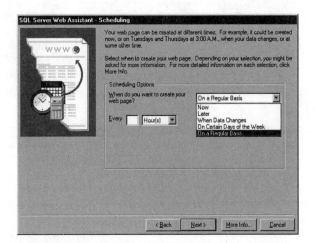

Part
V
Ch
23

Setting Page Options   There are two different dialog boxes with information about final formatting. Formatting options include headings for the page, column names on the resulting document, or changing the title or output location of the resulting HTML code. These are the steps you'll be using to create the database-related HTML you set up. See Figures 23.19 and 23.20 for examples.

FIG. 23.19
Review the formatting options carefully. These are the items that will be used to manage the content, appearance, and other facets of your HTML's presentation.

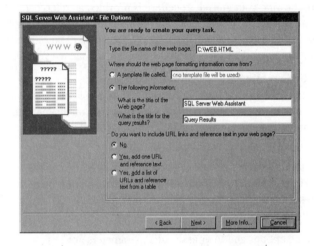

FIG. 23.20
If you are relying on the engine to do formatting for your tables of data, be sure to select the "Include column or view column names with the query results" when you set up the Wizard's Web page.

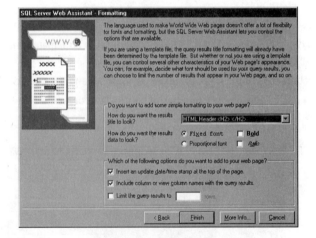

After you've made any changes you need, you can select Finish to generate the code that will be used to execute the different operations that manage the Wizard and its pages. Now, whenever the page is referenced by a browser, the HTML generated by the Wizard will be the results. The user will be able to see the new view you've constructed and will be assured of up-to-date information.

TIP One thing you'll want to consider including on every page you generate is a link to another page on your site. For example, you may want to always include a link with the following attributes:

Description: Return to Home Page

URL: `http://www.<your site>.com/default.htm`

It's a good idea to come up with a set of links that you include on each page on your site. These may be back to the home page, back to a search page, and to a copyright page, for example. Consistency across your site will make it much easier for users to navigate and understand.

Seeing the Results in SQL Server

It's helpful to review your SQL Server installation to understand what's happening when you implement a Wizard-generated Web page. There are a couple of things that have happened when you create a page in this manner.

- A master stored procedure is inserted into your database.
- A page-specific stored procedure is inserted into your database.
- A new task is created to be run by the SQL Executive at the intervals you requested.

The master stored procedure, sp_makewebpage, is created in the database you're setting up. This is used by the Wizard to create the code necessary to generate the page. You won't be making changes to this or the other stored procedures, and if you ever want to re-create it, you can run the Wizard again and create another page in the same database. This will create the stored procedure for you.

The page-specific stored procedure is created with a name that begins with Web_ and includes a unique numeric name that includes the date it was created. In the example shown in Figure 23.21, you can see that the stored procedures created to support the demonstration pages are named Web_96042622390211 and Web_96042700554612. If you review the stored procedures, you'll see that they're encrypted, so you won't be able to make any changes to them directly. Of course, the easiest way to make any changes you need is to remove the stored procedures and their associated tasks from SQL Server and then re-create them using the Web Page Wizard.

FIG. 23.21
Be sure not to remove the stored procedures from the database unless you also remove the corresponding task entries from the task scheduler.

By selecting Server, Tasks... from the menus, you can review the tasks that have been created to run the page at the intervals you set up. Figure 23.22 shows what you'll see. You can quickly determine that the Web pages are queued up and ready to go.

FIG. 23.22
After the Wizard has finished, the task is entered into SQL Server for processing as you established.

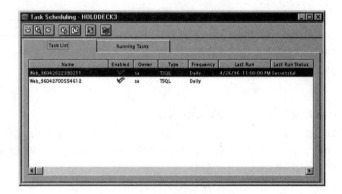

You can also check to make sure a Web page generation process is occurring as you'd expect by clicking the History button from the Task Scheduling dialog box. When you do, you'll see the dialog box shown in Figure 23.23, which indicates the times the procedure has run and whether it was successful. It's a good idea to start with the history review process in any diagnostics you need to run in the future should you encounter problems. In most cases, you can quickly determine exactly what's wrong by just doing some quick investigation with the Task Scheduler.

FIG. 23.23
You can verify that the pages are being generated successfully by reviewing the History logs.

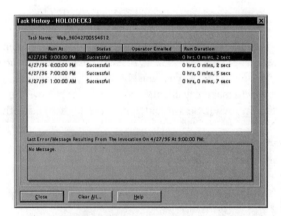

Keep in mind that you can also change the frequency at which your page is generated by modifying the task scheduling options. If you double-click the page you want to modify, you can set all the different options that control how often the page is generated. This might be helpful if you find that, after installing several pages and your site traffic picks up, you need to lessen server load a bit to provide better throughput at peak times. Simply change the times at which the pages are generated, and you'll be set.

Seeing the Results on Your Web Site

Implementing the page(s) you create on your site is a simple matter. You need to create a link to the pages or publish the URL to your user base. After the page is created by the SQL engine, it appears just as any other HTML document. Listing 23.7 shows the sample page created by the Web Page Wizard.

Listing 23.7 A Sample Page Created by the Wizard—(Web.html)

```
<HTML>
<HEAD>
<TITLE>SQL Server Web Page Wizard</TITLE>
<BODY>
<A HREF = /default.htm>Back to top of site</A>.<P>
<HR>
<H1>Query Results</H1>
<HR>
<PRE><TT>Last updated: Apr 26 1996 10:43PM</TT></PRE>
<P>
<P><TABLE BORDER>
<TR><TH ALIGN=LEFT>au_id</TH><TH ALIGN=LEFT>au_lname</TH><TH
➡ ALIGN=LEFT>au_fname</TH><TH
➡ ALIGN=LEFT>phone</TH><TH ALIGN=LEFT>address</TH><TH ALIGN=LEFT>city</TH><TH
➡ ALIGN=LEFT>state</TH>
➡ <TH ALIGN=LEFT>zip</TH><TH ALIGN=LEFT>contract</TH></TR>
<TR><TD NOWRAP>172-32-1176</TD><TD NOWRAP>White</TD><TD NOWRAP>Johnson</TD><TD
➡ NOWRAP>408 496-7223</TD><TD>
➡ <NOWRAP>10932 Bigge Rd.</TD><TD NOWRAP>Menlo Park</TD><TD NOWRAP>CA</TD><TD
➡ NOWRAP>94025</TD><TD
➡ NOWRAP>1</TD></TR>
<TR><TD NOWRAP>213-46-8915</TD><TD NOWRAP>Green</TD><TD NOWRAP>Marjorie</TD><TD
➡ NOWRAP>415 986-7020</TD>
➡ <TD NOWRAP>309 63rd St. #411</TD><TD NOWRAP>Oakland</TD><TD NOWRAP>CA</TD><TD
➡ NOWRAP>94618</TD>
➡ <TD NOWRAP>1</TD></TR>


...
<Edited for brevity see disk file for full listing>
...


<TR><TD NOWRAP>899-46-2035</TD><TD NOWRAP>Ringer</TD><TD NOWRAP>Anne</TD><TD
➡ NOWRAP>801 826-0752</TD>
➡ <TD NOWRAP>67 Seventh Av.</TD><TD NOWRAP>Salt Lake City</TD><TD
➡ NOWRAP>UT</TD><TD NOWRAP>84152</TD>
➡ <TD NOWRAP>1</TD></TR>
<TR><TD NOWRAP>998-72-3567</TD><TD NOWRAP>Ringer</TD><TD NOWRAP>Albert</TD><TD
➡ NOWRAP>801 826-0752</TD>
➡ <TD NOWRAP>67 Seventh Av.</TD><TD NOWRAP>Salt Lake City</TD><TD
➡ NOWRAP>UT</TD><TD NOWRAP>84152</TD>
➡ <TD NOWRAP>1</TD></TR>
</TABLE>
</BODY>
</HTML>
```

When you view the page, all of your SQL table data will be placed into an HTML table. The links you specified will be shown at the top of the page prior to the data from the site. Figure 23.24 shows what the top portion of this sample page looks like when presented in the browser.

FIG. 23.24
The sample Web page includes information from the Pubs database and a link back to the site home page.

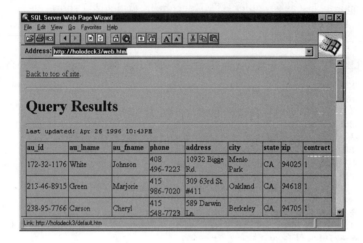

A great use of the Web Page Creation is to query the IIS logs that can be placed into SQL Server. For more information, see the next section that will show how this can be used to remotely monitor your site.

Logging IIS Accesses to ODBC Databases

Perhaps one of the biggest improvements you can make to your system administration abilities is to log your IIS access activity to an ODBC database. This is because you can start amassing excellent information about your site, including what information people are retrieving, how frequently they're visiting your site, and more.

As mentioned earlier in this chapter, to allow IIS to access your database, you'll need to set up a System DSN. After you've completed this, you can create the database, table, and user that you'll need to establish the Internet Service Manager for the Web, FTP, and Gopher services you're using.

▶ **See** the "Building ODBC Data Sources" sections for SQL Server and Access, found earlier in this chapter, for more information about setting up the System DSN, **p. 636**

To change logging to use your ODBC database, first double-click the service from the Internet Service Manager that you want to set up. In the example shown in Figure 23.25, you can see the logging options for the Web Services. Note that all the different services use the same logging tab, so after you've set one up, you'll understand how to establish the remaining services.

Before you can point the services to the ODBC database, you'll need to create the database and corresponding table. Table 23.3 shows the column information for the table that will be used for the logging.

Table 23.3 Table Structure for Logging Table

Column	SQL Data Type*	Access Data Type	Size
ClientHost	Char	Text	50
UserName	Char	Text	50
LogDate	Char	Text	12
LogTime	Char	Text	21
Service	Char	Text	20
Machine	Char	Text	20
ServerIP	Char	Text	50
ProcessingTime	int	Number	Integer
BytesRecvd	Int	Number	Integer
BytesSent	Int	Number	Integer
ServiceStatus	Int	Number	Integer
Win32Status	Int	Number	Integer
Operation	Int	Number	Integer
Target	Char	Text	200
Parameters	Char	Text	200

Note: Nulls are allowed for all columns in the case of SQL Server.

You may recognize this information from the discussions about installing and setting up the server components as the table structure maps directly to the different components of the standard log file when logged to ASCII files.

You set up the log table to be used by all the different services you're logging for. Notice that the Service column will show exactly what was being done by the user and what operation was being performed by the server. Listing 23.8 shows the SQL Server script for creating the table.

Part V
Ch
23

Listing 23.8 The SQL Server Script to Create the Logging Database—(makelog.sql)

```
/****** Object:  Table dbo.LogTable     Script Date: 4/28/96 10:04:11 PM ******/
if exists (select * from sysobjects where id = object_id('dbo.LogTable') and
➥ sysstat & 0xf = 3)
    drop table dbo.LogTable
GO

CREATE TABLE LogTable (
    ClientHost char (50) NULL ,
    UserName char (50) NULL ,
    LogDate char (12) NULL ,
    LogTime char (21) NULL ,
    Service char (20) NULL ,
    Machine char (20) NULL ,
    ServerIP char (50) NULL ,
    ProcessingTime int NULL ,
    BytesRecvd int NULL ,
    BytesSent int NULL ,
    ServiceStatus int NULL ,
    Win32Status int NULL ,
    Operation char (200) NULL ,
    Target char (200) NULL ,
    Parameters char (200) NULL
)
GO
```

Now that the table exists for logging information, you can indicate where to log information for each of the services. From the Internet Service Manager, double-click the service you want to update. Select the Logging tab to work with the different logging options (see Figure 23.25).

FIG. 23.25
The next step to begin using ODBC for logging is to select the ODBC option and indicate the login and database information.

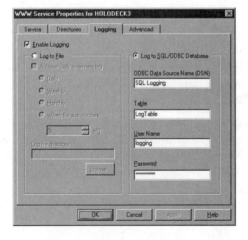

After you've selected the Log to SQL/ODBC Database radio button, you'll be able to access the different setup fields for the logging. It's a good idea to set up a different database to manage the logging. If you do, you'll be able to more easily manage the logging information separately from the other information on your system.

In the example, a specific database, table, and user have been created to use for the logging. If you create a user, be sure you set the rights to at least Insert when you establish them on the table. After you apply the changes, stop, and restart the service. You'll be logging all server accesses to the database.

N O T E If a user is accessing your server by using the FILE: protocol, the accesses will not be logged. These types of URLs are accessed by the client and handled by the client. Although the server will be providing the file to fulfill the request, it will not show up in the database. This is one detriment to using the FILE: type URL. If you want to be able to log accesses, consider making all links standard HTTP: type URLs, rather than providing direct links to the files. ■

When the logging is established, you can begin querying the database real-time to determine the activity on your server. In the next sections, you'll see some ways to provide this information in an easy-to-use and meaningful manner.

Sample Queries to Use in Reviewing Logs

The log data can quickly become overwhelming unless you can wrap it in some meaningful queries. Some good information to know about your site includes information about the following, just as a start:

- What pages are most popular?
- What time of day are people accessing the server?
- Who is accessing the server (by IP address)?

In the sample query in Listing 23.9, you can see that the database is examined to find out exactly this information, providing summary information for hits against the server.

N O T E For the following scripts, you'll need to change the database table that they reference to correctly identify your system configuration. Replace "wwwlog" and "ftplog" with the logging database you use for your system logging. ■

Listing 23.9 A Sample Script to Use for Server Reporting—Web Access— (www.sql)

```
SELECT "Total hits" = count(*),"Last Access" = max(logtime)
FROM wwwlog
SELECT ""

SELECT "Hit summary" = count(*), "Date" = substring(logtime,1,8)
FROM wwwlog
GROUP BY substring(logtime,1,8)
```

continues

Listing 23.9 Continued

```
SELECT ""

SELECT "Time of day"=substring(logtime,10,2), "Hits" = count
➥ (substring(logtime,10,2))
FROM wwwlog
group by substring(logtime,10,2)

SELECT ""

SELECT "Page" = substring(target,1,40), "Hits" = count(target)
FROM wwwlog
WHERE
    (
      charINDEX("HTM",target)>0
    )
GROUP BY target
ORDER BY "hits" desc
```

In Listing 23.10, a similar script provides good feedback on FTP accesses, showing what files users are accessing on your system. Again, it's important to understand what types of things people are finding most, and least, helpful on your site.

Listing 23.10 A Sample Script to Use for Server Reporting—FTP Access—(ftp.sql)

```
select "Summary of volume by day"

select substring(logtime,1,8), sum(bytessent), sum(bytesrecvd)
from ftplog
where  bytessent > 1000
group by substring(logtime,1,8)

select ""

SELECT "Time of day"=substring(logtime,10,2), "Hits" =
➥ count(substring(logtime,10,2))
FROM ftplog
group by substring(logtime,10,2)

select ""

select "Target" = substring(target,1,40),
       sum(bytessent),
       sum(bytesrecvd),
       count(substring(target,1,40))
from ftplog
where bytessent> 1000
group by Target
order by sum(bytessent) desc
```

Keep an eye on your site and always be looking for things that can be removed or demoted to less prominent presence on your site, while at the same time providing room for more new content that people are looking for on your site.

Reviewing System Logs Online

Of course, a great use of the IDC is to combine all of these different activities—logging, the IDC, the Web Page Wizard, and dynamic Web Page creation—to provide excellent feedback information online. Setting up the page is easy enough. You simply use the Web Page Wizard to query the database you've set up for logging and it is easy to call up as well, because it's established as a Web page.

Using this technique, you can create a Web page similar to the one shown in Figure 23.26 that will let you review your site activity while online.

Part

V

Ch

23

FIG. 23.26
Keeping the site activity only a hyperlink click away is a good way to put the database query capabilities to use at your site.

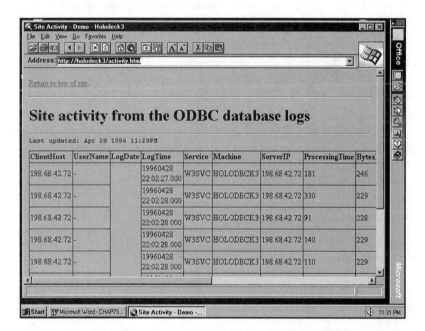

From here, it's a matter of pruning your Select statement to deliver more selective information. One idea would be to change the listing to return only the hits against the server by minute, for example. Then, by using an IDC link, you can offer the user the ability to drill down into a given time slice to gain more detail about an activity.

Another approach to this is to provide summary information by user with links to detailed log information for that user. The initial HTML page will show all users. The viewer can select the user to review and click the name. The next HTML page shows the user's access times individually. By clicking a specific access time, the reviewing party can see the details about what was accessed by that user during that session.

Integrating the IDC and drill-down informational research like this can really bring great leverage to you as an administrator. Remember, too, that you can place these pages into a protected subdirectory, making them available only to authorized users of your system.

Configuring IIS to Wait for SQL Server to Start

If you're using SQL Server for your logging, you may notice that when you restart the server, the IIS service is unable to begin logging to SQL Server. You'll receive an error message if you select the World Wide Web service from the Internet Service Manager that indicates that the logging configuration is invalid.

This comes from the fact that SQL Server requires more time to start than do the Internet services. Because the services start and immediately attempt access to the logging system, they are unable to get to the database because SQL Server is still starting. To avoid this, you'll need to make an entry in the system registry that tells IIS to wait on SQL Server when it starts the services.

From the Registry, select the following key:

```
HKEY_LOCAL_MACHINE\System\CurrentControlSet\Services\
➡ W3Svc\DependOnService
```

Add a new service as part of this key for each application you need to have IIS wait on. With SQL Server, the service name is MSSQLSERVER. You'll also want to update the Gopher and FTP service keys. They reside in the same key location, but you'll need to substitute either GOPHERSVC or MSFTPSVC for W3Svc in the preceding code. The resulting keys are

```
HKEY_LOCAL_MACHINE\System\CurrentControlSet\Services\
➡ GOPHERSVC\DependOnService
```

```
HKEY_LOCAL_MACHINE\System\CurrentControlSet\Services\
➡ MSFTPSVC\DependOnService
```

For each of these, you can set the DependOnService value(s) to include the appropriate processes.

Note that if you have selected logging to SQL Server and do *not* perform these steps, the logging will fail to start, and you'll end up with no logging occurring for your site. It is very important to set up these keys as soon as possible after you begin using SQL Server to log your site accesses.

Additional Emerging Options

Internet development tools are evolving so quickly it's nearly impossible to keep up. This book references the Reality Check site in every chapter as a point of reference to additional resources on new technologies that were released or standardized after going to print. Be sure you check in at the Reality Check site frequently to see what's new. The URL for the site is **www.pobox.com/~swynk**, and it contains information on all sorts of technologies, including those briefly mentioned here.

Database access is one of the most hotly developed areas on the Internet. This is due to the obvious fact that if you are to use your existing systems to their fullest potential, you'll almost certainly be referencing existing or new databases. This chapter has focused on the IDC and HTX combination as a good way of accessing this information. There are additional means of getting to this information, including your choice of scripting languages.

Microsoft has been pushing hard into the Active Server components and technologies. This approach moves the processing to the server for some or all of the content customization, including database access, for your pages. This brings back the whole approach that has been emphasized so heavily with SQL Server, that of providing client/server applications as an efficient way to use both your server and the client systems.

Choosing the Right Approach

There is a lot of debate right now about the "right" approach to providing database access to users. The choices fall into two distinct areas: providing client-side access to server-based databases and providing server-resolved access to server-based databases.

This might seem strange, but the issues really come down to how well defined and controlled your audience is. The choice is how the connection to the database will be handled. Because Microsoft is providing the software, and because they have a Web Browser, if you can ascertain that all users of your systems will have a Microsoft product, you can pretty much pick and choose between the approaches.

If, on the other hand, you can't absolutely promise what browser will be used, you'll need to consider using a server-based approach. A big benefit of the IDC approach is that it's server-based and completely browser independent. When it was first released, it was the *only* way of getting to databases; now it's become what amounts to as the lowest common denominator.

When you move to very recent browsers, like Internet Explorer 3.0 and upcoming promised versions of Netscape's product, you get some additional options, outlined next.

Active Server Pages, Advanced Data Control, and ActiveX Data Objects

Most of the options that you have available to you are moving to using DAO-like statements in VBScript or other scripting languages. These statements are getting added functionality that lets them reference server-based objects that are handling the server-side connection to the database. For example, consider Listing 23.11, taken from one of the sample files provided with IIS.

Listing 23.11 *ADO1.ASP*: Sample VBScript for Database Access

```
<HTML>
<HEAD><TITLE>ActiveX Data Object (ADO)</TITLE><HEAD>
<BODY>
```

continues

Listing 23.11   Continued

```
<H3>ActiveX Data Object (ADO)</H3>
<%
   Set Conn = Server.CreateObject("ADODB.Connection")
   Conn.Open "ADOSamples"
   Set RS = Conn.Execute("SELECT * FROM Orders")
%>
<P>
<TABLE BORDER=1>
<TR>
   <% For i = 0 to RS.Fields.Count - 1 %>
      <TD><B><%= RS(i).Name %></B></TD>
   <% Next %>
</TR>
<% Do While Not RS.EOF %>
   <TR>
   <% For i = 0 to RS.Fields.Count - 1 %>
     <TD VALIGN=TOP><%= RS(i) %></TD>
   <% Next %>
   </TR>
<%
   RS.MoveNext
   Loop
   RS.Close
   Conn.Close
%>
</TABLE>
</BODY>
</HTML>
```

The first thing you'll notice is the CreateObject method referenced as a server object. The ADOBB object, based on the server, provides the information needed to connect to the server based on the connection information provided in the Conn.Open call. After the connection is opened, the server is ready to receive statements. You may recall from the chapters on developing with SQL Server that you initiate a recordset by setting up the SQL statement that is used to define the recordset.

This is accomplished with the EXECUTE method, establishing the results to work on. You can then reference the results set exactly as you do with standard DAO calls. You'll recognize the balance of the logic as being identical to how you work with the DAO in Visual Basic or other languages you use with the objects and collections.

Once you're working with the information in your database in this manner, it's a simple thing to populate the page and get the data formatted the way you need.

Sneaking a Peek at the Advanced Data Connector

As of this writing, a new technology has started to arrive from Microsoft, the Advanced Data Connector. The ADC, available from the Web at **Error! Reference source not found.**, is a new client/server development model for web-based database development.

Traditionally, the challenge facing the web-based application developer is that of data handling at the client and server sides of the application. It was not possible to keep an active, open session on the server because of the inherent limitations built into the HTTP protocol. HTTP was designed to let you make a request, have the request fulfilled, then have no further communication until you make another request.

With the IDC, you gained the ability to query and ODBC data source. This is a very good way to query a database independent of the browser. It's also a low-overhead approach to working with the database. Of course, the downside to this is how limited you are in terms of what you can do with the information because the results are static and you're forced to manage the logic to perform any updates.

In the ideal world, you'd be able to manipulate the database as you do others, using the DAO. The DAO objects and methods give you full access to the database, tables and queries or views. This is where the ADC comes in. The ADC gives you access to these types of methods.

The ADC gives you an interface to the remote data sources in ways similar to the traditional Visual Basic approach. Specifically, you have a control that is responsible for the connection to the server, and you can manipulate either that control, or others dependent on it, to retrieve and work with the database information. The ADC is based on the OLEDB specification for working with databases and business objects. You can find more about OLEDB at **http:// www.microsoft.com/oledb**.

Understanding the Core ADC Components

The ADC includes several core components, shown in Table 23.4.

Table 23.4   ADC Core Components

Virtual Table Manager (VTM)	You can think of the VTM as "faking out" the data objects, giving them a logical table to work with that represents the data returned from the server.
AdvancedDataControl object	This control, and the AdvancedDataSpace object, lets you set up forms that are bound to the database columns or fields. This is like the datacontrol in VB.
AdvancedDataSpace object	As with the AdvancedDataControl object, this control helps set up the environment to support the use of bound controls over the Internet.
AdvancedDataFactory object	The data factory is responsible for communicating over HTTP and working with the VTM to create the locally cached virtual tables, making them accessible to your application. This is the query and update interface to your database.

continues

Table 23.4 Continued	
ADISAPI	ADISAPI (Advanced Data Internet Server API) is the API used by IIS to work with ODBC and the server-side datafactory objects.
Advanced TableGram Streaming Protocol (ADTG)	The ADTG is the internet-shortcomings-aware protocol that is used to shuttle the information between the client and server systems.

With all of these objects, you might wonder how this will affect the code you write for these web-based applications. The good news is that the code is much like Visual Basic and you will be able to leverage much of your education, testing, and experience to date with VB in your development of these applications. The bad news is that the HTML is getting longer, but you probably have expected that by now.

Reviewing an Example HTML Page

In the following listing snippets, you can see an abbreviated listing from the sample application provided by Microsoft with the ADC documentation. It gives you a good look at building a form that not only uses these concepts, but also a grid from Sheridan that helps display the information from the server.

N O T E In the following listing, portions of the code that have been removed are represented in the code by a set of ellipses, "..." ■

```
...
<PRE> First Name      <INPUT NAME=SFirst SIZE=30> </PRE>
<PRE> Last Name       <INPUT NAME=SLast  SIZE=30> </PRE>
<PRE> Title           <INPUT NAME=STitle SIZE=30> </PRE>
<PRE> E-mail Alias    <INPUT NAME=SEmail SIZE=30> </PRE>

<INPUT TYPE=BUTTON NAME="Find"           VALUE="Find">
<INPUT TYPE=BUTTON NAME="Clear"        VALUE="Clear">
<INPUT TYPE=BUTTON NAME="Update"        VALUE="Update Profile">
<INPUT TYPE=BUTTON NAME="Cancel"         VALUE="Cancel Changes">
```

Standard form definition tags are used to set up the form. In these opening HTML statements, the input forms are implemented and named. They can be later referenced for database updates and queries as needed.

The next section, outlined by the <OBJECT> tags, initiates the Sheridan grid control. Note that this control is assumed to be at the location specified on the server. The reference to Request.ServerVariables("SERVER_NAME") lets you find out the server name that is currently working with the Internet Explorer client.

The balance of the properties, for example AllowAddNew, are specific to the control and let you configure the control to suit your needs.

```
<OBJECT CLASSID="clsid:BC496AE0-9B4E-11CE-A6D5-0000C0BE9395"
     ID=Grid1
     CODEBASE="HTTP://<%=Request.ServerVariables("SERVER_NAME")%>/MSADC/Samples/
Sheridan.cab"
     HEIGHT= 125
     Width = 495>
     <PARAM NAME="AllowAddNew"    VALUE="TRUE">
     <PARAM NAME="AllowDelete"    VALUE="TRUE">
     <PARAM NAME="AllowUpdate"    VALUE="TRUE">
     <PARAM NAME="BackColor"      VALUE="-2147483643">
     <PARAM NAME="BackColorOdd"   VALUE="-2147483643">
     <PARAM NAME="ForeColorEven"  VALUE="0">
</OBJECT>
```

Next, you must set up the AdvancedDataControl object so that it provides the connectivity to the backend database. This object is linked to the Grid control above with the BINDINGS property. The properties for this object include the connect string that will be used to gain access to the remote database. As with the grid control, this object will be downloaded from the server, so you'll need to make sure you have it installed at the location indicated in the CODEBASE parameter.

 TIP Note the ID property in particular as this is what you'll use to refer to the control later when you move around the virtual dataset.

One thing to keep in mind is that the ODBC data source you indicate for the CONNECT property is a data source located and defined on the server, not on your workstation. This data source must be defined as a system data source and must be available in order for you to connect to the database.

This is one control measure that helps to make sure you're aware of all connections to your database and what their intent is. With this in mind, you'll want to make sure your ODBC configurations are as specific as possible. If you're providing SA-level access to data on your server, you're asking for problems as these approaches to working with the database become more prevalent.

```
...
<!-- Non-visual controls - AdvancedDataControl -->
<OBJECT CLASSID="clsid:9381D8F2-0288-11d0-9501-00AA00B911A5"
     ID="SControl"
     CODEBASE="HTTP://<%=Request.ServerVariables("SERVER_NAME")%>/MSADC/
msadc10.cab"
     WIDTH=1 HEIGHT=1>
     <PARAM NAME="BINDINGS" VALUE="Grid1;">
     <PARAM NAME="Connect" VALUE="DSN=ADCDEMO;UID=guest;PWD=guest;">
     <PARAM NAME="Server" VALUE="http://<%=Request.ServerVariables("SERVER_NAME")%>">
</OBJECT>
```

Finally, now that the objects are initiated, you can work with the objects and the results set and perform the operations that you need to complete your application. The first SUBroutine, the LOAD routine, will run immediately on loading of the form. This routine populates the grid control with the initial results from the database. The `.Refresh` method is used to accomplish this, just as it is when the control is based in Visual Basic.

```
...
<!— VBS scripting for composing queries, updating profiles, and retrieving
search results. —>

<SCRIPT LANGUAGE="VBScript">

Dim myQuery

SUB Load
      Grid1.CAPTION = "Arcadia Bay Corporate Phone Directory"
      'Initialize data grid with column names only.
      SControl.SQL = "Select FirstName, LastName, Title, Email, Building, Room,
➥ Phone from Employee where 2 < 1 for browse"
      SControl.Refresh
END SUB
```

If the user clicks the FIND button, you can see a great example of how a query is issued against the database and how it is used to return the results of the query. The query is built in the variable myQuery. This string variable will contain the select statement that will be submitted against the grid control.

If you work down through this listing, you'll see that the query is using the .Value properties for the fields defined on the HTML form. These properties are inserted into the string if they are non-blank, then a percent-sign, "%" is appended, making the entry a wildcard.

Finally, the .SQL property of the grid control is set to the value of the myQuery variable and the grid is refreshed to show the results of the query.

```
...
'Implement "Find" button - composes a dynamic SQL query to be processed by the
database and returns matching records to be bound to the SGrid object.

SUB Find_OnClick
      myQuery = "Select FirstName, LastName, Title, Email, Building, Room, Phone
 from Employee"
      'Check QBE fields and compose a dynamic SQL query.
      IF (SFirst.Value <> "") THEN
          myQuery = myQuery + " where FirstName like '" + SFirst.Value + "%'"
      END IF
      IF (SLast.Value <> "") THEN
          myQuery = myQuery + " where LastName like '" + SLast.Value + "%'"
      END IF
      IF (STitle.Value <> "") THEN
          myQuery = myQuery + " where Title like '" + STitle.Value + "%'"
      END IF
      IF (SEmail.Value <> "") THEN
          myQuery = myQuery + " where Email like '" + SEmail.Value + "%'"
      END IF
      myQuery = myQuery + " for browse"  'Mark recordset for editing.
      'Set the new query and then refresh the SControl so that the new results
 are displayed.
```

```
        SControl.SQL = myQuery
        SControl.Refresh

END SUB
```

If you're familiar with the DAO approach to database objects and methods, the navigation routines will look very obvious to you. You'll notice the following statements in the next few subroutines:

```
SControl.MoveFirst
SControl.MoveNext
SControl.MovePrevious
SControl.MoveLast
```

Each performs as it does with the DAO, moving the logical record pointer around the dataset. The SubmitChanges method sends all updates to the server. When you call this method, the virtual tables are not updated, though they will likely reflect your changes as the control is bound to the data source.

N O T E One thing to keep in mind as a difference between this and Visual Basic data-bound controls is that the information is not updated until you call the SubmitChanges method. To restore your dataset to its original state, use the CancelUpdate method. This will drop all changes you've made to the dataset. ■

```
'Submits edits made and pull a clean copy of the new data.
SUB Update_OnClick
        SControl.SubmitChanges
        SControl.Refresh
END SUB

'Cancel edits and restores original values.
SUB Cancel_OnClick
        SControl.CancelUpdate
END SUB
```

There's an interesting trend here that you've either noticed or will notice soon after you implement these types of pages on your Web site. There's a fair amount of code, ActiveX controls, and logic running behind this type of application. This is a far cry from the typically light-interaction-based systems that HTML is currently sporting on the Internet.

Be careful in your use of this technology. Only use the active connection and dataset pooling capabilities in those cases where another approach simply won't cut it. It's recommended that you consider the IDC approach first, if only for it's smaller footprint at both the client and the server.

Because you can mix and match your approach to different portions of a given application, be sure you keep in mind that each page you design and develop should be considered alone relative to the best approach to the data management.

The ADC is the technologically and functionally superior model to use for developing applications. The downside is that it requires the use of Internet Explorer for the Visual Basic scripting, as of this writing, and it's heavy on the initial downloads of the various ActiveX controls. It may be better suited for intranet application development in cases where an application usage is casual.

In cases where you are building an application that will be used quite a lot, the initial download of the components is not much more than a typical installation of other software and may play out to be less of an issue in the design considerations.

Finally, be sure to review the DAO appendix for details regarding different methods that are supported. Also, check the Microsoft site frequently as more methods are added and additional controls become available. This is a technology that can bring some solid tools to the mainstream, frequently used web-based application development arena.

Reality Check

The IntelliCenter Reality Check site **www.intellicenter.com** puts into play nearly all of the different techniques listed here, including the ODBC logging. The review of the logs is a very frequent operation and is used to help drive course and online materials content from a marketing stance, as well.

By putting content online and announcing its availability both to internal student users and the customer community at large, IntelliCenter is able to see what types of materials interest people and what other classes and activities might be of interest to customers.

In addition, as class students are assigned accounts on the IntelliCenter system, the usage statistics help drive the online research content. By looking after the content that is most requested on their system, it's possible to increase the online research materials to meet demand.

Database access is used, along with the IDC interface, to provide transcripts of the classes taken by a student or a company's students, with access to the information guided by the individual that is signing in. A corporate leader from the company, as designated by the company, can review the different classes that have been taken by his or her employees. At the same time, an employee can review his or her own records and can gain access to online materials that relate to the classes taken to date.

At the Integra site (www.integra.net), IDCs and HTXs are used extensively to provide download opportunities for trial versions of software. In addition, several Active Server pages have been put into use on the intranet, where we have more control over the user's browser. We've implemented several different databases, from tracking schedules to managing distribution lists and phone numbers. All of these are in SQL Server tables, accessed with the ADO approach.

From Here...

As you can see, the IDC is a very powerful extension to the IIS environment. Chances are good that after your initial installation of IIS to provide access to static HTML content, you'll quickly find that database-driven information is even more popular with the users you are serving.

This chapter touches on a number of different things. More information is provided about these topics in the following areas:

- See Chapter 22, "Developing Applications to Work with SQL Server," for more information about building applications to work with SQL Server.
- See Que Publishing's *BackOffice Intranet Kit* for more information about setting up and configuring IIS's Web, FTP, and other services.

Part
V

Ch
23

Creating and Using Cursors

Perhaps the biggest feature that Microsoft added to SQL Server 6.0 is back-end, or server-side, cursor support. Cursors provide a way to manipulate data in a set on a row-by-row basis rather than the typical use of SQL commands that operate on all the rows in the set at one time.

Specifically, Microsoft added a full implementation of back-end cursors, which are cursors that the database manages. These cursors have an easy access method from front-end application development tools and platforms such as SQLWindows and PowerBuilder. You could use cursors in previous releases of SQL Server, but those cursors were provided by the DBLibrary layer, not the server; for this reason, Microsoft refers to these new cursors as *back-end* cursors.

Cursors provide a way to do result-set processing inside the server without the need for a client program to manage the data sets on which you are working. For example, before SQL Server 6.0, it was difficult to write a fast-performing application that had to perform multiple actions on a set of data. The reasons for this difficulty were that you had to return each row in the data to the front end, and that the client application was responsible for initiating further activity on each row. Cursors provide a way for advanced Transact-SQL stored procedures to do all this processing without needing to return to the client. ■

> **CAUTION**
>
> Cursors can be terribly hard on your application's performance. They are, by their very nature, much slower to execute and respond than standard set-based operations. Make certain that you've exhausted set-based operations before you look to cursors, and make sure that you're not only considering their ease of use, but also the performance issues inherent their use.

Distinguishing Between Front-End and Back-End Cursors

With SQL Server, two types of cursors are available for use in an application: the *front-end,* or *client,* cursors, and the *back-end,* or *server,* cursors. These two types of cursors are quite different, so distinguishing between them is important.

N O T E Microsoft refers to back-end cursors, or cursors that the creates and manages, as *server cursors.* To avoid any confusion from this point on, unless this book specifically refers to cursors on the client or server, the term *cursor* refers to a cursor created in the database server. ■

When writing an application, you'll often find that you need to perform a given operation on a set of data. To perform such set-based operations, you usually can use an Update statement when you need to change data values, or a Delete statement when you need to remove data values. These set-based operations often provide great flexibility in an application, if a Where clause can appropriately define the required tasks.

Suppose that in the Pubs database, you want to change the ZIP code to 94024 for all authors who live in Menlo Park. To do so, you can use the simple Update statement shown in Listing 24.1.

Listing 24.1   24_1.SQL—Using *Update* to Change a ZIP Code

```
Update      AUTHORS
Set   ZIP = '94024'
Where City = 'Menlo Park'
Go
```

On the other hand, what if you need to perform different kinds of operations on a set of data? Two solutions are possible: You can perform multiple operations on exclusive sets, or you can get the whole set of data and, based on values in the set, perform the required operations. This second solution is the concept behind cursor-based processing.

Relying on the set-based updates and deletes can be inefficient, because your updates might end up hitting the same row more than once. Alternatively, you can create a view of data in the database called a *cursor.*

One of the best advantages of cursor processing is that you can perform conditional logic on a particular row of data in a set independently of the other rows that might be in a set. Effectively, you are issuing commands or SQL on single-row data sets. Complex applications often require this granularity of processing. In addition, this granularity offers several benefits:

- *Performance.* Set-based operations tend to use more server resources than cursor operations do.

- *Better transaction control.* When processing sets of data, you can control what happens to any given row independently from the others.

- *Special syntax.* WHERE CURRENT OF cursors allow positioned updates and deletes that apply to the row that you are currently fetching. Such cursors directly hit the table row, so you have no need for an index.

  ▶ **See** the section "Updating Rows" in Chapter 8, "Adding, Changing, and Deleting Information in Tables," for more information on updates, **p. 225**

- *Efficiency.* When you're performing several operations on a large data set, such as calling multiple stored procedures, having the database process the data and perform all actions per row is more efficient than performing each task serially on the entire data set. The reason for this efficiency is that data is kept in memory caches.

Part
V

Ch
24

Understanding Client Cursors

Before releasing SQL Server 6.0, Microsoft realized that its customers needed to be able to process data and to scroll backward and forward through a result set. Customers needed this scrolling functionality to support complex applications that users needed for browsing data fetched from the database.

At the time, Microsoft couldn't incorporate the server-based cursors that some of the other vendors supported, and so chose to mimic some of these cursors' behavior in Microsoft's client application programming interface (API) to the SQL Server database, DBLibrary.

N O T E Microsoft inherited the DBLibrary client interface from Sybase to interact with the SQL Server database. DBLibrary is a set of commands and functions that you can execute in C to perform operations on the database. With SQL Server 6.0 and later releases, Microsoft changed its preferred interface to the database to be that of Open Database Connectivity (ODBC). For more discussions on interfacing with the database from client applications and programming languages, see Chapters 22, "Developing Applications to Work with SQL Server," and 23, "Understanding SQL Server and the Internet." ■

To achieve this functionality, Microsoft added client cursors to the data sets on the client side.

These cursors work by having DBLibrary interact with the database how it normally does: by fetching data from the tabular data stream (TDS) as quickly as the client requests. TDS is the method of communication that DBLibrary uses to fetch data from the database. Typically, DBLibrary discards any data that it fetches from the database, and then gives the data to the client application, relying on the client to perform any additional work. With cursors activated, DBLibrary caches these records itself until the client cancels the cursor view on the data.

This caching has several limitations:

- SQL Server has no way to control or minimize the locks held on the database. Therefore, any locks are held for all data pages in the cursor, not just the affected data pages. This is because SQL Server is basically unaware that anything other than a select activity is occurring on the data.
- The caching can consume client-side resources very quickly if it involves large sets of data.
- The caching is inefficient when processing large amounts of data because all the data is sent across the network unnecessarily.

Client cursors were just a stopgap measure until Microsoft could complete the real work of server cursors. Server cursors provide all the same benefits of client cursors without any of the overhead or limitations. Aside from backward-compatibility issues, there are few good reasons to use client cursors in an SQL Server 6.5 application.

When used, server cursors usually have five states, as described in Table 24.1.

Table 24.1 The States of Existence of SQL Server Cursors

State	Explanation
DECLARE	At this point, SQL Server validates that a valid cursor will populate the query. SQL Server creates in shared memory a structure that has the definition of the cursor available for compilation at the OPEN phase.
OPEN	SQL Server begins to answer the DECLARE statement by resolving the query and fetching row IDs into a temporary workspace for the use of the client, should it decide to fetch the rows that this cursor has identified.
FETCH	In this state, the cursor returns the data so that any required activity can be performed.
CLOSE	SQL Server closes the previously opened cursor and releases any locks that it might be holding as a result of opening it.
DEALLOCATE	SQL Server releases the shared memory used by the DECLARE statement, no longer permitting another process to perform an OPEN on it.

Using SQL Server Cursors

To use a cursor in SQL Server, you need to follow the states described in Table 15.1. This section explains the steps that you must follow to use a cursor effectively in your applications.

You first must declare the cursor. Then you can open the cursor and fetch from it. During a cursor's fetch phase or state, you can perform several different operations on the cursor's currently active row. When you finish working with a cursor, you must close and deallocate it so that SQL Server does not waste resources managing it any further.

Declaring a Cursor

Declaring a cursor is quite similar to requesting data using a standard Select statement. Note that the Select statement that you use to declare a cursor can't include any of the Transact-SQL extensions such as COMPUTE, COMPUTE BY, or SELECT INTO.

The syntax for declaring a cursor is as follows:

```
DECLARE name_of_cursor [INSENSITIVE] [SCROLL] CURSOR
FOR Select_Statement
[FOR {READ ONLY ¦ UPDATE [OF Column_List]}]
```

> **N O T E** Because cursors must fetch row values into variables inside the stored procedure or command batch, you can't use the asterisk (*) in your Select statement. In the data tables, you must use named columns that correspond one-to-one with the variables used in the FETCH clause. ■

The options for the Transact-SQL command DECLARE CURSOR are as follows:

- name_of_cursor. The cursor's name must comply with the database's standard object identifier rules.
- INSENSITIVE. Actions of other users do not affect a cursor that you create with the INSENSITIVE keyword. SQL Server creates a separate temporary table of all the row data that matches the query, and uses the table to answer requests on the cursor. You cannot modify insensitive cursors by using the WHERE CURRENT OF cursor syntax; therefore, such cursors impose index update hits when any updates are done.

> **CAUTION**
>
> Be careful when using the INSENSITIVE keyword in defining a cursor. An application that uses this keyword might encounter problems of inaccurate data if the application has high transaction loads on the underlying table or tables on which the cursor is being opened. If you are writing a time-driven application, however, INSENSITIVE cursors are required. An example of this might be "tell me what our balance sheet position is as of right now, regardless of outstanding or in-process transactions."

- SCROLL. The opposite of the INSENSITIVE keyword, the SCROLL keyword enables the cursor to read from committed updates and deletes made by other server processes. The SCROLL keyword is also required if the application needs to do anything other than fetch the data sequentially until the end of the result set.
- READ ONLY. As its name implies, this option prevents any modifications of the cursor's data. Internally, this option has a great effect on how SQL Server chooses to retrieve the data and usually makes SQL Server more likely to hit any available clustered index. Unless you need to modify data for which the cursor is declared, you should use the READ ONLY clause. Use of this clause improves performance substantially.
- UPDATE. This option is the default on a single table cursor such as that which you create when issuing a select without any join conditions. A cursor that you declare in this fashion allows the use of the WHERE CURRENT OF syntax.

Listing 24.2 shows a basic cursor declared to fetch data from a single table (EMPLOYEE) in the Pubs database.

Listing 24.2   24_2.SQL—A Cursor Declared to Retrieve Information from the *EMPLOYEE* Table

```
Declare Cur_Empl Cursor
For    Select EMP_ID,    LNAME,
             JOB_ID,     PUB_ID
       From  EMPLOYEE
       Order By EMP_ID
Go
```

The Cur_Empl cursor, as shown in Listing 24.2, makes an application no more flexible than a simple SELECT on the data would. However, if the application requires absolute row positioning, as shown in Listing 24.3, you can add the SCROLL keyword to the Declare statement to make the cursor behave much more differently than a table SELECT.

Listing 24.3   24_3.SQL—A Scrollable Cursor Declared to Fetch from the *EMPLOYEE* Table

```
Declare Cur_Empl_Scrollable SCROLL Cursor
For    Select EMP_ID,    LNAME,
             JOB_ID,     PUB_ID
       From  EMPLOYEE
       Order By EMP_ID
Go
```

Opening a Cursor

After you declare a cursor, SQL Server reserves handles for its use. To use a cursor and fetch data from it, you must open the cursor using the following syntax:

```
Open Cursor_Name
```

In the preceding examples, the code required to open the cursor would have been either one of the following:

```
Open Cur_Empl
```

```
Open Cur_Empl_Scrollable
```

When a cursor is opened, SQL Server resolves any unknown variables with their current state. If you declare a cursor with a variable in the Where clause and then open the cursor, the value used to resolve the query is the value that the variable holds when you open the cursor, as shown in the example in Listing 24.4.

Listing 24.4   Declaring and Opening a Cursor

```
Declare      @nHighJobID integer,
             @nLowJobID  integer
Declare Cur_Empl_Where Cursor
For   Select      LNAME, FNAME
From  EMPLOYEE
Where JOB_ID Between @nLowJobID And @nHighJobID
/* Note that if the cursor were to be opened now,
probably no data would be returned because the values
of @nLowJobID and @nHighJobID are NULL */
/* Now we set the values of the variables */
Select      @nLowJobID = 3,
      @nHighJobID = 10
/* open the cursor now */
Open Cur_Empl_Where
...
```

> **N O T E** You can determine how many rows the cursor found. To do so, evaluate @@Cursor_Rows. If the number of rows is negative, the cursor hasn't yet determined the total number of rows. Such might be the case if the cursor is still serially fetching the rows to satisfy the cursor definition. If the number of rows is zero, there are no open cursors, or the last cursor that was open was closed or deallocated. ■

Fetching a Cursor

After you open a cursor, you can fetch data from it. Unless you declare a cursor with the SCROLL keyword, the only kind of fetching permitted is serially or sequentially through the result set.

The syntax for the FETCH statement is as follows:

```
FETCH [[NEXT ¦ PRIOR ¦ FIRST ¦ LAST ¦
      ABSOLUTE n/@nvar ¦ RELATIVE n/@nvar ]
FROM] cursor_name
[INTO @variable_name1, @variable_name2]
```

The options for the Transact-SQL command FETCH are as follows:

- NEXT. The NEXT keyword is implicit in normal fetching operations. It implies that the statement returns the next available row.
- PRIOR. If you defined the cursor with SCROLL, the PRIOR keyword returns the prior record. Stored procedure-based applications usually don't use this keyword unless they're responding to some kind of error condition by logically rolling back the previous row update.
- FIRST. This keyword fetches the first record of the result set found by opening the cursor.
- LAST. This keyword fetches the last record of the result set found by opening the cursor.

- ABSOLUTE n. This keyword returns the nth row in the result set. If you specify a positive number, the statement counts rows from the top of the data set. If you provide a negative value for n, the statement counts the number of rows from the bottom of the data set.

- RELATIVE n. This keyword returns the nth row in the result set relative to the current record most recently fetched. If the number is negative, the statement finds the row by counting backward from the current row.

N O T E In SQL Server 6.5, Microsoft has enhanced the syntax of the FETCH ABSOLUTE and FETCH RELATIVE statements by enabling you to substitute @ variables for n. The only variables that you can use are those of types int, smallint, or tinyint.

- FROM. SQL Server provides this unnecessary keyword to make the code slightly more readable. The keyword indicates that the next word is the cursor from which the statement is fetching.

- INTO. SQL Server provides the INTO keyword for stored procedure use. When you specify this keyword, temporary variables hold the data that the cursor returns. You can use these variables for evaluation or other purposes. The data types of the variables in the INTO clause must match exactly the datatypes of the cursor's returned columns. Otherwise, the clause generates errors.

Closing a Cursor

Closing a cursor releases any resources and locks that SQL Server might have acquired while the cursor was open. To close a cursor, use the following syntax:

```
CLOSE cursor_name
```

A closed cursor is available for fetching only after it's reopened.

Deallocating a Cursor

Cursors keep track of your location in the database and maintain an active, open structure of pointers to the next and previous row information.

Deallocating a cursor completely removes any data structures that SQL Server was holding open for a given cursor. Deallocating a cursor differs from closing a cursor; after you deallocate a cursor, you can no longer open it.

To deallocate a cursor, use the following syntax:

```
DEALLOCATE cursor_name
```

An Example of Using Cursors

The previous sections discussed all the separate elements that you use to work with cursors in SQL Server. This section shows how you put together all the elements.

Listing 24.5 is an example of the use of cursors in action. Refer to the comments in the script (placed between /* and */) to get a good understanding of what the cursors are doing. However, to summarize, the following steps are taken:

1. Drop the procedure and recreate it if necessary. This step ensures that the current procedure is the one that executes. Note also that if you have SQL Enterprise Manager generate the code for a stored procedure, any such statements that drop the existing stored procedure are generated automatically.

2. Create a cursor to find the information that you need. Doing so allocates the memory structures and sets up the cursor so that you can retrieve information from it in later logic.

3. Open the cursor and retrieve the first sets of information from it.

4. In the loop, retrieve information from the cursor until the logic to determine books on order completes. Return the results to the calling application.

5. End the procedure, cleaning up on the way out.

Part

V

Ch

24

On the CD

Listing 24.5   24_4.SQL—Using Cursors to Process the *STORES* Table in the Pubs Database

```
/* In this example, we will be working with the stores table
of the pubs database.
To illustrate the cursors most easily, we will create a stored
procedure, that when executed:
- declares,
- opens,
- fetches, and
- processes
the data returned from a cursor. */
/* First we drop the procedure if it exists. */
If exists( select object_id( 'proc_Stores' ) )
    Drop Procedure proc_Stores
Go
/* Step 0: Declare the procedure. */
Create Procedure proc_Stores
As
/* Step 1: Declare some working variables. */
Declare     @nOrderCount     integer,
    @nSQLError      integer,
    @nStorCount     tinyint,
    @sState         char(2),
    @sStorId     char(4),
    @sStorName      varchar(40),
    @sCity          varchar(20)
/* Step 2: Turn off result counting.
Turns off unnecessary "0 rows affected messages" showing on the front-end */
Set NoCount On
```

continues

Listing 24.5 Continued

```
/* Step 3: Declare the cursor that is going to find all
the data.
This step causes SQL Server to create the resource
structures required to manage the cursor. */
Declare Cur_Stores Cursor
For     Select      STOR_ID,      STOR_NAME,
            CITY,           STATE
    From      STORES
    Order By     STOR_ID
/* Step 4: Open the cursor.
This step causes SQL Server to create the initial result set
and prepare the data for returning to the fetching process. */
Open      Cur_Stores
/* Step 5: Perform the first fetch.
Fetch data from the cursor into our variables for processing
and evaluation. */
Fetch     Cur_Stores
Into      @sStorId,     @sStorName,
    @sCity,             @sState
/* Step 6: Initialize counters. */
Select      @nStorCount = 0
/* Step 7: Fetch and process loop.
Process the data while the system variable @@Fetch_Status is = 0
(meaning that a row has been fetched from the cursor) */
While @@Fetch_Status = 0
Begin
    /* Step 8: Increment counter */
    Select      @nStorCount = @nStorCount + 1
    /* Step 9: Do a quick operation to determine books on order */
    Select      @nOrderCount = Sum(QTY)
    From      SALES
    WHERE     STOR_ID = @sStorID
    /* Step 10: Return a result set to the front-end so that it knows
    what is happening */
    Select     "Store ID" = @sStorId,
        "Store Name" = @sStorName,
        "# Books on order" = @nOrderCount
    /* Step 11: Continue fetching.
    If no rows are found, then @@Fetch_Status will be set to a value other
    than zero, and the looping will end. */

    Fetch     Cur_Stores
    Into      @sStorId,     @sStorName,
        @sCity,             @sState
End
/* Step 12: Clean up - deallocate and close the cursors.
Note that for a stored procedure, this is really unnecessary because
the cursor will no longer exist once the procedure finishes execution.
However, it is good practice to leave the procedure cleaned up */
Close      Cur_Stores
Deallocate Cur_Stores
/* Step 13: Send a totaling result.
Send total count of employees to front-end */
Select "Total # of Stores" = @nStorCount
```

```
/* Step 14: Turn on counting again */
Set NoCount On
/* Step 15: End procedure */
Return 0
Go
/* Now we execute it to see the results. */
Execute proc_Stores
Go
```

When you run this program, the output looks like the following:

```
Store ID Store Name                                # Books on order
-------- ----------------------------------------  ----------------
6380     Eric the Read Books                                      8
Store ID Store Name                                # Books on order
-------- ----------------------------------------  ----------------
7066     Barnum's                                               125
Store ID Store Name                                # Books on order
-------- ----------------------------------------  ----------------
7067     News & Brews                                            90
Store ID Store Name                                # Books on order
-------- ----------------------------------------  ----------------
7131     Doc-U-Mat: Quality Laundry and Books                   130
Store ID Store Name                                # Books on order
-------- ----------------------------------------  ----------------
7896     Fricative Bookshop                                      60
Store ID Store Name                                # Books on order
-------- ----------------------------------------  ----------------
8042     Bookbeat                                                80
Total # of Stores
----------------
             6
```

TIP Sorting variables alphabetically in large procedures makes finding the variables much easier. In addition, you can sort the variables by datatype as well, so that finding them is even easier. This sorting occurs automatically if you prefix variables with a datatype indicator such as s for strings, n for numbers, or dt for dates and times.

Using Nested Cursors

A stored procedure can have multiple layers of cursors that you use to provide flexible result-set processing. An example of having more than one cursor active is when you're opening a cursor, as shown earlier in the Cur_Empl example. In addition to the cursor that you've already reviewed, you can add nested cursors to impose some additional conditional logic and perhaps open a second cursor to perform additional work with the data set.

Listing 24.6 shows some possibilities with nested cursors and provides an example of retrieving the employee record and then using that information to retrieve detail records for the employee.

On the CD

Listing 24.6 24_5.SQL—Using Nested Cursors

```
Create Procedure Maintain_Employees
As
/* First declare variables that are going to
be required in this procedure */
Declare     @dtPubDate    datetime,
            @nEmplCount   smallint,
            @nEmplID      empid,
            @nFirstHalf   smallint,
            @nRowCount    integer,
            @nSecondHalf  integer,
            @nSQLError    integer,
            @nYtdSales    integer,
            @sLName       varchar(30),
            @sPubID       char(4),
            @sLastType    char(12),
            @sType        char(12)
/* Now declare the cursors to be used.
Note that because variables are used in the
where clause on the second cursor, it is not
required that the second cursor be declared inside the first.
Take advantage of this functionality so that unnecessary
declaring of cursors does not take place (this will
save resources on the server). */
Declare Cur_Empl Cursor
For   Select EMP_ID,    LNAME,
             PUB_ID
      From   EMPLOYEE
      Order By EMP_ID
Declare Cur_Titles Cursor
For   Select  TYPE,   PUBDATE, YTD_SALES
      From    TITLES
      Where   PUB_ID = @sPubID
Order By TYPE
/* Open the outer cursor and fetch the first row */
Open  Cur_Empl
Fetch Cur_Empl
Into  @nEmplID,    @sLName,
      @sPubID
/* Initialize counters */
Select      @nEmplCount = 0
While @@Fetch_Status = 0              /* Fetch only while there are rows left */
Begin
      /* increment counter */
      Select @nEmplCount = @nEmplCount + 1
      /* Return a result set to the front-end so that it knows
      what is happening */
      Select      @nEmplID,    @sLName
      If @sLName < 'D'  /* Skip all the D's by using a GOTO */
            Goto Fetch_Next_Empl
      /* Now open inner cursor and count the different types
      of books for this employee's publisher */
```

```
        Open Titles
        Fetch Titles
        Into  @sType, @dtPubDate, @nYtdSales
        /* Reset totals */
        Select @nFirstHalf = 0,
               @nSecondHalf = 0,
               @sLastType = NULL
        While @@Fetch_Status = 0
        Begin
               If @sType != @sLastType AND @sLastType != NULL
               Begin
                      /* Send back a total record to the front-end */
                      Select @sLastType, @nFirstHalf, @nSecondHalf
                      /* Reset totals */
                      Select @nFirstHalf = 0,
                             @nSecondHalf = 0
               End
               If @dtPubDate <= '6/30/95'
                      Select @nFirstHalf = @nFirstHalf + @nYtdSales,
                             @sLastType = @sType
               Else
                      Select @nSecondHalf = @nSecondHalf + @nYtdSales,
                             @sLastType = @sType
               Fetch Titles
               Into  @sType, @dtPubDate, @nYtdSales
        End
        Fetch_Next_Empl:          /* Label to skip inner loop */
        Fetch Cur_Empl
        Into  @nEmplID,    @sLName,
              @sPubID
End
/* Deallocate and close the cursors. Note that for a stored
procedure, this is really unnecessary because the cursor
will no longer exist once the procedure finishes execution.
However, it is good practice to leave the procedure cleaned up. */
Close Cur_Empl
Deallocate Cur_Empl
Deallocate Cur_Titles
/* Send total count of employees to front-end */
Select @nEmplCount
/* End proc */
Return 0
```

 TIP SQL Server treats object names case-insensitively, regardless of the sort order defined for the server. You can take advantage of this and make your code easy to read by using upper- and lowercase emphasis when possible.

However complex this example might seem, using cursors is really not too difficult if you follow the basic steps outlined in the previous examples and throughout this chapter.

Part
V

Ch
24

Processing Cursors from Front-End Applications

A key consideration of using cursors in an application is how they can be accessed from front-end programming tools such as SQLWindows or PowerBuilder.

If the cursor returns a single set of data, which is the most common type, most front-end application languages cannot distinguish the data from that returned by a normal SELECT statement. Typically, the tool has a function for executing SELECT statements. This function is designed to work with a single set of data and, therefore, probably will work fine with stored procedures or cursors that return a single result set.

Most tools provide special functions for referencing data that comes from a cursor if the cursor and its associated processing returns more than one result set. A common construction might be something like this SQLWindows example snippet:

```
...
Call SqsExecuteProc( hSql, 'proc_Stores', gsResults )
While SqsGetNextResults( hSql, gsResults )
While SqlFetchNext( hSql, nReturn )
...
```

The execution of the stored procedure is followed by looping that forces the return of results to the front-end and then the fetching of the data in each result.

Most programming languages have similar functionality available. Whatever programming language you choose for your development should be capable of supporting anything that SQL Server can return. For a more detailed discussion on several client/server programming tools, refer to Chapter 25, "Accessing SQL Server Databases Through Front-End Products."

Reality Check

Cursors are, at first glance, a great feature for your applications. Indeed, cursors offer good funcionality for your application if you need to provide database-browsing capabilities but don't want to develop this type of functionality on your application's client side.

Because of their inherent functionality, cursors bring quick payback on the development cycle, but can harm the application's performance. Although the effect depends on your implementation, including the hardware on which the server is running, cursors can have a significant negative impact on your application's overall throughput.

From Here...

In this chapter, you learned about SQL Server's new server-based cursors and how you can use them to provide much more processing power to your applications without having to return to the client for help. According to Sybase's performance-tuning group, whose understanding of SQL Server's cursors is quite intimate, server cursors provide greater performance than all other results-set processing mechanisms, including embedded SQL in a C application running on the server.

The reason for this high performance is that cursors don't require any networking. Unless you can't model in stored procedures the type of work that you're doing—which might be the case with arrays—you should move all batch operations to cursor-based procedures running on the server.

From here, you can refer to the following chapters to implement what you've learned:

- Chapter 14, "Managing Stored Procedures and Using Flow-Control Statements," explains how to start embedding cursor processing in your stored procedures.
- Chapter 25, "Accessing SQL Server Databases Through Front-End Products," provides a full explanation of how your front-end tool of choice interacts with the database when using cursors.

Part

V

Ch

24

Accessing SQL Server Databases Through Front-End Products

▬ **How to use some of the most popular client/server tools with SQL Server**

In this chapter, you will see how to use SQLWindows, Delphi 2, and Visual Basic 4.

▬ **How to configure ODBC for use with SQL Server**

In the section "Configuring ODBC for SQL Server 6.5," you'll learn how to install the connectivity required for accessing SQL Server through front-end tools.

▬ **Tips and tricks for client/server development**

SQL Server's client interface from three popular languages is explored with sample applications that show how to develop smart applications.

With SQL Server 6, Microsoft introduced a new client-side interface through *open database connectivity*, or ODBC. Rather than using the old DB-Library approach that was created by Sybase, Microsoft decided to create a new access path through ODBC.

As custodian of the ODBC specification, it was easy for Microsoft to tailor the ODBC interface, making it no longer truly "generic" and, in fact, optimizing it for SQL Server access. With this new interface, there is no longer the stigma of slow performance associated with ODBC access. Microsoft still supports the DB-Library interface for backwards compatibility, but it seems that their primary focus is on making ODBC *the standard* for database access. ■

Configuring ODBC for SQL Server 6.5

ODBC is a way of connecting various data services to different front-end applications in a consistent manner. ODBC has undergone several revisions since its inception in 1991.

ODBC is configured through a Control Panel applet: ODBC or ODBC32. Configuring under Windows NT Workstation or Server version 4.x or later and under Windows 95 will look identical. Under Windows for Workgroups, or Windows NT Workstation or Server versions 3.51 or earlier, the dialog boxes contain the same information; however, there may be some difference in the shading of values and the layout of the dialog box close/minimize/restore options.

To configure ODBC for use with Microsoft SQL Server 6.5, follow these steps:

1. Install the ODBC drivers that ship on the SQL Server 6.5 CD-ROM.

2. Choose Settings, Control Panel from the Start menu. See Figure 25.1.

FIG. 25.1
Windows NT Workstation's Control Panel is really just a window with several icons in it.

3. Double-click the ODBC icon to display the ODBC configuration dialog box shown in Figure 25.2.

FIG. 25.2
ODBC's Data Sources dialog box lists available ODBC data sources that have had drivers loaded.

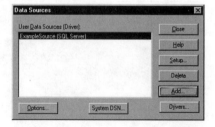

4. The Add Data Source dialog box, shown in Figure 25.3, is where you add new sources of data to be accessed via ODBC. In SQL Server's case, you add a new data source for each SQL Server that you have on the network. In this case, you can configure a default installation to access the PUBS database.

   Click the <u>A</u>dd button in the Data Sources dialog box.

FIG. 25.3

Notice that SQL Server is listed at the bottom of the Installed ODBC <u>D</u>rivers list box in the Add Data Source dialog box.

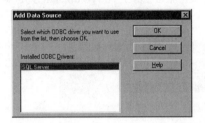

5. Select SQL Server from the list and click OK. The ODBC SQL Server Setup dialog box appears. See Figure 25.4.

FIG. 25.4

The <u>O</u>ptions button displays the bottom half of the ODBC SQL Server Setup dialog box.

6. Enter a name for the data source, such as **LocalServer**. The name can be anything meaningful to you.

7. Enter a description of the ODBC data type—that is, **MS SQL Server 6.5**—so that you can determine what source of data this ODBC service is providing without having to rely on its name.

8. Enter the name of the actual SQL Server where the data resides. If SQL Server is running locally on Windows NT, it is possible to enter **(local)**, and the ODBC driver will find the server using the Named Pipes protocol.

9. Enter a network address or network library if your network/database administrator indicates that one is necessary. Generally, these can be left on "(Default)" and the ODBC driver will find the server when first connecting.

10. Enter a database name that the ODBC service should connect to, such as **PUBS**. Some ODBC client programs lack the capability to change databases via ODBC commands, so it may be necessary to specify a data source for each database you want to connect to on the same server.

11. Unless there is a good reason to override the defaults of language and code page translation, they should be left as defaults. The completed SQL Server Setup dialog box is shown in Figure 25.5.

FIG. 25.5

The ODBC SQL Server Setup dialog box is complete and ready to add a new data source for ODBC.

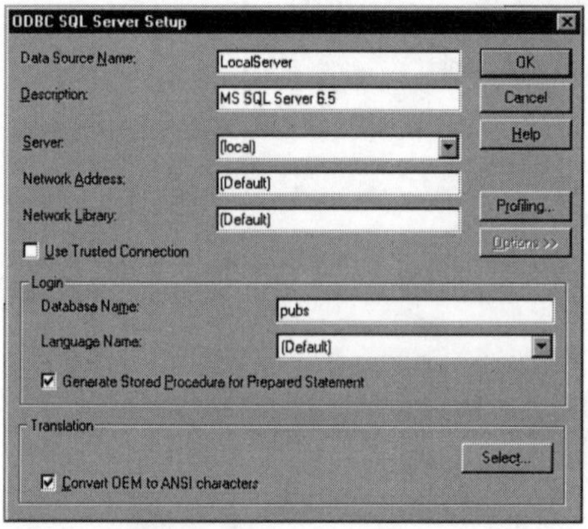

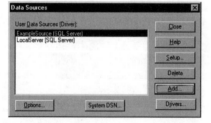

12. Click OK to add the data source. After clicking OK, the new server will be added to the list of available data sources. See Figure 25.6.

FIG. 25.6

The new entry, LocalServer, is in the User Data Sources (Driver) selections.

Using Gupta's SQLWindows

Gupta's SQLWindows is a classic front-end tool that has been around since the late 1980s. Since that time, it has acquired various drivers written natively to provide communications to different DBMSs. Most recently, ODBC was added with SQLWindows 5.0. However, because Microsoft revised ODBC with the release of SQL Server 6, Gupta was required to address the new functionality provided in the ODBC driver and put out a special release. Consequently, in order to connect to SQL Server 6.5 from SQLWindows, you must use version 5.0.2.

On the CD

All the source code that follows for the SQLWindows application can be found in
SWINDEMO.APP on the enclosed CD-ROM.

Establishing a Connection

Connecting or preparing SQLWindows for use with SQL Server 6 involves using Gupta's
query and report writing tool, Quest, to set up statements in a private INI file with connection
information about the ODBC data source. The GUPTA.INI file can be found in the directory
that is indicated in the WIN.INI file by the SqlWinDir option.

Preparing SQLWindows for SQL Server 6.x To use Quest to prepare the ODBC interface,
perform the following steps:

1. Install SQLWindows from the CD-ROM.
2. From the program group that SQLWindows installed in, double-click the Quest icon. See
   Figure 25.7.

FIG. 25.7
The Database Explorer
lets you work with the
different attributes of
the ODBC configuration.

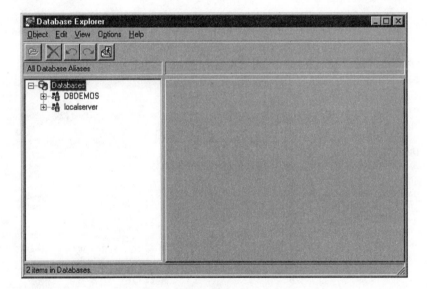

3. From the Utilities menu, select Database and then click Add. This displays the Add
   Database dialog box shown in Figure 25.8.

FIG. 25.8
The New Database Alias
dialog box in SQL
Explorer has MSSQL
selected.

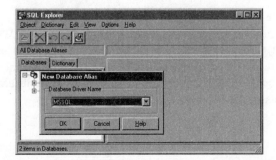

Part
V
Ch
25

4. Select the LocalServer database, or the name that was entered previously for an ODBC data source.

5. Enter the user that is going to be used to connect to the database—for example, **SA**. Note that user names and passwords are case-sensitive.

6. Enter the password that is required for the user entered in step 5.

CAUTION

SQLWindows and Gupta's other products, such as Quest, require that you enter a password for the database that you are connecting to. If you do not enter a password, Gupta will pass in the default password of sysadm. You *must* configure a password for the users that will access the database via ODBC.

Remember that the default installation of SQL Server is to install SA with no password. This must be changed.

---

7. Click OK to test the connection and to confirm that the user and password were entered correctly. If it's successful, the LocalServer database will be added to the list in the main Quest window shown in Figure 25.9.

FIG. 25.9

A completed database definition is ready to be applied by using the SQL Explorer from Delphi 2. Note that there is a highlighted arrow pointing to the database being worked on, indicating that it has not been activated yet.

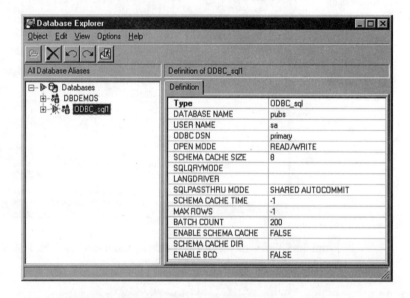

Connecting to SQL Server 6.5   Connecting to SQL Server using SQLWindows is relatively straightforward. SQLWindows has three reserved words that are used to specify the user ID, password, and database that is going to be connected to. Listing 25.1 shows the setting of the variables with hard-coded values. In your application, you would probably have some kind of dialog box that you use to achieve the same result.

**Listing 25.1 SWINDEMO.APP—Connecting to SQL Server Using
SQLWindows'** *SqlConnect( )* **Function**

```
Pushbutton: pbConnect
. . .
    Message Actions
        On SAM_Click
            Set SqlUser = 'sa'
            Set SqlPassword = 'dell'
            Set SqlDatabase = 'LocalServer'
            If NOT SqlConnect( hSql )
                Call SalMessageBox('Failed to connect to SQLServer!',
                                    'Demo - Warning', MB_IconAsterisk)
```

hSql is a local variable of type Sql Handle that is defined on the form.

Preparing and Executing SQL Statements

SQLWindows provides a simple interface for executing. The same interface is used to prepare
and execute queries on all database server types. Listing 25.2 shows the execution of a simple
SELECT to count the number of objects and place the results in the data field on the screen
dfCount.

**Listing 25.2 SWINDEMO.APP—Executing a SQL Statement on SQL Server
Using SQLWindows'** *SqlPrepareAndExecute( )* **Function**

```
On SAM_Click
    Set sSQL = '
            Select      count(*)
            Into        :dfCount
            From        sysobjects'
    If NOT SqlPrepareAndExecute( hSql, sSQL )
        Call SalMessageBox( 'Failed to execute a select from the SQLServer!',
                            'Demo - Warning', MB_IconAsterisk )
    If NOT SqlFetchNext( hSql, nReturn )
        Call SalMessageBox( 'Failed to fetch on the select from the
                            SQLServer!', 'Demo - Warning', MB_IconAsterisk )
```

Notice the use of the SQL Handle, hSql, is in all activity that involves the database. The SQL
Handle is the logical entity through which all database interaction is performed.

Using Stored Procedures and Command Batches

In SQLWindows, there are some extension functions used for executing stored procedures on
the server. These functions are prefixed with the letters Odr. To add this functionality to an
application, include the Gupta-supplied include file, ODBSAL.APL, which should be located in
the root Gupta directory.

Part
V

Ch
25

A simple stored procedure is used to test stored procedure execution. Listing 25.3 shows the code for the stored procedure.

Listing 25.3   SWINDEMO.APP—Simple Stored Procedure Used to Test Stored Procedure Execution in SQLWindows

```
create proc ConnectivityTest
as
Select      Count(*)
From        Sysobjects
Where       Type = 'U'
```

Listing 25.4 shows results are fetched and returned to the same dfCount data field.

Listing 25.4   SWINDEMO.APP—Executing Stored Procedure on SQL Server Using SQLWindows' *OdrExecuteProc( )* Function

```
On SAM_Click
    Set sSQL = 'ConnectivityTest'
    If NOT OdrExecuteProc( hSql, sSQL, ':dfCount' )
        Call SalMessageBox( 'Failed to execute a select from the SQLServer!',
                            'Demo - Warning', MB_IconAsterisk )
    If NOT SqlFetchNext( hSql, nReturn )
        Call SalMessageBox( 'Failed to fetch on the select from the
                            SQLServer!', 'Demo - Warning', MB_IconAsterisk )
```

Centura SQLWindows

Centura Corporation, formerly Gupta Corporation, changed its name to Centura Software Corporation in March 1996. Along with the name change comes a whole new development tool: Centura.

As a new product, Centura is remarkably stable and feature rich. It is fully code compatible with SQLWindows and yet adds full 32-bit engineering to its arsenal. The new user interface embraces Windows 95's Explorer model. See Figure 25.10.

In addition to beefing up its development tool, Centura sports new class wizards that support three-tier programming through three of the most popular architectures: Novell's QuickTuxedo, Open Environment Corporation's DCE-based QuickRPC, and QuickCICS. See Figure 25.11.

Finally, Centura adds a new tool for the developer. The Database Explorer is similar to Delphi 2's and allows easy browsing of all the key attributes. It even includes editable tables that allow you to directly manipulate the data in the database.

FIG. 25.10

The SQL Explorer has the new database highlighted and its name has been changed to LocalServer.

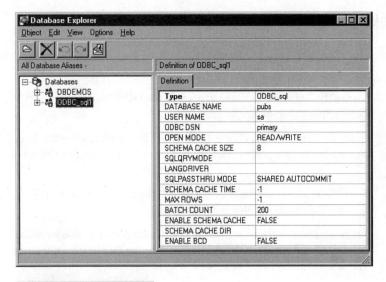

FIG. 25.11

When you open the connection to SQL Server, you'll be prompted to log on.

More Information and Examples

Gupta has provided two instructive sample applications, ODBSAL1.APP and ODBSAL2.APP, that can be found in the \SAMPLES directory below the Gupta directory. These examples show in more detail how to connect to the database and perform various operations on them.

Using Borland's Delphi 2

Borland's Delphi 2 is a strong client/server application tool that helps ease the way to working with ODBC data sources. Based on Pascal, Delphi 2 is the newest version of Delphi that was originally released in 1996. Delphi 2 is a 32-bit development environment that has received much praise for its ease of use and integration.

All the source code that follows for the Delphi 2 application can be found in DPHI20.PRJ and DPHIDEMO.* on the CD-ROM.

Part
V

Ch

25

Establishing a Connection

Delphi 2 has native drivers for SQL Server 6.5 that are shells over Microsoft's ODBC. The simplest way to prepare Delphi 2 for use with a database is to use the Database Explorer applet that ships with Delphi 2.

To use the Database Explorer to prepare the ODBC interface, start Delphi and select Database, Explore. See Figure 25.7.

From the Object menu, choose New. Select the configuration you have set up for your SQL Server. In the example, MSSQL is used for SQL Server. Click OK when finished. See Figure 25.8.

Click the editable portion of the DATABASE NAME property in the right pane and enter the name for the database to be referenced: **PUBS**.

Enter the name of the user that will connect by default to this database in the USER NAME property in the right pane: **sa**. In addition, update the ODBC driver settings as needed for the properties listed in the dialog box. See Figure 25.9.

N O T E   Though used in these examples for ease of presentation, you should always avoid using the SQL Server SA account for database development. Create a new user and set it up for appropriate access to the system. ■

From the Object menu, select Apply to activate this database. You will notice that the arrow goes away. Figure 25.10 shows the new database is available and ready for use.

N O T E   If you want to change the alias name for this database from the default of MSSQL*X*, where *X* corresponds to the number of default databases installed so far, highlight the database in the left pane of the Explorer. From the Object menu, select Rename. Enter the new name for the database alias and press Enter. ■

To test that everything is configured correctly, click the plus sign to the left of the database alias name to expand the Explorer view. This will display the Database Login dialog box, as shown in Figure 25.11.

Enter the **sa** password. The Explorer tree will expand, indicating the various components of the SQL Server that are available for manipulation via SQL Explorer.

Understanding the Delphi 2 Database Model

In its most common use, Delphi 2 has a layered approach to interfacing with databases. This layering provides several levels of abstraction from the database itself, allowing a generic application programming interface through common objects.

Delphi 2 has a number of classes that can be used to actually manipulate the data. These classes are responsible for executing the appropriate queries to perform any manipulation required. The classes that can be used vary from TTable, which is used for representing a table, to `TQuery`, which enables a custom query to be presented to the controls that make up the user interface. These data interface classes are typically not seen on the form.

These physical data sources are then mapped to a class that is responsible for interfacing with user interface objects/controls, such as data fields and lists. This interface is performed through a nonvisual class, `TDataSource`, which transfers data from the physical data class to the visual objects and data-bound controls that you place on an edit form.

Manipulating the data in `TQuery` or `TTable` to fetch records, update them, and so forth, can be performed by invoking the methods that they have or by adding a Navigation control to the edit form. `TDBNavigator` is a class that interacts with `TDataSource` and provides the standard Next, Previous, Insert, and Update buttons to manipulate the data on the form. By placing one of these controls on an edit form and then hooking—either at design time by setting its property or at runtime by adjusting its property to the required data source on the form—you will have all the necessary components to build an edit window to a data structure. This structure can be either a query or database table.

Finally, in Delphi 2 it is necessary to add controls to view/edit the actual data. Delphi 2 provides all the standard edit controls, including list boxes and combo boxes, that have properties that enable them to be hooked to a particular `TDataSource`. Placing the control on the form and setting its `DataSource` and `DataField` properties is all that is required.

About the Sample Application DPHIDEMO

The sample application provided here demonstrates a simple edit form to the authors' table in the PUBS database. This application took less than 10 minutes to write and shows how easy it is to use Delphi 2.

The application demonstrates the use of basic `TTable.Table_Authors` to read directly from the database table. On top of this class is `TDataSource.MyDataSource` that performs the data source manipulation. There are data fields on the form that enable editing of the basic name and address information in the table. They are all of class `TDBEdit`.

Finally, to control the interaction with the database, `TDBNavigator.MyNavigator` is hooked to `TDataSource.MyDataSource`. To upgrade the application and to learn a tiny part of Delphi 2, some code executes whenever the form is resized so that the Navigator control stays "docked" to the bottom of the window. The code in Listing 25.5 shows the simple code behind the form.

Listing 25.5   DPHI20.PRJ—Dynamic Form Resizing with Objects that Paint Inside the Form's Boundaries

```
procedure TForm1.FormResize(Sender: TObject);
begin
    MyNavigator.Top := Form1.ClientHeight - MyNavigator.Height;
    MyNavigator.Width := Form1.ClientWidth;
    end;
end.
```

Perhaps the nicest feature of Delphi 2 is that the data access can be tested during design. The TTable class has a property of Active, which, if enabled, will connect to the database and present data to the controls if they are hooked via a TDataSource. This enables you to at least see something of what the application is going to look like at runtime.

Preparing and Executing SQL Statements

Delphi 2 represents ad hoc queries through the class TQuery. TQuery is a nonvisual class that has properties that enable it to be attached to a database. The SQL property is provided to enable the setting of the required SQL statement. TQuery then interacts with a TDataSource just like TTable.

In the sample application, the Active property is set to True when the Titles button is clicked. This causes the SQL to be executed in TQuery.MyQuery and the Grid control to be populated with the results of the SELECT statement. The Grid control, TDBGrid.MyDBGrid, is hooked to the data source for presentation of the query results.

Clicking the Titles button executes the default SQL that was set in TQuery.MyQuery at design time. The Publishers button dynamically changes the SQL and executes it. Listing 25.6 shows what is required to do this SQL changing at runtime in Delphi 2.

On the CD

Listing 25.6   DPHI20.PRJ—Setting a SQL Statement in a Delphi 2 Control and then Activating (Executing) It

```
procedure TForm1.Button2Click(Sender: TObject);
begin
    MyQuery.Active := False;
    MyQuery.SQL.Clear;
    MyQuery.SQL.Add( 'Select * from publishers');
    MyQuery.Active := True;
end;
```

Using Stored Procedures and Command Batches

Delphi 2's implementation of stored procedures and command batches is identical to that of the general query execution principle. A StoredProcName property is provided to enable you to hook the object with a stored procedure in the server. The TStoredProc is then attached/hooked to a TDataSource and accessed normally through other data controls.

More Information and Examples

A nice feature of Delphi 2 is that class-specific help is invoked whenever F1 is pressed during design if an object is highlighted. This will make it easy for you to find out about the properties and methods of the Delphi 2 classes provided by Borland.

Also, check out the Delphi forum on CompuServe where you will get a lot of help from other Delphi users, along with their Web site, which hosts several discussion forums, online service bulletins, and additional downloadable samples. They can be found on the Internet at **http://www.borland.com**.

Using Microsoft Visual Basic 4 and 5

Visual Basic 5 (VB5) is Microsoft's latest incarnation of the BASIC standard. VB5 begins the major overhaul of the different application-based environments like PowerPoint, Excel, and Word to include VB. In addition, it provides the links from developing stand-alone applications and tools for the Internet.

As a general tool, it has great features and has a huge install base. VB also includes some form-wizard-like features, allowing VB to generate some generic VB forms that you can use as a starting point for your development efforts.

As mentioned in Chapter 22, "Developing Applications to Work with SQL Servers," VB also supports the use of the object libraries for access to SQL Server. These are important advancements and provide a solid footing for VB in client/server application development.

All the source code that follows for the Visual Basic application can be found in VB4DEMO .FRM and VB4.VBP on the CD-ROM.

Understanding the Visual Basic Database Model

Visual Basic and Delphi 2 have a similar approach to data access. Data access is controlled by a data object that resides on a form. Unlike Delphi 2, VB does not use truly nonvisual object classes or container classes. Instead, it is possible to alter the visible property of the data object to hide it if you want.

You can work with databases a number of different ways in VB. First, if you need to have a series of fields bound to the database, and want to have the connection provide the process of updating the field automatically, you can use the data-bound control. The data control lets you indicate the connection properties and then link controls on your form to the control and its associated columns.

The other alternatives to working with databases in VB include the use of objects and their associated properties, collections, and more. Accessing SQL Server using these approaches is outlined in Chapter 22, "Developing Applications to Work with SQL Server" on developing applications for use with SQL Server.

Connecting to SQL Server

Because the data-bound controls in VB are dependent upon the ODBC configuration, you must first set up an ODBC driver and its associated properties. Once you've completed this, you can bind the control to the ODBC installation and configuration. When the application is run, it uses this information to connect to SQL Server and work out the connection details.

You can use the Data Form Designer Wizard to create a data form. This will also create a connect string for you that you can use in connecting to the database in other portions of your
application.

The connection string that is used by the ODBC connection includes all of the information
necessary to log onto and use the SQL Server in question. The syntax for the connection
string is

```
ODBC;DSN=LocalServer;UID=sa;PWD=dell;
➥ APP=Data Form Designer;WSID=DELL_NT_SERVER;DATABASE=pubs
```

The information in this string can also be set at runtime by altering the Connect property
of the Data control.

Preparing and Executing SQL Statements

VB's Data control can be used to either represent tables or process queries directly. The
RecordSource property can be set to either a table name or to a query. The following code
snippet demonstrates a pushbutton changing the query used to populate the Data control.

In turn, the Data control acts as a DataSource for a DBGrid control that is also on the form.
Performing the Refresh method of the Data control causes the query to execute and the grid
to be populated:

```
Private Sub Command3_Click()
    MyDataSource2.RecordSource = "select * from titles"
    MyDataSource2.Refresh
End Sub
```

About the Sample Application VB4DEMO

The sample application that is included on the CD-ROM demonstrates a basic form that enables browsing and editing of the authors table in the PUBS database. The application has an
Update button that interfaces with Data.MyDataSource and invokes its UpdateRecord method,
as follows:

```
Private Sub Command1_Click()
    MyDataSource.UpdateRecord
End Sub
```

In a similar fashion, the Delete button removes a record from the table. By default, the typical
toolbar provided with the data control does not provide for deletion of records.

Instead, you must resolve the reference manually by referring to the Data control's Recordset.
You need to reference the Delete method:

```
Private Sub Command2_Click()
    MyDataSource.Recordset.Delete
End Sub
```

From Here...

In this chapter, you learned about the basics of ODBC and how to configure it on a workstation. In addition, you were introduced to three different approaches to client/server application programming and connectivity: Gupta's SQLWindows 5.0.2, Borland's Delphi 2, and Microsoft's Visual Basic.

Each of the products covered in this chapter is strong in certain areas and weak in others. Choosing one of these development tools should be done after carefully evaluating a project's needs.

- Chapter 22, "Developing Applications to Work with SQL Server," provides additional information about developing applications for use with SQL Server.

- Chapter 26, "Upsizing Microsoft Office 97 Applications," covers information about how you can migrate Access-based applications to the client/server environment of SQL Server.

Part

V

Ch

25

Upsizing Microsoft Office 97 Applications to SQL Server

Learn how to build applications that integrate your Microsoft Office components with SQL Server

Microsoft Access has significant database capabilities built in to it that can be perfect for a client-side-only application. In some cases, it's helpful to integrate these solutions with SQL Server as the application grows.

See how to painlessly migrate your Access application to SQL Server, without changing code in the Access application

By combining the components in SQL Server and Access, you can create full-blown client server applications. By carefully upsizing your application, you can even create these applications in a way that you won't have to change any code, reports, or macros.

Microsoft Office 97 brought into being a comprehensive solution for developing applications based in the productivity tools that make up the suite. Office 97 now has Visual Basic throughout the suite, from Word to Excel to Access. In each of these environments, you have the ability to develop complete applications based on the language.

Throughout this book, you've seen how to set up and work with SQL Server, but in this chapter, the focus is more on interacting with SQL Server, rather than administering the server itself. Much of the access to SQL Server can be standardized into a discussion of the Data Access Objects, and there are special considerations when working from Access. By and large, the ability to work with data from a SQL Server can be a good addition to your applications. In addition, by using some client/server techniques to work with information, you can leverage the processing power of the SQL Server system in your applications.

This chapter focuses on two distinct areas. First, you'll see how to move your databases from Access to SQL Server and how to work with databases and tables that are based in SQL Server from within Access.

The second area of focus is that of developing an application in VB that can work with database tables. Each of these will be highlighted here. ■

Upsizing to SQL Server from Access

As of this writing, an upsizing wizard for Access 97 is not yet available. You can check back with the Microsoft Access site, located on the Web at www.microsoft.com/access, and download the utility after it becomes available. The Upsizing Wizard is currently available for Access 95 and Access 2.

The upsizing tools help you migrate a database schema to SQL Server by moving your tables and relationships to SQL Server-based objects. The utilities will move your tables to the server by exporting them and creating the necessary indexes and other supporting objects. In addition, triggers can be created that will enforce any relational integrity rules you've implemented in Access.

What results is a system in Access that contains linked tables that reference the tables in SQL Server. See Figure 26.1 for an example.

FIG. 26.1

When you link to tables in SQL Server, they are shown with the link icon but can be accessed with your standard Basic instructions.

The wizard will not create stored procedures for you to take the place of data manipulation you may be performing in your Access Basic code. In these cases, you'll want to work through the information in this book on stored procedures and compare it to the types of things you're doing in your Basic code. Wherever possible, consider moving database manipulation statements and processes to stored procedures and out of your code.

In the next sections, you'll see how you can manually migrate your tables to SQL Server. You'll also see how to create the links you'll need to work with the tables as seamlessly as possible.

Using Microsoft Access with SQL Server

Microsoft Access gives you an excellent development environment with many of the capabilities of SQL Server available for testing and implementation planning. Because Access is a smaller engine and not truly client/server, its use as a server system in a larger implementation is somewhat limited, but it still provides an unmatched development environment for database work.

TIP This chapter is by no means a complete tutorial on the use of Microsoft Access. For detailed operation information, how-to assistance, and the like, be sure to get a copy of any of several books from Que, including:

● *Access 97 Expert Solutions*, by Stan Leszynski, 1997

● *Special Edition, Using Microsoft Access*, by Roger Jennings

This chapter is meant to provide a quick overview of what you'll need to do to work with database and table information shared between Access and SQL Server.

Access gives you a good user interface in which to develop the tables and relationships. There are some differences in how Access works with databases, including items at both the physical storage aspect and slightly different terminology when discussing some items. Some examples are:

■ With Access, there is no concept of a device as in SQL Server. The rough equivalent to the SQL Server device would be the hard disk drive on which the database is created. Databases in Access are stand-alone files, typically with an .MDB extension.

■ With Access, views are called *queries*. As with SQL Server, you can create updateable queries, you can select rows from a query, and you can create multi-table joins represented in a query.

■ In SQL Server, individual columns represent specific data items within a row. While data item groups are referenced as rows in Access, columns are referenced as fields.

■ Data types do not use the same name and are physically different in many cases between SQL Server and Access.

There are others, but these are the key differences that will likely help in your use of SQL Server with Access. If you have an application in Access, it's represented by up to six different elements. See Table 26.1 for a quick explanation of the different components and whether it's something you'll likely be upsizing or converting to SQL Server.

Table 26.1 Basic Elements of an Access-Based System

Element	Description and Upsizability
Tables	Same as SQL Server. This is probably the single most important item that you'll be upsizing. Tables represent the rows of information in Access that you want to convert to SQL Server.

continues

Part

V

Ch

26

Table 26.1   Continued

Element	Description and Upsizability
Queries	Queries will likely need to be converted, but it will be a largely manual task to do so. This means you'll have to review the SQL behind the query and create the appropriate view on SQL Server. Remember, too, that you can LINK to a view on SQL Server and use it as you would a table, assuming you declare an "index" on the view.
Forms	Forms will not be converted to SQL Server. Remember, in the client/server model, the client system is responsible for the management of the user interface; the server has responsibility for the management and manipulation of the data.
Reports	As with forms, this item will not likely be converted. Of special note, however, is any report based on a query. In Access, you can code the query into the report. To get the best results, you'll want to review the property sheets for the report, convert the hard-coded query, and make it a view in SQL Server. Then, in the query, reference the new view. Performance will be enhanced, the report will run the same as it did with the hard-coded query, but the result is a client/server implementation of the report.
Macros	Macros are strictly an Access item. Macros may be calling on Queries, and they may be issuing some higher level commands that are worth reviewing. As with Reports, you don't want to have a macro that relies on a query that you can place into SQL Server for better performance.
Modules	Modules are rarely an automatic decision to upsize. What this means is that you need to consider each and every procedure and subroutine to determine what's best upsized. With the modules, you have several options. You may be converting a subroutine to a stored procedure, a view, or a dynamic query. It will depend entirely on the processing you're doing in the database. Remember to make changes in short batches and continue testing. It's important as you start working with the core functionality of your system that you test it thoroughly before moving on to the next conversion goal.

Upsizing an application usually takes on several different steps, outlined in the next sections.

Upsizing Access Applications—An Example

When you convert pieces of your application to use SQL Server, it can be helpful to do so in stages that let you test each step of the way. In these examples, you'll see how to convert portions of the Northwind Traders demonstration database. The sample database is provided with Access as a learning tool and can be installed when you set up Access on your system.

CAUTION

Moving your information to SQL Server should be done at a time when other users are not on your system. During the process, if information is added to the Access tables, it will not be reflected in the SQL Server tables. In addition, there is no easy way to re-synch the tables to gather any information that had been missed in the transition. Be sure you have exclusive use of the database if dynamic changes are typically made to the system.

Moving the Tables to SQL Server The first step is typically moving your tables and their associated data to the SQL Server system. This is done pretty simply in Access, by using the Export functionality built in to the system. To start, open the Northwind application and select the Tables tab. See Figure 26.2.

FIG. 26.2
The Northwind system lets you work with a largely functional ordering system and includes several tables to work with.

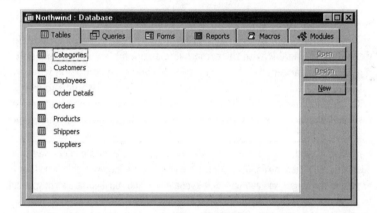

The first thing you'll do is select a table and then right-click it. Select Save As/Export from the resulting menu. Select To an External File or Database from the dialog box that results. This enables you to send the information to an alternate destination, rather than copying it within the current database. See Figure 26.3.

FIG. 26.3
You can use the Export option to make copies of data in an existing Access database. For sending information to SQL Server, however, you'll need to send it to an external database.

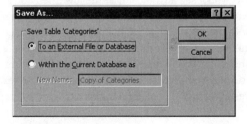

When you make your selection and click to continue, you'll be presented with a dialog box that prompts you with the type of export you want to perform. As you can see in Figure 26.4, you need to select the type of export you want to perform.

Part V
Ch
26

FIG. 26.4

The option to export to SQL Server is supported as an ODBC setting. ODBC is the last selection on the Save as type list box.

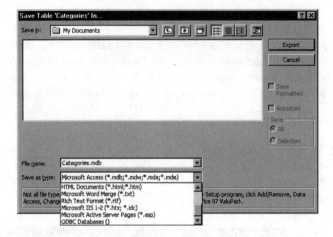

When you select ODBC, you'll be asked to specify the name of the table you'll export to. The default will be a table with the same name as the table you're exporting. For most systems, it's a good idea to accept the default name. This will save confusion when you're linking to the table later. Finally, you'll be prompted to select the ODBC data source you'll use to connect with the database on SQL Server. In Figure 26.5, you can see that you are able to select from all installed data sources, or you can create a new data source for the conversion batch.

If you'll be using this in a production environment, you'll save trouble later if you create a new data source for the linked tables. Write down the name and use it only for this task. That way, if a user name or password changes, you can update it in one place, and you'll update all of your links using that DSN to get to SQL Server.

After you select the ODBC DSN to use, the export process will begin. You'll be asked to log in to the server first, allowing you one final chance to select the database you want to use. To use the option, select the Options >> button on the dialog box. In the example shown in Figure 26.6, the Northwind database is used for the export.

During the export process, you'll see an indicator in the lower-left corner of the Access workspace that will tell you the status of the process. After the process is completed, the table will be on SQL Server, with the structure and data intact. As you can see in Figure 26.7, the table now shows up in the Enterprise Manager. You should always confirm that the table was converted without a problem. Perhaps the best way to do this is to run a simple `select * from table` and compare the results from Access with those from SQL Server. Repeat this export process for each table, resulting in a total of eight tables exported to the server.

FIG. 26.5
Select the appropriate DSN you'll use to gain access to the database and tables you need.

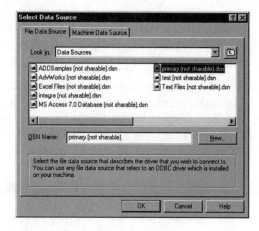

FIG. 26.6
When you log in, you'll have the opportunity to select which database you want to export into.

FIG. 26.7
You should verify that each table has exported to the database you planned before you continue with the upsizing of your application.

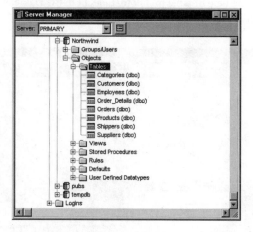

Part
V
Ch
26

At this point, there is no difference in your Access application. You've exported only the structures and data to the SQL Server system. The next step is to make the SQL Server tables those that are referenced when your application is run. Doing so requires that you first rename your existing tables, then create the links to the SQL Server-based information.

From Access, rename each table by right-clicking it and choosing the Rename option from the menu. Simply add "OLD" before the existing name and press Enter. You can use anything you'd like here. The key is to keep the old table (so don't delete it) and to rename it so you can create the active links that point to the SQL Server. When you're finished, you'll have a list of tables that resembles those shown in Figure 26.8.

FIG. 26.8

By renaming each table, you leave yourself the option of falling back to the original tables without a problem.

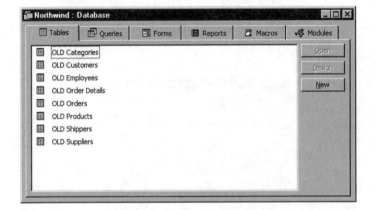

The last step to begin using your now-SQL Server-based tables is to link to them from Access. Right-click the Tables form and select Link Tables... from the menu. Once again, you'll be prompted for the table and type of table to link to. Select ODBC Databases () from the Files of type list box (see Figure 26.9).

FIG. 26.9

As with the export process, you'll be using an ODBC data source for the linked tables from SQL Server.

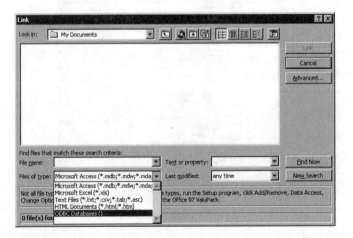

Select your ODBC data source, and you'll be prompted to log in to SQL Server. Remember, if you're using a different database, select the Options >> button to select it prior to completing the login. As soon as you log in, Access will display the list of tables from the database. You'll notice, as shown in Figure 26.10, that each table has a DBO prefix, representing the database owner.

FIG. 26.10

Access will automatically query SQL Server to determine what tables are available.

You'll also notice that any file name characters that were allowed in Access, but not in SQL Server, will be replaced to be correct for SQL Server. In the example, the Access table "ORDER DETAILS" was updated to be named "ORDER_DETAILS." Click each table you want, or in this case, click Select All. Next, click the OK button to begin the linking process. As each table is linked, you will be prompted to indicate the unique identifier for it. The list of fields, or columns, that you see will be taken from the table, and you'll need to highlight the index field or fields (see Figure 26.11).

FIG. 26.11

If you can, select the same fields for your key on the linked fields as you have for the original tables.

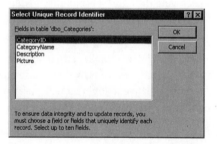

Be sure you select a field or combination of fields that will result in a unique key to the table. This is required in order to have an updateable table from Access. In many cases, as is the case with the Northwind sample database, several different elements may be required to create a unique key on the table. Be sure you have your database schema handy when you link to the tables.

N O T E The information you provide for the index is used to create a pseudo-index, based in Access. This index is used to work with SQL Server to provide the information to uniquely identify a row for updates. The index is not created in SQL Server, so you won't see it on the table if you review the objects associated with the table in SQL Server. ■

If you make a mistake, or later find that the indexes don't provide the functionality you need, you can always unlink the table and re-link it. After you've linked the tables and provided the information to identify the index, Access's tables will be updated to show the new links. You'll notice a globe next to each of the SQL Server tables, indicating that it's accessed externally. Figure 26.12 shows the results of linking the tables to the Access database.

FIG. 26.12

Once added, the linked tables are shown with a different icon next to them.

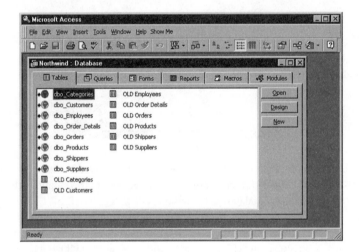

Of course, you've probably noticed that the tables came in with names that aren't quite right. You need to rename the tables, removing the "dbo_" prefix that's been added to them. As before, you can rename them by right-clicking them, selecting Rename, and removing the prefix. The result is a series of tables with the original names but linked to SQL Server.

At this point, you should run your application and make sure it still performs as you expect. If you have any problems, check the file names you've provided and make sure the SQL Server information you've provided is accurate relative to login names, passwords, and so on. If you have any trouble at all, do not continue in the upsizing until you've corrected the problem.

You may notice that you already have better performance on the application. It's interesting to see that even by moving the data to SQL Server, you can obtain some benefits, even without optimizing Select statements, queries, and other functions.

After you're satisfied that you've successfully converted your tables to SQL Server, you can review the queries to see which ones are likely candidates for translation into a view or stored procedure in SQL Server.

Reviewing the Queries—Making Views Converting your queries to SQL Server is not quite as straightforward as exporting and linking to tables, but it can certainly be faster than writing the views from scratch. The basic premise of moving the queries to SQL Server is that you'll create a view in SQL Server, then link to it just as you do a table. Because Access sees queries and tables as functional equivalents, this is another place you can make the changes to the data, make no changes to the application, but still get the benefits of a client/server implementation.

In this example, you'll convert one of the queries from the Northwind database, Order Subtotal, to a view. Then you'll see how to reference the view and use it in your applications. Of course, the goal of this is as mentioned earlier: no code change—only a change in the source of information.

To begin, select the Queries tab in Access. Select the Order Subtotal query and click Design. You'll be presented with the query designer, probably in Design mode, looking like that shown in Figure 26.13.

FIG. 26.13
In the default design mode, you can visually design the query by dragging and dropping fields to the query. This, however, isn't the best way to work with the query for creating the associated view.

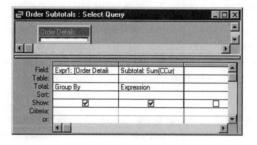

The first thing you'll want to do is change to SQL mode for the query. You can do this in one of two ways. First, you can select View, SQL View from the menus. This will change the display to the associated SQL statements that represent it. You'll get the same result from the second approach, selecting the View drop-down list and selecting SQL View. In either case, the result is that Access will give you the SQL statements, like those shown next:

```
SELECT DISTINCTROW [Order Details].OrderID AS Expr1,
Sum(CCur([UnitPrice]*[Quantity]*(1-[Discount])/100)*100) AS Subtotal
FROM [Order Details]
GROUP BY [Order Details].OrderID;
```

There are a couple of things you'll notice right away from this statement. First, it has references to the tables enclosed in square brackets. Because Access allows you to have spaces in your table names, brackets are used to delineate the names. These aren't allowed in SQL Server, and neither are the spaces in the object names.

You may recall from the work in linking the tables to SQL Server that the names that contained a space were changed to include an underscore character in place of the space. In this example, the table that was changed during the linking demonstration is referenced and will have to be updated to include the underscore.

N O T E Even though you updated the name of the object reference in Access, what you really
updated was the shortcut to the table in SQL Server. The table in SQL Server still contains
the underscore, even though the reference in Access has the space in the object name. ∎

Part
V

Ch
26

You'll need to change DISTINCTROW, inserted automatically by Access, to DISTINCT. SQL Server won't recognize the DISTINCTROW function provided by Access.

Another thing you'll notice is the use of the CCUR function, one that converts numeric values to currency representation. This will have to be either replaced or coded around to format the information as you'll need it.

> **TIP** In this case, the value will be left unconverted as it's used in reports. The Access report writer will format fields for you, saving you the need to format it before using it.

The final thing you'll need to change is the trailing semicolon on the statement. SQL Server doesn't need this and will point it out as a syntax error on the statement.

The first step you can take in testing statements like this is to cut and paste it in to ISQL/W and run it. See what the results are and step through the changes you need to make to get the right results set. In this example, the first thing that's pointed out is a syntax error, as outlined here:

```
Msg 170, Level 15, State 1
Line 1: Incorrect syntax near '['.
```

This error is referencing the brackets around the object names. Remove the brackets and re-run the query to find the next item you need to consider. Of course, when you remove the brackets, change the object name as well so it includes the underscore character. If you don't, SQL Server won't see the table. The result is shown next:

```
SELECT DISTINCT Order_Details.OrderID AS Expr1,
Sum(CCur(UnitPrice*Quantity*(1-Discount)/100)*100) AS Subtotal
FROM Order_Details
GROUP BY Order_Details.OrderID;
```

At this point, you have two final things to update. You need to remove the reference to CCur, and you need to remove the final semicolon. When you do, the results set will start off like that shown in Listing 26.1.

Listing 26.1   Sample Output Listing

```
Expr1         Subtotal
-----------   -----------------------
10248         440.0
10249         1863.39987182617
10250         1552.60003662109
10251         654.060005187988
10252         3597.89990234375
10253         1444.79998779297
10254         556.62003326416
10255         2490.49996948242
10256         517.800003051758
10257         1119.89994049072
10258         1614.88000488281
10259         100.799999237061
10260         1504.64999389648
```

```
10261       448.0
10262       583.999996185303
10263       1873.79995727539
10264       695.625
10265       1175.99995422363
10266       346.559997558594
10267       3536.60000610352
10268       1101.19993591309
10269       642.200012207031
10270       1376.0
10271       48.0
```

By comparison, the same query run against the linked SQL Server table from within Access produces the results shown in Figure 26.14.

FIG. 26.14

The results are the same in the newly modified SQL query that will be used for the View. The only exception is the formatting of the information.

Expr1	Subtotal
10248	$440.00
10249	$1,863.40
10250	$1,552.60
10251	$654.06
10252	$3,597.90
10253	$1,444.80
10254	$556.62
10255	$2,490.50
10256	$517.80
10257	$1,119.90
10258	$1,614.88
10259	$100.80
10260	$1,504.65
10261	$448.00

You're ready now to use this query as the basis for a view. In SQL Enterprise Manager, right-click the Views in the Northwind database. Select New View from the menu to get the dialog box that lets you provide the SQL statements that will comprise the instructions for the view. Cut and paste your SQL statement in to the box after the AS clause. Change the <View Name> to be the name by which you want to know the view.

 TIP Even if you have to place an underscore in the name of the view where a space exists in Access, you should name the view as close to its original name in Access as possible. This will make debugging and tracking down table/view links easier when you're debugging your application.

In Figure 26.15, you can see an example of the view with the name updated and the code pasted in.

Press the "play" button to run and store your new view in the database. When it runs, it will be tested for syntax validity, compiled, and stored. You won't get any results back from the query until you open it explicitly. If all goes well, the query dialog box will be cleared, and you'll be able to create another view if needed.

Part

V

Ch

26

FIG. 26.15
Use the tested SQL statement as the basis for your new view.

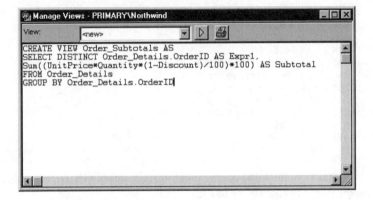

At this time, you've got the view in the SQL Server system, and you're able to use it in a query. You can test the view in ISQL/W by simply issuing a `select * from order_subtotals` statement. The results should match those shown earlier in the test run of the query.

Now the fun begins. What remains is linking the application to the new view and testing the application. Again, the goal is that you don't have to change any code in the application but only the objects referenced in the Access user interface.

Perhaps surprisingly, Access will allow you to link to the view just as you do a table in SQL Server. When you walk through the link process, you'll notice that the view is listed, along with the other tables that are available, automatically (see Figure 26.16).

FIG. 26.16
In the link tables options, views are listed right alongside available tables.

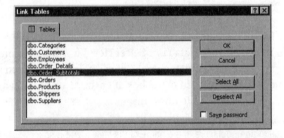

When you combine this with the fact that Access treats queries and tables the same logically in your application, you can quickly see that you'll be able to link to the view and run your application. Link the view to your Access application as you would a table.

Before you can rename the view to the name of the original query, you'll need to rename the query. As with the tables that were linked in earlier, rename the query with an OLD prefix, keeping the query around should the need arise later. After the query has been renamed, rename the newly linked view to the name of the query. In this case, it's `dbo_Order_Subtotals` that should be renamed to `Order Subtotals`.

Now is the time to test. Keep in mind that queries have the potential to be a more difficult testing proposition. It's a bit less obvious in your application where they're referenced. They can be called from reports, modules, and macros. In addition, you can have forms that reference the query. In short, be sure you fully test your application from every conceivable angle before you roll out a converted application to a production environment.

Creating Client/Server Systems with Microsoft Access

Microsoft Access is not a client/server system in and of itself. Applications you develop with it are not inherently developed with both client and server components of the solution. You can, however, use Access as a development tool, providing the user interface for applications. The tools it offers give you good leverage creating your applications, such as the report writer, the query tools, and so on. These are all helpful development tools.

When you create the application, consider first doing so in Access against a database that you can test against, break, and repair. By doing so, you can use Access for what it's best for and still use SQL Server to manage the database aspects of your work.

You've seen throughout this chapter how you can convert those items that should be server based to SQL Server. Tables, queries, and views are objects best managed by SQL Server, and they're easily converted to SQL Server after you've designed them.

Access basically becomes a development environment, giving you tools to manage the interface that is presented to the user and letting you work with SQL Server on the back-end.

Creating Pass-Through Queries

When you create queries in Access and then submit them to SQL Server, they are first parsed for the ODBC connectivity layer and then submitted to SQL Server as a sort of temporary stored procedure to be run. The results are returned to your application, and you can work with the data from there.

What happens if you want or need more control? What if you want to call a stored procedure and use the output from it directly? That's where pass-through queries come in. In Access, you can create a pass-through query that bypasses the translation and submits exactly what you indicate to SQL Server. To set up a query for pass-through operation, first open the query by highlighting it and clicking Design. Next, select Query, SQL-Specific, and finally Pass-through from the menus. When you do, you're presented with the SQL statement equivalent of the query, as shown in Figure 26.17, for the Invoices query in the Northwind database.

Pass-through queries let you call stored procedures, reference views, and use other features of SQL Server that might have been unavailable using the more typical query from Access. To run a stored procedure, for example, you can just use the EXECute command and call out the stored procedure.

FIG. 26.17

When you choose to make a query a pass-through query, Access will switch to SQL mode so you can edit the statement if needed.

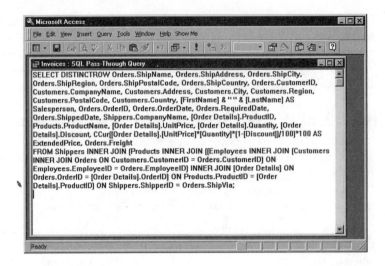

```
Microsoft Access                                             [_][□][X]
File  Edit  View  Insert  Query  Tools  Window  Help  Show Me
```

```
Invoices : SQL Pass-Through Query                           [_][□][X]
SELECT DISTINCTROW Orders.ShipName, Orders.ShipAddress, Orders.ShipCity,
Orders.ShipRegion, Orders.ShipPostalCode, Orders.ShipCountry, Orders.CustomerID,
Customers.CompanyName, Customers.Address, Customers.City, Customers.Region,
Customers.PostalCode, Customers.Country, [FirstName] & " " & [LastName] AS
Salesperson, Orders.OrderID, Orders.OrderDate, Orders.RequiredDate,
Orders.ShippedDate, Shippers.CompanyName, [Order Details].ProductID,
Products.ProductName, [Order Details].UnitPrice, [Order Details].Quantity, [Order
Details].Discount, CCur([Order Details].[UnitPrice]*[Quantity]*(1-[Discount])/100)*100 AS
ExtendedPrice, Orders.Freight
FROM Shippers INNER JOIN [Products INNER JOIN [[Employees INNER JOIN [Customers
INNER JOIN Orders ON Customers.CustomerID = Orders.CustomerID] ON
Employees.EmployeeID = Orders.EmployeeID] INNER JOIN [Order Details] ON
Orders.OrderID = [Order Details].OrderID] ON Products.ProductID = [Order
Details].ProductID] ON Shippers.ShipperID = Orders.ShipVia;
```

```
Ready
```

For example, to call the stored procedure `AccessProc` from a pass-through query, you can use the following statement:

```
exec accessproc
```

When you do, the stored procedure will be executed, and the results will be presented from the query. It's a simple thing to incorporate this type of logic in your application by creating the queries you need or by establishing your queries in Access Basic to be pass-through queries.

Reality Check

Access is a great tool. It provides the capability for corporate developers to create solid, database-centric applications that can be put into production. The applications can include security and can be quick and easy to use. It's a natural way to introduce and "test market" an application with users in the business environment.

Once completed, upsizing the application to SQL Server can make a good application even better. Performance can be improved, security can be added, and the open availability of the application's information can be expanded, providing corporate-wide access to the application if needed.

In practical applications, using Access as the development and test platform works well. We've used this approach at several sites with good success. The issues that don't tend to get ironed out appropriately in test situations that rely on Access include the following:

■ Performance issues on indexing and heavy-insert type applications—This will generally have to be revisited when you move to SQL Server because you'll have more opportunity to optimize the system. You can look to better indexes and other server-side processes to help with the performance in SQL Server, whereas these options are not available at the same level in Access. You can add indexes in Access, but they may have completely different results.

- Fine-tuning queries, views, and stored procedures—By working hard to optimize your stored procedures and other Access-migrated objects, you can significantly improve performance over the initial conversion effort. After the initial conversion and testing have been completed, re-examine your stored procedures and views. Make sure they're coded to take advantage of as many SQL Server features as possible to make them operate efficiently. Be sure to review the chapters in this book on triggers, rules, defaults, and other automated capabilities of SQL Server. Again, by shifting around functionality as much as possible, you'll be able to let the system do much of the work without specifically calling for it.

  One example is that of hard-coding "trigger-type" transactions. Don't do the check from one table against another manually to determine whether a delete will be allowed. Instead, implement a rule or trigger that will enforce the relationship for you, saving you time and coding in the stored procedure.

- Security—Don't forget that when you migrate your application, you still must handle the security on the SQL Server side of the system.

After your first application is converted, you'll come up with additional items that pertain to your development style that need to be reviewed. The best thing you can do is make a list of these items and make sure you check them on each and every system you upsize.

From Here...

In this chapter, you've seen how to move an Access-based application to SQL Server while still maintaining compatibility with the code you have based in Access. You'll do best by your application if you add the special things possible in SQL Server to your database. These include those items in the following closely related chapters:

Part
V

Ch
26

- Chapter 10, "Managing and Using Views," covers how you can further modify the queries that you upsize from Access for use in SQL Server.

- Chapter 11, "Managing and Using Indexes and Keys," will help explain how you can optimize the storage and retrieval of the data in the tables in your system.

- Chapter 13, "Managing and Using Rules, Constraints, and Defaults," can help point out the things you can be doing in SQL Server automatically, without stored-procedure-level coding to ensure data integrity in your system.

- Chapter 15, "Creating and Managing Triggers," covers how you can control how SQL Server manages the information updates to your system, preventing unwanted updates or deletions from your system, regardless of the client-side application used to make the changes.

- There is a mailing list available that works with Office-related development issues. Send e-mail to listserv@peach.ease.lsoft.com and put SUBSCRIBE msoffice-l *firstname, lastname* in the body of the message, including your name as indicated.

Appendixes

Mail-Enabling Your SQL Server

As this book goes to press, Microsoft is readying the release of Exchange Server version 5.0 and has just released Release Candidate 1 of the system. With this in mind, with an eye toward making sure you have the latest information about using SQL Server with Microsoft Exchange, we've decided it would be best to provide this information as an after-the-fact update to this book. The update is free, and is available via several different means.

First, you can visit the author's Web site at **http://www.pobox.com/~swynk** or **http://www.swynk.com**. The updated appendix will be available both as a Microsoft Word file and as an on-line document.

You can also send e-mail to **swynk@swynk.com** and put SQLMAIL UPDATE in the subject of your message. When you do, you'll get a copy of the file e-mailed to you. You can also include comments and suggestions to that e-mail address.

The appendix covers all aspects of connecting to mail from SQL Server, including the following:

- How to start your mail session. This includes how to work around the limitation in SQL Server with the relationship between your SQL Mail login name and the profiles you set up in Exchange.

- Using `xp_startmail` to start the mail session. Alternatively, you can use the SQL Enterprise manager's mail icon to stop and start services.

- How to use the extended stored procedures, including `xp_findnextmsg`, `xp_readmail`, `xp_sendmail`, and `xp_deletemail`. These extended stored procedures let you work with the mail queue, both in reading and sending mail directly from SQL Server-stored procedures.

- How to stop mail services by using both SQL Enterprise Manager and the `xp_stopmail` extended stored procedure.

This up-to-date appendix will provide you with sample procedures and code, as well as complete practical descriptions and notes about applying the extended stored procedures to your mail-based solution. ∎

Understanding RAID

Redundant Arrays of Inexpensive Drives (RAID) currently has six implementations to provide a set of physical devices that will offer better data device integrity and performance. Those levels are described in this appendix. ∎

Level 0

RAID Level 0 is basic data striping across multiple physical devices. The *striping* refers to the fact that multiple drives are allocated for data as a group. The data is then placed across the drives evenly so that each drive has a portion of the data. Striping provides better performance than single drives because multiple I/O threads from the operating system are allocated to servicing each drive. In addition, multiple physical reads and writes can occur simultaneously on the separate physical devices.

RAID Level 0 does not provide any fault tolerance and is purely a performance enhancement.

Level 1

RAID Level 1 is device mirroring. As discussed in Chapter 5, "Creating Devices, Databases, and Transaction Logs," mirroring provides an absolute duplication of the data on any given physical device, on the mirror device. Mirroring can, depending on physical implementation, improve read performance if both drives are read in parallel and data is returned to the operating system in a single stream composed of the parallel reads. Mirroring generally imposes a slight performance cost when writing because two writes are done instead of one.

Mirroring is fault-tolerant and an automatic and complete switch generally handles media failure by switching over to the mirror device.

Level 2

RAID Level 2 is an error-correcting algorithm that employs striping across multiple physical devices. It is more advanced than Level 0 because it uses error correcting "parity" data that is striped across the devices, and copes with media failure on any particular device in the stripe set. The parity data, however, consumes several disks and is quite inefficient as a storage mechanism.

RAID Level 2 is generally not used because it does not offer significant performance benefits over the straight mirroring implementation of Level 1.

Level 3

RAID Level 3 is a different implementation of the striped, parity algorithm. It differs from Level 2 by using only a single device in the stripe set for storing the parity data.

RAID Level 3 offers some performance boost to reads and writes since it's using only the single volume for parity.

Level 4

RAID Level 4 is the same as Level 3, except that it implements a larger block or segment storage size. This means that the basic unit being striped is large in size and generally gets better performance due to the more advanced modern physical devices that are able to read and write bigger blocks of data in a single I/O operation. RAID Level 4 stores the parity information on a separate device from the user data that is striped across multiple physical devices.

RAID Level 4 is an inefficient algorithm and is generally not used.

Level 5

RAID Level 5 is currently the most commonly implemented RAID level. It is a striped implementation that stores parity information on the same striped drives. This allows an individual device to fail and the other devices in the stripe set contain enough information to recover and keep processing. The parity information for any particular device is always stored on another device in the stripe set ensuring that if media failure occurs on a particular device that its parity data is not affected.

RAID Level 5 uses the same large block algorithm as Level 4, and is quite efficient. Level 5 will offer performance gains to reads and writes, until media failure occurs. When media failure occurs, reads suffer because the information on the failed device must be constructed from the parity data stored on the other devices.

App
B

Understanding the SQL System Tables

SQL Server is built by using the "practice what you preach" motto. The entire system, from the tables you create, to the columns in those tables, to configuration options that control SQL Server's operation, is stored in relational tables within the system.

These tables, installed automatically when you install SQL Server on your system, contain the information that SQL Server needs to manage and operate your system. In this appendix, you'll get a better idea about what's in each of these tables. While it's not typically necessary to manually modify these tables, it can be helpful to understand the purpose of each, and what you can expect each to contain.

Starting with Table C.1, each table provides a table name and a brief description of the purpose of the table. ■

Table C.1   SQL Server System Tables

Table Name	Description
Sysalternates	Maps the user's name for a given database. The name is looked up in the table, based on the `suid`, then validated as being allowed access when the user logs in.
Sysarticles	Manages the articles available for publication when you're using replication. You can review this table, and the articles represented by the rows in the table, by using the system-provided `sp_article*` stored procedures.
Syscharsets	Contains the different character data sets available to SQL Server. For example, on a default installation, the character sets shown in Listing C.1A are installed on your server. This table only exists in the master database, and sysconfigures references one row of the table, determining which character set is in use on your system.
syscolumns	Contains one row for each column defined in every other table or view. The rows define the datatypes and behavior of each of the columns in the other tables.
syscomments	Syscomments is used to document the tables in your system. The rows in the table contain information regarding each rule, default, trigger, and constraint. They also outline the stored procedures in your system. The TEXT column of the table contains the SQL statement that makes up the object. If the SQL statement is too long for a text column, or 255 characters, there can be more than one row in the table, essentially pieced back together when they are needed. A given object definition can take up to 255 rows for its definition and associated SQL statement.
sysconfigures	Set for your SQL Server. For example, as mentioned above, it references the character set definition, from the syscharsets table in use. This table is found only in the master database.
sysconstraints	All constraints, and the type of constraint they represent, are defined in this table. Types of constraints, determined by the status column, can be Primary Key, Unique Key, Foreign Key, Check, or Default.
syscurconfigs	Much like sysconfigures, syscurconfigs contains the values that represent the configuration of the system. Sysconfigures contains the values that are the current *saved* values, while syscurconfigs contains the values currently in effect. If you make changes, the syscurconfigs table contains those changes until the next time you restart your server.
sysdatabases	As the name suggests, sysdatabases contains one row for each database in your system. You can select * from sysdatabases to see each database defined in your system, along with the different attributes that define it.
sysdepends	Outlines all dependencies between stored procedures, tables, keys, and so on.

Table Name	Description
sysdevices	Sysdevices contains a single row for each device on your system. The row defines the type of device and its associated configuration parameters. When you install SQL Server, two floppy disk devices, one master database device, and one disk dump device are defined automatically.
sysindexes	Contains one row per index defined for a given database's tables. Indexes defined include both clustered and non-clustered. Sysindexes has replaced the previous syskeys table, though syskeys is still included for legacy systems.
syslanguages	For each language known to SQL Server, there is a single row in this table. It is important to note that English is always available and not included in the listing.
syslocks	When locks are issued against a table, they are represented by a row in this table. The table is built dynamically when you query it, so it is more of a view than a static representation of the locks currently held. Remember that, when you view this table, the locks shown were in effect when the query was issued but may have been released in the time since the query. The TYPE column indicates the type of lock, as shown in Table C.2. If any of the locks appear with 256 added to them, it indicates that the lock is blocking another user. You can query the spid to determine what process is holding the lock.
syslogins	There is one row in the syslogins table for each login for the system. This table also indicates the default database for a user, along with the other configuration options, including disk allocations, for the user.
syslogs	Syslogs contains the transaction log, which is the heart of the SQL Server recovery systems.
sysmessages	Containing roughly 2,200 rows, this table contains all the text messages that you receive when SQL Server issues an alert, error message, or informational message.
sysobjects	From tables to indexes, this table contains the information that defines the objects in your system, including their object ID and type of object.
sysprocedures	Contains the information that serves as a reference into the syscomments table.
sysprocesses	As with several other system tables, the sysprocesses table is built dynamically when you query it. It contains information about all current processes being managed by SQL Server at the time of the query.
sysprotects	Provides the security parameters for users of the system. It provides the information on what types of restrictions are applied to user IDs.

App
C

continues

Table C.1   Continued

Table Name	Description
syspublications	Contains one row for each publication defined in your system as a replication object.
sysreferences	The sysreferences table contains information on all foreign keys in your tables.
sysremotelogins	This table controls remote procedure call user access to your SQL Server. There is one entry in the table for each login allowed to access your system and run remote stored procedures.
syssegments	Defines the fragments that make up your database storage subsystem.
sysservers	The inverse of sysremotelogins, sysservers defines the servers on which you can run remote stored procedures.
syssubscriptions	Lists the subscriptions on your system when you implement replication.
systypes	For each datatype in your system, there is one row in this table. This includes both user-defined datatypes and those provided by the system. By default, those types shown in Table C.3 are installed on your system.
sysusages	As your database grows, each page of the database is recorded in sysusages. The table contains a row for each portion of each database on your system.
sysusers	This table, which is database-specific, contains one row for each user allowed access to the database. It contains information about the group the user belongs to, which will relate the security information as it relates to that database/user combination.

Listing C.1A   Default Character Sets

```
ISO 8859-1 (Latin-1) - Western European 8-bit character set.
Code Page 850 (Multilingual) character set.
Code Page 437 (United States) character set.
Code page 1250
Code Page 1251
Code page 1253
Code page 1254
Code page 1255
Code page 1256
Code page 1257
Code page 949
Code page 950
Code page 936
Binary Sort Order for the CodePage 850 Character Set
Case-insensitive dictionary sort order for use with several Western-European
languages including English, French, and German. Uses the ISO 8859-1 character
set.
Code page 932
```

Table C.2 Type of Locks

Value	Description
1	Table lock, exclusive
2	Table lock, shared
3	Intent lock, exclusive
4	Intent lock, shared
5	Page lock, exclusive
6	Page lock, shared
7	Page lock, update – if the page is updated, this lock will change to an exclusive lock
8	Extent lock, exclusive
9	Extent lock, update
10	Extent lock, next in sequence
11	Previous extent lock

Table C.3 Default Data Types

binary	bit
char	datetime
datetimn	decimal
decimaln	float
floatn	image
int	intn
money	moneyn
numeric	numericn
real	smalldatetime
smallint	smallmoney
sysname	text
timestamp	tinyint
varbinary	varchar

App
C

Understanding SQL Trace

SQL Trace is a graphical utility used to monitor database activity. The monitoring can be done in real-time or on particular users, applications, or hosts. This utility can be used only with SQL Server 6.5 servers. ∎

Starting SQL Trace

The name of the SQL Trace executable file is SQLTRACE.EXE and it is located in the SQL Server BINN directory. By default, the SQL Server 6.5 installation will place a shortcut to SQL Trace in the SQL Server program group. This (or another) shortcut can be used to start the utility or it can be started from the command line. Figure D.1 shows SQL Trace immediately after it is started.

FIG. D.1

When started, SQL Trace will prompt the user to log on.

After successfully connecting to a database, the user is prompted to select which defined filters should be started (see Figure D.2). If no filters are defined, this dialog box does not appear.

FIG. D.2

Filters can begin monitoring a database as soon as the user successfully logs in to that database.

Filters can now be added, deleted, edited, started, stopped, and paused. In addition, several other utilities can be started from within SQL Trace:

- ISQL/w
- SQL Enterprise Manager
- Windows NT Performance Monitor

N O T E   When starting an ISQL/w session from within SQL Trace, ISQL/w will attempt to log in with the login information used to connect SQL Trace to a SQL Server database. ■

Using SQL Trace

The SQL Trace interface is divided into two sections:

- Active Filter Pane
- Filter Status Pane

Activities that meet a filter's criteria are displayed in the active filter pane. The name of the filter being displayed is shown in the title bar. Later, in the "Setting Up a Filter" section, filters will be explained in more detail.

At the bottom of the SQL Trace window is the filter status pane. This pane is made up of several items that display information about filters defined for the current server. Figure D.3 shows a SQL Trace window with an active filter pane and filter status pane visible.

FIG. D.3
The filter status pane can be toggled between visible and invisible.

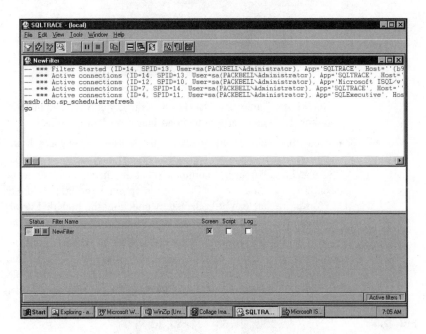

The filter status bar tracks the following information about defined filters for the current server:

- *Status*—Graphically represents the state (started, stopped, or paused) of a filter.
- *Filter Name*—Displays the name that was assigned to the filter when it was defined.
- *Screen*—If you check this option, an active filter pane is displayed for that filter.
- *Script*—Checking this option will cause the activity monitored by the filter to be saved as an SQL script.
- *Log*—Checking this option will cause the activity monitored by the filter to be saved in a log file.

Setting Up a Filter

To create a new filter, follow these steps:

1. Either select New Filter from the File menu or click the New Filter button (refer to Figure D.3). The New Filter dialog box appears (see Figure D.4).

FIG. D.4

Filters can be added or deleted form the New Filter dialog box.

2. Enter a Filter Name as well as any specific Login Name, Application, or Host Name to monitor. To monitor all connections, leave the default <All>.

3. Choose the Capture Options page at the bottom of the dialog box. The SQL can be captured as screen output (View on Screen), SQL script (Save to Script File), log file (Save as Log File), or any combination of the three. Each connection can be monitored separately by using the Per Connection option. In addition to the commands issued, performance data can be collected by checking the Include Performance Information option.

4. Select the Events page and choose the events for which to capture data. As shown in Figure D.5, the Events page also enables you to filter SQL and RPC statements. The SQL and RPC filters are used as string values for which to search. Multiple values can be entered and separated by a semicolon, and the percent sign used as a wildcard.

FIG. D.5

SQL and RPC statements that contain a specified string value can be filtered.

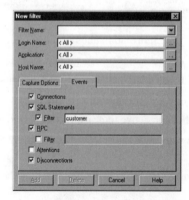

5. Click the Add button to add the filter to the defined filters for the current server.

SQL Trace is a simple but powerful tool. You can use it for many purposes. You can debug applications more simply by using SQL Trace to monitor SQL statements issued from an application. You can address performance issues by recording a particular user's activity. And you can enhance security by checking for dangerous activity on a server. ●

How to Become a Reality Check Site

Throughout this book, you've seen references to the "Que Reality Check Site." The concept behind this site is to provide a checkpoint of sorts on the techniques and technologies presented in a given chapter so you can see how it works where the rubber meets the road.

The Reality Check site has implemented many of the different tasks outlined in a given chapter, and you can review them online at the site to see how they work. The other aspect of the Reality Check is to provide additional feedback on any bumps in the road that may be encountered along the way when you implement the different techniques in a given chapter.

You can have a Reality Check site as well and display the Reality Check logo on your site, too. If you're interested, just send a quick note to **swynk@pobox.com** and indicate your site's URL if it's on the Internet. If your site is an intranet-only implementation, state that in the message.

In addition to the address, provide information on what types of techniques from the book you used at your site. You don't need to go into the gory details, but do let us know what you've implemented. We'll take a look and issue you the logo, complete with the HTML you can use to add the logo to your pages.

In addition, we'll put a link from our site to yours for other people to reference. This will create a network of sites that can be used to review different approaches to the intranet implementations.

The criteria for having a Reality Check site are simple. You must do the following:

- Implement the Reality Check logo in its unaltered state on your server should you decide to show it. The logo will be unobtrusive on your pages and will simply indicate your "membership" in the program.
- Use at least one technique from the book on your site.
- Display the Reality Check logo on your home page.

You can combine your use of the Reality Check site approach with the WebReference materials to gain access to some great technical resources that you can use to ensure your success as the Webmaster for your site.

For examples of existing Que Reality Check sites, you can visit both **http://www.integra.net** and **http://www.intellicenter.com**. ■

Case Study: New York Metropolitan Museum of Art

by Jay Hoffman
Gallery Systems
New York, New York

I began developing software for the art world in 1981 with my first application, *The Museum System*, which is used to catalog art objects. The Museum System stores information about art, including a picture of the object that can be displayed on a PC monitor.

The Museum System is used at more than 75 art galleries in the United States and Europe. U.S. institutions that use the Museum System include The Detroit Institute of Arts, The United States Holocaust Memorial Museum, The United States Supreme Court, The American Craft Museum (New York), and New York University's Grey Art Gallery.

I had decided to develop a similar, but more robust, system that would store information in a Microsoft SQL Server database when the Antonio Ratti Textile Center of The Metropolitan Museum of Art contacted me. The Met wanted me to develop an application that would combine the tracking of movement and preparation of textiles for storage in its new textile facility.

N O T E Objects in museums—even objects publicly displayed—are often temporarily removed by curators or art historians for research purposes. In addition, a number of objects can be removed from display to be lent to other museums. As well as the obvious information that must be kept about art objects, such as who the artist is and when the object was created, the current location of objects must also be kept. ■

The new application that I was to develop for the Met included a read-only version running on PC workstations in an area of the museum accessible to visitors. Visitors would be able to explore the textile database and view images and related data about the textiles. ■

Selecting Microsoft SQL Server for Windows NT

Many departments (including mine) within the Metropolitan Museum of Art that were already using other Microsoft products were pleased with the features and performance of the Microsoft products. The Museum staff's experience with Microsoft's word processor, spreadsheet, and PC database is the reason that I initially considered Microsoft SQL Server.

I also needed a database that could eventually store information about a nearly unlimited number of art objects, though the immediate needs only required the cataloging of less than 100,000 art objects for the textile project. Microsoft SQL Server looked as if it could meet the current needs of the textile project, as well be used to store much more data about additional art objects in the future.

Anticipating Time Required for the Project

There are several phases in the textile project, with the total time for completion specified to be one year and nine months. The first phase was completed on time, and the second phase is moving along nicely. The textile project will probably evolve into a second project with a much longer time frame.

The museum recognizes that it must eventually catalog all objects within the museum's collection so that the information about art objects can be easily and quickly retrieved. Such a project would also have to be completed in phases and would take considerably longer. It's easy to project that the museum should eventually catalog on a computer system information about its entire collection, which is far more vast than the textile information.

Choosing a Computer System

I selected a Sequent 3000 with two Pentium processors for the database server platform. The Sequent system permits me to add additional processors. I anticipate that there will only be a need to add two additional processors in the future when the museum requires additional processing capabilities.

N O T E A product such as Microsoft SQL Server is designed to leverage the power of the Windows NT operating system (see Chapter 2, "Understanding the Underlying Operating System, Windows NT"). SQL Server is written in sections that execute as separate threads under Windows NT.

The greater the number of processors within the computer system, the greater the number of threads, or application code, that can execute simultaneously. Purchasing a computer system to which you can add processors as the processing demands of the system increase over time makes it less likely that you'll have to uproot your applications and move them to a larger computer. ■

Number of PC Client Workstations Supported

At this point in the project, the exact number isn't determined, but the number of PC workstations should be somewhere in the range of 12 to 60. The client workstations will be primarily used by the curitorial and conservation staff for scholarly purposes.

The PC workstations will be located on desktops in offices of the museum as well as in a public area. The size of the Sequent server and its expansion capability should permit the server to easily satisfy the number of clients within the range specified.

Part of the plan is to provide up to six workstations that are connected to the server in a public access area that can be used by visiting scholars or the general public. A visiting scholar or a member of the public will be able to use the PC workstation to retrieve information on textile objects in the database, using one of the public workstations. A museum visitor can make the same query that a member of the museum research staff could make to obtain information about the textiles.

For example, a query could be made based on the culture or period of an object, and all matching objects that would be displayed in a thumbnail sketch of the object found. The access to objects for the PC workstations in the public area will be limited to read-only. Information stored about the textiles cannot be changed from the PC systems that are located in the public area.

Structuring the Database

I allocated half a gigabyte of storage for the database, and calculated the initial allocation of space for the database to catalog data for 42,000 art objects, the tapestries. I didn't require half a gigabyte of space for the storage of information about the existing objects. I wanted to ensure that I had plenty of room to add data for more objects that the museum would subsequently acquire. In addition, the museum hadn't completely defined the amount of information that would be cataloged for each tapestry.

The amount of space that's used for the storage of actual data is only 200M, and I expect that the final amount of space required for data about the 42,000 textiles will be 300M to 400M. I defined the storage for the database and the transaction log on different logical and physical devices, which is the usual recommendation for the best performance.

Actually, 300M to 400M is a relatively small amount of space to use for the storage of data about 42,000 art objects. A relatively small amount of space is required for the storage of the information about the tapestries because the images of the tapestries are stored externally to the SQL Server database, as separate files.

Rather than defining the column of a database table as an image datatype (an appropriate datatype for the storage of pictures), I chose a format that permitted the greatest flexibility for subsequent access by other applications. By storing the pictures of the tapestries external to the SQL Server database, I achieved maximum flexibility in their use: their access from other applications and retrieval systems that may require use of the pictures.

The format I chose for the storage of the pictures is the Kodak Photo CD format, which actually stores multiple copies of each graphic of a tapestry, each in a different resolution. This is one of the advantages of the Photo CD format. Subsequent applications, that may be written can choose one of the formats to display the graphic on the screen.

The current retrieval and display application normally displays the graphics with 4 million colors, which is required for scholarly research and proper representation and identification of the art objects. The objects also look more pleasing at a resolution that provides several million colors rather than the 256 colors more commonly used for graphics in computer applications.

I built a table that contains a column to link the object number to the slide or image number of the picture of the tapestry. The Photo CD format actually provides five virtual resolutions, though the application primarily uses two: one of the Photo CD formats and an additional black-and-white format. The application uses a black-and-white TIFF format that permits 256 shades of gray and the 24-bit Photo CD format that provides millions of colors.

An outside vendor scans the pictures of the tapestries and delivers the scanned images to me on compact discs (CDs). The multiple resolutions of the Photo CD format are also useful because they permit the use of client systems that support different hardware, which may vary in the resolutions that they can display because of different video cards. I'm trying to define a standard client system that permits a resolution of 1024×768 and displays images in at least 32,000 colors.

One of the capabilities of the retrieval system permits the display of up to 12 small so-called thumbnail representations of the tapestry pictures at a time on the screen. The thumbnail display supports only 256 colors, though the full-screen display of the tapestry permits a display of several million.

All the client systems are Intel-based PCs that are currently running Windows for Workgroups. Both the PCs and the operating system were already in place at the museum when the tapestry project was conceived, and it was decided to use them as the client system rather than replace them.

The network connectivity that is a part of the Windows for Workgroups configuration permitted a simple conversion to a server-based NT domain system. The existing Windows for Workgroups configuration was one of the reasons for implementing the storage of information for the tapestry project using Microsoft SQL Server on Windows NT.

I'm considering upgrading the client system to run Windows NT Workstation instead of Windows for Workgroups. I'll probably do this by using Visual Basic 4 in order to take advantage of the more powerful client system that NT Workstation provides. Alternatively, it's possible that some of the clients will be upgraded to Windows 95, which, like Windows for Workgroups or Windows NT Workstation, permits a simple connection to the database server.

Using Application Packages to Define the Database

The application that I'm creating for the tapestry collection at the Met is a direct evolution of my existing DOS-based application, The Museum System. As a result, I was also aware of the design issues involved in the type of database required. The Museum System effectively served as a prototype for the tapestry application.

Number of Tables Defined in the Database

I should need 50–75 tables in the database, though some of the tables are quite small in keeping with the type of information in the tables. Many of the small tables are authority tables in which information stored about the tapestry varies depending on the department of the museum.

Islamic art is different from Asian art, twentieth century art is different from European sculpture and decorative art, and the information that is kept about each tapestry is different depending upon its origin (and hence the department that has ownership of it).

Even the same type of information that is sorted about an art object can vary. For example, the dynasties of China are different from the dynasties of Egypt, and though they are similar information, different information must be stored for each.

The differences in the information recorded for art objects also affect the entries that appear in the user interface for the tapestry application. For the example, the names of dynasties on drop-down menus must be different for Chinese and Egyptian dynasties.

Formally Defining Primary and Foreign Keys for the Database Tables

I feel strongly that the database is defined correctly, and it does make sense to define primary and foreign keys. Though SQL Server will permit relational joins and triggers to be performed in the absence of key definitions, such definitions provide a descriptive structure to the database. Moreover, the formal definition of keys anticipates what may become a requirement of Microsoft SQL Server in subsequent versions for the definition of other objects dependent upon keys, such as triggers.

Defining Indexes on Tables

Both clustered and nonclustered indexes are defined for the database tables. Generally, the smaller tables that are referenced less frequently have as few as one or two indexes defined for them. The main tables, which are referenced frequently, have several indexes defined for faster joins and retrieval.

Using Storage Optimization Techniques

The Sequent server that we're using has a disk array, and we're currently making use of volume sets to optimize data access. I'm also considering using other optimization techniques, such as striping without parity to improve performance, which I may or may not implement later in the project.

App

F

Using Fault-Tolerant Techniques

The database is backed up daily. The images are stored on CDs, so there's no need to back up this nonvolatile media. The database information isn't considered critical enough to make use of additional fault-tolerant mechanisms, such as mirroring, at the database, operating system, or hardware level. Although not a fault-tolerant mechanism, replication may be later used to make the information about the art objects available at other institutions around the world.

Allocating the Temporary Database in RAM to Optimize Performance

I initially tried allocating the temporary database tempdb on a logical device defined in memory. For the type of queries and access that we're doing, it didn't seem to provide much of an improvement in performance. I've gone back to using the hard disk for the temporary database.

Using Triggers the Database

I use triggers in the usual way: to maintain the referential integrity of the database tables. In addition, I use triggers to maintain an audit trail about changes that are made to data about the art objects. Some columns, of course, can't be changed by anyone, and appropriate security is provided to prevent unauthorized updates.

I also use a trigger to generate a row ID for entries in some tables to uniquely identify the rows, retrieving a value from another table. I also considered generating a unique row number using the timestamp datatype or the max function to return the largest row number in the table and then incrementing the value to use as a new row number.

The Front-End Query Application

I'm writing the application in Visual Basic by using ODBC to access the database. I'm using ODBC because I want the platform independence it provides. Visual Basic makes it easy for me to pull up the 50–500 objects that a user may want to browse through once they've chosen an initial object.

I'll also permit the SQL Server database to be accessible from front-end products, such as Microsoft Access. I've already permitted the access of the database using the Attach Table feature of Microsoft Access. Users have local Access tables on their clients in which they can initially store information about objects.

Through Microsoft Access, they can also attach to the SQL Server database and update the data rows. They may also need to combine the data that they've stored within the local Access tables with information from the SQL Server database.

We're also testing the use of the report writer Crystal Reports to be used to access the SQL Server database as well as Access databases. To simplify the user's access, I've set up views in SQL Server. I use the views to permit users to access multiple tables—as many as twelve tables—without having to be aware of the structure of the SQL Server database and the SQL syntax required to reference so many data sources.

Administrating the Database

The server will be located in the Textile Center, which is under construction; so for convenience, the administration of the database will be performed through the provided client administrative applications that come with the Microsoft SQL Server product.

Archiving Data

Currently, there's no plan to perform on-site or off-site storage of archives of the data. The concerns of the museum are different from those of a commercial environment. In a sense, the graphics images of the art objects are already a back up of the original art object itself, the tapestries.

If the CDs that contain the representations of the objects were lost, they could always be exactly recreated from the art objects. The focus to this point in time, as it should be, has been on the security and preservation of the objects themselves.

As time goes on, the museum will probably implement an archive strategy for safeguarding the information that is kept about the objects. We will be replicating the data to other institutions, which can also be used as backup copies of the data.

Existing Repositories of Information

The storage of data about art objects was started in 1988, and data was stored in dBASE III. Within the museum as a whole, each department has started committing the information that they have cataloged about art objects onto computer systems. Other PC databases were and are in use for the storage of data throughout the museum.

I've sometimes had to write custom programs for the conversion of the data from the PC databases to SQL Server. Fortunately, I often have been able to use Microsoft Access to read the data from another vendor's PC database and write it out to the SQL Server database.

Dial-Up Access to the Database

Initially, there won't be any dial-up access provided to the database, although it will be provided at a later time.

App

F

N O T E The main window of the retrieval portion of the textile project application will display a miniature view of the tapestry in a rectangle that can be seen in the upper-right portion of the window. Information that is often retrieved about a tapestry is automatically displayed in several fields of the window.

For example, the name of the tapestry is shown in a Title field, which is defined as a list box. Multiple lines of information can be stored and subsequently displayed within the Title list box field. The classification of the art object will subsequently permit other art objects to be recorded and displayed when the application is used for cataloging other objects within the museum.

A Medium Label Copy field displays information about the characteristics of the tapestry (such as its composition). Two remaining fields that display data are the Date/Period and the CreditLine (which shows the manner in which the museum acquired the tapestry).

The image of the tapestry itself can be displayed in an enlarged view in a high resolution (several million colors), permitting as detailed a view of the tapestry as permitted by current technology. The image also can be displayed in a small representation using the Make Thumbnail. In addition, the contrast and brightness of the tapestry can be adjusted to permit alternative representations of the image for research purposes. ■

Data Access Objects 3.5 API

The Data Access Objects interface to database development gives you an easy-to-use, object, method, and property interface to your database. The DAO makes working with database tables a good deal easier and the API is largely the same from Visual Basic to C to Java, and even when working with newer advanced objects for developing on the Internet.

This appendix is meant as a dictionary into the different capabilities published by the DAO for use in your applications. Some objects may or may not support these methods, especially as they relate to database-centric controls. Always be sure to use these as a guideline, but the documentation with your specific controls should serve as final authority on the capabilities offered.

In this appendix, some options are language-specific, but most are generic across implementations. You'll be able to tell which are specific to a given language based on the definition provided. ■

The DBEngine Object

The DAO 3.5 Object Model (see Figure G.1) must be created to perform any operations using DAO, except the new ODBC Direct functions. You also need to cast the DBEngine object to its interface when constructing a new instance of this object.

FIG. G.1

The DAO 3.5 Object Model.

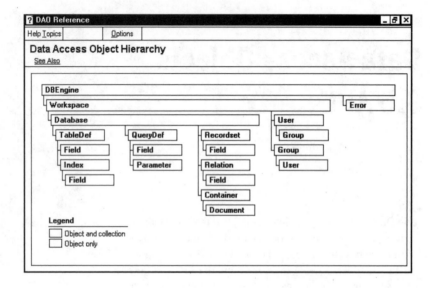

Constructor   DBEngine dao_engine = (_DBEngine) new dao_dbengine();

You need to use the ILicenseManager interface to create the instances (unlike RDO), because DAO requires a license to use.

Methods   *dbEngine._30_CreateWorkspace(String m_Name, String m_User, String m_Password)*

Returns: A Workspace Object.

Table G.1   Arguments

Argument	Data Type	Description
m_Name	String	Sets the name for the Workspace object.
m_User	String	Sets the default user account for the Workspace object.
m_Password	String	Sets the default password for the Workspace object.

dbEngine.**BeginTrans( )**

Begins a new Transaction.

dbEngine.**CommitTrans(int)**

Ends all Transactions for a single Workspace by saving the changes to the data source.

dbEngine.**CompactDatabase(String m_OldDB, String m_NewDB, Variant m_Locale, Variant m_Options, Variant m_Password)**

Copies and compacts a Jet database.

Table G.2   Arguments

Argument	Data Type	Description
m_OldDB	String	The full path to the database.
m_NewDB	String	A different path to the (new) database.
m_Locale	Variant String	CollatingOrderEnum constant. The password can also be changed by specifying dbSortPDXIntl & ";pwd=password".
m_Options	Variant int	DatabaseTypeEnum constant.
m_Password	Variant String	Specifies the password to use if the password is not set in the local argument.

dbEngine.**CreateDatabase(String m_Name, String** m_Locale **, Variant)**

Creates a new (physical) Jet database.

Table G.3   Arguments

Argument	Data Type	Description
m_Name	String	The absolute path and name of the database.
m_Locale	String	This specifies the collating order for creating the database, can also be used to specify the password: dbLangSpanish & ";pwd=NewPassword".
m_Options	Variant	DatabaseTypeEnum constant.

dbEngine.**CreateWorkspace(String m_Name, String m_User , String m_Password, Variant m_Type)**

Creates new Workspace object.

Return Type: A Workspace object.

App

G

Table G.4   Arguments

Argument	Data Type	Description
m_Name	String	Sets the name for the Workspace object.
m_User	String	Sets the default user account for the Workspace object.
m_Password	String	Sets the default password for the Workspace object.
m_Type	Variant	A variant containing a WorkspaceTypeEnum constant.

dbEngine.**getDefaultType( )**

Returns: A value of WorkspaceTypeEnum corresponding to the default Workspace Type that any new Workspace objects will be created with.

Return Type: int

dbEngine.**getErrors( )**

Returns an Errors collection for this object.

Return Type: An Errors object.

dbEngine.**getIniPath( )**

Returns the path to the INI file.

Return Type: String

dbEngine.**getLoginTimeout( )**

Returns the default login timeout.

Return Type: short

dbEngine.**getProperties( )**

Returns the Properties Collection for this object.

Return Type: A Properties object.

dbEngine.**getSystemDB( )**

Returns the path to the System Database, useful only on Microsoft Jet databases.

Return Type: String

dbEngine.**getVersion( )**

Returns the version of the Jet engine.

Return Type: String

dbEngine.**getWorkspaces( )**

Returns the Workspaces Collection for this object.

Data Type: A Workspaces Object.

dbEngine.**Idle( )**

Allows the Jet engine to perform background processing immediately—similar to thread.sleep().

dbEngine.**ISAMStats(int, Variant)**

Action:

Table G.5   Arguments

Argument	Data Type	Description
	int	
	Variant	

dbEngine.**OpenConnection(String, {Optional} Variant m_Prompt, {Optional} Variant m_ReadOnly, {Optional} Variant m_Connect)**

Opens a connection to an ODBC data source.

Return Type: A Connection object.

Table G.6   Arguments

Argument	Data Type	Description
m_Name	String	Sets the name for the connection.
m_Prompt	Variant int	A DriverPromptEnum constant.
m_ReadOnly	Variant Boolean	True if the connection is to be opened for read-only access.
m_Connect	Variant String	An ODBC connect string.

dbEngine.**OpenDatabase(String, {Optional} Variant m_Prompt, {Optional} Variant m_ReadOnly, {Optional} Variant m_Connect)**

Opens a database.

Return Type: A Database object.

App
G

Table G.7   Arguments

Argument	Data Type	Description
m_Name	String	The name of the Jet database or ODBC DSN.
m_Prompt	Variant int	A DriverPromptEnum constant.
m_ReadOnly	Variant Boolean	True if the connection is to be opened for read-only access.
m_Connect	Variant String	An ODBC connect string.

dbEngine.**putDefaultPassword(String m_Password)**

Sets the default password.

Table G.8   Argument

Argument	Data Type	Description
m_Password	String	A password.

dbEngine.**putDefaultType(int m_DefaultType)**

Sets the default type of Workspace object that will be created next.

Table G.9   Argument

Argument	Data Type	Description
m_DefaultType	int	A constant matching a value in WorkspaceTypeEnum.

dbEngine.**putDefaultUser(String m_UserName)**

Sets the default user account for new Workspaces created with this *dbEngine* object.

Table G.10   Argument

Argument	Data Type	Description
m_UserName	String	The user account to use by default for new Workspaces.

dbEngine.**putIniPath(String m_IniPath)**

Sets the Registry key from which to read settings.

Such as: dbEngine.putIniPath("HKEY_LOCAL_MACHINE\SOFTWARE\Microsoft\Jet\3.5\ISAM Formats\FoxPro 3.0").

Table G.11	Argument	
Argument	**Data Type**	**Description**
m_IniPath	String	A registry key or path to an INI file.

dbEngine.putLoginTimeout(short m_defaultTimeout)

Sets the default login timeout.

Data Type: short

Table G.12	Argument	
Argument	**Data Type**	**Description**
m_defaultTimeout	short	The timeout value, specified in seconds.

dbEngine.putSystemDB(String m_SysDB)

Sets the Microsoft Jet Workgroup access file.

Table G.13	Argument	
Argument	**Data Type**	**Description**
m_SysDB	String	Path to the System database.

dbEngine.RegisterDatabase(String m_DSN, String m_Driver, Boolean m_Silent, String m_Attributes)

Registers a new ODBC data source.

Table G.14	Arguments	
Argument	**Data Type**	**Description**
m_DSN	String	Data Source Name.
m_Driver	String	Friendly name of the driver as shown in the ODBC Administrator. (Not the file name.)
m_Silent	Boolean	Set to true if you don't want to show the ODBC Register Data Source dialog box. (This will be ignored if you don't provide complete information.)
m_Attributes	String	A list of keywords to be added to the Windows Registry.

App
G

dbEngine.**RepairDatabase(String m_DBName)**

Attempts to repair a Jet database.

Table G.15   Argument

Argument	Data Type	Description
m_DBName	String	Absolute path to the Jet database file.

dbEngine.**Rollback( )**

Action: Ends all transactions created by this DBEngine object by throwing away the buffered changes.

SetOption(int m_Parameter, Variant m_NewValue)

Overrides registry settings.

Table G.16   Arguments

Argument	Data Type	Description
m_Parameter	int	A SetOptionEnum Constant.
m_NewValue	Variant	The new value of the parameter.

The Error Object

Constructor   Error m_objError;

Methods   int getNumber( );

Returns: The error number.

Return Type: int

String getDescription( );

Returns: A description of the error.

Return Type: String

String getHelpFile( );

Returns: The path to the help file associated with the source of the error.

Return Type: String

int getHelpContext( );

Returns the help context ID.

Return Type: int

String getSource( );

Returns the source of the error.

Return Type: String

The Workspace Object

Constructor *Workspace* m_objWorkpsace = *dbEngine*.CreateWorkspace(String *Name*, String *User*, String *Password*, Variant *Type*)

Methods *Workspace*.**put_30_UserName(String m_strUser);**

Sets the default user account for this Database object.

Table G.17	Argument	
Argument	**Data Type**	**Description**
m_strUser	String	Name of the default user.

Workspace.**getDatabases();**

Returns the Databases Collection.

Return Type: A Databases object.

Workspace.**CreateDatabase(String m_Name, String m_Locale, Variant)**

Creates a new (physical) Jet database.

Table G.18	Arguments	
Argument	**Data Type**	**Description**
m_Name	String	The absolute path and name of the database.
m_Locale	String	This specifies the collating order for creating the database, can also be used to specify the password: dbLangSpanish & ";pwd=NewPassword".
m_Options	Variant	DatabaseTypeEnum constant.

Workspace.**getLoginTimeout();**

Returns the default login timeout for this Database object.

Return Type: int

Workspace.**putLoginTimeout(int m_iLoginTimeout);**

Sets the default login timeout for this Database object.

Workspace.**getUsers();**

Returns the Users collection for this object.

Return Type: A Users object.

Workspace.**put_30_Password(String m_Password);**

Sets the default password for objects created through this object using DAO 3.0 Syntax.

Table G.19   Argument

Argument	Data Type	Description
m_Password	Variant (String)	Sets the password for the new user account.

Workspace.**CreateUser({Optional} Variant m_Name,   {Optional} Variant m_PID, {Optional} Variant m_Password);**

Returns: A new User object.

Table G.20   Arguments

Argument	Data Type	Description
m_Name	Variant (String)	Sets the name for the user.
m_PID	Variant (String)	An identifier 4-20 characters in length— alphanumeric.
m_Password	Variant (String)	Sets the password for the new user account.

Workspace.**BeginTrans();**

Begins a new transaction for this Workspace.

Workspace.**CommitTrans(int);**

Ends all transactions within this workspace by saving the changes made.

Workspace.**OpenConnection(String m_DSN, Variant m_VOptions, Variant m_vReadOnly, Variant m_vConnect);**

Returns: A new Connection object.

Table G.21   Arguments

Argument	Data Type	Description
m_DSN	String	The Data Source name.
m_vOptions	Variant (int)	Any combination of DriverPromptEnum constants and/or RecordsetOptionEnum.dbAsyncEnable.
m_vReadOnly	Variant(Boolean)	Sets the access to read only if True.
m_vCoect	Variant (String)	A variant containing an ODBC connection string.

Workspace.**getDefaultCursorDriver();**

Returns the default cursor for Recordsets opened on this Database object.

Return Type: int

Workspace.**putDefaultCursorDriver(int m_CursorDriver)**

Sets the default cursor for Recordsets opened on this Database object.

Table G.22   Argument

Argument	Data Type	Description
m_CursorDriver	int	A constant of CursorDriverEnum type.

Workspace.**getIsolateODBCTrans()**

Returns: The Isolation Level for this Database.

Workspace.**getName();**

Returns the name for this Database object.

Return Type: String

Workspace.**putName(String m_dbname);**

Sets the name for the database object.

Returns a new Database object.

Table G.23   Arguments

Argument	Data Type	Description
m_Name	String	The name of the actual database file or DSN.
m_vOptions	Variant (Boolean)	True for exclusive access, False for shared access.
m_vReadOnly	Variant(Boolean)	Sets the access to read only if True.
m_vConnect	Variant (String)	A variant containing a connection string.

Workspace.**putIsolateODBCTrans(short m_dbIsolationLevel);**

Sets the whether or not the transactions are isolated.

Table G.24   Argument

Argument	Data Type	Description
m_dbIsolationLevel	short	A value of 0 or 1.

Workspace.**Close();**

Closes the open Database object.

Workspace.**OpenDatabase(String m_dbName, Variant m_vOptions, Variant m_vReadOnly, Variant m_vConnect);**

Returns a new Database object.

Table G.25   Arguments

Argument	Data Type	Description
m_dbName	String	The name of the actual database file or DSN.
m_vOptions	Variant (Boolean)	True for exclusive access, False for shared access.
m_vReadOnly	Variant (Boolean)	Sets the access to read only if True.
m_vConnect	Variant (String)	A variant containing a connection string.

Workspace.**Rollback();**

Rolls back any transactions pending for the current Workspace or Connection.

Workspace.**CreateGroup({Optional} Variant m_Name, {Optional} Variant m_PID);**

Creates a new group.

Table G.26   Arguments

Argument	Data Type	Description
m_Name	Variant (String)	Name of the new group.
m_vSQL	Variant (String)	PID of the new group (4-20 alphanumeric characters).

Workspace.**getType();**

Returns a DatabaseTypeEnum constant.

Return Type: int

Workspace.**gethEnv();**

Returns the ODBC Environment handle.

Return Type: int

Workspace.**getConnections();**

Returns the Connections Collection for this Database.

Return Type: A Connections object.

Workspace.**getProperties();**

Returns the Properties Collection for this Database.

Return Type: A Properties object.

Workspace.**getGroups();**

Returns the Groups Collection for this Database.

Return Type: A Groups object.

Workspace.**getUserName();**

Returns the user account with which this Database object was accessed.

Return Type: String

The Database Object

Constructor   *Database* = *Workspace*.**CreateDatabase( );**

-or-

Database = *Workspace*..OpenDatabase( );

Methods   *Database*.**Close( );**

Closes an open Database object.

Database.**CreateProperty(Variant m_PropName, Variant m_vType, Variant m_vDataType, Variant m_vDDL);**

Creates a new Property.

Return Type: A Property object.

App

G

Table G.27	Arguments	
Argument	**Data Type**	**Description**
m_PropName	Variant (String)	The name of the new Property.
m_vType	Variant (int)	A member of the DataTypeEnum constants.
m_vDataType	Variant	The initial property value.
m_vDDL	Variant (Boolean)	True if this property is a Data Definition Language property.

Database.**CreateRelation(Variant m_RelationName, Variant m_vPrimary, Variant m_vForeign, Variant m_vAttributes);**

Creates a new relation object. (Jet Workspaces only)

Return Type: A Relation object.

Table G.28	Arguments	
Argument	**Data Type**	**Description**
m_RelationName	Variant (String)	The name of the Relation to be created.
m_vPrimary	Variant (String)	Name of the primary table in the relation.
m_vForeign	Variant (String)	Name of the foreign table in the relation.
m_vAttributes	Variant (String)	A member of the RelationAttributeEnum constants.

Database.**CreateQueryDef(Variant m_Name, Variant m_vSQL);**

Returns a new QueryDef object.

Table G.29	Arguments	
Argument	**Data Type**	**Description**
m_Name	String	The name of the new QueryDef.
m_vSQL	Variant (String)	A variant containing a SQL Statement.

Database.**CreateTableDef(Variant m_dbName, Variant m_vAttributes, Variant m_vSource, Variant m_vConnect);**

Returns a new TableDef object.

Table G.30   Arguments

Argument	Data Type	Description
m_dbName	String	The name of the actual database file or DSN.
m_vAttributes	Variant (int)	A member of the TableDefAttributeEnum constants.
m_vSource	Variant (String)	Sets the source table name for the TableDef.
m_vConnect	Variant (String)	A variant containing a connection string.

Database.**Execute(String, Variant);**

Executes a SQL statement or QueryDef object.

Table G.31   Arguments

Argument	Data Type	Description
m_Source	String	The SQL statement or name of a QueryDef.
m_vConnect	Variant (int)	A member of the RecordsetOptionEnum constants.

Database.**getCollatingOrder();**

Returns the collating order for this Database.

Return Type: An int matching a value in LanguageConstants.

Database.**getConnect();**

Returns the connection string used to create this Database object.

Return Type: String

Database.**getContainers();**

Returns the Containers Collection for this Database.

Return Type: A Containers object.

Database.**getRecordsAffected();**

Returns the number of records affected in the last Execute method.

Return Type: int

Database.**getName();**

Returns the name for this Database.

Return Type: String

App
G

Database.**getDesignMasterID();**

Returns the GUID for the master replica Database.

Return Type: String

Database.**getRecordsets();**

Returns the Recordsets Collection for this Database.

Return Type: A Recordsets object.

Database.**getReplicaID();**

Returns the Replica Collection for this Database.

Return Type: String

Database.**getTableDefs();**

Returns the TableDefs Collection for this Database.

Return Type: A TableDefs object.

Database.**getQueryDefs();**

Returns the QueryDefs Collection for this Database.

Return Type: A QueryDefs object.

Database.**getQueryTimeout();**

Returns the QueryTimeout Collection for this Database.

Return Type: A Connections object.

Database.**getRelations();**

Returns the Relations Collection for this Database.

Return Type: A Relations object.

Database.**getTransactions();**

Returns whether or not this object supports transactions.

Return Type: Boolean

Database.**getConnection();**

Returns the Connection object for this Database.

Return Type: A Connection object.

Database.**getProperties();**

Returns the PropertiesCollection for this Database.

Return Type: A Properties object.

Database.**getUpdatable();**

Returns whether this object allows changes.

Return Type: Boolean

Database.**getVersion();**

Returns the version of the Jet engine used to create this Database.

Return Type: String

Database.**MakeReplica(String m_ReplicaName, String m_Description, Variant m_vOption);**

Creates a replica of the database.

Table G.32   Arguments

Argument	Data Type	Description
m_ReplicaName	String	The path and file name to the replica.
m_Description	String	Description of the replica.
m_vOption	Variant (int)	A member of the ReplicaTypeEnum constants.

Database.**NewPassword(String m_OldPassword, String m_NewPassword);**

Changes the password of the database.

Table G.33   Arguments

Argument	Data Type	Description
m_OldPassword	String	The old password.
m_NewPassword	String	An alphanumeric string representing the new password.

Database.**OpenQueryDef(String m_Name);**

Returns an existing QueryDef object.

App
G

Table G.34   Argument

Argument	Data Type	Description
m_Name	String	The name of the QueryDef stored in the database.

Database._30_OpenRecordset(String m_Source, Variant m_vType, Variant m_vOption);

Returns a new Recordset object (using DAO 3.0 syntax).

Table G.35   Arguments

Argument	Data Type	Description
m_Source	String	The name of the actual database file or DSN.
m_vType	Variant (int)	A member of the RecordsetTypeEnum constants.
m_vOption	Variant (int)	A member of the RecordsetOptionsEnum constants.

Database.OpenRecordset(String m_Source, Variant m_vType, Variant m_vOption, Variant m_vLockType);

Returns a new Recordset object.

Table G.36   Arguments

Argument	Data Type	Description
m_Source	String	The name of the actual database file or DSN.
m_vType	Variant (int)	A member of the RecordsetTypeEnum constants.
m_vOption	Variant (int)	A member of the RecordsetOptionsEnum constants.
m_vLockType	Variant (int)	A member of the LockTypeEnum constants.

Database.putConnect(String m_ConnectString);

Sets the connection information for this object.

Table G.37   Argument

Argument	Data Type	Description
m_ConnectString	String	Semicolon-separated string of Connection parameters.

Database.PopulatePartial(String);

Repopulates a partial replica with fresh information.

Table G.38   Argument

Argument	Data Type	Description
m_Target	String	The name of the target database to replicate with.

Database.**putDesignMasterID(String m_GUID);**

Sets the GUID for the Design Master in a replication environment.

Table G.39   Argument

Argument	Data Type	Description
m_GUID	String	The GUID of the master design database.

Database.**Synchronize(String m_Target, Variant m_Direction);**

Sets the target and the direction of synchronization between two database replicas.

Table G.40   Arguments

Argument	Data Type	Description
m_Target	String	The absolute path to the replica database file.
m_Direction	Variant	A member of SynchronizeTypeEnum constants.

Database.**putQueryTimeout(short m_Timeout);**

Sets the default query timeout for this database.

Table G.41   Argument

Argument	Data Type	Description
m_Timeout	short	The number of seconds to wait before timing out a Query.

The Connection Object

Constructor   connection object = Workspace.OpenConnection()

Methods   **void Cancel();**

Action: Cancels a pending update.

void Close();

Closes an open Database object.

CreateQueryDef(Variant m_Name, Variant m_vSQL);

Returns a new QueryDef object.

Table G.42   Arguments

Argument	Data Type	Description
m_Name	String	The name of the new QueryDef.
m_vSQL	Variant (String)	A variant containing a SQL Statement.

void Execute(String m_Source, Variant m_vConnect);

Executes a SQL statement or QueryDef object.

Table G.43   Arguments

Argument	Data Type	Description
m_Source	String	The SQL statement or Name of a QueryDef.
m_vConnect	Variant (int)	A member of the RecordsetOptionEnum constants.

String getConnect( );

Returns the connection string used to create this Database object.

Return Type: String

int getRecordsAffected( );

Returns the number of records affected in the last Execute method.

Return Type: int

Database getDatabase( );

Returns the Database object for this connection.

Return Type: A Database object.

int gethDbc( );

Returns the ODBC connection handle for this Connection.

Return Type: int

String getName( );

Returns the name for this Connection object.

Return Type: String

getRecordsets( );

Returns the Recordsets Collection for this Database.

Return Type: A Recordsets object.

getQueryDefs( );

Returns the QueryDefs Collection for this Database.

Return Type: A QueryDefs object.

short getQueryTimeout( );

Returns the default query timeout for this Connection.

Return Type: short

Boolean getStillExecuting( );

Returns True if the asynchronous query is still executing.

Return Type: Boolean

Boolean getTransactions( );

Returns whether or not this object supports transactions.

Return Type: Boolean

Boolean getUpdatable( );

Returns whether this object allows changes.

Return Type: Boolean

OpenRecordset(String m_Source, Variant m_vType, Variant m_vOption, Variant m_vLockType);

Returns a new Recordset object.

Table G.44   Arguments

Argument	Data Type	Description
m_Source	String	The name of the actual database file or DSN.
m_vType	Variant (int)	A member of the RecordsetTypeEnum constants.
m_vOption	Variant (int)	A member of the RecordsetOptionsEnum constants.
m_vLockType	Variant (int)	A member of the LockTypeEnum constants.

App
G

void putConnect(String m_ConnectString);

Sets the connection information for this object.

Table G.45   Argument

Argument	Data Type	Description
m_ConnectString	String	Semicolon-separated string of Connection parameters.

void putQueryTimeout(short m_Timeout);

Sets the default query timeout for this database.

Table G.46   Argument

Argument	Data Type	Description
m_Timeout	short	The number of seconds to wait before timing out a Query.

Recordset Object

Constructor   *recordset = recordset.*OpenRecordset()

*recordset = tabledef.*OpenRecordset()

*recordset = querydef.*OpenRecordset()

*recordset = Connection.*OpenRecordset()

*recordset = Database.*OpenRecordset()

Methods   **void _30_CancelUpdate();**

Cancels any pending updates.

void _30_MoveLast();

Moves the cursor to the last record in the Recordset. (No option to run asynchronously.)

void _30_Update();

Saves the changes made to a Recordset.

void AddNew();

Adds a new record to the Recordset.

void Cancel( );

Cancels a MoveLast or OpenRecordset method call.

void CancelUpdate(int m_Type);

Cancels pending updates. Allows for you to specify the type of updates.

Table G.47   Argument

Argument	Data Type	Description
m_Type	int	A member of the UpdateTypeEnum.

Recordset Clone( );

Clones the current Recordset Object (except for the Indexes).

void Close( );

Closes the Recordset object.

QueryDef CopyQueryDef( );

Returns a new QueryDef object that is a copy of the query used to create the Recordset object.

Return Type: A QueryDef object.

void Delete( );

Deletes the current record from the Recordset.

void Edit( );

Copies the current record to an Edit Buffer, and saves the changes made to the buffer. Use the Update method to save the changes permanently.

void FillCache({Optional} Variant m_iRows, {Optional} Variant m_vBookmark);

Table G.48   Arguments

Argument	Data Type	Description
m_viRows	Variant (integer)	The number of rows to hold in the cache.
m_vBookmark	Variant (String)	The bookmark to begin filling the cache from.

void FindFirst(String m_SearchCriteria);

Moves the cursor to the first occurrence of the specified string.

App
G

Table G.49   Argument

Argument	Data Type	Description
m_SearchCriteria	String	A string value.

void FindLast(String);

Finds the last record that matches the string value specified and positions the cursor on that record.

Table G.50   Argument

Argument	Data Type	Description
m_SearchCriteria	String	A string value.

void FindNext(String);

Returns the next record matching the specified search string, and sets the cursor to the record's position.

Table G.51   Argument

Argument	Data Type	Description
m_strSearch	String	The search string.

void FindPrevious(String m_SearchCriteria);

Find the record previous to the current record that matches the string value specified and positions the cursor on that record.

Table G.52   Argument

Argument	Data Type	Description
m_SearchCriteria	String	A string value.

int getAbsolutePosition( );

Returns the ordinal position of the current record.

Return Type: int:

Variant getBatchCollisions( );

Returns an array of bookmarks indicating the records where the collisions took place.

Return Type: Variant

int getBatchCollisionCount( );

Returns the number of collisions encountered in the last Batch Update.

Return Type: int

int getBatchSize( );

Returns the number of statements that can be sent to the Server at once.

Return Type: int

Boolean getBOF( );

Returns whether or not the current record is the beginning of the Recordset.

Return Type: Boolean

Boolean getBookmarkable( );

Returns whether or not the Recordset supports bookmarks.

Return Type: Boolean

SafeArray getBookmark( );

Returns the bookmark of the current record.

Return Type: SafeArray

SafeArray getCacheStart( );

Returns the bookmark of the first record in a dynaset-type Recordset object to be locally cached from the ODBC data source (Jet Workspaces only).

Return Type: SafeArray

int getCacheSize( );

Returns the number of rows that can be held in the cache.

Return Type: int

Variant getCollect(Variant m_vFieldName);

Returns the value of a field.

Return Type: Variant

Table G.53 Argument

Argument	Data Type	Description
m_FieldName	Variant (String)	The name of a field in the Recordset.

App
G

Connection getConnection( );

Returns the Connection associated with this Recordset.

Return Type: A Connection object.

Variant getDateCreated( );

Returns the date the base table was created.

Return Type: Variant

short getEditMode( );

Returns EditModeEnum constants value.

Return Type: short

Boolean getEOF( );

Returns true if the current position of the cursor is at the end of the recordset.

Return Type: Boolean

Fields getFields( );

Returns the Fields Collection for this Recordset.

Return Type: A Fields object.

String getFilter( );

The setting or return value is a String data type that contains the WHERE clause of an SQL statement without the reserved word WHERE.

String getIndex( );

Returns the index being used by this Recordset object.

Return Type: String

Indexes getIndexes( );

Returns the Indexes Collection for the current Recordset.

Return Type: An Indexes object.

int gethStmt( );

Returns the ODBC statement handle.

Return Type: int

Variant getLastUpdated( );

SafeArray getLastModified( );

Returns a bookmark of the last modified record.

Return Type: SafeArray

Boolean getLockEdits( );

Returns the locking in effect, True for Pessimistic and False for Optimistic.

String getName( );

Returns the first 256 characters of the SQL statement used to create this Recordset.

Return Type: String

Boolean getNoMatch( );

Specifies whether the last search or seek operation returned a match.

Return Type: Boolean (False if a match is found)

int getODBCFetchCount( );

Returns the number of records fetched at one time from the server.

Return Type: int

int getODBCFetchDelay( );

Returns the estimated latency of the last ODBC fetch.

Return Type: int

Database getParent( );

float getPercentPosition( );

Returns the position of the cursor as being a percentage relative to the entire Recordset.

Return Type: float

Properties getProperties( );

Returns the Properties Collection for this Recordset object.

Return Type: A Properties object.

int getRecordCount( );

Returns the number of records in the Recordset.

Return Type: int

short getRecordStatus( );

Returns a value matching a RecordStatusEnum constant.

Return Type: short

Boolean getRestartable( );

Returns whether or not the Recordset supports the Requery method.

Return Type: Boolean

Variant GetRows(Variant m_vNumrows);

Returns an array of records.

Return Type: Variant array

Table G.54 Argument

Argument	Data Type	Description
m_vNumrows	Variant (int)	The number of rows to return with this method.

Boolean getStillExecuting( );

Returns whether or not an asynchronous operation is still executing.

Return Type: Boolean

String getSort( );

Returns the parameters of the ORDER BY clause in the SQL Statement that created this Recordset object.

Return Type: String

Boolean getTransactions( );

Return whether or not transactions are supported for this Recordset.

Return Type: Boolean

short getType( );

Returns a constant of RecordsetTypeEnum constants.

Return Type: short

int getUpdateOptions( );

Returns the type of Update options that are being used with a Batch update.

Return Type: int (of type UpdateCriteriaEnum)

Boolean getUpdatable( );

Returns whether or not the Recordset supports changes.

Retun Type: Boolean

String getValidationText( );

Returns the text of the message your application displays if the value of a Field object doesn't satisfy the validation rule (Jet Workspaces only).

Return Type: String

String getValidationRule( );

Returns the update, insert, or delete constraints on the object.

Return Type: String

void Move(int m_iRows, Variant m_vBookmark);

Moves the cursor a specified number of rows from this bookmark, or from a specific bookmark.

Table G.55   Arguments

Argument	Data Type	Description
m_iRows	int	The number of rows to move. (Can be positive or negative.)
m_vBookmark	Variant	A bookmark to begin the move from.

void MoveFirst( );

Moves the cursor to the first record in the Recordset.

void MoveLast({Optional} RecordsetOptionEnum.dbRunAsync);

Moves the cursor to the last record in the Recordset.

Table G.56   Argument

Argument	Data Type	Description
dbRunAsync	int	Use to enable asynchronous execution of this method.

void MoveNext( );

Moves the cursor to the next position.

void MovePrevious( );

Moves the cursor to the previous record.

Boolean NextRecordset( );

Loads the next batch of records (from a different query) into the Recordset object.

App

G

Return Type: Boolean (True if more Recordsets are available)

Recordset OpenRecordset(Variant m_vOptions, Variant m_vLockType);

Opens a Recordset on this Recordset of the same type, except for TableType recordsets (which return a dynaset type).

Table G.57   Arguments

Argument	Data Type	Description
m_vOption	Variant (int)	A member of the RecordsetOptionsEnum constants.
m_vLockType	Variant (int)	A member of the LockTypeEnum constants.

void putAbsolutePosition(int m_Ordinal);

Sets the position of the cursor to a specific record using the ordinal value of its place in the Recordset.

Table G.58   Argument

Argument	Data Type	Description
m_Ordinal	int	The row number to which to move the cursor.

void putBatchSize(int m_BatchSize);

Sets the number of statements sent to the server in each Batch.

void putBookmark(SafeArray m_Bookmark);

Sets the bookmark for the current record.

Table G.59   Arguments

Argument	Data Type	Description
m_BookMark	SafeArray	A string of bytes representing a unique ID — a bookmark.

void putCacheSize(int m_nRows);

Sets the cache to a specified number of rows.

Table G.60   Argument

Argument	Data Type	Description
m_nRows	int	The number of rows to hold in the cache.

void putCacheStart(SafeArray m_Bookmark);

Sets the bookmark of the first record in a dynaset-type Recordset object to be locally cached from the ODBC data source (Jet Workspaces only).

Table G.61   Argument

Argument	Data Type	Description
m_Bookmark	SafeArray	A bookmark.

void putCacheSize(int m_nRows);

Sets the cache to a specified number of rows.

Table G.62   Argument

Argument	Data Type	Description
m_nRows	int	The number of rows to hold in the cache.

void putCollect(Variant m_vFieldName, Variant m_vValue);

Sets the value of a field.

Table G.63   Arguments

Argument	Data Type	Description
m_FieldName	Variant (String)	The Field Name to populate.
m_vValue	Variant	The field value.

void putConnection(Connection m_objConnection);

Sets the Connection object for this Recordset.

App

G

Table G.64   Argument

Argument	Data Type	Description
m_objConnection	Connection	The Connection object to associate.

void putFilter(String m_strFilter);

The setting or return value is a String data type that contains the WHERE clause of an SQL statement without the reserved word WHERE.

Table G.65   Argument

Argument	Data Type	Description
m_strFilter	String	Filter criteria in the SQL WHERE clause.

void putIndex(String m_Index);

Sets the index for the Recordset.

Table G.66   Argument

Argument	Data Type	Description
m_Index	String	The name of an index object in the indexes collection.

void putLockEdits(Boolean);

Sets the locking for the Recordset, True for Pessimistic and False for Optimistic.

void putPercentPosition(float m_Position);

Moves the cursor a specified percentage of the way through the Recordset.

Table G.67   Argument

Argument	Data Type	Description
m_Position	float	The percentage to move through the recordset.

void putSort(String);

Sets the Sort Order for a dynaset or snapshot style Recordset.

Table G.68   Argument

Argument	Data Type	Description
m_SortString	String	A string representing the parameters of the SQL ORDER BY clause.

void putUpdateOptions(int m_UpdateOptions);

Sets the update options for a Batch update.

Table G.69   Argument

Argument	Data Type	Description
m_UpdateOptions	int	A constant of the UpdateCriteriaEnum.

void Requery(Variant);

void Seek(String m_Operand, Variant m_Key1, Variant m_Key 2...Variant m_Key13);

Locates the next record matching the values in the Key fields and positions the cursor on the new record.

Table G.70   Arguments

Argument	Data Type	Description
m_Operator	String	A logical operand.
m_Key	Variant	Up to 13 values corresponding to fields in the Recordset object's current index, as specified by its Index property setting.

void Update(int m_UpdateType, Boolean m_forceUpdate);

Saves the changes made to a Recordset.

Table G.71   Arguments

Argument	Data Type	Description
m_UpdateType	int	A value matching a member of UpdateTypeEnum constants.
m_forceUpdate	Boolean	Set to true to overwrite any changes made since the recordset was fetched.

The TableDef Object

Constructor

Methods   Field CreateField({Optional} Variant m_vName, {Optional}, {Optional} Variant m_vDataType, Variant m_vSize);

Table G.72   Arguments

Argument	Data Type	Description
m_vName	Variant (String)	The name of the Field to be created.
m_vDataType	Variant (int)	A member of the DataTypeEnum constants.
m_vSize	Variant (int)	The size of the Field (Read/Write only for a Text field, up to 255).

Index CreateIndex(Variant m_vName);

Creates an index for the TableDef.

Table G.73   Argument

Argument	Data Type	Description
m_vName	Variant (String)	The name of the Index.

int getAttributes();

Returns the attributes for this TableDef.

Return Type: int (of type TableAttributesEnum)

String getConflictTable();

Returns the path to the conflict table if one exists.

Return Type: String

String getConnect();

Returns the connection string used to create this Database object.

Return Type: String

Variant getDateCreated();

Returns the date the table was created.

Return Type: Variant

Fields getFields();

Returns the Fields collection for this TableDef.

Return Type: A Fields object.

Indexes getIndexes();

Returns the Indexes collection for this TableDef.

Return Type: An Indexes object

Variant getLastUpdated( );

Returns the last time this table was updated.

Return Type: Variant

Variant getReplicaFilter( );

Returns the SQL WHERE clause (or Boolean value) used to filter the data that is replicated.

Return Type: Variant

int getRecordCount( );

Returns the number of records in the TableDef.

Return Type: int

Variant getLastUpdated( );

Returns the last time this table was updated.

Return Type: Variant

String getName( );

Returns the Name of the Variant

Return Type: String

String getValidationRule( );

Returns the update, insert, or delete constraints on the object.

Return Type: String

String getValidationText( );

Returns the text of the message your application displays if the value of a Field object doesn't satisfy the validation rule (Jet Workspaces only).

Return Type: String

Properties getProperties( );

Returns the Properties collection for this TableDef.

Return Type: A Properties object.

String getSourceTableName( );

Returns the source table of this TableDef.

Return Type: String

void putAttributes(int);

Sets the Attributes for this TableDef.

Table G.74   Arguments

Argument	Data Type	Description
m_vOption	Variant (int)	A member of the RecordsetOptionsEnum constants.
m_vLockType	Variant (int)	A member of the LockTypeEnum constants.

void putConnect(String m_ConnectString);

Sets the connection information for this object.

Table G.75   Argument

Argument	Data Type	Description
m_ConnectString	String	Semicolon-separated string of Connection parameters.

void putName(String);

Table G.76   Arguments

Argument	Data Type	Description
m_vOption	Variant (int)	A member of the RecordsetOptionsEnum constants.
m_vLockType	Variant (int)	A member of the LockTypeEnum constants.

void putReplicaFilter(Variant);

Sets the filter (A SQL WHERE clause) or sets the replication to all records, or none.

Table G.77   Argument

Argument	Data Type	Description
m_vFilter	Variant	A Boolean or String value.

void putSourceTableName(String);

Sets the Source of the TableDef.

Table G.78   Arguments

Argument	Data Type	Description
m_vOption	Variant (int)	A member of the RecordsetOptionsEnum constants.
m_vLockType	Variant (int)	A member of the LockTypeEnum constants.

void putValidationRule(String m_Rule);

Table G.79   Argument

Argument	Data Type	Description
m_Rule	String	A member of the RecordsetOptionsEnum constants.

Recordset OpenRecordset(Variant m_vOptions, Variant m_vLockType);

Opens a Recordset on this Recordset of the same type, except for TableType recordsets (which return a dynaset type).

Table G.80   Arguments

Argument	Data Type	Description
m_vOption	Variant (int)	A member of the RecordsetOptionsEnum constants.
m_vLockType	Variant (int)	A member of the LockTypeEnum constants.

void RefreshLink( );

Refreshes the Connection information for a linked table. (Used to update the Connection string after changing it with the putconnect method.)

The QueryDef Object

Constructor   *QueryDef = Database*.CreateQueryDef()

Methods   **QueryDef _Copy( );**

void Cancel( );

Cancels a MoveLast or OpenRecordset method call.

void Close ( );

Closes the open QueryDef object.

void Compare(, short[]);

CreateProperty(Variant m_PropName, Variant m_vType, Variant m_vDataType, Variant m_vDDL);

Creates a new Property.

Return Type: A Property object.

Table G.81   Arguments

Argument	Data Type	Description
m_PropName	Variant (String)	The name of the new Property.
m_vType	Variant (int)	A member of the DataTypeEnum constants.
m_vDataType	Variant	The initial property value.
m_vDDL	Variant (Boolean)	True if this property is a Data Definition Language property.

void Execute(String m_Source, Variant m_vConnect);

Executes a SQL statement or QueryDef object.

Table G.82   Arguments

Argument	Data Type	Description
m_Source	String	The SQL statement or Name of a QueryDef.
m_vConnect	Variant (int)	A member of the RecordsetOptionEnum constants.

int getCacheSize();

Returns the number of rows that can be held in the cache.

Return Type: int

String getConnect();

Returns the connection string used to create this Database object.

Return Type: String

Variant getDateCreated();

Returns the date the table was created.

Return Type: Variant

Fields getFields();

Returns the Fields collection for this TableDef.

Return Type: A Fields object.

int gethStmt();

Returns the ODBC statement handle.

Return Type: int

Variant getLastUpdated();

Returns the last time this QueryDef was updated.

Return Type: Variant

int getMaxRecords();

Returns the maximum number of records that can be retrieved from the server in a single fetch.

Return Type: int

String getName();

Returns the Name of the integer

Return Type: String

short getODBCTimeout();

Returns the ODBC timeout in seconds.

Return Type: short

Parameters getParameters();

Returns the Parameters collection.

Return Type: A Parameters object.

Variant getPrepare();

Properties getProperties();

Returns the Properties collection for this QueryDef.

Return Type: A Properties object.

int getRecordsAffected();

Returns the number of records affected by the last Execute method call.

Return Type: int

Boolean getReturnsRecords();

Returns whether or not this QueryDef returns a recordset.

Return Type: Boolean

String getSQL();

Returns the SQL property of the QueryDef.

Return Type: String

Boolean getStillExecuting();

Returns whether or not an asynchronous operation is still executing.

App
G

Return Type: Boolean

short getType( );

Returns a constant of RecordsetTypeEnum constants.

Return Type: short

Recordset _30_OpenRecordset(String m_Source, Variant m_vType);

Returns a new Recordset object.

Table G.83   Arguments

Argument	Data Type	Description
m_Source	String	The name of the actual database file or DSN.
m_vType	Variant (int)	A member of the RecordsetTypeEnum constants.

Recordset _30__OpenRecordset(String m_Source, Variant m_vType);

Returns a new Recordset object.

Table G.84   Arguments

Argument	Data Type	Description
m_Source	String	The name of the actual database file or DSN.
m_vType	Variant (int)	A member of the RecordsetTypeEnum constants.

Recordset OpenRecordset(String m_Source, Variant m_vType, Variant m_vOption,);

Returns a new Recordset object.

Table G.85   Arguments

Argument	Data Type	Description
m_Source	String	The name of the actual database file or DSN.
m_vType	Variant (int)	A member of the RecordsetTypeEnum constants.
m_vOption	Variant (int)	A member of the RecordsetOptionsEnum constants.

OpenRecordset(String m_Source, Variant m_vType, Variant m_vOption, Variant m_vLockType);

Returns a new Recordset object.

Table G.86   Arguments

Argument	Data Type	Description
m_Source	String	The name of the actual database file or DSN.
m_vType	Variant (int)	A member of the RecordsetTypeEnum constants.
m_vOption	Variant (int)	A member of the RecordsetOptionsEnum constants.
m_vLockType	Variant (int)	A member of the LockTypeEnum constants.

void putCacheSize(int m_nRows);

Sets the cache to a specified number of rows.

Table G.87   Argument

Argument	Data Type	Description
m_nRows	int	The number of rows to hold in the cache.

void putConnect(String m_ConnectString);

Sets the connection information for this object.

Table G.88   Argument

Argument	Data Type	Description
m_ConnectString	String	Semicolon-separated string of Connection parameters.

void putMaxRecords(int m_nMaxRecords);

Sets the maximum number of records to return in a single recordset.

Table G.89   Argument

Argument	Data Type	Description
m_nMaxRecords	int	The number of records to return.

void putName(String m_Name);

Set the name of the QueryDef object.

App

G

Table G.90	Argument	
Argument	**Data Type**	**Description**
m_Name	String	Sets the name of the QueryDef.

void putPrepare(Variant m_vPrepared);

Sets the QueryDef to call either SQLPrepare or SQLExecDirect on execution.

Table G.91	Argument	
Argument	**Data Type**	**Description**
m_vPrepared	Variant (int)	A member value of QueryDefStateEnum.

void putODBCTimeout(short m_sTimeout);

Table G.92	Argument	
Argument	**Data Type**	**Description**
m_sTimeout	short	ODBC Timeout (in seconds).

void putReturnsRecords(Boolean m_HasRecords);

Sets the value determining if the QueryDef returns a Recordset.

(Note: Setting this to True and then using DDL won't cause a recordset to be returned.)

Table G.93	Argument	
Argument	**Data Type**	**Description**
m_HasRecords	Boolean	Value denoting whether the QueryDef returns a Recordset.

void putSQL(String m_SQL);

Table G.94	Argument	
Argument	**Data Type**	**Description**
m_SQL	String	SQL Statement.

The Parameters Object

Constructor   *Parameter = Parameters*.getItem(*Name*)

Parameter = Parameters.getItem(*Index*)

Methods   *Parameters*.**getDirection();**

Returns the direction of the parameter, matches a value in the ParameterDirectionEnum constants.

Return Type: short

Parameters.**getName();**

Returns the Name of the Parameter.

Return Type: String

Parameters.**getProperties();**

Returns the Properties collection.

Return Type: A Properties object.

Parameters.**getType();**

Returns a member of the DataTypeEnum constants.

Return Type: short

Parameters.**getValue();**

Returns the value of the Parameter.

Return Type: A variant containing the value of the parameter.

Parameters.**putDirection(short m_Direction);**

Sets the direction of the Parameter.

Table G.95   Argument

Argument	Data Type	Description
m_Direction	short	A member of the ParameterDirectionEnum constants.

Parameters.**putType(short m_DataType);**

Sets the data type of the Parameter.

App

G

Table G.96   Argument

Argument	Data Type	Description
m_DataType	short	A member of the DataTypeEnum constants.

Parameters.**putValue(Variant m_vValue);**

Sets the value of the Parameter.

Table G.97   Argument

Argument	Data Type	Description
m_ vValue	Variant	The Parameter value.

The Relation Object

Constructor   *Relation = Database*.CreateRelation()

Methods   **Field CreateField({Optional} Variant m_vName, { {Optional} Variant m_vDataType, Optional} Variant m_vSize);**

Table G.98   Arguments

Argument	Data Type	Description
m_vName	Variant (String)	The name of the Field to be created.
m_vDataType	Variant (int)	A member of the DataTypeEnum constants.
m_vSize	Variant (int)	The size of the Field (Read/Write only for a Text field, up to 255).

int getAttributes();

Returns the attributes for this TableDef.

Return Type: int (of type TableAttributesEnum)

Fields getFields();

Returns the Fields collection for this Relation.

Return Type: A Fields object.

String getForeignTable();

Returns the name of the Foreign Table in the relation.

Return Type: String

String getName( );

Returns the name for this Connection object.

Return Type: String

Boolean getPartialReplica( );

Returns whether or not the Relation is enforced during synchronization.

Return Type: Boolean

Properties getProperties();

Returns the Properties collection.

Return Type: A Properties object.

String getTable( );

Returns the name of the primary Table object, a QueryDef or TableDef.

Return Type: String

void putAttributes(int m_Option);

Sets the Attributes for this Relation.

Table G.99   Argument

Argument	Data Type	Description
m_Option	int	A member of the RelationAttributeEnum constants.

void putForeignTable(String m_ForeignTable);

Sets the name of the TableDef or QueryDef that will be the Foreign Table in the Relation.

Table G.100   Argument

Argument	Data Type	Description
m_ForeignTable	String	The name of a QueryDef or TableDef.

void putName(String m_Name);

Sets the Name for this Relation.

Table G.101   Argument

Argument	Data Type	Description
m_Name	String	A name.

App
G

void putPartialReplica(Boolean m_Enforce);

Determines whether or not the relation is enforced during synchronization.

Table G.102   Argument

Argument	Data Type	Description
m_Enforce	Boolean	True if the relation is to be enforced.

void putTable(String m_Table);

Sets the name of the TableDef or QueryDef object you are using.

Table G.103   Argument

Argument	Data Type	Description
m_Table	String	The name of a TableDef or QueryDef.

The Field Object

Constructor   *Field = Fields*.getItem(Variant *name*)

-or-

Field = Fields.getItem(Variant *index*)

Methods   int _30_FieldSize( );

void AppendChunk(Variant m_vChunk);

Used to break up large data types during submission to the data source. Improves performance and decreases load on the network.

Table G.104   Argument

Argument	Data Type	Description
m_vChunk	Variant	The piece of data you want to send.

CreateProperty(Variant m_PropName, Variant m_vType, Variant m_vDataType, Variant m_vDDL);

Creates a new Property.

Return Type: A Property object.

Table G.105 Arguments

Argument	Data Type	Description
m_PropName	Variant (String)	The name of the new Property.
m_vType	Variant (int)	A member of the DataTypeEnum constants.
m_vDataType	Variant	The initial property value.
m_vDDL	Variant (Boolean)	True if this property is a Data Definition Language property.

Boolean getAllowZeroLength();

Returns whether or not the Field allows zero-length strings.

Return Type: Boolean

int getAttributes();

Returns the attributes for this Field.

Return Type: int (of type FieldAttributesEnum)

short getCollectionIndex();

Returns a short value equal to the index of this Field in the collection.

Return Type: short

Field.**getCollatingOrder();**

Returns the collating order for this Database.

Return Type: An int matching a value in LanguageConstants.

Boolean getDataUpdatable();

Returns true if the data in the Field is updatable.

Return Type: Boolean

Variant getDefaultValue();

Returns the default value of the Field.

Return Type: Variant

int getFieldSize();

Returns the size of the Field.

Return Type: int

String getForeignName();

App
G

Returns the name of the Field in a Foreign table that is the foreign key in the Relation.

Return Type: String

Variant GetChunk(int m_Offset, int m_Bytes);

Used to break up large data types during retrieval to improve performance and decrease load on the network.

Table G.106   Arguments

Argument	Data Type	Description
m_Offset	int	The byte offset at which to begin retrieval.
m_Bytes	int	The number of bytes to retrieve each time.

String getName();

Returns the name of this Field.

Return Type: String

short getOrdinalPosition();

Returns the ordinal position of this Field in the Fields collection.

Return Type: short

Variant getOriginalValue();

Returns the original value in the case of a collision during a Batch Update.

Return Type: Variant

Properties getProperties();

Returns the Properties collection for this object.

Return Type: A Properties object.

Boolean getRequired();

Returns whether or not this Field requires non-null values.

Return Type: Boolean

String getSourceTable();

Returns the name of the source table for this Field.

Return Type: String

int getSize();

Returns the size of the Field.

Return Type: int

short getType( );

Returns a constant of RecordsetTypeEnum constants.

Return Type: short

Variant getValue( );

Returns the value of the Field.

Return Type: Variant

Boolean getValidateOnSet( );

Returns true if the Field Validation Rule is checked when the Field's value is set.

Return Type: Boolean

String getValidationText( );

Returns the text of the message your application displays if the value of a Field object doesn't satisfy the validation rule (Jet Workspaces only).

Return Type: String

String getValidationRule( );

Returns the update, insert, or delete constraints on the object.

Return Type: String

Variant getVisibleValue();

Returns the newest value in the case of a collision.

Return Type: Variant

void putAllowZeroLength(Boolean);

Sets the value that determines whether this field allows zero–length strings.

void putAttributes(int m_Attribute);

Sets the Attributes for this Field.

Table G.107   Argument

Argument	Data Type	Description
m_Attribute	int	A member of the FieldAttributeEnum constants.

void putForeignName(String m_Name);

Sets the name of the Foreign table in a Field Constraint.

Table G.108   Argument

Argument	Data Type	Description
m_Name	String	The name of a QueryDef or TableDef.

void putName(String m_Name);

Sets the name of this Field object.

Table G.109   Argument

Argument	Data Type	Description
m_Name	String	The name of the Field object.

void putOrdinalPosition(short m_Ordinal);

Sets the position of the Field in the Fields Collection before it is appended.

Table G.110   Argument

Argument	Data Type	Description
m_Ordinal	short	Sets the position of the Field.

void putRequired(Boolean m_ValRequired);

Table G.111   Argument

Argument	Data Type	Description
m_ValRequired	Boolean	Set to True if a value is required of this Field.

void putSize(int m_Size);

Sets the size of the Field object before it is appended.

Table G.112   Argument

Argument	Data Type	Description
m_Size	int	The size (in characters) of a text field.

void putType(short m_DataType);

Sets the data type of the Field before it is appended.

Table G.113   Argument

Argument	Data Type	Description
m_DataType	short	A member of the DataTypeEnum constants.

void putValidationRule(String m_Rule);

Sets the expression that is checked when data is updated.

Table G.114   Argument

Argument	Data Type	Description
m_Rule	String	The expression, in the form of a valid SQL WHERE clause expression.

void putValidationText(String m_ValidText);

Sets the message to use when a client activates a Validation Rule.

Table G.115   Argument

Argument	Data Type	Description
m_ValidText	String	The message seen when a validation rule is activated.

void putValue(Variant m_vValue);

Sets the Field value.

Table G.116   Argument

Argument	Data Type	Description
m_vValue	Variant	The value of the Field.

void putDefaultValue(Variant m_DefaultValue);

Table G.117   Argument

Argument	Data Type	Description
m_DefaultValue	Variant (String)	Default Value for the Field if not specified in the SQL statement.

App

G

void putValidateOnSet(Boolean m_ValidateNow);

Allows you to set whether the field is validated when the value is set, or when the Update takes place.

Table G.118   Argument

Argument	Data Type	Description
m_ValidateNow	Boolean	True, if you want to validate the fields as they are set.

The Index Object

Constructor   *Index = Indexes*.getItem(Variant *name*)

-or-

Index = Indexes.getItem(Variant *index*)

-or-

Index = TableDef.CreateIndex(Variant *fieldname*)

Methods   *Index.* **CreateField({Optional} Variant m_vName, { {Optional} Variant m_vDataType, Optional} Variant m_vSize);**

Table G.119   Arguments

Argument	Data Type	Description
m_vName	Variant (String)	The name of the Field to be created.
m_vDataType	Variant (int)	A member of the DataTypeEnum constants.
m_vSize	Variant (int)	The size of the Field (Read/Write only for a Text field, up to 255).

*Index.*CreateProperty(Variant m_PropName, Variant m_vType, Variant m_vDataType, Variant m_vDDL);

Creates a new Property.

Return Type: A Property object.

Table G.120   Arguments

Argument	Data Type	Description
m_PropName	Variant (String)	The name of the new Property.
m_vType	Variant (int)	A member of the DataTypeEnum constants.

Argument	Data Type	Description
m_vDataType	Variant	The initial property value.
m_vDDL	Variant (Boolean)	True if this property is a Data Definition Language property.

*Index.***getClustered();**

Returns True if the Index is clustered.

Return Type: Boolean

*Index.***getDistinctCount();**

Returns the number of unique keys in the index.

Return Type: int

*Index.***getFields();**

Returns the Fields collection for this Index.

Return Type: A Fields object.

*Index.***getForeign();**

Returns True if the object is a foreign key.

Return Type: Boolean

*Index.***getIgnoreNulls();**

Returns True if null values do not have an entry in the Index.

Return Type: Boolean

*Index.***getName();**

Returns the name of the Index.

Return Type: String

*Index.***getProperties();**

Returns the Properties collection for this object.

Return Type: A Properties object.

*Index.***getRequired();**

Returns True if the field cannot contain null values.

Return Type: Boolean

*Index.***getPrimary();**

Returns True if this is the primary Index.

Return Type: Boolean

*Index.*getUnique();

Returns True if this is a unique index.

Return Type: Boolean

*Index.*putClustered(Boolean m_Clustered);

Sets this index to be clustered.

Table G.121   Argument

Argument	Data Type	Description
m_Clustered	Boolean	Set to True to indicate this index is clustered.

*Index.*putFields(Variant);

Sets the Fields in the Index.

Table G.122   Argument

Argument	Data Type	Description
m_Fields	Variant (String)	Sets the Fields in an Index.

*Index.*putIgnoreNulls(Boolean m_Ignore);

Sets the property that determines whether the Index ignores null values.

Table G.123   Argument

Argument	Data Type	Description
m_Ignore	Boolean	Set to True to ignore null values in the Index.

*Index.*putName(String m_Name);

Sets the name of this Index.

Table G.124   Argument

Argument	Data Type	Description
m_Name	String	The name of the Index object.

*Index.***putPrimary(Boolean);**

Sets the Primary Index.

Table G.125	Argument	
Argument	**Data Type**	**Description**
m_Primary	Boolean	Set to True to make this the Primary index.

*Index.***putRequired(Boolean m_Required);**

Set to True to require that Fields be non-null.

Table G.126	Argument	
Argument	**Data Type**	**Description**
m_Required	Boolean	Determines whether null values are allowed.

*Index.***putUnique(Boolean m_Unique);**

Sets this index to be a unique index.

Table G.127	Argument	
Argument	**Data Type**	**Description**
m_Name	String	The name of the Index object.

The Group Object

Constructor

Methods   User CreateUser({Optional} Variant m_vUserName, {Optional} Variant m_vPID, {Optional} Variant m_vPassword);

Creates a new User.

Table G.128	Arguments	
Argument	**Data Type**	**Description**
m_UserName	Variant (String)	The name of the new User.
m_vPID	Variant (String)	A unique identifier for this User.
m_vPassword	Variant (String)	A password up to 14 characters in length.

Users getUsers();

Returns the Users collection for this Group.

Return Type: A Users object.

Properties getProperties();

Returns the Properties collection for this object.

Return Type: A Properties object.

String getName();

Returns the name of the Group.

Return Type: String

void putName(String m_GroupName);

Sets the name of the Group.

Table G.129   Argument

Argument	Data Type	Description
m_GroupName	String	The name of a group.

void putPID(String m_PID);

Sets the PID of the Group.

Table G.130   Argument

Argument	Data Type	Description
m_PID	String	A 4- to 20-character long sequence of alphanumeric characters.

The User Object

Constructor   *User = Users.*getItem(Variant *name*)

-or-

*User = Users.*getItem(Variant *index*)

-or-

*User = Database.*CreateUser()

Methods   **Group CreateGroup(Variant m_GroupName, Variant m_PID);**

Creates a new Group.

Return Type: A Group object.

Table G.131   Arguments

Argument	Data Type	Description
m_GroupName	Variant (String)	The name for the new Group.
m_PID	Variant (String)	The unique ID for the Group.

void NewPassword(String m_OldPassword, String m_NewPassword);

Creates a new password for the User object.

Table G.132   Arguments

Argument	Data Type	Description
m_OldPassword	String	The old password.
m_NewPassword	String	The new password.

Properties getProperties();

Returns the Properties collection for this object.

Return Type: A Properties object.

String getName();

Returns the name of the User object.

Return Type: String

void putName(String m_UserName);

Sets the name for a User.

Table G.133   Argument

Argument	Data Type	Description
m_UserName	String	The user name.

void putPassword(String m_Password);

Sets the password for the User.

App
G

Table G.134   Argument

Argument	Data Type	Description
m_Password	String	An alphanumeric string up to 14 characters long.

void putPID(String m_PID);

Sets the PID of the User.

Table G.135   Argument

Argument	Data Type	Description
m_PID	String	A 4- to 20-character long sequence of alphanumeric characters.

The Container Object

Constructor   *Container = Containers*.getItem(Variant name)

-or-

Container = Containers.getItem(Variant index)

Methods   *Container*.**getAllPermissions();**

Returns the sum of the permissions on the Container (matching members of the PermissionsEnum constants) including the inherited permissions.

Return Type: int

Container.**getDocuments();**

Returns the Documents collection for this Container.

Return Type: String

Container.**getInherit();**

Returns True if the Documents placed into this Container will inherit permissions from this Container.

Return Type: Boolean

Container.**getName();**

Returns the name of the Container.

Return Type: String

Container.**getOwner();**

Returns the name of a User object that is set as the owner of this Container.

Return Type: String

Container.getPermissions();

Returns the sum of the permissions on the Container (matching members of the PermissionsEnum constants) excluding inherited permissions.

Return Type: int

Container.getProperties();

Returns the Properties collection for this object.

Return Type: A Properties object

Container.getUserName();

Returns the user account with permissions on this object.

Return Type: String

Container.putInherit(Boolean m_Inherit);

If True, causes all Documents created in this Container to inherit its permissions.

Table G.136 Argument

Argument	Data Type	Description
m_Inherit	Boolean	True—Inherit permissions, False—do not.

Container.putOwner(String m_UserName);

Sets the User account that has ownership of this object.

Table G.137 Argument

Argument	Data Type	Description
m_UserName	String	The name of a User object.

Container.putPermissions(int m_Permissions);

Sets the permissions for this Container.

Table G.138 Argument

Argument	Data Type	Description
m_Permissions	int	A member of the PermissionEnum constants.

App
G

Container.**putUserName(String m_User);**

Sets the user account for this container.

Table G.139   Argument

Argument	Data Type	Description
m_User	String	A user account.

The Property Object

Constructor   *Property* = *Database*.CreateProperty(*name, data type, value, DDL*)

Property = *Document*.CreateProperty(*name, data type, value, DDL*)

Property = *Field*.CreateProperty(*name, data type, value, DDL*)

Property = *Index*.CreateProperty(*name, data type, value, DDL*)

Property = *QueryDef*.CreateProperty(*name, data type, value, DDL*)

Property = *TableDef*.CreateProperty(*name, data type, value, DDL*)

Property = *Properties*.getItem(*name*)

Property = *Properties*.getItem(*index*)

Methods   *Property*.**getInherited();**

Returns whether or not this property is inherited.

Return Type: Boolean

Property.**getName();**

Returns the name of the property.

Return Type: String

Property.**getProperties();**

Returns the Properties collection.

Return Type: String

Property.**getType();**

Returns a PropertTypeEnum value.

Return Type: int

Property.**getValue();**

Returns the value of a property.

Return Type: Variant

*Property.*putName(String);

Sets the name for the Property.

Table G.140	Argument	
Argument	**Data Type**	**Description**
m_Name	String	A name.

*Property.*putType(short m_DataType);

Sets the data type of the property.

Table G.141	Argument	
Argument	**Data Type**	**Description**
m_DataType	short	A member of the DataTypeEnum constants.

*Property.*putValue(Variant m_vValue);

Sets the Property value.

Table G.142	Argument	
Argument	**Data Type**	**Description**
m_vValue	Variant	The value of the Property.

The Document Object

Constructor   *Document = Documents.*getItem(*name*)

*Document = Documents.*getItem(*index*)

Methods   *Document.*CreateProperty(Variant m_PropName, Variant m_vType, Variant m_vDataType, Variant m_vDDL);

Creates a new Property.

Return Type: A Property object.

App

G

Table G.143   Arguments

Argument	Data Type	Description
m_PropName	Variant (String)	The name of the new Property.
m_vType	Variant (int)	A member of the DataTypeEnum constants.
m_vDataType	Variant	The initial property value.
m_vDDL	Variant (Boolean)	True if this property is a Data Definition Language property.

*Document.***getAllPermissions();**

Returns an int that is the sum of all of the PermissionsEnum constants representing the permissions on this object.

Return Type: int

*Document.***getContainer();**

Returns: String with the name of the Container object associated with this Document.

Return Type: String

*Document.***getDateCreated();**

Returns the date this Document was created.

Return Type: Variant

*Document.***getLastUpdated();**

Retunrs the last date the Document was updated.

Return Type: Variant

*Document.***getName();**

Returns the name of the Document.

Return Type: String

*Document.***getOwner();**

Returns: A String with the name of a user account that is the Owner of this object.

Return Type: String

*Document.***getPermissions();**

Returns the sum of the permissions on the Container (matching members of the PermissionsEnum constants) excluding inherited permissions.

Return Type: int

Document.**getProperties();**

Returns the Properties collection for this object.

Return Type: A Properties object

Document.**getUserName()**

Returns:

Return Type: String

Document.**putPermissions(int m_Permissions);**

Sets the permissions for an object.

Table G.144   Argument

Argument	Data Type	Description
m_Permissions	int	A member (or sum) of the PermissionsEnum constants.

Document.**putOwner(String m_Owner);**

Sets the user account who has ownership of this object.

Table G.145   Argument

Argument	Data Type	Description
m_Owner	String	A user account.

Collections in DAO – Part One

- Fields
- Groups
- Indexes
- IndexFields
- Properties
- QueryDefs
- Relations
- TableDefs
- Users
- Workspaces

App

G

Table G.146   Methods Supported by These Collections

Method	Argument List	Description
Delete	None	Deletes the collection member.
Append	(Object)	Appends the object to the collection.
getItem	(Variant)	Returns the collection member at the specified index.
getCount	None	Returns the number of members in the collection.
_NewEnum	None	
Refresh	None	Enumerates the members of the collection.

DAO Collections – Part Two

- Connections
- Containers
- Databases
- Documents
- Errors
- Parameters
- Recordsets

Table G.147   Methods Supported by These Collections

Method	Argument List	Description
getItem	(Variant)	Returns the collection member at the specified index.
getCount	None	Returns the number of members in the collection.
_NewEnum	None	
Refresh	None	Enumerates the members of the collection.

_DynaCollection

Table G.148   Methods Supported by These Collections

Method	Argument List	Description
Delete	None	Deletes the collection member.
Append	(Object)	Appends the object to the collection.

Method	Argument List	Description
getCount	None	Returns the number of members in the collection.
_NewEnum	None	
Refresh	None	Enumerates the members of the collection.

_Collection

Table G.149 Methods Supported by These Collections

Method	Argument List	Description
getCount	None	Returns the number of members in the collection.
_NewEnum	None	
Refresh	None	Enumerates the members of the collection.

Constants

Java Package: com.ms.com

_DAOSuppHelp

int LogMessages;

int KeepLocal;

int Replicable;

int ReplicableBool;

int V1xNullBehavior;

CollatingOrderEnum

int dbSortNeutral;

int dbSortArabic;

int dbSortCyrillic;

int dbSortCzech;

int dbSortDutch;

int dbSortGeneral;

int dbSortGreek;

int dbSortHebrew;

int dbSortHungarian;

int dbSortIcelandic;

int dbSortNorwdan;

int dbSortPDXIntl;

int dbSortPDXNor;

int dbSortPDXSwe;

int dbSortPolish;

int dbSortSpanish;

int dbSortSwedFin;

int dbSortTurkish;

int dbSortJapanese;

int dbSortChineseSimplified;

int dbSortChineseTraditional;

int dbSortKorean;

int dbSortThai;

int dbSortSlovenian;

int dbSortUndefined;

CursorDriverEnum

int dbUseDefaultCursor;

int dbUseODBCCursor;

int dbUseServerCursor;

int dbUseClientBatchCursor;

int dbUseNoCursor;

DatabaseTypeEnum

int dbVersion10;

int dbEncrypt;

int dbDecrypt;

int dbVersion11;

int dbVersion20;

int dbVersion30;

DataTypeEnum

int dbBoolean;

int dbByte;

int dbInteger;

int dbLong;

int dbCurrency;

int dbSingle;

int dbDouble;

int dbDate;

int dbBinary;

int dbText;

int dbLongBinary;

int dbMemo;

int dbGUID;

int dbBigInt;

int dbVarBinary;

int dbChar;

int dbNumeric;

int dbDecimal;

int dbFloat;

int dbTime;

int dbTimeStamp;

DriverPromptEnum

int dbDriverPrompt;

int dbDriverNoPrompt;

int dbDriverComplete;

int dbDriverCompleteRequired;

EditModeEnum

int dbEditNone;

int dbEditInProgress;

int dbEditAdd;

int dbEditChanged;

int dbEditDeleted;

int dbEditNew;

FieldAttributeEnum

int dbFixedField;

int dbVariableField;

int dbAutoIncrField;

int dbUpdatableField;

int dbSystemField;

int dbHyperlinkField;

int dbDescending;

IdleEnum

int dbFreeLocks;

int dbRefreshCache;

LanguageConstants

Generic dbLangArabic;

Generic dbLangCzech;

Generic dbLangDutch;

Generic dbLangGeneral;

Generic dbLangGreek;

Generic dbLangHebrew;

Generic dbLangHungarian;

Generic dbLangIcelandic;

Generic dbLangNordic;

Generic dbLangNorwDan;

Generic dbLangPolish;

Generic dbLangCyrillic;

Generic dbLangSpanish;

Generic dbLangSwedFin;

Generic dbLangTurkish;

Generic dbLangJapanese;

Generic dbLangChineseSimplified;

Generic dbLangChineseTraditional;

Generic dbLangKorean;

Generic dbLangThai;

Generic dbLangSlovenian;

LockTypeEnum

int dbPessimistic;

int dbOptimistic;

int dbOptimisticValue;

int dbOptimisticBatch;

ParameterDirectionEnum

int dbParamInput;

int dbParamOutput;

int dbParamInputOutput;

int dbParamReturnValue;

PermissionEnum

int dbSecNoAccess;

int dbSecFullAccess;

int dbSecDelete;

int dbSecReadSec;

int dbSecWriteSec;

int dbSecWriteOwner;

int dbSecDBCreate;

int dbSecDBOpen;

int dbSecDBExclusive;

int dbSecDBAdmin;

int dbSecCreate;

int dbSecReadDef;

int dbSecWriteDef;

int dbSecRetrieveData;

int dbSecInsertData;

int dbSecReplaceData;

int dbSecDeleteData;

QueryDefStateEnum

int dbQPrepare;

int dbQUnprepare;

QueryDefTypeEnum

int dbQSelect;

int dbQProcedure;

int dbQAction;

int dbQCrosstab;

int dbQDelete;

int dbQUpdate;

int dbQAppend;

int dbQMakeTable;

int dbQDDL;

int dbQSQLPassThrough;

int dbQSetOperation;

int dbQSPTBulk;

int dbQCompound;

RecordsetOptionEnum

int dbDenyWrite;

int dbDenyRead;

int dbReadOnly;

int dbAppendOnly;

int dbInconsistent;

int dbConsistent;

int dbSQLPassThrough;

int dbFailOnError;

int dbForwardOnly;

int dbSeeChanges;

int dbRunAsync;

int dbExecDirect;

RecordsetTypeEnum

int dbOpenTable;

int dbOpenDynaset;

int dbOpenSnapshot;

int dbOpenForwardOnly;

int dbOpenDynamic;

RecordStatusEnum

int dbRecordUnmodified;

int dbRecordModified;

int dbRecordNew;

int dbRecordDeleted;

int dbRecordDBDeleted;

RelationAttributeEnum

int dbRelationUnique;

int dbRelationDontEnforce;

int dbRelationInherited;

int dbRelationUpdateCascade;

int dbRelationDeleteCascade;

int dbRelationLeft;

int dbRelationRight;

ReplicaTypeEnum

int dbRepMakeReadOnly;

int dbRepMakePartial;

SetOptionEnum

int dbPageTimeout;

int dbLockRetry;

int dbMaxBufferSize;

int dbUserCommitSync;

int dbImplicitCommitSync;

int dbExclusiveAsyncDelay;

int dbSharedAsyncDelay;

int dbMaxLocksPerFile;

int dbLockDelay;

int dbRecycleLVs;

int dbFlushTransactionTimeout;

SynchronizeTypeEnum

int dbRepExportChanges;

int dbRepImportChanges;

int dbRepImpExpChanges;

int dbRepSyncInternet;

TableDefAttributeEnum

int dbAttachExclusive;

int dbAttachSavePWD;

int dbSystemObject;

int dbAttachedTable;

int dbAttachedODBC;

int dbHiddenObject;

UpdateCriteriaEnum

int dbCriteriaKey;

int dbCriteriaModValues;

int dbCriteriaAllCols;

int dbCriteriaTimestamp;

int dbCriteriaDeleteInsert;

int dbCriteriaUpdate;

UpdateTypeEnum

int dbUpdateBatch;

int dbUpdateRegular;

int dbUpdateCurrentRecord;

WorkspaceTypeEnum

int dbUseODBC;

int dbUseJet;

Obsolete Features Still Supported

- All CreateDynaset methods
- All CreateSnapshot methods
- All ListFields methods
- All ListIndexes methods
- CompactDatabase statement
- CreateDatabase statement
- DBEngine.FreeLocks
- DBEngine.SetDefaultWorkspace
- DBEngine.Password
- DBEngine.SetDataAccessOption
- Database.BeginTrans
- Database.CommitTrans
- Database.Rollback
- Database.DeleteQuerydef
- Database.ExecuteSQL
- Database.ListTables
- Database.OpenQuerydef
- Database.OpenTable
- FieldSize
- Index.Fields
- OpenDatabase statement
- Querydef.ListParameters

App
G

H

What's on the CD?

In this appendix, you will learn about the materials included on the *Special Edition Using Microsoft SQL Server 6.5, 2nd Edition* CD-ROM that accompanies this book. It contains applications, tools, and demonstration products. ∎

Third-Party Products

Following is a brief description of the products and demos from third-party vendors that you'll find on the CD.

N O T E The products on the CD are Demos and Shareware. You may have some difficulty running them on your particular machine. If you do, feel free to contact the vendor. (They'd rather have you evaluate their product than ignore it.) ■

NetScanTools™, www.eskimo.com/~nwps/programs.html. NetScanTools is a shareware application that brings many classic UNIX network client utilities into an easy-to-use Windows® environment: Name Server Lookup (NSLOOKUP), Ping, Traceroute, Finger, Whois, Time Sync, Daytime, Quote, Chargen, Echo, Ident Server, Winsock Info, Services and Protocols database checks, NetScanner, Hosts file Management and "What's New At NWPSW"—a barebones URL grabber.

WebTrends, www.webtrends.com/. WebTrends analyzes the log files created by your Web servers and provide you with invaluable information about your World-Wide Web site and the users that access it. WebTrends is compatible with log files created by ANY Web server (Microsoft IIS, Apache, CERN, NCSA, O'reilly, Lotus Domino, Oracle, NetWare, etc...)

SQL Server Frequently Asked Questions (FAQ)

The Microsoft SQL Server FAQ is available online at the author's web site, **www.swynk.com/ mssqlfaq.asp**. The questions and answers are provided from the many newsgroups and mailing lists available in support of SQL Server. Be sure to check back frequently for updates, and feel free to suggest topic areas for inclusion in future updates of the FAQ.

Using the Electronic Books

The following books are available to you in HTML format that can be read from any World Wide Web browser that you may have currently installed on your machine (such as Netscape Navigator or Mosaic).

> *Special Edition Using Microsoft SQL Server 6.5, 2nd Edition*
>
> *Special Edition Using Microsoft BackOffice*
>
> *Special Edition Using Windows NT Server 4*
>
> *The BackOffice Intranet Kit*

If you don't have a Web browser, we have included Microsoft's Internet Explorer for you on the CD.

Reading the Electronic Books

To read the electronic books, you will need to start your Web browser and open the document file INDEX.HTM located in the main directory of the CD. Alternatively, you can browse the CD directory using File Manager or Windows Explorer and double-click INDEX.HTM.

Once you have opened the INDEX.HTM page, click on the cover of the book you would like to read. You can access any book's contents by clicking on the highlighted chapter numbers or topic names. The electronic book works like any other Web page; when you click on a hot link, a new page is opened or the browser will take you to the new location in the document. As you read through the electronic book, you will notice other highlighted words or phrases. Clicking on these cross-references will also take you to a new location within the electronic book. You can always use your Browser's forward or backward buttons to return to your original location.

Installing the Internet Explorer

If you don't have a Web browser installed on your machine, you can use Microsoft's Internet Explorer 4.0 on this CD-ROM.

Microsoft Internet Explorer can be installed from the self-extracting file in the \EXPLORER directory. Double-click the Ie4setup.exe or use the Control Panel's Add/Remove Programs option and follow the instructions in the install routine. Please be aware you must have Windows 95 or Windows NT 4.x installed on your machine to use this version of Internet Explorer. Other versions of this software can be downloaded from Microsoft's FTP site at **http://www.microsoft.com/ie/download**.

Finding Sample Code

This book contains code examples that include listing headers (for example, see Listing 10.1) and the On the CD icon:

On the CD

Listing 10.1   10_01.SQL-Creating the Authors2 Table and Indexes

This listing indicates that this particular *code snippet* (or example) is included electronically on the CD. To find it, browse to the \CODE subdirectory on the CD and select the chapter directory where your code is located, then find the file name that matches the one referenced in the listing header (in this example, 10_01.SQL).

Index

G

Complete and Return this Card
for a *FREE* Computer Book Catalog

Thank you for purchasing this book! You have purchased a superior computer book written expressly for your needs. To continue to provide the kind of up-to-date, pertinent coverage you've come to expect from us, we need to hear from you. Please take a minute to complete and return this self-addressed, postage-paid form. In return, we'll send you a free catalog of all our computer books on topics ranging from word processing to programming and the internet.

Mr. ☐ Mrs. ☐ Ms. ☐ Dr. ☐

Name (first) ☐☐☐☐☐☐☐☐☐☐☐☐ (M.I.) ☐ (last) ☐☐☐☐☐☐☐☐☐☐☐☐☐☐☐☐☐

Address ☐☐☐☐☐☐☐☐☐☐☐☐☐☐☐☐☐☐☐☐☐☐☐☐☐☐☐☐☐☐☐☐

☐☐☐☐☐☐☐☐☐☐☐☐☐☐☐☐☐☐☐☐☐☐☐☐☐☐☐☐☐☐☐☐

City ☐☐☐☐☐☐☐☐☐☐☐☐☐☐☐ State ☐☐ Zip ☐☐☐☐☐ ☐☐☐☐

Phone ☐☐☐ ☐☐☐ ☐☐☐☐ Fax ☐☐☐ ☐☐☐ ☐☐☐☐

Company Name ☐☐☐☐☐☐☐☐☐☐☐☐☐☐☐☐☐☐☐☐☐☐☐☐☐☐☐☐

E-mail address ☐☐☐☐☐☐☐☐☐☐☐☐☐☐☐☐☐☐☐☐☐☐☐☐☐☐☐☐

1. Please check at least (3) influencing factors for purchasing this book.

Front or back cover information on book .... ☐
Special approach to the content .... ☐
Completeness of content .... ☐
Author's reputation .... ☐
Publisher's reputation .... ☐
Book cover design or layout .... ☐
Index or table of contents of book .... ☐
Price of book .... ☐
Special effects, graphics, illustrations .... ☐
Other (Please specify): _____ ☐

2. How did you first learn about this book?

Saw in Macmillan Computer Publishing catalog .... ☐
Recommended by store personnel .... ☐
Saw the book on bookshelf at store .... ☐
Recommended by a friend .... ☐
Received advertisement in the mail .... ☐
Saw an advertisement in: _____ ☐
Read book review in: _____ ☐
Other (Please specify): _____ ☐

3. How many computer books have you purchased in the last six months?

This book only .... ☐   3 to 5 books .... ☐
2 books.................. ☐   More than 5 .... ☐

4. Where did you purchase this book?

Bookstore .... ☐
Computer Store .... ☐
Consumer Electronics Store .... ☐
Department Store .... ☐
Office Club .... ☐
Warehouse Club .... ☐
Mail Order .... ☐
Direct from Publisher .... ☐
Internet site .... ☐
Other (Please specify): _____ ☐

5. How long have you been using a computer?

☐ Less than 6 months   ☐ 6 months to a year
☐ 1 to 3 years   ☐ More than 3 years

6. What is your level of experience with personal computers and with the subject of this book?

	With PCs	With subject of book
New	☐	☐
Casual	☐	☐
Accomplished	☐	☐
Expert	☐	☐

Source Code ISBN: 0-7897-1117-6

**7. Which of the following best describes your
   job title?**

Administrative Assistant .... ☐
Coordinator .... ☐
Manager/Supervisor .... ☐
Director .... ☐
Vice President .... ☐
President/CEO/COO .... ☐
Lawyer/Doctor/Medical Professional .... ☐
Teacher/Educator/Trainer .... ☐
Engineer/Technician .... ☐
Consultant .... ☐
Not employed/Student/Retired .... ☐
Other (Please specify): _____ ☐

**8. Which of the following best describes the area of
   the company your job title falls under?**

Accounting .... ☐
Engineering .... ☐
Manufacturing .... ☐
Operations .... ☐
Marketing .... ☐
Sales .... ☐
Other (Please specify): _____ ☐

9. What is your age?

Under 20 .... ☐
21-29 .... ☐
30-39 .... ☐
40-49 .... ☐
50-59 .... ☐
60-over .... ☐

10. Are you:

Male .... ☐
Female .... ☐

**11. Which computer publications do you read
    regularly? (Please list)**

_____
_____
_____
_____
_____
_____
_____
_____
_____
_____

••

Comments: _____
_____
_____

Fold here and scotch-tape to mail.

Check out Que® Books
on the World Wide Web
http://www.quecorp.com

As the biggest software release in computer history, Windows 95 continues to redefine the computer industry. Click here for the latest info on our Windows 95 books

Make computing quick and easy with these products designed exclusively for new and casual users

Examine the latest releases in word processing, spreadsheets, operating systems, and suites

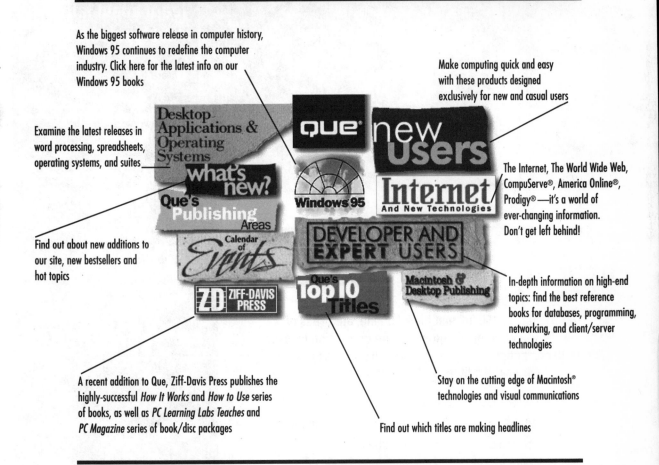

The Internet, The World Wide Web, CompuServe®, America Online®, Prodigy®—it's a world of ever-changing information. Don't get left behind!

Find out about new additions to our site, new bestsellers and hot topics

In-depth information on high-end topics: find the best reference books for databases, programming, networking, and client/server technologies

A recent addition to Que, Ziff-Davis Press publishes the highly-successful *How It Works* and *How to Use* series of books, as well as *PC Learning Labs Teaches* and *PC Magazine* series of book/disc packages

Stay on the cutting edge of Macintosh® technologies and visual communications

Find out which titles are making headlines

With 6 separate publishing groups, Que develops products for many specific market segments and areas of computer technology. Explore our Web Site and you'll find information on best-selling titles, newly published titles, upcoming products, authors, and much more.

- Stay informed on the latest industry trends and products available
- Visit our online bookstore for the latest information and editions
- Download software from Que's library of the best shareware and freeware